Choices...Memoirs of a Sportswriter

By Bill Tangen

ISBN 0-7414-2433-9

Published by:

PUBLISHING.COM

1094 New DeHaven Street, Suite 100
West Conshohocken, PA 19428-2713
Info@buybooksontheweb.com
www.buybooksontheweb.com
Toll-free (877) BUY BOOK
Local Phone (610) 941-9999
Fax (610) 941-9959

Printed in the United States of America

Printed on Recycled Paper

Published March 2005

ACKNOWLEDGMENTS

Phil Chase, Teresa Martin, Chris Farlekas, Phil Dusenbury, Jackie Beck Bush, Janice Osborne.

IN APPRECIATION

Muhammad Ali, David Chaudoir, Deborah Seager
(G.O.A.T. Inc., Berrien Springs, Michigan).

Muhammad Ali, David Chaudoir, Deborah Seager
(G.O.A.T. Inc., Berrien Springs, Michigan).

ADDITIONS:

Since the Foreword and early chapters of this book was written, three more grandchildren were born.

Joining Russ, Sarah, Ashley and Jeremy, are Brooke, Kyle and Jackson. Brooke and Jackson reside in South Carolina while Kyle lives in Pennsylvania.

FIGHTING TO SURVIVE

He repossessed cars one night and covered a high school basketball game the next.

Bill Tangen became a newspaper sports editor who perfected his talents into reaching the top. He wound up being named 1977 New York State Sportswriter of the Year (scholastic wrestling).

The former athlete covered Port Jervis High School twins who went on to become NCAA mat champions and freestyle gold medalists at the 1984 Olympics.

He sat in a hotel room, across from heavyweight boxing champion Muhammad Ali, and kidded with him in September of 1976. "I'll switch places with you," Ali had told Bill. "I will drive your car home and you fight Ken Norton."

Bill watched and listened to "The Greatest" and then wrote a revealing column that uncovered the real Ali, the man behind the mask.

In the late 1990s, Bill began a downhill spiral that was fueled by alcohol addiction. On July 4, 2000, he stood at death's door and refused to turn the knob. Miraculously, he was given a second chance at life and is making the most of it.

This book began with handwritten notes being scrawled on scraps of paper, in a Bronx, New York veterans hospital. Bill wanted his grandchildren to know who their "Poppy" is and was. He chronicles his life in a compelling and humorous way. From childhood escapades through military service in Southeast Asia, to his marriage, arrival at the sports desk and beyond, you share in his incredible journey. .

This real life story will make you laugh, make you cry and tug at your heartstrings. You will see a real life story through the eyes of an award-winning journalist

The messages are simple. Nostalgia is healthy, overwhelming odds can be overcome and dreams do come true.

Bill has touched countless athletes, parents, coaches and fans. Now he touches you with this down to earth account of what a fight for survival feels like. Like Muhammad Ali, Bill Tangen has had his glove raised in victory.

DEDICATION

Bill Tangen lives in Matamoras, Pa., with his wife Christine. The couple has two grown daughters, Tracie Lynn and Dawn Melissa, plus seven grandchildren.

Bill is a former police reporter and sports editor of the Port Jervis Union-Gazette and continues to be a freelance writer, maintaining his interest in local and national sports.

He was sports editor at the Sullivan County Democrat in Callicoon, New York (1978) and has written for the Pike County Dispatch (Milford, Pa.), Times-Herald Record (Middletown, New York), The Scranton Times (Scranton, Pa.) and Wilkes-Barre, Pa. newspapers The Times-Leader and The Citizen's Voice.

He attended the prestigious American Press Institute in Reston, Virginia in 1976, and was named New York State Sportswriter of the Year in 1977 at Onondaga War Memorial in Syracuse, New York, for his scholastic wrestling coverage.

This book is dedicated to his wife, Christine, who stood by his side through thick and thin. Her inspiration, strong religious beliefs, and love helped to save his life.

TABLE OF CONTENTS

1. Welcome to the Bronx 1

2. Family Tree Has Missing Limbs 30

3. Discovering Sports 58

4. Her Name is Christine 73

5. Goat to Hero 98

6. Welcome to Texas, Boy! 125

7. Plattsburgh, N.Y. -- Paradise on Earth 146

8. I am a Rock I am an Island 180

9. The Repo Man 232

10. Wedding Bells 252

11. Muhammad Ali: Man Behind The Mask 295

12. 15 Minutes of Fame 312

13. Life is for the Living 332

14. We Come This Way But Once 362

FOREWORD   By Bill Tangen

Memories, pressed between the pages of my mind. Memories, sweetened through the ages, just like wine.

Those words were sung by "The King of Rock and Roll", Elvis Presley, during a 1968 television special that marked his comeback.

He had disappeared from the public eye, largely due to the emergence of an English group known as The Beatles.

Presley had a choice of whether to remain a virtual hermit or to change his musical direction a bit and perform again. Long live the king!

Life is made up of countless choices that can mold memories, some good and some bad.

The choice of whether or not to write this book hung in the balance for years and years.

It was always put on the back burner as there were other things to do, that seemed more important. And, I figured some day I'd get on with it.

After all, who really cares about what this person has seen, done and experienced in more than 54 years of life?

For the first 23 years, I never knew there was writing ability in this body.

One day I was repossessing cars and the next I was in a high school gymnasium covering a basketball game.

There was a choice of staying at the Middletown, New York bank, or going to the Union-Gazette newspaper as a police reporter and sportswriter. The year was 1970.

It's almost too much for my mind to fathom that this occupation held plenty of opportunity for me and resulted in plenty of success.

It afforded me the chance to meet and interview heavyweight boxing champion Muhammad Ali and basketball star Willis Reed, to cover Olympic gold medal- winning twins from Port Jervis, New York, (1984 freestyle wrestling), and to be named New York State Sportswriter of the Year in 1977 for scholastic wrestling coverage.

Sportswriting was, is and always will be the ideal job for me. I fell in love with it instantly and its appeal to me has never dwindled.

Many times while growing up, I had heard that making decisions would wind up being a tough part of adult life. And, what I had heard, really came true.

There have been ups and downs during this 30 plus years of journalism.

I could just escape from my years of real life experiences and act like they'd never occurred.

My life hasn't exactly been that of a glamorous Hollywood star, in fact, it's been kind of ordinary.

Then again, an ordinary lifestyle has been known to receive some jolts, composed of unpredictable ebbs and flows. Kind of like a graph of zigzag lines.

Ever look at a story from the past and wonder what made the main subject of the piece tick? Who was he? Did he have kids and where was his home?

Or how about a faded photograph? You know, the images that suddenly escaped their long time hiding places in the attic of the Aunt Carols and Uncle Joes of our land.

Those faces looking back at you are a real mystery aren't they?

Maybe the clothes will define the era, but without identity, the folks wearing those clothes remain a lifelong secret.

Were their memories sweetened through the ages just like wine?

Before I head to "Boot Hill", I have decided to explain just what I did in life.

So, sometimes I'll be looked upon as a hero of sorts and of course, sometimes I'll be a villain.

It has been said that your personality is formed by the people you have come in contact with over the years.

If that is true, my personality is a real mixed bag, a mind-boggling puzzle just screaming to be solved.

Rather than have family and friends wonder about some of the things I did, including my human feelings and reactions to various happenings, I choose to bring them out in the open.

So someday when these words are comprehended by someone in an attic, at least they'll know that the lock box of secrecy and memories has a key.

There is no real choice here. It would be selfish to simply ignore what I believe is a mandatory task, that being, to share with folks, while I'm on this earth and after.

So, from a tricycle on Brooklyn Street to a seat across from Ali's Concord Hotel bed, I will tell my story.

Tomorrow evening, July 21, 2001, Christine, my wonderful wife of 30 years, and yours truly, will attend my 36th Port Jervis High School reunion.

In this class, there are doctors, lawyers and probably Indian chiefs. And, I'm sure each will have a story.

This is dedicated to Christine and our children, Tracie, who lives in Pennsylvania and Dawn down in South Carolina.

And of course to our grandchildren, Sarah, Ashley, Russ and Jeremy. I could never forget my dad and mom, Jerome and Emily, and my sister Anne.

This is who Bill Tangen is and was.

These are the memories, pressed between the pages of my mind.

And yes, because of my family, these memories have been sweetened through the ages just like wine.

Bill Tangen
July 20, 2001
Matamoras, Pennsylvania

INTRODUCTION

Being a sportswriter for more than 30 years, I guess it would be fitting to condense play-by-play happenings into lowlights and highlights in a peaks and valleys type format.

But that's not what I'm all about.

It's true that some of my pleasures are good oldies, music, sports, collecting tins and other containers, flirting with waitresses and yes, jotting down or retaining statistics and trivia like Mickey Mantle having a lifetime batting average of .296 with 536 homers and Joe Jones singing "You Talk Too Much."

Some think statistics are for losers, but I don't buy into that.

After all, I am a statistic, having somehow refused to walk through death's door when I probably had no more than a 50-50 chance of surviving.

Beer had finally taken its toll and the lethal results may have been mere minutes away. No more wife, no more grandkids, no more friends. A simple three pitch strikeout and those dearest to me would be stranded on base.

Some stories or books start at the beginning, coast to a middle and then wax hot for a spine-tingling explosive climax.

But this isn't a "who-dunnit" that keeps you on the edge of your seat. I already know who the culprit was and came face to face with the enemy much like Dirty Harry would.

"Well, punk, how lucky do ya feel? Make my day."

I choose to address the beginning of my life fairly early in the book. And that beginning was at St. Francis Hospital, in Port Jervis, New York, 54 years and 119 days ago.

People used to ask me how long I spent in the United States Air Force and I'd answer "three years, four months, 14 days, 11 minutes and 10 seconds, not that I was counting."

I haven't guzzled down a beer in one year and 35 days, and that is the most incredible statistic I have ever had the pleasure to view.

I'm one of the lucky ones who hasn't experienced the compulsion to go back. In fact, sometimes I drop into a bar for a ginger ale or two. In my younger years, I almost lived in bars, stopping by the friendly neighborhood taverns on the way, during and after work.

Now, just a few minutes in a place like that and I'm ready to leave. I'm happy to be alive and free to make choices. Really there is no choice in this situation, and that may be why I feel no pressure or compulsion to crack open a can of Milwaukee's Best Beer.

No, I had no guarantees to survive the 12th round when I was out on my feet and hoping to reach the end of the longest most grueling fight of my life. First, I had to make it through the whole fight, then I had to wait around for the decision and in the end, remarkably, I not only survived the fight but had my glove raised in victory.

If I were a cat, I came within a whisker of losing my ninth and final life.

But I was taken in and tended to during this scary and stormy experience. I was revitalized with a will to live that I hadn't felt in years. I actually began to sleep at night and to feel real emotions as day by day, the cobwebs went away and my mind cleared.

No, this publication isn't about drinking. But if it had continued, you wouldn't be reading this.

The game of life was almost over for me, but it wasn't my time yet. There was more to do on this earth and I look at the whole ball of wax differently now.

I have true feelings now, a lot of my facade has been chipped away, much of my defenses let down, instead of shielding a very private person.

I no longer hide in a make believe world where floating in a sea of suds was the only real choice available to me.

The gut-wrenching walks across the bridge into New York State on Sundays waiting with sweaty palms, a sick stomach and anxiety for noon to arrive, are gone but never forgotten.

When it hit 12 o'clock I could get my fix, "hair of the dog" would ease my nervousness within an hour and the merry-go-round would continue in motion.

I can never have the past back, never make amends for all those times I sat in a bar instead of playing with my kids. But in this case, it is "better late than never" that I can appreciate the things that life has to offer.

Am I afraid of a relapse? No, but as I mentioned in one of the three alcoholics anonymous meetings I have attended since getting sober on July 3, 2000, I "respect" the word relapse. However, I refuse to be intimidated or scared by the fact that there definitely is another drunk left in me.

I'm far from overconfident and realize that there could be another visit to death's door. And this time, the door will open.

I think I was involved in a battle between angels and demons and in the end, the angels prevailed.

They were flying outside the window of a bedroom in my house as I hallucinated away the day and night of July 2, 2000.

On this day, I was going through pure hell on earth in a frustrating contest that involved good versus evil.

I had always been the guy rooting silently for the underdog to emerge as the victor. And looking back, I had been the underdog in this final 12-round fight to the finish.

I'm not a religious man, but I do feel that the will to live came in there somehow. Who had given it to me, when my brain was soaked and fried in alcohol? I doubt I even knew who I was on July 4 and for a couple of days after that. Something had taken place when I was too sick and weak to go on.

I regard myself as a lucky person who is now living on borrowed time and am making the most of it.

Sure I still get upset picking up after the dog and cats or fuming when I'm having a bad day or things aren't going my way. But I have to stop sometimes and think where I had been and all of a sudden, things didn't seem so critical or important.

I've been told many times over the years that I possess writing ability and am a talented writer. I never really believed it though and closed my ears to that line of thought.

Please toss me just a quarter for every byline I slapped on a story. Yes, alot has happened since April 8, 1947, when I was born at St. Francis Hospital.

I've been a New York Yankees baseball fan since my grandfather, William Clancy, pointed me in that direction at the age of seven in 1954.

The New York Giants of the National League were my favorite team in the 1954 World Series against the heavily favored Cleveland Indians, a big winner in the American League.

The Giants upset the Indians in four games straight and my favorite player, Dusty Rhoades hit a couple of home runs.

"We have to make you a Yankee fan," Papa had told me. "And Mickey Mantle will be your favorite player, Billy. He's a good one."

I'm named after William Clancy, my mom's step dad. He called us "Big Bill and Little Bill." And though he died nearly 40 years ago, I'll never forget him.

In Chapter 1, this book will begin with a byline.

I went down to Yankee Stadium a few times with Papa and it seemed "The Mick" would hit a homer for me whether it be left or right handed.

He wound up my baseball idol. I lived and breathed for the talented kid from Commerce, Oklahoma.

This dateline is the most important of my life. It is located a stone's throw from "The House That Ruth Built" at 161st Street and River Avenue.

It was the home of Mickey Mantle.

Bill Tangen
August 6, 2001

CHAPTER 1

Welcome to the Bronx

BRONX, N.Y. - The date is Thursday, July 6, 2000.

A nearby voice asks if I know where I am.

Looking around what appears to be a hospital room, and trying to recall where the last place was that I lay my tired body, my mind seemed to control the mouth and words that came from it. "Montrose" was the quick reply.

It was the female voice of a doctor, nurse or nurses aid I decided, not being able to focus on the face.

My confused and jumbled up mind was about to be thrown for another loss.

"Mr. Tangen, you are at the VA (veterans) hospital in the Bronx, New York. Do you remember anything?"

Somehow, as if by magic, I had changed hospitals from Westchester County's Montrose facility, to the area of New York that the Yankees call home.

I vaguely remember being with my wife at Montrose as we waited for me to be admitted.

Thoughts of getting into a wheel chair to be moved upstairs or saying goodbye to Chris, near the room I'd be observed in, never went into my memory bank.

That date at Montrose was the morning of July 4, 2000 and I had just been driven by my wife for help, help that wound up being of paramount importance. Little did I know that this ride and her recognizing my desperate straits, were the first of a three-pronged effort that would ultimately save my life.

The other two pieces to the life-saving puzzle were Montrose social worker Jackie Beck and psychiatrist Dr. Sheikh, seeing that I needed an immediate transfer to the Bronx, July 5 and Bronx doctors who slaved over me in an emergency room for hours.

My brain was soaked in alcohol and I'd been hallucinating since Sunday when I heard music and the voices of a radio station that only existed in my head.

The voices were so real that I was hearing weather forecasts and a

1

Mamas and Papas song that kept playing over and over.

That was just the tip of the iceberg, because the following day, Monday, my first official day of sobriety, I was to witness people coming after my wife and me with knives.

Earlier Tuesday morning, I was literally running around the neighborhood with no socks on.

I had entered the back seat of a neighbor's car twice, thinking I was in a police car and on the way to headquarters in Port Jervis, N.Y. for stealing car parts with an employe of an area car dealership.

Fantasy and reality had blended into one, and for the next few days I can only guess what things actually occurred and what had only happened in my brain.

I ate breakfast at Montrose, Tuesday, and saw a patient either throw his food on the floor, or smack another patient in the head with a tray.

For over a year, I figured that to be a hallucination, but in July 2001, Jackie told me it actually had occurred.

I may have subconsciously known that an ambulance was transporting me from Montrose to the Bronx.

Hallucinations included my daughter, Tracie, and son-in-law, Mike, being in the ambulance with me. Could they have been in my mind as my dying body was being moved?

In this hallucination, and upon my arrival in New York City, I wound up in a Rite Aid store.

At the store, I was expecting to get back in the ambulance for a ride back to Matamoras, Pa., where I reside.

Instead, a major accident had taken place just down the street, and I was left waiting with no way out of the city.

Something was being done to my arm (IV perhaps?), like a needle going in, but it kept falling out.

Bob Corvino, the head football coach at Port Jervis High School, was having the same thing done to him.

My conclusion to that thought was that my family and athletics were both firmly imbedded in my mind.

Here I was, stranded in New York with no money or way home.

I didn't want to phone Mike to come all the way back to get me and, are you ready for this? The cost of what Corvino and I were having done at Rite Aid was $700 each.

Bob will be pleased to find out that he put my services on his credit card, and I promised to get half the cost from my wife and back to him as soon as possible.

So now, I had a ride home with the Port football coach and his wife, Betty.

Next thing, I was in my back yard sitting on the porch steps.

The steps are where I have sipped plenty of cans of Milwaukee's Best beer until I pulled the plug on drinking at 11:47 p.m., July 2, 2000.

I had always sensed that my final sip would be taken at either 11:47 (my flight number at Lackland AFB, Texas, boot camp) or at 11:59 p.m., the last possible moment before the next day and a fresh start.

Those two times had been logged into notebooks for years and years as I tried, without success to kick the drinking habit.

Chris and a lot of other people were at my home, as there was going to be a party involving workers from K-Mart and the Rite Aid stores.

Sitting on the steps, the needle kept coming out of my arm and some hospital worker kept telling me what to do, to keep it in.

We were invited to Joe Viglione's house (former Port football coach) to eat, as his mother was going to make up a big batch of spaghetti.

Keep in mind, that all of this seemed so real.

We weren't sure whether or not to attend, even though this was a genuine Italian feast to take place just a block away.

Of course, I suggested we go and pick up some beer, but my wife contended that she would get it.

Perhaps while I was wrangling with a needle that kept popping out, in actuality, the ambulance ride from Montrose to the Bronx VA emergency room was taking place.

I'm told that a CAT scan was administered and that my liver and kidneys were breaking down.

Over a year later, on July 18, 2001, at 10:45 a.m., I came face to face with one of the people who saved my life.

"Your body was dying, Bill," Jackie Beck said in a Montrose hallway. "But your brain didn't want to give up."

Jackie explained the goings on that preceeded the move to the Bronx.

"You were seeing and hearing things that we didn't," she said of herself and several staff members.

"We observed and listened to you," she continued. "One conclusion was that you were schizophrenic, but I didn't think so. Your past didn't have that and alcohol was your only problem. I believed you were psychotic."

Schizophrenic is delusional behavior, while being psychotic is a mental disorder affecting the total personality.

"You had alcohol poisoning and we had watched you and what was going on," she went on. "Some times we know what is happening within 72 hours, but with one guy, it was five days."

This professional kept looking at me and smiling.

"You are lucky to be alive and here today," she asserted. "It makes me feel so good to see that you made it all the way back."

Jackie said I became very irritated at the situation I was experiencing.

"You were looking in a mirror at yourself," she stated. "And, were upset that we couldn't see a female relative of yours (sister), named Anne. 'Can't you see her? She's right here' you kept saying while looking in the mirror at yourself."

3

Jackie said she didn't want me to panic as an ambulance was being arranged.

"I entertained you as they were preparing," she said. "We didn't know if we'd ever see you again."

This is what 35 years of hard beer drinking had resulted in.

I was the two-fisted drinking man a la baseball player and manager Billy Martin and writer Jimmy Breslin.

I'd been in a couple scrapes with the law, but always managed to land on my feet. And my writing always seemed the thing that kept me going.

But sometime after 9:30 a.m. on July 4, 2000, I was en route to an emergency room. I would join the other two million people in the Bronx, not as a permanent resident or Yankee baseball player, but as a very much in trouble patient.

I had been a dynamic writer and loved sports. Now I was on an emotional roller coaster that was threatening to jump the tracks and kill me.

My organs had come a whisker from shutting down. My brain was short-circuiting.

As Jackie Beck said in a phone call to my wife, "Bill had a near death experience."

And so, at the age of 53, I was all but ready to pack it in.

Jackie called it absolutely the worst case she had seen in five years.

It seemed very typical of me. Everything I did seemed to be dramatic and this was no different.

Before leaving Montrose for the Bronx, I was in an observation room, alone.

I was the only one that occupied the room, which contained about eight beds, four to a side.

I put my gear, such as shaving cream and toothpaste on the floor near the foot of my bunk and lay down for awhile.

Staring at the wall and mind torn in a thousand directions, images suddenly appeared like magic on the wall, which had been transformed into a large screen television set.

There was a game show on the screen. It was a show that had a spinning wheel that was located on the floor.

Three of the contestants, standing at various points on the wheel, were Derek Jeter and Andy Pettitte of the New York Yankees and Michael J. Fox. Meanwhile, in the studio audience David Letterman appeared. His mother and step-brother were also on the show.

In the glass enclosed office (which does exist) was the publisher of a paper I worked for back home.

She was typing on a computer and ignoring my pleas to be let out of the room, so I could go and meet two doctors who were waiting for me downstairs.

These visions were happening either on July 4 or the morning of July

4

5. My last drink had been the evening of July 2.

Someone either real or imagined, told me that I had to go to the cafeteria down the hall in order to eat.

The last thing I remember, prior to being in the Bronx, was sitting at a cafeteria seat and watching people.

Meals were brought to the tables by workers at Montrose.

The next thing I recall is being told I was in the Bronx.

I had experience tons of hallucinations back home before I ever reached Montrose.

The final day of consuming beer for me (July 2, 2000) was my 18th straight day of drinking.

Earlier in the day, my sister had driven her truck, to Rite Aid for a 12-pack of Milwaukee's Best beer (cans). It was to be the final 144 ounces of beer I would ever consume.

Sitting out in her back yard, and hearing the constant music in my head, the realization was there, that I was too sick to travel.

Beer had always calmed me down in the past and why couldn't it happen again.

There had been so many Sunday mornings that I agonized for noon to arrive, so that I could exorcise the demons that were ruining my body.

Many times I'd walked the bridge that links New York and Pennsylvania, dehydrated, weak from puking and wondering if I'd pass out and maybe even die before I could introduce alcohol into my system. I had been a "hair of the dog" kind of guy, ever since my Air Force days.

Prior to the 18 straight days, my drinking had been on cruise control for 78 consecutive days, from Sunday, March 26 through June 11. That bender had been preceeded by 10 sober days.

Prior to my final binge, I layed off suds from June 12 through June 14.

Back on June 30, I had fallen in my garage and banged the back of the old noggin pretty good in what I figured to be a blackout. And, I began spitting solid blood for about an hour.

The day and night of July 3, I experienced terrifying hallucinations.

Some happened while I lay in bed and others while sitting on the back porch and later walking over to Port Jervis for a 40 ounce bottle of beer I'd never get to open.

I sat on that porch, where I used to happily drink, looking at a clothes line in the dark.

Suddenly, dead animals appeared on the clothes line. But when I ventured off the steps and blinked my eyes, they went away.

Under the line, live horses, deer and even elephants were walking around. Again, if I blinked, the vision was gone but upon blinking again, they reappeared.

There had been no drinking in close to 24 hours at this point, but walking around, I stumbled two times over dead deer who were laying on the ground.

This was the real onset of nightmarish thoughts and obvious short-circuiting of the brain.

To this day, I can't believe that I actually was able to walk, in the dark, over a mile each way, to get a 40 oz bottle of Silver Thunder Malt Liquor (beer) at a Port Jervis convenience store.

It would be hours and hours, including the overnight period, that I went through visions, sounds and unbelievable nervous energy that had me up and down the stairs dozens of times and rooting through cardboard boxes in a bedroom, looking for hidden people who might be out to get my wife and me.

The countless hallucinations were sharp, clear, vivid and most of all believable to me.

They include all of these scary and tension-filled thoughts.

*I was issued a fine by the local police department ($125) for not picking up after my dog (although I always do in real life).

Carrying a flashlight to the scene of the alleged crime, I could find no waste and walked to the police department to explain that fact. I was let off with no fine.

I don't know if I was actually on a dog walk when these visions occurred. But if anyone would have asked, I'd have told them that it really happened.

*During the daytime of July 3, I looked out the bedroom window at a car parked in the driveway.

My wife, daughter and grandchild had gone to eat lunch (in reality).

However, when I squinted and blinked, I saw four heads in the car including my wife, daughter, grandchild and my mother. I blinked again and the people were gone.

*Chris and I were in a motorcycle type club that made Hell's Angels look like child's play.

You had to endure plenty of pain and take unbelievable risks, including maneuvering around in high places and running endurance races with a stop watch monitoring you.

Meetings were at my house and then there was a hideout type place where members went, at the dead end of a road.

The road was guarded by club members (male and female).

If you did something wrong, you literally received kicks in the ass by people in the club.

There was constant physical and mental torture going on and there was no way you could quit or resign from the club.

If you tried, the leader of the club would either have you killed, or sever limbs or fingers from your body.

*My sister Anne and myself stayed over at Atlanta Braves pitcher John Rocker's house.

Rocker is the guy who really did lace into New Yorkers in a Sports

Illustrated story and wound up being suspended from baseball.

His house was near a hospital, and I recall that a neighbor and fellow sports fan, Ray Wagner Sr., was there as well.

A psychiatrist dropped by and some black guy that worked with him, talked me into signing a form, that wound up trapping me into going to the hospital.

My sister was crying because she thought she, not I, needed the shrink.

She was up near the ceiling, standing near clothes and hangers that slid on a rod.

Decked out in a long dress, she refused to come down from there and liked being the center of attention.

She was pissing me off, because I wanted her safely down from there and she was holding me up from scouting out the hospital's parking lot for my wife's car and my clothes, which were in the car.

Rocker was extremely tired, and the next morning he was leaving on a road trip.

I aggravated him because all night long I was trying to fix door locks in his house. This kept him awake and robbed him of valuable sleep.

Rocker's brother, father and mother weren't thrilled with me either.

Rocker left in the morning, caught a flight and on the radio, we heard him hit a first inning homer.

Wagner drove a big truck into the driveway at the side of the house and later, we all sat around a dining room table while sitting in "lazy boy" type chairs.

Sometimes you could see people's faces and other times you couldn't, because material from the top of the chair was long enough to be placed over your face.

There is a rather large black employee who worked in the dining hall at Montrose and I'm wondering if I had any contact with him during my visions and while in the process of departing for the Bronx.

Could he be the black guy that got me to sign forms, in my hallucination?

*The night before leaving for Montrose, I was sure there were two midgets hiding in the cedar closet of the bedroom.

From the closet, I could hear voices coming from boxes (with lids) that were being used for storage purposes.

The same was true of a second closet in the room.

The hallway light was on and the bedroom door pulled open.

I was constantly reassured by my wife, Chris, that there was nobody hiding in the confines of the boxes and closets, but I didn't believe that to be true.

And so, I spent my time, literally racing in and out of my bed, to open lids to boxes, until every last box was examined.

Even then, the torment wouldn't end.

The overnight period was spent stopping people from entering windows in the room, plus running up and down stairs to halt those who tried to sneak in my front or back door.

The desperados came in waves, first just one or two people trying to trick me. Then countless killers who wanted my wife and myself dead.

Sweat poured down my face and back as I dealt with each case.

My heart hammered out of my chest. And, in retrospect, I wonder how close I could have been to suffering a heart attack.

*A guy I know, who owns an area dealership, was backing me for vice-president of that torture-driven motorcycle gang. He was president of the club.

I had to run from my home in Matamoras, Pa., to a bridge that connects Pennsylvania and New York (over the Delaware River), in a certain amount of time, which was being calculated on a stop watch.

The bridge was just one check point on a long and grueling run that would end at the gang's hideout near the end of a dead end street, at what used to be Joyland Beach, in Port Jervis (N.Y.).

Telling the dealership fellow that I had heart problems and couldn't risk the run, and must resign from the gang, didn't go over well. I feared repercussions from gang members.

Trees out in front of my house served as perfect camouflage for gang members who wanted to be hidden.

There was a go-cart-like vehicle under a front bush and bees buzzing near it.

Near my picnic table were two girls, who were talking. I could see them, then blink, and they were gone.

The dealership guy had all kinds of initiations ready for me, including driving his car in my neighborhood.

It was my job, to quickly see which way he was approaching my house and quickly take off, on foot, to catch him before he could drive past me.

As my hallucinations had me running, I later learned that in the real world, I was running around the neighborhood at like 6:30 a.m., July 4th, in my stocking feet.

I actually did get in a neighbor's car, which was located in his driveway.

Dennis walked me home that horrible morning, and watched me sweat, profusely.

He later told me he was worried that I was going to die right in front of him.

He delivered me, out of harm's way, to my wife, for the impending trip to the hospital.

*In the daytime of Monday, July 3, 2000, I saw five or six small angels and demons flying outside the bedroom window and talking to me.

All but one of the flying visions were of the male gender.

The female liked me, but the others kept shouting the word "loser" in buzzing unison, as they made fun of me.

"If I was a loser, I wouldn't be speaking to you," I told them, probably out loud

I carried on a conversation with them, and from time to time, they would fly away, only to return moments later.

"I'm tired, I have to sleep now," I explained.

As they flew away, I recognized that one of them had the voice of Hank Young, who passed away quite some time ago.

It may sound far out, but could it be that my nearly-destroyed mind, was trying to tell me that Hank Young was reaching me, to let me know that I was fighting for my life and had to be strong?

*The night before leaving for Montrose, a girl named "Linda" was in the back bedroom of our house.

I was downstairs, but heard her voice pleading with me to come upstairs.

I refused to do so, instead figuring that when I could no longer hear her voice, I would be safe.

Linda informed me that if I didn't follow her orders, she would have the power to make my dog (now 17), Penny, die.

When I said "no", an exact replica of Penny, as a puppy, lay dead on the hardwood floor, between the living room and dining room.

Sitting on the edge of the coffee table, I focused (the best I could) on my dog, as she lay sleeping on the couch. Then my eyes moved to the floor, where that exact image appeared.

My heart began hammering out of my chest and I became filled with fear and dread.

Was my dog, who sat next to me as a pup, during the 1984 Olympics, really dead, either on the couch or floor? And what about Linda, was she real or imagined?

Suddenly, as if by magic, the dead dog disappeared.

I kept telling myself that a jumbled mind was making me see and hear these horrible visions and voices. Yet something inside of me, said that some of this could be real.

Paranoia had been my constant companion for many hours already. However, as I look back, hallucinations increased, as time without beer, was going by. At some point later on, I decided that somehow getting money and reaching a store for alcohol, was of paramount importance.

It seems that Linda was running for some type of high political office, (are you ready for this) against God. Seeing that Linda represented evil and God is good, this thought had to be reverting back to that demons versus angels game.

She threatened that if I endorsed God for this office, she would make the dog die.

At that point, I remember actually saying a prayer, out loud, to God. I told him I believed in him and suddenly Linda's voice began fading away.

From downstairs, I could barely hear her, as she spoke through the wall, located at the foot of our shower.

I remained mum, but when I moved even an inch, she could see me, thereby knowing that my ears still heard her speak.

It was shortly after this that I actually walked down to my sister's house and borrowed enough money to buy a 40 oz. Silver Thunder bottle of beer, over in Port Jervis.

"You scared me," Anne said, after I had been sober for awhile. "Your eyes were wild and you looked right through me. You demanded the money and frightened me. I knew something was really wrong."

At roughly 11 p.m., the night of July 2, 2000, I was headed, on foot, for the bridge, knowing that this beer purchase was probably the last of my life.

My battle plan, like it been been so many times, was to knock off the drinking prior to midnight and to get a clean start the next day.

I remember seeing, and talking to, what I regarded as "young punks" on the bridge as I started across the Delaware River.

And, like it had been for hours, the sights and sounds continued, and they were to accelerate during this little jaunt.

*On this walk from hell, houses and mountains were talking to me.

As I walked by houses in Matamoras and over in Port, the house, in a loud and eerie voice, would either say "Linda" or "no Linda", over and over, as if trying to influence my decision about who I wanted to win, evil or good.

Not wanting to verbally tell anyone what my decision in this "election" would be, I suddenly focused on

people, who were intent on coming after me and inflicting bodily harm.

The unsteady and hallucination-filled walk suddenly became a jog and then an all out sprint for my life.

I maneuvered around cars that were parked on the street and had numerous obstacles to deal with, on this dash.

These frenzied savages, hunted me and had one obvious common denominator in mind, to seriously hurt or kill me.

In my twisted and spinning out of control mind, I told myself that the "Linda decision" would come at midnight, as I sat home with a bottle of beer in hand.

If I decided to quit drinking, then July 3 would be the official date of sobriety, or I could opt to build on the 40 ouncer and continue on a merry-go-round of denial.

I have no clue how I managed to count out the correct money for my beer purchase.

But now, beer in hand, I weaved toward the bridge after being confronted on Brown Street, by a kid with a knife in his hand.

By the time I reached the Matamoras Police Department, just four blocks from home, I saw two policemen outside the station, near their cars.

"They are after me," I told one, as I pointed up the street. "Please take me home, I live only up a few blocks."

The cop gazed at what I was holding and then to where my finger was pointing. "There is nobody there," he said. "But he was there just a second ago," I replied. "He must be hiding."

Fantasy and reality were clashing again, this time in front of the police. Leave it to me, in having that problem result in a brush with the law.

The cop would not give me a ride home.

"You have been drinking and I don't want to see you get into trouble," he said. And with that, he confiscated the bottle of beer.

To this day, I wonder what would have happened, had I made it home with the beverage.

Would I die of a heart attack or stroke, with bottle in hand? Or was it possible to take my own life, in this tormented and twisted struggle that involved my very existence?

In the area of midnight, Chris was to arrive home from her job, at the Vernon (New Jersey) A&P, to see a profusely sweating, hunted and mentally tormented man, who was totally out of control.

Still ahead of me, during the overnight period, were visions of people on ladders trying to enter the window, located in the back bedroom of the house.

The bedroom I stayed in, used to be occupied by my oldest daughter, Tracie.

My wife, not wanting to smell the rank odor of booze night after night, more or less remanded me to the other room, months and months prior.

I referred to the room as "the drunk tank". And for the most part, that is exactly what it was.

One thing should be addressed here.

It would be a misconception to indicate that drinking dominated my life since the teenage years. That simply is not true.

The consequences of heavy drinking didn't emerge totally, until the 1990s. Especially the last half of the decade.

Prior to that, I was in tip-top shape mentally and covered my athletic events in a professional manner.

In the 1990s, I began skipping assignments when I became too drunk or hung over. After all, it has been proven, that alcoholism is a progressive disease.

When I was high, reeking of alcohol or experiencing "the sweats", I was very seldom seen at a game.

I refused to expose myself to the embarrassment of the situation and would rather beg off the event completely, rather than show up sick.

After seeing my condition, Christine knew that this wasn't the ordinary shape she was used to finding me in.

"You were a mess," she recalls. "You never slowed down and had me up all night. And in the early morning, I found you outdoors, in socks and sweating terribly. I told the neighbor (Dennis), that I was taking you to the hospital."

At the time, I was probably already in delirium tremens (DT's) and had alcohol poisoning.

As the minutes and hours ticked by, a normal alcohol withdrawal would have been taking place. But I felt no such sensation. In fact, I didn't feel at all. I barely noticed that my heart was pumping a mile a minute, sweat was pouring off of me, plus visions and sounds were totally enveloping me.

It was morning, when the car pulled out of the driveway, with a destination of the Montrose facility, located across the Hudson river, more than 45 miles away.

*In my mind it was suppertime. And on the way there, I told Chris that some very tall trees, along Interstate Route 84 east, were "waving at me and some of them were walking."

Chris said later, that I seemed to know I was in trouble and wanted any help that was available.

"I was afraid I'd have a hard time getting you there," she said. "I agreed with you, no matter what you were saying, just to get the trip over with."

She saw me "scared and afraid" for hours, a condition she had never seen me in, during our almost 30 years of marriage.

To this day, I owe my life to Christine Diane Goble Tangen. Without her, I would not have survived.

*Being in my fictional gang, felt totally real.

Ray Wagner, Tim (a neighbor) and his oldest son, plus others in the group, were regular people in the daytime, but turned into absolute hell raisers at night.

Quitting the gang, meant being tortured or killed, so there was no way out of this hell on earth. I was trapped.

Meetings were on Thursday nights and a big and brutally mean black guy, was the gang's president.

His presence, in my crackling brain, made my heart pound all the faster.

He regularly raped the women in this sick club, and often stabbed fellow members, or cut off parts of their bodies, when they had disobeyed orders.

*On July 3, while lying in bed, I knew that any moment someone was coming through the bedroom door, and would be stabbing me in the stomach area, with a long knife.

I couldn't bear to watch the knife go in, and when I closed my eyes, the person, the knife and the pain were instantly gone.

*Doctor Frank Simpson is a well-known veterinarian in Port Jervis, and a helluva nice guy.

But in my hallucinations, he appeared at my side yard picnic table.

As I gazed out the window, I saw him talking softly to someone, and then glancing up to my room. In an instant, I knew he was conspiring to come up those stairs and that my life would be in danger

*While staring at the bedroom ceiling, I could make the light fixture in that ceiling move and return to its original position, just by blinking my eyes.

*In the early morning hours of July 4, the Port Jervis police were coming to pick me up and take me to city hall for arraignment (burglary).

I was told to be by the side of my street in 10 minutes.

Each time the police cruiser came by the house, it speeded up and I couldn't catch up to it.

I was in my socks (no shoes) and was running and out of breath. (This probably was occurring as I really ran around my neighborhood).

Gary Scales, a childhood friend and usher at my wedding, dropped by the house and told me he was in trouble with the law, too. He had also been busted for burglary (in Milford, Pa.) and was also to be picked up.

He slowly was reading a list of charges against him and I was frantic, worrying about the time, and how we had to be by the road soon.

I had already missed getting in the cruiser on a couple of attempts and knew that with each time I was late, more jail time would be added to my sentence.

During all of this foolishness, the owner of a local car dealership, wanted to use the bathroom.

While in the room, he scribbled some notes on the floor, tipping me off on what to say to the police.

Matamoras Pa. Police Chief Joe Roeder was one of the cops that was to pick me up. But that changed, and it would be his dad, coming to transport me.

"Fish" Scales decided to drive his own car, and suddenly my fate was to change.

Instead of a police station destination, Chris would be taking me to a detox. And, in reality, she was taking me to Montrose, where I would be issued hospital "greens" and asked endless questions.

*While in the bathroom at Montrose, I looked around for a way to escape. I had heard a doctor talking to my wife, outside the bathroom door, And, I looked around the room for any way I could get out of there.

In the real world, she never uttered a word to a doctor outside that door. The hallucinations were continuing in the facility, although Chris says I appeared quiet and very much in control.

She did notice though, that I was grinning at nobody in particular.

*I think I ate lunch in the Montrose cafeteria and while there, noticed that Ralph Smith, a former neighbor from Lyman Avenue in Port Jervis, was at a nearby table.

Another hospital patient gave me some change, so I could use a pay phone to dial up John Rocker's house .

Two things occurred in that cafeteria, which I later figured to be hallucinations. At a visit with Jackie Beck over a year later, I learned the one had actually occurred.

I saw a guy advance across the cafeteria floor and bash another person in the head with his tray. And in another instance, a patient bitched about the food being "no good," said he wouldn't eat it and dumped it on the floor. I picked up dishes and food off the floor, of one of the trays that had been misused.

The tray on the head maneuver, actually did happen.

*In the large observation room, where I was first assigned to sleep, I saw David Letterman, through the small window of a shower room door.

He was on an exercise bike and was nursing some type of injury.

I wanted to speak with him and do an interview, and he tried to unlatch the locked door with his foot, while on the bike.

He complained about "the woman in the office" never being around, to let him out.

I waited at a table, with pen, paper and questions ready, to do the interview, once he was out of the room. However, he slipped away when I wasn't looking.

On July 5, 2000, not much more than 24 hours after arriving at Montrose, I was transported to the borough that the Yankees call home.

I was in the Bronx VA emergency room for countless hours, as doctors and nurses probably toiled feverishly, to save my life.

I recall none of the ambulance ride or emergency room. The next thing I remember, was being asked if I knew where I was.

In a blue notebook where I took notes after being released, is a written notation of having reached 108 days of sobriety.

"I have attended one Alcoholics Anonymous meeting, in Milford (Pa.), on Sunday, August 27," the words explain. "Some guy was celebrating 90 days of sobriety."

At that point in time, (at the meeting) I was in my 56th day. As I type these words, I currently have been sober for one year, three months and 15 days (as of Oct. 16, 2001). And, I was the guy that couldn't reach 90 consecutive days, 87 being my longest attempt.

I remember being at a meeting in Montgomery, N.Y., in my 87th day.

A girl had "slipped" and went back to drinking. As she cried, she was consoled by fellow AA members. That went into my memory bank and on the 88th day, I was swilling suds again. I realized that I would still be accepted, even if I screwed up. So, why not?

As a teenager in high school, I was an athlete (basketball guard, track and field long jump and triple jump) and never touched beer, or any kind of alcohol, for that matter.

Prior to my teen years, the only contact I had with beer, were small glasses of Schaefer, consumed with food, at Matante's house (old lady friend of my dad's family). And, it was always just one small glass per meal.

I figure that these days, there is no choice to be made, of whether to drink or not.

Should I decide to pop open a beer, I have no idea how long I would last, before getting a non-reversible death sentence. That is a hell of a price to pay, for sloshing down the suds in order to get high.

*Weeks before experiencing the horrible visual hallucinations, I had them to a lesser degree, as I was hearing songs in my head.

I went through the whole nine yards, including the weather forecast, and a DJ announcing things. And of course, I "enjoyed" a whole list of songs, including a Mamas and Papas tune that played over and over.

By plugging my ears, the sound diminished, but the songs followed me to every room of the house and even outside, when I went for walks.

The second or third time I heard these songs, I thought "man, I am having hallucinations, how can I get rid of this?"

Dennis and his wife, next door, played oldies music while they worked outside, beautifying their yard.

And I recall putting my fingers in my ears and walking to the bedroom window, to make sure there really weren't songs playing outside, on the radio. But the tunes were originating from me.

One night, my wife arrived home from work, while I was hearing religious music.

As she tended to the hamsters, I repeated words to the songs as I heard them. The terrible situation was driving me to distraction and I kept telling myself "this isn't really happening, so try to calm down."

*The first real visual hallucination happened during the winter.

I had a New York Jets football game on TV upstairs, while working in the cellar. And, suddenly I decided to go upstairs and check on the score.

When I reached the landing to the cellar, my calm demeanor was transformed into panic.

There was some type of table on the landing, that was preventing me from reaching the closed door.

I was blockaded in my own house, and was sure there were burglars upstairs, who had quietly sealed me off.

While I sweated profusely, I scrambled across the top of the table, opened the door and quickly ran out the back of the house.

Figuring the burglars to still be inside the house, and worrying that

15

they would kill my cats and dog, Penny, I literally sprinted to the local police headquarters. Nobody was at the site, so I ran a short distance, to my sister's house.

Phone calls were placed to my wife, (who was at work), and the police.

While Chris traveled home from the Vernon, New Jersey A&P, in a panic of her own, the police arrived and went to my home. Of course they found nothing.

I flatly refused to go in the house until it had been completely searched. The only thing on the landing, was an empty Milwaukee's Best beer can.

Had I imagined this thing? No way.

For days and days, I stuck to my guns, really believing that someone had entered my dwelling and left, table and all, while I was at my sister's house.

A scary fact about that night, was the fact that I had consumed less than eight cans of beer that day. Had the days, months and years piled up and taken this type of toll?

I looked up "hallucinations" on the internet to see if this could be what I was experiencing.

A definition I found was "an apparent perception of an external object when no such object is present."

Other information on the subject, showed that substance abuse can be a cause of hallucinations .

Counter stimulation, includes "using headphones or reading out loud (to counter the sounds). And, for an increase in external stimulation "play music."

Also on the internet, "withdrawal" is described as "severe anxiety, tremors, hallucinations and convulsions."

While I don't remember leaving Montrose or arriving in the Bronx, I'm told that I had to be restrained, spent plenty of time in the emergency room (while my wife tried to learn my status), and nearly didn't make it.

My liver and kidneys were damaged, I was given an MRI, and woke up in a hospital room, with an IV in my right wrist. Bottles hung from a contraption at the right side of my bed, and beyond them, appeared a panorama of Bronx, N.Y.

Somehow, emergency personnel had countered an alcohol-filled brain.

I was a very sick person and was extremely lucky to even have the opportunity to open these eyelids and try to focus on the surroundings.

It was Jackie Beck, my guardian angel social worker, who went to any length, in keeping my anxious family informed of my situation.

I firmly believe that hours before, when my fate was in doubt, I had made the choice to fight for my life. And, someone, or some force, answered my prayers.

My body had become accustomed to a phenomenal amount of beer.

Most days, I was good for at least (12) 12 ounce cans of Milwaukee's Best beer, while also adding a 40 ounce bottle of Silver Thunder Malt Liquor. I averaged 18 ounces of beer an hour, for like 10 hours. Then, this same cycle would begin all over again, the following day.

During these difficult days on end, I usually continued to function, writing stories, doing things around the house, and always contemplating where and when I would secure my next supply of alcohol.

I suffered through hangovers and withdrawals, that reduced me to a bundle of nerves. There were numerous trips to the bathroom and my eyes looked like road maps. When I wasn't sick, I was high as a kite, usually turning up the music, to block out the reality of life.

Getting the money to continue this existence, wasn't a piece of cake.

My sister helped me out countless times, because she identified with what I was going through.

It seemed like every day, I would be borrowing $5.09 (the price of a 12-pack) from her, and heading to the store for my next fix.

A lot of times the going was real rough, especially on the trip over a bridge and across the railroad tracks, to a Rite Aid store in Port Jervis.

Most of the time, on these horrible mornings, I would stop on the way home, sit at a chair in her back yard, and slowly sip my first can. Sometimes the can wouldn't stay down, and would come up violently, just as cold as when it went down my throat.

It would take two cans and about 30-45 minutes, for the nerves to calm, and to be able to start functioning like a human being. Many times I scared Anne, because of how sick I appeared and acted.

Sometimes I would beg for money from my wife, and that process seemed to take unbelievable time, as my body craved alcohol. One time, I thought I had successfully lifted a couple of dollars from Chris' pocketbook, only to find myself detected through a clear shower curtain. I was not above any devious plan, to secure money.

I sat in diners while she ate breakfast, but couldn't touch a bite myself.

Instead, I fidgeted in my seat, wondering if I could make the half hour without getting sick. Sometimes, I would have to leave the premises to get air. My life had become a mess.

While in the Bronx, thirst and the television were my constant companions.

I left my TV on all night (private room), and sometimes woke up at 5 a.m. or so, with CHIPS on the screen. I watched the Mets-Yanks subway series (Yanks' Roger Clemens beaning Mike Piazza), and it was strange being here, with a game taking place almost within my sight, at Yankee Stadium.

At night, the twinkling lights of the Bronx, from houses, buildings and cars, were beautiful. I gazed out there and wondered what life was all about, why had I been spared?

My strength was lacking and I felt very shaky and uneasy, as I slowly made my way to the bathroom, or to take a shower, across the hall.

I looked forward to meals and hoarded orange juice, so that it would last into the night. And, I swigged ice water like it was going out of style.

There were countless blood samples taken, and blood pressure was monitored constantly. This was the perfect place, for Dracula and his vampire friends to hang out.

The uniform of the day, was green pajamas and blue slippers. I still have a pair of the slippers, with the black soles, as a reminder of where I had been, in body, and in the progression of my life.

A nurse named Bernadette Daria, was especially nice, and smuggled me in orange juice at night, on two different occasions.

This setting was to be my home from July 5 through July 12.

Except for the guy who was shouting every day and night from down the hall, this was to be my first escape into solitude. And, even though I was restricted, phone calls from my wife and daughter in Pennsylvania, plus youngest daughter in South Carolina, helped me move forward.

My doctor's name was Rita M. Sachdev, and I believe she was the first face I recall seeing, upon coming back to the real world. She was the one who asked me if I knew where I was. This petite lady, who sported a winning smile, asked just a couple of questions, and told me to get some rest.

Genuine concern showed on her face that first day, and she was happy for me, the day I boarded a bus back to Montrose.

I lay in the Bronx bed, weak, yet serene, not knowing what in God's name, the future held for me.

A trip back to Montrose was a certainty, and a rehab requirement was probably in the cards. But that wasn't on the front burner yet. I moved from bed to window, observing another twinkling light show, as the Bronx completed another day, and settled into quiet darkness.

I became comfortable in the Bronx, and was delighted when the IV was removed and there was freedom to move about, and shower as much as I wanted.

Finally able to shave, nurses were no long greeted by a "wolf man" but someone who began looking and feeling, years younger.

Soon, the day to leave the Bronx (July 12), arrived. I was to depart, by bus, in the afternoon for Montrose.

All went smoothly, until I was informed that civilian clothes were needed to make my getaway. And of course, my clothes were locked up, back at Montrose.

Halloween arrived early in that Bronx hospital, on this summer afternoon.

Battling the clock, and weak as a kitten, I accompanied a nurse, down the elevator, to a huge room filled with used clothing and shoes.

This was no time to inspect items for the perfect wardrobe. And so, the race to make the bus, was on.

I briskly walked to the bus, decked out in checked shorts (I never wear shorts), a short-sleeved Marlboro shirt (I don't smoke), no socks, and black tie shoes (one had no shoelaces), that were the size of canoes.

I wobbled off the bus at Montrose, like some bowery bum, disorientated and hopelessly lost.

Once I got my bearings, after roughly walking (shuffling in my canoes) 10 city miles, I wound up in the room where this all started, just over a week earlier.

The next step, was issuance of another set of green pajamas, and being led back to that big observation room, where I had "talked" to David Letterman.

This move from the Bronx to Montrose, should have been filmed as a comedy.

At the Bronx, I had been in a private room on Floor C.

My main responsibilities were knowing where the TV remote was, waiting for food and drink, and gazing out the window.

Then, suddenly, it was over, and I was leaving with a dizzy head, and looking like a circus clown.

Letterman's "exercise room", actually turned out to be a shower facility and bathroom.

Patients "sneaked" cigarettes in to the room, nervously looking around, not wanting to get caught by nurses or employees.

The fact that I had been lucky enough not to go through death's door, hadn't really sunk in yet.

My mind didn't seem to belong in my body, I felt like someone else, not me. I just couldn't comprehend the seriousness of my situation.

As I processed back in, my mind focused on Jackie, Lori (who had helped serve lunch), and Marty, a nurse who no doubt remembered me as a raving lunatic. Soon, I would be back in their midst.

I had to meet, at a large rectangular table, with doctors, nurses, social workers and for all I know, the entire population of New York State. I was under the microscope, big time.

I was observed, watched and listened to. Notes were taken, and any flaw, twitch, or hesitation, was probably detected immediately.

"Is this man alright? Is he sane or insane? Can we ever let him out into the world?" That is what I believe they were thinking, as they perused me. As I recall, all I wanted was out of this facility. So, I made sure I didn't show nervousness, and that I comprehended what was going on.

This little task, was far from easy. In reality, my mind was still far from sharp, and I was extremely unsteady on my feet. In one test administered, I was to stand on one foot and lift the other. I could only do so, for just seconds, before wavering sideways. That shaky balance, along with a test for my memory, weigh- ins, plus blood pressure and blood samples, were viewed, relentlessly.

Somehow, I had started out with Jackie Beck as my social worker, on the first visit to Montrose. But now, I had been placed in the hands of Sam Cohen.

It wound up being a big break for me, because when he learned all beds were occupied at the 31-day rehab I would be attending, he indicated there was a possibility, I could go home for a couple of days, before returning to Montrose. That was an opening I began exploiting immediately.

Jackie was far from happy with this development, afraid that I would "fall through the cracks" as she put it, and be back out there drinking again.

I stayed at Montrose two nights, the second in an area with psych patients, one of whom, insisted he was going to have a baby.

On the evening of July 13, I walked to the TV room and watched a movie, "Christine", a flick about a car (Plymouth) that made a teenager become possessed. Meanwhile, I was obsessed with a "Christine" too, my wife, who would be picking me up the next day.

I had already been through one memorable July 14, in my life.

On July 14, 1967, I left Plattsburgh AFB, New York, en route home on leave, before shipping out for Andersen AFB, Guam (Pacific), which was scheduled to be my home for 18 months.

This July 14, I was up early, as medication was being dispensed in the hall.

I sat in the cafeteria, waiting and waiting, to eat, as patient after patient was having blood drawn. I had to have it done, one last time.

Finally, 11 a.m. arrived, and Chris was in the hall, waiting for me.

We hugged endlessly. I think it was then, that I finally comprehended that this reunion, wasn't a sure thing, just nine days prior. My days away from home, seemed like years, and yet, it had been less than two weeks.

I went off to a room to shed my greens, and changed into civilian jeans and white sneakers. It felt great, just to be dressed differently.

When Chris and myself hugged Jackie, a certain warm feeling came over me. There were three people near tears, as I said my goodbyes, promising, and fully intending, to return for the 31-day rehab, beginning July 27.

Jackie was very worried that without a support system, such as the 31-day rehab, I would be back drinking in a month or two.

I reassured her (and myself, silently), that the drinking was all done. And during my final hug with this attractive lady, I knew in my heart, that a brand new life was already underway.

I had been living a life of choices all my life. But the biggest one of all, was waiting for me outside the front gate of Montrose.

I gave Jackie my word, that the alcohol was finished and that I would come back to Montrose. I wound up batting .500, and that one hit in two plate appearances, was damn important.

We stopped at a Boston Chicken, in Middletown, to eat on the way home.

I still felt very nervous and it was hard swallowing the food. The excitement of the day and the prospect of this new life, were taking their toll.

Our daughter Tracie, her husband Mike, and granddaughter, Sarah, stopped by the house, later on. They all seemed happy and relieved to see "Poppy" home.

There was a Montrose doctor's appointment set for July 20, and I was to return there one week following that, to begin the rehab, at 8 a.m. in building 54.

July 20, I traveled back across the Hudson River to Montrose for an examination, that I found out, wasn't needed.

A small foreign, female doctor, (from the Philippines), with a quick reassuring smile, viewed her computer screen for all of my information, then turned to me.

"You don't need to be looked at," she said. "This is remarkable. Your liver is much better, and your kidneys and cholesterol are both fine." My weight, that morning, had been 180 pounds

She congratulated me on the fact that my grandchildren weren't going to lose their grandfather. And that there was more living to do, for me. She wished me luck on my upcoming 31-day rehab. At this point, I was in my 18th day of sobriety.

Chris and I enjoyed lunch at a Cracker Barrel in Fishkill, on the way home.

Tenseness was starting to subside, but my mind kept fast forwarding a week, and to a 31-day task, that I wasn't eager to tackle.

Other than a few days in Reston, Virginia, for a sportswriters seminar, at the American Press Institute (1976), I hadn't been away from home, since the military.

I wouldn't have the luxuries of my TV, papers to read in the cellar, or walks with Chris, to Turkey Hill (store) at night. I flat out, didn't want to go.

If anyone tells you, that quitting the drinking of beer, will reduce your weight, run as far away from them as possible.

At least in my situation, weight began to accumulate, as I began eating well, for the first time in years and years.

As of Nov. 16, 2000, I was 5 7 ½" and 205 pounds. And now, Nov. 13, 2001, about 18 more pounds have been tacked on.

I figure that this obstacle can be overcome, and have a 155-pound goal in mind, for sometime in 2002.

The toughest challenge I ever had to meet face to face, had occurred over 16 months prior, so this is certainly attainable.

Tracie dropped off some yummy dinners for me after I had returned home, as my strength began to return.

Those first uncertain days, I would look at those back steps, where day after day went by, with me on the top step, staring off into space with a cold can of beer in my hand. To me, it seemed that happened so long ago, and not to me, but to a person that I didn't know.

In my mind, there was no choice to be made about whether to drink or not.

Back then, I would mull it over in my mind, especially after a string of sober days, and then head for the suds.

How had I managed to live through all that pain and suffering?

How many times had I walked or driven to stores, with loads of empty beer cans, just to get enough money to get my next 12-can fix?

On the green chair, in the back bedroom, I had assembled all the things I'd be taking back to Montrose.

I eyed the underwear, socks and razors and thought about how the hours were slipping away.

I phoned the head of the rehab program, Dr. Warren Goldfarb, two times on Tuesday, July 25, two days before I was scheduled to be screened at building 52D2.

Dr. Goldfarb was in charge of a large program at Montrose, conducted in a building, that the facility's regulars referred to as "on the hill."

He came across, as a hurried disciplinarian, said I'd be allowed $15 spending money, and there would be no outside visits. I was to arrive with my VA Card and DD Form 214 (honorable discharge from the service).

In my mind, there would be no chance to go "over the hill" from the building "on the hill."

My mind was being made up, I was turning thumbs down, on going back to Montrose.

Waiting until later that evening, to make a second call to the rehab chief, I figured that at 6:45 p.m., he would be gone and I could get off the hook, by talking to a tape machine.

A message was left, stating that I wouldn't be attending Dr. Goldfarb's alcohol program.

Jackie Beck didn't waste any time following up this dramatic decision.

The next day, Goldfarb got to her, and she in turn, left a message on my machine, almost begging for me to get back to her.

She was baffled about the sudden change of heart, and was concerned to say the least. There is no doubt, that on her end of this situation, she worried herself sick, that I had picked up a beer.

She was instantly relieved, the second she heard my voice on the phone. She could tell, that I hadn't gone back to what had nearly killed me.

Her expertise in the mental health field was tested that day. And she passed with flying colors.

"There are resources I can pursue," she explained. "The 31-day program may have been too constrictive." No truer words have ever been uttered.

The people I came in contact with, at Montrose and the Bronx, had genuinely cared about me. And that trend was continuing.

The word "choices" comes to mind again, here.

I was free from the rule of Montrose completely now, and had thrown myself to the wolves, without a formal support system. It was sink or swim, and now, it was all up to me.

There was absolutely no craving for alcohol, a liquid that in my case, had proved to be nearly lethal. The word "relapse", didn't exist in my vocabulary, and it was getting through to me, that life was fragile and can be snuffed out in the blink of an eye. A can of Milwaukee's Best, would be the start of a certain death sentence.

On the afternoon of my 136th day of sobriety, Nov. 15, 2000, I phoned Jackie, to let her know I was okay. Also, there was curiosity on my part, regarding my behavior, prior to being transferred to the Bronx.

"You were psychotic," she said. "You were really upset that we (the staff) couldn't see and hear what you did."

This guardian angel of mine, then related a fairly recent happening, that made me glad, that I had indirectly helped someone, who had been sharing my agonizing confusion, pain and suffering.

"A guy came in about a month ago," she asserted. "He wasn't as bad as you were, but was on the brink. Because of our experience with you, we sent him right out, instead of playing the waiting game."

It was comforting to know, that another person was quickly taken care of, and that there wasn't much of an observation period for him.

Again, Jackie afforded me reinforcement, by pounding into my head, the seriousness of what my situation had become at the Montrose facility.

"You were very toxic," she explained. "Your whole system, including your brain, were short-circuiting. It was life threatening. You should be very happy to be alive."

She said how good I sounded on the phone, and that she was moved, just hearing my voice.

Wishing me a happy Thanksgiving, we ended our conversation. I felt rejuvenated and powerful, after this little talk. Jackie Beck was continuing to be very important in my life.

As of Dec. 16, 2000, I had attended just two Alcoholics Anonymous meetings (Aug. 27 and Dec. 5), in 166 days of being sober.

On the last day of November, Chris and I had hopped in the car and driven to Montrose, in hopes of surprising Jackie.

However, she was absent, due to a family emergency.

Instead, Marty, one of the folks who saw me at my worst, and wound up discharging me, shook my hand.

"You weren't doing too good," he smiled sheepishly, in describing how I had been before the Bronx.

I probably think about alcohol, each and every day of my life. This progressive disease, reduced me to a sweating, wild-eyed raving lunatic, and nearly took away my life.

For some reason, which I refuse to question, I was given a second chance, and don't think for one moment, that I have taken that chance for granted.

It hits home with me, a lot these days.

Sometimes, when I am in the back bedroom, I remember how I used to refer to this room as "the drunk tank." It was here, where I passed out, went through the shakes, gasped for cold air when I was sweating profusely and finally "saw" angels and demons outside the window and "heard" music.

Yes, I do realize how tenuous my life became. I am cognizant of the life-saving efforts of first, my wife, then Jackie and her co-workers, and finally the staff at the Bronx. I was lucky, fortunate, spared and blessed.

I had no "death wish", although I do admit, that the "Death Wish" movies, starring Charles Bronson, are among my favorites.

Like his character, Paul Kersey, I too lurked in the shadows, many times in my life.

I was an excellent skip tracer as a bank employe (car loan collections), and usually got the payment I wanted, or wound up driving or towing the vehicle.

Sometimes, I got away in the dead of night, heading to police headquarters with paperwork for another successful repossession. My delinquency percentage was excellent, but I was, and still am, for the underdog, whether it be overcoming odds to make car payments, or winning a basketball game, when you were supposed to lose.

Many memorable events have shaped my life.

Mickey Mantle homers down in the Bronx, were always a highlight as I grew up. When I was at Yankee Stadium with my Papa, Bill Clancy, it seemed "The Mick" would always deliver, with a solid shot over the outfield wall.

I remember the awful poison ivy I suffered with as a kid, fishing the banks of the Delaware River. Many times I played softball games, covered in calamine lotion.

The March night, in 1961, when my dad lost an eye and nearly died as a result of an auto crash, and the evening Papa passed away in my living room, remain vivid, etched in time, forever.

A highlight, included a last second desperation basket, against Ellenville, when I played for the Port Jervis Junior Varsity basketball team, in 1964. That bucket, from two steps inside midcourt, tied the game (one second remained when I released the ball), and sent it into overtime.

In the second overtime, my foul shot with 16 seconds remaining, proved to be the game winner.

My name was all over the local radio station that night, and written up in the daily Union-Gazette newspaper that I would some day work for, as sports editor.

The single most memorable moment, is marrying Christine Diane Goble, on September 12, 1970, in Matamoras, Pa.

The night before, high school friends Gary "Fish" Scales, and John Hensz, plus Air Force buddy Frank Ott, accompanied me to Bamberger's Bar, in West End (Port Jervis), for a few suds.

Following our wedding reception, and bound for JFK Airport in New York, Chris and I had to drop off an old lady friend of her parents, in Middletown. Right away, I knew this marriage was really going to be something off the beaten path, yet special, all the same.

Tracie Lynn Tangen came into the world, on March 29, 1972, and her sister, Dawn Melissa, arrived January 11, 1974. These two dates, accompany September 12, 1970, as the three most important dates of my life.

In September of 1976, I interviewed and joked with heavyweight boxing legend Muhammad Ali.

This talented individual, formerly known as "The Louisville Lip" was as controversial a figure as you can ever imagine.

Yet, as he trained for his title defense, at Yankee Stadium, against Ken Norton, I uncovered the man behind the mask.

The Ali I grew to know, at the Concord Hotel, walked a crying baby in the middle of the night, would have preferred pushing his daughter on a swing in the park rather than boxing, and was a sincere man.

He stood up for what he believed in, by sticking with his religion and not going in the service, and I admire the fact that he stated these beliefs, no matter how unpopular they were.

I had gotten to know his trainer, Angelo Dundee, and drank with him after one of Ali's Concord workouts, at King Arthur's Court.

"Ali loves reading your stories," Angelo told me. "He is like a big kid, and can't wait to read about himself. You want to meet him tomorrow?"

And meet him I did.

This guy had enough charisma to fill the Grand Canyon. His infectious smile, serious talk about the upcoming fight with Norton, and sincere demeanor, captivated me easily.

Years back, I had been the only kid on Bus 9 in West End, to pick the former Cassius Clay to beat the rugged Sonny Liston.

Everyone figured me to be slightly out in left field, with my outrageous prediction.

25

I took all the barbs, and the day after the fight, I took all their money.

I had always wanted to meet two people in my lifetime. The pair were Cassius Clay and Elvis Presley.

I pursued a pair of Presley tickets, through Ticketron, prior to his 1971 concert at Madison Square Garden. I kept getting put on hold, and like an impatient 24-year-old, gave up the quest. I am still kicking myself, today.

Presley was a threat to me as a teenager. His damn mug smiled out from the jacket of his latest album, and girls I went out with, had their knees turn to jelly. There was no competing with this "pretty boy."

It was years later, that I realized this kid from Tupelo, Mississippi, was something special. From "All Shook Up" to "Kentucky Rain" and beyond, he was and still is, in my mind, the best to ever come down the pike.

My choices of people I'd like to meet, a singer and a boxer, weren't bad.

Presley was already established, but the cocky kid from Louisville, Kentucky, was a brash, young type, who loved making predictions about when his opponent would fall. I liked his ridiculous attitude and how he exuded confidence. And, the day I shook his hand, I will never forget.

Terry VonIgnatius, a friend I smuggled in to meet Ali, was spellbound for the whole interview.

When we got home he phoned his wife from my house.

"I have been to the top of the mountain, I have met the great Muhammad Ali," he said into the mouthpiece. His wife, Nancy, had a quick response. "When you get down, the garbage needs to be emptied."

On November 19, 2001, just before Thanksgiving, I talked with Jackie, by phone.

As usual, it was great to hear her voice, and to let her know that all was well, with the sportswriter from Pennsylvania.

Two days later, on the day before Thanksgiving, Chris and I took the laundry over town to Port Jervis and ate breakfast at Joe's Coffee Shop on Pike Street.

In need of a haircut, I walked from there, to the barber shop. Not wanting to wait for five other people, I left the place, on foot, bound for the laundromat.

On the way there, I eyed the New Bauer Inn bar, on Jersey Avenue. This is the place, that had been my second home from early 1969 and right up through half of the 1990s.

Many would think that walking into a bar and ordering a ginger ale, would be deadly, for a heavy hitter like me. But, I firmly believe that each of us is totally different, in that regard.

I walked past the neon sign that graced the window, took a deep breath, and hung a left in through the door. I just had to take a look at the dwelling, where I spent hour after hour, drinking mugs of Schaefer, playing the jukebox, and sometimes shooting a game of pool.

George and Louise Noroian own the Bauer, a landmark in our area, that sports plenty of tradition.

When the Erie Railroad was big in town, there are stories that this tavern was jammed to the rafters, as railroaders cashed their checks, on Friday nights. Back then, Port Jervis was a buzzing little city, with more than 10,000 population.

I hung out in this place when prior owners Ben and Marie had the business. It is the site of my famous dog caper of 1984.

When Ben and Marie had the bar, Ben acquired a small spaniel mix pup, while on one of his bar-hopping escapades up in Sullivan County.

Realizing they had a dog at home, it seemed the pup may not fit in, and the small brown and white dog, with the tiny round brown spot on its head, was shuttled between their house and the bar kitchen.

Wanting to give the dog to a good home, I was asked about taking the animal, one evening, when I heard yipping from the kitchen and inquired about the barking.

Armed with a small fur ball, and buoyed by a beer high, I showed up home and was greeted, at the back door.

Trying to at least have Chris look at the dog, she said in no uncertain terms "we can't keep the dog. We have too many cats...take the dog back."

It tore my heart out, taking the little cuddly thing back to the car and into the lonely bar kitchen.

The next day, I said to my wife, "what if the dog goes to a home where it is treated badly, or nobody wants it?" She then indicated, that if the dog didn't find a home... She never got to finish the sentence, because I was on my way to bring Penny Ann (circle on the head), home.

She was heading for 18 years old in November 2001, hobbled by what may be a cracked or broken bone, in her back left foot. This gentle and loyal dog, for years a favorite of neighborhood kids, still remains my best friend, and it is Chris' name on a tag, that graces Penny's collar.

This is the bar, where my big claim to fame, was bowling a 300 on the bowling machine, in the back room.

I would sit here for hours, laughing with people, listening to good tunes and sometimes standing in the doorway, mug in hand, watching rain splash down into the pools that had formed puddles.

George and Louise, were both from Brooklyn and each possessed a witty demeanor and big city business sense. I felt very much at home, in this dwelling.

When I ran short of cash, I would ask George for a small loan and then settle up on payday. Very seldom, did I get turned down.

Entering the inside of the tavern, was a strange experience. I walked to a bar stool, like I had done so many times over the years.

I ordered ginger ale for $1.25, from a slender girl bartender. Then I started to slowly focus my eyes on objects in the room, while loud and nerve-jangling music filled my ears.

There were about 10 people in the tavern and only one face, that I recognized. It didn't lack for activity, but this felt very foreign, to me.

Letters that formed the words "Happy Thanksgiving" appeared from behind the bar, near where mugs hung from hooks by the big mirror.

Above the cash register and on the mirror, were various signs, that informed the general public, about food and drinks.

The television to my left was on, but people didn't seem to notice, as they chattered and filled their mugs from beer pitchers.

I thought, "gee, this is the place where I got Penny." And later, I visualized how Penny and I had stayed up until all hours in 1984, to watch Port Jervis' Ed and Lou Banach, win gold medals in the Olympics, at Anaheim Convention Center. Had the place changed or was it me? I walked out the door knowing, that it was a combination of both.

After Thanksgiving, I walked across the same railroad tracks, where I lugged 12-packs and sometimes 40 ounce bottles of beer, one and two times a day.

My arms got used to the 12 extra pounds of transported burden. My legs, weary from the effects of alcohol abuse, would somehow carry me over the tracks and across the bridge, to the safety of my house, and the isolation of my very being.

On this day, I carried a bag that contained potpourri spray, garbage bags, four dish cloths and a puzzle, for one of my grandchildren. I thought how ironic it was, that in less than 17 months, the goods contained in the plastic bag, had changed so dramatically.

It is so easy, to be humble and thankful for what I have now. It doesn't take Thanksgiving Day to make me reflect on what was, and what is.

As I walked by the Flo-Jean Restaurant and toward the bridge, my mind wandered to the memories of my ex-brother-in-law, who had died of a heart attack at the age of 51, less than a week prior.

Back in the early 1970s, Jim Finlay married my sister, Anne, and they had a son, Shane, currently a damn good musician, down in Panama City, Florida.

My recollections raced back to nearly 30 years prior, way back to our Silver Grill bar days.

Once, we were all fired up in "the grill" on a Friday night, and I talked him into riding north, all the way to Plattsburgh, New York, where I had been stationed in the Air Force.

We had a real great reason for traveling almost five hours from Port Jervis. That reason was, to get a beer and listen to a good band at Brodi's.

There was one thing wrong with this 270-mile jaunt. By the time we arrived in the city, all the bars had closed.

Jim gave me his trademark grin, and we nodded off in the car for a rest, beer in hand, not a care in the world.

As dawn arrived, we attempted to joke through cotton mouths. And a few hours later, we were back home, hung over, and looking like something the cat dragged in.

Through my sportswriting, I had covered this excellent athlete in softball and also golf tournaments. Toward the end of his life, he was still wowing them, with his long ball golfing ability.

Just recently, I had gone into the Flo Jean, where he tended bar. It was a Saturday night (karaoke night), and we both got some chuckles out of some guy, that was murdering the song "Margaritaville."

"Fin" moved behind the bar with a Hawaiian type shirt on, a ladie's man, with a constant smile and joke for everyone.

"Bill, doesn't just drinking ginger ale bother you,?" he asked. "No, Jim, it really doesn't," I replied. "If I get tired of the atmosphere or the people around me, I'll just go home."

That was the last conversation we ever had.

When I had walked out of the Montrose VA, with my wife, on that sultry July day in the year 2000, the biggest choice of my lifetime, was at my fingertips.

And we passed the bars and neon beer signs, as we went through the small town and headed for the Newburgh-Beacon Bridge.

I look at that decision now, as no decision at all. The choice had already been made and there would be no agonizing or second guessing.

I sat at my picnic table this morning, November 25, 2001.

It was a breezy, warm and overcast day. My wife, a church organist, was due home any minute.

Yes, it was a Sunday. And, not so long ago, my eyes would have been on the clock, just waiting for noon to come, so I could stay on the merry-go-round and pop open a Milwaukee's Best.

"Sunday Morning Comin Down," by Kris Kristofferson, had always been a favorite song of mine. Lots of the words described the wretched way I felt on Sundays. I liked the song and I had lived the part.

I glanced out to the nearby street, then looked at my dog in the side yard and took a swig of coffee.

There is no way, I can replace the lost days, months and years, that happened in the past.

But I can truly say, through thick and thin, good and bad, as I sit here today, I am happy to be alive.

CHAPTER 2

Family Tree Has Missing Limbs

I guess starting at the beginning, might be a good idea.

William Jerome Tangen was either born or hatched, at St. Francis Hospital, in Port Jervis, New York, the morning of April 8, 1947.

He entered the world, as the first child, of Jerome and Emily Clancy Tangen.

Jerome Tangen was born in Port Jervis, on May 9, 1922, the son of Frithjof M. Tangen and the former Palmyre Verkindere. Dad was the second oldest, in a family that included seven children, including six boys.

In his life, he was destined to be an aerial gunnery instructor in the Army-Air Force, touched soil in 47 of the 48 contiguous states (only New Hampshire missing), and became a successful insurance agent, in Port Jervis.

He became politically active, becoming Deputy District Governor in the Lions Club (District 20-0), and running unsuccessfully for Mayor of Port Jervis, in 1995, at the age of 73.

Mom was born in New York City, July 7, 1924. She was put up for adoption, and never knew her natural parents, or her real name, for that matter.

That all changed in 2001, when she forced herself to open a letter, that contained adoption information, that had remained unopened by her, for 75 years.

"When I got married, my mother (Anne Murphy Clancy) told me I was adopted and offered to give me some information," Mom told me. "To me, she was my mother, and I was not interested."

On Mother's Day of 2001, (May 13), my mom told me she opened the letter, after much soul searching.

Emily Anne Clancy, was originally, Lydia Theurer. And at this point, we are pursuing mom's birth certificate from New York, in hopes of learning at least what her mother's first name was. This is an important limb in my family tree. And, maybe it isn't too late, to salvage that long lost limb.

Mom was officially adopted by William Arthur and Anne Mary

Clancy on November 6, 1926, with the final order of adoption, coming out of children's court in Middletown, New York.

I was named "Bill" after my grandfather, who I recall as a patient, gentle man, standing over 6-foot tall, with white hair, and possessing love, for Notre Dame football, New York Giants football, and New York Yankees baseball. It was "Papa" who gave me my real first taste of sports.

It was also Papa, who played catch with me in the yard, read me comic books, and took me to Yankee Stadium, to see Mickey Mantle and his Yankee teammates play Major League Baseball.

To this day, I remember what my young eyes took in, as I riveted my stare inside the awesome ballpark.

The natural beauty of the lush green and manicured grass, blended in with the rich, brown color of the infield dirt. Monuments out in deep centerfield, gleamed in the sparkling sun. And the big scoreboard, beyond the fence, seemed so huge, to a small and spellbound boy. And, of course, there was the solid echo of bat meeting ball, as the teams took batting practice, and I prayed to catch a foul ball.

At the top of the third deck in right field, was a light blue facade.

It was that facade, that the powerful switch-hitting man in uniform number 7, nailed with a towering home run that was just 18" shy of going out of Yankee Stadium.

While he smacked that homer lefty, "The Mick" also is credited with creaming a 565-foot homer, righty, at Washington, off Senators pitcher Chuck Stobbs.

The monuments, which symbolized Yankee tradition, were looked at fondly, not only by Yankee fans, but Major League supporters, in general.

Once, the unpredictable Boston Red Sox and Cleveland Indians center fielder, Jimmy Piersall, got so upset in a game, he walked over and halted the action, as he sulked, while sitting at the foot of the monuments.

The monuments were moved years ago, behind the outfield fence, to "Monument Park." And, there for all to see, is the plaque of late baseball hall of famer, Mickey Mantle, a kid from Oklahoma, who wore his Yankee pinstripes proudly, and captured New York's heart.

One night in September 1962, Papa died, at our house, sitting in his favorite chair. I was 15 years old.

While I was watching the television show "Route 66" at my girl-friend's place, Bill Clancy, the guy that read me "Peter Porkchops" comic books, and was my hero and best friend in the world, took his last breath, at age 76.

Papa, at least got to see the conclusion of a great home run chase (1961) of Babe Ruth's 1927 Major League record 60 round trippers (154 games).

Roger Maris and Mantle, Yankee teammates, chased Ruth's ghost.

And in the end, it was Maris, who crashed 61 homers (162 games) while Mantle came up lame, but still bashed 54.

The evening Papa passed away, my dad knocked on the back door of my girlfriend's home. She escorted him into the living room and I knew something was very wrong.

He said just two words to me. "Papa died."

This was a perfect example of the way my father was, about most everything. Short and to the point.

Dad seldom had time for me, when I was growing up, as he worked relentlessly, to support his family.

He never went swimming, didn't drive until I was about eight years old, seldom saw me play basketball in high school and never told me he loved me. To say I feared my father and his discipline, right through my teenage years, is the understatement of the century.

That all came to a screeching halt, when I got out of the service and during a shouting-filled drunk, begged him to say the words "I love you." He may have said them, just to shut me up. But deep in my heart, I know he meant the words he had so much trouble saying.

I realize now, that being one of seven children of a strict father, effected he and his brothers and sister. He was all business, and upon arriving home from work, looked over our property, and complained about how playing wiffle ball, was ruining the grass. He was always the head of the household and when you screwed up, it was dad you had to face. He was and still is, a perfectionist with a capital "P".

In early 2001, I asked my father, about what his life was like, growing up. He had mellowed sufficiently enough to divulge some information.

"My father (Frithjof) would sit at the table with a cup of coffee and say nothing," Dad recalled. "He was very mechanical minded and made his own tools (stationery engineer). He didn't want anyone to know how he did things at work (employed Deerpark Brewery, Port Jervis). He had job security that way, and a lot of the work he did was on Sundays, when nobody was around to watch him."

Dad wouldn't say it, but indicated that Frithjof's kids had felt the sting of his discipline plenty of times, in their young years. "It's not like today, when you can't touch a kid," he asserted.

My Aunt Pat (the former Pat Davis), toiled for endless hours, in trying to get some kind of background on the Tangen family. She married Dad's younger brother, Bob, who is my favorite uncle.

Like Dad, Frithjof was one of seven children. He was born in Boda, Norway (north of the Arctic Circle) and was the son of Oskar and Marn Tangen. Frithjof, the youngest child, moved with the rest of the family, to Drammen, Norway (near Oslo), when his father relocated, due to his job.

Young Frithjof's mother was the former Marn Hansen and his dad was a lawyer, handling land claims for the government.

Their children were, Oskar, Herman, Monhil (girl), Raymond, Dorothy, Ruth and Frithjof.

My grandfather, who I met one time in my life, had brothers who came to this country and had dairy farms in Albert Lea, Minnesota.

Frithjof also had seven kids, including, Jack (deceased), Jerome (my dad), Raymond (whereabouts unknown), Sonja (Port Jervis), Bob (New Jersey), Rene (Oregon) and Denis, who has lived on the West Coast.

Frithjof went to sea, at the age of 14, as a Merchant Marine (World War 1). The Navy took over the Merchant Marines and Frithjof served for 12 years.

He married Palmyre, who was born in Lille, France. I would never meet my grandmother.

Although he was Norwegian and his wife French, Frithjof, known as "Fritz", insisted that while living in the United States, English, be the only language spoken by his family.

"He felt very strongly about that," Dad recalls.

Ruth Tangen wound up knowing seven or eight languages and graduated from two universities.

She was head interpreter for Bell Telephone Labs and interpreted all formulas, for use in the New York City labs.

Ruth, who went back to Norway periodically to further her education and keep up with her job, was born Sept 2, 1897, and died in June 1983.

Palmyre's brother, Oscar, was married to Elsa, and had a beautiful home in France.

He was a Socialist, connected with the government and his position was that of an ombudsman.

Oscar is said to have been a good friend of Charles DeGaulle and carried messages between London and Paris, during World War II. For that reason, Germany was on the constant lookout for Oscar. And it wasn't to shake his hand.

Palmyre was born in France, but met Fritz in Bay Ridge, Brooklyn, N.Y. This is where they both obtained U.S. citizenship.

Following the service, Fritz worked in the silk mill and at Deerpark Brewery before and after prohibition.

Dad's sister Sonja, says the brewery was open, even during prohibition and she recalls carrying lunch to her father, when the noon whistle blew.

It is said that New York State Troopers would come to Fritz' house at night, so he could go to the brewery, in order to load trucks with beer, to go over the mountain to New Jersey.

In 1927, before the stock market crash, Fritz went to California in a Stanley Steamer. He bought the car from someone in Sparrowbush, who was afraid of it. On the way out west, he experienced trouble with a burned out boiler.

At the same time that Fritz went to California, Palmyre visited France to see her mother. Dad, Jack and Raymond, made the trip as well.

My dad, was schooled in Hallauin, France (Lille Province) and spoke French before learning English.

To this day, Dad remembers going to his Uncle Oscar's house and leaning against red paint. "I was five or six years old and the paint was all over my back," he says.

While staying in France for about six months, Dad went to school and lived at his grandmother's house. But the day came, when Dad would be coming back to the U.S.

Palmyre and the kids, left France on an ocean liner, the U.S.S. President Harding.

"There was a terrible storm," Dad asserts. "It was a choppy ride and I fell on my head. The vessel was forced to Halifax, Nova Scotia, instead of New York."

By the early 1920s, all ocean liners had been changed to combustion engines. Liners were breaking the 40-knot mark, and the "golden era" of ocean liners had arrived.

By planes, trains, automobiles and ocean liners, Dad traveled all over the world in his lifetime. He saw not only France, but other places including Mexico, Canada, Korea, Japan and Belgium.

Another thing about his time in France, is recalled.

"I remember getting a present for Christmas," he says. "It was a doll made out of sweet bread."

As for the President Harding, it was a vessel that started out being named, the Lone Star State. It went into trans-Atlantic service (NY-Bremen) with United States Lines, the year Dad was born (1922). It was renamed the Taft after one voyage and the Harding after two more.

Sold to the Belgian line Societe Maritime Anversoise in 1940, and renamed the Bruges, it was bombed by German aircraft in the River Scheldte on May 14, 1940. It was beached and burned and the wreck was dismantled in 1952, after 93 sailings.

Fritz, a charter member of the VFW of Port Jervis (1936) and in Florida, went to Rochester, N.Y., after the brewery was raided, during prohibition. There, he was a stationery engineer and shoemaker.

The brewery was officially back in business again, in the 1930s.

Dad was alive for the roaring 20s, the depression, prohibition, the stock market crash, Charles Lindberg's 1927 33 ½ hour solo flight, from Roosevelt Field, Long Island, to LeBourget, just outside Paris, France. And, he was five years old, when Babe Ruth smacked home run number 60, for the New York Yankees.

Dad went to high school in Port Jervis and later was on the track team at Warwick High School, where he graduated in 1940.

Later, he became a gunnery instructor (aerial gunner) and Sergeant Major, in the Army-Air Force.

Dad was officially discharged on my birthday, April 8, 1947, at

Mitchell Field, N.Y.

He had served in Korea, and just over three years later, on June 25, 1950, the Korean War began, when Communist North Korea invaded U.S.-supported South Korea.

By the time the war had ended in 1953, the U.S. had 54,000 dead and 103,000 wounded. More than 400,000 South Koreans perished in what is labeled "the forgotten war." A million North Korean and Chinese people died.

Of Fritz and Palmyre's seven children, Jack was the oldest (October 30, 1920). He died in March 1982, from emphysema. His wife was Opal (June 12, 1925-October 4, 1997), and her son Tom, predeceased her (June 10, 1946-Aug. 24, 1993). The other children were Jack Jr., Linda, Cheryl and Brian.

I remember Uncle Jack, Aunt Opal and the kids, when we visited them up in Rochester, N.Y.

They lived across from an airport, and I recall that my uncle worked at Brighton Bowl.

I remember Jack Jr. playing organized baseball, Opal being strict and that they owned a horse named "Jillio." There was plenty of wilderness behind their house, for tree forts and things that kids like.

Uncle Jack was a well-known chef in Rochester. He was in charge of American Airlines food service in the northeast, and moved around the country, in that capacity.

Dad relates a story that his older brother once told him.

"Jack was walking home from work in Rochester, (to Dad's knowledge Jack never drove) at two o'clock in the morning," he says. "A police cruiser pulled up alongside him and a cop asked where he was going. He answered "what's it to ya?", and he was then taken to police headquarters."

This trait of not mincing any words and instead, being straight and to the point, seems to run in the family.

Dad's youngest brother, Denis, once owed Dad a dollar or two. When Denis got around to paying the money back, Dad told him not to worry about it...to forget it. Denis' reply? "Well, I'll throw the money in the street then."

Denis was a cool customer. He reminded me of a quiet James Dean type, a slender, good looking guy, who wore his belt buckle left of center. He had perfectly combed hair, said very little, and when in Port Jervis, hung out at the bowling alley, when ladies were bowling. I think he had his eye on one or more of the bowlers. It is believed, that Denis settled down with a woman named Phyllis.

Uncle Buddy (Rene real name) is the most interesting of my uncles by far, and had to be the family's genuine "Rebel Without a Cause."

Buddy was a real joker and needler, always into heavy equipment, machinery, tools and the like. And, I think he was in the Army for more than one hitch.

Dad says Buddy took the Army very seriously.

When he was in the service, his tank was going to be assigned to someone else. I guess Buddy didn't much care for that idea, because he walked away. We're talking about walking away from the service, completely.

I remember him having a motorcycle crash and hurting his back real bad, maybe even breaking it.

He was a comedian who loved to tease, and also possessed a bizarre sense of humor.

Buddy babysat for me once, when I was small. Notice the word "once." He took great delight in scaring the living hell out of me.

He put a scary horror movie on TV, turned the lights out, made horrible sounds and told me there were monsters in the house.

Matante, the French lady who I called "my aunt", was a very strict disciplinarian, and she was very "old school."

But Buddy took none of Matante's guff, instead teasing her unmercifully and staging rebellion against any orders she might be barking.

One time she was lecturing me about something, when stocky and feisty Uncle Buddy dropped by Matante's house.

He said his quiet hellos and listened to Matante go on and on. When she had concluded her forceful tirade, Buddy looked me right in the eyes.

"Don't listen to her," he said. "What does she know?"

When Matante tried to come down on him, he grinned widely, until her face was flushed in red. "Hop on your broom and away you go," he said.

With the old French lady (or witch in Buddy's mind) shouting in his ear, he cheerfully strode toward the front door, happy he had spoken his piece.

Once when I lived in West End (teen years), Dad was having trouble with the neighbors.

They were the type, who had to have the property looking "just right" and despised when I played basketball out back. If the ball went near their precious grass, either the husband or wife, was quickly at the scene of the crime. And if a car tire strayed an inch too far right in the driveway, there was trouble.

Once when winter was approaching, Dad told them to roll up their grass and keep it in the cellar until spring arrived. He made the mistake of telling Buddy about his hard-assed neighbors.

Being the guy Buddy was, the next time he was at our house, he jumped out of the car, walked a few steps and promptly demonstrated how motorcycle boot marks look on a lawn.

I guess you could add the word "disrespectful" to Buddy's resume. He is probably the first person I recall, other than Dad, who had the courage to stand up for what he believed in. Rebel or not, Buddy stories remain in my memory bank. It seems like yesterday when he was here.

From what I am told, Buddy lives out in Oregon. Dad got Thanksgiving and Christmas cards from him, so at least he lets us know he is alive. Reportedly, he has a wife and daughter, Jeanette.

The last time I saw him was in 1974, but in the near future, I'd like to pop in on Uncle Buddy and maybe scare the hell out of him. Hey, maybe I'll have him sign a copy of this book.

I remember Dad's lone sister, Sonja, (born in 1932) from back on Hammond Street, in 1952 or 1953, when I went to grade school.

My sister, Anne, was a baby then, and it's easy to recall Sonja holding her and hugging her. Meanwhile, she had little use for me and I was referred to as "a little snot." I was all of six years old, but I never forgot.

Uncle Bob (born 1934) and Aunt Pat (they were married April 14, 1956), of New Jersey, were by far my favorites.

Bob, who is older than Buddy and Denis, is my dad's closest brother.

He is a Navy veteran, (January 1952-December 1955), who is into submarines big time. Every now and then, when they just had two kids (Ronnie and Eric), they would come up to visit and I'd show Ronnie how to play basketball.

Bob never talked down to me, even though I was a kid. He and Dad would each tell humorous stories about "the old man" for hours on end.

Once Uncle Bob picked up one of those little water objects that you turn upside down, and a substance that resembled snow, would fall. In the plastic and oval casing, was a lone figure.

"Look Jerry, it's the old man looking for a job," Bob said, and the brothers would laugh, till they nearly cried.

Back in the 1950s, on Hammond Street, I remember Bob getting out of the Navy and staying with us for awhile. He had Navy tattoos on his arm or arms, and one was of a Japanese or Chinese guy (Bob was overseas).

Pat was slender and real good looking. She never had a bad word for anyone and had a great sense of humor. I always looked forward to their visits. Ronnie, now heavily involved in car racing (has worked NASCAR pit crews and driven), never forgot how patient I was, showing him how to shoot a basketball.

Bob and Pat wound up with four sons, including David and Jonathon. Eric, who was a carpenter and Sparrowbush, N.Y. Fire Chief, passed away in 1993.

In all fairness, I have to admit that Sonja, at least acknowledged me.

I was quite small, when she was married to Gene Niles, in 1954. I think they had four children, and I've met the oldest, Gene Jr. His dad, an electrician, passed away in 1990.

Of Dad's siblings, Raymond had to be the oddest one. Like Bob and Pat, he surfaced once in a blue moon, and always on a Sunday.

Dad was never a big drinker. He would have a few beers at Lions Club events, or something like that, but there was seldom alcohol in the house.

Sunday was "work day" around the home, for my father. He would put on Army-Air Force type attire in cooler weather, or an old sweater or long sleeved shirt, if the temperature dictated it. When he was at work, and at all other times, the uniform of the day was and still is, shirt, tie and sports jacket. He is always dressed immaculately.

Back in the West End years, Ray would show up, with his wife, Hilda, and kids, Scotty and Pam (I'm told they went on to have five kids).

Dad would be out doing yard work, and they would slip into the house and make themselves at home.

There was usually a six-pack of beer on ice, for Sundays. However, that modest supply was in serious jeopardy, when Ray and his crew arrived on the scene.

While Dad wrapped up whatever segment of work he had at hand, and headed inside, Ray was usually already firing down beers, while the rest of the family chowed down, on food from the fridge. "Pushy" and "arrogant" are words that come to mind, in this situation.

On one occasion, they stopped by when Dad and Mom were in the house. While Dad and Ray spoke, Ray's wife suddenly cut into the conversation. "Aren't you going to at least offer your brother a beer?" she blared at Dad.

Ray never paid any attention to me, except for one time. Dad told him I needed a part (chain link) for my bicycle.

Dad says Ray went to the back of his station wagon and lugged out tools and tool boxes. Tim "the tool man" Taylor (television show Home Improvement) would have been green with envy.

After hauling all this hardware out onto the sidewalk, he discovered he didn't have the part that was needed. And so, without a word, he began loading the equipment back into the car.

Ray is a little under three years younger than Dad, and nobody has heard from him in a good 40 years. Like I may have mentioned, this is not a tight-knit family.

Some believe he wound up out west, maybe in California.

I found information on a Raymond Tangen, in Montana, who had died May 8, 2000, at age 75, but his birth date, probably is not that of Dad's brother. Dad recalls Ray's date of birth as December 12, 1925.

Fritz was born November 22, 1891, in Norway and died in January 1970. He had remarried, after my grandmother (who I never met) died and relocated to Fort Pierce, Florida.

I met my grandfather, Fritz, just one time, when I was a little guy.

He was trying to get Jack and Dad to financially be involved, in the purchase of a bar-restaurant, in Middletown, N.Y. (Hotel Middletown). I played bumper pool, while they talked near the bar. That was the one and only time, that I got within five feet of my grandfather. To this day, I wonder how he and my grandmother could have been so mean, to never want to see their grandchild.

It seems that some of the bricks are missing from the building, when it comes to the Tangen family. But even on Palmyre's side, there were some strange people.

Victor Derammalaer (who I called Uncle Vic), was from Palmyre's side of the family, and Matante was his second wife (lucky Vic).

I couldn't have been more than two or three years old, when he used to take me for walks. I remember he was a little but sturdy guy, who wore suspenders, a hat and glasses. I also recall that his biggest passion in life, was stepping on ants.

Vic held some patents on silk weaving and owned a butcher shop in Port Jervis. He also had a speakeasy on the top of Pike Street. There was a hat shop in front of the building and a bar in the rear. In addition to these ventures, Vic was a partner, in a Paterson, N.J. silk mill.

Dad says he saw cigarettes being sold in the front of the "store." And, he remembers a question he asked Vic.

"I asked him how many years old the whiskey was," Dad explains. "And he answered, 'you mean how many hours?'"

Matante was referred to by Dad, as "the aunt." I stayed over night, at her big red brick house, at 5 White Street, many times, after Uncle Vic died.

She ate vegetables that she grew in the garden, was a fine cook, and there was always a glass of Schaefer beer, at the dinner table. "Eat everything on your plate," she would say. "There is no garbage can here." Once, she had a big rabbit, I named "Harvey." One day, the rabbit was nowhere to be seen. And shortly there after, we were sitting down for a rabbit dinner. Let's just say, that suddenly nobody had an appetite, except for Matante.

I became real attached to her wolf-collie mix dog, Doxie, a big brown, yellow and black, longhaired animal, with those big, brown eyes. I petted the dog and fed it. I also dumped water on Doxie, from an open door, in the upstairs of the garage. And, I got caught, by Matante.

We took long walks down Hamilton Street where there were railroad tracks and open fields, with high green grass, for as far as you could see. Years later, in the early 1960s, this became Port Jervis Senior High School athletic fields.

As a teenager, I would long jump and triple jump near the area, and inside the high school, wearing uniform number "3", I was a fine guard, on the Port JV basketball team.

Palmyre was a small woman, according to Dad. "She was 4-10" or 4-11"," he says. "She had naturally smooth complexion and it looked like she had rouge on, but she didn't."

The grandmother that I never even got to touch, died in the mid 1950s, around the time that Dad suffered a heart attack.

Fritz and Dad, were among those at Palmyre's funeral, up in Rochester. "It was about 40 below zero, near the lake," says Dad. "It was really cold."

Just like a baseball player, with a great day at the plate, I went a perfect 4-for-4, when it came to having nearly zero contact with my grandparents.

Mom's dad and mom were unknown, I saw Fritz from a distance and never saw Palmyre. I batted .500 in the foster grandparent category. Grandma Anne Clancy, died Oct. 6, 1948, when I was less than 18 months old. But Papa saved the day. He made up for all the attention that I missed out on. He was always there for me, never too busy, never with an unkind word.

Papa was known to party from time to time. And if he had his share of alcohol, he would hug me, and say we were Big Bill and Little Bill. "If you hear my name, after I'm gone, you tell them 'that was my pop,'" he told me. And, I promised I would. It has happened over the years, and I have honored Papa's request.

My wife and myself, know what it's like to be a grandparent. Tracie has two girls (and a child on the way), while Dawn has two sons. We have been truly blessed, to be able to hold them, feed them, play with them. I hope that someday, they will say "that was my Poppy."

Christine has been the greatest thing that ever happened to me.

To say that I love her, would be a terrific understatement. I have no words to describe what I feel for her. It is too much to comprehend. Words just won't do. I definitely know I would die for her, without even thinking about it.

Much of her influence, has helped to break a Tangen trait. I do want to be there, for my grandchildren, to share their lives, their hopes and dreams. I'm not afraid to say "I love you" and that is a real plus, in my life.

Although Dad, never physically showed me his love, I know it was there. It came through in the things he did for me. I just had to read between the lines. And that caring, came from a guy, who lived under Fritz' roof. The Fritz that didn't have the time of day for me.

Dad showed me a Bible, that was given to his father, when Fritz was 15 years old. He carried that Bible, out to sea, at that tender age.

"My father got torpedoed twice," Dad noted. "He sailed on both English and American ships. On one of those hits, he was in the water for more than 20 hours."

I wonder if that experience stuck in Fritz' mind, and he decided not to teach my father how to swim. I never saw Dad go swimming, but I think he told me about him falling in water somewhere, and that may have been a bad happening that turned him against getting in the water again.

As a child, Dad recalls seeing his father's service uniforms, with all the stripes on the sleeves.

"First, there were the three of us children," Dad said, on his 79th birthday. "And, when we were on our own, the other four came along. The younger children, didn't know much about us, and we didn't know about them."

In order from the oldest were, Jack (deceased), Dad, Ray, Sonja, Bob, Buddy and Denis. Dad keeps personal contact, with only Sonja and Bob.

I don't mean to portray Sonja as a mean person. On the contrary, she has been good to my dad, brought up her kids well, and perseveres, although suffering through some medical problems. It's just that through the years, I never got to know her.

When Dad was young, and stayed at Matante's, he would see a girl, at a nearby house.

"She had long, blond hair, and was riding a blue bike," Dad muses. Years later, when I was on furlough, I saw her, with her father, at the Flo-Jean Restaurant."

The girl with the blond hair, became his wife (my mother), and her father, was none other than Papa.

When I was small, I remember Dad whistling in the bathroom, while he shaved. He always dressed immaculately for work, and it is from him, that I got my perfectionist demeanor. The discipline comes from him, and the writing ability, may be passed down from Mom, who worked for the Union-Gazette newspaper in Port Jervis, years before I did. While Dad was, and still is, a shirt and tie type, I am a white sneakers and jeans kinda guy.

Dad was a real comedian in the morning. He never ate breakfast, but made time to tease my sister and me, sometimes urging us to get moving, and off to school.

He would sing his short jokes, or blurt out certain phrases, usually to piss us off.

"Everybody out of the pool," he would shout, to wake us up. "Hit that apple."

In West End, he called our gray cat, Penny, "Woody the puddy." And he would sing, "Woody the puddy, how could he? He killed his own grandma." When Penny wasn't Woody, he was called "Catso."

Sometimes, we'd hear Dad say "Good, good, good, a head of wood." And then, like I sometimes do, he'd laugh at his own words.

If Dad had a few beers on the weekend, he would call me "Roscoe" and to make my mom mad, he would call her "Martha" or "kiddio."

Dad never hit me, no matter how bad I'd been. And when I got out of the service, he had a rough time with me. After all, I was now under his roof again, after being away 16 months.

He would give me an hour to be in, like say 1 o'clock, and tell me "don't get involved" and "don't celebrate too much." Then he would

41

reiterate. "I lock the door at 1, so get home by then." "Great Dad, what day?" would be my sarcastic, smart-assed answer.

Just before shipping out for overseas, I wrecked one of Dad's cars, twice in one day. And, of course, it involved beer drinking and a girl named Patsy.

John VanGraafeiland, who I didn't like at first glance in Plattsburgh, had become a close buddy. He was shipping out for Vietnam and me for Guam.

So in July of 1967, I racked the car up in the afternoon, going up to Sullivan County, to apologize to the cute, little, brown-eyed girl. That night, on the way home from hearing a band, I ran it off the road again, this time with Van in the car. He cut his nose on the dash, and the beautiful green, 1964 Plymouth Fury convertible, all of a sudden, resembled an accordion.

How Dad had any sense of humor over that one, I'll never know.

"Billy, what the hell did you do to the car?" I heard him scream, the next morning, as my head throbbed, with the pain of a killer hangover. "I had to swerve to miss a deer," I said. "Looks to me, like there were two deer," he shot back. "Both sides of the car are destroyed."

When my sister, Anne, would come in, well after her curfew, he would slap her ass up the stairs, with his slipper, while shouting "beero" in her ears. Anne still chuckles about those nights. "I had to scream and yell, like it hurt bad," she smiles. "Then, I'd jump in bed, put a pillow over my head, and laugh, until tears came down my face."

Once, when I was small, I remember Dad arriving home from work, with his briefcase. I asked what was in it, and he had a simple reply. "A wildcat is in there," he said, as I walked away quickly.

When there would be the rumble of thunder on a summer day, he said the noise was "the elves bowling." I maintained that the loud and frightening sound, was being caused by "gluppies."

Dad never doled out much advice, but was there, if you requested some.

He always told me that buying a house, would be my biggest expense, and that a car, would be the second highest. He always advised me to "travel light" and to not hang on to too much stuff. And, he hit the nail right on the head, when he said "nobody can stop time."

When I was in basic training at San Antonio, in 105-degree August heat (1965), his letters would reinforce the fact, that the days were going by.

I thought I had an ulcer during boot camp, and he had to fly down to Texas, when I went to a hospital for tests. Luckily I didn't have an ulcer and returned to flight 1147. But he was there for me, when I needed him most.

The only vacation our family ever went on, was to Illinois, after Dad had a heart attack, in the mid 1950s. Mostly because of doctor's orders for him to "relax", we went to see an Air Force buddy of his, Wayne Archer, and his wife, Marion, and kids.

Dad still keeps things light. To cause a ruckus, would be "raising cain" and when you complained about your job, he says "what do you want to do, sell bananas on the street corner?"

After nearly losing sight in both eyes, in an auto accident, at the start of the 1960s, he bounced back, right away.

Minus his right eye, he came out of the hospital and bought a new car. He got right back up on the horse that had thrown him.

I picture the night he bowled a 236 at Minisink Lanes and the afternoon he smacked three hits, in a Lions Club softball game in Milford, Pa. He did this and a lot more, with vision in just the left eye. My mom was driving on a slippery road the night of the accident, but Dad never blamed her for anything. He never once complained about his misfortune, or felt sorry for himself.

Dad has always had the courage of his convictions, and takes orders from no man. He is disciplined, yet fair, and is not "one of the good old boys." He goes down in my memory, as a rebel with a cause.

Dad ran for Lions Club District Governor (District 20-0) two times, against well known Dr. Frank Sears of Middletown, and Curt Smoyer of Kingston, in 1965. He lost the battle both times, but in each case, won the war. Because he challenged the usual hum-drum "your side of the Hudson River and then my side" silliness, there was a fair and democratic vote. His perseverance and beliefs, gave people a choice. This proves again, that without doubt, life is filled with choices.

It was Dad, who first questioned, and then challenged the usual Lions Club procedure, of having a district governor from one side of the Hudson River and then the next time, selecting from the other side. There hasn't been another election, since that 1965 race.

At the age of 73 (1995), Dad ran for Mayor of Port Jervis, N.Y., against Republican Mayor R. Michael Worden. He disagreed with many of Worden's ideas, and instead of just bad-mouthing, he tried to do something about it. He debated Worden, tooth and nail, but was fighting a losing battle.

Worden had a political machine, and wasn't about to be knocked off. Dad's advanced age, was definitely a detriment, and he was solidly defeated, 2,024 to 556.

Dad taught me to fight fair, fight hard, and never quit or give up. At times, I can be stubborn as a mule. Can we guess where this trait comes from?

Mom says she can never remember being an unhappy or lonely child. And, she knows for sure, that Bill and Anne Clancy, loved her very much.

The couple had lost a son at birth and decided to go the adoption route.

At first, Papa was against seeking a child, as he continued grieving over the loss of his baby boy. In simple English, he just wasn't coping very well.

Anne said that she pleaded with him day after day, until he finally gave in.

Mom notes that Papa wouldn't hold her, for nearly six months. But one day, my grandmother exclaimed, "look Bill, she is smiling. Just hold her."

From that day forward, Mom says she had Papa, wound around her little finger. She was now, daddy's little girl. The song "Daddy's Little Girl" remains a favorite of my mother.

When Mom reached three years old, it was found that she had asthma very badly. It was acute on certain occasions, and at times, she was bedridden, instead of being able to go out and play with other children.

Anne had a big sand box, with benches all around it, built for her daughter. She painted animals on it and Kenny, a next door neighbor on Kingston Avenue, would come over and play.

One day, while playing in the sand box, Kenny turned to Mom and said, "know what? Your mommy and daddy aren't your real mommy and daddy. You got adopted. My mom said so."

Mom, who was nicknamed "Mimi" and "Dolly," says she ran to her mother while crying her eyes out, and told her what the boy had said.

"Mimi," her mother said. "Kenny was right in a way...but let me tell you how much luckier you are than him."

Anne, a school teacher by trade, held her daughter in her arms and said comforting words. "When Kenny was born," she began, "his mom and dad had to keep him, because they had no choice. But when we adopted you, we picked you, because we loved and wanted you so much. So you see, Dolly, that makes you luckier than Kenny."

Mom's first pet, was an Irish Setter, named "Rory." She asserts that the dog died a year later, mysteriously. "Rory was found in a farmer's barn, way out of town," she notes. "Then, my dad's sister, gave me a brand new puppy, a Boston Bulldog. Her dog, had pups and she gave us one. I named him Boots, and oh did I love him."

A black and white cat joined the family, one night during the Christmas season, when her "meow" was heard on the side porch. "Dinah" became a good companion to Boots. When Eenie, Meanie, Miney and Mo were born, Boots faithfully washed the kittens and rounded them up for Dinah.

Tragically enough, years later, Dinah got caught in a swinging door that led to the kitchen. She wound up paralyzed and had to be put to sleep.

Mom did alright in school, but was absent a lot because of the asthma.

When she was a senior at Port Jervis High School, she attended

Ursaline Academy in the Bronx, just above Yankee Stadium, on 163rd Street. She also studied Voice, on 57th Street, at the studios of Maestro Astolfo Pescia. He was brought here, by Grace Moore, diva of the Metropolitan Opera.

Moore chose six of the maestro's students, to spend the summer (1940s) at her home, in Faraway Meadows, Newtown, Connecticut. And, Mom was one of the half dozen.

She studied Voice and Italian after high school, during the early months of 1945. She had broadcasts (piano and voice, semi-classical) on radio stations WGNY (Newburgh, N.Y.) and WKIP (Poughkeepsie, N.Y.), on Sundays.

Later, Mom attended Vermont Junior College, in Montpelier, studying Music Theory and Advanced Voice.

Following college, she got a New York job, in the underwriting department of the Insurance Company of North America. After a year living at the YWCA, Mom returned home, to work at her dad's insurance business.

During this time, my grandmother lost her hearing, gained a lot of weight and became housebound.

A former music teacher at PS 149, in Brooklyn, she had been in charge of the first all-boy orchestra.

Although her health was declining, and she wouldn't leave the house, she stayed home, playing the piano, with a yardstick between her teeth. The stick extended to the sound board of the piano, so she could "hear" the music.

Mom said that one night after work, her and Papa went to the Flo-Jean Restaurant to relax and enjoy a cocktail and dinner.

It was at this historical restaurant, along the banks of the Delaware River, that Mom met an Air Force Sergeant, who was on furlough. He was quiet, efficient and confident. And, someday, he would become her husband, and my dad.

During a conversation, the two came to realize, that they knew each other from years and years prior.

"Back then, he (Dad) thought I was a stuck up snob," Mom says. "He soon found out, that I wasn't. During his furlough, we started to date."

Dad and Mom both agree that they were married two times, the first by a Justice of the Peace, in either Teaneck or Hackensack, N.J., and the second, at St. Mary's Church in Port Jervis.

Mom always said that their wedding anniversary was July 2. But, on a couple of occasions, she has indicated that there was another date involved. What the dates and places were, I have no real idea. My parents say that Papa and his wife, were present at the New Jersey ceremony.

Dad left Mitchell Field, Long Island, N.Y., shortly before I was born. He had been in charge of 24 units, at the 308th Bomb Wing, in Korea.

This baby, with blue eyes and blond hair and weighing more than eight pounds, entered the world, at St. Francis Hospital, at about 8 a.m., April 8, 1947.

Dad and Mom were living in my grandfather and grandmother's house, at 57 Kingston Avenue, at the time. And so, that was to be my very first home.

Other places I lived while growing up included: 10 Prospect Street, 36 Kingston Avenue, 32 Brooklyn Street, 75 Hammond Street and 6 Lyman Avenue.

I don't remember my first three residences, as I was way too young to recall them. However, Dad fills me in, on my first days home, after leaving the hospital.

"You cried all night and kept people awake," he laughed. "Nobody got any sleep and we all dragged around the next day."

It was determined, that the reason I was wailing my little head off, is that I had a spasmatic stomach.

I was taken to the doctor that delivered me, Dr. Clare Kenny, and he tried to figure out a way to stop my around-the-clock crying. "Give him a boiled egg," he told my mother.

Deciding not to employ the boiled egg treatment, my parents arranged for me to see a specialist in Middletown, 16 miles away.

I simply couldn't hold down milk, and it was decided that my formula would be changed. Once that switch was made, 57 Kingston Avenue, became a house that contained five Rip VanWinkles.

I am told that Anne Clancy, my grandmother, really loved me a lot. She only got to enjoy me for a small amount of time. On October 6, 1948, Anne Murphy Clancy passed away of cancer.

I know for a fact, that Papa never got over her loss. He showed me her picture, sitting on a blanket in the woods. That, and what I have been told about her, are the only real link I ever had with my grandmother. Papa was 62 years old when she died and Mom was only 24.

After his wife died, Papa moved out of 57 Kingston Avenue, and rented it, to a railroad engineer, who had taken on the job of helping convert trains from steam to diesel. The Erie Railroad was very big in Port Jervis, in those days. The railroad had replaced the D&H Canal.

Dad remembers the landlords he had, back before he bought the house at 75 Hammond.

"Rudy Berthiaume was the landlord at 10 Prospect," he says. "That house used to be the Deerpark Hospital. And, Sam Goldman owned 36 Kingston. That was over a Grand Union store. He also owned Goldman's Market, on Orange Street."

I do remember some of my exploits on Brooklyn Street. That is where I first rode a tricycle, cut my head open by falling off a rocking horse and rode my toy steamroller through a busy city, all by myself, at the age of about three.

"Jim Cole, a milkman (Diamond Dairy), owned the Brooklyn Street

46

house," Dad says. "He later became the mayor of Port Jervis."

After Brooklyn Street, came Hammond Street. While I boxed as a toddler at the prior address, I started becoming an athlete at this location.

This is where I batted rocks in the driveway for hours, played wiffle ball in the back yard and sandlot baseball, in the corner field. As a boy, I ate, drank and slept sports and their statistics. I lived for athletics and soon enough, I began collecting trophies in softball and bowling.

There were some real quirky stories, that occurred at 75 Hammond. Once, I got into Dad's white paint, and proudly printed the name "Tangen" on the back sidewalk, near the garbage cans. When he started screaming at me, I swore I didn't know who had done it.

The list of schools I went to, is easy enough. I began the elementary grades in kindergarten, at Church Street School. The school was located around the corner and up at the top of Church Street hill and I was there for six grades.

When we moved to West End, I went to West End School for sixth grade. Later the junior high grades (seventh, eighth and ninth) were attended at Port Jervis High School (now the middle school) on East Main Street.

A brand new high school was built out on Route 209 in the early 1960s and that is where I completed my final three years of schooling.

On the other hand, Dad went to 11 schools, that were located in two states and two countries.

He started at Matamoras Grammar School (1927), where Chris, her mom and our daughters Tracie and Dawn went. Then it was on to East Main Street and Sullivan Avenue schools in Port Jervis (1928).

From there, he was educated in France, at L'ecole in Halluin (Lille).

Once back in the states, Dad went to St. Michael's and St. Ambrose schools in Rochester (1931-33). Then it was back to Port, for St. Mary's and Church Street schools (1934), on to the Port Junior High (1935-36) and the high school (1937-39). One final move brought him to Warwick High, where he graduated in 1940.

September 17, 1942, Dad enlisted in the U.S. Army Air Corps., as an aviation cadet. He was sworn in at the Federal Building, Rochester, and received a three-day pass to wind up his business affairs. Three days later, he reported to the Fort Niagara Reception Center, Niagara Falls, N.Y., for processing. He remained at that location for 3-4 weeks.

In the fall of 1942, he was shipped by train to Camp Mills, outside of Mitchell Field, Long Island, N.Y. While there, Dad was injured in basic training, when a Corporal in charge, decided to have the obstacle course run in reverse.

He wound up at the base hospital, where his left rib cage had to be strapped up. He was then sent back to the barracks, a converted garage with no heat.

Dad left by train in late October 1942, to San Antonio Aviation Cadet

Center (Texas), for air crew cadet training. He was grounded due to injury and told to report to the dispensary. He became permanent party (SACC) and was made a clerk-typist and a PFC. He made Corporal several weeks later, under a 1st Lieutenant, in the Mess Department (three mess halls).

Soon, he and the Lieutenant, were transferred on base and Dad was left in charge of setting up a new office. The Lieutenant got moved again, and Dad was promoted to Sergeant and sent to the Main Mess Office, where he received a civilian secretary and an assistant. He became in charge of the Mess Maintenance Department, replacing a Captain and overseeing 42 mess halls on the base.

In 1944, after two years on the ground and in spite of a Major's promise that he would receive Staff Sergeant stripes, Dad signed up for aerial gunnery training and shipped out to Tyndall Field, Florida. "After all," he says, "I did sign up to fly in the Air Force and that was my objective." He arrived at Tyndall in the summer of 1944 and had to go through, what amounted to, another basic training segment (two months).

Most of his flight training was over the Gulf of Mexico, and part of the assignment, was watching for foreign submarines. He successfully completed training and anticipated going to the 8th Air Force (England), with members of his squadron.

However, Dad was called to the Orderly Room and told his training marks qualified him for instructor training. He requested assignment to the 8th Air Force, but was informed he had no choice in the matter. He was going to B-24 Arial Gunnery Instructors School, in Laredo, Texas. Laredo is known as the Mexican border "Gateway City."

While training at Tyndall, Dad was indirectly involved in the crash of a B-24, that was on a training mission. The aircraft was one of three, including Dad's, that were in flight formation while undergoing combat flight training.

The ill-fated aircraft developed engine failure. While 10 trainees bailed out, four fliers went down with the ship and were killed. In addition, one trainee died when his parachute didn't open.

"I remember our Colonel going to the rigger shop on the base and pulling the rip cords on all the parachutes, as a result," Dad asserted. "Meanwhile, the rigger had to repack them all."

At Laredo in late 1944, Dad underwent B-24 instructor training and graduated with gold instructor wings, that were displayed on his right sleeve. He made several flights in B-24's over Texas, during his time in Laredo. Following his Texas schooling, Dad was sent back to Tyndall, as an instructor. He taught French, Chinese, Turkish and Americans in the classroom. Enlisted personnel as well as officers, including Lieutenant Colonels, attended classes and listened to Dad's instruction.

In early 1945, Dad signed up for B-29 aerial gunnery instruction training at Harlengen, Texas. Once completing the course, he went on to

Greensboro, North Carolina, McChord Field, Washington and Alamagordo, New Mexico, where the Atomic Bomb had just been tested. "I stayed there just one night, as all the water on base had dried up," he explained. "I went home on a 90 days delay in route and then reported to Seattle. (he signed up for one additional year of service and reported to Seattle for overseas deployment to Japan)."

After Japan (Tachikowa and Zama), he reported to Kimpo Air Base, 308th Bomb Wing (H), 5th Air Force, Seoul, Korea, as a command level Personnel Sergeant Major (A-1 Section). Dad worked directly under a Captain and Major and had three enlisted men in the same department.

As a section head, he met with the Commanding General and other department heads every Monday morning, to discuss strategy.

In the Spring of 1947, Dad left Kimpo for the states by ship, following a stop in Japan. The trip took 10 days, and he was assigned to Fort Slocum, New Rochelle, N.Y., where he awaited discharge. That discharge came in early April, at Mitchell Field, Long Island, N.Y.

A lot of people, never get a chance to speak with their parents about the past. And even though being a writer, I just let things ride for a long time, not wanting to pry. That all came to a screeching halt, in a Bronx, N.Y. VA hospital.

Mom's adoption and Dad's service years, are just two of the things that I have learned about my parents. It may be selfish, but this gives me a solid foundation about who I am.

I suddenly feel Mom's pain and suffering about being given up for adoption. Why was she cast aside? Did her real mom and dad love her, or was she regarded as a burden?

The love she was given from my grandmother and Papa, now reaches me. I know grandma held me, I just wish I could have been older.

The discipline and tough love of my dad, plus the emotions and expressed love of my mom, are the things that Anne and I grew up with. There were some tough times for sure, but some happy and humorous stories come from our upbringing, too.

Beginning July 19, 1946, Dad kept a diary of his train ride from Greensboro, North Carolina to Seattle, Washington. Also included in the small, blue memo book, and written in fountain pen, is his voyage from Seattle to Yokohama, Japan.

After reading this journal, I realize that I have inherited a great deal of my writing ability from him. He describes things in an interesting and matter-of-fact way, and takes you behind the scenes, placing you where the action is.

I have done the same thing in the world of sports, on countless occasions. I can take you behind the locker room door. There you can hear the shower dripping as it echoes off the walls and around the locker-filled room. You can see the tears and sweat that follow a hard-hitting football game and the eye-watering sharp aroma of liniment in the air.

In a column about Ali, you were with me in his hotel room, watching him recline on his bed, as he joked about how pretty his face was. You can see the vitamins on his dresser top, the area where he views tapes of prior Ken Norton fights and the white terrycloth robe he is wearing. One second his voice reflects the rigors of his endless training and the next he is jumping out of his bed, to spread a prayer rug on the floor. His charisma fills the room…he is "The Greatest."

In digesting Dad's train ride across the states, I see a 24-year-old man who handles responsibility well. He is proud to serve his country, is drinking in all that his eyes can focus on, and realizes he is experiencing this trip, never to pass this way again in his lifetime.

This ride by rail, is filled with the lonely hours of being away from home, and the uncertainty of what lies ahead in Seattle and Yokohama, Japan. Most of the time on this train, including the changing of engines and the endless card games, are about as boring as watching grass grow or paint dry.

Back in the 1960s, a folk singer named Arlo Guthrie, from Coney Island, N.Y., came on the scene. The son of well-known singer Woody Guthrie, Arlo hit the big time in 1966, with the song "Alice's Restaurant." It was a tune about a real life experience in Stockbridge, Massachusetts. Arlo got busted for littering in that town and apparently got the hard core criminal treatment by local authorities. So he made his trying experience, into a popular record.

Guthrie appeared on the first day of the Woodstock Festival in Bethel, N.Y., (30 miles from my home) in August 1969. This festival of peace and love, is said to have attracted a half million people. He joined artists such as Joan Baez, Blood Sweat and Tears, Country Joe McDonald and the Fish, Creedence Clearwater Revival, Jimi Hendrix, Janis Joplin, The Who, Crosby, Stills, Nash and Young, The Grateful Dead and Melanie.

To me, this musical genius, captured Dad's railroad ride perfectly, in a 1970 song entitled "The City Of New Orleans." That is the name of the train in the song, and Arlo makes you feel a variety of moods, experienced by the passengers. In my dad's case, the boring journey would have been enough to make Harpo Marks start shouting obscenities.

The words that Guthrie sang, speak for themselves.

"Rolls along past houses, farms and fields. Passing trains that have no names, freight yards full of old black men and the graveyards of the rusted automobiles.

Good morning America how are you? Don't you know me I'm your native son. I'm the train they call the City of New Orleans, I'll be gone five hundred miles when the day is done.

Dealin card games with the old men in the club car. Penny a point ain't no one keeping score. Pass the paper bag that holds the bottle. Feel the wheels rumblin' 'neath the floor.

Nighttime on the City of New Orleans. Changin' cars in Memphis, Tennessee. Halfway home, we'll be home by morning. Through the Mississippi darkness. Rollin down to the sea."

The rhythm of the rails is what he felt, when he was put into motion in Greensboro. A long trip by rail and sea awaited. Here is how he so vividly captured those moments, more than 55 years ago.

"July 19, 1946. Greensboro, N.C. En route to Seattle. First leg to Yokohama, Japan. Army sleepers ride like boxcars. Up at 6 a.m. and in Tennessee. Started in Greensboro, then Knoxville, Tennessee, Louisville, Kentucky, East St. Louis and St. Louis, Missouri."

"July 20, 1946. Travel through Mo. Following the Mississippi River and passing through farmlands, under water from rain. Contrast to the tobacco farms of Kentucky. River dams and boat locks. Hannibal, Mo., Iowa-farmlands and corn. Burlington, Iowa is a beautiful railroad station, nice town. Then Cedar Rapids, Waterloo. Half hour stop at Manley, Iowa. Drilling to limber up. Busy guarding car."

"July 21, 1946. St. Paul, Minnesota by 2 a.m. Wheat fields at Breckenridge, Minn. Great Northern Railway rest of the way. Fargo, North Dakota 10:30 a.m., level plains. Headed toward Montana. Arrive Minot, North Dakota 3:30 p.m. 125 miles from Montana border. Entered Montana 7:30 a.m. Wide open country-rolling hills used for cattle grazing. To arrive at Whitefish morning of July 22."

"July 22, 1946. Middle of the Rockies in a.m. Crossed Idaho border 1 p.m. Eagles nests here and the water looks green. Priest River, Idaho, then through mountains 6 p.m. in Spokane, Washington (on border). Quincy, Wash., headed for Seattle."

"July 23, 1946. Seattle 5 a.m. Railyards till 10 a.m., then trucks to camp. Post is in Ft. Lawton, Wash., just outside Seattle, in mountains. Beautiful scenery. Barracks overlooks Puget Sound."

"July 30, 1946. Informed at Ft. Lawton ship out tomorrow."

"July 31, 1946. Roll call every hour. Going to the pier in groups of 16 (400 men), truck number 4. Ship in Seattle pier 37. Ship "General McRae" troop ship, is newly painted. Bunks in tiers of four. Lights out 10 p.m. Sail at 11 a.m. Aug. 1, 1946."

Dad's voyage from Seattle, had a roadblock thrown in right away. His log book started on July 19 and would end over a month later, on August 23.

"Aug. 1, 1946. Will be a typist. Others KP and guard duty. Head up Puget Sound to the Pacific. Passed out books on the Japanese language. 60 miles up Puget Sound, trouble in engine room. Dropped anchor. Back to Port of Seattle. Need repairs."

"Aug. 2, 1946. Working in Orderly Room. Repairs taking place. Can see Mt. Ranier in distance."

"Aug. 3, 1946. Left Seattle 1:30 p.m. Port Angelus."

51

"Aug. 4, 1946. Most guys sea sick. White caps."
"Aug. 5, 1946. 15 knots. 800 miles from Seattle."
"Aug. 6, 1946. Noon. 1,054 miles from Seattle. Foggy. 8-9 more days to Yokohama. 6 hours earlier than New York now. 1,500 miles from Seattle. Guys playing blackjack."
"Aug. 9, 1946. Over half of trip done. Crossing International Date-line."
"Aug. 11, 1946. 1,536 miles to go."
"Aug. 12, 1946. 1,100 miles to go. Over 3,000 from Seattle. 15 hours ahead of New York. In North Pacific."
"Aug. 13, 1946. Weather warmer."
"Aug. 14, 1946. Saw schools of porpoise and whale. 200 miles to go to Yokohama. Slept on deck."
"Aug. 15, 1946. Passed lighthouse at 4 a.m. Seeing Japanese carriers and other war ships. Can see Fujiama. Yokohama 9 a.m. Going to Fourth Replacement Depot, 26 miles southwest of Yokohama, near Zama."
"Aug. 23, 1946. Went to Tachikowa by truck. Boarded C-46 transport plane. Four planes are carrying 60 men. 9,000 feet over the ocean, 140 mph. 5 hours, destination Kimpo, 20 miles from Seoul, Korean capital. Permanent station 5th AF 308th Bomb Wing, probably 6 months. Assigned Section A-1, Sgt. Major Post Personnel Section."

Although Dad didn't elaborate much, he gave you the facts and told you what he saw and knew about his trip. This is much the way he is in real life. He cuts straight to the chase, without beating around the bush.

One thing I can say about my father. You always knew where you stood with him. The discipline he gave me while growing up, has gotten me through some real tough times. In fact, 19 years to the day, that he was on the Pacific Ocean and had 1,536 miles to go, I was at Lackland Air Force Base, San Antonio, Texas, in boot camp. My training instructor was an ex-Marine named Stacy Young. I still have a tough time absorbing the fact, that I made it through his mental and physical rigors. Later, I put up with 16 months overseas, close to 14 of them on an island 4-8 miles wide and 32 miles long. I still have nightmares about "The Rock", otherwise known as Andersen AFB, Guam.

I have been to various places with Dad in my lifetime.

There was the trip to Illinois, a period when we bowled on Sundays, a couple of baseball games in New York, and horse racing at Monticello Raceway. None of those events can compare with Sunday, August 26, 2001 though. That is the day that he went back in time, over a half century and once again was aboard a B-24 plane. Some of the people who came to Montgomery Airport, listened to his fascinating stories about being an aerial gunner. He had turned back the clock and was in his young 20s again.

For $7, a person could look at and go aboard the B-24 or B-17 planes. I was a shutter bug that day, getting pictures of Dad as he talked with several World War II and Korean veterans. One of them, a guy named John, from Mayfield, NJ, had also been an aerial gunner.

Dad came equipped for this event, carrying a case that contained genuine Air Force material from the 1940s. Included were patches that he had kept from his time in the service. Curious people edged closer to see and hear what it was all about.

The fellow in charge of the plane exhibit, Randy Duncan, from the state of Washington (who reminds me of former Yankee Don Mattingly), was very interested and became quick friends with my father. "We have to keep this kind of thing going," Duncan said. He noted that it wasn't just about the planes, but centered on the men from all those years ago. "It is all about guys like you," he told Dad, "who helped to make these memories."

It was a sunny day with blue skies when we left Port Jervis around 2 p.m. About 4:30 p.m., we returned from a trip into the past.

In Montgomery, Dad looked up the back steps and then ascended a B-24 (J). It was a later version of the plane he had been on (H), but that didn't matter. He was right at home with his surroundings. I guess it was like riding a bicycle. It is something you never forget.

This experience, complete with a 27-shot roll of film that I photographed of the event, is priceless. "I laid on my belly for hours at a time, when in an aerial gunner's position," he explained. "I couldn't see my hands." Dad had to operate in a small, confined area and obviously, claustrophobia didn't come into play. "You get used to it," he said matter-of-factly.

On the way home, Dad started telling some Air Force stories, which is something he very rarely did.

He told about being threatened with being busted, when he was in charge of an office in Texas. "I didn't report for physical training because I was needed at the work place," he recalled. "The Major said he would take care of it, but he never did. Later, a staff car pulled up near the barracks and there was a two hour meeting over it. All I got, was suspension to quarters for 24 hours. So after that, I transferred to another area. There was no sense in staying where I got in trouble."

Earlier, back in Montgomery, Dad was telling someone a story about a guy that outranked him, as he prepared to board an aircraft. "You can't take that on board," an official told him, regarding a briefcase Dad was clutching. "If this briefcase doesn't go, I don't go," was his reply. The final words of that conversation were, "Go ahead then, get on board."

Dad knows that his aerial gunnery days were a long time ago. For years, I was never even given a tidbit of information, regarding any of Dad's past, including those Air Force years.

But his journal describing the train trip to Seattle and his Pacific sailing aboard the "General McRae" were written, while Mom was back home, pregnant with me.

Coming home from Montgomery, Dad talked about getting five medals from the government, that are due him. He also spoke about his views on life and death.

"People worry about dying," he said. "They stop working or retire and wind up sitting on the front porch. A year later, they are dead."

An oddity in the family tree, surrounds the date September 17, 1942. That is the date Dad enlisted in the service, while also being the birth dates (not the same year) of both Aunt Sonja and Uncle Bob.

The thing I will most remember Dad for, is how he provided for his family without complaint, while toiling almost every day of his working life. He is always seen wearing an immaculate shirt and tie, day in and day out. This professional person, never stuck his nose in my business and was always there for me.

He always told me to "travel light" and his reassuring words "nobody can stop time", got me through a demanding boot camp in Texas and nearly a year and a half in the Pacific. At both locations, I could count on both Mom and Dad sending me letters from home.

Mom was the person who brought cookies and refreshments out to my friends and me, while I was growing up. She could break up fights, play catch with the best of them and would buy me my next wiffle ball.

She came to most of my high school basketball games, whether they were home or on the road.

Once while I was playing for the Plattsburgh Panthers base softball team, I competed in a tournament, while nursing a near strep throat. It was Mom who traveled close to five hours and helped to make sure I was okay when I came off the softball field.

Both parents were there when I made a last second basket against Ellenville that sent a junior varsity game into overtime. My foul shot eventually won the memorable event. My chest was bursting with pride, not so much that I had come through in the clutch, but because they were there to see it happen.

The local radio station, WDLC Port Jervis, kept saying that it was a desperation shot from just inside half court by "Jerry Tangen", that sent the game into overtime. Leave it to Dad to be given credit, when all he did was sit in the bleachers.

Regarding sports, Dad was a follower of Ted Williams (Boston Red Sox), but knew that Mickey Mantle was my idol. We saw both on the same field, at Yankee Stadium. I believe it was Williams' last appearance in New York. I was also fortunate enough to see Bob Cousy of the Boston Celtics, in his last pro basketball game, against the Knicks, at the old Madison Square Garden.

Dad was never real serious about baseball. He called power hitter Harmon Killebrew "Harmon drink-a-beer" and Mantle "Mickey Moose."

Mom doesn't kid when it comes to baseball. She is a die-hard Yankee fan, just like Papa was, and worships Derek Jeter (shortstop). She calls him her "Little Jeter" even though he stands 6-3, has a rifle arm and is a productive hitter, who can supply the long ball on occasion. I shake her up all the time, by throwing Mike Piazza of the New York Mets, in her face.

My folks are from a very disciplined era and it was captured in a 1998 book, entitled "The Greatest Generation" by broadcast journalism professional Tom Brokaw (NBC).

The South Dakota native, believes that Dad and Mom are from a generation that is the greatest any society has ever produced. Those folks came of age during the Great Depression and Second World War.

In the Spring of 1984, Brokaw went to Normandy (northwest of France) to report an NBC documentary on the 40th anniversary of D-Day. D-Day marked the massive and daring Allied invasion of Europe, that was the beginning of the end of Adolph Hitler's Third Reich.

Brokaw said he underwent a life-changing experience by walking the beaches with American veterans, in their 60s and 70s, who came back for the anniversary. He became grateful for what they had done and was back for the 50th anniversary as well.

That generation is to be respected, that is for sure. However, they were so much in control, that they sometimes hurt the feelings of their offspring, probably without meaning to.

"Little pitchers have big ears" and "children should be seen and not heard" were two sayings that really made young people feel wanted and good about themselves. Parents felt it was noble, for a kid to take the blame for something that someone else had done wrong, because it was the proper thing to do. That is pure hogwash, in my opinion.

They could dispense advice and inform their kids of important things too, as demonstrated by these gems. "Don't smoke it will stunt your growth...tuck your shirt tails in or you will get a cold...don't touch a frog or you will get warts...wash behind your ears...don't swim after you eat or you will drown."

On a serious note, we should be proud of that generation. Regarding the service, World War II and the Korean War produced awful casualties. But Vietnam was no picnic either.

There were enough U.S. deaths in Vietnam (58,169) to fill Yankee Stadium to capacity. And still, it is only referred to as "The Vietnam Conflict."

This unpopular "conflict" affected our whole country. Boys had to change into men overnight. They were in the jungles of a far off land, hopefully for 12 months, not even knowing what they were fighting for. But each and every female and male, did their country proud, fighting for America. The reward for many of them, was to be spit on, when they came back home. For shame!

While on temporary duty at Utapao Airfield, Thailand, I saw the B-52s go out on bombing missions every night. I flew near or over Vietnam twice, and to this day, I can't forget how green the countryside was down below. A classmate of mine at Port Jervis High, Jack Tedrick, wrote these words in my 1965 blue and white yearbook. "Enjoy your vacation in Vietnam."

In my early days as a newspaper reporter in 1970 and 1971, I covered the police beat and sports. I would place phone calls every morning to police agencies, to see if there had been activity overnight.

One of the troopers that treated me decently, was Trooper Edwin Pearce at the Milford, Pa. barracks. He was always willing to help and had a cheerful disposition. No doubt, his personality changed some in 1972.

On March 29, 1972, Edwin and Rosemary Pearce's son, Edwin "Jack" Pearce, a former classmate of my wife's at Delaware Valley High School (Pa.), was shot down in Laos. The Air Force Sergeant, an aerial gunner, was one in a crew of 14, from the 16th Special Operations Squadron, attached to Ubon Airfield, Thailand.

The AC130A gunship "Prometheus" left Ubon on an armed reconnaissance mission over Laos, was shot down and burst into flames.

Emergency beepers could be heard from the area of the aircraft and it has been said that some survived the crash, by parachuting out of the ill-fated plane. In 1973, Pearce was declared Missing In Action. A few years back, a tooth believed to be linked to Jack Pearce, was sent home for burial. He had been declared dead. To this day, the Pearces refuse to accept that type of thinking.

Jack's dad, the trooper, fought in World War II and was captured by the Nazis. He spent two years as a Prisoner of War, in Stalag 17. Call it a gut feeling or just positive thinking, but Edwin and Rosemary refuse to give up.

Jack Pearce, born December 8, 1947, may be one of many in the 50-56 year-old age group that could still be alive in Southeast Asia.

Pearce was shot from the darkness of the sky at 0300 on March 29, 1972. At 2:36 p.m., March 29, 1972, Tracie Lynn Tangen came into the world at St. Francis Hospital. For one family, a door was about to close and for a young couple, just seven miles away, a door to the life of a new born baby girl opened.

Three guys that I knew from my high school days at Port Jervis, Tom Case, John Ripel and Jerry Evans, became casualties of Vietnam.

Evans, from Wurtsboro, N.Y., was a year younger than me (born November 6, 1948), and from the class of 1966. A PFC in the Marine Corps., hostile small arms fire on the ground, claimed his life on September 11, 1968, at Quang Nam, South Vietnam. He was only 19 and had been in country just 29 days.

I remember him as a good-looking, shy, blond guy that the girls swooned over. His name is on panel 44w line 23 of "The Wall."

Going back to my family tree, Mom still doesn't know her mom or dad's first name. It has been weeks since she sent in another request and payment for her birth certificate. Hopefully, the information she is entitled to, in the form of her birth certificate, will finally reach her hands.

Seeing where my roots are and where I came from, is a fascinating journey into the past.

I have learned quite a bit about my dad and mom's side of the family. Fritz set the tone for my dad's side, with a loner type attitude. Never confuse the description "tight knit" with my family.

Uncle Buddy, the teasing motorcycle guy that scared the hell out of me as a boy, takes top billing in the list of relatives who had an impact on me.

Way back in the 1950s, he left me with a solid piece of advice. "Don't let your battleship mouth overload your rowboat ass."

CHAPTER 3

Discovering Sports

We moved to 32 Brooklyn Street in 1949, when I was only two years old, and left in 1952. By the time I was three, I was riding a tricycle and teaching a cat named "Mouser" how to eat his cat food correctly. With me on all fours in the kitchen, Mouser watched in amazement as I chewed his food with great gusto. It may have been around this time, that Listerine was invented.

As a toddler, I fell off a rocking horse and had to have stitches in my forehead. Maybe that head injury stayed with me for life. At least that could serve as an excuse for some of the crazy things that have happened to me over the years.

It wasn't a matter of simply falling off the toy horse as a normal child might do. I had to go a step farther and put the toy on a slanted outside cellar door and proceed to topple onto my little noggin.

There was substantial blood. Mom says I screamed loudly while also yelling "my horsie threw me."

It seems that "Billy" had a knack for getting into trouble, much of the time. With a reservoir runoff brook occupying the side of our apartment house, there was plenty of mischief for me to get into, once I was four and five years old. However, when younger, I pulled some surprises that my parents still talk about a half century later.

I'm told that one of my favorite toys was a steamroller. As a child I rode it for hours on end. There was the sidewalk out front and on the side (near that infamous cellar door), to ride on. And, as Mom would find out, there was the whole city of Port Jervis available to me.

Mom would stop by Papa's insurance office at 32 Ball Street on occasion. I always loved being spoiled by Papa and looked forward to each meeting. Then came a day when a little boy decided to take the bull by the horns and hit the open road.

This unaccompanied journey was my first big caper and it got rave reviews, to say the least. It covered roughly 10 city blocks and included two stops on my steamroller route.

First was a visit to the Colonial Inn, a historical hotel and bar-restaurant on West Main Street, about four blocks from home. Papa lived in an apartment here and I went looking for him. Obviously the adult that told me he was at his office, thought Mom was close by.

Undaunted by failing to connect, Billy The Kid proceeded through the heart of town, hopped off the steamroller and went inside the building he had recognized from prior visits.

I'm told that Papa greeted me with his customary good humor and was happy to see me. "Where is your Mommy, Billy?" he asked. "Oh, she will be coming later," I replied seriously. The resulting phone call to Mom must have been a dandy. She probably set some type of speed record in reaching the office.

"I wanted to spank you," Mom explains. "But instead I hugged you very tightly."

The first two sports I was exposed to were demolition derbies and Friday night boxing. I would sneak down the stairs and quietly watch the television as cars demolished each other. Soon, I got interested in boxing as I watched Jimmy Powers broadcast the Gillette-sponsored fights.

My favorite fighter was a guy named Frankie Ryff. I liked the way he looked in his dark trunks as he punched relentlessly. The record books tell me Ryff was still fighting in 1959. He was on the cover of Ring Magazine in May 1955. Back in 1954, he knocked out Ralph Dupas in the eighth round in Brooklyn. But on July 20, 1959, Dupas returned the favor in New Orleans.

Dad was friendly with an insurance special agent, named George Milot. He was my Godfather and would visit us from time to time. When George dropped by, we would have a "real" boxing match. I would come out in my red trunks and bathrobe, just like Frankie Ryff. And, George would let me punch his hands with all my might.

This was my first real exposure to the sport of boxing. I still can't comprehend that some day, I would stand next to Joe Louis and shake the hands of Sugar Ray Robinson, Ken Norton and Muhammad Ali.

Dad says that George Milot talked of how his dad died at a young age. "He (George) believed that he wouldn't live a very long life," Dad once told me. And that is exactly what happened as Milot died of a heart attack at the age of 43.

My playmates on Brooklyn Street also lived in the same house. Keith, Charlotte and Howard Griffin were my constant companions. I still have pictures of me on my bike and surrounded by them, near a big tree that bordered our property. Keith was a little bit older than me and always wore a sailor hat. His dad had been in the Navy. Our days were filled with adventure and non-stop fun, whether it be going to Heussy's store for a popsicle, riding bikes or playing in the canal.

Al Mosher lived down the block and across the street. I never really associated with him in those days but occasionally waved hello. In my teen years, he became friends with Fish and then we became acquainted. Al played a mean guitar and became part of "The Five Dimensions" band that played at the Pinehurst Casino, near Highland Lake, back in the summer of 1965. Those days, plus the summers of 1966 and 67, were the greatest of my life.

I was constantly told not to go near the canal. It could be a dangerous place for us kids, with its four foot high cement walls. Since I was told to avoid that spot, I, of course did the opposite and sneaked in it whenever possible.

This reservoir runoff brook is a concrete structure that empties into the Neversink River. A block away, on Canal Street, the brook goes under the road. We used to take jaunts down the brook and under the road, if we could avoid the eyes of our parents.

Ann Buckley lived in an upstairs apartment with her husband, Dutch. The two were real nice to us kids, and every weekday we would go up the outside steps and into their apartment to watch the Howdy Doody television show. We all liked Howdy, Clarabell the clown, Buffalo Bob, Flub-A-Dub, Mr. Bluster, Chief Thundercloud, Dilly Dally and Princess Summerfall Winterspring. There was one obstacle though as we waited to see Howdy. Kate Smith always stood between us and our favorite show.

Ann would always offer us candy and that probably helped in getting us through Kate's "When The Moon Comes Over The Mountain" song. That is how her program always ended and we counted the seconds until she was finally through. Kate Smith passed away in 1986. I wonder how many times she sang that song in her lifetime.

One day our gang decided to go into the brook area and up under Canal Street. We were caught though by parents and were remanded back to the house. Meanwhile, Ann Buckley came on the scene and began firing a .22 rifle under the road. Word has it, that we were playing in the company of rattlesnakes or copperheads.

Once I was playing out back while Dad worked near me. Dark clouds moved in and a rumble of thunder was heard in the distance. "You better go inside Billy, it's going to rain," Dad said. I ignored his advice and stayed outside. Soon enough, the sky illuminated with lightning and a deafening crack of thunder followed. The "gluppies" were after me and I ran crying into the house. "I don't like this rain" I wailed. Oddly, the opposite became true in my life. I love rain pouring down on the roof, splashing through the trees and into deep puddles. Watching it against a street light or in headlights of a car, are very pleasurable to me. The 14 months I spent on Guam included its share of rain. At night, I peered through the louvers of the barracks, watching the rain against the dazzling lights of the cars that were heading back toward the base.

As a kid, I hated onions, peas and red cabbage. The onions were especially gross and tasted yucky to me. One time they were on my plate and Mom made me eat them anyway. I told her onions would make me sick. She insisted though and somehow I got through the task. Not a half hour later, Mom was cleaning up after me. Just as predicted, I had gotten sick all over the place.

While onions are still not a favorite of mine, I will have occasional onion rings. Peas are no problem now, but red cabbage is still a no-no. If I had to pick the two things I despise the most, it would be liver and olives.

All of you people that tell me "you haven't had liver cooked the right way" can take a long walk off a short dock. It was, is and always will be, a pungent, strong and revolting taste that makes shoe leather seem yummy.

On Guam there was always one night a week of liver at the chow hall. And of course, that night fell on the day before we got paid. There was no going to the Filipino Club for chopped steak or to the BX for a cheeseburger. With just change jingling in my pocket, I had no choice other than shuffling into the damn chow hall. Early in my overseas tour, I took a bite of liver and promptly spit it back onto the plate as I looked around the room. And from that day forward, on liver night, I loaded up on cottage cheese bathed in French dressing. This concoction still is made in my home, from time to time.

Eventually, Dad convinced me to believe that the loud claps of thunder I thought were those horrible "gluppies" was actually nothing more than the elves bowling. But there was a worse problem than gluppies, lurking down at the end of my block.

In the summer, we would walk and ride our bikes for ice cream or popsicles at the store, located around the corner on Orange Street. But a band of wild kids that I called "the freshies" were throwing sticks and rocks, swearing and scaring us to death. They had faces caked in dirt, ripped clothes and acted like barbarians. We were taught to never go in the road, but this rule went by the wayside whenever we had to get around those freshies. With this obstacle standing in the way, I learned at a young age, that the world could be a scary place to live in.

Mouser was an alley cat who came in to eat from time to time. He was white with a touch of gray as I recall, and stayed outside overnight. Every now and then, Mouser would disappear for a day or two. One time he returned home via the canal, dragging a trap from his paw. It wasn't long before Mouser was just a memory.

Dad tells me that there was a day when I threw papers in the canal and the neighbors (across the canal) called the police on me. I'm sure that a 4-year-old was a definite menace to society and it's good to see that the neighbors halted this dangerous criminal.

I remember Mom discussing names for a baby that would be coming to live with us. And on March 15, 1952, a premature Anne Elizabeth Tangen was born at St. Francis Hospital. She was the apple of Mom's eye and of course I became a jealous child.

During our upbringing, the five years difference in age split us into two different crowds. We fought like cats and dogs but I always protected my sister if she got into any problems with others. If my folks got into an argument, I would take her outdoors and away from the noise. When we were five and 10 years old, Dad called us "the 5 and 10" (a store chain).

I was a jock in high school and hung out with two different types of groups (athletes and non-athletes). I ignored my sister for years and it probably wasn't until I reached my 40s that we became tight. She shares my gregarious traits, has the same smart-assed attitude I do and possesses a sense of humor that makes me laugh. We both make fun of certain people and are great at imitations.

They say "you can never go back." I don't agree.

While memories of the past are just that, you can return to the very spot where those memories originated. I plan to do that with Hammond Street, Lyman Avenue in West End, way up in Plattsburgh, where I was in the Air Force, and have already done it with Brooklyn Street.

On the morning of Feb. 18, 2002, I went back in time a half century, with Chris at my side. The house on Brooklyn Street is still there, although aluminum siding now covers the brown exterior that I remember as a young boy. As you look at the front of the dwelling, the brook still borders it on the right.

The other side of the brook used to be the Karst property. You enter that land between pillars, located at the end of the street. If you look to the right, you can see Canal Street, where Ann Buckley took aim at the snakes.

The front yard is tiny and at the left side of it stands a rusted pipe and spigot. I wonder if that was present when I resided here. Across from that are the slanted outside cellar doors that I took my toy rocking horse on. The doors are now painted brown. Three large trees still stand on the property. One of them is where my picture was snapped with the Griffin kids.

Three cars are parked here this day. One of them leaves though, holding passengers who probably wonder who the hell we are. The back yard where I visualize high grass, is now all dirt and fenced in. It appears that the same slate sidewalks remain in front and on the side, leading to the porch.

32 Brooklyn Street is both foreign and familiar at the same time.

Through the eyes of a young and energetic boy, this place was the ideal playground. Games of hide and seek, exploring the canal, running like the wind, chasing a dream. This was nothing short of paradise to a hyper kid who hadn't even picked up a basketball yet. My fountain of youth always gushed the fun of today and the innocent promise of tomorrow. Fast forwarding 50 years seemed very strange. I was looking back at a little blond-haired boy who kept people on their toes, but was lucky enough to be loved. It was my old stomping grounds and the first location I remember in my life. But Billy felt more like a character I had read about in a story from long ago.

I walked down the street toward our car. Past where Daisy the dog had growled at us so many years before. Daisy, owned by Emogene and Morgan Sweeney, never did care for my gang. We never teased the small and furry long-haired animal, but she bared teeth just the same.

My eyes scoped out the scene to the right. There is a paved parking lot here now. But long ago, bratty girls and boys with unruly hair claimed this territory. I can still hear the freshies with their high-pitched wailing and screaming voices.

Behind me I had walked the area and recaptured some special memories. At the same time, I had gazed down at a brook that now resembles a mini junk yard. Wrappers, empty soda bottles and a discarded McDonald's bag spoiled the scenery. I had focused on the steps up to where Buckley's apartment was and even recalled the words "Say kids, what time is it?" and all of Howdy's loyal viewers answering "it's Howdy Doody time."

We moved to Hammond Street in 1952 and stayed until 1958. This is where baseball, football and basketball started to occupy a large part of my life. Papa lived in a downstairs apartment here and I recall going down to listen to spring training baseball games on his radio. This is where I hopped up on his knee to listen to the interesting comic books that he would read in an unhurried and gentle style.

When Papa worked, he worked. But he knew how to laugh it up and party with the best of them. Secretaries at his office were always informed when the tall man with white hair would be taking a day off. "They all knew," Dad recalled. "He would go out and have his drinks. And after a couple of days of that, he always stopped the drinking by having a big meal."

One time he drove into the driveway and fell asleep with the car still on. Dad got up from his bed and went down to escort "Bill" inside. Another time he got all fired up and ordered a brand new car from his good friend Henry Ruderman at the Pontiac dealership. "Just switch cars in the driveway," he said. The next day, he went out to go to work and asked "whose car is this? where did my car go? I want it back."

On another occasion Papa was said to take a short cut on one of his driving escapades. There was an alleyway between Front and Balls streets and he figured, what the hell, why waste time? So, he barreled his Pontiac through that alley, ripping chrome off both sides of the car.

Sometimes I would stay overnight with Papa. However, he would have nightmares and be screaming "help, help!" into the night and scaring me to death. Mom says some of the nightmares were about being robbed and another was about falling from his outdoor porch at the Colonial Inn (which really happened).

Papa introduced me to the Yankees and I also began being interested in local sports. He was known throughout Port Jervis as a fair, decent man with a heart of gold. If a customer couldn't afford an insurance payment he would spot them the money until they could make it right. He was an organizer of a yearly Elks Port Jervis football banquet that honored Red Raider players. He was my Papa and there will never be another.

As an 8-year-old, I played Little League baseball for the Yankees and wore number "7", the same as Mickey Mantle. I was the youngest kid on the team and was very small in size. I got to bat only a few times, but my manager, Johnny Schoonmaker, a former sportswriter and mayor of Port Jervis, treated me kindly. My lone hit was a bunt single that I beat out by sprinting to first base. Schoonmaker laughed and laughed with the little kid who got his hit. "Willie whiskers...you ran like a jack rabbit," he told me.

The next year, Jazz Seeber, a hard-nosed former Port athletic star, took over the Yankees. He dripped with discipline and wanted to win at all costs. We practiced on freezing cold days and he yelled if you complained about your hands stinging from connecting with the ball. Baseball became agony for me. I was completely turned off and didn't return the following year.

In the service, I was a softball centerfielder in Plattsburgh, nicknamed "quail" for my speed and always batting with aggressiveness. Here and on Guam, players, coaches and fans were incredulous to hear that the guy consistently batting over .300 and gracefully patroling the outfield, never played high school baseball. Instead, I had been a long jumper and triple jumper on a powerhouse track team.

While I preferred playing sandlot baseball to Little League, Schoonmaker and John Bell were the best friends a young kid could ask for. Mr. Bell, an Indians manager, took time to hit fly ball after fly ball to me in the outfield. He had two future Port Jervis athletes for sons, Frankie and "Little John." I wound up playing basketball with Little John and later covered him as wrestling and football coach at Minisink Valley High School.

Baseball games down at the corner of Church and Hammond streets were lots of fun. In one at bat, I hit a towering fly ball to left field that found a resting place on the top of a telephone pole. I never forgot that home run and for years recalled it as being a long shot. That vision was shattered in my adult years when I happened by the field and saw how tiny it was. Like the old Bee Gees song "now we are tall and Christmas trees are small."

On Hammond Street I had lots of friends. Tom Beirne, a diehard Brooklyn Dodgers fan, and Lester Buchanan, were two of them. Then there was Stuart Peck, an intellectual kid and his older brother Peter. Stuart, a science whiz, once set the kitchen linoleum on fire to see if it was combustible. It certainly was, and the fire trucks all responded in a timely manner.

Beirne and I played wiffle ball for hours on end. He was always the Dodgers and I was the Yanks. Three big things happened in 1955. Port Jervis got pounded with a flood in August, compliments of Hurricane Diane, the Yanks lost the World Series to the Dodgers and I hit Tom Beirne in the head with an empty whipped cream bottle as I sat on the top of my garage roof.

The Delaware River jumped its banks during the flood as rowboats became the main mode of transportation. Southpaw Johnny Podres beat the Yanks in game seven and the whipped cream bottle caught Beirne square in the forehead. When I saw all the blood I took off toward Tri-States, knowing I could never return home. How would life be as a fugitive?

Time seemed to heal the rift between Beirne and me, although for days and days he laid guilt trips on me by talking about his stitches while pointing to the band aid on his head. Simply put, we were playing catch and he couldn't handle one of my throws from up above. The moral of the story is to always be prepared for the next ball or whipped cream can that is thrown to you.

I must have badgered Dad for weeks on end to take me fishing. He finally got tired of my begging and decided we'd go in mid-August. While the rains of Hurricane Diane poured down, I alternately looked at his Ted Williams fishing pole and out the window. This trip to the river just wasn't meant to be. And in an odd twist, the river came to us. I can still see Papa sitting on his front porch rocking chair, flatly refusing to go to higher ground. He was stubborn at certain times and was ready, willing and able to go down with the ship.

I continued to bat rocks in the driveway. If the game was at Yankee Stadium I'd hit them toward Hammond Street and if it was a Yankee away game, the pebbles would be hit over the back yard. At both "stadiums" were houses. And when I really smacked one, sides of houses and roofs would be targets. The "ping" of contact with a dwelling sent me scurrying inside my garage to a safe hiding place.

I guess the first girl that I ever had feelings for was grade school classmate Sally Gallondorn. Matante and a school friend, Mike Castle, both lived near Sally. So, after school Mike and I would go and terrorize Matante and then move on to Schultz Street (where Sally lived), under the guise of visiting another friend, Doug Casterlin.

At the 35th high school reunion, Castle brought up the blond and pretty Sally Gallondorn. "You wrote all over her driveway "Billy Loves Sally" Mike laughed. "Don't you remember?" As Sally danced nearby with her husband I smiled back. "No Mike, I don't remember that at all."

Friday nights were fantastic in those days. Especially if the Port football or basketball teams were playing at home. Sports had started becoming very important to me and even got me in trouble from time to time. We neighborhood kids had little money to spend and what we could save out usually went for wiffle balls, baseball cards, the movies or ice cream and snacks.

One such visit to Glennette Field to see the Port Red Raiders in action, always stuck in my mind. On this occasion, we were caught red handed as we tried to sneak into the game without paying.

Years later, I covered many games at Glennette Field as coaches Viglione and successor Corvino guided state-ranked teams. Night games were always my favorites as the football was teed up under the dazzling brilliance of lights. People of all ages buzzed in the bleachers and congregated around the cinder track that borders the historical gridiron. Many times I walked behind the home stands and to a nearby fence as the hands of time rewound back to the mid 1950s and froze there.

I am now that young kid from Hammond Street that worships Red Raider football. All roads lead to Glennette Field for Friday night home games. A bunch of us chatter with great expectations as we walk up Church Street toward East Main. Our heroes, quarterback Dick Pencek, fullback Vince "Barrel" Pagano and the rest of the Raiders are just moments away from tangling with the enemy.

One of the big capers of the day, was sneaking through the fence that parallels the Port bleachers. All you had to do, was time things right and hope to go undetected.

Patrolman Frank Masanotti was the cop assigned to Glennette Field detail. The trick was to slip through the hole in a damaged fence when he wasn't looking. We were silently enveloped into the shadows near Sylvia and Hatch's "Campus" (a teen hangout near the high school) and entered the world of risk and adventure.

The hole was big enough for all members of our nervous gang to fit through, one at a time. Our lookout had his eyes riveted beyond the fence. We took a deep breath and proceeded to break the law as the National Anthem was just beginning. We never heard the words "by the dawn's early light."

As if by magic, one Frank Masanotti appeared out of nowhere. For years, the tall guy with the humorous personality and big smile, was a magician during his time off. But this had been one of his most impressive tricks.

The policeman with the shiny badge and the painfully visible nightstick had made the pinch. Needless to say, we were scared beyond belief. Our eyes spied the handcuffs that dangled from the law enforcement belt. What would jail be like at the tender age of eight?

Brandishing his big flashlight and training it on our faces, he walked forward. "Look you kids," he bellowed, while trying to keep a straight face. "You don't go sneaking through the fence while the Star Spangled Banner is playing. You sneak through it when it's over."

With that, he turned on his heel and resumed his Glennette beat as if he hadn't seen a thing. There would be no jail time after all.

Years later, Masanotti became Port Jervis Police Chief and I was a police reporter and sportswriter for the Union-Gazette newspaper. We laughed about the incident more than once.

Nobody can really make time stand still. Black leather jackets, hot cars, cherry cokes and Peggy Sue have passed into oblivion. The infamous fence is still there, but Chief Masanotti is no longer with us, although his memory will never die.

Other memories at Hammond Street include getting a brown two-wheeler bicycle for my birthday, my sister getting her head caught between rungs of a railing and meeting boxer Sugar Ray Robinson.

Robinson, who many still consider the best pound-for-pound fighter ever, trained at Greenwood Lake. Robinson was training at the Long Pond Inn, for a fight against Carmen Basilio. I remember Sugar Ray skipping rope to music, sparring in an outdoor ring and later, greeting people who had attended.

We went into a lounge after the workout and it wasn't long before the handsome boxer with the polite and easy going attitude, came through the screen door. He took the time to hold my baby sister in his arms and played a game of pool with me. He gave me an 8x10 glossy picture and signed it "keep on punching--your friend Ray Robinson." This was my first encounter with a professional athlete and I was mighty impressed by this kind man.

One winter, while Dad and Mom were at a convention, Matante came to babysit. We had a major snowfall and gleefully jumped out of second story windows while Matante freaked out.

At school, I was a decent student and spelling was my favorite subject. I was winning spelling bees and also excelling in sports. Lester Buchanan and I became friends, although he and his dad, a fire chief, liked hunting and I knew nothing of the sport. The two of us kept fifth grade teacher Mrs. Winkler on her toes. Lester was the rugged type that acted tough and commanded respect. He was kind of like "Fonzie" from the television show "Happy Days", right down to the black leather jacket. Doris Winkler told me "Billy, stay away from him. He is a bad influence and your grades will suffer." Of course given a choice between being an excellent student and becoming slightly wild, Les won me over easily.

One lunch hour, we headed down Church Street for home. I would be gobbling down my customary peanut butter and jelly sandwich and then going back to my fifth grade class. However, this particular day, Les was hatching an exciting plan that would prove I had actually started taking a walk on the wild side.

"Hurry up and eat your lunch and then come down to my house," he said. "Nobody will be home and I know where my father keeps the whiskey." Before I could even think, we were firing down shots and then having to run up the hill to make it to school on time. We both completed the day with a dazed look in the eyes and smiles on our faces. I had passed the test with flying colors. While Les laughed it up, my eyes caught the glare of an icy stare from Mrs. Winkler. There was no doubt, that I had begun to tread on thin ice.

The "bad influence" later became a Port athlete, served in the Army and became a policeman. The way people change is really unpredictable. I remember reading a story on musician Billy Joel. He went to high school in Hicksville, Long Island and got this sparkling review from one of his teachers. "Billy, you'll never amount to anything," the teacher is believed to have said. Joel never did graduate but still was invited to his 10th class reunion. He had a real good reason for declining to attend, seeing as though he was scheduled to play Carnegie Hall that evening. Needless to say, that teacher wouldn't be a threat to Jeanne Dixon.

Softball and basketball began emerging as favorite sports for me. In 1957, I had played recreation Pint Size Division softball for Church Street (first base). We made it into the championship game under the lights at Glennette Field, where we were beaten by perennial titlist West End.

West End was loaded with talent and had many power hitters. One was a big left handed batter named Jerry Decker. Opponents were intimated by his raw power. I was on the receiving end of that fury in the big game, when he sent a screaming line drive down the first base line. I had no time to react but somehow got my glove up in a split second to rob him of a double or more. While fans applauded the play, I tried not to show that my left palm was screaming out in pain and swelling by the second.

A year later I was in the championship game again, this time as a pitcher for West End, where I had moved in the summer of 1958. Oddly enough, my mound opponent was none other than former teammate Les Buchanan. We won the title, 5-4, and I garnered that season's Most Valuable Player award for going 10-1 on the mound and batting .426.

My second year as a Yankee in Little League, I had a teammate named Johnny Dudko. I remember him as being a quiet kind of kid and I had an uneasy feeling when I was around him.

Jazz Seeber had this rule that forbid his kids from playing softball or swimming the day of a game. That made a helluva lot of sense to me, since all I did was sit his bench anyway. So I decided to put my time into becoming a softball star. Sometimes I had to change my name (for newspaper stories) in games played the same day as Little League contests. That worked for awhile.

However, Seeber found out what I had been doing and gave me a good ass chewing. Someone had ratted on me and word had it that the someone was Johnny Dudko. I recalled that a couple of times he had been among the spectators that watched me play softball. And, he verbally warned me that I was breaking a Yankee Little League rule.

In July 1958, Dudko was sexually abused and brutally murdered while fishing in Port Jervis. The 34-year-old killer was charged and sent to prison. Johnny was taken before he ever really got a shot at life. He was just 10 years old.

From wiffle ball to sandlot baseball, softball and witnessing high school athletic events, Billy was becoming totally involved in sports. I memorized Major League batting averages and knew standings in baseball and football by heart.

But Port Jervis high school basketball was to become my love and obsession. The reason for that can be explained in two words "Alex Osowick."

"Ossie" still holds the Port Jervis and DUSO League single game scoring record for pumping in 62 points against Monticello in 1958. Long before this amazing accomplishment, I had faithfully prided myself in being his number one fan. Years later, he became head varsity basketball coach at Port and I interviewed him many times. Osowick, in my opinion, is the greatest pure shooter to ever come out of this area.

While Osowick remains on the top of the totem pole in my eyes, one of his players, 1971 graduate Rich Saul, is pound for pound the finest high school basketball player I have ever had the pleasure to watch.

I stop to think and my mind takes over. The brain stores an incredible amount of information and visual images. This awesome human tape recorder is about to be clicked into the rewind mode again. The time machine stops in 1958.

Out here in the bitter cold of winter one is expected to complain about the freezing temperature and stomp his feet to generate some heat. But when you're a kid 10 years old and your basketball hero will be performing in just a little while, the Sahara Desert at high noon couldn't provide a warmer feeling.

Sure there are other things in life besides Port Jervis varsity basketball. At the Strand Theater, Clint "Cheyenne" Walker is featured in his first big motion picture entitled "Fort Dobbs." Another flick, "Jamboree", is playing with a star-studded cast that includes Fats Domino, Jerry Lee Lewis, Buddy Knox (that's the fellow that sang "Party Doll"), Jimmy Bowen, Charlie Gracie and The Four Coins.

Over at the Tri-State Theater, "Deep Six" with Alan Ladd and "Abbott and Costello Go To Mars" are on the agenda. For those who want to drink, dine and dance, there is always the Time Out in Sparrowbush, where Carmen's Trio furnishes the music.

To a staunch Red Raider hoop fan, those movies and any other event, rank a distant second to watching Alex Osowick gun down the enemy.

He stands 6-4" tall, says little and does it all. Many people confuse Osowick's quiet disposition for conceit. But this crew-cut shy and determined scoring machine is the farthest thing from being stuck on himself. When he unleashes a corner jump shot or hook shot, the ball

69

seems to have eyes for the basket. His hook shot is second to none. He is smooth as silk in releasing it and to try preventing the attempt, means fouling him.

The loyal fans who stand here tonight waiting for the doors to warmth and competition to open, fool around with each other as a means of dealing with the bitter cold. There are laughs and catcalls. Even though the evening is frosty and you can see your buddy's breath when he talks, a certain unexplained electricity crackles in the air. The little guy of 10 knows that tonight is going to be a special one.

He imitates Alex's every move. He mimics that deadly hook shot and practices for hours on end. Many times it is dark when he arrives home for supper and his parents just can't understand how a young high school athlete named Alex Osowick can have such an effect on their son.

Through the grapevine the kid learns that when Ossie was young, he took his mother's lampshade off the lamp, turned it upside down, nailed it up and made a basket out of it. The kid figures that if Alex used a lampshade, that must be the right thing to do. The sight of the kid's father trying to find a missing lampshade is an event in itself.

The little fellow secretly dreams and fantasizes about being the next Alex Osowick. This pint-sized boy eats, drinks, sleeps and talks basketball. Port basketball statistics are a way of life.

While the kid slumbers, perhaps dreaming of scoring that champion-ship-winning bucket, the room is enveloped in darkness. However, under the bedside table lays a scrapbook that is a shiny ray of light to the young Rip VanWinkle. It contains all of Port's basketball games to date. You could be out of town for weeks, but 20 minutes in this book and you'd know exactly how Coach Pat Farace's charges were faring.

Suddenly the long line of fans moves toward the concrete steps and through the big yellow doors. It is Friday night in Port Jervis, and the Raiders are moments away from getting acquainted with visiting Monticello.

Funny how all roads lead here. Black leather jackets, ducktail haircuts, saddle shoes, bobby socks and maybe even a beatnik or two are seen. Cigarette smoke billows skyward and a car peels out on East Main Street. The freezing night is a thing of the past and suddenly the brisk air is replaced by warmth. The aroma of sweat mixed with the sound of chattering people and bouncing basketballs dominates the scene. There is a feeling of unity as hundreds of spectators become one.

Port arrives on the court decked out in impressive red satin warmup suits with black numerals on the sleeves. During pre-game practice, warmup jackets are discarded by the five starters and the small kid's blue eyes are riveted on the big red number "7". If a net could feel pain, it would cringe with fear as Osowick fired up shot after shot that ripped the chords with a swishing sound.

Two hours later, Ossie is being carried around the gymnasium on top of his teammates' shoulders. He has outscored the entire Monticello team by zeroing in for 62 points in a stirring 98-61 Port win. The victory hikes Port's final regular season record to a shiny 14-2. Osowick tossed in 24 of 42 field goal attempts (all from long range) and clicked on 14-15 from the foul line to smash the DUSO League scoring record.

In Port basketball history there never has been the type of scoring extravaganza that took place on Feb. 28, 1958.

Union-Gazette Sports Editor Mike Kowal captured the event perfectly with these words: "A superhuman scoring effort, which sapped every bit of precious strength out of his body, saw Port Jervis scoring wizard Alex Osowick climax a glorious and colorful 3-year DUSO basketball tenure on the high school floorboards last night where Mr. Basketball of Port Jervis stuffed 62 incredible points into the nets to destroy all existing records as the Raiders cuffed Monticello, 98-61."

Ossie tacked up two league scoring championships and splashed 1,455 career points. He did that in just three seasons (60 games) and three decades before there even was a 3-point shot in basketball.

All special things wind up fading into the past. And, Feb. 28, 1958 was no different.

The enthusiastic kid with the blue eyes turned 11 years old today. It is April 8, 1958, and he expects the usual birthday party with family and presents. But this day will contain something that the birthday boy still has trouble comprehending.

Alex Osowick arrives at the party, ducking his tall athletic body under the top of the doorway. The kid's mother arranged this unbelievable surprise. This momentous happening remains in the boy's memory forever. Alex and the kid are both shy, but by the end of the evening they are comfortable with each other.

He could have broken my heart.

Instead he chose to shrug off the bleakness of the situation and made a young fan happy on his 11th birthday.

Sometimes I get the feeling Alex Osowick is playing again tonight. He'll peel off that warmup top revealing that big number "7" and proceed to handle the enemy again with his graceful style and accurate shooting touch.

Now that I look back I see how perfectly Ossie fit into the events of the 1950s. It was an innocent era and a fun time to be alive.

True, the Russians were acting up back then and at school we had to cover our heads and hide under our desks during air raid drills. Some people really freaked out and built air raid shelters that contained food and drinks. But there was a joyful feeling back then, too. This was a time when you didn't have to lock doors to the house. Walking down streets at night didn't turn into a fight for survival. Drugs were something you purchased at the pharmacy.

Dad had bought that house on Hammond Street in October of 1952.

The white apartment house was sold on July 16, 1958 and eight days later, we moved to a brown home up on 6 Lyman Avenue in West End. It had a nice big and shady grove in the back that was dotted with apple trees. More tall green and blue trees lined the side of the house that faced West Main Street.

While I lived here I became a good high school basketball player, discovered girls, managed to graduate with my class, was engaged twice, smashed up Dad's car twice in one day and met my future wife when I was just a sophomore in high school.

CHAPTER 4

Her Name is Christine

I didn't even have to ask her name. There it was, spelled out in white letters on a black Delaware Valley class of 1965 jacket. The name said "Chris."

This slender and long-haired girl was from a Pennsylvania school located across the river from Port Jervis, New York. DV and Port were bitter basketball rivals in those days and crowds would flock to the respective gymnasiums for one home and one away game.

During my junior year of school, one of the favorite pastimes on Friday and Saturday nights in Port Jervis, was pursuing and teasing girls from DV. We would follow them in and out of stores like Woolworth's, Newberry's or Penney's and make wise cracks while joking around.

I was already seeing a girl from Port named Charlene, but going steady didn't mean I was dead. Although Charlene and I were nearly inseparable, I did find some time to be with my friends. And it was during these periods, that I managed to have sporadic contact with the smiling and quiet Chris Goble. In my wildest dreams, I could never believe that someday this pretty girl would wind up my wife and life's soul mate.

When I first moved to West End, I kind of felt my way around the new surroundings. I was suddenly among strangers and guys my age had already picked their best buddies. My friends were back across the tracks in the Church Street area.

The first kid I met in West End lived on the street behind us. He was a dynamic and inquisitive little guy named Hollis Farr. As fate would have it, years later I became engaged to his sister. After marrying Chris in 1970, I covered a talented wrestler at Port who would pull out close decisions and nearly qualified for the New York State Tournament. That grappler's name was none other than Hollis Farr.

In the early days in West End, Hollis was a constant thorn in my side. He carried out the "sister's little brother routine" with gusto. It seemed it was always tough to manage being alone with a teenage girlfriend. Hollis made it a virtual impossibility.

Early on, girls were not my top priority. Basketball, softball and

73

bowling were my main loves and I worked hard at those sports in order to reach the top.

It wasn't long before I began making friends in sixth grade. Eddie Hutchins, Jack Tedrick, Gary Scales, John Hensz, Roger Gottleib, Bill Hankins and Pad Kroger became buddies. Gary (nicknamed Fish) and John (Henszie), wound up being ushers at my wedding while Pad was my best man.

In high school, I was the first of my West End group to go steady. As a junior in 1964, I sat next to Charlene on Bus #9 during Monday through Friday trips to and from Port Jervis Senior High School. Thom McKeeby was the interesting and humorous bus driver and got a kick out of the young "steadies" on his bus. He was driving that vehicle the day all the kids got on me about the Cassius Clay-Sonny Liston fight. "Liston will kill Clay," they shouted. I simply smiled and said "Clay will be our new heavyweight boxing champion."

After Clay shocked the boxing world and I won my wagers, I often daydreamed about what it would be like to meet him someday. I wonder what the odds were against that ever happening.

I tried to never turn my back on my friends. And, that began causing friction between Charlene and me. We were too young to be tied down and her mom tried constantly to get that point across. We didn't listen though and instead, believed that we were meant to be.

Before I began getting serious with her, I played countless wiffle ball games in my side yard. Fish and I ran around my block (track meets), played basketball by the hour and started becoming close friends. We were both comedians and would do most anything for a laugh. We were constant companions on the weekends and even had a boxing match in front of neighbors on a Saturday morning.

Fish didn't play organized sports that much. We were on the same track team but his love and expertise was slanted more toward music. We bowled on the same church recreation team and sometimes I even started staying overnight at his house (up in his furnished attic).

Fish and I were both raised in the Catholic religion. He went to church most Sundays while my participation began to dwindle. Of course I would do anything to get out of school, so when we had "religious instruction" I would attend, just to escape from classes.

I found that behind my garage was a great place to hide from unwanted visitors. My priest, Father Leddy, used to go to my house and seek me out. This is in the days of "if you don't go to church, God will strike you dead." I always kept a step ahead of him and even evaded Matante a few times. "He was just here a minute ago," my mother would say, incredulously. "Now where can he be?"

I found that one of the biggest chores on Lyman Avenue would be raking apples out in that grove. So I'd have to put down my basketball and retreat out there with rake and empty buckets. After awhile it became a tedious and time-consuming task. I would try to ease the burden by stopping every now and then and firing the green apples into the containers, while pretending I was attempting a game winning basket.

I really got to love life on Lyman Avenue. We were in a really nice neighborhood and still close enough to walk to downtown Port. There was a big lot on the side of the house where I played wiffle ball against Fish and Pad. I was always the Yankees and when it was Mantle's turn to bat, I would hit both lefty and righty.

Hitting toward the trees that bordered the house was used for Yankee home games. To smack a home run, the ball would have to be hit in the top half of the trees. Away games were played facing the neighbors' small home.

Mr. and Mrs. Carlson were from Sweden, I believe. Old Oscar couldn't see very well, but he sure could hear a ball reverberating off the side of his house or off his roof. The second the house was struck, he appeared on the scene, walking up his driveway while saying "my shingles, my shingles." We knew for sure, that he wasn't referring to his medical condition.

Some of the neighbors included the Visertas, Morans, Hawkins', Tanczyns, Romeos plus Dutch and Ann Buckley. Behind us were the Tippens', Charlene's family and the Krogers. On the corner, in an upstairs apartment lived Grant (Gramp) Wykoff. Fish and I used to go up to his apartment to visit him and his dog "Nipper." We went there to joke with the old guy, who was known to fire down a drink or two. "Don't bite em good, bite em bad" he used to tell his old black dog. One day, Gramp was all fired up and blurted out "get the hell out of here." We wasted little time exiting that place and running down the steps.

I began accumulating bowling and softball trophies as I grew older. In 1960, my bowling team took second in the Church Recreation CYO League and I carried a 113 average. That same year, I became a Hudson Valley Bowling Proprietors Association finalist. Our team took third place in New York State and I managed the high team triple (419).

In softball, West End won back-to-back Senior League championships in 1962 and 1963. Despite battling poison ivy between my fingers and toes for part of August, I managed to bat .267 in 1962. We won the title, 5-4, after scoring four runs in the seventh inning.

John Duryea was one of my teammates and he basically ran the team. His brother Roger was a fine outfielder and hitter and our lineup was powerful from top to bottom. I came to find out that West End was a perennial champ because of two things, talent and being organized. Everything was done for the team rather than individually. In 1963, I played short field and we defended our title with an 11-8 victory under the lights at Glennette.

Some Sundays our family would go bowling out at Minisink Lanes. My highest game ever bowled is a 242 while Dad rolled a 236 and Mom a 193.

I played basketball outdoors continuously, even in the snow and ice of winter. There was also a basket hung up inside our garage and I would duck in there in the event of a downpour.

I would play records out near my basketball court while my gray cat, Penny, laid close by. Much of the time I hoped Charlene would hear the records from over in her yard. Music sooths the savage beast and the combination of good tunes and a basketball, sent me into heaven.

In my move from Church Street to West End school, I had the novelty of being taught sixth grade by a male teacher. We all feared Richard Donald would be tough on us, but instead he was a kind guy who liked to talk baseball. Mr. Donald even had us over to his house for a Halloween party.

At this party was a female classmate named Sharon Wood. I had been attracted to Sharon right from the beginning of the school year. I remember that she was a slender and sexy blond and wore a leopard outfit at the get together.

Somehow I found out that she lived at a large red brick house at 95 West Main Street. The house was located on a hill, just past the railroad bridge. I was invited to go there, following the next school day. Visions of Sharon and I winding up as a couple, filled my head. That bubble would burst soon enough.

Upon arrival at the residence, I found that this quiet and pretty girl was a wolf in leopard's clothing. She had an extremely wild side and as I recall, she was into firing bee-bee guns at targets in her back yard. Buffalo Bill I wasn't, and I headed for home much wiser from this experience.

Pad had a grandfather that must have invented the word discipline. He was a retired railroad worker who ruled the home of his daughter (Pad and Dutch Kroger's mom) with an iron hand. The boys' dad and mom had divorced and "Gramp" Kroger was an unbelievable authority figure.

God forbid if you ever hit a ball in his garden and then went in there to retrieve it. I got caught more than once by the big hulk of a man with the pipe hanging from his mouth. "Now Bill, I'm not gonna tell you again," he began. "Leave the ball here in the garden. I will get it back for you." I started to heed his advice and it wasn't long before balls were returned to my yard on a daily basis.

I feared Gramp just like all the neighborhood kids. But when I started to mature, I found him to be a strict yet fair man. He ran that house almost like a factory. His grandkids grew up to respect authority. He made sure of that.

It was Pad, five years older than me, and a non-athlete, who somehow became proficient at wiffle ball and basketball. His love was fishing though and he soon was taking me to the Delaware River in quest of rock bass, sunfish, eels and catfish. He untangled my line by the hour and was one of the most patient people I have ever met. A few years after I got married, I hired him as a part time sportswriter and we took the sports section straight to the top. There had never been and still isn't, a sports section like the one we put out.

We did most of our fishing right there in West End at a place called "Buckley's Rock." You walked up West Main Street and behind some houses to reach this rock that was situated partially in the river. Years after leaving West End, I returned to my boyhood haunt. Things had changed as properties were posted. Reaching the river was an exercise in futility as property owners tossed you off their land. We finally reached the rock by paddling a rowboat to it.

Fish, Henszie and Tedrick also fished from time to time. With Pad the fishing was serious, but with these guys it was a comedy show.

Once Henszie, Fish and I were casting our lines off of Buckley's Rock. Suddenly Henszie gave out a loud scream. "My watch, oh no, my watch fell in the river." Fish and I howled until tears came down our faces. It was no laughing matter for Henszie though. He had set a pocket watch down on the rock and somehow knocked it down into the water. "My grandfather gave me that watch," he moaned. "I gotta try to get it back."

While we laughed our heads off, John stripped down to his underwear and started diving underwater in search of the time piece. Each time he surfaced he said "damn, I can't see it." We lost our minds and caved in from laughter. I think some of the bass and sunfish even got a chuckle or two.

Fish Scales missed his calling. This guy was without a doubt the funniest kid I ever knew. He was a laid back type who valued his privacy. When at his house, he would play dinosaurs or bounce a ball in his basement. When I came to call on him, his dad, Roy, answered the door the same way every time. "Come in, come in," he would say. "He (Fish) is downstairs bouncing that ball again. That is all he ever does, he should be studying."

Gary (Fish) could imitate people, make ridiculous faces and was a hoot on the tape recorder. We did skits on tape and then laughed at our silly accomplishments. These days we both agree that "Fish and Willie" were far ahead of their time. We were the first Saturday Night Live show, way back in the early 1960s.

One late afternoon, Jack Tedrick conjured up a real devious plan while we were fishing. Jack had his boat and we were all fishing a ways away from Buckley's Rock. "Hey Gary, I think the fish are out there," he said pointing farther out in the river. "I'll take you out to that rock and you can try to get some."

Fish reluctantly agreed to the plan and got into the boat. Jack paddled out to the rock, located in the middle of the river. "Here take the tackle box too," Jack smiled. The trap had been set.

Fish got out of the boat with his pole and tackle box in hand. A look of anticipation was pasted on his face. Meanwhile, with a big splash, Jack began rowing feverishly away from the site. He howled with delight, laughing his way back toward shore. "You are on bunghole island," he shouted out to Gary. "And the river will be rising pretty soon."

Fish became livid as he stood out there stranded in the river. Finally, Jack gave in and went to retrieve the tricked fisherman. Jack Tedrick had a strange sense of humor and this prank had been a real scream.

Jack used to cut out paper dummies in junior high school, make a noose out of the window shade string and put the dummy behind the shade as the sun shined into the classroom. Another time, he threw a paper airplane out the window with a message on it that said "send help to room 310B." He was also famous for making up signs like "I been sick" and taping it to kids' backs as they walked the school halls between classes.

I passed sixth grade easily and settled in for a summer of sports and fun. Soon enough, it was time to experience seventh grade and the thrill of being in junior high. Port Jervis High School was on East Main Street at the time, and we were to be the babies of the school.

Al Mickel was my home room teacher and I had him for a science course too. It seemed every year I would wind up with Mickel. By the time I graduated, he had gained my respect as a decent teacher.

During those memorable school years, Fish's grandmother on his mom's side, came to live in his house at the corner of West Main and Gariss streets. At the time, Junior Walker and the All Stars were a well known musical group. "Ma" as they called her, was feeble, her mind wandered and she used a walker. It didn't take Fish long to come up with "Ma Walker and the All Stars."

Fish didn't laugh it up much in Joe Pepin's Math class. Pepin was a young and short, crew cut, dark-haired disciplinarian. He flashed a quick pearly white smile and quickly had it vanish. Part of his results in the class came from intimidation. He doled it out to see how much you could take. Pepin was involved in sports and knew I was a future basketball player. I got along with him great and he called me "Willie."

Gary was having a tough time picking up the arithmetic. And, when Pepin gave a test, you better be prepared. While I was no great shakes in that class, Fish floundered horribly. When the tests came back, Pepin would sometimes write a notation at the top of the paper. It could be "good job" or "you can do better than this." In the case of Fish, the red letters spelled out "you need a doctor."

Roy and Florence Scales weren't real happy with Gary's test paper and the written note at the top of the page. He tried to explain that Pepin picked on him and he deserved better grades. One day after school, Mrs. Scales tried to get down to the bottom of the problem. She phoned the school and asked to speak to Joe Pepin.

While Pepin made his way to the phone, Fish ran into his room and hid. Pepin had absolutely thrown the fear of God into my buddy. We still talk about Mr. Pepin to this day. I think he lives in the state of Florida.

During junior high, I managed to mingle with a much older crowd at "The Campus" located next door to the school. The place was packed to the rafters at lunch time as Sylvia and Hatch served up delicious tuna or egg salad sandwiches on hard rolls. The juke box was great, as sounds of Chubby Checker, Sam Cooke (Chain Gang) and Elvis Presley were heard wall to wall. Saddle shoes, pony tails and black leather jackets were everywhere. This structure contained what the 1950s and early 60s were all about.

While Principal Lou Horsman, assistant Ted Archer and legendary football coach Al Chase exuded discipline, some teachers carried that power too far. That was the case in the late Mel Gotleib's class.

Gotleib kind of looked like a big ape, so we called him "Zippy." He would lumber into the room at the start of class and each day became a carbon copy. "Open up your books and read," he would say. No instruction filled this class time, just boring reading. If you got caught talking, he would roll up his morning newspaper and beat you in the head. What an enlightening educational experience.

Passing ninth grade was a good feeling. The 10th, 11th and 12th grades had been moved to the "new school" out on Route 209. I would be among the third class (1965) to ever graduate from here.

Back in ninth grade, I had worked hard to gain a starting berth on the Port JV basketball team. Coach Bob Boening began to notice talent emerging and promised me I would be getting a start in mid-February. I never received that thrill of being on the court for the opening jump ball.

I was shooting baskets over in Joe Viserta's driveway one day, when the ball bounded toward the front bumper of his dad's old car. His old man affectionately referred to this weathered automobile as "the shit box."

I hit the inanimate object squarely on the right knee. A sickening feeling immediately reached the pit of my stomach and I realized this was no common bump or bruise. I could barely maneuver back across the street to my house and the knee blew up like a balloon. I lay in a hospital bed from February 10th through 15th of 1961, as the knee was tapped of fluid a couple of times. I was treated with heat and had to have the knee under an object containing a light bulb, that resembled a mini green-house. Until the doctor would give me written permission to resume basketball, I was sidelined. The permission didn't come and I ended the season in misery, by having to watch my team play while I sat in street clothes.

Hospitals and doctors have never been my favorite things in life. Years before, I had been diagnosed with a duodenal ulcer and even had to stay at Matante's for a few days to slow down and take medication. I was a high strung and emotional kid and was always on the move. Every now and then Mom and Dad would get into an argument and I couldn't deal with that pressure. It always seemed to occur on a Friday or Saturday night after the two had gone out, to relax or to a Lions Club function.

Dad would always work at least part of Saturdays at his insurance office. He would stop off on the way home at the New Bauer Inn, the bar that became my second home years later. Mom could always track him down though. Lots of times Dad made business contacts in these type places. "It is good for business," he used to say.

Mom was an expert at securing babysitters on a moment's notice. In my younger years, Janet Pepper or Judy Riker would sit with Anne and me while later on it was Ann Hensz or Judy Wagner. Mom always felt left out if Dad was at a place without her. I can't count how many times she joined him on a Saturday afternoon and evening. It was when they got home, that the bickering would begin. Mom was a good needler and kept on and kept on. While Dad was always ready to call it a night, Mom refused to let issues drop. Dad would become irritated, Mom would keep taunting and pretty soon we had a full-fledged Saturday night or early Sunday morning argument on our hands.

Anne would start crying, I would beg for the fight to stop and it just kept progressing. Alcohol was a very big factor in these episodes. Partly because of these fights, I vowed to never pick up a drink and that vow, except for the few ounces of Matante's beer, held up until just before I left for the Air Force in 1965. I was 18 years old before I ever experienced a drunk.

Sometimes I would have Anne get dressed and I would go outdoors with her, near the fireplace by the picnic table in the grove. The next day, neither Mom or Dad would mention the night before, although I asked questions about it and was stonewalled time after time. Without alcohol involved, those nightmarish weekends never would have taken place.

I got to play plenty of baseball during these teenage years. After school and during the summer all roads led to Bamberger's, near the end of West End, close to the Delaware River. Bamberger's was a historic hotel, bar and restaurant. Right next to it was a perfect field for baseball. The hotel was at our back when we strode up to home plate. Our target was always the railroad tracks, which was a pretty good poke. Al Cron's house was out near right field, so he could see when a game was formulating.

We would play home run derby here by the hour. I began becoming a power hitter both right and left handed. Tedrick, a righty and Henszie, a lefty hitter, could also connect for plenty of distance. Many times trains were dormant on the tracks and our long homers resulted in the inconvenient and dangerous task of climbing between box cars to get the ball.

The right field grass near Al Cron's house had grown really high and I patrolled that area one afternoon. A fly ball was hit, I reacted and as I glided under the ball, my right knee was ripped open in pain. An old and rusty piece of lawn equipment was the villain and I had opened a gaping hole that was spurting blood. That little adventure resulted in the emergency room and stitches.

Back when I was 10 years old, I remember watching the New York Giants lose to the Baltimore Colts in the 1958 NFL title game at Yankee Stadium. I saw the game on Papa's TV at the Colonial Inn. Alan Ameche scored the winning touchdown for the Johnny Unitas-quarterbacked Colts. Sports was taking up a big part of my life. And later, even stitches in my leg or water on the knee, couldn't dull my will to participate, watch and read about sports.

Fish and I collected 45 rpm records by the barrelful. We were always hanging out at Burger's Music Store on Front Street. Bill Burger would always be whistling as he paced around the store. He had a big smile on his face when we came in, because we were two of his best customers. My first record was "The Wayward Wind" by Gogi Grant. Later I got into The Beatles, The Beach Boys and all the 1960s surfing songs. I had stacks of records in cases and tacked to my bedroom wall. I recall that "Locomotion" by Little Eva, was Henszie's favorite song and that I couldn't beg, borrow or steal "Green Door" by Jim Lowe, from Fish.

My mother treated Pad like he was her own son. He even came over to my house and took what he wanted to eat or drink out of the fridge. That type of activity would never go on at his house.

Mom suffered from asthma for as long as I can remember. She was taken to the hospital countless times by the ambulance. Each time she looked horrible and I worried that she would never be coming back. Maybe it was my prayers that helped her pull through each time.

Anne and I still talk about some of the mishaps that occurred during holidays. One time, Mom dropped a turkey on the floor on Thanksgiving and another time she sliced off a knuckle while cooking a ham for Easter. Our family never sat down at the table for a regular meal. Dad would always be served on a tray as he watched TV on the couch. He put in grueling work days at the office and was an excellent provider for his family.

When we walked over town, we would cross the railroad bridge and hang a right onto the "toe path." Then you wouldn't have to continue climbing West Main Street hill in order to reach the downtown area.

The toe path ran along what was the site of the D&H Canal many years ago. The canal disappeared from view when the railroad came into the Port Jervis area.

One time I was heading for Papa's to watch some sporting event. Instead of taking the toe path, I kept walking up the hill because that was a more direct route to his apartment.

Suddenly, I saw a group of unruly youths hanging out on my side of the street, across from where Sharon Wood lived. They saw me in the dusk and began bolting toward me in a menacing fashion. Being outnumbered roughly 5-1, I quickly careened down a wooded hill that connected to the toe path. In my haste at getting away, I ripped a hole in my right palm. As was the case with my knee, blood spurted all over the place, my heart hammered out of my chest, I sweated profusely and I began feeling faint.

The sight of blood really didn't bother Papa all that much. In fact, anything short of death was treated like a minor paper cut. He told me to go into his bathroom and wash the cut out and then suggested band aids. Putting a band aid on this injury was like the little Dutch boy putting his finger in the dike. Again, I was taken to the emergency room and stitches were taken.

I had started to get interested in boxing and soon Henszie and I each had our own pair of gloves. John was bigger and more muscular than I was, so it was decided that Fish and I would meet in a 15-round fight in my side yard on a Saturday morning. Fish seemed like no big obstacle to me. He was funny, a bit timid and laid back. There should be no problem in roughing him up and having my hand raised in victory.

Fish trained at Henszie's down near the river and one day I dropped in to talk about the fight. From what I saw, this win would be a piece of cake. I turned on my heel and smiled as I returned home, confident in the event that was a couple of days away.

While Tedrick was a practical joker, he was also a real intelligent kid. The son of a man who was into blueprints and land surveying, he drew up some plans for a boxing ring. Tedrick did the job to his own specifications and a nifty ring now appeared in the side yard.

The day of the fight arrived. Neighborhood kids arrived on this sunny Saturday morning to see the two of us slug it out. I can still see old man Viserta across the street, screaming for us to kill each other.

Walter Finch, a young kid from down the street, was supposed to be working my corner. He was responsible for getting me my water between rounds. I knew it was going to be a long fight when I dragged my tired and sweating body to my stool after the fourth round. Fish and I had each gotten in some good shots in that round and expended lots of energy. I was as hot as West End Beach in August. It warmed the cockles of my heart to reach the corner and see Finch guzzling down the last of my precious water.

"You moron," I shouted at him. "What the hell are you doing?" And simply enough, he toweled off his mouth, instead of my body, and said "I was thirsty." Battling a case of cotton mouth, I headed out for round five.

I had some silk type boxing trunks on, while Fish was decked out in multi-colored shorts that we still refer to as "the rainbow trunks." We looked classy as we each looked for an opening that could bring this fight to a quick close. Neither of us ever figured to get into the all-out brawl that was starting to shape up.

We had both agreed before this fight, not to hit the other with any damaging punches. Fish was content to just throw ineffective punches here and there. He seemed to just want to go through the motions. Once we started mixing it up out in the ring, I abandoned that type of thinking. I wanted to take him out early. His southpaw style was hard to figure out and it amazed me that Gary, that funny kid from down the street, was getting in some stinging punches. By the time it was over, we both sported swollen faces plus tired arms and legs. It had been a grueling outing, much more than I ever imagined. I managed to gain the 15-round decision and not by a very wide margin. The moral of this story is "don't judge a book by its cover." While I had planned to cross Fish up and come after him, he became a real wolf in sheep's clothing. That fight resulted in great memories that last to this day.

Long before I ever went to high school, life at 6 Lyman Avenue was about to change forever. The family was in a usual routine and nothing seemed out of the ordinary. But then one of those infamous weekend nights, and with a babysitter in our home, our four lives were thrown into mass chaos.

Mom and Dad were attending a Lions Club function and Anne Hensz was sitting for us. A buddy of mine, Dave Shive, a reverend's son and real hell raiser, was staying overnight with me. For some reason, that was meant to be, because on this hellish overnight I nearly lost my father in an automobile accident.

I recall the phone ringing and it woke me up. Never thinking much of it, I went back to sleep. In what must have been the wee hours of the morning, I awakened again to the sound of my mother crying downstairs. I listened for a second and then quickly vaulted out of the bed and down the stairs.

"Everything will be alright," she kept repeating. "Daddy will be fine." Mom's dress was completely saturated in blood. I feared the worst, but at least I knew Dad was still alive.

On the way home, with Mom at the wheel, the car had skidded off the slick roadway, crossed a sidewalk and smashed into the side of a porch. The corner of the porch came through the windshield and pierced my father's right eye (cornea). He was in critical condition and his life was hanging in the balance. Just like that, the guy that whistled in the morning, joked with us about getting up for school and called me "Roscoe" if he had a couple of beers, was fighting for his life. The date March 19, 1961, was to be etched into my mind forever. There was genuine worry that Dad would not survive and later, that he would lose vision in both eyes. In the end, the scary and near fatal car crash had cost him his right eye. Monday, the accident and a picture, were front page news.

I attended church later that Sunday morning with Dave Shive. Reverend Shive had the congregation pray for the life of my father. Later, I saw the twisted front of Dad's Chrysler in the junk yard where it had been towed. We had gone to the car in hopes of getting some things out of the front seat. This site is where an uncouth and heartless son of a bitch talked about my father as if he was a goner. "He isn't expected to make it," the jackass said loudly.

Dad never talked about his brush with death. I remember playing the instrumental entitled "Strings" on my record player during the time Dad lay in Horton Memorial Hospital (Middletown). One of Dad's favorite songs of the day was "North To Alaska" by the late Johnny Horton. Before the accident I remember him liking that song and always saying "mush you huskies." He left the hospital and immediately bought a new car. Life went on.

Arrival at the Port Jervis Senior High School was both exciting and intimidating at the same time. The older students looked down on us babies of the school. Now my classes were in the same building where basketball practices and games would be taking place. The exterior was a combination of glass, light brown brick and aqua. There were long hallways that contained dark gray lockers and the new smell still permeated throughout.

I had been a sophomore for just a few days when Papa passed away on that awful evening of September 14. When I arrived home, he was still sitting in his favorite chair and looked to be fast asleep. I had never been around death before and walked back into the kitchen rather than stay in this uncomfortable scene. It seemed time suddenly had frozen or at least changed to slow motion.

It was 1962, the year that Jack Nicklaus joined the pro golfing tour and began stealing Arnold Palmer's thunder. Two other visible personalities included our young and vibrant President, John F. Kennedy and blond sex symbol Marilyn Monroe. Papa was interested in both and when he started to become a bit frail, Mom would read him stories about the mysterious death of Marilyn. Kennedy and Monroe were accused of being romantically involved and it made for plenty of quiet speculation.

Papa had been a big Kennedy guy from day one. He made no bones about the fact that he wanted the Democratic senator from Massachusetts to knock off Vice President Richard M. Nixon. Dwight D. Eisenhower's term was coming to an end and there would be new blood running the country.

Many Protestants disliked Kennedy, a Brookline, Mass. native, mainly because of his Catholic religion. They feared there would be no separation of church and state and shuddered at the thought of Kennedy taking over and the Pope running the United States. Their worst fears were realized in November 1960 when Kennedy squeaked by Nixon for the nation's most prestigious spot. JFK, a Navy hero (World War II, South Pacific) and his beautiful wife, Jacqueline, were headed to the White House in January.

Kennedy swayed some of the voters by appearing handsome and confident in four television debates. Meanwhile, Nixon sweated profusely under the heat of the TV spotlights. In the end, JFK tabbed 34,227,696 popular votes to 34,107,646 for Nixon, a virtual dead heat. Kennedy officially clinched the victory and his quest to become the 35th President, by downing Nixon 303-219 in electoral votes.

Many of those who condemned Kennedy earlier, became believers as time went on. Kennedy's handling of the Cuban missile crisis was one strong point. But he had laid down the foundation for his exciting time as President, way back on Inauguration Day, January 20, 1961. "We observe today not a victory of party but a celebration of freedom," he had said. Later, he spoke the words that sank in to a whole nation. "And so my fellow Americans...ask not what your country can do for you...ask what you can do for your country."

Young Americans like myself, were proud of JFK and the country. We took pride in day to day activities and there wasn't all that much protest going on. Kennedy was big on touch football games on the White House lawns and he stressed physical fitness to all Americans young and old. At high school, I earned two red, white and blue oval Senior Merit Fitness USA patches. Those in gym classes had to do so many situps, pushups, pullups and the like to earn the badge. I was young, slender, about 5-7" tall and 115 pounds. Most of all, I was in super shape.

One of the things I remember most about the night Papa passed away, were the vultures who congregated in front of their houses or walked toward ours when they learned something had happened inside. It tore at my very fiber and stung my eyes with tears. I couldn't just stand by and let this mass display of disrespect continue. And so, I went out on the front porch and told these fine folks exactly how I felt.

"What is wrong with you people?" I screamed. "Don't you have any respect? Get the hell out of here." Mom remembers that instance and how I dressed up, went to Gray Funeral Home on Ball Street and stayed by Papa's casket until the very end.

I had lost the gentle man that made me laugh through my childhood tears. No more would I hear that soft voice that complimented me or how "The Mick will hit one for us Billy." Papa seldom got upset with me. But if I raised my voice to my mom, he injected himself immediately. "Don't talk to your mother like that," he would say. I would walk away heartbroken that my hero had made me feel bad. It was the worst feeling in the world to disappoint Papa. We were and always will be "Big Bill and Little Bill."

Every now and then I would stop in my dad's insurance office, usually to "borrow" some money. Years back, when Papa and Dad both had insurance agencies, I would sit at their desks on Saturday mornings and take messages while they went out on calls. Papa would always give me a dollar while Dad forked over a 50 cent piece. I grew to learn that Papa was very generous while Dad taught me the value of money.

In later years, one of Dad's secretaries, a pretty and intelligent lady named Jackie Mack, was always nice to me when I stopped by the office. One time she mentioned a girl that lived near her in Matamoras. "That Christine Goble is a very nice girl," she said. This may have been the very first time that I ever heard my future wife's name mentioned. But it wouldn't be the last. I quietly wondered who that girl was and then simply pushed it out of my mind.

Jackie's husband, Jay, was a dance instructor and used to watch me play JV basketball for Port. His friend, Leroy Stucker, and Art Gray, a funeral director who later became mayor, were in the stands, during home games my junior year. They offered me plenty of support and encouragement plus tossed out a tip or two for me to use in games. Years later, two of these men, Mack and Gray would become employers of mine.

In my sophomore year, I competed on the track team in addition to starting all 18 of our JV basketball games. I also took regents courses that required that I get a 65 on the final exam. In regents, you could get fantastic grades all school year or bomb out and fail miserably on tests. Either way, it required a 65 on the final, to pass the course. Long jumper Jim Swingle taught me that putting a high hurdle in front of the long jump pit would help develop height. Basketball wound up being a nightmare but my sophomore year education-wise was devastating. With girls, fun and sports on the brain I was a mediocre student and when finals came I flunked five subjects. Summer school was not an option for me.

Although Delaware Valley was in Pennsylvania, it was located close to us. There was an intense basketball rivalry between the two schools. Gymnasiums were packed to the rafters for both the JV and varsity games when we collided. In the 1962-63 season, my Port team lost twice to the Warriors. We were beaten 26-17 at home and got ripped off over at their place, 32-30.

Billy Oliver and I were guards on the team. And at DV, under those dim lights that made the atmosphere appear greenish, we had our foe on the ropes. Their school spirit was second to none. DV had its own band for home games and the words "fight, fight, fight for Delaware" rang out and reverberated against the walls. There was a stage at an end of the gymnasium that contained bleacher seats. If you were an opposing player at the foul line at that end, you could expect waving hands and whistles aimed at distracting you. This is the court where DV guys like Hallie Orben, Jim Crellin and Billy Carroll worked their magic.

Charlene and my mother attended all of my games, whether they were home or on the road. They were among the screaming fans on this particular night across the river. We had already lost to DV once, so why not even up the score in front of their fans?

We nursed a razor thin lead as the clock ticked down to the final buzzer. During a time out, our coach, Tom Hoppey, told us to use the clock and force DV to foul. Victory was well within our grasp and all we had to do was stay away from making some silly mistake that would cause us to turn the ball over. Or so we thought.

The gym, bulging at the seams with a capacity crowd, was in bedlam when play resumed. The spectators were seeing a nail biting game that could go either way. I whipped the ball to Oliver and he returned the pass as the black minute hand on the oval time clock moved toward the one minute mark. Our other three players were covered pretty well on defense, so Billy and I were content just to waste time out front. Suddenly a referee's whistle pierced the air. It also wound up piercing our hearts. They were taking the ball away from us. But why?

Confusion suddenly reigned and a vacuous feeling enveloped me. In Pennsylvania rules, a team must make a move toward the basket within a five second period. While we froze the ball, there was no movement toward the basket. And a referee was counting the seconds. DV was given possession of the ball as the noise decibel went through the roof.

Our team was a young one and during this season, we would always find a way to lose. That precedent was being set on this spine-tingling evening in the winter of 1962. DV seemed cool under pressure while we appeared and acted frazzled. The momentum had switched in an instant and DV proved very opportunistic.

Coach Bob Rhoades' team came at us with a vengeance. A layup and foul shot later, it had been decided. The final buzzer sounded and we trudged off the court with our heads bowed. A win over DV was not meant to be and it really ate at my gut to have given this game away. What I didn't know at the time, was that this razor thin reversal was just the beginning of an agonizing schedule that resulted in the season from hell.

While George Reidinger and Ray Orben of DV helped sink our version of the Titanic, there was a kid on that team named Corbin Case. "Corby" would wind up my boss at H.D. Case Motor Sales over a decade and a half later. I was in the parts department and Corby learned the business from his father, Howard, who went by the name Doug.

Coach Hoppey was a kind, fair and patient basketball mentor. I listened to what he said and used many of his ideas and strategies a season later. I first met him during recreation softball days when he was an umpire. He did not deserve a team whose only win would be over Ellenville, 43-42. The Blue Devils returned the favor later in early 1963, 27-23. We were simply inexperienced and overmatched. With maturity came the wins in 1963-64, 12 of them in 18 outings.

Playing on a basketball team is quite an experience. In my opinion it builds discipline by teaching a person how to blend into a unit. Contributing through teamwork develops character even if the results are disheartening. There are good times, bad times and humorous moments that players never forget. An away game at DUSO League power Kingston remains vivid in my memory bank.

At the time, the recollection of our Kate Walton Field House visit wasn't a bit funny but loaded with embarrassment. Hoppey knew we were probably in for an old fashioned ass kicking but tried to be philosophical about the impending game.

Before we hit the court for layup drills, he took us aside and gave us an inspirational pep talk. "They (Kingston) are no better than we are," he boomed in an enthusiastic voice. "Sure they are unbeaten, but that doesn't mean anything. They put their trunks (shorts) on the same way you do, one leg at a time."

By halftime, we were ecstatic with our performance. We were ahead of an undefeated team, 16-15, and unbelievably enough, this was happening on their home court. I remember toweling off and thinking that Kingston indeed hopped into those trunks the very same way we did. They could be had. They would be had.

The second half arrived and we were dealt a cruel, sobering and punishing blow. We were outscored 29-5 in a humiliating loss. Who was that guy that was getting around me and driving the lane for baskets? I don't remember him. What had happened? We were shocked. My mind snapped back to the first half when we were in the lead. Some of their players on the bench were smiling anyway and that hadn't made sense. The pieces to the puzzle were finally starting to interlock. The team we led at the half, was the second string and those grinning from ear to ear were the usual starters. This had been a great con job by Kingston and their regulars came in and ripped us apart.

A season later we got sweet revenge at Port Jervis. We had lost to Kingston earlier and they came to town 16-1. They left town a 58-53 loser in a monumental upset. Their defenders watched me like a hawk and it was the only game of my junior year that I didn't score. Instead, the plan was to go to Jack Brady and he responded with 28 points. Every dog has his day.

I still eat oranges whenever I get a chance. You see, if you played basketball for Port back then, it was a cold day in hell when you would taste an orange at halftime. Game after game the team manager would come into the locker room during intermission with a delicious looking tray of sliced oranges. "Take those things out of here," our coach would say. "The way they played, they don't deserve oranges." To this day, I wonder if those oranges were really wax replicas.

One time in my sophomore year, we were behind by 20 points at half time. "Tangen, did you take a layup in that first half?" the coach screamed in disgust. From the back of the room came a voice "no, is there one missing?" We all broke up on that one. In the second half we were broken up some more. By the other team.

For away games, the JV and varsity teams would travel on the same bus and cheerleaders on theirs. After we began losing on the road, coaches dangled a carrot in front of our noses, for incentive. "If both teams win on the road the same night, each team can ride home with the cheerleaders," our skipper said. We were real excited about traveling with the JV girls . Unfortunately, I'm still waiting. Both the JV and varsity squads finished with rotten 1-17 records and the wins were at home.

We were a tense team during the 17-loss campaign, losing some tight heartbreakers and being blown out too. When opponents clamped on a full court press, we treated the ball like a hand grenade and did great impressions of Don Knotts. Actually, we were perfectly capable of getting nervous without the full court defensive pressure.

I remember a game at Newburgh when one of our players toed the foul line and took a deep breath. He bounced the ball a couple of times and promptly fired the ball over the backboard. They must still be talking about that one on the banks of the Hudson River.

Another time, one of our tall players maneuvered inside and got fouled. He also went to the charity stripe and concentrated. His results were equally embarrassing as the ball barely grazed the bottom the net. These exercises in free throw shooting futility would have made a great comedy show. The attempt that went over the backboard in Newburgh got some wonderful reviews. "Hey, where are you shooting for the moon?" was one of the barbs tossed. The other attempt occurred at home. Players on our own bench laughed their heads off at the ridiculous shot. "Nice shot," one of them said. "It touched nothing but net."

My best times in 10th grade were playing basketball, goofing around with Fish and spending time at Charlene's house. One time my sister and I were invited over to her house for dinner. I was nervous as a cat and promptly elbowed over a full glass of milk. Anne was really cool though. She stared at Charlene's father, George, and said "Gosh, you have such nice teeth." I guess it is safe to say that the two of us were not Waldorf Astoria dining material.

I struggled with regents horribly. Far from a dumb kid, I just couldn't comprehend the material very well. And the time I should have been studying, was spent shooting baskets, long jumping, hanging at Fish's house or watching TV with Charlene. And too, there was always the movies and hamburgers at Homer's.

I feared a second round of summer school and wondered how many subjects I would be flunking. Two years prior (eighth grade), I had failed a couple of subjects and had to return to school while other kids played ball or fished. On that occasion, Gary, my lifelong buddy, was right by my side because he had failed also.

In those younger years, we were carefree and life was a happy time. Even summer school didn't break our spirit. Between classes we walked down Pennsylvania Avenue and did homework on somebody's front lawn. This site became our own private study hall and we didn't give a rat's ass whose property it was. Talk about nerve!

I guess every young boy comes in contact with a bully at some time or another. My cross to bear came in the muscular shape of one Tony Sicuro. Tony was a rugged kid who was pretty wild and loved to needle through intimidation. One day, he began to pick on me for no reason at all.

"Hey chicken shit," he said. "Wanna fight? I'll kick your ass." I got along with everyone and just couldn't put my finger on why Sicuro didn't like me. "I have nothing against you," I answered. "Why fight?" The intimidating went day after day until I had absorbed all I could take. His imposing figure was enough to make coffee nervous, but I accepted his challenge. "Don't back down," Fish had said. "He will respect you if you show up and fight him."

The confrontation was set for the next day, behind the visiting bleachers and in the woods of Glennette Field. The night before, I tried to figure ways to get out of this unpleasant task that was mere hours away. I was trapped and there was no backing down. The hours flew by and in class I saw Tony smiling across the room at me. I could see he was savoring the moment as he smacked his open palm with a fist.

Sidney Quick was Tony's buddy in summer school. The two of them, Fish and a few others made the trek under the trees near the Neversink River. "Do you want to box or wrestle?" Sicuro queried. I thought for a few seconds and pictured my nose splattered on my face. "Wrestle," I said in a firm and unwavering voice.

This fight lasted less time than the second Cassius Clay-Sonny Liston title fight. I was immediately tossed to the ground and put in a defensive position. Tony had me in a headlock and slipped one of his strong arms over my ear and squeezed. The pain was unbelievable but I was determined not to quit. "You give up?" he said from above. When he heard no answer, the pressure became stronger. At the risk of breaking an ear drum, I yelled that I was through.

I regained my feet and figured I'd be slowly walking away, defeated and embarrassed. But remarkably enough, that didn't happen. "Hey Tangen, wanna come to the river and swing on the rope with us?" Sicuro asked. We all made our way down the river bank and took turns swinging out over the narrow and murky Neversink. The thick brown rope was tied to a big tree limb high above the water. This challenge seemed like nothing, compared to what I had just been through.

Fish had hit the nail squarely on the head. By taking up the challenge and not backing down, I had gained Tony's respect. My chest swelled with pride that afternoon as Gary and I walked to the post office to see his father, Roy. I had lost the battle but won the war. There was nothing "chicken shit" about me.

My grades for the sophomore year more resembled point totals in a basketball game box score. I had bombed out big time by failing five regents courses. Way back in 10th grade, I was already seriously threatened with not graduating with my class of 1965.

I still remember the June 1963 nights when Al Mosher played guitar in Margaret Tierney's West End store while Fish and I chuckled in the background. Brian Bushweller, a Port senior, got a charge out of us young clowns, but never made fun of us. He was a very intelligent and humorous person. Once at school, he turned in a blank verse poem for a class assignment. The piece of paper he gave the teacher, was completely blank. Meanwhile, we were fighting for our academic lives. A few days later, we learned our fate.

Viglione had gone around our World History class predicting what each student would get on the regents. He looked at me and said "maybe you'll get a 40, if your lucky." It seems to me, Vig hit the mark right on the nose.

That summer, I applied myself to school work with all four feet. But there was still plenty of time to enjoy the warm weather and fun that is associated with being a carefree teenager. Charlene and I continued to go nearly everywhere. During the school year, we sometimes skipped school and went down near the river. These were days that could never be recaptured.

One time Dave Shive and I were swimming in the Delaware River just off Bamberger's Rock. It was nearly nightfall and we looked up the bank to the street and saw Beth Bushweller (Brian's younger sister) and a friend of hers, peering down at us. Before you could say "strip tease" Dave and I had shed our bathing suits and given the girls a good look. They screamed in mock horror while we laughed our asses off. Life was good in West End during the summer of 1963.

I even tried smoking that summer. Dave and I sneaked into my garage and he had a pack of Marlboro cigarettes. He lit his and passed the matches to me. "Smoke one of these and you'll be a man of the world," he said, laughingly. I took a drag, coughed and didn't like the bitter taste. Other than to win bets in bars, I never took a drag on a cigarette again.

While I had a handful of failures, Fish had flunked two subjects and Henszie one. "Why can't you be like Henszie?" Roy Scales asked his son. "He only failed one." Fish looked at his dad and answered. "Henszie is a year older than us, he should do better. At least I didn't fail five like Bill." I guess this is what is called being put on a pedestal.

It had been quite a school year. Fish and I were even allowed in Tom Roberts' record room. Tom, who went in the Marines after high school, was a sharp dresser and made us sit quietly to hear some of his tunes. It as Tom Roberts who went to Bamberger's with me the night before I arrived at boot camp in Texas. He was with me for the first drunk of what would be many.

During the regular school year, we had to take a segment of square dancing for physical education. Being the shy boys we were, many of us flat out refused to do-si-do and swing our partners. So instead of taking part in this ridiculous activity, with girls from another gym class, we hid in our lockers. We were far away from the promenades of our land. And of course, we got in big trouble.

Summer school became more fun than a chore for me. For History, I had a crew-cut disciplinarian named Bob Dickinson. The first day, he asked me if Viglione had been my World History teacher during the regular year. I'm sure Dickinson already knew he was, but he just asked to make it official. I was an athlete at this time and very quick on my feet. Vig liked football players for obvious reasons, and I wasn't one of them. The next basketball season, Coach Al Wilgard (wrestling) lured Bill Oliver away from basketball and onto the mat.Wilgard

tried like hell to secure me as a lightweight wrestler, but I declined because of my love for basketball. Wilgard called me "round baller" and "T-Bone" for the rest of my high school days.

Bob Dickinson, without a doubt, is the finest teacher I ever had. Even in taking college courses, I never came across such a positive and inspiring person. He made you want to learn by presenting the course as a challenge. He rewarded positive results with a verbal pat on the back. "I knew you were a better student than your grade showed," he told me. "You are proving it."

Dickinson gave me the push I so desperately needed. And, he got me on the right track with reassuring and sensible words, not a rolled up newspaper that smashed into the skull.

Pat Farace, the Port varsity basketball coach, was another teacher who made you want to study. Sometimes he would lecture in a firm voice that begged for your attention. His fiery demeanor was the same one he used on the basketball court. It was under Pat Farace, that Port went 14-2 and Osowick scored 62 points.

Dickinson still jokes about when he coached the Port varsity golf team. In 1963, he was the skipper of a fine Raider squad that included Rich Lefferts, Glenn Roderman and Rick Spears. The team defending DUSO League champions. Two years later, under Hugh Spangenberg, Spears won the New York State Intersectional Golf Championship. He played in The Masters at Augusta, Georgia, the U.S. Open in San Francisco and became a star at the University of Florida. Later, he became a professional golfer. "That team (1963) really needed me," Dickinson joked. "Like I was really going to teach Rick Spears a lot."

While going through summer school, "Tie Me Kangaroo Down

Sport" by Rolf Harris was on the radio quite a bit. Surfing songs like "Surfin U.S.A." and "Surfer Girl" by the Beach Boys plus Jan and Dean's "Surf City" were heard blaring from the convertibles of the day.

Songs were a big part of our lives. You just couldn't beat "The End Of The World" (Skeeter Davis), "Puff The Magic Dragon" (Peter, Paul and Mary), "Have You Heard" (The Duprees), "Popsicles and Icicles" (The Murmaids) or "I Wonder What She's Doing Tonight" (Barry and the Tamerlanes).

I did great in summer school and entered the 1963-64 year as a junior, but was officially half sophomore and half junior. There was much catching up to do. I had switched from Regents courses to local ones, and didn't have the pressure of a 65 facing me on the finals.

In my junior year, I would fall in love with my English teacher, the willowy Miss Pearce, find a degree of fame on the basketball court, stand Christine up after a game, continue going steady and fight raging hormones. I caught fish in the Delaware, got my New York State driving permit, and became a decent long jumper under the watchful eye of Coach Gordie Short and fellow cinderman Jim Wilkerson.

I continued to blast my 45 records on the back porch while shooting baskets by the hour. I had the apple detail down pat in the grove and looked forward to the challenge of my junior year. Things got off to a spectacular start when President John F. Kennedy gave a speech on September 24, 1963, in neighboring Milford, Pa.

Kennedy dedicated Grey Towers, the mansion that had been the home of Pennsylvania Governor and legendary conservationist Gifford Pinchot. He dedicated it as the Pinchot Institute for Conservation Studies.

Students were bussed in from Delaware Valley and Port Jervis high schools. It was a sunny day and the grounds were beautiful. There was green grass, rolling hills, trees and blue sky. Kennedy arrived by helicopter and walked through the woods to a podium located out in the natural woodlands.

His hair appeared reddish in the shimmering sun, he was immaculately dressed and his teeth gleamed as he plunged into an inspiring speech. Cameras clicked everywhere and TV crews dotted the landscape. He showed some of the wit that became one of the trademarks of his presidency. He appeared taller than he did on TV or in the newspapers. The place was absolutely jammed with people of all ages, colors and religions. I left the site with a feeling of patriotism for the United States. I had just seen the President of the United States in person.

Two months later, JFK was gunned down in Dallas, Texas. He was only 46 years old and left a pretty wife and two young children, Caroline and John John, 3. Never before or after, had we such a vibrant and inspiring man lead our land.

At school, an announcement was made and we were allowed to go home early. Kids walked the halls in somber moods, crying and sharing their grief. The 35th President of the United States was still alive as far as we knew. We all held out a flickering of hope that he wouldn't be taken from us. There was just no possible way we could conceive of him dying.

I will remember November 22, 1963 forever. It was the monumental type happening that made time stand still in a frozen and heartbreaking picture laced with gloom and despair. It had the empty and powerless feeling that Americans experienced in the Oklahoma City tragedy and the World Trade Center terrorist attacks. Gunning down President Kennedy was gunning down all of us. And this unspeakable act was taken personally as a collective feeling of a nation. Everything moved in slow motion. It was the only thing on the minds of those within and outside the walls of Port Jervis High School.

Somehow we moved out the exits and to televisions in the calming solitude of our homes. Kennedy had addressed a breakfast sponsored by the Forth Worth (Texas) Chamber of Commerce, and was in a motorcade that was en route to the Dallas Trade Mart

Television anchorman Walter Cronkite interrupted the afternoon soap opera "As The World Turns" at 1:40 p.m. eastern standard time with a sketchy bulletin that there had been an assassination attempt and that Kennedy had been struck by at least one bullet. "Three shots were fired at President Kennedy's motorcade in downtown Dallas," the bulletin began. "The first reports say that President Kennedy has been seriously wounded by this shooting." I, like so many others, said a silent prayer that a miracle would occur and that this energetic and handsome man would soon be joking with us again and making us feel so much a part of his presidency. Of course we were spitting in the wind and hoping the saliva wouldn't be felt on our face, like the biting and cold slap that was ultimately coming. Cronkite had the unpleasant task of delivering the shocking news that John Kennedy was no more. He brought most of the world to its knees with a sickening punch in the stomach that didn't hurt as much as the human heart ached.

"From Dallas, Texas, apparently official. President Kennedy died at 1 p.m. (Parkland Hospital) Central Standard Time, an hour ago."

People from all lands were in total shock. They wanted someone to change the bulletin and say it was a cruel joke. But on this black Friday, there was no joke. Faith in mankind had been dealt a severe and lethal sucker punch. Just when a nation believed, it sank into a river of bitter tears that flowed for days and days. The man with the gleaming teeth and redish hair that shimmered in the bright sunshine of Milford, was with us no more.

Kennedy's killing is still debated. The details are rehashed over and over again. Did Lee Harvey Oswald act alone? Was this assassination a conspiracy? Who was behind this horrible killing? It is easy to see that people of my generation and older, will never find out for sure.

Oswald, charged with the killing, was himself fatally shot by nightclub owner Jack Ruby. Oswald was in the basement of the police and courts building and was to be transported by armored car to the courthouse. Live television cameras caught Ruby shooting Oswald during the transfer. Life went on with heartbreaking emotion.

Christine kept a diary during her high school years. She figures the first time that I laid eyes on her was less than seven weeks before Kennedy was shot. I am mentioned in her entry for October 11, 1963. "I think Bill saw me," she notes. She was with friends Susan Brush and Nancy Lambert on Pike Street and then in Homer's for food and drink. It's great to see that I was so mature in those days. She wrote that some friends and I chased them through the underpass that leads to Pennsylvania.

On October 17, Sue Ricciardi, who worked the counter at Newberry's in Port, weekend nights, told Chris on a DV school bus, that I liked her (Chris). It's good to be reminded that I was running around Port telling people that I liked this girl from DV. Does this mean I was in some sort of love after less than a week?

She kept notes on me that would make a private investigator green with envy. Chris said October 25, I was talking to some kids about her, and a day later, we met during the Port Jervis Lions Club-sponsored Halloween Window Painting Contest. Chris, in her third year of participation in the contest, was painting a window on Sussex Street. Chris had come up with the idea of what her and friends would draw and wound up placing in the competition.

Two days later, Chris received a Halloween card from me and a couple of days after that, I got one in the mail from her. The future wife and husband were communicating and I felt an instant connection to her. She was a slender, quiet girl with a nice smile and long dark hair. To me, Christine Goble represented a nice looking girl from Delaware Valley. She was kind of mysterious and was a challenge to my male ego. I appeared conceited to certain people, although deep down, I was a fun loving person who liked to laugh and joke.

I have to admit that I was remiss in certain areas. Let's just say that I was not really a man of my word. Reliability and I didn't go in the same sentence. Chris was to learn that a few years later, when I would promise to phone or pick her up and didn't follow through. These days, "reliability" is my middle name.

My mother saw the card I had received and asked Jackie Mack about the girl from over Matamoras way. Of course Jackie have Chris a glowing recommendation. She had seen the girl either riding her blue bicycle in the neighborhood or observed her doing chores. Chris' father, Ernest, was a hard working type who had strong arms and hands.

Ernie was a strict disciplinarian who expected his daughter to toe the mark at all times. The blue house Chris, Ernie and wife Marion lived in, at 810 Avenue M, was built by Ernie. He would come home from work at a shoe factory, and get busy on constructing the one story home. He didn't have a high school diploma, but made up for it with a keen intelligence when it came to electricity, mechanics or working with his hands. He would go on to become a self-taught clock maker, dabbled in citizen band radios and was known as "Mister Fix It."

On November 1, 1963, I met Chris under the clock near a Port Jervis bank. I walked her, Sue Brush and Ann Davis back home. Bill Thomas, a friend of mine, was along for the laughs. Five days later, we gabbed on the phone for an hour and a half, and it wasn't long after that, when Christine Goble peddled all the way to West End with a hand written letter for me. The length of that correspondence rivaled that of the Declaration of Independence.

Through the rest of November, we talked on the phone or met in Port. On the 16th, we went to a football game and walked around town with Fish. And on the final day of the month, a few of us went bowling at night and then adjourned to Homer's. In her diary, Chris made a note of part of her attire. "I wore a furry white top," it says.

My favorite time of year had rolled around. Players on the Port JV basketball team were a year older and already knew what the agony of defeat felt like. Bob Boening, who had replaced an ailing Farace as varsity coach the year before, was back coaching the JV team. I would be starting at guard for the second straight season. Instead of Oliver in the backcourt with me, Chuck Bierlein would be starting. Oliver was now an outstanding wrestler.

I still recall the exciting feeling I got in my stomach while being driven to a home game. We drew nice sized crowds and I loved being on center stage. Charlene, my mom and friends like Fish, watched me whether I was at home or on the road. I had the nervous anticipation of excelling on the basketball court. And, I felt in my heart, that a winning season was on the horizon.

Chris notes on December 3, 1963, that in eight days, Port would be meeting DV. I now had two girls to impress, one a diehard Raider fan and the other from the rival school. Five days before the December 11 showdown between neighboring teams, Chris shook hands with me and wished me good luck. That evening I told her I was heading home for an early bed, but she learned that I had lied and gone to Charlene's house. I realized that regarding girls, leading a double life was a potentially dangerous situation. So I remained going steady and basically flirted with Chris and led her on.

The first of two dates against DV, took place on our home court. Between the JV and varsity games, I managed to see Chris and was all smiles. We had defeated the Warriors, 35-28, behind 11 points by Jack Brady. I tabbed seven points including three field goals. Reidinger led the visitors with 12 markers. We led 23-22 through three periods and then increased the margin. Corby Case had three points for them. On opening night, we had tied our entire win output for the prior season.

On December 24th, Chris got a nasty letter from me, saying that I liked Charlene and was remaining with her. Three days later, she wrote in the diary "I want to see him (me) so bad." Four days later she did, and I ignored her. I had been rotten to her in late 1963. But under four years later, the light of true love began to flicker between us.

CHAPTER 5

Goat to Hero

Andy Warhol, one of the giants of 20th century art, has been dead for over 15 years. The Pennsylvania native is remembered for many accomplishments, but the following quote of his, is a well-known one. "The day will come when everyone will be famous for 15 minutes." In my case, the time under the dazzling spotlight of fame, occurred at the tender age of 16 and on my home basketball court.

The 1964 game against the Ellenville Blue Devils, in front of a packed gymnasium, seems like it occurred yesterday. Just over 13 years later, I nearly gained 15 more minutes of fame when I was named New York State Sportswriter of the Year for scholastic wrestling coverage. About 10,000 mat fans filled Onondaga War Memorial in Syracuse, for the 1977 New York State Intersectional Wrestling Tournament finals. My name was announced, but I was a few miles away at Danzer's on Erie Boulevard West, chomping down burgers and drinking imported beer. As I sat relaxing with Chris, Fish and his wife, I had no inkling that I had been selected for the award.

Neil Kerr, of the New York State Sportswriters Association, had sent me a letter prior to states. He talked about the fabulous Banach brothers from Port Jervis and said there were "other reasons" why I should be present at the event. I never did pick up on that reason.

While I have known others who vigorously campaigned to win this prestigious award, I never opened my mouth regarding it. There was no way in hell I ever figured that the state would recognize the writer of a 5,000 circulation daily newspaper. Frank Carrozza, Minisink Valley wrestling coach extraordinare and sports personality Phil Dusenbury accepted the award for me. Later, Lou Banach won Port Jervis' first state wrestling title while Port surged to the team championship.

Following that 1963-64 opening season win at home against DV, we knocked off Middletown, 35-26. Jerry Calvario had seven points for us while Brady and myself each bagged six. The season before, we had made more turnovers than Pepperidge Farm and got about as much respect as Rodney Dangerfield. We were off like a herd of turtles that season, but this start had everyone excited and in a positive mood. Then came the second game against DV.

I remember that Ron Robacker was the JV basketball coach for the Warriors. He wore glasses then and was fairly new to the school system. Robacker would go on to become athletic director and one of the winningest high school boys soccer coaches in Pennsylvania history.

We returned to that dimly lit gymnasium where we had been ripped off a year earlier. The DV band and fantastic school sprit were still very prevalent. People chattered as they crammed into the gym. Two exciting basketball games between neighboring rivals was on tap. This was the place to be on a Friday evening.

As I laced up my sneakers for the impending battle, I was bothered by an off court dilemma. As usual, Mom, Charlene and Fish were in attendance. And, following the JV contest, I would be taking my usual seat next to my girlfriend. There was one fly in the ointment though. "Mister Basketball" had opened his big mouth and promised Christine he would sit with her. During the layup drill, I looked at two opposite sides of the gym. Over here was Charlene and over there, Christine.

I was the monkey in the middle of this mess. The situation would be enough to make Clint Eastwood come unraveled and lose his cool. I blocked out the nerve wracking situation and prepared for 32 minutes of basketball.

It was a spine-tingling game from start to finish. We had beaten DV by seven points at home, but the Warriors evened up the score with a 49-42 victory. We came on strong at the end, by outscoring DV 24-16 in the final quarter. However, we trailed 11-3, 26-11 and 33-18 at the first three buzzers. Paul Hendershot went wild for DV with 23 points while Jim Launt had 10 markers for us. I was next in line with seven points.

For the second straight year, I had a knot in my stomach when I walked off the DV court. To say I was upset, would be the understatement of the year. I showered quickly, dressed and left the locker room. Well wishers said we would turn things around and get on the winning track again. People slapped my back and shook my hand. I looked for Charlene and hoped I wouldn't see Christine. Across the playing surface, a slender long haired girl waited for a jock who wasn't coming. Chris saw me in a hallway as we tried to maneuver through a mob of people that made us resemble sardines in a can. "I said something to you and got a one word answer," Chris recalls. "I went home and wrote you a very long letter."

As I look back on those days, I see a talented basketball player who had a tough time staying humble. All 115 pounds and 5-foot seven inches of me lived to career down the lane, hit a basket and be fouled. I could pull up for the 15-foot jump shot, played non-stop defense and was accurate from the free throw line. Except for a lack of height, I had all the tools and planned on starting in the backcourt on the Port Jervis varsity team with Spears, during my senior year. Rick was a fine all around athlete. He possessed driving and scoring ability. I could take some pressure off him and was a capable scorer if he were double teamed.

While I possessed a good personality, it wasn't beyond me to exhibit a selfish demeanor that included a rude streak. I had been cold hearted and immature to a nice and sincere girl who was embarrassed and heart broken by my actions. Not only was she waiting for me to join her, but all her friends saw her let down and mistreated as well.

I had pride in my basketball uniform and used to eye it up on its hanger, before home and away games. We were black and red on the road and white and red for home games. My uniform number was "3", the same as Tex Harding who had played a few years before me. The away uniform was a little looser on top, but the home top and trunks fit like a glove. I used to tape my wrists and the tops of my socks with adhesive. I carried that trait all the way overseas to Guam.

Years before I played, I had watched Osowick, Harding, Tom Coleman and Gibby Romaine like a hawk. I went to some of the away games, and at one, I saw Coleman make a reverse layup that looked so smooth and cool. I decided that move was going to go in my shot assortment. And it did.

I was the first on the JV team to use a behind-the-back pass. My ball handling was slick and if I was being overplayed on my right side, I wouldn't hesitate to flip a tricky pass from behind to an open teammate. Coach Boening, who we called "Hawkeye" watched me very closely. I knew he was just waiting for an errant behind-the-back toss, to put the kabosh on the showy type play. He never got the chance, because I only used the tactic once or twice a game and made sure the pass was accurate.

Music was a big part of our basketball team. Transistor radios played in our locker room before and after games. When we were on the road, songs that came out in 1963, like "All Alone Am I" by Brenda Lee, "You're The Devil In Disguise" by Elvis or "He's So Fine" by The Chiffons could be heard on our bus.

If we lost an away game, Boening was not a happy camper. The radio had to be kept down low or not on at all. We would whisper and crack low toned jokes. The tittering of our laughter would reach Boening's ears and we all went on Hawkeye alert. "Watch out, Hawkeye's watching," we would say. "Shhhhhhh."

Henszie and Mr. Boening did not hit it off. For some reason, the teacher had Henszie cast as a smart ass and didn't care for him. One time the two got into it toward the end of a class. The bell rang and John picked up his books and headed for the door. Boening cut off his path and smacked the books out of his hands and onto the floor. John could never figure out how I could play basketball for Bob Boening.

After I suffered the water on the knee injury two years earlier, it was Boening who came up to the hospital to visit me at night. He told me to hang in there and my day would come. He was true to his word and my junior season became one that is still firmly imbedded in my mind.

If the team had a bad night on the foul line, you could bet we would be shooting free throws by the truck loads the next day at practice. If he wasn't pleased with our play in a game (win or lose), we would scrimmage continually. There would be no breaks in the action and Boening would not say one word. He ran us ragged to prove a point. Most of the time, his tactics worked. He knew how to get the best out of us and that result showed in the 12 wins.

My favorite referee was the late Joe Palone. He was a little fella who exuded his love for basketball with a friendly smile. He would hand me the ball to hold for him, prior to the game opening jump ball. Once the action began, he was a disciplinarian with a keen knowledge for the game. If I questioned a call, he would make a face at me and quietly say "come on now, you know you did it." I was always happy to see Palone on the scene for our games. I was lucky enough to never foul out of a high school basketball game. Palone was very perceptive and sly as a fox. I tried driving the lane and slapping my own leg one night, in order to draw a foul. I tried the tactic two times and came out 0-2. "Every time you head down the key, I'm watching your hand," he grinned. "But nice try, anyway."

I had been hooked on basketball for many years. Way back when, I'd played at the YMCA on Pike Street in Port Jervis. One of the referees there, was Savey Orlando, a policeman. I was small in stature but could shoot with the best of them. Jim Trotta, a big fella, was our team captain and I didn't get to start games. I remember standing in the corner and saying that some day, I would show them all. Plenty of those days occurred in my junior year.

Miss Pearce, that foxy lady English teacher made my heart pound a mile a minute. "You gonna come to the game tonight?" I would ask in class. "I may stop by, just to watch you play," she would smile back. One time I got her to talk about her personal life. She had a boyfriend and I think she was planning on getting married. All the girls in class were jealous of the beautiful Miss Pearce. You can take a wild guess about what my fantasy was. But first, we had to get rid of that damn boyfriend.

We did bounce back from the DV loss by defeating Poughkeepsie (49-27) and Liberty (57-50). I managed to hit double figures in both games by splashing 10 against the Pioneers and 14 in the Liberty victory. We went for win number five in six outings on a Friday night, at home, against Ellenville. This event was the highlight of my high school cage career.

It was a physical and tight ballgame with oodles of emotion. We led 13-7 at the first buzzer but fell behind 24-22 by intermission. Needless to say, a fresh tray of bright oranges, cut to perfection, was brought into the locker room and left immediately. The familiar words rang off the walls, ceiling and gray lockers of the room and echoed off the tiled floors. "Take those oranges away. They don't deserve them."

Trailing 38-29 after three periods, we mounted a furious fourth quarter rally that tied the wild and wooly affair, 45-45. The gymnasium was in an uproar when we caught up and sent things into overtime. Neither team would give an inch in the extra session. I recall my mouth being very dry as we continued using an air tight man-to-man defense. The teams played at breakneck pace and at times playground basketball, complete with fast breaks and one-on-one matchups, took place. I was in great physical shape in those days, but I dragged a sweaty and weary body to our huddle as we trailed 54-52 with just one second left in the game.

We had the ball, full court to go, under Ellenville's basket. Moments earlier, I had missed a one-and-one foul shooting situation that I believed had cost us the game. Boening's piercing eyes went from one player to another. Martin DeMond, Bob DeVore, Tom Cherry, Chuck Bierlein, Jack Brady, Jim Launt, Jerry Calvario and Bill Tangen all tried to hear his voice through the loud cheering.

I hung my head in disgust, just knowing that I had cost us a possible win. "Bierlein, you take the ball out and look for someone open," he shouted. The paper said that Brady was the guy that inbounded the ball during this scene of mass chaos. Spectators were on their feet for the climax of a pulsating contest. My palms were sweaty as I headed down court and tried to get open. My eyes were focused first on my parents and Charlene and then on the blue-and-white uniforms of the enemy. We had come too far to let this one get away. It would be a tragedy to walk off this court a loser. I don't believe I have ever played a better all around basketball game than on this night.

The odds against us scoring on this last play of the second overtime were overwhelming. Somewhere up above, there was a God that didn't want me to be a goat on this night. I was destined to evade the unpopular tag and instead would bask in victory, as a hero.

I shook loose of my defender on the left side just over midcourt as a high arching pass was thrown. The clock wouldn't start until the ball touched a player. That player was to be me. In one motion, I caught and released the ball in a desperation heave that left my right hand with a prayer attached to it. Through a maze of hands and moving bodies, I saw the ball headed toward the rim and backboard.

The sound in the gym was deafening as the ball banked off the white, wooden backboard and dropped cleanly through the net. The impossible had taken place. We had tied the game 54-54 and sent the game into a second overtime. I was delirious with excitement. My heart was thumping uncontrollably and I couldn't help but smile and pump my fist in the air. Somehow, we had survived and were heading into another extra session. At the opposite end of the gym from where I made the shot, the black scoreboard showed a 54-54 deadlock. I had no idea where any of my extra energy was coming from. I popped another stick of gum into my cotton mouth and went back into the battle.

The final three minutes felt like slow motion. And when I drew a foul with just 16 ticks left on that clock and the scored still tied, 56-56, bad thoughts started to fill my mind. I had missed a critical free throw earlier and figured it would cost us the game. I toed the line and spun the ball in a backwards dribble a couple of times, set and heard nothing but net. That shot proved to be the difference in a nail biting 57-56 win.

For a long time people talked about "the shot." Even as recently as the 1990s, a couple of the Kean boys, Cy and Bernie remembered that night. I was having a beer with Scott Robinson once and someone in the bar recalled the play. "It was lucky and I still remember it," I said to Scott. "I know," he replied. "I was the team manager."

I couldn't wait to see the story and box score in the paper the next day. And it was there for everyone to read. "The Jayvee (game) was a real thriller- diller with Port's Jayvees going through two overtimes before they could shade the Ellie Juniors, 57-56. A foul shot by Bill Tangen, with about 16 seconds left in the second OT won it for the Porters."

The article went on. "One of the highlight plays in this game was a spectacular basket accomplished by Port with only one second left in the first overtime. Port trailed, 54-52 and had the ball out of bounds under their opponents' basket with just one second left. Jack Brady took the ball and fired a court length pass to Bill Tangen who grabbed it and flipped it in just before the buzzer sounded."

Of course in reality, the pass length was just over half court. But the results were what counted. For at least 15 minutes, I had received my touch of fame. Ellenville never forgot the heartbreaking loss and couldn't wait to see me up in Ellenville. While I had 14 points (including 10 free throws) in the earlier triumph, Ellenville covered me like a blanket and gained revenge. I got just four points in a 51-36 defeat. I had snapped back to reality and had returned to the real world with this harsh slap in the face.

Some of the other wins came over Fallsburgh twice (47-36 and 24-21), Monticello (30-27), and Kingston in a stunning upset, 56-53. Kingston had beaten us earlier in the season up at their place, 44-17 (I got eight points). I turned into a passer in the Kingston win in our last home game of the season. I was scoreless but had several assists. Kingston had entered 16-1 with the same squad that had swamped us earlier on the schedule. My final high school basketball game ever, was the three point verdict at Fallsburgh. I managed just one field goal in a defensive battle with the Comets.

The year 1964 proved to be a memorable one. I was playing catchup in the classroom but wasn't bombing any subjects like in my sophomore year. Still, I would have to tighten my belt as a senior, skip basketball and hope to make it out of school in June of 1965.

As a junior, Harold Goewey was one of my teachers. I had him for Business Arithmetic and Retailing during my final months at Port. He was known as "Harry" and there were a million Goewey stories that were passed down from older kids who had already been in his class.

"Harry" had white hair and an easy going smile, plus prided himself in his knowledge of clothes and shoes. While he talked a good game, students ran roughshod over him with numerous jokes and pranks. Let's just say that Goewey tried to be in charge of his classes, but unruly people such as myself, stymied him continually.

In Retailing, he would pass around a suit so that we could visually examine and touch the fabric. He walked around the class in squeaky alligator shoes and once the suit made the rounds, it was returned up front, tied in knots.

On the first day of trout season, many of us decided that at a certain time, we would all run to the windows of the room, look out at a bordering brook and start shouting "Harry, look at those trout." He would get very angry with us when we had no discipline. "Shut your wobbly mouths," he would say. "Guess you don't want to learn anything. You just want to wind up being bums."

One day Harry was talking about cork board and that opened up a new can of worms. Ted Kuykendall and a few others, including me, starting screaming "cork board" in high pitched and silly voices. "Isn't this awful. Can't be serious for once," Goewey said in a disgusted tone. Spit started to escape the corner of his lips. There was always an abundance of saliva when Harry got upset.

"Awe come on Harry, you know we all love you," somebody said. The teacher looked at us with a blank stare. Suddenly, his anger turned into a big wide grin and he turned 20 shades of red. Guys like Ted, Ken Felter and Hank Dunn were great kidders and got the best out of Goewey. "We really like that smile Harry, please don't get mad at us," another voice pleaded. Goewey snapped back to reality quickly. "Let's get to work," he barked. "We don't have time for this drivel."

The serious complexion of the room changed in a heartbeat. Several in the class had come up with other examples of boards and began shouting "bulletin board", "ironing board" and "ouija board", which was a Kuykendall offering that cracked the class up. This shrill tirade of foolishness had us all overcome with laughter. Tears ran down my face. This class was the funniest I ever attended in my life.

Goewey stuttered and stammered to attempt getting some form of discipline back into the class. We were too far gone though. He squeaked over to the phone in his alligator shoes, and said loudly, "I am calling the office right now. You will all have detention."

Goewey picked up the receiver and was set to complain to the front office. "Hello....hello," he said. The class was in stitches and total chaos prevailed. There was poor Harry, for all of us to see, holding a receiver with a curled wire that had been snipped off with a big pair of scissors, moments earlier. When he saw this, he went nuts, screaming and yelling his way out the door and down the hall to the principal's office.

When school wasn't in session, Goewey worked at a place called the Red Apple Rest, on the way to New York. We always got him talking about that. We also teased him about a woman substitute teacher we had, Miss Chris. "Hey Harry, we hear you and Miss Chris got something going," we'd say. "Is she any good?" He would cut us down with that icy stare and shout back "You all have dirty minds. You will never amount to anything."

Jay Mack told Fish and I that once he was out and about with his son Jay Jr. and they came across Mr. Goewey, who Jay had in high school, before us. The elder Mack, it is said, had his son meet Goewey with a resounding kick in the shins.

There were tough times in high school, but the funny times are recalled too. In Tom Hoppey's Science class, we all raised hell when he wasn't in the class. Henszie and Fish were acting up on the other side of the room one day and I stood up to wave at them or throw a spit ball. Hoppey arrived back in the room and I sat back down. Nothing but air was under me though, because Barbara Georgi had pulled my seat away from the desk. I plunged to the floor with a great clattering, my desk falling on me and my books flying all over the place. Nothing we did surprised Hoppey. He just looked away until we were ready to begin learning again.

Early one school year, we had a teacher who passed around a sheet of paper and instructed us to write down our last name first and then our first name. When the sheet came back, the teacher read the list of students aloud. "Nimble, Jack B." was announced. Jack Tedrick had struck again. Then came a real life offering that was no joke. "Long, Dick." Over on the other side of the room, Richard Long blushed.

Hanging out at Tierney's store, kidding while getting our hair cut by Joe Pagano and fishing the Delaware were all part of West End life. So was going to Vern Warneke's store on West Main Street. Vern was a nice guy with a foreign accent (German) and we could hardly understand him. The crew I traveled with, used to go in there just to gaze at his wife, who had some set of breasts on her.

Fish and I worked for Vern part time and we were responsible for bringing up empty bottles from the cellar and replenishing soda. These were really carefree days in my life. Near Tierney's, was a big dwelling with some real whackos living upstairs. This weird kid named Cody used to open the window, hang his head out of the second story and begin reciting the Bible from memory. He had big buck teeth and obviously wasn't all there. His father's name was Everett. He was a short and grizzled unshaven man who probably didn't have a bath for a month. Most of the time, he reeked of alcohol and boasted about how tough he was.

Everett was mean, loud and belligerent. This man was no Ward Cleaver, if you catch my drift. While we snickered over Everett, Cody was an absolute riot. A few of us friends would sit by the side of the store and wait for Cody to open the window, located across the street.

Cody went through his Bible readings (I forget which testament) and screamed "wee, wee, wee" to get some laughs. When we left for the night, he would shout down to us "hey kid where are you going?" Pagano would give us a full rundown of anecdotes that took place when Cody's father came by his shop for a haircut.

"Hey Scales," he would say to Fish. "Your buddy Everett was in the other day. I had to wash the dirt out of his hair before I could cut it." Pagano was a great barber and a cool guy. He never looked down on us teenagers and joked constantly.

Cody was always after us to come upstairs and visit him. So one night, we were crazy enough to take him up on the offer and climbed the stairs to the second floor. We found a small place with an old wood stove near the middle of the room. Everett was on the scene also and he was babbling on and on about how he beat up some guy. "I whipped him too," he shouted. He teetered on wobbly legs and began yelling at Cody. Before we knew it, he staggered to the stove and ripped the stovepipe off, turning it into a lethal weapon. As soot fell all over the place, Fish and I bolted down the stairs taking them three and four at a time.

While the good times went on and on, my crowd knew that school was important. That, we figured, is all that stayed between us and unbridled happiness. Graduation would mean total freedom. There would be no parents on our backs and we could pursue a job, college or military service. Way back when I was a junior, I was already thinking of joining the Air Force. Little did I know that the Vietnam "conflict" would be raging when I got out of school in June of 1965.

I loved it when my parents and sister were nowhere to be found on a weekend. Paradise to me, was eating a tuna sandwich and tomato soup on a cold or snowy day while I watched basketball on TV. Even in the winter, I would play my records outdoors while I shot baskets after shoveling off the driveway.

In February of 1964, The Beatles performed on the Ed Sullivan Show. The four young men from England had captured America's heart. Paul, John, George and Ringo arrived at JFK Airport in New York on February 7, 1964. They had recorded "She Loves You" way back on June 6, 1962 and "I Wanna Hold Your Hand" on October 17, 1963. Long hair and Beatle boots were suddenly the "in thing" if you were a teenage boy. The Beatles were part of a British invasion that rocked the music world. Parents bitched and moaned over the bad influence The Beatles were bringing the youth of the land.

While parents raved on and on, at least they were finally leaving Elvis alone. But Elvis was suddenly overshadowed by the mop tops and wasn't real happy about that. It is said that The Beatles visited Graceland on one occasion. They waited, and waited and waited some more for him to come in the room. "The King" was merely showing these musicians who was still boss. Later, they all got together for an impromptu jam session. I would have loved to be one of the walls of that room.

Before I knew it, my senior year arrived. I realized a tough battle lay ahead for me and that it wasn't going to be easy to make it out on time, with my class. I had always loved playing basketball. It was my passion, my hobby and my life. I had walked into guidance counselor Guy Shaw's office knowing that roundball was probably all finished.

"Cat sakes," Shaw said as he gave me a toothy grin. "You have really come along." The jovial guy with the gray crew cut turned serious. "You have a choice to make, Bill. You know what happened in 10th grade when studies were neglected. You have no room to screw up. None at all."

It tore my heart out to watch Bierlein in the backcourt with Spears. I at least had wanted to have a chance to beat him out for the other guard slot. Instead, I was faced with having to pass all seven subjects to graduate. I accepted the cards that were dealt to me. Life would go on. By the way, the basketball team went 4-14 without me.

I continued going steady with Charlene and Fish remained my best friend. We used to make tapes on a reel-to-reel tape recorder and laughed at our own foolishness. Fish had some old 78 rpm records and we incorporated them into our skits. We were even doing this kind of stuff after I went in the service. We laughed and laughed after making tapes of Sergeant Blackbird and Goomba George, the nation's first black president. We weren't prejudiced, but no race was exempt from our deranged minds.

Life was simply hilarious and fulfilling in the teen years. We shot baskets by the hour, played baseball and football, plus fished for eels and catfish off Buckley's Rock. And we studied hard in school. I could suddenly see the light at the end of the tunnel.

Charlene and I shared plenty of time together. And, it appeared that once high school was over, we would be headed to the alter. Every now and then, this girl Christine would come into my life though. On April 28, 1965, I talked to her on the telephone. A month later, Barbara Cleveland, a friend of hers, tried to coax me into taking Chris to her senior prom at DV. I hemmed, hawed and got off the hook. She was crestfallen that I didn't want to take her. Any future with her, looked bleak at best.

During the weekends, I would be indolent, watching sporting events or sitting on Buckley's Rock. One summer, a transfer from the state of

Florida, Nancy Buckley, arrived on the scene. Her dad was none other than Dutch Buckley. She and her sister, Penne, stayed at his house, along with the step mom, Ann Buckley.

Nancy was a tomboy but was good looking. This girl and Mom hit it off great and there were days that Nancy did her own ironing in our living room. I remember a song at that time was "Bread and Butter" by The Easy Beats. I didn't much care for the song, but started caring for Nancy. She tried to tag along with me sometimes, but I would sneak away and trudge off fishing. We did go to one football game together, but the word got back to Charlene. From then on, I played it cool.

Music was great in 1965. It was a spectacular time to be a senior in high school. "Satisfaction", by The Rolling Stones, "Mr. Tambourine Man", by The Byrds, "Help", by The Beatles and "Eve of Destruction", an offering by Barry McGuire, blared on car radios. When Dad would let me drive the 1964 Plymouth Fury convertible, I had a regular record studio at my finger tips.

Most parents loathed "Eve of Destruction". At Christine's house, her mother, Marion, made light of the song. Other older folks weren't that kind and said the tune was ruining the youth of America. Of course I played the song every available moment and learned the words immediately. "Look at all the hate there is in red China, then take a look around at Selma, Alabama, you can leave here for four days in space but when you return it's the same old place." Those words and "hate your next door neighbor, but don't forget to say grace," rang so true. McGuire was exposing hypocrits for what they were. It is obvious that the truth does hurt.

"Unchained Melody", by The Righteous Brothers and "We Gotta Get Out Of This Place", by the Animals were some favorite songs. I heard both from nearby juke boxes while marching in a scorching Texas sun in August. The Righteous Brothers song made me long for home while The Animals recording seemed to be a rallying cry for me to complete basic training and get the hell out of San Antonio forever.

My senior class was an intelligent and very athletic one. I look back at the blue and white yearbook entitled "Archives". I was slim and had a dirty blonde crew cut in those days. Under my mug shot are these words. "P.J.H.S. athlete...Gary's pal...pleasing personality...never a dull moment...always smiling...hails from West End...that's sharp." Apparently, I used the words "that's sharp" quite a bit, or maybe I knew those words were going in the yearbook so I began using them in every other sentence.

There is a picture of Linda Faller, who was the 1964 Thanksgiving Day football queen. The year before, Kathy Kean had won that title. I would have a tie in with both. Faller was the daughter of Doctor Harry Faller, our family physician. One of her brothers was Mark, who would go on to become a fine athlete at Port (football, fourth in state wrestling), and then coach the state title wrestling teams at Port that was paced by the fabulous Banach brothers.

Kathy wound up being a secretary at my dad's insurance office. I would invent reasons to drop by the office, just to see her pretty face. I bought a car from her dad, city clerk Cyrus Kean and the Kean kids came to my wedding. Later I covered some of the boys in Port sports and Fran Kean as an Eldred baseball and girls basketball coach.

The 1964 football team (our class) went 6-2 under Viglione, and wound up in a three-way tie for the DUSO crown. Bill Hallock, John McKechnie, Bill Blasberg, Ed "Ziggy" Rutan, and Spears, all from my class, made all-DUSO. Juniors John Bell and Dave Simmons also made the elite squad. While I later covered Bell as Minisink football and wrestling coach, I have also written about Simmons. He came back to Port as a teacher, is the current varsity wrestling coach and guided Port's Jason Jones to Port's fourth individual state mat championship in 2001.

The season before (1963), Port had gone 7-0-1 and tied for the DUSO crown. They beat Brentwood, Long Island on the road, 24-21, and tied co-champion Newburgh 14-14, at Glennette Field in an epic football game. While flanker Jim Perrego, Spears, Bell and halfback Ray Schultz were offensive stars, defensive back Oliver, lineman Brian Seeber, and the DUSO League's "top defensive player" co-captain Joe Nolan, shone on defense.

That 1963 team had the distinction of beating Thanksgiving Day rival Middletown, 27-7 while my class lost to the Middies, 33-26. Port-Middletown football was one of the oldest rivalries in the nation. The series began in 1897 and 104 games were played. The last holiday contest between the two was in 1969 and tradition was ended when Port joined the Orange County League.

Thanksgiving Day always included an 11 a.m. meeting between the two schools. One year the game would be played at Glennette Field and the next at Wilson Field in Middletown. It was the Erie Bell game and all the pride in the world revolved around the outcome. The Erie Bell, symbol of victory, had come off an Erie Railroad train in 1953. Its home was always the trophy case of the winning school. The railroad runs through both cities and this rivalry was known all over the country. Generations of Raiders and Middies met on the gridiron in the fabled history. And then suddenly, the rivalry was no more. A Taco Bell now occupies the land where Wilson Field used to stand, behind some beautiful trees, as you enter Middletown.

My class starred in wrestling too. Al Wilgard had started wrestling at Port in 1962-63. Already he was getting results as Port went 8-1 in 64-65 and captured the DUSO regular season and tournament titles. At the tournament, 10 of 12 weight classes saw Raiders in the finals. Rich Santiago, Eric Keyes, Oliver, Steve Drapala and his brother Mike Drapala all won tourney crowns. Later, Mike Drapala became a Section 9 champion and went to states. The year before, Charlie Bayer had become our first sectional kingpin.

While basketball was my favorite and track a close second, Nolan and Drapala were varsity standouts in football and wrestling respectively. It would be the three of us who Dad drove north to Albany, New York, in August of 1965, for induction into the Air Force.

In golf, Spears anchored an 8-2-1 squad that included John Werner, Paul Corso, Tom Laidley and Sam Cuddeback. Rick, "Mister Athlete" at Port Jervis, went on to cop the New York State Intersectional title. Spears would go on to star at the University of Florida, and Werner, a 1966 grad, moved on to Rutgers.

While basketball was my love, I did manage to be an integral part of an awesome track team in my senior year.

We had been Section 9 and DUSO Village champions the year before, a year that lanky junior John Kinney ran a 4:38 mile and senior Jim Wilkerson leaped 21-feet in the long jump. Wilkerson was a lean and graceful jumper who also played basketball. While Jim Swingle had put a high hurdle in front of me as a sophomore (to develop height), I watched everything Wilkerson did and learned plenty. It was my ambition to someday snap the 20-foot barrier.

Gordie Short was without a doubt, the fairest and most disciplined coach I have ever seen. He was Port's athletic director then and he is the best mentor I ever performed for, in any sport. He made all of us on the track and field team work extremely hard to reach our goals. He had expertise in all phases of the program, from the sprinters to the long distance men to the field events people. There is one thing I learned about Short, from way back when I competed on varsity as a sophomore. He was a stickler for conditioning and there wasn't an opponent invented yet, that could be in better physical shape than we were.

We ran and ran in the parking lots of the school during pre-season pactices, as we were molded into condition. Like the mail, we went through rain, sleet and snow to get Short's desired results. Fish and I groaned during school hours, just knowing that when the final bell rang, we would be outside sweating our guts out again.

The runners were equipped with faded red hoods while field event participants wore gray sweat pants and tops. After our initial warming up segment, runners would adjourn down to the cinder track at Chase Field while we would head for the long jump pit. Fish was an average athlete and a lot of fun to be around. He didn't compete in the away meets, but was always present when we were at home.

Once May rolled around and the weather got hot, long jumpers like Fish, Carl Popstein, Martin DeMond, Ziggy Rutan and me, practiced hard but played hard too. There were lots of laughs down at the pit, located down a hill from where the track was located. There was a city dump next to our area and the Neversink River ran behind the sawdust pit and behind a bank of weeds and trees. Are you with me so far?

In our book, heat plus river equals swimming. We kept a sharp watch for Gordie, who was known to amble down to check on us with his whistle around his neck. Rutan was always telling us wild stories about Mustangs, wild women and some girl named Carol Ann. Ziggy's Tales of Terror became very well known. He was a fine athlete and was the main swimmer from our little group. Many times he would emerge from the river, dripping all over the place. I think Gordie knew we took an occasional dip. As long as Port Jervis was winning track meets, he was kept happy.

The whole school felt the pride of our track program. In my senior year, we won almost all the time and were the cream of the crop in meets involving lots of teams. We scored over 100 points against Middletown and had a winning reputation. Other teams feared the Raider cindermen and they had justifiable cause.

The team began the season on a roll and stayed that way. We shattered school and area records regularly and never gave losing a thought. Kinney was a premiere miler who had run a 4:18.8 mile during the indoor track season at the Westchester County Games. Kinney used to do a paper route in the morning and ran before school. He was a Jim Ryun era runner who strived for perfection. He set track records all over the place, yet his success never went to his head. John, who would later become one of my editors at the Gazette, ran a 4:19.3 in the Penn Relays for a third place.

It was Gordie's final year as track coach and we made sure he went out with a bang. He won all five of our dual meets against Nyack, Middletown, Suffern, Monroe-Woodbury and Poughkeepsie. If you had to describe our track team in one word, that word would be "depth".

We won the area's biggest competition, the Hudson Valley Relays. Our two mile relay team, consisting of Gerry Carlton, Terry Britt, Rich Haring and Nelson Keyes, snapped a meet record by 12 seconds. We also were entered in the prestigious Englewood Relays that season.

Filled with inspiration, we captured the DUSO Village Track Meet. Our sprint medley relay team of John Piccolo, Tim Card, Kevin Hipsman and Haring, established a new league mark of 3:59.3. Hipsman learned from Gordie and is the current Port Jervis boys and girls track coach.

Carlton set a new record of 10:09 in the two mile, and just for laughs one day, Kinney entered the half mile and blazed to a new league and school record of 1:56.8. In 1965, we extended Gordie's winning streak to 26 out of 27 dual meets (in four years) and won our fourth straight Village DUSO crown.

We wound up second to Newburgh in the City DUSO Track Meet, but four of our runners set records. Carlton ran an awesome 9:48.2 two mile, and Kinney a 4:18.9. Both smashed DUSO and Wilson Field marks. Meanwhile, Keys ran a 1:58 half mile.

We copped the Section 9 Class B Meet on our home track. New York State Meet (Cornell University, Ithaca, N.Y.) qualifiers included George Gardner (shot put), Carlton (two mile) and Kinney (mile). At states, Kinney grabbed a third in a clocking of 4:15.2.

I enjoyed a fine season, although I never did get to snap 20-feet in the long jump. I did eclipse the mark on one excellent jump, but fell back after landing. Getting my steps down to perfection, hitting the take off board just right and getting maximum height, were always on my mind.

I lost an early season long jump competition to Anton DeVries of Delaware Valley and beat the highly regarded Steve Faller of Middletown, plus tied him in the triple jump. I did eclipse 39-feet in the triple (39-4) and hit 19-5 in the long jump, before the season was out.

Faller became my dentist in Matamoras and we used to kid about the long ago day when his Middletown team met us in Port. Tragically, Steve died of a heart attack in 1989 at the age of 42. He had touched many people in his life and as a writer I was torn between remaining quiet in respect, or producing a column about Steve's life and how I felt about him. Although this fine human being had just passed away, the story appeared in a local paper just 12 days later, on May 11, 1989.

Plenty of tears spilled over this piece. It was filled with humor, yet tugged at the heart strings. Somewhere up in heaven, Steve, a football referee, called a good game then fired a sub-par round of golf. He then sat and read the column in the 19th hole, and a smile came to his handsome face. Here are some parts of the story.

"I entered the triple jump competition with an undefeated record and so did the guy in the blue and white uniform. Somebody told me that he was also unbeaten, so I figured this might be a rough battle. After all the flashing spikes gleaming in the afternoon sun, the graceful kicks into the air and sawdust flying everywhere, Bill Tangen and Steve Faller still had unbeaten records--we had tied for first place. That's the first day I shook hands with Steve and as fate would have it, it wouldn't be the last.

He was a professional from day one. When he used the drill, water would fly up onto the lenses of his glasses but he persevered with a satisfied smile until the job was done. He checked my kids' teeth and always kept the little folks happy and at ease. Dr. Steve made friends quickly. To know him was to love him.

One day I had an appointment and came prepared. I pulled the worn newspaper clipping out of my wallet, the one from the 1965 Port-Middletown track meet. "Well, I'll be Billy, you're the same guy that tied me," he said incredulously. "No, you're the guy that tied me," I replied, and we both had a good laugh. Then we compared birth dates. "April 1947," I said. "Me too," he retorted. "April 17th." I had to go one step up on him and I did. I was nine days older.

I debated for awhile whether or not to put out this column, especially because Steve's wife, the former Catherine Ptak, son John and countless friends are so grief stricken at this time. And then I knew I was only kidding myself. Doc would have wanted this to be done, to share his feelings, memories and wit, to pass on his love of mankind.

Steve Faller left us with so many memories in his short 42 years and 12 days. Put quite simply, a little bit of all of us went with Steve. We'll be a little more tolerant with our fellow man. We'll find the bright spot in the darkest cloud. We'll not be afraid to show love and yes, we'll persevere, no matter how tough life can get, or how much the odds are stacked against us. Thank you for getting through to us, Doc. We will miss you an awful lot. We love you."

In 1965, Gordie counted on me for first place finishes in the long jump. Inevitably, the day before a track meet he would appear on the top of the hill, clipboard in hand. He mapped out projected points for the impending meet and left no stones unturned. "Bill, can you get me a first place?" he would ask. "Yes" would be my answer, and then I would go out and do it.

A ways into the season, he appeared on the horizon and walked slowly down the hill to the long jump pit. Something seemed very wrong, because he walked at a slower gait and seemed more thoughtful about the approaching track meet against Monroe-Woodbury. I expected the usual query but my suspicions were found to be justified when he said "Bill, can you get me a second place?"

I had shrugged off the loss to DeVries and had a mind set that didn't allow the word "lose" or "second" to be part of my vocabulary. I was easy to get along with, amiable and very content with the way the season was progressing until that unbelievable question. "You mean a first place, don't you Mr. Short?", I blurted out. "No, Bill, you heard me right. I need you to get me a second," he replied.

Before I could question him anymore, he got to the point. "The kid you will be facing is named Dennis Gurrant. He is an exceptional athlete and an excellent long and triple jumper. He breaks 20-feet very easily and may only jump once or twice against you and that should be enough for his first. Monroe-Woodbury is playing us in baseball too. So he may get done quickly and then run over to the baseball field and play in the game."

My eyes must have glazed over, because Gordie laughed and said "hey, don't worry about it, just get me that second place, okay?" I nodded as if in a trance and went on with practicing my jumps. I wondered who in hell this Dennis Gurrant was and hoped that Gordie was just kidding me. My mind snapped back to reality though, when I realized that Gordon Short was no "Mister Chuckles". He was far from being a comedian or joker. Most of the time, he kept a serious and disciplined demeanor.

I look back and see wins over Middletown (102-34), Suffern (88-48) (Tedrick took second in the discus) and Monroe-Woodbury (88-39). We did a number on Monroe, but Gurrant was everything Gordie said he'd be.

The day of the meet I got down to the long jump area early and began limbering up. I saw the Monroe-Woodbury bus arrive and their purple and white clad team pile out of the vehicle and head down the bleachers to our cinder track. Then I saw an imposing sight that has stayed with me all these years.

Dennis went around 6-2 I think and had to tip the scales around 200 pounds or so. He had short kinky hair and walked in big strides. His attitude made Gordie look like Good Time Charlie. He was quiet, had eyes of coal and was totally focused on the task ahead. That task, was like a walk in the park or taking candy from a baby. I watched his short exhibition and marveled at his tremendous athleticism. He was top notch and knew it. I don't think we exchanged five words.

Our school record in the long jump was 21-feet, set in 1964 by Jim Wilkerson. That record stood the test of time for 35 years until Steve Rhoades leaped 21-9" in 2000. These days, the New York State qualifying standard is 22-feet. It shows how much more talented jumpers of today are.

Gurrant never removed his gray sweats. He quickly got his steps down to the take off board and didn't even take a practice jump. When the competition began, he kept the sweats on as he walked back to the place he would begin his sprint. It took one jump to beat me that May afternoon. He barreled down the runway, hit the board and took off into space with spikes churning in the air. He landed gracefully and attendants measured the jump at 22 feet 10 inches. Before I could congratulate Dennis Gurrant, he was heading up the hill, with his cousin George, to play baseball. Never before and seldom after, has there been a jumper in our area, quite the caliber of Gurrant.

He competed in some invitational meets and I think he eclipsed the 24-foot mark. That same year, Bob Beamon of Jamaica, Queens, leaped 25' 3 ½" on June 12, 1965 at Downing Stadium, Randalls Island, Manhattan, NY. I am almost positive that Beamon and Gurrant wound up tangling at a meet that season. Beamon later notched a 29' 2 1/2" in the 1968 Olympics at Mexico City.

I saw Gurrant four days after he whipped me. He had an off day but still won at the Hudson Valley Relays with a distance of 22 feet 1 ½". Meanwhile, I grabbed a fourth place (19-5"). My jump of 19-feet was enough to win against Suffern and 18-11" beat Middie jumpers. At the DUSO Track Meet, we were second to Newburgh, while Kingston, Ellenville, Middletown and Poughkeepsie completed the field. I managed a fifth place finish while Kinney won the mile in a new meet record of 4:18.9.

When Chris went to school at Orange County Community College in Middletown, she met a classmate named Helen Burgunder from Central

Valley. Chris knew that a guy named Dennis Gurrant had beaten me. Helen knew the name also. He was her boyfriend.

This young long and triple jumper never got a chance to live a full life. I believe it was a New Year's Eve, that Dennis lost his life in an auto accident. It is a tragedy that Helen Burgunder will never forget. She lives in Arizona now, and the two old college chums, Helen and Chris met out there in 1988.

If you ask most of our guys from the 1965 track team what their most vivid memory was, the answer would come as a surprise. It wasn't all the wins or the fabulous times recorded by Kinney. While Gordie didn't laugh it up all that much, he had a team of talented clowns. Our bus rides to away meets are still legendary.

We usually came out on the winning end of the score, so why travel home like a bunch of sad sacks? One day we won a prestigious meet that involved plenty of teams. Some school and meet records were snapped and we hopped on the bus delirious with happiness. Some of the guys asked if we could stop at a store in a nearby town, to get some soda and munchies. Gordie was proud of our accomplishments and figured he would reward us with a booming "yes." This was the beginning of a wild and crazy ride back to Port Jervis.

Kinney, Fran Bender, John Garrity, Tom Bayer, Dennis McCullough, Tom Geib, Lou Stewart and the rest of our team were enjoying our first place finish. We chattered happily on the road after the store stop, as the bus headed toward Port Jervis. Everyone from sprinters John Piccolo and Kevin Hipsman, to field events people George Gardner and Bunny Kean, either saw or heard about what transpired on our team bus, that memorable afternoon.

It seems that potato chips and soda weren't the only purchases made in that store. We were men who had just been successful, and beer came out of that establishment too. When you take some happy campers and add alcohol, anything can happen. The party on wheels rolled on.

The gradually increasing creschendo reached fever pitch out on a major highway. There was a reason why the laughs became much louder. Some of the guys decided to liven up the trip home. So they dropped their pants in the back of the bus and "mooned" the car behind us. Songs like "There's A Moon Out Tonight", "Moon River" and "Blue Moon" became traveling medleys for us and all was right with the world.

Suddenly, Gordie was looking to the back of the bus as it maneuvered off the road and onto the right shoulder. "There is a woman pulling us over," he shouted. "Anybody want to tell me what this is all about? She looks upset."

Everyone clammed up big time. There wasn't a murmur and you could hear a pin drop. We eyed each other or looked at the floor. We realized that big trouble was lurking just moments away. Silently, I knew we would not tell on a teammate or teammates. We had become such a sports "family" that we stuck together through thick and thin. Gordie gave up trying to get an answer from us, and left the bus to talk with the woman. When he got back aboard, there was hell to pay. It was bad enough that a mooning went on. But we had three strikes on us. The driver was a woman, there was a child in the car, and if you can believe this, she was a New York State Trooper's wife. Game, set and match!

"That woman is very upset," Gordie screamed. "Who are the ones who stuck their asses out the back window?" It was one of the toughest things I've ever done in my life, suppressing a laugh at those words. Guys snickered into their open hands and tears ran down cheeks. I nearly pissed my pants it was so serious, yet so funny.

Nobody uttered a word. None of us fessed up to what had just occurred. It seemed just a matter of seconds went by, before we reached the grounds of Port Jervis High School. This turmoil was far from over and we were about to be grilled more than a well-done cheeseburger. Fran Bender provided a startling explanation point to this little saga. While trying to conceal a quart of beer, as he left the bus, he dropped the bottle and it smashed all over the place. Gordie was absolutely livid.

He herded us into the gymnasium and made us sit in the bleachers. For a long time, he said nothing. Then he started talking about how disgusted he was and he pointed out that the day's successes were ruined. He stared at us and he paced. Every so often he would look into the crowd and shout out a name. "Who is the liar, Garrity?" he shouted. "Who is the liar Geib?" Again, we tried to stifle laughter.

Gordie said we would sit there all night if somebody didn't take the blame. Finally a couple of the guys admitted their guilt. I felt bad for Bender too, cause he was the nicest guy on the team and was probably hiding the beer for someone else. Gordie wanted to get down to the bottom of the beer story too. A couple of my teammates owned up to that also. One of them went a bit too far though when he uttered these immortal words. "We didn't buy the beer Mr. Short, we stole it."

From that day on, "who is the liar, Garrity?" became a battle cry. We said it all the time and broke into laughter, even though suspensions were handed out. The bottom line is that this team accomplished a lot and is recalled as a record breaking squad. "Blue Moon" remains one of my favorite songs.

The days flew by and soon it was time to view my report card. I was really sweating Miss Altenhofen's Bookkeeping class and was afraid that a failing mark in that class would prevent me from graduating on time. The key to my future was in my hands as I sat at a desk in Room 204. And just like that, I slipped the card out of its holder. I had gotten an 82 in Bookkeeping and finished with a 70 average. I averaged 81 in English, 87 in Business Arithmetic, 79 in Typewriting, 74 in Retailing, 68 in Printing and 90 in Physical Education. On June 29th, 1965, I would be graduating from high school.

It was the 96th annual commencement and was staged at Glennette Field, beginning at 7:30 p.m. A total of 204, including 96 girls, had successfully made it through school. Valedictorian Neal Kaplan (95.78 average) and Saluatorian Carol McAllister (94.30 average) gave speeches. Principal Willard Lloyd and Assistant Principal Russ Faiello were on hand for the festivities. I walked up on the stage and got that precious document that freed me from the prison walls of high school forever. They say you only remember the good times and that is a bunch of bunk. But as I stood there in black graduation garb, a world removed from my precious white, black and red uniform number "3", a feeling of uncertainty about the future entered my mind. In six weeks I would be off to Air Force boot camp in San Antonio, Texas. I must admit the good memories of the teen years began to invade my head.

It had all begun years ago with the sneaked whiskey and run up Church Street with Lester Buchanan. Numerous softball and bowling trophies followed and talking the Yankees with Papa was a daily thing. I wished he had been alive to watch me sink that shot against Ellenville. He always used to say "when you feel good, I feel good." He would have felt kind of great on that memorable evening.

I remember when the Russians were acting up and threatening war with the United States. I expected an attack in the night and everyone running screaming into the streets. Grade schools didn't relieve the anxiety but only added to it, by refusing to explain things while you crouched under your desks. Looking back, it was an age of innocence. But it was also a silly era when kids sometimes were either ignored or looked down at, like second class citizens.

Billy Joel ends many of his concerts with the words "don't take any shit from anybody." While some may regard the message as a vulgar one, I see the words as enlightening. I had begun to think that way at a young age. While I may smile it up and play the game, my mind would be clear. I would have the ability to sift out the true from the fairy tales and the genuine people from the phonies. While not always possessing common sense, I do have a pretty good gift for reading people for what they are. That worked real well in the working world, where I interacted with both decent and ridiculous human beings.

How can I ever forget assistant principal Ted Archer lurking around the hallways and inflicting punishments for lack of discipline? And what about John Metcalfe? I had him for both Shop and Printing. He was a tall guy with a blonde crew cut and a strange but funny sense of humor. There were vises dotted throughout the shop and he had a rule about them. He screamed at the top of his lungs "don't touch the vises." You could probably hold Metcalfe, Archer and 10 other teachers hostage in the library, but as long as you didn't touch the vises, you would pass the class.

Of course Art class and Biology immediately came to mind. Hillis

McIlnay tried to soften the blow with a smile. "You have got to be the worst Art student I've ever had," he said. I looked at my Art paper that is supposed to show some type of perspective and nodded my head in agreement. When I attempted to draw people they looked like "stick people." No doubt Tracie gets her drawing ability from Chris, because it sure didn't come from this side.

Henry Howard tried to be patient with me in Biology. Reaching Biology problem conclusions in that class was baffling to me. When Fish helped me with a Biology notebook I figured things would get better. Then someone stole my notebook from a cabinet in the classroom. I told Howard and knew he didn't buy the excuse. Sadly, I had told the truth and came up empty. There was no way to make him see all the hours and hard work that I had expended in order to make a go at it. I wondered if real life as an adult would produce the same futile results.

I recall John Donnelly, a young, fair and cool English teacher. Pepin was a favorite of mine because of his demeanor and self-confidence. Health teacher William Romalho was a disciplinarian and knew his subject well. It was Romalho who was courteous enough to say "please" and "thank you" in the toughest situations. To this day, a little bit of Romalho's classy actions come through in how I deal with people.

Back in junior high, I still see lanky custodian Mr. Lewis going about his duties. I don't think I ever heard Mr. Lewis talk. He would hang out in the boiler area and watch you come into the school as his keys jingled from his belt. This guy was not "Mister Personality." The cafeteria ladies always got a charge out of my crowd. We put on a free show for them every day. Cho cho popsicles and Rockets (ice cream) were the favorites of the day. And it was extremely uncool to buy your lunch, as far as our little group was concerned.

If anyone bought their lunch, Tedrick would look at you as if you had a contagious disease. He would scrunch up his face and say "what is that garbage?" as he eyed the tray's contents. The day Fish forgot his lunch is my all time favorite cafeteria memory. I still see Henszie offering part of his lunch to Gary. But my pal wasn't about to chow down on those sardine and ketchup sandwiches on raisin bread. Fish nearly barfed on the table and decided to skip lunch and just settle for dessert.

Our commencement seemed to go quickly and before I knew it, we were moving that tassel from one side of the mortarboard hat to the other, signifying that we were official graduates of Port Jervis High School class of 1965.

I walked through the gates of Glennette Field and out into the real world. It was a world where homework assignments were never given out. There were no book reports, study halls or failing grades. There would be no more leaping out of bed and rushing to the bus stop. I felt light as a feather and free of pressure. It was great to be alive in June of 1965. The music was great, cars were cool and girl watching was a must.

Responsibilities ebbed to an all time low. I nearly had to pinch myself to make sure I wasn't dreaming.

Chris graduated indoors at Delaware Valley High School, Pa., on June 4, 1965. I guess that would make her about three weeks smarter than me. We had absolutely no connection then. There was no communication between us and it seemed we'd never even see each other in the future. It appeared as if Charlene and I would someday get married and have children. But first, I had a service commitment to honor.

Chris had gotten her first job at the age of 16, cleaning motel rooms during the summer for 75 cents a room. She applied and was accepted for employment at the Port Jervis Atlantic and Pacific Tea Company (A&P) in June 1965. She worked until going to Orange County Community College in Middletown, where she majored in Secretarial Science. Meanwhile, Chris was already working as an organist at the Epworth Methodist Church (three Sundays a month) where she made $42 per month. That money tided her over until she resumed work at the A&P. She admits that boys and looking forward to annual vacations were her hobbies. In June 1968, she would graduate from college with a two-year degree.

Her parents were very strict and didn't really believe in her getting a college education. "They wanted me to work, work, work," she says. "They didn't have faith in me when it came to college. My father finally agreed to college and paid for my first semester."

While I was over on Guam and counting days until my discharge, my wife to be, wanted the luxury of her own car. While she finished school in January of 1968, she was working three jobs including a full time one at Eddy Farm Hotel in Sparrowbush. She ordered a bucket seat burgundy 1968 Plymouth Barracuda Fastback with an automatic 318 engine in March 1968, at Culver Motors, after saving up $800 for a down payment. Back in 1965, she had read in our local newspaper that I was gone to Texas. What a difference just over three years would make.

In 1965, the first combat troops arrived in Vietnam. There was probably a good chance that Tedrick's yearbook notation would come true and I would be in that country sooner or later. Some other happenings that year included the Dodgers knocking off the Twins in the World Series (4-3), Montreal beating Chicago for the hockey Stanley Cup (4-3), and Luck Debonair winning the Kentucky Derby.

Alabama and Michigan State topped the NCAA football polls, The Sound of Music premiered, and Bill Cosby ("I Spy") became the first African American to ever headline a television show. James Baldwin's book, "Going to Meet The Man" came out and Edward White II became the first American to walk in space (June 3). Winston Churchill and Nat King Cole died and Dick Clark was going strong. Rod Serling's "Twilight Zone" was a must see on TV.

The summers of 1965, 1966 and 1967 were the best in my life. After graduation, I continued to mature and was faced with plenty of decisions and choices. Should I get up at 10 or 11? What clothes should I wear on wild car drives over the famed Hawk's Nest (Route 97), and which girls should I impress? I guess you get the idea. "Fun Fun Fun" was not just a Beach Boys song, it became my lifestyle. With a 1964 aqua Plymouth Fury convertible sometimes at my disposal, I would don my shades and head for the hills with the radio blasting. Mom always tried to separate Charlene and me in the front seat. Soon, she wouldn't have to, because it would be Fish, Henszie and I who headed to Mongaup, along the Delaware River, in search of girls and fun.

I used to ride over the Hawk's Nest with Bob Thiele in his 1961 Chevy Impala convertible, as "Baby The Rain Must Fall" played on the radio. Now it was my turn to be at the controls and it was a complete ego and power trip.

Fish was the guy who got the rest of us interested in this section of Sullivan County. He had this girl he liked, named Linda, and it went from there. It seemed lots of people were related to each other in close-knit families. For us guys from Orange County, it was a case of the grass being greener on the other side of the fence. The ladies we sought went to Eldred High School and lived in a picturesque area that was bordered by waterways and mountains. It seemed like a science fiction episode here, as Mongaup, Pond Eddy, Yulan, Barryville and Eldred seemed to be trapped in the time warp of the 1950s. It was a great way to be trapped.

Bob Liptak, a member of the Invaders band (drummer) with Henszie and Fish, used to accompany us on some of our journeys to God's Country. All was going well, and I felt extremely free and happy. That all came to a screeching halt when I got hooked on a girl named Nancy, one of two pretty sisters. Henszie, of course, had to be spellbound by the same female, and the competition was on.

Neither of us would give ground. I wanted to be alone with her, but it was impossible. When Nancy's mom and dad weren't around, her little brother was. He was a blonde kid that was always on the move and traveled from room to room. I'm really glad I treated Donnie well, cause he grew to be a man who resembles Paul Bunyan. He is tall and rugged and I doubt many people have ever screwed around with him.

One day I got really frustrated about this situation and tried to figure a way out of it. Nancy's mom was home at the time and although she protected her daughter with iron hand, she seemed to like me. I asked if it would be alright to take Nancy for a ride in the convertible. "Sure," she replied. "As long as John can go along too."

So with me steaming under the collar, we walked to the car and hopped in. "Satisfaction" by The Rolling Stones, the number one hit of the times, was blaring out of the speakers. Nancy was in the front seat with me but Henszie was assuming his role of chaperone well. He leaned forward to check where my hands were. "So this is real life," I thought. I felt like an amoeba under a microscope as the car pulled out of the driveway and headed from Mongaup to Eldred. If I only knew then what I know now. I never figured to be headed for a writing career.

Classmate Rick Spears went on to become a professional golfer and before that, was on television in the U.S. Amateur Tournament, which was won by Lanny Wadkins. Rick played in the U.S. Open and Masters and I covered him several times, including Orange County Golf Club Middletown, where he fired a 65 and at Montclair, New Jersey, where he played in the same field as Chi Chi Rodriguez.

Roger Duryea went the state police route as a trooper. He married the former Yvonne Flannery, another classmate of mine. They were "Duke" and "Dutchess" in the yearbook. These were two good looking kids who were destined to wind up with each other. Chris and I saw them at Tom and Jill Vicchiariello's house once, and recalled a day in the past.

I had been driving east on Route 84 when a police car suddenly appeared on my bumper. The lights went on and I pulled off to the side of the road. A New York State Trooper in full battle regalia, approached the car with sun glasses on. "License and registration," he barked. "What are you doing you little bastard?" There stood my old softball teammate Roger Duryea with a big grin pasted across his face. "Just wanted to keep you on your toes," he said with a laugh. Roger and I had once watched the World Series with other troopers at the New Bauer Inn. "I hope the police aren't out there," I had said before leaving the bar. "We are the police," Duryea replied. Years later, I covered his son, Steve, as he played for the Port Jervis baseball team. He was a good ballplayer just like his dad had been.

Stanley Siegel was an intelligent, yet humorous kid. To know him was to like him. He would walk around saying "there's fungus amongus." It couldn't have been in his craziest thoughts, that he would wind up in city government. And yet, in November 2001, he was elected Councilman-at-Large for the City of Port Jervis. In other words, he is the guy that serves directly under Mayor Ross Decker. It proves good guys do finish first.

I never knew that any writing ability at all was hidden in my body. In fact, I figured to be someday taking over my Dad's insurance agency. But he really didn't have the patience to teach me and I had other interests.

One of the great things about hanging out in Eldred, was the Pinehurst Casino. On weekend nights, this was the place to be for sure. Al Mosher was in a band called "The Five Dimensions", along with four cool guys from Staten Island, N.Y. The four, Bill Koonz, Dougie Kurtz, Jeff Grotz and Bob Ellard came up here and were absolutely awesome. I have never heard a more dynamic or talented rock and roll band in my life. The music blared out the front windows and doors and into vehicles that were passing by in the warm summer air. Drivers had to wonder if

The Byrds or The Searchers were inside the casino, because "Tambourine Man" and "Needles And Pins" were played to perfection. The bar bulged at the seams with tune- happy patrons.

I slept late, thought "physical labor" was some guy in Mexico, and soaked in life without the rigors of high school. Music was a panacea for any ills or bad moods that came my way. While Charlene was less than happy with my lifestyle, freedom flowed over me like a tidal wave of relief. Going steady or being tied down with commitments, suddenly didn't feel cool. I was serene, content, satisfied with life. I eagerly looked forward to each new day in a summer brimming with joy. It doesn't get any better than this.

Wiffle ball and fishing had been replaced by car rides north and bottles of Budweiser. "Can't Help Myself" by The Four Tops and "Cara Mia" by Jay and the Americans, made the WMCA radio Fabulous 57 Survey. It's simply amazing that I even survived that sizzling summer. In retrospect, I figure I wasn't the only one watching the dates fly by on the calendar. Dad and Mom may have been counting the hours until they could finally breathe easily. They could only control me so much and once I drove slowly down Lyman Avenue and turned right onto West Main Street, I entered the world of terrific teenage times.

There was that straightaway on the way to Eldred, where I accelerated the vehicle to 100 and 110 miles an hour. I had to see what the car would do, and I had nearly no conception of fear. I looked through the tint of the sunglasses at the beauty summer can bring. I was intelligent enough to realize that this was a once in a lifetime experience. There would be a day when all this was over. I hated the thought of all these great times ending and thirsted for more.

Those Pinehurst nights are a memory that is permanently etched in my mind. The Five Dimensions were spectacular. Just picture Eddie and the Cruisers (movie) and music from the Jersey shore. This was the type image they portrayed, long before the movie was even thought about. Their emphasis was on 60s rock, but they could throw out some 50s music with a loud or soft accent that would silence the most severe critic.

Fish was always eying the front windows at Pinehurst. He was underage for drinking and didn't turn 18 until October 31, so his plan was to jump out of a window if the cops suddenly came into the joint. Sweat poured from drummer Ellard's face as his wild hair flew in his eyes. His drums had chains wrapped around them. Ellard was the neatest thing since sliced bread.

Big Gypsy and Little Gypsy accompanied the band. They were sexy looking girls with long, dark hair and everyone noticed them. Between sets, the casino crowd, packed in like sardines, escaped out to the parking lot where hot cars and hotter girls could be found. Ellard spent a lot of time under a car and he wasn't fixing anything that was mechanical. Four feet showed in the moonlight. While Ellard was the wild man of the group, Koonz was the calm and methodical type and Dougie the quiet member. Grotz and Mosher could make guitars sing.

The owners of the casino were fairly old and kept telling the band to turn down the amps. Instead the amps got turned up. Some big guy they called "Ox" was calling the Air Force the "Air Farce" and began receiving riveting stares from me. Nearby, a guy walked by with dog tags jangling from his neck. "That is gonna be me soon," I thought.

Sometimes the band played at the roller rink in Yulan. The rink was a spacious place with high ceilings and the chattering of excited teens. When the Dimensions played, the place was packed to the rafters. I danced with Barabara Dunlap and cracked jokes with her neighbor Tom Mollema, more than once at the rink.

In early August, I had my final 1965 night at the Pinehurst Casino. "Satisfaction" had dropped to number two on the survey and "What's New Pussycat" by Tom Jones was third. The number one tune in the land was "I Got You Babe" by Sonny and Cher. My time home was dwindling and I already felt the void that was rapidly approaching. There would be no Charlene, Nancy, Fish or The Five Dimensions. My longish hair would be shaved and the sunglasses would be turned in for dogtags. A big change was right around the corner.

That final night at home, slugging down beers with Tom Roberts, was a real happening. Nothing like puking in the kitchen sink the night before you leave home. I woke up early with a monumental hangover that included a pounding headache. I had gotten drunk for the very first time and vowed it would never happen again.

I battled a genuine case of cotton mouth as Dad drove Mike, Joe and me north to Albany, N.Y., the site of our enlistment. We were sworn in at the state capitol and stayed at the Wellington Hotel that night. I gazed out the hotel window and saw Dad's car, a small dot down below, wind its way through the Albany traffic. He was going home and we were going to God knows where.

We never did use our free meal ticket that evening. Instead, all three of us sacked out for a few hours. Later, we planned to have a look around town. However, the lounge downstairs pulled us in like a magnet. I got sloshed for the second straight night. The next day I was nervous as a cat and hung over on my first flight ever, from Albany to Newark, New Jersey. The plane was a small Mohawk and I swear I saw the wings flapping in the breeze. I envisioned the pilot wearing an old time uniform complete with leather cap and goggles. Would I crash before I ever saw Texas? It seemed at the time, that this would be an easier fate than suffering through a monumental hangover.

While our aircraft floundered around in turbulence, my stomach was doing flip flops. I was far from gleeful on this maiden voyage and had a sardonic attitude regarding the loss of my summer freedom. Once in Newark, the three amigos transferred to a larger plane, and had stops in

Atlanta, Georgia and Houston, Texas. We continued west, and finally touched down in the heat and darkness of San Antonio. We were in the land of the Alamo and I felt as if I'd been through that battle. My aching an tired body dragged down the steps and into the terminal.

Soon an Air Force Sergeant appeared and rounded us up. Outside was a large bus with the words "Lackland AFB" written above the windshield. The sarg herded us toward the vehicle with eyes black as the Texas night. "We're going to Lackland," he screamed. "Now get your sorry asses on the bus…now!"

CHAPTER 6

Welcome to Texas, Boy!

I had arrived at my destination in one piece.

Looking down at the pretty blue runway lights as my plane touched down on Texas soil, gave me solace. The curtain came down on a happy summer and weeks of anticipation. Suddenly, it seemed all of that was a mere dream as I gazed into humid conditions and a pitch dark sky.

Sergeant Stone, my Air Force recruiter back in Port Jervis, had told me how easy basic training would be. "It will be a piece of cake," he said through gleaming teeth. Then he continued with some more of his clever jokes. "It's just like a country club. You will come back home and thank me for this opportunity."

While "Stoney" had a likeable demeanor, there were many times in the fives weeks of boot camp, that I wanted to strangle him. In the place of a piece of cake, was a steady diet of harassment. The country club was a two-story barracks where we were shouted at, intimidated, smacked around and disciplined. Boys walked into this dwelling and men marched out, weeks later.

Those comforting blue runway lights stayed with me for my entire enlistment. Evenings, I would look out at them from a window of the barracks and wonder if there was a nearby fence that would spell freedom. I could silently sneak into the night, climb the barrier and head off into oblivion, never to be seen or heard again. The mind can play plenty of amusing tricks when you're hopelessly confined.

Later, those blue lights followed me to Thailand where B-52's took off on bombing missions over Vietnam. On the island of Guam, I saw those lights for 14 months. On the runway most days, was a Pan American Airways plane. And one day that aircraft would be mine, to escape the jungle for "the world" (United States). The military, its rigors, pettiness and prejudices, would be left far behind as the island became a dot far below. The lights and runways were a constant companion and a source that represented tranquility, relief and hope.

The strangeness of Lackland clung to me like a rude relative who wore out his welcome. I felt puzzled, bewildered, dominated and lonely. I possessed an ego that had become inflated by girlfriends and sports. They

125

say everything is bigger in Texas and I immediately started feeling inferior by a huge and stern military system. The Sergeant barked loudly at us and once we were herded onto the bus, our minds began working overtime. My skin was clammy, sweat rolled into my eyes and there was no air to breathe. The bus pulled up to the main gate of Lackland AFB and another chapter of my life began.

I had never felt this exhausted in my young life. Many of the guys rubbed their eyes and yawned. Through bleary eyes, I began to process in as the hot Texas sun began to make its appearance. I was just a zombie going through the motions and the procedure seemed endless.

Surely when this tedious task ended, they would finally allow us to sleep for at least a couple of hours. This type of thinking would be nipped in the bud and stopped cold. The realization that there would be no sleep, was like a giant door slamming shut with a sickening bang.

"You were determined to get the Air Force over with as soon as possible," Fish reminded me many times over the years. "Vietnam was going on and the draft was here. You didn't want to waste any time and knew you wanted to leave right after school was over."

It is strange how we both took the same path. While I became an airman August 10, 1965, Fish followed in January 1967. When I speak of Texas and the hazing that went on there, he can relate.

Air Force boot camp in August, is hotter than three whores in a closet. As the saying went, "everyday is a holiday and every meal is a banquet." Day 1, saw a bunch of raw recruits, dressed in every color in the spectrum, heading toward their barracks. The guy marching us to this location, made just one statement about what lay ahead for us. "Your training instructor will be Sergeant Stacy Young. He is the toughest and meanest son of a bitch on the base."

Flight 1147, 66 of us who were mostly from New York, arrived in front of barracks 6116. It was August 11, 1965 and I will never forget this day. A mountain of a man waited for us near the front screen door. He stood more than six feet tall and had to tip the scales at close to 300 pounds. Young was mean looking, had piercing eyes and a nasty disposition. "Well I'll be God damned, my babies are here," he spit out. "They tell me most of you are from New York. I hate New York."

Young stared at each one of us, surveying his new flight of "rainbows" (civilian clothes) with hatred in his eyes. Then he gave the statement that so many recruits have heard at Lackland. "I'm gonna be your mama, your papa and your girlfriend. But don't fuck with me."

Young pointed in the direction of the barracks. "One of my strictest rules is to never, ever see grass in my barracks," he glared. "For every blade of grass I find, you will give me 25 (pushups)." The rugged man walked a few steps, bent over and ripped a handful of grass from the front yard. He opened up the front door and tossed the green blades inside. "Now get down and give me those damn pushups."

Life with Sergeant Young was pure hell. He must have violated plenty of Air Force regulations in whipping us into shape. He wanted us to be the finest flight that ever came through Lackland and would leave no stone unturned to accomplish that goal. One thing I have to say in defense of this mountain of a man. You knew exactly where you stood with him. You were just a number and a thorn in his side. He physically and mentally harassed us into oblivion.

There would seldom be a break in the action. We double timed everywhere, to and from chow, to the rifle range and to the drill pad. At night, lights were out, but we sat on the barracks floor with flashlights, reading "The Code of Military Conduct" or studying security instructions plus customs and courtesies of the Air Force.

He had us go through the obstacle course at night, marching us quietly to the site. He was obsessed with posting the fastest time on the base and he wanted us prepared. That first evening at Lackland, gave us a taste of what was to come. We fell out into the front yard, enveloped in darkness, with our duffel bags and military clothing. With flashlights in one hand and ink stamps in the other, we marked all our clothing with our Air Force serial numbers. Even though it is nearly 37 years later, I still remember the number, including the last four digits "9849."

We had to throw everything we owned on our bunks to be inspected. Playboy magazines, combs, pens, razor blades, knives, candy and gum were suddenly out in the open. The items were confiscated immediately and the transformation from civilian to military life continued.

Young told us he had some type of affiliation with the Cleveland Browns football team. Looking at his stature as he tossed foot lockers around like toothpicks, made me a believer. While marking our clothes in the yard resembled a humorous Three Stooges film, the next morning was no laughing matter.

I laid motionless in my top bunk (second floor) but was suddenly rousted from sleep by bright lights overhead and an awful voice shouting "get up you bastards. Hurry up, we have a lot to do today." Nothing would ever be serene with Young in the picture. He demanded perfection and he wanted things done immediately if not sooner.

Nolan was one of four squad leaders in the flight and I was lucky enough to be in his squad. We never let on we knew one another. We briskly marched to breakfast in the dark and waited to enter the chow hall. In the early days, brogans hit the pavement at various times, but soon enough, 132 feet pounded the ground in unison . Sergeant Young disciplined us right away, and as time went by, we became a finely tuned military instrument.

Meals at the chow hall was a big joke. It was a race against time and you had to inhale your food as quickly as possible. I concentrated some on the food, but when my pith helmet was off and I was sitting in the chow hall, I had chocolate milk on my mind. Young made us march in the wicked Texas sun with a minimum of water breaks. My canteen became a best friend and just getting a swig of water was a huge luxury.

All meals ended the same way, with Young shouting "flight 1147 get out." We stood near dumpsters outdoors and our squad leaders asked Airmen their security instructions. I think there were about 10 of them that you had to know by heart. Nolan always asked me the same exact one, and to this day, I will never leave my post without being relieved.

It wasn't long before we became real acquainted with fire drills. One typical training day, Young wasn't pleased with the way we were marching. "Fuck it, get in the grass," he said. "Give me 25." He did this over and over again and then gave us a hint of what was coming later on. "You babies are gonna be doing some fire drills," he barked.

That night we burned the midnight oil again, studying and learning while brandishing our flashlights. We had buffed the barracks floor with a blanket and everything appeared in order. The flight had duck walked around the inside of the barracks for what felt like hours. Punishment was doled out regularly and harassment was a way of life. Our feet hurt from marching and we prayed that a few hours of sack time would arrive. Once we finally slipped under the covers and heavy eyelids closed, a three ring circus began with plenty of loud noise, whistles and bright lights.

The words "fire, fire, fire" pierced the air as we leaped from bunks, swiftly put on our brogan shoes and wrapped a blanket around our legs. The trick in this fire drill, would be to get out to the front of our barracks in record time. Being on the top floor, I had a flight of steps to run down. Guys were everywhere, fighting to reach the stairs and to get out the screen door.

Young stood near the front door and dared anyone to brush him on the way by. Some of the big guys couldn't help but touch him lightly. They were rewarded by a backhand that had to sting. A stop watch monitored the time for 66 Airmen to reach that small front yard. He shook his head in disgust and berated the flight. "We'll run these fuckin fire drills all night or until you get it right," he wailed.

Seconds after lights were turned out, we were again whistled and shouted from our bunks. This repetition continued hour after hour. The number 27 sticks in my head for some reason. I recall that someone said Sergeant Young was out to break some kind of base record for fire drills. I don't know if that is true, but I do know Young wanted to see stamina and mental toughness. He secretly told other flights to laugh at us when we marched by them, made us watch him drink soda in the blistering Texas heat while we had none, and intimidated us constantly. There was no getting away from this man, because he slept in the same barracks as we did.

Some nights if you listened closely enough, you could hear some guys weeping themselves to sleep. Drapala, Nolan and I were in excellent physical shape. Al Wilgard (wrestling), Joe Viglione (football) and Gordie Short (track) had prepared us well. Still I asked myself the same questions every morning when I was routed from my bunk "What the hell have I done? Can I make it through this boot camp? Is there any way out?"

Once Young told us that if anyone wanted out, to come and see him. I figured what the hell, it's worth a try and went to see what that was all about. Needless to say, he wasn't serious and threatened to kick me through a wall. "Boy, what is that on your face?" he said, pointing to a mole on the left side of my cheek. "Is that hair I see coming out of that mole?" I nodded my head in an affirmative manner. "From now on, your gonna dry shave, boy, and I'm gonna watch you shave that mole. Now get the hell out of here."

Young constantly played mind games with us. If you were on barracks guard at night, nobody was to be allowed entry to the barracks. No matter what the rank or reason, you were expected to politely tell the person they weren't allowed to come inside. We were approached nightly by many individuals, many of them pissed off officers. Basic training would be one big test, my father had told me before I left home. He had hit the nail squarely on the head.

Nolan and the other three squad leaders had unbelievable pressure on them. They were picked on, roughed up and had to answer to Sergeant Young when members of their squad screwed up. At night, Young would sit in his office and shout out a squad leader's name. That means the leader had to sprint to Young's door while wearing shower clogs. "Is that a woodpecker at my door?" he used to shout. "Knock hard, God damn it." As a training instructor, Sergeant Stacy Young took the cake when it came to whipping a group into shape. Although I despised him, I had to admit that he took immature boys and molded them into confident men.

One evening Young beckoned Nolan to his office because one of Joe's guys wasn't marching well. Young sat in his office like some kind of king when he called for someone to report to him. Joe made the fatal mistake of showing up without his shower clogs on. We all heard Young shouting and then there was plenty of noise coming from the office. Had Young struck Joe? All we could do was listen in silence and hope we weren't next.

I did learn a few things while in Texas. Donnie Charleston, a mild-mannered black recruit, taught me some tricks that would help me memorize things. We had to know all the enlisted and officer ranks in order from Airman Basic up to Chief Master Sergeant and Second Lieutenant to General of the Air Force. The order of Generals had me a bit confused but Charleston came to the rescue. "Be my little General," he said simply. I asked what he meant and he was happy to explain. "Be is Brig General, my is Major General, little means Lieutenant General and of course General of the Air Force (four stars)." To this day,

Charleston's short cut has helped me countless times in the sports field.

Our flight had plenty of New Yorkers in it, but we were a mixed bag. Another black Airman, Joe Cross, made us laugh after lights were out. He did a great impression of Sergeant Young. "Oh fuck it. God damn it, get in the grass," he would say as the whole second floor chuckled. Once the activities of the long day had finally concluded, there was a degree of solitude at Lackland. That is when I would look out at the blue runway lights at neighboring Kelly Field and dream of an escape plan. How high is the fence and how many guards are watching that runway?, I wondered.

Like anyone away from their state for the first time, I missed home and was just a step short of homesick. We did receive mail and I wrote letters with whatever time we were given. Young never let up on us, but we started adjusting to his leadership. We would go out in the sun, marching and drilling. Upon returning to our barracks bay, we would find the contents of foot lockers dumped all over the floor and bunks tipped over. "Clean up this God damn mess," Young would say, and then retreat to his office. Young delighted in our misery, but by now we were getting used to all of his tactics. I did my job everyday and tried to stay out of his way. In my head was an unseen calendar with a date in September circled. That would be the day I could finally get out of this rotten place.

Dad had taught me to never volunteer for anything in the Air Force. My voice was eternally quiet when volunteers were sought. We worked liked dogs from before the sun came up, until long after it set. Many times I fell into my bunk exhausted and overtired.

While Nolan, sporting salt and pepper hair, had a solid linebacker physique, Drapala was a lean and athletic wrestler type. He had a sly kind of smile that tipped you off that something was going on in his head. Far from a dummy, "Drap" was figuring out a way to get out of some of the marching. He volunteered to do the laundry for the whole flight, In hopes that he could gain some extra sack time.

I still see him busily hustling around the washers in the middle of the night. He had taken a risk by assuming this responsibility and hoped it would pay off. Yawning and bleary eyed, he got a small amount of sleep. However, his feet hit the floor right along with ours, as each grueling day began. Drapala possessed a great sense of humor and he needed that trait, to cope with the tasks he faced.

I was really sweating the 17th day evaluation. We would be watched in lots of different areas, including first aid. I wasn't sure I could make it through and realized that not cutting the mustard would result in being set back to my third day of training. That chilling penalty was on many minds when the day finally rolled around. I made it through the test alright and had my sights set on the day I would ride back through the gates of Lackland AFB.

Young never softened. He promised us everything in the world and gave us nothing. He would purposely steer us to an area of soda machines and halt our marching. "Sure is a hot day," he would say. "You babies want a nice cold soda?" In one voice, we shouted "yes sir." Young would look at us, give a fake grin and shake his head. "Well you aren't fuckin getting one," he would say. Then he would swill down his soda in front of us. "Maybe someday I'll let you go to town (San Antonio) and see the Alamo," he said. The odds were better that Davy Crockett, coonskin cap on his head and musket in hand, would return to the Alamo before we would see it.

I was never into rifles or hunting in my life. But at Lackland, I was introduced to either an M-1 or M-16 rifle (I forget which). There was this little matter of qualifying on the rifle range that became a big obstacle for me. I had to be able to describe components of the firearm and be familiar with how it worked. Soon terms such as clips, windage and clicks became part of my vocabulary. We had a session of "dry fire" and then had to march way out to the edge of Lackland to qualify.

I did my very best from the standing, sitting and prone positions. Young patrolled the area like a warden and I prayed my score would be high enough to pass. When I went to take down my target, it was evident that I would be headed to remedial training. While zeroing in on a basket from 15 or 20 feet out was no problem for me, hitting the target was.

Joe Viglione's saying of "fool me once, shame on you, fool me twice, shame on me" came to mind. I was confident that I wouldn't be going down in flames a second time. I completed remedial training and was ready to take a second crack at qualifying. The night before heading back out to the rifle range, I had a tough time sleeping. I gazed at the runway lights off in the distance and wondered just what the hell I had gotten myself into. Hopping on the top bunk, I tried blocking out what was lying ahead of me. Before I knew it, the overhead lights came on, Young was shouting his head off, and feet were hitting the floor. My day of reckoning had arrived.

I was decked out in the usual fashion for my date with destiny. I wore white tee shirt and boxer shorts, fatigue tops and bottoms, black socks, brogans, pith helmet and a web belt that had my canteen attached. Once out on the range, another item would be added to my gear. That item was a sharp pencil.

We were issued rifles and were all set to walk over to the firing line. On a nearby table were scorecards and pencils for tallying up results from targets. I had found a flaw in the military system and the wheels in my head began turning instantly. The pencils would also be used for circling bullet holes in our targets, once the firing was completed.

I adjusted my rifle settings, closed an eye and peered through the scope. The attempt at qualifying had begun. It was tough to figure whether or not I was getting desired results. I remained calm, with shallow breaths and keen concentration. I know dirt under my target had been hit a couple of times, either by my bullets or from rifles to the left or right of me. Suddenly, it was all over, firing had ceased and it was time to walk to my target and begin circling bullet holes. The target would be brought back to the firing line and points from the circled holes would be written on the scorecard and then tallied for a final score.

I had noticed when this exercise started, that Young was not present. That took lots of pressure off of me and it was about to make a big difference on this sunny morning. Had he been there, he would have been breathing down our necks, walking from target to target, his eyes missing nothing.

I spied my target long before reaching it. My eyes strained to see if it appeared that enough bullets had made their mark on the white and black sheet of paper. My first reaction was that I was a borderline case when it came to qualifying or not. I began circling the bullet holes and sneakily added some "insurance holes" courtesy of my pencil. Young wanted us sharp at all times and thinking was a vital part of our daily regimen. My thought process had produced a backup system, just in case things weren't working out well. I removed my target and headed back toward the firing line with sweaty palms and a racing heart.

The Sergeant who tallied my target smiled as he worked. "Airman, looks like you qualified," he asserted. "You may have a couple of bullet holes here from those who were firing from your left and right." I returned his smile and my heart beat slowed. Airman Tangen had beaten the system.

Keep in mind, that I went through basic at a time when Vietnam was going crazy. I pictured myself being sent to Nam after Texas. I would be "in country" and on patrol with all the gear I needed. Uniform, check. Hand grenades, check. Canteen, check. Sharp pencil, check. If I came face to face with a north Vietnamese soldier, it would be rifle against pencil. My mind snapped back to reality from that silly vision. I had done what I had to do and done it my way.

Qualifying on the rifle range had been a big break for me. An even bigger one was right around the corner though, when I learned that Sergeant Young had left us and was taking on a new flight of rainbows. We now had another training instructor and he was actually human. "Dipshit" is about the worst curse word we ever heard out of him. We had been well drilled by Young and his replacement inherited a flight that operated on automatic pilot.

The days were winding down and one afternoon, after mail call, I got my orders. While Joe and Mike would be going to technical school at Lowry AFB, Colorado (munitions), without a leave, I would be heading home on leave and then on to March AFB, California. I had put in for New York but wound up assigned to southern California. Being 3,000 miles from home didn't seem to matter though, as I looked forward to getting back to the Empire State for a couple weeks of leave.

Going through the airport at San Antonio was a delight. We had been told to stay away from new guys that were just heading to Lackland. My parents, Charlene and all my friends awaited my arrival back east. My date of rank to A3C (Airman third class) was September 22, 1965. I wore the stripe proudly and had proven to be a basic training survivor. Like Dad had said, nobody can stop time.

The first signs that I was back in my geographic area, were "New York" license plates on the yellow cabs and the hustle and bustle of JFK Airport. I fixed my eyes on people in a hurry and felt the excitement of the impending trip home. I would be going by railroad up to Port Jervis, about 70 miles away.

I arrived back at Lyman Avenue physically fit, content and looking forward to my time at home. It wasn't long before I made contact with Charlene and Fish. The rugged training had transformed a boy into a man in just under six weeks.

I saw Christine twice while I was home on leave, waving at her from the car both times. Being home was heaven after the pure hell in Texas. I spent time with Charlene and laughed it up with Fish. The leave was going by quickly and I knew that come early October, I would be far away in southern California.

It was on this leave, that I was introduced to the hazards of a wine drunk and hangover. Fish and I decided to party one day in the attic of his house. I think Kenny Aber and a couple of other friends may have dropped by too.

We had hit a liquor store earlier in the day and purchased some real rot gut wine. We chugged it down like it was water and it didn't take long to feel the buzz of a high. Fish chuckled and fooled, with purple teeth evident. The taste was kind of bitter but what the hell, the results were exhilarating. We laughed until we cried and started tossing furniture around the attic. The two of us had totally lost control and escaped into never-never land. Every now and then Fish will still say "remember the day we wrecked the attic?" and we'll smile at the memory. I still refer to that day as "the great wine hangover of 1965." Its impact was felt forever as it is the one and only time I ever got drunk on wine.

It was still daylight when I arrived home and fell on my bed. I looked up and saw a ceiling that was spinning. Dizziness had arrived and I could barely make it to kneel before the porcelain God in the bathroom. I heaved and heaved until there was nothing left to come out. Then the dry heaves came and was accompanied by an awesome case of cotton mouth. My eyes scorched out of their sockets and the softest of voices hurt my head so bad, I felt like I was close to death. Hour by hour I suffered the consequences of the earlier drunk. Finally, I began to feel a little bit better. I resolved to never again get drunk on wine and have kept that vow for over 37 years.

The time flew by and the day came when I had to bid farewell to the northeast and head out west. California had always appeared like a glamorous place to me. Trends were set out west and then moved eastward. The jet stream moved west to east. It was the land of Hollywood movie stars and motion pictures. It seemed that everything occurred first out there, and the thought of California, set off visions of palm trees, surfing, sunglasses and pretty, tanned women.

Being from New York, I viewed myself as a man. I was able to accept responsibility and could get a drink at 18. I would be arriving, via Braniff Airlines, to a land where I would be regarded as a kid. The drinking age was 21 out there and the people I'd try to mingle with, were all older than me. Many looked down at my youth and immaturity, rather than accepting me. It was on the soil of California, that I found a world filled with sarcasm, conceit and selfishness.

The First Sergeant was a disciplinarian named Sergeant Morant. He was a no-nonsense kind of person, who I knew enough to stay away from. March AFB, Riverside, California, was a Strategic Air Command base. I remember it being immaculate on the base with palm trees and neatly kept homes dotting the landscape.

I stayed overnight in a transient barracks and then processed in the next morning. I walked across a field in a bright sunshine with my orders and pay records under my arm. I was not only processing into the base, I was going to my duty station. I would be an in and out processing clerk at March.

My immediate supervisor would be Staff Sergeant Richard Banta and the head of the shop was Sergeant Paul Sisneros. Sisneros was a very quiet man who had little patience with the immaturity of green Airmen. He was the type to calmly explain something one time and one time only. Banta was a sharp contrast to Sisneros. He laughed with gusto, giggling at jokes in a high-pitched manner. I immediately felt out of place here, although Banta was easy to get along with.

I was to reside in an open bay barracks that was located near the Base Exchange (BX). It had stone floors and there were 20 or 25 of us in the room. The first thing I noticed, was that there were no double bunks. You had your own locker and bed area that afforded just a hint of privacy. The first person I met in the barracks was Don Hoveiler, who lived near San Francisco. Don, like many of his fellow Californians, was hooked on his home state. Don liked the new song "California Dreamin" by The Mamas and Papas and soon, asked to borrow my record player to listen to some tunes. I agreed and we became instant friends.

News of my arrival preceded my appearance and I had the tag of "another New Yorker" placed on me. Also in our bay, was one David Garzone who was from Staten Island, N.Y. Dave wore sandals, sunglasses, was loose as a goose and made enemies of Californians. He loved New York and crowed about it constantly.

When you are from New York or "back east" and are out in California, prepare to be labeled. I was eyed suspiciously and had two strikes against me instantly. Not only was I from New York, and was probably carrying knives and explosives in my uniform, but I was only 18 years old. People from other parts of the country just don't get the fact that there is a New York City and a New York State. Subways, theaters, museums, ritzy hotels, 42nd Street, hookers and pickpockets reside in the city. Up where I live, I am surrounded by mountains, rivers and lakes. Grass is something to mow, more than it is something to smoke.

More than once I heard the question "how far from Yankee Stadium do you live?" After being hit with this several times, I had a ready made answer. "You go a half block, turn left, travel 70 miles east then south and there it is, Yankee Stadium."

I was in California less than a month when a blackout gripped parts of the east. The blackout started at 5:16 p.m. November 9, 1965, when the northeast power system at Ontario, Canada, failed (Ontario-New York border at Niagara Falls). This event affected 30 million people for up to 13 hours. Electricity ceased, people were stuck on elevators and mass chaos resulted. When a single line from the Niagara generating station tripped, New York, Ontario, most of New England plus parts of New Jersey and Pennsylvania went dark.

Out in California, they read about it in the Los Angeles Times. People in our barracks didn't give a hoot, except the only New Yorkers, Garzone and me. "Screw New York," I heard a voice say from across the room. That sentiment kind of sums up the times I spent out on the West Coast.

I was attached to the 22nd Bomb Wing, 15th Air Force, at March. The base had a rich history, as it came into existence, as March Field, on May 20, 1918. I was to serve here from October 1965 until March of 1966. Everything was "just so" at March. There were formal parades every other day it seems, and people treated this installation as if there was no other in the world. While the pride displayed was admirable, some natives looked down their nose a lot. The words "snooty" and "pompous" come to mind when I think of the type attitudes I encountered both on base and off.

Once I was on a bus from Los Angeles back to Riverside and met a cute girl who lived in Rialto. I wore four rings in those days, two on each hand. We kidded back and forth and had a nice talk until this question. "Where are you from?" When I answered "New York" she said "oh" then turned around in her seat and ignored me.

Riverside is a city that now has a population of 255,166. Riverside County is located east of Los Angeles between San Bernardino (locals call it San Berdoo) and Escondito, along Highway 60, near Lake Perris. Citrus fruit is big here and it is a diversified industrial hub. The University of California at Riverside is a popular site for a college education.

The cities of Indio, Hemet, Pomona, Chino, ElMonte, Ontario, Palm Springs and Indian Wells are all in this area. While March AFB was a vital cog in Riverside's economy, the base was selected for realignment in 1993, and became March Air Reserve Base on April 1, 1996. Currently standing adjacent to the base, is March Field Air Museum.

In this section of California, the rainy season includes November. I remember waiting for a bus into town, on November 22. On this, the second anniversary of President John F. Kennedy's death, it was pouring rain and since there were no sewers, small lakes were popping up on the roadways and properties on base. It was the night of the Cassius Clay-Floyd Patterson heavyweight title fight at The Sands Hotel in Las Vegas, Nevada.

Patterson, trained by the legendary Cus D'Amato, was a crowd pleaser who was very light for a heavyweight. He was a classy former champion who didn't brag and wore the invisible white hat of the good guy. Clay, the mouthy and predicting kid from Louisville, who had stopped the villain champ Sonny Liston in Miami Beach for the crown, would now be cast as the bad guy who wore a black hat. Clay entered the ring fresh off a one round title rematch knockout of Liston, at Lewiston, Maine, less than six months earlier, on May 25, 1965.

Instead of the sultry weather of Texas, the rain was refreshing on my face as it poured down on people awaiting the bus. Someone had a radio and the upcoming Clay-Patterson fight was the top sports story on the airwaves. I had mixed thoughts on the fight as I admired Patterson, yet knew how brash and exciting Clay was.

It is so ironic that less than 11 years later, I would stand and interview D'Amato at the Concord Hotel as he watched Ali train. When I asked him about Ali's impending battle against Norton at Yankee Stadium, Cus never hesitated in his prediction. "Ali is too much of a man for Norton," he told me from his seat near ringside. "He'll knock Norton out." This legendary white-haired fight man, later became a father figure and manager to heavyweight terror Mike Tyson. He was an open encyclopedia on boxing and was very interesting to talk to.

Prior to that memorable 1965 fight, Patterson had proclaimed his mission to reclaim the heavyweight crown for Christian America. Clay had converted to Islam, became a black muslim in 1964 and had changed his name from Clay to Ali. Patterson, who continued to call Ali Clay, had the public support for this event.

Ali, a lightning fast 24-year-old, proved to be too vicious for Patterson and was superior in the ring. "Come on American. Come on 'white' American," Ali reportedly taunted during the battle. The fight was stopped in the 12th round and when it was over, Patterson praised Ali, and called him by his new name. The former Olympic gold medal boxing winner, whose first fight had been against Tunney Hunsaker in October of 1960, had shown the boxing world again.

At March AFB, located about an hour from LA, I would be ignored and feel lonely, ridiculed and miserable. I became sick of hearing of "sunny California" and how you could surf and see snow on the same day. I wanted to trade palm trees for maple trees and experience northeastern weather. I had no idea how long I would be trapped in this laid back atmosphere. Neil Diamond's "LA's fine but it ain't home" from the song "I Am I Said" fits perfectly.

In California, I would purchase an engagement ring for Charlene at Kirk Jewelers in Riverside, see the movies "Red Line 500" and "Sons of Katie Elder", plus see singer Jack Jones and actress Melody Patterson of the TV show "F Troop", in person at the base theater.

I would also try to fit in with a couple of Airmen older than me, be refused alcohol while on a date, and wind up hustled by a pretty blond in LA. This only gets better. One of the Airmen I tried to befriend, ripped me a new ass on a Brunswick pool table outside the base, to the tune of a couple of hundred dollars. That little event came just days before I was going home on leave, for Christmas.

The two Airmen that were in my flight at Lackland AFB, Gerald Cline from North Carolina and Allen Girardin who hailed from Massachusetts, were also sent to March. These guys had been out of high school a couple of years and were rapidly becoming close friends. I made out fairly well one-on-one with the duo, but when they were together, I couldn't penetrate the friendship. I guess they saw a young guy who was just getting his feet wet in the real world. I could see they were ignoring me and joking at my expense. After awhile, I stopped trying to eat chow with them or hang out at the movies or pool hall. My final jaunt to the pool hall with them, is the one I will remember the rest of my life.

They wanted to go to the movies, but I insisted on playing pool. I was relentless from the start and in the end, I got what I deserved. The three of us played for small amounts of money, but Girardin, who I later heard had grown up near pool halls, saw a big fish just waiting to be hooked. "Lets make it interesting," he had suggested at one point. All I could see, was easy money that would help with my trip back home. I bit, hook, line and sinker.

Allen let me get a few wins here and there in 8-ball and 9-ball. Suddenly he surfaced with a couple of "lucky wins" as he put it. I found myself playing "double or nothing" and the stakes were going up. Once I got down around $200, he wanted to call it a night, collect his money and head for the base.

Being in desperate straits I begged him to play one more game. He didn't want to, but relented. Everything rode on one game of pool. I never got a shot. I had been wiped out, and money wise, I was in bad shape to go on leave. My mom was suffering from asthma and experiencing attacks back in Port Jervis. She, Charlene and all my friends were waiting for me to get back there for the holidays. I swallowed my pride and asked Girardin for a break. I never figured him to agree, but he showed a great deal of class, by cutting the amount I owed him in half. "If I ever see you playing pool for money again, I'll kill you," he said, with the most serious face I ever saw. I thanked him up and down and walked out the front door of the establishment. I had learned a hard but valuable lesson, and it has stayed with me for life.

I snagged a date with a WAF (female Air Force person) one day, in an unexpected development. A girl that worked across the street had spoken to me a few times and the opportunity presented itself. She was a lady from Idaho and she had a car. I grabbed a shower at the barracks and dressed in some nice clothes and she picked me up in the early evening.

We rode around Riverside for awhile and looked at the happenings going on. We passed "The Playpen" and "The Brass Rail" restaurant-bars and decided to go in one of them for a drink. The drinking age in California was 21 and I was only 18. I worried some about getting nailed, but figured I looked of age. Chalk that assumption up as a big mistake. Both of us were carded at the door and only the WAF got the go-ahead to order a drink. She felt bad for me and we retreated back to the car. I pouted as we wound up at some place that served ice cream. Once again, the baby of the barracks had come up short. Little did I realize that these type setbacks would be only a memory in a few short months. Fate would be taking me back to my home state, in March of 1966, for my next assignment. What morale was lacking at March, would me made up for in spades at a place called Plattsburgh AFB, New York.

I returned home for leave on December 24, 1965, and got engaged to Charlene for Christmas. The girl with the strawberry hair and dimples, wanted to get married after she graduated in 1966, but I hoped to hold off until I was discharged from the Air Force. Three days before I got home on leave, Christine sent me a Christmas card. For some reason, and I believe it to be destiny, her name was always coming up.

I returned back out west, to a place I barely tolerated. There were cliques everywhere in the barracks. The groups banded together, drank a few beers and laughed it up every night. I was never offered a beer or allowed to penetrate their sarcastic inner circles. I was sick and tired of drinking soda and one evening, asked if I could have a beer. These wonderful people provided the beer, but collected a buck for it. With friends like these, who would need enemies?

One morning, I processed in an Airman who was reassigned from Lackland AFB. "Ever hear of Sergeant Young?" I said, just to make conversation. "He was my TI," the guy said. "He pushed one of the guys down a flight of stairs and is being court martialed." Either this guy is breaking my cookies, or Young is really in disciplinary trouble, I thought.

I met the most memorable person I ever processed in, before going home on leave at Christmas. Mary was a short and pretty blonde-haired

WAF. She had a confident air about her, but I could tell she was simply lost. I knew instantly, that given the chance, I would take her out in a heartbeat. As luck would have it, I would get my chance to be with this petite lady from Massachusetts. We talked casually as I finished up her paperwork. She talked of her home in New England and I told her a few places on base that I hung out. Our paths crossed that night.

Mary had a thick New England accent and was dressed immaculately. We met at a recreation center type place and walked around the base. Soon, it began to rain and we ducked into the dugout of a nearby baseball field. I looked out at the muddy infield and wondered if this night would be a lucky one. I didn't want to scare this female away and was a gentleman with a capital "G". It seemed to me there was an old saying that said nice guys finish last. I wanted to defy those words and be a nice guy that finished first.

Mary had said earlier that day, that she wanted to see LA. I was off weekends and had been going to LA about every two weeks by bus and staying at the Mayflower Hotel. At the Mayflower, I escaped the unhappiness of military life, wore civilian clothes, ate good food, had a shower to myself and a television at my disposal. I had learned the ropes, regarding travel to and from LA, plus was familiar with some of the territory. It was decided that we would leave the next morning for LA and return at night. I walked back to my barracks with a satisfied smile on my face. I looked up into the rainy evening and thought that I was finally going to turn things around in California.

We departed Riverside in the morning and arrived in the big city after a few stops along the way. Mary's eyes took in the sights as we pulled into the bus station. She looked fresh, pretty and was filled with boundless enthusiasm. The hint of perfume touched my senses and made me glad to be alive and free from military life.

I enjoyed her company and accommodated her desires. We walked the streets of LA all afternoon. While my idea of a great time was watching a game-winning basket or home run, Mary was into the magnificent things that life has to offer. Gift shops, flower arrangements, art studios and the latest fashions were high on her list.

I began to realize that this petite and classy woman could be down to earth, yet enjoyed the finer things in life. Our dinner didn't take place in a fast food joint. As we motivated around the LA streets, she pointed out a restaurant that was located on top of a tall building. "That is where I want to eat," she proclaimed. I wasn't about to buck the system at this point and the two of us dined together in a cozy and intimate atmosphere. This delightful lady with the "pock the cah" accent, felt safe with me. I regarded our hours together as an investment of sorts. Rather than looking across the table at her, I would rather be hugging this cutie and looking into her blue eyes. I figured there would be plenty of time for that during the evening hours.

While I appeared content on the outside, wheels were turning in my head about what would be next. I knew that neither of us had to be back at base that night and didn't work until Monday morning. I also knew the bus schedule from LA to Riverside by heart.

Earlier, I had told Mary that we didn't dare miss the last bus back to Riverside. Of course the time I gave her, was fictitious and when we arrived at the bus station, it was too late. I feigned horror when we found out we were stranded. "Damn, they must have changed the schedule," I said as I hid a wide smile behind my hand. "I guess we'll just have to find a place to spend the night."

While in southern California, I passed up pro basketball games in Inglewood, Disneyland in Anaheim, and the Riverside 500 (which was a stone's throw from the barracks, I could hear the engines). There was no way I would be giving up a Saturday evening at the Mayflower Hotel, with a vivacious and attractive blonde.

The Mayflower Hotel was located just a couple of blocks away and I had told Mary that I stayed there frequently. In my most impressive voice of the day, I casually laid out the sleeping arrangements. "We can save a lot of money by just getting one room," I said innocently. "You can take the bed and I will sleep in a chair or something. Then we will get a bus out of here in the morning."

Mary didn't answer but looked into the distance. She seemed upset that she had to stay in LA overnight. "I'll pay for the room," I said, as we neared the front door of the Mayflower. "You know you can trust me." I silently hoped that my spiel had worked and approached the desk with a positive attitude.

Suddenly, Mary stepped in front of me and spoke up to the desk clerk. "We need two rooms," she said as she gave me a quick glance. My bubble had been burst and wind let out of my sails. In one swift action, this girl had squelched a day that was filled with good times. I meekly nodded in agreement and the situation was resolved.

I smoldered as we entered an elevator to our rooms. She was located on another floor and got off the elevator first. "I'll see you in the morning," she said. "I'll call your room," I answered. Once settled in the room, I turned on the television and dialed up her number. "Come on up, there's a good show on television," I said. For all I knew, the worst program to ever hit modern TV was on the screen. "No thanks, I'm tired and want to get some sleep," she retorted. I tried to be resilient and took one last shot. "I want to share some more time with you, Mary, please come up." The last ditch effort proved futile and I climbed into bed dragged out from the day, depressed and most of all pissed off.

We ate breakfast downstairs and I gave one and two word answers to any questions she might have. "When does the bus leave?" she asked. "Soon," I answered. "Did you sleep well?" "Are you mad about something?" "no" and "yes" were my replies.

I didn't look at her and held a grudge all the way back to Riverside. I avoided her stares and looked straight ahead. She continued to ask why I was upset and finally I couldn't hold back anymore. "Thanks for nothing," I blurted out. "Your company was great last night." In my mind I had been hustled for a whole day and evening. I had given unselfishly of my time, plus bought dinner and snacks. The only consolation was the fact that she paid for her hotel room. We got off the bus in Riverside and parted ways forever. "Live and learn," I thought, as I slowly climbed the barracks stairs.

I did get to do a great deal while living in the west. A bus took me down to San Diego one weekend. I got to see LaJolla, where rich people's homes bordered scenic sea cliffs above the Pacific Ocean. Sea lions and harbor seals were as much a part of this culture, as the diversified lifestyle that helped make the city become known as "the jewel of southern California."

Famous Torrey Pines Golf Course, city- owned since 1957, sits on 327 acres of land, overlooking the Pacific. There are two 18-hole championship golf courses here and this establishment hosts the annual Buick Invitational PGA Tournament, each February. LA and Hollywood had been 58 and 65 miles away respectively. San Diego, a naval town north of Tijuana, Mexico, was about 100 miles from the base.

In San Diego, I stayed overnight at former West End neighbor Walter Finch's house. It was Finch, a thin kid who had to use crutches as a child, who drank my water the day I fought Fish. We went out to Balboa Park where flag football seemed a way of life. The West Coast lifestyle was markedly different than I was used to. I began to long for back east.

"LA's fine the sun shines most the time and the feelin is lay back. Palm trees grow and rents are low but you know I keep thinking bout makin my way back." Neil Diamond absolutely had it right.

While I was living the "bitchin" California life, Chris was fooling around with a ouija board one evening. According to a January 1966 entry in her diary, the future was being decided. This cardboard swami said she would ride by my house on May 2, 1966, go out with me four days later and marry me April 9, 1973. She batted 0-3 that night, and in actuality, we got married over two-and-a-half years sooner than the predicted date.

My mom's asthma continued to flare up while I was gone from home. It seemed she was much better, regarding health, when I was close by. Meanwhile, I was miserable much of the time, living a boring life of GI parties (cleaning the barracks) and personnel work. One day, I had reached the limit of my patience and decided to do something about it.

I put in for a permissive reassignment to the east coast, although I figured my chances of attaining that goal rivaled that of a snowball surviving in hell. Dad had the same type of perseverance I did and got the ball rolling back in Port Jervis.

I was trying for this change of duty station because of my mother's health problems. A reassignment of this type, swaps Airmen from two locations and is at the convenience of and is no expense to, the government. Sergeants Sisneros and Banta doubted that the request would ever be approved, but I never gave up hope.

Dad wrote a letter to the Air Force on January 26, 1966, requesting that I be moved. He stated that his wife was under doctor's care for the treatment of chronic bronchial asthma. He mentioned that my entry into the Air Force had helped accelerate asthma attacks and said that having me closer to home could relieve her anxiety and help her condition. She had been in the hospital three times since my enlistment began. My father requested that I be moved to Stewart AFB, Newburgh, N.Y., about 40 miles from my home.

The Air Force, like any other service branch, consists of miles and miles of red tape. Everything is "hurry up and wait" from chow hall lines to dental appointments. It seemed like forever that I waited for some type of answer in the reassignment matter. I inquired a kazillion times about my status and people in assignments were getting tired of seeing me.

My supervisors and co-workers had one hell of a surprise waiting for them. They were doubting Thomas' from the get-go and gave me no hope of heading back east. Then one day I received the greatest message I'd gotten since passing all my subjects as a senior. I was going home.

The orders were cut March 3, 1966 and were signed by First Lieutenant Cynthia Little. I would be leaving the 92508 zip code of the 22nd Combat Support Group and heading for the 380th Strategic Aerospace Wing, zip code 12903. Whatever days it took to reach Plattsburgh would be charged as leave. I would make sure I'd have a few days at home, before heading up to the north country of New York State.

I had a few days left at March AFB and came to work with an easygoing smile on my face. The lifers really hated an Airman getting a break. Some who had made my life miserable, either ignored me or made disparaging remarks. Either way, I was getting my wish to return to the land of the four seasons and I'm not talking about Frankie Valli and his group. While Lackland had been extremely rigorous, March introduced me to an atmosphere where officers were gods and enlisted men were for the most part, callous and arrogant toward younger personnel. This scenario played out for my whole enlistment, although along the way, there were exceptions to the rule.

Sergeant Morant, the big First Sergeant with all the discipline, never said congratulations or good luck in the future. "It is cold up there and you'll see lots of snow," he smirked. "You'll be out on that damn flight line shoveling snow that is up to your ass." Many times during my enlistment, I would be accused of being derogatory and having a bad attitude. But I was the same guy, who would later receive a letter of appreciation from southeast Asia (Thailand) and become highly recommended for reenlistment. I never kissed ass in the service and was regarded as a rebel of sorts. I never knuckled under to ridiculous requests and to this day, am proud of my service to this country. I will still, never kiss the feet of some blowhard, even if they are in a supervisory position.

Sergeants Banta and Sisneros gave me a pretty good Airman Performance Report, but I figure part of that, was because I was a reflection of their teaching expertise, and they wanted to look good. I learned quickly, that service people covered their own asses constantly. Many times, any type of discipline from higher grades, resulted in a "yes sir, no sir, three bags full" mentality. I realized from the start, that this type of life would never be for me. I wanted to put my time in, learn a trade, and get the hell out.

"A3C Tangen performed a variety of tasks, completing each thoroughly," Banta wrote. "He worked many hours overtime to help eliminate the backlog of accumulated records during October and November of 1965." He lauded my loyalty to my supervisors, ability to get along with everyone, and willingness to do anything to get the job done.

Sergeant Sisneros concurred with the report. "Airman Tangen continually strives to increase his knowledge of the Personnel career field," he noted. "I feel this airman has the aptitude and attitude to increase his potential in meeting the requirements of the Air Force."

The Captain in charge, said he observed my performance daily. I think I saw him a handful of times, smiling from his desk chair. In the Air Force's eyes, I guess that means I was being observed. I laughed off the Captain's short statement, knowing that one of my requirements was to play the game.

I said farewell to Hoveiler, Garzone and a couple of others in that dreadful barracks. Hoveiler continued to talk up how great California was, while Garzone would break in and start singing "I'll take Manhattan, the Bronx and Staten Island too." They used to fight over the most petty of things. While Hoveiler's face would turn a crimson red, Garzone chortled about how mad Hoveiler got, pissing him off all the more. After I got out of service, Garzone showed up at my dad's office one day, driving a small sports car. He wore his customary dark shades, shorts and sandals and offered me some weed. God only knows whatever happened to this laid back, yet feisty, man.

I never cracked the cliques at this location. My talent in sports went totally unnoticed. They played favorites constantly here, and I lost interest in even watching basketball or softball. There was no wine, women or song at March AFB. The place I was going to, in New York's Adirondack mountains, would be an exact opposite and would prove to be the greatest thing that ever happened to me.

I was driven to Riverside by a foxy black WAF who was now working in the office. Every time she bent over, Sergeant Banta would have a hormone attack. And when she left the building, Banta would start describing her and laughing in those high-pitched tones. Banta was a good guy and we tolerated each other just fine. Sisneros stayed quiet and distant, only smiling occasionally. I was ecstatic to be getting out of that atmosphere. I tossed a few bucks to the WAF and walked away and into the bus terminal. This ride to LA would be the best I ever experienced. The destination was LA International Airport rather than the Mayflower. And I would never see March AFB again.

I landed at JFK and was back in the land of New York license plates again. I sniffed the crisp, cool air and thanked God I had returned to my native state. I would be going home to my girlfriend, family, friends and as many beers as I felt like consuming. Life had turned good in March of 1966.

Chris' diary shows that she saw me with Charlene on March 18, which means I wasted little time circulating around Port Jervis. The TV program "Get Smart" with Barbara Feldon and Don Adams was an entertaining show at the time and the music of the day, included some of the best songs I've ever heard.

In 1966, "The Ballad of the Green Berets" by Staff Sergeant Barry Sadler, wound up being ranked first on the Musicradio WABC Top 100 list. "Hanky Panky" by Tommy James and the Shondells, "96 Tears" by ? and the Mysterians, "You Can't Hurry Love" by The Supremes and "19th Nervous Breakdown" by The Rolling Stones, were all blaring from car radios.

Little did I know, I would soon wind up in a bar-restaurant in Platts-burgh, named Brodi's, listening to a spectacular band called The Falcons. They captured many 1966 songs with precision, like "Summer in the City" by The Lovin' Spoonful, "Sloop John B" by The Beach Boys and "Devil With A Blue Dress On" by Mitch Ryder and the Detroit Wheels.

One day I was suffering through the boredom of March AFB, clicked my heels three times, said "there's no place like home" and like Dorothy and Toto, found myself back home. This unreal happening, kept me ecstatic for my days in Port Jervis. Being with my girlfriend, plus family and friends, was like a dream come true. All dreams come to an end though and soon enough I was heading up to a place called Plattsburgh, N.Y., which was about 279 miles north, and just over an hour south of Montreal, Canada.

The car ride north seemed to take forever (it was before Interstate Route 87 was completed). The scenery was spectacular once we left the Albany area. The Adirondack Park includes about 3,000 lakes and ponds and 2 ½ million acres of protected wild lands. There are 105 towns and villages in this great mountainous park, which is the largest in the continental United States. It contains some of the continent's oldest rocks.

Towns and villages like Lake George, Lake Placid, Saranac Lake and

Ausable Forks were either driven through, or spelled out on the green and white signs. When we got off Route 87, and entered Route 9 north, the beauty was simply spectacular. I had traded the freeways of southern California for the natural beauty, tranquility and serenity of northern New York.

When we reached Keeseville, in Essex County, the trip was winding down to an end. We were just 17 miles away from our destination, and minutes later, we passed into Clinton County. Soon, I found myself at the gate of Plattsburgh AFB and was waved through.

I had no idea what waited for me beyond the gate. There were two sides to the base, one on each side of the highway. Where I was headed, the buildings appeared much newer. With the wave of the white-gloved Air Policeman, a new world was opening for me at the tender age of 18. As it turned out, Plattsburgh would be a shining jewel in my Air Force enlistment.

The palm trees, Pacific Ocean, surf boards, freeways, "bitchin" times and laid back attitudes of southern California, faded into a blur of oblivion.

This must have been the feeling that Billy Joel experienced when he recorded one of his numerous hits. I was truly in a "New York State Of Mind."

CHAPTER 7

Plattsburgh, N.Y. -- Paradise on Earth

My arrival and departure at Plattsburgh AFB is a study in contrast.

I arrived on this historical base, as a young and vibrant teenager and left nearly 16 months later, as a confident man, who was bound for Southeast Asia's Guam. The countries of Japan, Thailand and Taiwan would also be on my travel itinerary, before returning back to Travis AFB, California, for discharge on 23 December 1968.

There couldn't be a bigger change in my environment from my early days here, to the waning hours before I bid Plattsburgh a sad goodbye. This North Country area was simply beautiful and my experiences in the military gave me great memories to laugh about and cling to, for the rest of my life.

I sniffed the crisp air and just sensed that all would go well up here, in northern New York State. I would find that the people I worked and partied with and the people who lived in this city, were lots of fun and for the most part, sincere.

On holidays, people from Plattsburgh would take in base personnel that were too far away from home to be with their families. They would share meals and companionship that was both heart warming and inspiring. Plattsburgh State Teacher's College was located here and Montreal was just an hour up the road. It was an interesting blend that occupied Plattsburgh on a Friday or Saturday night. The interaction between these diversified groups, military, collegiate, Canadians and residents, would make a shining example in courtesy, for any human being.

From an open bay barracks of smug Airmen in California, I walked into the world of two-man rooms in New York. The floors were black and green checked (linoleum type material), there was plenty of locker space, a sink in the room, and there was a bathroom with toilet and shower that separated adjoining rooms. These accommodations would nearly rival your favorite motel.

I walked into my new room and was met by a smiling Airman named Bob Logan (from Waukesha, Wisconsin) as the sound of Christian music drifted from a record player. I took a mental note not to swear in Logan's presence and immediately felt uncomfortable.

More than 15 months later, I walked away from a room occupied by myself and one John VanGraafeiland III. We had been paired the final weeks of our tour at Plattsburgh, because we were both uncontrollable wild men who partied our asses off and kept unbelievable hours. He was bound for Vietnam and me for Guam.

I had a total of three roommates in "The Burgh". Sandwiched between, was Chris Lynn, a sharp troop and practical joker from Bethlehem, Pa. While Chris and I were humorous types who would short-sheet your bed in the wink of an eye, even Chris, begging for sleep, was glad to see me wind up with VanGraafeiland.

The belly laughs and joking that occurred in this barracks were of legendary proportions. I still see Pat Kelly eating six pizzas to win a contest, "Van" and I miserably failing a surprise inspection, Lynn and I sabotaging beds next door and Earl Braddee answering the hall phone and then walking away with shaving cream in his ears, from the receiver. And, of course, there was the old "flower bed trick" pulled on me by Lynn and Tony Sewall of Maine. The explanation of that unbelievable event will come a little bit later.

Outside our little barracks world, far away from the sophomoric pranks of 1966 and 1967, was a very historical air force base.

Plattsburgh had been a military installation for over 150 years (one of the oldest in the country). The base is located on the western shore of well known vacation destination Lake Champlain. In 1609, Samuel de Champlain, French founder of Quebec, Canada, discovered the lake for France and fought the Iroquois Indians near its southern end. In 1954, the military site became known as Plattsburgh Air Force Base.

In 1954, a ground breaking took place on January 29, for the Strategic Air Command bomber base. The first aircraft, a KC-97, landed there on November 7, 1955. Muskets, cannons, FB 111s, KC-135s and all types of aircrafts wound up at this site.

The 380th Strategic Aerospace Wing, my unit, began on October 28, 1942 at Davis-Monthan Field in Tucson, Arizona. It was activated in Plattsburgh on July 11, 1955 and left for good in 1992.

In September of 1965, one of the wing's B-47s, named "Pride of the Adirondacks", left Plattsburgh for SAC's 14th bombing and navigation competition at Fairchild AFB, Washington. Six days later, the aircraft returned and was being hailed as the "world's best B-47." The plane was commanded by Major Charles W. Patrick, while Captain John W. Wilcox was the co-captain and Major Robert Wickland the navigator.

On December 14, the last three of Plattsburgh's B-47s left the base in 15 minute intervals. These aircraft were headed for storage and the fabled era of the medium bomber in the North Country, had come to a close.

The "Pride of the Adirondacks", however, was to become a permanent fixture near the main gate at Plattsburgh AFB. It was put on display at the entrance to the base, on February 8, 1966 and stood in memory of the crews and maintenance men who flew and supported B-47s.

I saw this permanent monument of the nation's defense in the North Country, many times over the course of my tour of duty. Never did I ever have an inkling that this plane had won a satisfying world competition.

The jet was dedicated in ceremonies March 21, 1966. More than 300 spectators turned out to honor the plane. This same day, represented the 20th anniversary of the 380th Strat Aerospace Wing and 10th anniversary of the first B-47 coming to Plattsburgh.

While everyone from the base commander to Plattsburgh Mayor Frank Steltzer acknowledged this Monday event, I was home packing my stuff for Wednesday's arrival up north. They phased out the B-47s and brought in the B-52G aircraft, which stayed until 1970. I was phased in, listening to that Christian music and wondering what I'd gotten myself into. It didn't take long to find out.

My official processing in, took place over on the old side of the base, in a majestic red brick building. These offices, where I would be working in Military Pay, were a beehive of activity. The energy level was unbelievable and I immediately felt at home here. The boring and tedious days at March AFB were long gone and replaced by a vibrant and uplifting atmosphere.

I began my tasks without an immediate supervisor and under the sometimes watchful eyes of Tech Sergeant Richard Kaczka (pronounced Kaska). My boss to be, Airman William D. Lehman (A1C), was down in Texas on temporary duty.

Sergeant Kaczka did his best to issue a welcome and get me set up at a desk. Meanwhile, I saw paperwork stacked everywhere, personnel having their pay records checked out and the phone ringing off the hook. This frenzied pace made the time pass quickly that first day and watching Kaczka run the place was worth the price of admission.

Everybody mispronounced his name. Finally he gave up and answered the phone "Sergeant Kazaka, can I help you?" Guys from the next large room (In and Out Processing section) busted Kaczka's cookies constantly and he became frazzled and beside himself. With the wild Columbo-like hair, he ran across the office with his blue tie in his mouth. "God damn it Lehman, where are you?," he said to the wall.

Lehman had been due back at Plattsburgh from his Texas stint, but hadn't arrived yet. It would be a few days before I came eye to eye with him for the first time. So while I acclimated myself to the new surroundings, I began to hear more and more about what my new boss was like.

"Wait until Willie Lehman gets back here," Braddee, from Uniontown, Pa., said. "You will wish you never heard the name Plattsburgh." A few of the others nodded in agreement and one guy added "He is a hard ass and will be awful to work for. I feel real sorry for you."

Suddenly, I dreaded the day that Lehman would come into view. I thought of what Dad drilled into my head many times, and realized that nobody can stop time. Soon enough, a sharply dressed three-striper in a 1505 uniform (tan color, short-sleeved top), walked through the door and into the Military Pay section. He had a brown crew cut and a front tooth missing. In later years, his image put me in mind of Marine Sergeant Vince Carter (Frank Sutton) from the Gomer Pyle TV show. "It's about damned time, Willie, where the hell you been?," Kaczka shouted. The look on Lehman's face, told me that he and Kaczka were friends. "Just got in," Lehman said in a slight drawl. "How long is it gonna take these damn guys to process me back in anyway?"

Willie Lehman was from Mooreland, Oklahoma and was in his second hitch in the Air Force. While he appeared to be a career-orientated person, and extremely good at his job, I would find an individual that was exactly the opposite of what Braddee had said. He was far from the tyrant that the jokers in the records section had described. They had given me "the business" and pulled the wool over my eyes.

I sat in the corner virtually unnoticed until Kaczka, spewing words a mile a minute, glanced my way. For my couple of days on base, Kaczka had referred to me as "Junior Bird", I guess because I was young and new to Plattsburgh. I hoped he wouldn't use that terminology in my introduction to Lehman.

"Hey Willie," Kaczka offered. "Look over here, I got you a brand new Junior Bird." I turned 50 shades of crimson and shook Lehman's hand. In my wildest dreams, I never figured that this crew cut 5-8" Oklahoman would have such a lasting impression on me. I would wind up looking up to him as the big brother I never had, and even followed him over to Guam in 1967.

"You process in yet?", Willie asked. I nodded in the affirmative, as he moved toward the door and waved at me to follow him. "You haven't officially processed in, until you have cleared through Ma Branson's," he winked while gazing at Kaczka, who was now grinning ear to ear.

Ma Branson was a slender and kindly white-haired lady that stood behind the bar at Branson's and welcomed Willie. It was easy to see that she thought of Willie as a son and doted over him until he had his beer. The egg salad sandwiches in this establishment were legendary and the atmosphere was fantastic. You didn't hear four-letter words flying out of mouths here, even though the clientele was primarily from the air base.

You could look out the front window and see the fence and the old side of the base. Traffic moved by at a steady pace and for that afternoon, time stood still. Lehman wouldn't let me buy a beer that day, and when we walked out the front door, sporting the glow of many swallowed suds, I had been officially "processed in" to Branson's.

In the early days here, I came home about every other weekend.

Some from the base "booked" south toward Albany and New York City while others "hatted" north to Canada. A popular question around the barracks on Fridays was "you bookin or hattin?"

Soon, I moved across the corridor of the second floor to a room occupied by Chris Lynn, my new roommate. He came from the area that made Bethlehem steel and was about a year older than me. I still remember heading south with him on many Friday nights. While "I Got Rhythm" or "96 Tears" reverberated from the radio, we laughed and joked as the miles went by. Sometimes, John Wallace and John Corcoran would come along and we'd have a meeting of the "Mystic Nights of the Baltic Sea", a fictional group that discussed happenings on the base.

I was still seeing Charlene on my trips home, but Plattsburgh was starting to grow on me and it already was feeling as if I belonged there on weekends. At Brodi's Bar, The Falcons band was out of sight and dancing with all the girls plus drinking free beer agreed with me. Soon, the excursions home began to dwindle. I was fitting in fine at my new base and there were many adventures ahead.

Willie and I hit the taverns quite a bit, but I also was in an athletic-orientated crowd as I played squadron softball and basketball plus base team softball. They took sports seriously here, and I was on a dynamic base softball team that played all over this section of the Adirondacks plus Canada.

I played base team centerfield and teammate Jim Stephens gave me the nickname "Quail" because of my speed. To become the starter in center, I had to beat a fiery, diminutive guy name "Mike." This competition could have gone either way and I was honored to be selected. He sulked, the same way I would have, if I'd been beaten out.

In charge of Military Pay was a Warrant Officer, R. T. Bower. Bower reminded me of the actor Leo G. Carroll (Topper). He always answered the phone "ah Bower" and we all mimicked him behind his back. Lehman, Stephens and H.R. Bears, from Carthage, New York, all did great Bower imitations.

I played softball games for the Panthers in a Plattsburgh tournament, where my picture, being nipped at first base, graced the front page of the local paper. Decked out in the black and yellow colors made me feel proud when we played down in Hudson Falls or up north. Once, we were scheduled for a big tourney up in Verdun, Canada.

The orders for the event were cut June 24, 1966, and authorized by the deputy director of admin services. Lefty power hitter Jim Pribble, super infielder Carl Price, pitcher Sonny Shields and myself were on the orders. Three players went north and I was the unfortunate one who had to stay behind, working overtime, for none other than R.T. Bower. I pleaded and pleaded with him to let me go, but he wouldn't change his mind. "Ball playing isn't as important as catching up this paperwork," he said. "You can't go." No doubt that Bower's favorite TV show had to be

"Victory at Sea." He was another of those stubborn old guys who lived for the service, and nothing else seemed to matter. I seethed for days over his decision and flat out refused to acknowledge him.

Braddee and I both played on the squadron team, 380 GHS (Group Headquarters Squadron). Many of our players competed on the base squad as well. We were a well-balanced squadron contingent that possessed pitching, hitting and defense.

Lehman had a passion for fishing and wasn't much into other types of competitive sports. At Plattsburgh and on Guam, I can still see him handling a fishing pole in the barracks and pretending he had a fish on the other end of the line. He would gently move the pole up and down so the flexible tip would bend just a bit. "I got the son of a bitch," he shouted as he began "reeling him in." The one thing that struck me as being odd, is the fact that he couldn't swim.

Three things stand out when it comes to the Plattsburgh softball days. I hit between .300 and .350 and was a threat to steal. Most of my hits were singles and doubles although I'd tagged a triple or two. One game I lofted a hard hit fly to left center that I figured would either be caught or smack off the fence. The ball kept carrying though and I was in unfamiliar territory running out a home run.

One game, Stephens, a rugged hitter, bashed a single and stole second on the next pitch. He slid into the bag too late and his right ankle snapped into a compound fracture. He screamed in pain and I got a sour feeling in my stomach. His ankle and the bones were a mess and it sunk into my mind, that this could happen to me on one of my steals. It took a long time for this horrible vision to go away.

It didn't take Lehman long to see that I was a good ballplayer. He was an immaculate dresser and showed up for our games shaved and showered. He was in the stands for a game that became the talk of the base for a long time.

We were playing a services squadron team and they had a really talented athlete in left field named Joe Wadsworth. He could hit with the best of us, was a good fielder and had a rifle arm. While Joe had all these weapons, there is one thing he didn't possess and that was self control.

A fan in the bleachers that ran along the third base line started to get on him during the course of the game. Wadsworth said nothing but cut the loudmouth down with an icy stare from his position in the outfield. The jackass persisted in running his mouth and finally Wadsworth reached his boiling point.

In one swift move, Wadsworth leaped the outfield fence and ran to some nearby trees. He ripped a branch off a tree and began sprinting toward the unruly fan with vengeance in his eyes. They intercepted Joe before he could smack the guy with a huge branch. From that day on, Joe was known around the base as "branch Wadsworth."

There were many cool stories that came out of my stay up north. I knew this guy named Frank Ott by sight, but never traveled in his crowd. Later, we became close friends on Guam and the Mineola, Long Island joker wound up an usher at my wedding. One of his favorite tales came from his time in Plattsburgh.

He had a friend named Lee Galen that was a burly, no-nonsense type. Lee liked swilling down the suds like we all did, and took the drinking seriously. Ott relates that one night Lee was drinking a mug of Genesee beer as he walked downstairs. He slipped, fell down the flight of stairs and broke his back. "He held onto the mug though and didn't spill a drop," Ott said. "He was extremely proud of that fact and was marveling about it when the ambulance came to take him to the hospital."

If you wanted a cool place to drink beer, fraternize and listen to the best jukebox around, Filion's was the location. Situated in town near a bridge, the bar was down in a dimly lit cellar. It had the intimacy of drinking in your own house and the place was usually packed with guys from the base and wild and crazy girls.

One night, my buddies and I were soaking up the suds when a big mouthed girl, who knew everything about everything, parked herself at our table. She rambled on and on, and we tried our best to tune her out. She began being abusive and our nerves were about to shatter. As she got up and went to the ladies' room we noticed that our pitcher was nearly empty and needed a refill. Her glass was also empty and at the same time, one of the guys had to take a leak. Are the pieces to the puzzle starting to fit yet?

There were two refills, including one in the pitcher and another in the mug. To any person who enjoys a good beer, I would highly recommend that they didn't touch that mug. Talking a mile a minute, our female friend returned to her perch and eyed her full glass. "Do you like the beer?", one of the guys said, as she hoisted it to her lips. She took a slug and replied "it's good beer, a little salty, but it is definitely Genesee." The laughter coming from Filion's, had to be heard way up the road at the base.

Soon, our rowdy crew piled in a car for the ride back to the barracks. Rounding a corner, we pulled over when a pretty girl was seen standing at the curb. One of our honorable Airmen thought quickly and said "hey baby, wanna screw?" She never flinched or hesitated in her reply. "No, but my brother does, bring your mother."

The next day, I returned to Filion's to get a little hair of the dog and ease my hangover. Those at the table next to us were drinking "scahoobies", and like a fool, I asked what the dark concoction in the pitchers was. "This appetizing thing is a mixture of beer and wine," a man told us. "Here, try a glass." I took a sip and then thought better of this venture. The great wine hangover of 1965 was still fresh in my mind.

Outdoors, a girl was threatening to jump from the nearby bridge into the water below. I sidled up near her and gently tried to persuade her not to. "Nothing can be that bad," I reasoned. "Now get down and come on inside and have a drink." I spoke with her a good 30-45 minutes, hoping to not only gain her confidence, but secure a very pretty dark-haired drinking partner.

Finally, the girl gave up the idea of jumping, leaped to the sidewalk and turned on her heel. Instead of heading toward Filion's, she walked the other way, turning to look over her shoulder. "You son of a bitch," she said to me. "Why didn't you leave me alone?" Once back inside, I learned that this was a normal Sunday ritual with this person and that those in the bar, were used to her carrying on and drawing crowds.

Another time a whole bunch of guys were informed about a "gang bang" that was going to take place near the base. I went to this "event" out of curiosity more than anything else. I watched guys come and go from the house where this woman was. The front porch light went out when a guy entered and went back on when it was the next guy's turn. When I went in the front door, I found a girl with tears coming out of her eyes. She was the one that originally wanted this activity and yet she seemed miserable. I told her to knock it off for the night and she thanked me. Of course I returned to one of the cars, bragging about how great it had been.

Braddee was a lady's man if there ever was one. He would literally take hours for shower, shave and getting dressed. When he left the barracks to go out on the town, he was totally ready. It was Braddee who introduced me to Brodi's and Filion's. We also hit Muron's (a college bar) and a couple of other places.

For awhile I took rides across the base to work, with Braddee. Earl was one of those who possessed charisma. He knew everybody in the world, from the Air Policeman at the gate to the Airman that gave 5 BX (physical conditioning) tests. His habitual lateness started getting to me though and I began riding to work with Sewall or Joe Banco.

Banco was as sharp as an Airman could appear. He was good look- ing, with short blond hair and blue eyes. He never slouched and his uniform was always immaculate and pressed. This fellow from Altoona, Pa., was as punctual as an individual could possibly be. When it was time to get in the car, you better be there.

He told a story to me that he swears is true. "My mother needed to go shopping back home," he said. "I asked her how long she would be. When she said 45 minutes, I came back to pick her up. When she was nowhere to be seen, I went home." Now that folks, is being a stickler for being on time. He said this so seriously, I just had to believe it.

Everybody on the second floor at the barracks teased Braddee. He had what seemed like zillions of phone calls. The phone was always some girl looking for him. Sometimes he would return to his room, towel around waist and mouth filled with toothpaste, to get dressed. Later a car would pull up and sure enough, a girl would pick him up.

Earl had a girlfriend in town named Sharon. Her dad wound up being the mayor for six years and her family was aces. Once it was the day before payday and Earl and I wanted to go slug down a couple of beers. We drove to Sharon's house and she wrote him out a check. I marveled at how Braddee smooth-talked people. But as time went on, I felt bad for her. We became really close friends and had many laugh-filled times together. Her friend "Bunny", myself and whoever happened to be with me, would be on the move and in a carefree kind of mood.

On one occasion, a bunch of us, including VanGraafeiland, rolled up our pants and waded in a pond at Plattsburgh State Teacher's College, near Sharon's Brinkerhoff Street house. I told her to watch out for the invisible tree frogs who were all around us. She looked up in the trees and we all cracked up.

While "sloppin the hogs" with Braddee (picking up girls in bars) was a fun pastime, sports took up some of my time. When Jimmy Hunt of New Jersey processed in from Italy, another dimension was added. Jimmy was a mod kind of guy and had a tremendous sense of humor. He was a short, diminutive fellow with a quick laugh and he could match wits with the best of them. He bolted on everyone from the First Sergeant to his new friends.

It was Hunt, with an eye on the latest fashions, who transformed me into a polka dot, hip huggers and bell bottoms wearer. To say we appeared in cool threads and were on the flashy side, is the understatement of the year. Soon, those who laughed at us, began turning up in similar attire. I was becoming a trend setter of sorts and we frequented Brodi's and then, ended many an evening laughing at "The Honeymooner's" on Jimmy's TV.

Chris Lynn was a good roomie. We played pranks on each other quite a bit and joined forces to terrorize the barracks. Our next door neighbors, Jack Jones and a big guy named Creighton, were gone for the weekend and had a nice surprise waiting when they got back. There was nothing keeping us from entering their room through the connecting bathroom and we did so, with wide grins on our faces. We disassembled their racks (beds) and were awakened in the night when their beds came crashing to the floor.

I did a real good Willie Lehman imitation. When he got drunk, he sounded like he had marbles in his mouth. "Tangen," he would say. "What the hell you doing?" And so of course, Lynn put me up to doing his voice one afternoon after work. "Do Lehman," he encouraged. "You do a real good Willie Lehman." And so, I cleared my throat while standing in the doorway to our room.

I went through a good Lehman episode, complete with some stuttering and a weaving kind of walk. Lynn broke out in hysterical laughter and tears came out of his eyes. I knew the little skit was funny, but not that hilarious. Suddenly I turned around to see Lehman standing behind me. Chalk up another victory for Chris Lynn.

Plattsburgh was a blend and mix of comedians and serious people who made my time there fly by. From Joe Padula's New York City accent to Robert Flood's class, I had found my second home. Some of the loudest cackles came at the expense of some black guys from the first floor. It wasn't a racial thing by any means, when they ripped apart us white guys or we joked about them.

"Brother" Allen and brother Boney should have had their own comedy show. On Fridays they would be in a hurry to get the hell out of Plattsburgh. We watched and chortled when the big and chubby Sergeant Allen came running down the hall with his big green cigar in his mouth. Boney ran behind him, sometimes with a stocking over his hair.

When we didn't have enough money, the guys entertained themselves in the barracks. Some ironed uniforms or watched TV, while others like Joe Pohdan, sang into his beer bottle and George Wickman from California, wandered around resembling George Carlin. Wickman was the first cool guy I ever met from California. Instead of bad-mouthing the East Coast, he thought Plattsburgh was great.

It wasn't all fun and games up at this base. By night, I was either firing up basketballs, hitting softballs, downing beers or chasing the ladies while sporting four rings on my fingers. I hung out with some girls from the town and others from Montreal and one of them referred to me as "her little Ringo." The daytimes were not always a piece of cake.

Our First Sergeant, Milton Lacher, was a disciplinarian who I never saw smile. The slender Sergeant in glasses was an intimidator from the word go. He delighted in watching Airmen pull bay orderly. "Make sure you empty the Major's waste basket," he would say. "And then buff that third floor."

The officer in charge was Major Byrum, who we heard had once smashed up a plane. He sat in his office and listened to Lacher rant and rave. A group of us called the Major "crash Byrum" and said he was secretly trying to fly his desk.

As far as I know, Bob Balmos and myself were the only two Airmen on base, who were from Port Jervis. Bob, who I remember as a fine bowler back home, got here before me, but traveled with a different crowd. Braddee and Hunt were the two I spent the most time with. Earl would always prepare well for a big night on the town. "Gotta catch some z's Tang," he would say, looking at his bed. His roommate, Paul Kalinowski would just shake his head. He knew that Braddee always controlled his own life and other lives as well.

I never had to go through the physical exercises of 5 BX, which was a requirement. Braddee signed off on Rick Robinson's airman's records and "Rickeroo" a part-time DJ at WIRY radio, would reciprocate by helping Earl and his friend.

Sergeant Lacher had no use for sports. His stern ways turned all the guys off and we looked for ways to screw him up. Once he caught me listening to records in my room and went bananas. "Your supposed to be buffing the floor," he screamed. "Now get busy."

Very few people volunteered for Vietnam. But one day the news began circulating that old zebra stripes was going to be taking a little excursion to "the bush." I doubt he put in a volunteer statement, but I could be wrong about that. All I know is that Wayne Hjermstad, a real good guy and cheery assignments clerk, smiled extra wide when these orders were cut.

"It's only 12 months, you'll be back in the states before you know it," someone said to Lacher one day. The head honcho didn't smile back at those smart assed words. Everyone was overjoyed when Lacher departed, but we were skeptical of the new first shirt, Sergeant Stull. However, it didn't take long for Stull to get the morale of our barracks moving in the right direction.

It happened to be softball season when Stull arrived. He watched the team play a night game and the old urge to play ball again, gripped him. "Do you think you could use another pitcher?" he asked me. I nodded my head positively and he grinned from ear to ear. The next day I was on bay orderly again, but I traded my broom for a softball glove and my talent for emptying trash, for a chance to catch Stull's wicked curve ball. He removed his 1505 shirt and threw in a tee shirt. This individual was as down to earth as he could be and he proved that being classy got results.

I was promoted to A2C on 1 June 66 and celebrated with vigor. I guess there was a status factor to the promotion, but I was more interested in the extra money. We had become one big family at the barracks and you had to constantly be on guard for various pranks. Sewall, in his thick Maine accent, made fun of the town I was from, by shouting "Port Javis" with the beady eyes of a mental patient. When you walked away from him, he'd shout after you "later for your raunchy ass."

Lynn became known as "Little Adelord" because his disciplined by-the- numbers boss was named Adelord J. Bourassa. It seems every day there was another humorous anecdote to be discussed. Lehman hung out mostly at Branson's and down the street at another bar, where a girl named Rosie was the bartender. Meanwhile, I hung mostly at Brodi's and Filion's.

Lehman partied a lot but was always sharp when it came time to report for work. One day, he was just dying to tell me something that happened to him the night before. I egged him on and this "Okie" with the calm disposition, spilled his guts.

Lehman was never one to be impressed by the gay population. He kept his distance and remained quiet about lifestyles. He had ventured north of Plattsburgh to a bar and was downing a few, when he began watching a pool game a few feet away. "They were saying things I didn't like," Willie explained. "They definitely weren't straight. So I walked up to the pool table and knocked the pool balls all over the place."

Willie left the bar on foot and was in desperate need for a ride back to Plattsburgh. "This car pulled up on Route 9 and I got in," Lehman asserted. "It was those same damned guys from the pool game. I was going to jump out of the car but they swore they were busting my balls on purpose, and that I had them wrong. We drove to Branson's and drank the night away. Mike Branson (Ma Branson's son) was there, and he was friends with them. I felt like a real ass when I found out they were good guys."

Once I got in a real tight spot at Brodi's. It was a Saturday night and I had dates with a girl from town and another from Montreal. I spaced the times out so they wouldn't overlap. Well, you guessed it...one lady got there late and the other early. This dilemma became a nightmare when my girlfriend from back home surprised me by unexpectedly arriving on the scene too. I left one of the girls as I was allegedly on my way to the bathroom, and darted toward my girlfriend. I hid behind customers near the dance floor as I maneuvered around tables while noting locations of all three women.

After a hello kiss, I told her I was going to get a beer and quickly ducked into the bathroom. On the way there, I told the third lady of the three, that I got called into work and quickly hugged her while keeping tabs on the other two.

Looking in the bathroom mirror, I wondered how I was going to completely wiggle out of this precarious and potentially dangerous situation. The Falcons came off their break and began playing tunes again. I really wasn't hearing the music though. Instead, I began selecting music to be played at my funeral. Braddee seldom got shot down when it came to the ladies and I had wanted to work that same kind of magic. Faced with this predicament, I would much rather have been standing all alone by the bar, without a care in the world.

The wheels raced in my head as I quickly told the Montreal girl that "something came up and I have to leave quick." Swooping in on my girlfriend, like a wavering marathoner, I simply said "let's go for a ride and come back later." I hit the back door of Brodi's and disappeared into the dark Plattsburgh night. I looked up in the sky and simply thought "thank you God."

One weekend, I went with one of the guys to a party in Plattsburgh. Actually, there were only five of us there, two men and three women. He and his girlfriend adjourned to privacy in the house and the girlfriend's female roommate, a motherly type, seemed perfectly content to listen to music by herself. The third girl and I hit it off from the beginning. She said she was a Sergeant's daughter and liked to party. With Sonny and Cher singing in the background, I got to know her extremely well.

We stayed together all night on a fold out couch and in the morning I headed back to base. This vibrant girl was about a year or so younger than me. "It was the "or so" that made me a bit apprehensive about how close we had become.

A couple of days later, I administered a records check to an enlisted guy with the same last name as the girl. Later, I dug deeper into the Sergeant's records for any sons or daughters. The glaring black letters screamed out the first name of the girl I had been with. I swallowed hard, as I realized the gravity of the situation. I pictured myself coming eye-to-eye with this man. "So you're the son-of-a-bitch who was with my daughter," he would say, as he trained the barrel of a gun at my head. I shivered at the thought and put the records away.

Still wanting to see her again, I came across her in a bar called "Patches", which was another dark place with a good jukebox. She seemed very sad and distant, not acting anything like the girl I had hugged just a couple of weeks before. Later, a bombshell was dropped on me when I found out she was pregnant. I knew her situation made her sad. Later, I learned that some guy from base owned up to it and was going to marry her. I was being clearly educated about life, at the tender age of 19 and figure I matured a lot because of sobering stories like this.

Back at work, the usual comedy club type atmosphere prevailed. Kaczka was still munching on his tie, Lehman was making the job bearable and Sewall was acting up down the hall. Tony worked for a cool guy named Tom Plunket. Tom, who took his job seriously, was from Kingston, N.Y., about 58 miles north of Port Jervis on Route 209. Plunket was a few years older than Tony and did his best to keep some type of military atmosphere in their office. These guys, however, were the Abbott and Costello of the building.

I still hear Tom's voice booming "God damn it Sewall, get serious." Sewall sporting his long hair, which stuck out from under his military hat, (wouldn't cut it for anyone) just smiled. Plunket would be trying to drive a point home and Sewall, on purpose, would stare him down and then act like he had no idea what was going on.

One time I dropped by the office to see the place in disarray. Tom was beside himself, yammering like a lunatic. Nearby, Sewall laughed his ass off. Tony had rigged a ruler in Plunket's center desk drawer with an elastic band. Tom had casually opened the drawer and been struck in the gut by a ruler that shot out like a missile.

Trips back home were occurring with less frequency as I happily adopted Plattsburgh as my new residence. However one early evening I rode past Lake Champlain, the sixth largest fresh water lake in the United States, bound for a New Year's celebration. I rang in 1967 at Fish's house, just days before he left for basic training in Texas. His dad, Roy Scales, tried his best to control the wild activities of the party. Guests were grooving to the music and literally diving head first down the cellar stairs. The late Jan Baldwin walked on wobbled legs and Fish was the focal point of the amazing festivities.

Up in the kitchen, Roy told the others to take it easy and not to abuse the alcohol. "Look at Bill here, he can hold his liquor," he pointed out. I hid my right hand behind me when he said that, because my finger tips were cut from opening pop tops of beer cans.

Fish would be heading to Lackland in a few days and then Sheppard AFB, Texas, for six weeks of technical school. Before it was over, his enlistment would take him to Suffolk County AFB, N.Y., from May 1967 until March of 1969 and on to Watertown, N.Y., from March until September of 1969. He received a hardship discharge in September, because his mother, Florence, was very sick in a Middletown, N.Y. hospital.

Back at my base, Braddee and myself got a first hand look at what married life was like. We both went over to Sergeant Art Townsend's house for Super Bowl I (January 15, 1967), which pitted the grizzled National Football League's Green Bay Packers (13-2) against the American Football League kingpin Kansas City Chiefs (12-2-1).

Packer players like quarterback Bart Starr, Jim Taylor and Max McGee (seven pass receptions, 138 yards, two touchdowns), led Vince Lombardi's team to a convincing 35-10 win before 61,946 at Los Angeles' Memorial Coliseum. Coach Hank Stram's guys, like quarterback Len Dawson, Otis Taylor and Mike Garrett, were no match for the champs. We watched Townsend's wife and saw how they got along in their house. I had the feeling that someday I would settle down in this kind of manner.

Winters in the North Country resemble Alaska, except for the sled dogs. Most of the cars in the parking lot of the barracks, wouldn't start in 30 and 40 below weather. Sewall's trusty white and red 1960 Chevy convertible was equal to the task though. While other vehicles simply wouldn't respond, he stood by the driver's door of his faithful machine and barked out, "get your raunchy asses in the car, I'm leaving."

The ride to the other side of the base didn't take long. Some mornings WIRY Radio was on and we listened to a cranky old maid of a character called "Miss Lonely Hearts" bitch and moan about life. "She" had a rotten disposition and was down on everything. It was a great way to start another day of military life.

The end of my relationship and engagement to Charlene took place in April of 1967. We had grown far apart after I went up to Plattsburgh. While she wanted to get married right away, I didn't want that commitment until after my service days were over.

Things didn't end on a mature note. After an argument to end them all, she threw my engagement ring in my side yard, somewhere by an outdoor fireplace grill near the grove. I felt bad about the breakup but knew in my mind, that it was the best for both of us. I hadn't exactly been true to her, by running all over up in Plattsburgh. At the same time, she must have been getting tired of being somewhat tied down.

159

I spent that April evening on my hands and knees, with a flashlight, looking for the ring. After much swearing and duck walking around in the pitch dark, I found the ring. In the end, this California ring had the stone reset into another piece of jewelry. The diamond wound up in the possession of Jackie Mack's daughter.

The day came when Willie Lehman got his orders for overseas. He was going to a place called Andersen AFB, Guam, an island over in Southeast Asia. I saw him off at the terminal, figuring I would probably never see him again. "Be good Junior Bird," he joked, before departing. "Take care of all the women for me." Braddee and I wound up working in the same military pay office and it wasn't long before Staff Sergeant James Perry processed in and became our new boss.

Perry tried to make us mind him and was extremely disciplined. He had been in Vietnam and tried to lord it over us from the beginning. One day, while we were supposed to be working overtime, he caught Bradee and I with a couple of Canadian girls. "They are helping us out," Braddee offered with his teddy bear grin. Perry turned on his heel and walked out, totally disgusted with us.

Perry's bark was worse than his bite and soon he began to chill out. Whenever we would crack a joke, he would go "yuk yuk" in response. It was common for us to refer to Perry as "yuk yuk". Like, "Hey Earl, have you seen yuk yuk around?" Perry talked about the Mekong Delta, Ton Son Nhut and other Vietnam locales all the time. He wore his military blues everywhere, even into Brodi's, after Braddee forced him to go there. While I was slugging down free beer, dancing the "shing-a-ling" or playing kissey face, Braddee was busy embarrassing Perry over near the bar. "Tell us that Vietnam story again, Sarg," Braddee would joke. "And loosen up will you? You're in Plattsburgh now."

John VanGraafeiland III arrived in late 1966 and struck me as the most arrogant and self-centered son of a bitch I had ever met. Processing his military records was shear torture and we stared each other down more than once during the tedious session. Appearing extremely tired, irritable and possessing no patience, he just wanted to be anywhere other than at my desk.

"I had gotten in at 3 a.m.," he told me in May of 2002. "I was coming from Taiwan and was told I'd have a couple of days off. I didn't like Lacher right away. He dragged my ass up early in the morning and told me to go process in. When you saw me, I had not been to sleep in a long time."

"Van" had gone through boot camp and then on to Keesler AFB, Mississippi. After Taiwan, he hit the North Country and through bleary eyes, wasn't impressed with what he saw or how he'd been treated.

"I put in for Plattsburgh because of a girl from New York State," he said, in his pleasing voice, that sounds a bit southern (he once worked in Virginia). "In the end, we split up and I was stuck in New York."

Never judge a book by its cover. Van was a smooth as silk con man type, who was easy going and had a great sense of humor. He was never loud, possessed charisma and simply didn't give a rat's ass when it came to the military. "Mother fuck this and bullshit that," he used to say while playing Air Force games. "I feel kind of groaty (dirty) today, but don't really care. Know what I mean?"

When Lehman hit the gate for Guam, I hung out with Braddee, Hunt and VanGraafeiland. Leave it to me to befriend the three wildest people on the base. Van and I are different and yet very much alike. If you ask him how long he was in the Air Force, he will tell you "three years, nine months and 27 days." In Air Force statistics, and in our ideas about life in general, we are birds of a feather.

The days flew by at Plattsburgh. There was never a dull moment that I can recall and from the softball fields to Filion's, I was on cloud nine. Sewall, like VanGraafeiland, regarded the military as a necessary evil. There was a slender Chief Warrant Officer in our personnel building known as "Mr. Cleveland." He walked in a bent over fashion because of a bad back. Sewall showed his compassion for the situation by shouting out "straighten up you son of a bitch," and then hiding, so Cleveland couldn't see him.

My Airman Performance Report of October 3, 1966, was of a positive nature. Bower said I performed in "an excellent manner, was courteous and cheerful." Meanwhile, Lieutenant Larsen, Chief of the Data Control Section, said I was a "team worker who accepted a tremendous workload and overtime with a positive manner."

One time, while Lehman was still at Plattsburgh, he, Sewall and I went to a drive- in movie with some alcohol that Tony had transported from Maine to New York. "Go real easy on this stuff," he told Willie and me as we began imbibing. "It is potent stuff that will wipe you out. Just sip this, never drink a lot of it at one time."

I figured this concoction was the famous white lightning I'd heard about. I was pretty much on the money with that. It reminded me of apple juice or cider, but had a bitter after taste. Being a beer drinker, I was in unfamiliar territory. I began to drink the water glass of "hootch" quicker than expected. A couple of times, Sewall turned around in his seat and tried to slow me down, but to no avail.

I don't remember leaving the drive in. I do vaguely recall puking up green liquid and fearing for my life. I held onto my bunk for dear life and rode out an unbelievably gut-wrenching hangover. I was in bed for more than 48 hours and missed two days of work.

When I finally managed to regain my strength and the cotton mouth finally subsided, Sewall was there to say a couple of kind words. "You dumb son of a bitch. I told you to sip it. Then again, what should I expect? You're from Port Javis."

The year 1967, was great for music. "To Sir With Love" by Lulu topped the Musicradio WABC New York charts. We grooved to "Kind of a Drag" by The Buckinghams, "Light My Fire" by The Doors, "Ruby Tuesday" by The Rolling Stones and "Penny Lane" by The Beatles.

There is an old saying that indicates that familiarity breeds contempt. While I'm not a proponent of that type of thinking, I have to admit that wine, women and song were starting to become old hat. When you are partying in a downtown apartment with friends and a girl known as "Mousie", you have to stand back from the situation and measure where your at, in life's little battle plan.

Keeping with his professional approach to the military, Van had some business cards made up that were a big help to the nation's well-being. The card said that John D. VanGraafeiland specialized in used cars, whiskey, manure, nails, fly-swatters, racing forms and bongos. "Wars fought, governments run, bars emptied, virgins converted, orgies organized," the card concluded.

As I passed the one year mark in Plattsburgh, softball took center stage again. I continued to produce on the field of battle and was still in fine physical shape. It seemed there wasn't a ball that I couldn't run down in the outfield and I was comfortable at the plate as well.

One day a letter arrived with the familiar handwriting of Lehman in the upper left hand corner of the envelope. I had been contemplating a change of station from "The Burgh" ever since my engagement ended. I was tied to nobody and was free to do as I pleased. Seeing another section of the country or shipping out for overseas, suddenly started to sound attractive. You could snag an assignment to Vietnam in a heartbeat, just ask Lacher. The other place that was getting assigned was Guam.

"The weather here is nice and sunny," Lehman wrote. He had great penmanship and I can still see him tracing and retracing letters, to make sure they looked good. "I'm drinking here on the veranda," he asserted. "How are things back in Plattsburgh?" I read and reread the letter many times and wheels started turning in my head. Perhaps in the near future, I'd be drinking side by side with Willie on that veranda.

Chris Lynn and myself were moping around the room late one afternoon, bored to tears. There was nothing doing downtown and even if there was, payday hadn't arrived yet. Some souls in the barracks were ironing fatigues or shining shoes to pass the time.

"We haven't gotten Tony Sewall in a long time," Lynn announced in a matter of fact manner. "I know he's down there in his room. I got this idea, and if it works, it will really be something. You go downstairs (we were on the second floor) and lie in the flower bed under the window and I'll run to Tony's room and tell him you fell out of the window."

Unprepared for a double cross trick, I stupidly headed down the stairs and outdoors to the good old flower bed. I put on an academy award this day, complete with groans and sighs as I laid on my back in the dirt.

From time to time, I'd sneak a glance up to our window hoping to see Sewall's horrified face.

Sewall's mug finally did appear--but it showed laughter rather than concern. Seconds later, SPLASH! They had tricked the tricker with a pail of ice cold water.

Years later, Lynn and I stilled laughed at that day in the military. He wound up living in Bethlehem, Pa., in a beautiful home. His property was immaculate and well manicured. One thing stood out though, there were no flower beds under the windows.

It wasn't long before I visited Hjermstad down in assignments. I put in a volunteer statement that had choices of bases on it, that included England and Italy. Down further on the sheet of paper, I wrote in the word Guam. "I wouldn't count on England," Hjermstad said. "More than likely Bill, you'll be joining Willie on Guam."

My last Airman Performance Report at Plattsburgh was signed by Perry and Captain Larsen. Perry said I had a "strict attention to detail" He went on to say I was "courteous" and "diplomatic" in my dealings with military pay. Yuk, yuk. Larsen said I had "adapted to the pressures of the pay area" and was "an asset to the unit."

While my real orders for Guam (APO San Francisco 96334) came out in June, my favorite order was cut July 7, 1967 and read like this. "Temporary Duty Order--Military. Plattsburgh AFB, N.Y. To: Mother Branson's and return. Airman will proceed on or about 1130 hours on the 7th of July to Mother Branson's for lunch and heavy rehash and heavy, heavy drinks. Airman will return to assigned station no later than 1230 hours and should be fairly high." In a box to the left of the order that lists the purpose of the TDY, were the words "to get smashed at Mother Branson's."

The influence of Jimmy Hunt was definitely reflected in this order. When somebody talked too much or went on and on about pure drivel, Hunt would halt the useless conversation by saying "heavy, heavy rehash. I can't believe it." Jimmy is one of the funniest people I ever had the pleasure to meet. Any guy that wears polka dot shirts and likes Ralph Kramden, is worth his weight in gold.

Toward the end of my tour, Van and I wound up roommates. Those in charge of the barracks, believing that we would have a change of heart and suddenly take the military seriously, were living in a paper doll world.

Our main objective before leaving on July 14, was to fit as many empty beer cans as possible into our room lockers. Most nights we got totally wasted, as we built beer can pyramids on the floor. Once I was relieved of duty, all hell broke loose. It was one constant party and our dwelling took on the look of a horse stable. No eyebrows were raised when girls were smuggled inside at night. The rule of thumb was, when things involve Tang and Van, expect the unexpected. It makes me shudder to think that Van and I may have been role models to some of the younger Airmen.

One Saturday morning we were awakened by a knock on our door. One of our buddies informed me that there was a surprise room inspection going on. Van was drunk and disorderly on his bunk and I needed a shave. We both wreaked of alcohol as I scurried around trying to clean the sink and get dressed. Van threw on a fatigue top and slowly put on a pair of pants. I never got to sweep the floor and Van never got to put on his shoes. It didn't matter, because it looked like they were shined by a Hershey Bar.

"Comb your hair...hurry up," I told Van. "Oh screw em if they can't take a joke," he replied, through glazed eyes. We were a pair of rumpled individuals, trying to stand tall and look sharp near our bunks, when Major Byrum and company entered. Just think of Detective Columbo and his twin brother and you get the picture.

Any attempt to make us totally committed to the Air Force mission, would be a feeble exercise in futility. Byrum sniffed the stale air and looked totally disgusted. "These must be the two that are leaving soon," he said. "It looks like they deserve each other." He then made the fatal mistake of opening one of the locker doors. Empty Budweiser cans tumbled out at his feet and a pained look came over his red face. He quickly turned and walked back out into the hall.

A week later, on July 6, Van came home with me for some more partying. That is the jaunt where I smashed up the 1964 convertible twice the next day. I still remember Van, blood streaming out of his nose, as he walked in my house. "Let me do the talking," he said. I don't really know if Mom ever bought the story about Van and I fighting and him taking a shot to the nose. It all came out in the wash the next day, when my father went bonkers. We had hit a tree in the dark and walked away from the crash. I realize today, just how fortunate we were.

Willie Lehman, Hunt, Lynn, Sewall, Braddee and Hjermstad were all a big part of my life in the North Country. They all made my assignment go smoothly and helped me form memories to last all of my remaining days.

Mayor Steltzer, his wife, Virginia and daughter Sharon, all treated me great. In fact my wife, Fish and I visited them in 1969. In 1973, Christine, toddler Tracie and I stayed overnight at the mayor's house. This was a very happy home, with Virginia forcing us to eat something and telling us to go out on the town (she babysat our daughter). I remember Sharon's brother, red-haired Eddie (now in Maine) and younger sister, Gina (North Carolina) being nice kids. It had been six years since I had left, but I immediately felt at home.

Mayor Steltzer and his wife have been in North Carolina for about 29 years. Sharon went to college in New York State and later moved down there too. I spoke to Virginia and Sharon the afternoon of July 10, 2002.

All are doing well, although the former mayor has gone through four by-pass operations.

It was Mayor Francis Steltzer who joined 2,500 students, faculty and staff of Plattsburgh State College, at the main gate of Plattsburgh AFB, on May 6, 1970. There had been a candlelight memorial peace parade, following the tragic deaths of four students on the campus of Kent State (Ohio) two days earlier.

Plattsburgh State (established 1889) was ranked in the top 100 (of four-year public universities and colleges, 1998) out of 558 in the nation. Mayor Steltzer was well known by the city, air base and college. He is a 1942 graduate of Plattsburgh High School and returned there, to be inducted into its sports Hall of Fame. "He (Steltzer) was a fine athlete," Sharon said. "He got a college scholarship to St. Lawrence University."

Chris Lynn and I kept in touch over the years. He basically wound up bringing up his kids, daughter Lori and son Chrissy, by himself. One time we stayed overnight at his place for New Year's festivities. We laughed about the Plattsburgh days and the flower bed happening. In the morning, he turned chef and made some pancakes.

The Port Jervis wrestling team competes in the Bethlehem Catholic Holiday Wrestling Tournament around Christmas, so there were times that I saw Lynn and we'd bust each other about our home town wrestling teams. "Well, I see Port Jervis is here for the tournament," he said on one occasion. "The school roped off an area for the Port fans to park their tractors."

As a sportswriter, I saw some of the toughest teams around, in that event. Bethlehem, Freedom, Nazareth, Parkland, Liberty and Port high schools were always good on the mat. One time I stopped in a Holiday Inn for a sip of brewski prior to the championship finals. "I feel sorry for that kid from Port Jervis," I heard a voice say from a nearby table. "He has to wrestle Fred Williams tonight."

I quickly moved toward the table and joined the conversation. Williams, of Freedom, was a Pennsylvania state place winner, who was undefeated. I told them about a grappler by the name of Ed Banach who would meet Williams that night. The four guys at the table chuckled when I said Banach would hand Williams his first loss. No doubt they had long faces that evening, when the future Olympic gold medal winner came off the mat with a hard-fought decision over Williams, who wore a mask to cover an injured nose.

Port and Bethlehem met head-to-head in a duel match at famed West Point in the mid 1970s. And that knock-down-drag-out battle ended in a tie. Lynn and I had to agree that both wrestling programs were out of this world.

Chris and his kids would stop by the house whenever they ventured up Route 209 north from the Lehigh Valley. There was a day he pulled up in front of the house with a brand new sports car. "I was coming home from work and stopped at the local store," my former roommate explained. "Something told me to get a lottery ticket, and I did. I wound up winning big." As he pulled away from the house, I saw his rear license plate spelling out the words "rub off." Not only did he purchase a car, he put away money for his kids' education.

The last time I had any contact with Earl Braddee (pronounced Brady) was in 1967. Nearly 34 years later, on May 6, 2001, we talked on the phone. Earl was at one time, married 25 years, has kids and was in the restaurant business. He had lived in the Denver, Colorado area and seen lots of this country. Instantly, through the Pennsylvania-Vermont telephone cable, we were thrown into a time machine and rewound back to 1967. He was the guy that called me "rookie" when I first arrived at Plattsburgh. "You rink," he used to say while we typed out Military Pay Orders. "Just get the work out."

Earl is just a year or two older than me and we played a lot of basketball and softball together. This smooth operator, God's gift to women, couldn't believe we had made contact. "Hey Tang," he said. "I swear I was just talking about you the other day."

Van has been through some tough times health-wise but being the persevering guy he is, he'll be around a long time to come. As Billy Joel's song indicates, "Only the Good Die Young," so we don't have to worry about Van.

We never lost touch. The day we left Plattsburgh, he went home to the Washington, D.C. area for a couple days of leave. He shipped out to Vietnam while I was home for over a month, awaiting my assignment on Guam.

He wound up "in country" (Vietnam) on August 4, 1967, and was discharged exactly a year later, at McChord AFB, Washington. His time over in the war torn country was far from easy and there is no doubt that a different John VanGraafeiland came back from the war. He still has a great sense of humor and remains the king of wisecracks. He became my best friend in the service, and to this day, would take the shirt off his back for me, as I would him.

"We got shelled a lot and I slept in bunkers," Van recalls. "I was at Ton Son Nhut (air base) for six months during the Tet Offensive. I wound up at Phu Cat toward the end of my tour. Once I got short (days left in Vietnam), survival was what I lived for. I got discharged, flew home and eventually went to college."

John wound up getting married but that union broke up. He has a daughter that he hasn't seen since she was a child. His ex-wife remarried and Van didn't want to rock the boat by disrupting his daughter's life. In the past, Van, who has relocated near Buffalo, New York, used to crack open a beer with me on the phone. We would talk about everything under the sun, but I always maneuvered the conversation toward his kid and how he just "had" to see her someday.

"One of these days, she is going to come looking for you, buddy," I would say. "She is entitled to know who her real dad is." He would get silent on the other end of the wire, and I just knew that he was shattered by the whole damn situation.

Like his "business card" says, Van is flexible enough to do nearly any type of job. In 1976 I went down to Reston, Virginia, to the prestigious American Press Institute, for a seminar with some of the finest sports editors in the country.

Van was selling new cars at a dealership across the Potomac River from Washington, D.C., in Arlington, Va., and even did business with the Kennedys. We partied heavily in Washington and Georgetown and eventually stayed overnight in my hotel room at The Sheraton. He was the same old Van, nine years later, that is for sure.

We awoke on a morning that I had to get to my seminar, and he said "take it easy man, you got time. Let's order up some room service and get us a breakfast." Seems to me we washed down the eggs with a warm beer and went our separate ways.

One time, John showed up at my house in Pa. He was driving a late-model compact car with Florida plates on it. He methodically backed the car up to the garage door and gave me a mysterious look. Later, he scanned a United States map and paced the floor. I sensed his confusion and when he was ready, he told me what was on his mind. He worked for an agency that returned cars to sites all over the U.S. His latest task in this job, was to drive a car from Florida, back up north to where the owners had another house.

"I kind of got stopped on the way back up here," Van explained. "I went here and there, visiting friends and drinking some beer. The time got away from me." I helped this "desperado" by giving him 50 bucks and heading him to Interstate Route 84, a couple of days later. He continued to "hide" as he cruised the country. Finally one day he had absorbed enough mental and physical torture and checked into a hospital. He phoned the owner of the car and apologized. Van was beginning to get his life going in the right direction. A couple of weeks later, a check for $150 arrived from Van. His focus on certain things was becoming straightened out.

By the time I walked away from alcohol, Van either had quit or was damn close to it. He had wound up working two jobs that included a delivery job and driving a cab. "I drank a lot," Van admitted. "By 6 a.m., I had to be at the delivery job. It was a vicious cycle and my immune system was shot." My old roommate suffers from emphysema and had a horrible bout with Aspergillus, which is a fungus of the lungs. He is bouncing back nicely from all the setbacks and seems damn happy to be alive.

We talked on the phone on July 22, 2002 and he expressed great interest in this book and our Plattsburgh years. "Remember those tree frogs at that pond with Sharon Steltzer?", he said. "Those were some great times."

There are a million good "Van stories" but one of the best, is when he showed up at my house one Christmas Eve. He wheeled up to the house with a bottle of booze in his hand and a police car behind him. Talk about arriving in style. The police had showed him how to get to my house. "That cop is a good guy," Van said, as he walked up the front steps.

My girls were small then, and Santa was due the next morning. My wife played the church organ for a Christmas Eve service and later, I adjourned to Bill's Tavern with Van. We were having a good old time until Chris showed up at the bar. "You're going to a hotel room tonight, Van" Christine said. "It's time to leave now." Van obediently followed as we checked him into the Hotel Minisink. Earlier, he had "given me" about $150 or so in cash. The next day I returned the money and through clouded eyes, we had a good chuckle about the night before.

Van has been with a classy lady named "Teri" for quite a few years now. He had three cats at one time, including one he named "Kitty Cat." Van definitively wins first prize for originality. It has been 16 years (1986) since I have come eye to eye with John. I nearly saw him back in May of 2002, but he was sick and I talked to Teri on the phone instead.

Christine's mom, Marion, used to baby sit our daughters and every now and then, Van would phone and think he was talking to my wife. Mother and daughter had a nearly identical voice on the phone and even I couldn't tell the difference.

Apparently, Van and Marion had a couple of talks while we were out. She was a very quiet and shy person but I can see Van putting on a good show for her and making the lady laugh. "How is your friend Van doing?", she used to ask me with a wide grin on her face.

My mother met Chris Lynn, Van and Willie Lehman. She thought a lot of all three Air Force buddies and always wished them well.

Jimmy Hunt dropped by in the 1970s with a container of fine wine in his hand. He was dressed immaculately, as usual, and had his trademark smile as we traded old war tales. Hunt wound up in the clothing business (which is no surprise) down in New Jersey.

Hjermstad, the kind and low key assignments clerk, wound up sending himself to Guam (June 1968 until December 1969). Originally from Minnesota, he has been in South Dakota for four years as the reverend of a Grace Lutheran church. I spoke to him by phone on May 25, 2001, 19 days after I rapped with Braddee.

I have spoken to Tony Sewall by phone a couple of times. He still lives up in Maine and is in a deck and dock building type business. He is married to Diane and hasn't changed one damn bit. In June 2002, we went up to Ogunquit, Maine for a few days. One evening we hit the road and traveled north on Route 495. I phoned Tony from a rest area and we met him at a transit lot a few minutes later.

Since his favorite word back in Plattsburgh was "Port Javis", I made sure to wear a red and black Port Jervis wrestling tee shirt that former Raider state qualifier and current modified wrestling coach Ernie Jackson gave to me. I got out of the car in pristine Maine territory when Sewall's red pickup truck lumbered into the lot. The last time I saw Tony was in Okinawa in 1968. So 34 years later, on June 10, 2002 at about 8:30 p.m., a familiar figure walked toward me.

Again, it was the mid and late 60s all over again. He looks the same except the brown hair that used to peek out from under his hat, is now white. The comedian that used to shout out "ah, you ache" and "get serious" put his hand out and 34 years were extinguished.

Sewall is the youngest of six kids. His late father, Aldon Sewall, was the 1952 skipper of a famous yacht named "Escapade" owned by Wendel L. Anderson. Tony had been in the Air Force from November 1965 until September 1969. He got married in October of 1971 and worked at Blue Cross for 10 years. He always kept in touch with Tom Plunket, his former boss. "I showed him how great the fishing was up here," Tony noted.

"Tom was in my wedding and it was great to see him whenever we got together. A few years back (1997), he got a lump in his stomach that was like a brick." Tony's voice trailed off as he recalled a friend who will never be forgotten.

It didn't take long for the conversation to turn toward the drunken evening at the drive-in. While Chris, Tony and I sat eating at Cole Farms, I learned what mixture had done me in all those years ago. "You got ripped on apple jack," Sewall asserted. "That stuff fermented in a wooden barrel until it bubbled. I drove it 11 hours from here in Maine to Plattsburgh. I will never forget you lying there missing work. Lehman was a mess too. He crawled up the barracks floor on his hands and knees and told me he wanted a pizza. He didn't need any pizza, a bed was the only place for Willie that night."

The time in that booth at Cole Farms went rapidly. Chris took our picture at the establishment's entrance and we bid each other farewell. Who would ever believe that 34 years later, connection would be made between two of the three characters in the flower bed caper. We plan to meet again soon and I don't mean 34 years from now. As my wife and I got in our vehicle, Tony called back to us. "Later for ya," he said. Chris looked at me and exclaimed "now I know who Tony is. You talked about him a lot over the years. It seemed so strange hearing that drive-in story from him. You have told me that one many times."

At Plattsburgh, the base had been the official military support installation for the 1980 Winter Olympics, staged at Lake Placid, N.Y. That was the famous site where the Americans knocked off Russia in ice hockey. Fifteen years later, on September 30, 1995, Plattsburgh AFB officially closed. The closure came as a result of a realignment action that began back in 1993.

The site of the base is now occupied by the Plattsburgh AFB Redevelopment Corporation (PARC), created to fill a gap in the region's economy. It is designed to attract new businesses to the area.

On April 20, 2002, an earthquake with a 5.1 magnitude struck roads in northern New York. The quake, which occurred 15 miles southwest of Plattsburgh, cracked foundations and chimneys just before 7 a.m. on that Saturday morning. It rattled homes from Maine to Maryland and broke off a 100-foot section of road near Ausable Forks, in the picturesque Adirondacks. When all was said and done, $14 million in damage was reported.

I often wonder what this city of my youth, looks like today. Nearly three decades have gone by since I took in the sights and sounds of Plattsburgh. This place is where I smacked game-winning hits, swished 20-foot jump shots, swilled beer in Branson's and Filion's, heard a great band called the Falcons and felt a pail of water cascade onto my face.

The current mayor is Daniel Stewart. On May 3, 2001, he had front row tickets for an Elton John-Billy Joel concert up in Montreal. Anybody who likes these musicians, has got to be a good guy. I saw Joel twice at Madison Square Garden in New York City. He ran up and down ramps in his sports coat and sneakers, energizing the crowd with his brand of infectious music. John, like Joel, is a musical genius. From "Crocodile Rock" to "Candle in the Wind" you can't find a better entertainer.

They say you can never go back. But I returned to the place where I lived at age three and saw the brook, sidewalk, trees and yard where I played in my toddler years and beyond. Inside the house was a room where I laced on boxing gloves and pretended to be fighter Frankie Ryff. A quarter century later, I would sit in a chair and joke with Muhammad Ali. Who says dreams don't come true or that you can never go back?

Early tomorrow morning my wife and I will be headed north to the tranquil, serene Adirondacks. Lakes, rivers and streams dot this lush landscape, and it seems as though a ride north on Route 87, gives views of a giant picture postcard that has sprung to life. Sadly enough, it is true that the past is gone forever. But it is also a fact, that nobody can ever take away the memories.

Is "The Pride of the Adirondacks" plane still out by where the main gate of the base was? And what about Ma Branson's place. Is the bar still in the family name or did someone buy it?

I'm curious about the status of Filion's and what has become of Brodi's, Arnie's (restaurant) and Patches. I'll gaze at the bridge next to Filion's and remember that Sunday when a "lady" threatened to jump.

There was the Orange Julep on the outskirts of town, an eating place, similar to "Happy Days" hangout Arnie's. What about the motel where Mom stayed so many years ago when she came up to watch me play base team softball?

Of course there is the air base property (new and old bases). I wonder if my barracks is still there, or my personnel section office (Military Pay) where I became known as "Junior Bird", in the early days. A parade field used to stand right across from the building's front windows. If you come out the front door and hang a left onto the street, you begin the trek to the gate and over to Branson's. Maybe Mike Branson took over his mom's business and there are still great egg salad sandwiches to be had.

The pond is probably still there where Van, Sharon Steltzer and I splashed around and laughed about tree frogs. A trip to Plattsburgh wouldn't be complete without checking out WIRY radio and the Plattsburgh Press Republican and cruising past Mayor Steltzer's former house on Brinkerhoff.

Adulthood began for me in Plattsburgh. The ratio of girls to guys back then, still boggles the mind. The Falcons, who became The Franklin Brothers (Brodi's and Egg and Machine Shop in town) were fabulous. Fish, a bass player himself, got to hear them in 1969 and still marvels at their talent.

I left Plattsburgh and spent over a month with the girl I would marry someday. I went off to Southeast Asia and spoke with men who went on bombing missions. I returned home an older and wiser person who had learned that it isn't always what you know, but who you know, that counts.

Tomorrow I return to my second home. It has been 29 long years during which our second daughter was born, I became an award-winning writer and six grandchildren have come on the scene. For just one day, I will recapture my youth of the 1960s. I am the guy that nearly went to the Woodstock Festival in 1969 (less than an hour from home), but saw bumper to bumper traffic and instead, went to Plattsburgh with Christine. I am the guy that returns to "The Burgh" on July 25, 2002.

Entering Adirondack Park, north of Albany, is still exhilarating. Right away, roadside billboards seemed to go away and the huge trees and unspoiled environment took over. Green and white signs for Warrensburg and Pottersville appeared as the car continued north. I recalled when Route 87 ended at these towns and you had to get off the exit and continue on Route 9 north, where you faced oncoming traffic. As 87 progressed, they would take down barriers and trips back to the base would sometimes give you a new section of road to travel.

We were to meet a friend, Frances Murdock, at the Noon Mark Diner on Route 73, in Keene Valley. This witty and dear friend, had recommended the diner optimistically, but had to beg off, when she discovered a doctor's appointment would interfere with our arrival. I hope to see this classy Saranac Lake lady in the future.

We sat at the table of the clean and homey facility and gazed at the majestic mountains that dwarfed the buildings in the clean town. Our waitress was Amanda Senecal, a patient and pretty young lady with deep blue eyes that could make the color of Lake Champlain jealous. The 2002 Ausable Valley High School graduate had a great disposition and was proud of Peru, N.Y., where she lives. Headed for Plattsburgh State College in August, she had already visited her boyfriend's state, South Carolina, and was glad to get back to the crisp air of the Adirondacks. The Noon Mark, owned by Lola Porter, is just a stone's throw from Lake Placid. I already felt at home.

The food was spectacular, the atmosphere laid back and it was refreshing to hear Amanda's hopes and dreams for the future. "I live at home now," she said. "But some day I will be in the dormitory at school."

We talked about sports a little bit and she noted that her sister's boyfriend was a Section 7 wrestling champion, who had advanced to the state tournament in Syracuse. Then she recalled the morning of the earthquake.

"It happened around 7 a.m., rattled the dishes and knocked the refrigerator door open," she says. "Everything shook and it cracked our foundation. It was really scary." Amanda's positive attitude and love for where she resides, spells out a keen personal pride, and sent me toward the car realizing that I was roughly her age when I lived in Plattsburgh.

It was 1:25 p.m., when we approached exit 37 at Plattsburgh. On WIRY, "Twisting The Night Away" by Sam Cooke, was wailing. There were signs for Lowe's, Wal-Mart, Holiday Inn and EconoLodge. Taking Route 3, we saw a ton of traffic that reflected what Amanda had mentioned to us earlier. "You will see a lot of cars when you get there," she predicted.

Moving past Adirondack Plaza and Sherwin Williams on the left and Friendly's on the right, I saw a sign that said the temperature was 79 degrees. Soon Cornelia Street and then the college, came in to view. Somewhere in the area of all these businesses, was WIRY. At least the station used to be located out here somewhere.

Stop lights were everywhere and the steady stream of traffic went on forever. Finally, we turned left on Margaret Street and parked the car, near where Brinkerhoff intersects. Getting out of our silver vehicle, we saw a sign that told us Arnie's Restaurant was still very much alive. The green sign advertised Italian-American food (upstairs), just like way back when.

Arriving on Bridge Street, I looked down the road at familiar territory. At the corner of Bridge and City Hall Place, Fish had walked in the wind with me in 1969, lost grasp of money in his hands and had to run up and down the street retrieving bills that were blowing along the ground. I, of course, had laughed my ass off at him kneeling under cars in search of his money, while he swore up a storm.

This jaunt down Bridge Street, began my venture into the world of years gone by. It was to wind up a bittersweet jaunt, that tugged at my heart strings in more ways than one. I arrived at the bridge where that "lady" had threatened to jump so many years ago. The happenings of the 60s were now well kept secrets of the past. There was a treasure chest of great memories and rich history here, but sadly, it was lacking a key. Before this day would end, Christine would sum things up perfectly. "The structures have survived," she pointed out. "But the people haven't." Prior businesses, affected by the base closure, had disappeared. Many of the vibrant people, so vital to a good economy, had simply evaporated into thin air, as if they had never existed.

Looking to our left, we were relieved to see that the building housing Filion's was still there. Three generations have been associated with the business, but that is all finished now. Down below the bridge the water swirled, as I refocused my eyes to a sign on the side of the structure. The sign said "Bob's Games", and had an arrow pointing down the side, to a door I had entered countless times.

Walking down a slope and past the red brick and rock exterior, we went inside through an open door. The black railing where bouncers used to check ID's is still there and so was the lower stone walls that gave Filion's the intimate cellar atmosphere. It used to be real dark in here and it seemed extremely bizarre to be looking up at bright lights.

The bar used to be to the right while tables and rest rooms were at the left, near where the best juke box I had ever heard, was located. Two young guys, with smirks on their faces, were behind the counter and informed me that Filion's had closed "three or four years ago" and that a gun store had replaced it. Maybe they were just amused at the two people in their 50s, or that we had come back and mentioned the word "Filion's." I got bad vibes from their smart-assed attitudes and an eerie feeling about where we stood. The stone walls stood dormant, yet they begged to go back into the past when energy and perpetual motion marked eventful and fun-filled afternoons and evenings.

I felt a mixture of sadness, and bridled hostility at this hopeless situation. "Games" and these disrespectful young adults, didn't belong here. Clinking glasses, darkness, kids laughing and The Zombies record "Time of the Season" blaring in the background, did. These walls had heard and seen years of memories pass before them. However, days of a flashlight on an ID, flirting with the girls and howling at idiotic jokes were officially over.

This site had undergone a sickening transformation in my eyes. I experienced an empty and hollow feeling that is beyond description. I had expected lots of change up in this city, but the sobering reality was already hitting me between the eyes, like the excruciating pain of an exposed nerve.

I noticed "The Egg and Machine Shop" bar, where the former Falcons, turned Franklin Brothers, used to play, was gone. I gritted my teeth and headed south on Route 9, toward the former Plattsburgh Air

Force Base.

Approaching the old side of the base, I noticed that beyond the fence, historical red bricked buildings stood forlornly and without purpose. Countless dwellings, majestic in appearance, showed no sign of life. Curtains and shades had been taken down and there were no cars in the driveways. It looked like a Rod Serling movie that I viewed through misty eyes. I had no idea, that this was merely a prelude of things to come.

I began understanding that people were expendable, and that nothing is forever. I felt pangs of loneliness when I thought of what had occurred here. The usefulness of this base was over. It had become obsolete. I identified with every pissed off Plattsburgh person who suffered because the Air Force closed this once proud installation. The Air Force had simply walked away from a city that had embraced Airmen so thoroughly. This town unrolled the red carpet and invited those from California to Maine to come on in. When all was said and done, they got a slap in the face for their hospitality. I seethed with anger that the Air Force had abandoned the city and left much of it a shell of its former self, much like the housing I was to see on the new side of the base.

We hung a right to where the main gate used to be. I was pleased to see that the award-winning "Pride of the Adirondacks" plane, with the numbers "385" and "Plattsburgh" near its tail, still stood to the left, still guarding the North Country. Old times and new blended in, as the plane, a symbol of American pride, and a Dunkin Donuts, a symbol of donuts and coffee, were located across from each other.

Where the white-gloved Air Police used to wave folks onto base, stands a small shed with a sign that says "Welcome to PARC." It is unreal that I actually remembered the way to my barracks. We passed abandoned base housing that made the place look like an Arizona ghost town. No kids shouted, laughed, played ball, ran races or jumped rope. There were no swing sets, chairs near the porches, or swimming pools on this hot July day. Plattsburgh Air Force Base, in my eyes, was officially dead. We viewed the base theater where Chris Lynn used to work part time. The white letters are gone on the outside, but the outlines are still visible.

Earlier, we had passed the base hospital on the left, where the letters "380th Medical Group" were still attached. I recalled that this is where Lee Galen was taken after he had fallen down that flight of stairs, beer safely in hand. Progressing deep into what had been base property, we turned right, as if by instinct, and entered the paved parking lot where my barracks had been. My mood was somber but there was a faint hint of anticipation in the mixed bag of feelings. We didn't see a soul, as I waded my way back to that July day in 1967 when a Chrysler 300 picked me up here, for my ride home.

The faded gray black top surface was filled with pot holes and cracks from which weeds grew in the bright sun. I was afraid to look, but when I did, there stood my barracks, the second of three staggered dwellings with the "1942" building number still on it.

This is the place that I called home for nearly 16 months. To the left was the yard where Sergeant Stull and I fired a softball so long ago. The end fire escapes, where I used to enter and exit the second floor, were gone. Upon further examination, Christine pointed out that a short addition had been attached to the original end of the barracks and the fire escapes were now indoors. White letters on the outside wall of the former barracks, spelled out "Arnold Hall."

The roof was in need of repair and the first door I came to, had a gold padlock on it. There were still some white curtains in the windows but the main entrance was a mess. Pine trees grew uncontrollably next to the barracks and lazily swooped down to block the sidewalk. I slowly walked to the side of the place and looked up at the window on the second floor, that used to shield the room Chris Lynn and I shared. From there, I had moved across the hall for jocular and drunken times with John Van.

Looking down at where the flower bed used to be, I saw nothing but weeds and rocks. Like the rest of the base, this once pretty section, had been reduced to a sickening example of what neglect can do. It was almost impossible to comprehend that colorful and fragrant flowers graced this spot back in the 60s. My final view of my old homestead was that of a rusted and broken bicycle rack that seemed to announce a person's arrival or departure from heartbreak.

As we maneuvered out of the lot, I consciously stopped myself from looking back. The sight was too upsetting to be perused again. In the past, I had seen this area through the eyes of a 20-year-old young man. I was now 55, and people, like places, change.

Dennis Balch is a mutual friend of Fish and me. I played Little League baseball with him (Yankees) back when I was eight years old and he was 12. He hit the nail on the head when he heard of what I went back to. "You were very young then," he says. "You had no fear and never stopped to think of what you were experiencing. You figured that it would always be this way. And then you found out that it wasn't."

We left the former base and parked in a shopping plaza near Dunkin Donuts. Walking about two blocks, we approached Brodi's on McKinley Avenue. I had heard about this place from former Port Jervis track teammate Bob Pavlich. Bob said "definitely go to Brodi's," in 1966, when he heard I was going to the base up in Plattsburgh.

This is the site where I spent many Friday and Saturday nights. I would always start at Branson's and walk around the corner to Brodi's. If I struck out with the American and Canadian ladies at Brodi's (which was hard to do), I ended the evening at Filion's. As I eyed the premises, thoughts of The Falcons filled my head. Falcons and Brodi's were synonymous to myself and countless others. This is the sacred ground where husbands and wives shared their first dance or drink. Brodi's is no more.

"It must be gone 10 years," says an employee of nearby Bill McBride used cars. The mention of "Branson's" drew blank stares from a couple of people. "There is Joe's Bar, if that is the place you mean," one of them said.

What was Brodi's, is a gray brick and wood building. A white and pink sign on the wall says "Guibord's School of Dance." That business is a training school for the North Country Ballet Ensemble. Gym tots and gymnastics are advertised. Near the pink stone steps in back, are those same black railings on a back patio type porch, that I remember. Cars are parked here, and apartments can be seen at the rear of the building.

Beatrice Brodi had been the owner-operator of the establishment. She made it to over 80 years old but died June 13, 2000. Surviving were her husband, Mike, plus sons, Mike and Stephen. I looked into the sky and remembered how I had never been carded here, when in the Air Force at ages 19 and 20. When I returned in 1969, at age 22, I was carded in the doorway. When I showed a degree of anger, I was told "hey, smile, be glad we are checking the license, you look young and it won't always be this way." While I agree with that logic, I began thinking that maybe the water on Guam had something in it, that came from the fountain of youth. Instead of aging, I was getting younger all the time.

My mind snapped back to the present as Chris and I walked to U.S. Avenue (Route 9) in search of Branson's Bar. The green house is still there, with the large window in the downstairs front of the bar that gives great views of the roadway and old side of the base. A catcher's glove, ball and bat are attached to the front and a white and green sign says "Home of the Louisville slugger" and "Joe's Bar."

The place was closed, although someone was sitting inside at the bar. While Chris decided to head for the car and the air conditioning, I meandered up the road to a tavern called the Dry Dock Bar. I was hoping to find out about the former Branson's, plus learn whether or not Rosie, a bartender at Charlie's, was still alive and living in the area. Willie used to like Rosie a lot and he spent plenty of time at Charlie's, which I couldn't seem to find. She was, or still could be, my last living link here, to Plattsburgh AFB. I figure Rosie would be in her 50s or 60s.

Alana Hood, a lady with a nice personality, poured me a ginger ale and I talked to a couple of people in the establishment. None seemed to know about Charlie's, so I figured it had been torn down. I walked back down the street and noticed a black dog on the porch of Joe's. I wasted a few minutes, saw the dog had left and knocked on the front door.

Joe Proctor must have figured I was a salesman and he was inquisitive as to why I was there. Once he learned my mission, he was courteous and very helpful. I walked inside and was immediately transformed into the past. For once, things hadn't changed all that much. Time had stood still here and it was 1966 all over again. This was the place Willie had taken me first, on that cold March day. He used to play darts by the hour in here, and a dart board still hangs on the wall.

A pool table is in the front and the bar is in the same place. I glanced out the window, like I had done a myriad of times. Then, there was activity beyond the roadway, behind the silver colored fence to the old base. Now there were no people moving around. It was almost as if a nuclear attack had occurred and taken human beings from the site.

My mind drifted back as I looked at the bar and imagined I saw the kindly face of Ma Branson. She was the perfect model of a grandmother you would like to call your own. She was a slender white haired lady who wore glasses and possessed a calming demeanor. She smiled quite a bit and Willie was her pet. Since I became friends with Lehman, I was welcomed with open arms.

When Willie used to drink his limit and become edgy and aggressive, it was Ma who noticed right away. "Willie, don't be like that, you look tired," she used to say. "Why don't you go back to the base and get some sleep? I will see you tomorrow." Lehman always listened to her advice and there is nothing he wouldn't do for Ma Branson. She served egg salad sandwiches with pride and quickly became a favorite of mine.

In 1969, Fish and I drove up to Plattsburgh (in the winter) to spend a couple of days. He phoned our job, Arrow Shirts, in Chester, N.Y., from Branson's, to inform our boss that roads were snowy and we couldn't make it to work. We laughed our asses off as we chugged beers more than five hours away.

"She (Ma Branson) passed away some time ago," Joe said. "Her son, Mike, lives down in Orlando, Florida. Branson's was sold in 1971, Gene Gadway had it from 1971 until 1990 and I have had it since then."

Joe sipped his coffee from behind the bar and reflected on what the base closing meant to him. "We took a big hit," he says. "My son was in high school so I stayed with it and made due with the situation. Most businesses closed and left. Some kept opening, closing and opening again. Nobody really drinks around here anymore." This former serviceman had a connection with me and neither of us knew it for awhile. Then he announced that he was a bouncer at Filion's during the time I was at the base.

"Brodi's was sold in the early 1970s," Joe said. "They kept the same name and I think a couple of guys from a band bought it." My mind raced as I figured that perhaps Les and Rick, two members of the Falcons band, may have purchased the place. "There was great music in Brodi's and that name Falcons rings a bell," Joe asserted. "I worked for Bea Brodi for awhile. That was the place to be."

Proctor knew the story behind Charlie's, just up the street a couple of minutes. "Charlie's 6th Ward Tavern was torn down about eight years ago," he reflected. "Charlie has died and they leveled the place in one day. Now they park cars there." The name Rosie didn't sound familiar to him though.

We shook hands as if we'd been friends for years and years. Chris and I began to head out the front door and Joe wished us a safe trip. A half hour earlier, he had insisted that I go and bring Chris back into his tavern, which I did. It seemed only right, that we had touched base with the first bar I had walked into all those years ago.

Back near "The Pride of the Adirondacks," I had glanced at the Plattsburgh Press-Republican, a morning newspaper owned by Ottaway Newspapers Incorporated. Ottaway also owns the weekly Gazette in Port Jervis, which was formerly the Union-Gazette, the daily afternoon paper I worked for. I saw where Jim Dynko was editor of the Press-Republican and Bob Parks was publisher. I met the humorous and accomplished Dynko way back in the 1970s at an Ottaway seminar at Campbell Hall, about 25 miles from my home. Parks was a good guy that had been publisher in Port, when I dabbled into part time work there.

Before departing Plattsburgh, we drove across Route 9 to the old side of the base. I gazed up at the second floor of Building 34, where I was known as "Junior Bird." three and a half decades earlier. I flashed back to my first day, then wondered if Sergeant Kaczka was still alive, enjoying retirement while a tie hangs from his mouth.

I viewed what had been the parade field. The grass was still nice and green and soccer goals were evident, with nets shimmering in the brilliant sun. Viewing the base gymnasium next to Building 34, I remembered Jim Hickey, Gust Swensen, and Rick Robinson, who used to work there. I wore a gold colored basketball uniform in there, while representing the 380th Group Headquarters Squadron in games. I found it ironic that I couldn't recall my basketball or softball uniform numbers at Plattsburgh. On Guam, I was number "4" in a blue and red basketball uniform and "14" on the softball diamond.

There was a lump in my throat and my emotions were affected by this journey north. I loved this place so damn much, I could have found a way to silently cry, even without tear ducts. But on this day, I wouldn't have to hide tears. They simply would not come.

We headed the 2001 Silver Pontiac Sunfire south on Route 9 to Port Henry. From there, we took a one hour ferry ride to Burlington, Vermont and drove to Stowe. Suddenly great sorrow enveloped me as I realized that there were now two Plattsburghs. One is a busy and bustling city that is looking to place two major car dealerships near the base entrance and maybe build a major racing facility (possible NASCAR Winston Cup race someday) that could seat 30,000 to 80,000 people in the grandstand. The other is a section of city that has been hurt by the base closure.

Businesses began declining when service personnel were no longer there to order up a sandwich or belly up to the bar. While Bruce Springsteen's "Glory Days" seems to sum up my feelings of my high school athletic years, the 1967 tune "Little Bit of Soul" by The Music Explosion has a Plattsburgh feel to it. When in Plattsburgh, think 60s. We got on the ferry and looked at Vermont across Lake Champlain. The trip I had looked forward to, for so many years, seemed tarnished in a way. And yet, it almost seemed like I had gone back to see an old friend who just wasn't home. At least the thought was there, if not the fulfillment.

I took one last look at those incredible Adirondacks and turned around. I could smell the lake and the freshness of the air as the wind from the ferry's movement wreaked havoc with my hair. At Stowe, we would go up to "Smuggler's Notch" stay at "The Town and Country" and eat at the fabulous "Gracie's" in Stowe.

Back on the ferry, I had experienced one last thought regarding Plattsburgh. I had turned the time machine back to July 14, 1967, and I stood in the parking lot again, near the barracks, where weeds now peek through that hard surface of pavement. Van was in a black short-sleeved shirt and wore sunglasses. We shook hands and said we'd keep in touch over the years. I hopped in the gold Chrysler and headed for the Route 87 northway. I'd be going south for over a month of fun before shipping overseas.

I had written Chris a letter saying I'd be home. I looked forward to the relaxation that a leave can bring. And I wondered what spending time with this Matamoras girl would be like. The leave was a great one and I hated for it to end. Guam could hold on for awhile. We would listen to "Light My Fire" together. I was dating my future wife.

CHAPTER 8

I am a Rock I am an Island

The rest of July and good part of August 1967 was shear ecstasy to me. I could sleep as late as I wanted, raid the fridge whenever I felt like it and had great times with Christine, Fish and Paddie Kroger. There was never a dull moment as fishing, wiffle ball, swilling beer and picnic lunches took center stage. I remember the lunches, with the long and dark-haired pretty Chris, most of all.

I had met her the night after I got home from Plattsburgh and we went to Mount Carmel together. Mount Carmel is a yearly summer celebration in "The Acre" section of Port Jervis, where rides, cotton candy, sausage and pepper sandwiches and fire works became a part of life.

We walked toward her house, across the bridge in Pennsylvania, when it became late. I had a great feeling that I had stumbled into something really good and was glad I had written her a letter. The moon shone down on the tranquil Delaware River, stars twinkled and my young life was suddenly very satisfying. The only drawback in this memorable summer, was smashing up the Plymouth Fury and having no wheels during my leave.

Dad and Mom may have felt kind of sorry for me, because a few times I managed to use Dad's car to pick up Chris or take her home. Other times, she would arrive at my house in West End, in a taxi. We watched television, listened to music and sometimes walked the few blocks to Bamberger's for a drink.

The two things that stand out most of all, were sitting on a blanket in the grove (eating together) as "Light My Fire" played on the radio and the night I had to say goodbye. We would play pool out in my driveway (small table) those wonderful afternoons or we would shoot some baskets. The evening before I left for Guam, I felt like I had been hustled by the Air Force.

We had been at my house, listening to some old songs by some great groups. Jimmy Hunt had introduced me to this type of music and Chris enjoyed it as well. "Lovers Never Say Goodbye" by The Flamingoes had become one of our favorite songs. Every time we heard it together, I thought of what lay ahead of me. I blocked out the leaving part, but it kept invading my mind. "Only You" by The Platters seemed to soothe the awful reality of going away. It had become "our song" and remains our trademark tune to this day.

The last glimpse I had of Christine, before leaving for 16 months, was the vivacious, gentle girl walking toward her blue house in Matamoras. I had driven her home and given her a goodbye kiss. We had promised to write to each other and Chris said she would be waiting back here, for me to come home.

The summer I fell in love with Chrisine Goble was what kept me going over on the Western Pacific Island. I would be starting an 18-month tour, which amounted to 547 days. Chris was crying when I parked the car in front of her house. I had all I could do to control my emotions in this heart-wrenching scene. "Don't look back," I said to her as she walked away. I quickly maneuvered the car back out onto Avenue M, as tears filled my eyes.

Dad, Mom, Chris and I had gone for supper at Scully's Restaurant in Sparrowbush earlier in the evening. Later, Fish and Paddie came by the house to say their goodbyes. But it was Chris whose time I cherished and savored the most. "I had to get to you that summer, before you wound up with Gary (Fish)," Chris explains. "You were always on the move and it was hard to pin you down."

Fish was stationed at Suffolk County Air Force Base, N.Y., and when he found out I was headed home for leave, he planned on driving home weekends, although Port Jervis was way too far from the distance he was allowed to travel. Fish, a medic, was in hot water all the time at Suffolk County. He had caught hell already, for skipping training classes and was told to never skip again. The next weekend he came home anyway.

After I was out of the service, he would come home in the dead of winter and not want to go back to base. One time he had gotten a pass to come home and we had a dusting of snow. Instead of heading back to his base on time, he phoned Suffolk County to wangle more time off. "The town is closed," he told someone on the phone. "I'll get back there after they clear the roads."

Fish drove a white Opel car and had constant trouble with it. It seemed everything broke down on that vehicle. It became a convenient excuse for him on occasion. He was home one time and was having so much fun he hated going back to the base. Se he phoned again and said he was having car trouble but would get back there when he could.

Fish was already on thin ice with the big wigs at Suffolk County. When he got back to his duty station, a high-ranking officer sat our hero down in his office. "Well Airman Scales, what do you have to say for yourself?" he queried. "Wanna buy a car?" was Fish's answer.

The white Opel vehicle was a real piece of work. "This God damned car," Fish would say as he kicked it. Once he was broken down on the road and was beside himself. The car had a light flashing on and was making horrible sounds. He bitched at his dad about how unreliable his wheels were and Roy said "have you checked the oil?" Airman Scales thought for a second and replied "I didn't know I had to."

One afternoon in August, Fish and I sat in the grove and did some serious drinking. I mixed two kinds of beer in a big pitcher and we began to chug what Frank Ott used to call "golden life sustaining fluid." We were three sheets to the wind when we walked all the way downtown to get something to eat at Spero's on Front Street. Lou, an employe at the teen hangout, refused to get us a burger so we had to walk all the way back home in pitiful condition. Oh yes, one other thing. Fish was due to be back at Suffolk County that night and had to catch a bus.

I volunteered to go back with him but that got squelched by my father when I blurted that idea out. "If you go, don't come back," he said firmly. So Fish had to go it alone, first drunk, then hung over. He went by bus and railroad to reach his destination. En route he lay down on a bench somewhere and got tapped on the feet by a cop's billy club. He finally made it though and looked like something the cat dragged in when he finally arrived at his barracks.

One day a letter arrived from Guam. It was a long document all about the island and mentioned what type of clothing to bring to this tropical paradise. It was signed by Douglas B. Smith, who was my sponsor. A day or two later, a personal letter arrived from "Smitty" saying that the "cozy barracks" and wonderful impression I may have gotten from his official sponsor letter, was a crock. "Get out of this assignment if you can," he wrote.

I am not a person who likes surprises, so I was happy to be informed that my destination could be a place that was a bit unpleasant. Instead, what I would find, was an atmosphere at Andersen AFB that I would despise most of the time. In the end, I would spend 14 months on "The Rock." Let me clarify once and for all, that I am not against the island of Guam. It is a beautiful place and is currently a big tourist draw. Plattsburgh was a tough act to follow, I admit, but the living conditions and the way the lower enlisted grades were treated was pathetic.

I hated leaving Chris and my family behind. I never even got to see the final episode of "The Fugitive" TV show, starring David Janssen. That show aired from September 17, 1963 until August 29, 1967. It was with mixed feelings and emotions that I departed John F. Kennedy Airport in New York, bound for San Francisco International Airport. I left the continental United States a boy of 20, and returned 16 months later, a man.

Guam is across the International Dateline (14 hours ahead of the East Coast) and nine time zones away. The flight took 17 hours with a stop at Honolulu, Hawaii for refueling. It is 30 miles long and a maximum of nine miles across. The weather there is warm with trade winds, temperatures usually around 87 degrees and humidity in the area of 70 per cent. The dry season is January through June and rainy season the rest of the year. It is roughly 75 per cent of the way from Hawaii to the Philippines and is three times the size of Washington, D.C.

The terrain is of volcanic origin and coral reefs outline the island. Some of the villages from north to south include Yigo, Tamuning, Agana (the capital), Agat, and Merizo. Guam ceded to the U.S. in 1898, was captured by the Japanese in 1941 and was retaken by the U.S. in 1944. The barracks I would be residing at, out at a place in the jungle (eight miles from base) called Marbo, was made of rock. Shell marks from World War II could be seen on the side of it. Looking around my surroundings and where I was expected to live, must have resembled what it was like in 1944. I was scheduled to be here, trapped on an island way out in the Pacific, until my scheduled return to California on February 23, 1969.

Guam is the largest and southernmost island in the Mariana Island archipelago. Typhoons occur here, especially in August, and there are frequent squalls during the rainy season. America's day begins here first, and the area is known as the gateway to the west Pacific and Asia. The white sand beaches, palm trees, cliffs, and coral reef coastline look like an awesome Warner Brothers movie setting. It is so hard to believe that I would be subject to daily harassment here and begin counting days left on my tour, almost immediately.

To this day, I still have a recurring nightmare regarding Guam. The dream is always identical to others I've had over the years. I am walking on base as the sun beats down from a dark blue sky. Others think I have just arrived on the island and I frantically try to convince them that I have already put in my 16 months in the Pacific and don't belong overseas again ."I have already been here and done my time," I plead. But nobody listens and I feel trapped at Andersen all over again, knowing I have all those days ahead of me on a rock that I already lived on. I wake up restlessly in a cold sweat and immediately thank God aloud that this is just a dream and not reality. It has been 35 years since my plane descended on a tiny dot in the Pacific. Guam had such an impression on me, that it emerges in the form of dreams and will probably be part of me forever.

The original "rock" was Alcatraz Penitentiary, located just over a mile off the coast of San Francisco. While outside the prison (closed in 1963), seagulls and spectacular views are seen, the interior held hardened criminals such as Al Capone. I am not a hardened criminal. I may as well have been on Guam though, if the treatment received is any indicator. I figure four things were accomplished here. My job was done to the best of my ability (Airman's Records), I continued to shine in athletics, I made friends for life, and matured and survived with the realization that life can deal some rotten cards.

Andersen AFB is located at the northern end of the island. While I was here in 1968, 550,000 U.S. military personnel were in Vietnam. America's longest war came to an end when South Vietnam surrendered to North Vietnamese forces on April 30, 1975. I flew in the war zone on November 3, 1967, on my way to U-Tapao Airfield, Thailand, where I spent nearly two months. What I saw below, was green foliage and pretty green countryside. Killing would be the last thing you would ever suspect from viewing the scenery below.

Andersen AFB was named in 1949 in honor of Brig General Roy Andersen, who was chief of staff at Harmon Field, Guam, in 1945. That year (February), Andersen's plane disappeared on the way to Hawaii. Andersen was a strategic site, three hours away from Taipei, Taiwan (where I went on leave), Tokyo and Manila. Operation Arc Light (bombing missions) began here on June 18, 1965 and continued for eight years. Vietcong base operations plus enemy troops and supply lines were targeted. Eventually, the rapid buildup of B-52s and KC-135s (planes) on Guam began to sink the island and steps had to be taken to ease the burden.

The Guamanians who call this place home, appeared to always be smiling. It may have been because they knew they had a New York boy trapped for awhile. You could frequently hear the words "Hafa Adai" spoken, which is like saying good morning or how are you. While that may have been how the natives viewed life on the island, I would quickly begin fitting in with my fellow "inmates" by saying "Guam is good" and "I hate this fucking place" many times during the course of a military day. Is it any wonder that it didn't take all that long for me to be branded as a guy with a derogatory attitude?

I walked off the plane in a hot sun and looked toward the Andersen terminal. Once inside, a big guy wearing glasses extended his hand. "I see you made it to Guam," said Douglas B. Smith. Smitty had a booming voice, a radiant smile and a constant plan in his head. I had met the master of all con artists in my first few minutes on Guam. Hailing from Blue Ash, Ohio (not far from Cincinnati), he once told me his dad had been in politics there. Smitty was comical, smooth talking, calculating and one of the best needlers I would ever come across. The witty Airman got me out to a spot called "Marbo" and got me set up in one of the six barracks' located out there.

The floor was a dark brown, there were many double bunks separated by gray lockers (cubes) in the open bay barracks. You looked through louvers instead of windows to see outside. What you saw was a dumpster that smelled to high heaven, Airmen walking in the sun or rain (depending on what minute you looked out) and the Philippine Sea in the distance.

Smitty helped me secure my linens (including my pink bedspread) and smiled widely. "Well, my boy," he began. "It looks like you've been had." He said Lehman was on base and that I could catch up to him later on. "Red Williams (Sergeant in charge at barracks) will have your ass up with the rest of us in the morning," Smitty asserted. "We are up bright and early to clean up our cubes before going to work." I gave my sponsor a blank stare which got him laughing. "Take it easy my boy," he said. "You have only 546 days to go." Many times in the coming months, I would enjoy Smitty's humor and it would get me through some rough days.

Smith left me in my new surroundings with many thoughts racing through my head. My eyes fixed on a nearby gray locker that had a rebel flag attached to it. I counted out four double bunks in our cube and wondered where the other seven guys came from. It didn't take long to find out what the deal was, as I was informed by someone, that all seven hailed south of the Mason-Dixon line. "They're all pissed off cause the guy that left was from the South and they know a Northern troop is replacing him. They wanted to keep their cube totally Southern."

Knowing I had two strikes against me already, I met the first of the seven, Garland (Carl) Corrigan Butler III of Portsmouth, Virginia. "Well, I see you met Smitty already," the lanky and smiling Butler said. "And Willie Lehman is a friend of yours. He sleeps over there," he said pointing across the aisle. I was learning that Douglas B. Smith knew just about everyone on the island and he had pet names for the unsuspecting souls he came in contact with. Smitty had named Carl Butler "Tube" because he said Carl always got drunk on two beers.

Some of the other states represented in this cube, were Tennessee, Alabama, North Carolina and Georgia. Once I met all of my "neighbors", there was a getting-to-know- you period. They chuckled at my "accent" and had me repeat certain words so they could laugh again. I learned later on, that they were very skeptical of me because I was from New York. "We figured you might try to rob us in the night," one of them grinned.

Smitty reappeared sometime later, and saw me talking to Butler. "Hey Butler," he said. "Don't you know the Civil War is over? Get that God damned Rebel flag off of there." Butler threw his body in front of the flag in mock horror and retorted "You're nothing but a damn Yankee." As time went on, I developed friendships with my Southern buddies. "For a Yankee, you're not all that bad," Butler said one day. "We don't even think about where you come from anymore." They had long since removed the Confederate flag because a New Yorker had successfully penetrated their turf and the area wasn't totally Southern anymore.

In the evening I had some beers with Lehman and proceeded to chew his ass because of the misleading correspondence he had sent me. "I wanted you to suffer right along with me," he explained. "But, I never figured you were dumb enough to swallow that bullshit in the letter."

I found out Smitty had designated himself "the official greeter" of new guys on the base. He would give them an old fashioned pep talk about how nice the island is and then proceed to pump the guy for beers all night. Add me to the list of his victims. We sat in the Filipino Club (we called it the Flip Club, near our barracks), and downed the suds on my first night. It is there that I met my supervisor, a Tech Sergeant Anthony Gagliano from Massachusetts. Smitty was begging for him to give me off the next morning as I was so new. "Come on Gecko (nickname for Gagliano), give him a break," he said. But there would be no mercy shown, as I reported to the monstrous Building 21000 eight miles away, on base, the next morning.

When I returned to the barracks I saw a small lizard type thing on one of the louvers. "That's a gecko," one of the guys said. "They go on the louvers and ceiling but won't hurt you. They are after sweet things to eat, too." Wishing I could sack out the next morning, I pictured "Gecko Gagliano" on the louver and drifted off to sleep.

Smitty had warned me about the bosses that would be lurking at Building 21000. "They are snakes Bill," don't trust them, cause they will stab you in the back," he cautioned. One of my superiors was Senior Master Sergeant Wiley Price. He was a quiet guy who obviously didn't care much for young enlisted types. He constantly said "no" to requests and threw his weight around a lot. It didn't take long for me to get on his bad side.

One day he told me my hair was too long and I better get to the barber shop right after work. "Watch out for Price," Smitty told me. "I don't trust him as far as I can throw him. He will try to get you busted in a second." I was still getting acclimated to the island, where it seemed that everyone was named Guerrero. Price was adamant about his hair cut order, so I slugged down a few beers with Smitty and we both got the haircut of our lives.

Smitty suggested we fix Price once and for all. He had a plan all hatched and the two of us stumbled into the barber shop and got our heads shaved with a straight razor. Years before anyone ever heard of Michael Jordan, the two of us showed up for work the next morning bald as cue balls. Price ripped us for having "bad attitudes" and told us our day was coming. In the meantime, everybody at work laughed their asses off when Smitty and I appeared with our chrome domes. Misery loves company, and so we went everywhere together until the hair grew back in.

There were last names like Ruby, Kublik, Elkins, Gambaiani, Rooney, Pransky and Webster in the barracks. Smitty would walk down the aisle and quickly spit out "Ruba, Kuba, Elka, Gamba, Roona, Pranska, Websta, Tanga (pronounced like tango)." He would keep adding names and had a list a mile long that he would spew in a frenzied rush. One day he added "Newga" to the group. When queried about the addition, he pointed into the corner at a quiet person near his locker. "This is Newg" he said. "He is a new guy who just got here a couple of hours ago, Tanga. You're becoming a veteran of the rock."

Sundays, Lehman would drop by my bunk and announce that it was time to vacate the barracks. "Time to go to church," he would say. With that, we would begin walking down the road, in the middle of the jungle, toward Carman's Bar. Carman's was our "church" and we imbibed with gusto. Ott and I also were known to walk to Carman's and Mussel's Bar in Yigo (pronounced Jeego) on the way to base, usually at night. I would be flat broke when I approached Frank and talk him into getting dressed and going out. His compensation was flipping me a ten, drinking on it and getting the money back on payday. You just can't trust those guys from Long Island.

The Flip Club was the place to be when your money supply was low. For a decent price you could get a chopped steak and rice dinner and a couple of beers. I still hear those Filipinos running around the place shouting "choppa steak, choppa steak." When Typhoons approached the island, there were different levels of alerts issued. One of them stipulated that you had to remain wherever you were, until it was safe to go out. So of course when things got bad, I literally ran to the Flip Club so when I was stuck, it would be at the bar.

One of the great challenges every morning was getting to work on time and in one piece. About every 15 or 20 minutes the blue and late-running "Marbo bus" would appear out at Marbo and a huge crowd of GI's would literally fight their way on the bus while pushing, shoving and even punching to get a seat. The strong survived while those who gave up, were left waiting for the next bus and a repeat performance of the savagery.

If I was not in the mood to start the day with a fist fight, I would just hang out and arrive at work later on. Price would notice me arriving late. "Where you been, Tangen?" he would ask in his low and bland voice. When I explained the situation, he didn't want to hear it. "That is no excuse, just get here on time," he used to say. "I don't care how." The "don't care" are the key words here. Most of the lifers (in Air Force until retirement) on Guam, were venomous snakes, just as Smitty had told me. They lived in quarters with their families and didn't give a rat's ass how tough we had it in a rotten barracks located out in the middle of nowhere.

Sergeant Wayne Partie didn't fit the mold of the typical lifer. He was a laid back individual who had a refreshing sense of humor. Ed Merrick from Massachusetts (who did a great John Kennedy imitation) worked for him. It was kind of like a Plunket-Sewall thing all over again. Merrick, a slender curly haired man, was a comedian who livened up whatever room he happened to be in.

Partie invited a whole bunch of us out to his house one weekend. Now remember, the girls on the island were Catholic, and their fathers kept a close watch on things. The single guys climbed the walls for women and really shouldn't have even been allowed in mixed company.

187

After a few beers the guys loosened up and sexual innuendoes complete with four-letter words, flew around with regularity. I guess Mrs. Partie was used to the heathen mentality of the troops and Wayne just smiled through it all. Later, when we tried to apologize, he brushed it off easily. "Hey, you guys have it tough over here," he said. "We realize that."

One Sunday, Merrick had been to a fiesta (event with much food and drink) and arrived back at the barracks in wonderful condition. He had driven his compact car to the street in front of the barracks, left his car running in the middle of the road, and promptly came in and passed out on his bunk. When Smitty offered to help, Merrick opened his eyes and threatened to kick his ass all the way back to the states. Doug Smith went about 225 pounds and Merrick around 145. Merrick drifted off to sleep again and Smitty, with that booming voice, informed everyone in our bay of the situation. "Well gentlemen, there he lies, Easy Ed Merrick," the joker announced.

When we had money, there was no chow hall being visited. There was a place close to it, where you could get burgers, fries and soda. At weekend breakfasts, Lehman introduced me to ham and cheese omelettes. The meat in the hamburger had a real sharp taste to it, nothing like United States ground round. Like everything else on Guam (other than liver), I got used to it in time. Every day on the bus ride to work, I would pass a field of huge carubao (water buffalo) grazing on the right side of the road. It seemed to me, the herd was dwindling as the days went by, and I looked at my hamburgers with increased skepticism.

The joint next to the chow hall was open at all hours, so one time, in the wee hours of the morning, I arrived there in a sea of suds to grab some burgers to go. As I went up the outside stone steps to the third floor of the drab and gray barracks, I had a brilliant idea. I would share my food with good old Willie Lehman.

Lehman was asleep in his bottom rack, and so I shook him gently. "Hey Willie, I brought you a cheeseburger. Here man, eat up," I whispered. "It is four o'clock in the morning," Lehman said. "I want to get some sleep, get your ass in the bed." This pissed me off to no end, so I glared at him for two or three minutes. Finally I prepared to walk away and left with these final words. "Lehman, you're an ungrateful bastard." I heard Butler and a dozen other voices begin to laugh. I crawled up on my bunk and passed out with a cheeseburger on my chest.

At my job site there was a real blend and mix of Americana. The tanned Captain Robert Stillman was the head honcho of my section. Sergeants Ferguson and Bill Ferris (career Air Force), Ron Brewer from Texas, Bob Dodge, Californians Paul Gambaiani and Bernie Pransky, John Erdmann, Peter Rooney and Smitty were some of the people I worked near. Stillman pitched and I played third base on our weekend "beer team." Colonel Collins, the highest ranking officer in our section, also played on the squad.

Smitty had his own personal waiter in Bob Ruby, an Airman with one stripe, who had been in the Air Force for way more than four years. "Ruba, go downstairs and get me some coffee and doughnuts," he would command. "As an extra bonus, you may buy for all of us, today. God Ruba, you are a poor excuse for a human being. Now get going. And find time to sandblast those things you call teeth."

From day one, I learned to hate getting up for work. Red Williams, from Georgia, was a strict disciplinarian in the barracks. This early morning GI party was a real favorite of the guys. I still see Sergeant Doke shaking Lehman awake. "Let's see some action," Doke said. "I'll show you some God damned action," Lehman barked back.

"Hey sarg, I work nights and never get to bed until five o'clock," Jack Christoff said to Williams one morning. "Do I still have to get up with the others and police my area?" Williams hit Christoff with an icy stare and said "nobody gets out of this." Christoff shook his head in disgust and began sweeping the floor. Smitty had heard the whole thing and wasted little time in ribbing Jack. "Well, if it isn't Jack Pistoff," he said.

Life at the barracks was just plain miserable. People survived and went back to "the world" (United States) while new personnel joined us in Guam's morale capital at Marbo. A couple of guys left and were replaced by Jon Taylor, who we called "Tadpole" and another fellow with a hairy chest, who of course, became known as "Tamba." I also became acquainted with Bill Vokolos, Dennis Markman, Clark Gross, Perry Harris from South Carolina, Mel Greenblatt of New York and Bob Andrus, a great softball player, from Port Arthur, Texas.

I wrote letters to Christine nearly every day and that helped maintain my sanity. In the upper left corner of the envelope I sent, was a blue outline of the island. I would write next to that outline, the number of days I had left to go. After two months were gone on my tour, I found myself under 500 days. "If I had close to 500 days to go, I'd kill myself," a smart ass told me. "My day will come," I replied.

On the way to work I would always see a Pan American plane on the runway to my left. "That plane is going to the world," I would think aloud. "And one day, it will be my plane. I will be getting the hell off of this island for good." In reality, I would escape this place on two other occasions, once to Thailand and once to Taiwan.

Lehman and I played the Air Force game but had plenty of time for fun. He used to do officers' records checks and the brass got along great with him. Sometimes Willie would get a real serious look on his face and then ask me, "are you authorized?" He would walk around for a second, then stop at attention. Pointing a finger he'd say "you better be authorized."

Hum drum life on the island went on. But one day, excitement was about to come into my bleak and boring life. An assignment came down for U-Tapao Airfield in Thailand. Only two people in our section were eligible, a Staff Sergeant (four stripes, Jack Bynum) and myself, a two striper (Airman Second Class). Bynum, who later became my basketball coach, could have just accepted the assignment because of his rank, and cut me out. Instead, he wanted to be totally fair and gave me a chance to escape the island.

Bynum, an easy going black guy, fished a shiny nickel out of his pants pocket and said a coin flip would determine who would be headed to Thailand. "Call it," he said as the coin tumbled toward the floor. "Heads", I shouted as I crossed my fingers with hope. The stoic bust of Thomas Jefferson lay face up and I had officially gotten myself a plane ride.

The Saturday before I left, Marbo was in the midst of a near race riot. Some black guys from the barracks across the way, started throwing marbles at the louvers and taunting us to meet them outside. The Southern guys were more than willing to take them up on the offer. "Hey, this is just like back home," Butler said. The Air Police took forever to arrive, but managed to quell the situation, at least for that night.

James Boyle, who I had seen around before, was going on the same flight as I was. He was a Colonel's son and did everything by the book. He struck me as a proper type who was a favorite of officers because of his military bearing. Leave it to me to be stuck with a goody two shoes. As it turned out, I learned to never judge a book by its cover. There were two Jim Boyles--the military Boyle and the one who liked to have fun and enjoyed a good joke.

Lehman told me I was going to love Thailand. "You lucky bastard," he said. "You will be drinking in town with girls all over the place. I have been in Thailand and you are going to hate to come back here." Willie wound up being correct as I arrived in a make believe type world that included 10 cent cans of beer (the base beer garden) and wall to wall women at the main gate, who were just waiting for Airmen to head to town.

I looked down to watch the island of Guam get smaller and smaller beneath me, as my aircraft rose in the sky. "What a pretty place," I said to myself. "Too bad they ruined it with an Air Force base." Soon I was over Vietnam and then landing at U-Tapao Airfield. This base was a strategic installation that pounded away at Vietnam in night raids. I was located 116 miles south of Bangkok and directly west of Cambodia and South Vietnam.

I left a disciplined military atmosphere and entered a scene where we worked hard but partied our asses off. U-Tapao was straight out of the TV show MASH. Somewhere on this base, Hawkeye Pierce and B.J. Honeycut had to be lurking. When you saluted an officer, they either gave you the finger or told you salutes weren't needed here. The Major in charge, acknowledged us in his office and poured us a whiskey. Then we received our briefing, which was largely composed of how not to get venereal diseases that some of the Thai women carried. "They (the women) get tested regularly," the Major said. "And different color cards are given to show whether they are safe or not. Of course these girls have been known to switch cards, so you really don't know where you stand."

The officer concluded his little talk as Boyle and I joined him in a toast. "To the guys from Guam," he said. "The work is hard and the hours are long. But they will have to drag you out of here to go back to that island." We clinked glasses and the Major stood up. "I don't know about you guys, but I'm going back to the beer garden. You can find your living quarters later on. Now follow me, because cold beers are waiting. And that's an order."

While this Major was a real winner, the fellow in charge of me, was a black Major named Darl W. Stephens, the Chief of Personnel. He saw the job I did in Airman's records and sent me back to Guam with a nice letter of appreciation. The duty in the 4258th Strategic Wing was a sharp contrast from the 3960th on Guam.

Boyle and I went out on the town that night and we discovered some great bars. Girls, something we weren't used to, lingered wherever the eye would roam. We took a "baht bus" outside the main gate and immediately feared for our lives. We rode the primitive roads in the back of what looked like a small pickup truck, as the driver attained speeds that would rival that of the Indy 500. Once I saw a baht bus hit a pedestrian and the unfortunate soul lay bleeding in the road. Nobody made a move to help him though, because I was told it was against the area's religion.

A dynamic place that night was "The Brongo Bar" where an American GI did a great job on Chuck Berry's Johnny Be Good. We slugged down tall brown bottles of Singha beer and life was but a dream. It was explained to us that the alcohol content in this product could be anywhere from six per cent to God knows what.

Boyle and I lived in a hootch (screened in cabin) and had house girls to do our laundry and shine our shoes. One day I came back from work to find Boyle's rack bare and his belongings gone. I was told that his dad had died in the states and Jim was now on emergency leave. Suddenly I had the hootch all to myself but actually began to miss Boyle, who was a really good person. I reflected about how crazy my military life had become.

When I left the security of Plattsburgh, I began a precipitous slide into the chaos of Andersen AFB. A two-man room became an overrun open bay barracks with little or no privacy. A bathroom that joined two rooms changed into one large area with community showers. The showers in Thailand were much more comforting. Can you guess why? Here is a pretty good hint. The night I arrived, I was standing under a shower head when I happened to notice a person a few feet away. That individual just happened to be a house girl. I was to learn quickly, that there was nothing out of the ordinary to have three or four ladies in there with you. They soaped up and rinsed off with no embarrassment at all. Life and culture was very different in this section of the world.

The most excitement back on "the rock" was the weekend race skirmishes and the 1967 World Series. The Cardinals knocked off the Boston Red Sox four games to three as pitcher Bob Gibson, base stealer Lou Brock (52 thefts) and Curt Flood (.355 batting average) won the title, 7-2, at Boston, on October 12. Gibson struck out 10, hit a homer and tossed a three-hitter before 35,188 fans. It was also the year that Carl Yastrzemski of Boston, won the triple crown.

There was one major drawback in Thailand. I have never particularly loved snakes and saw just a couple in all my years of fishing the Delaware River. However, the venomous and deadly coral snake inhabited our area. Snakes weren't a problem on Guam but were a force to be reckoned with here. We were advised to wear combat boots and drape a blanket around the legs and ankles when walking along the gravel path to the shower building at night. The multi-colored coral snake is nicknamed "the two stepper" for a good reason. I was told that two steps after you are bitten, the venom hits your heart and you are a goner.

I wound up befriending a big and comical guy named Fred Zinn. Zinn, who I think had spent time in Plattsburgh, used to tease me about coral snakes all the time. We would be sitting outside, drinking a beer, and I'd hear a buzzing or chirping sound off in the weeds. "You know what that is," Zinn would say. "That's a two-stepper coming to say hello." This guy who looked and acted like Jay Leno, didn't amuse me with this kind of comedy.

A house girl named "Somechi" washed my clothes in a big soapy bucket while smiling constantly. How she stayed on her haunches for so long, is beyond me. Some of the other lady workers would stop by from time to time and helped Somechi with her duties. These women looked at pictures I showed them with puzzled and curious looks. Their eyes were big as pies when they viewed images of snow in New York. "Number one" (which means good), they would say in excited voices.

As I prepared for another work shift, I could smell burgers being cooked at a nearby base eatery. The chow halls here served fantastic food but the convenience of being right next to this place, lured me more than once. The beef tasted great and the milk was cold in this section of Thailand. I noticed there was no ketchup though and substituted plenty of mayonnaise along with lettuce and tomatoes.

I began my assignment here on the day shift. Stacks of paperwork appeared on all the desks at my duty station. It was very hot and fans swirling around warm air, was one of the constant sounds that became familiar. I was sapped by the heat and lost plenty of weight in my time away from Guam. For me, a work day meant work, play and sleep in that order. Sometimes one of those areas suffered and I found myself coming directly from play to work quite a bit. Unlike Guam, there was no time to compete in sports but it didn't really seem to matter.

In Thailand many of us acted out the words to a popular song. "If you can't be with the one you love, love the one your with." We all lived for the second we could escape work and enjoy a little bit of relaxation.

My job section had to be one of the most confusing on the base. The only thing missing was the guy from Saturday Night Live shouting "cheeesebuga, cheesebuga, cheesebuga. No coke pepsi." The three of us that worked this job were all named "Bill." Bill Dovel from New Mexico and Bill Carter from somewhere down South, both outranked me. Dovel was an aggressive worker while Carter was laid back and took things as they came. Both made my job comfortable and the lack of strict discipline helped us churn out the mountains of work.

Meanwhile, back at the ranch, I had a good thing going on "the strip" downtown. Like Ricky Nelson's song "Travelin Man" I had a girl in every bar (instead of port). Two stood out from the others though. A short little girl named Mollie, used to wait for me to arrive in the bar after work. She would take a tremendous high flying leap into my arms, give me a big kiss and immediately begin shaking me down for jukebox quarters. She focused her eyes on my blonde hair and blue eyes in fascinated amazement. When I was ready to head back to the base, she would shout "you no go," and then tears began rolling down her face. I would be lying if I said that I didn't like the wine, women and song of Thailand. I was far from being a prude, but really looked forward to the music and booze after a long work shift.

I had become a pessimistic person on Guam but was transformed into an affable kind of guy in Thailand. If I arrived at bars in the daytime, I would interact with the young kids who played outside in the dust and sub-standard conditions. It brought joy to my heart to play ball with these devilish little people. All they wanted was some good old fashioned attention. And I went out of my way to bring smiles to their faces. I looked forward to the childish voices saying "sawasdee kap" (hello and goodbye). As it turned out, mine weren't the only silent tears shed, when it was time to pay the fiddler and head back to Guam. I would be leaving behind countless friends from both America and Thailand.

Prior to coming here, I had played a little bit of basketball outdoors under the blue sky and cotton ball white clouds of Guam. Markman, from Minnesota, was an individual who was real deep and complex. He would be smiling one second and upset with something the next. I never had a problem with Denny, but a friend of his, named Gary, was a different story. This Gary person was an arrogant type, who was sarcastic and self-centered. He played a good game of basketball but his disposition was conceited and phony. He didn't care for me either, and he took that dislike a step further.

This lanky fellow happened to work in Military Pay, where the checks are actually sent out. Mine was supposed to be forwarded to Thailand for the duration of my temporary duty. It was extremely curious that I had trouble getting paid. Tracers were put out, but in the meantime, I had to write home for money plus get small partial payments at U-Tapao. There is no doubt that my pay had been sabotaged by Markman's rotten buddy. I confronted him upon arrival back on Guam and my oratory met with blank stares and fiendish grins. I vowed to get even with the son-of-a-bitch, but let it drop as time went by. I knew that someday and in some way, life would deal this jerk a severe jolt.

If you want to see a miserable Airman, just picture a guy in a far off land who is wandering around with no money and a set of irritated eyes. Licking my wounds from the military pay woes, I contacted a severe case of conjunctivitis (pink eye).

I felt like I had grains of hard sand in my eyes as the membrane covering them, became inflamed and resulted in swelling. As if this wasn't enough of a blow, the house girls all began yelling at me and calling me "number 10" (not good, real bad). I rubbed my hurting eyes and asked what in the hell I had done to deserve this type of treatment. They continued screaming at me and indicated that my interaction with Thailand's ladies, had caused my eye condition. If you want a real challenge, try defending yourself from a ridiculous verbal barrage, when there is a language barrier. I finally gave up, put a pillow over my head and let them rant and rave.

U-Tapao was constructed in 1965 and became operational in April 1967, just seven months before I arrived. In November 1967, there were 25 B-52's stationed here on 11,000 feet of runway, in this remote area on the Gulf of Siam. At night, I heard the cadence of the aircrafts' engines as they prepared for another bombing mission over Vietnam. The blue runway lights that caught my attention in Texas, were calming and serene. I wonder if pilots and crews, perhaps heading out for the final time, felt any comfort at all.

I was taken off the hustle and bustle of daytime work and began a two man night shift with Sergeant Jim Hoffman. The demeanor of Hoffman made Bill Carter seem like a raving lunatic. He said very little, was easy to work with, and kept things calm and efficient. They say opposites attract, and in this case, it was true, as Hoffman and I became fast friends. He was not a big drinker, but on nights off, we hit the bars on the way to Sattihip (nearest town to the strip). I would have to leave the ladies and drinks behind, in order to make my 10 p.m. shift. After dragging through the night, I would stumble back to the hootch and fall into bed. There was little sleep, because the house girls showed up with their excited banter. I suddenly identified with Jack Christoff and how the lack of sleep sucked.

What I recalled most about the night shift, was hearing some great oldies on the radio. The one that stood out from all the others, was Bobbie Gentry's "Ode To Billy Joe." Whenever I heard that tune and Gentry's sultry and sensual voice, I was instantly transformed from Thailand into southern sections of the U.S. where oppressive heat envelopes cotton fields. I felt the melancholy mood of a love gone forever and saw the hay being baled.

One of my daughters lives in South Carolina and that very song crossed my mind when I stood on her front porch in the shimmering morning sun. I gazed at nearby fields, barns and horse fences and felt the South. From grits and gravy to the famed Southern hospitality, this was the type of geographical background that lived in that song and my mind.

When I talk with a friend, Beth Virgin of Alabama, the tune sometimes enters my head also. She is in the land of Dixie where air conditioning is a way of life. Piggly Wiggly and Winn Dixie stores blend in with good old Southern fried chicken down there. When they say "good morning" they mean it. Most of all, family is an important ingredient in life, south of the Mason-Dixon line. That family vision came through in "Ode To Billy Joe" more than anything else. I realized that I wasn't just hearing the song, I was seeing it too. It sparked images of hard work, sacrifice, love and heartbreak on a sleepy, dusty, delta day. And even though I'm from the North, the South seemed like home to me, when I was all those miles away.

The Air Force mission was being fulfilled while I was in Thailand. The morale was simply spectacular as we waded through all that paperwork. When I had been on days, there was a rather bewildered Airman who showed up in our office without many of the documents he was supposed to have. His attitude became a bit testy as we did our best to take care of him. It was obvious he didn't appreciate our commitment and so we got even.

"Take these things over to Military Pay and make sure they open the white envelope," one of our workers told him. In that envelope, was a hand written note that said: "Tell this asshole to shape up. He has an attitude problem." We pissed our pants as he walked out the door and again when Military Pay called us up and cackled into the phone.

There was always plenty of humor going on to loosen up the troops. Back when Boyle had asked me what I thought the girls waiting outside the main gate were like, I said "they probably have black hair, brown eyes and speak Thai." That description fits just about everyone in the country.

My job performance never suffered here in the 4258th, as I welcomed any kind of challenge. Major Stephens pulled out all stops in trying to keep me in Thailand. He pleaded with Guam to extend my assignment and let me stay, as I was a valuable personnel link. His spirited campaign was futile though and I was notified that I would be going back to Guam in late December 1967. "Merry Christmas to me," I thought.

The letter of appreciation was impressive. "Airman Tangen is a fine example of the type of Airman desired in our line of duty," it said. "He worked many long and tedious hours here in Southeast Asia and always did so willingly and with true professionalism. Many times those hours were 0700 until 2200 at night. In addition, his ability to perform without close supervision was a tremendous asset and his Esprit de Corps aided immeasurably in the smooth operation of the unit."

The clock began ticking down to when I would have to say "sawas-dee kap" for good. I had grown close to a girl down on the strip named "Muli" and sometimes ate lunch with her at a shack behind the bar. She was a possessive and jealous type who had laid down ground rules right away. "You no go other girls," she had said from the beginning of our relationship. With piercing eyes she simply said, "Other girls number 10."

I continued to frequent other establishments but always had a sharp eye out for her "spies." When I asked a friend of hers what would happen if I cheated, she looked down under my shiny belt buckle and said "cut." Suddenly, getting out of Thailand started sounding like a good idea. My time in Thailand was drawing to a close and Muli somehow sensed that and made me promise to take her with me when I left. She couldn't comprehend that this type of request, was ridiculous. It was easier to just agree and go on with daily life.

My last lunch with her, was extremely tough. I had to act happy, although I knew that when night fell, I would be viewing the blue lights of the runway. She didn't act the same, and I saw a few tears escaping her eyes when I said I had to get back to work. I left with a heavy heart and took one last look at the shacks behind the bar. As I walked away, kids ran and played tag in the dirt. I picked up a ball, bounced it a couple of times, and fired a pretend jump shot at a non-existent basket. The crowd noise I used to crave, had been replaced by the innocent chattering of young voices, half a world away from the Port Jervis High gymnasium. Sadly, I knew that this basketball game had ticked down to its final buzzer.

Today, both the U.S. and Thailand have established diplomatic relations with Vietnam. There are no B52s in Thailand anymore and the 4258th Strategic Wing was replaced by the 307th just a few years after I left. But in 1967, the war was very real to us. Jeanne Dixon, who was right on with many of her predictions, reportedly said the Vietcong would infiltrate Cambodia and Laos in late 1967. She mentioned that they were centering in on U-Tapao Airfield and that there would be casualties. We had been placed on alert and given briefings on firearms and safety. Sand bags were now located near the hootches and I wrote a nervous letter home, informing my loved ones that I could wind up in the middle of some deadly action. Luckily enough, I never had to lift a rifle.

I had my share of angst when thinking about having to go back to Guam. As I watched the U-Tapao airfield whiz past me and the big bird lift into the air, I thought of the 1965 Simon and Garfunkel song and had to smile at how ironic the words were. It wasn't a winter's day but it was a deep and dark December. "And a rock feels no pain. And an island never cries."

Gone would be the optimistic spirit and refreshing will to live that I felt in Thailand. There would be no more kidding with house girls, drinking in the beer garden, baht bus trips to the strip, or happy squeals of young Thai kids. Instead it would be a return to fights at the Marbo bus, the backstabbing of certain lifers and the empty and rotten feeling of military harassment. This kind of depression made me feel that Billy Joe McAllister may have been on the right track by jumping off the Tallahatchee Bridge.

We were to refuel at Kadena AFB, Okinawa, on our way back to Guam. Flight plans became all shot to hell, when engine trouble forced us to remain in Okinawa. Kadena was a really clean base and had an immaculate Airman's Club. We had to stay all night so I was given quarters with a couple of other guys that I didn't know.

I immediately got the lay of the land and headed for Koza City, the nearby strip, where night life and girls took center stage. It was New Year's Eve 1967 and I was in a rotten mood, because I was forced to leave Thailand. I had enough money to tie on a good drunk, and that's exactly what I did. I bought drinks for the ladies and got into the swing of things. It was in the wee hours that I stumbled out of Koza City and back to the base.

My last recollection of the bar scene, was having a girl on each side of me at the bar. They paid plenty of attention to me and whispered interesting things into my ear. I had let my defenses down and drank in the festive atmosphere around me. My dread of going back to Guam eventually went away and so did my wallet.

The realization hit me like a knockout punch when the sun came up. I blinked through bloodshot eyes as I maneuvered to a bathroom and then began to get dressed. My two roommates (one who was a real ass) were still sacked out, and I started thinking of finding a coffee or beer somewhere. Hung over and sick to my stomach, the latter choice seemed like a logical antidote, to straighten out.

Reaching for my wallet on the dresser, resulted in nothing but air. My heart skipped a beat and the pulse quickened as I searched in my pants pocket, behind the dresser and under all the objects in the room. My wallet was gone. I retraced everywhere I had gone when arriving back at the barracks. I left no stones unturned but came up empty. "Oh God it was those girls," I thought. "One of them lifted the wallet."

The roommate I didn't care for, woke up and saw my frenzied state. He didn't appear too upset at my plight and he became a suspect. I remembered he had not been in his rack when I got back to the room. This jerk, vehemently denied stealing the wallet. I figure one of three things occurred. Either it fell out of my pants pocket in Koza City, the roommate took it, or a girl or girls grabbed it. I had heard horror stories of unsuspecting GI's being rolled here. Although money was gone, these GI's would sometimes find their wallets, containing all their important documents, in alleyways or garbage cans. I took a fast trip to Koza, to the area of the bars I had frequented. I found nothing.

Not only was I going back to a place I despised, I would be arriving on New Year's Day with no money and no military ID or social security cards. "Happy New Year to me", I thought as I dragged my weary body onto the plane. What would 1968 hold in store for me? As it turned out, the year was as diversified as can be imagined. At times it was painful, slow moving, and boring, yet those modes ended, with the sweet and exhilarating feeling of being a civilian again.

There were positive aspects to life on Guam. There were beautiful sunsets and scenic drives. Ferdinand Magellan discovered the island in 1521. I imagined what the place looked like in 1944 when the U.S. took it over again. Liberation day was July 21, 1944. I can see Red Williams storming the Japanese held island but stopping his heroic charge to check his watch. "Time to get the troops up," he would think in the darkness of early morning. "They have to clean up their areas."

There were traditional fiestas on the island and I would attend a couple of them as a guest. A fiesta includes religious and social activities built around honoring the patron saint of whatever village you are in. Other than fiestas, there was some entertainment around. Natives seemed to enjoy cock fights, which took place during the weekend. Only one chicken came out alive, while the other met his waterloo. While folks back home, considered boxing a brutal sport, they should check this one out. To me, this activity is sadistic and inhumane.

Guam is 800 miles from the equator and 1,500 miles from Manila. The island was actually on top of the tallest mountain in the world, rising from the deepest water. The Marianas Trench was 37,000 feet deep and 1,300 feet high, above the water.

Rusted remains of World War II tanks have been found here. There is a Spanish flavor on the island, which is filled with palm trees, jungles and breathtaking views of rock meeting ocean. Some of the villages include Dededo, Barrigada, Piti, Yona, Talofofo and Umatac.

Former Japanese soldiers have shown up here, years and years after the war ended in 1944. On January 24, 1972, Sergeant Shoichi Yokoi, who had been a tailor and then a military man, was captured. He wove cloth from tree fiber to make trousers and a jacket. He lived in a jungle cave for 28 years, near Talofofo. The heavily bearded man was anemic from a salt free diet and was found by hunters.

Yokoi had been listed as killed (September 30, 1944) but was very much alive. When he was found, he possessed scissors and a Japanese flag. Japanese soldiers preferred death rather than the disgrace of being captured alive. Yokoi died of heart failure, at age 82, September 22, 1997.

After a smooth flight, I felt the aircraft drop in altitude and saw the peanut-shaped island, surrounded by blue and green liquid, appear below me. Green palm trees swayed lazily in the breeze and near the coral reefs, the rocks glistened in the sun. Sharks inhabited the area beyond the reefs, but in my mind, the real sharks were located well within those reefs, and were attired in Air Force garb. I had left Thailand for the sounds and sights of "Hafa Adai", "Guam is good", KUAM radio, San Miguel beer (brewed in the tropics) and that awful open bay barracks.

I hauled my gear through the terminal and out front. "My God", I thought, "I'm back here waiting for that damn Marbo bus again." The runway passed on my right, as I proceeded out into the jungle and to that gray stone World War II barracks. Everyone crowded around when I walked to my bunk and tossed my belongings on it. I was asked about my flight, how life was at U-Tapao and of course about the girls. I looked at my friends and said the only words that came to mind. "I hate this fucking place."

I won my fight at the Marbo bus the next morning and made it to work on time. Sergeant Price glanced in my direction and said "how are you, Tangen?" I smiled back and said "much better, now that I am back in paradise." The one thing I will always remember about this office, is Bernie Pransky, a big black-haired guy, with great sarcasm, sitting there with a cheshire cat smile. "I love the Air Force," he would say. "Being here is such a great privilege. It is probably the best thing that has ever happened to me." We would both crack up and our bosses would shoot serious stares in our direction.

Danny Webster, from Tennessee, was a real joker. He was a tall, black-haired, good looking guy with a Jimmy Dean voice. He was also from the Bernie Pransky school of sarcasm. He would lumber up to you in the barracks with a face as serious as could be. "I feel so God damned good I might reenlist," he would say. That statement was always a favorite in the barracks.

Sundays were the day you could lie around, write letters, shine your shoes or just vacate the barracks. Some guys went off in "the boonies" for a day to block out military life, while others shot baskets or went to the base. Since Willie and I went to "church" at Carman's, we didn't stick around long. The song that always filtered through the open bay Sundays, was Johnny Cash's "Folsom Prison." We could sure identify with the words "and time keeps draggin on." Another favorite was "I Left My Heart In San Francisco," by Tony Bennett.

Lehman was the ring leader on the journey to Carman's. "Let's get going," he used to say, "we don't want to miss Mass." He was all of 24 years old (born May 13, 1943), but seemed much older than me. He wore black pointed type dress shoes and looked neat and clean on our walks through the jungle. Soon, he had recruited a bunch of bored barracks people who wanted to get away. We always hung our for a few hours at Carman's and Mussel's, located in Yigo, on the road to the base.

Mussel's was a favorite place of mine to be during the evening. They had a blonde bartender, older than me, who all the GI's were after. She had to be the wife of either an Air Force member or perhaps the husband was down at Naval Air Station, south of Andersen. There was also Marine personnel located down that way. They had a great jukebox that featured Jeannie C. Riley "Harper Valley PTA" plus Tommy James and the Shondells "I Think We're Alone Now" and The Young Rascals "How Can I Be Sure."

One time I was running short on cash, wanted to keep drinking and had to come up with some plan. Guys were betting on various things at the bar, so I figured a bet could be my way to make some quick money. "I'll bet you I can chug six 12 ounce bottles of Budweiser in under 10 minutes," I said. One of the men was interested in a $20 wager but lowered the time to five minutes. "Six minutes," I answered. "Six in six."

While I knew that winning the bet would mean some serious swilling of suds, I also had wheels turning in my head. I waited to hear the words "and you have to keep it down", but they never came. My plan was to swallow all the alcohol, but I realized I would be luckily afforded the luxury of heaving it back up, after I had consumed the final drop.

Everybody stopped what they were doing to view the wager and even the jukebox got turned down. I stood on the bar with my eyes focused on a clock that hung high in the air. The time piece had a second hand, so I could pace myself for the six minutes. The first three beers went down easily but the fourth was hard to toss down. By the time I hit number six, I had just 25 seconds left. I forced myself to fire down the remainder in two gulps.

While bar patrons cheered my victory, I sprinted out the front door to the parking lot. The cold liquid came back up the second I hit the lot. I looked like I had been through the war, but a crisp $20 bill was now sitting next to the empty brown beer bottles.

Bynum had welcomed me back from Thailand with open arms. He had heard I could shoot hoops, and asked me to come by the gymnasium, so he could take a look. When I reached the place, I noticed that Coach Bynum wasn't the only black guy to attend the team practice. In fact, I was the only white guy there.

Suddenly, I knew what a black guy on an all white basketball team felt like. A slender man with "Gunner" printed on an arm pad, fired up swishing jumpers from 20-feet out. Another player, nicknamed "Lefty" (Jack Leftwich) drove the lane and smiled as his layup kissed off the backboard and through the net.

Bynum immediately accepted me, while the rest of the team regarded me as an unknown quantity. I had joined a competitive and talented group, whose style was "run and gun." During layup drills I was fed a steady dose of James Brown music. "I feel good, I knew that I would."

I maneuvered myself into the starting lineup replacing Leftwich at one of the guard slots. Lefty and Bynum were best friends and for awhile it affected their relationship. "How could you do this to me?", I heard Lefty ask Bynum one day, when they thought I had left the locker room. "He is younger and quicker, Lefty," Bynum offered. "We need him out there, but you will get plenty of playing time."

As I began producing in points and assists, I gradually was accepted. It felt good to know I wasn't just a token white. I became affectionately known as "the blue-eyed soul brother," and even got all of that animated hand slapping down pat. Before a game, while the starting lineups were announced, we would all stand together and clap our hands loudly in unison. We were confident and filled with enthusiasm. I enjoyed every second of competing for this team. Young kids and their dads came to watch me, just like they would later in softball, and I was proud to have a sizable amount of fans behind me at games.

I hit double figures with regularity and Gunner and a guard named Baker, got used to my style play as I adapted to theirs. My teammates even tossed me a break during layup drills. Suddenly, from out of nowhere, came a couple of Beatles songs, that they worked into their soul music medley. "Man," one of the guys said. "Those damn Beatles just got to go. They got no soul or jive."

The team won lots of games and made the playoffs. Coach Bynum was real proud of us and let us know in his quiet way. Even Lefty, who continued to ride the bench, became my friend. When he was relating a story, he would stop in mid sentence and stare straight ahead with a real somber look on his face. "I'm serious as a heart attack," he would say, as we all broke out laughing.

Once we were playing a man-to-man defense and I was matched up against this guy named Moore. I always remembered his last name because of one thing that happened early in the game. The first time his team had to ball, he dribbled toward me, looked me in the eye and said "now I'm taking you underneath." I tried to stick with him but Moore, standing only 5-9", started with a stutter step, flew past me with a fake, and dunked the ball. I stood there in shock at what had just happened. "Get me some help with this guy or lets go into a zone," I said during a timeout. "Well I'll be," Bynum said. "You finally met your match. I told you black guys could jump."

Willie continued his love for fishing and could be seen time to time holding a rod and testing its weight. "I got him. Man this fish is huge," he would say as he pretended to hook his foe and reel him in. "Gotta keep the tip of this rod low," he said in a serious voice. "I don't want to lose him."

Work continued to be the usual grind as people processed in from the states in droves. I administered numerous Airman's records checks each and every day. I was becoming a veteran though, and somehow the days started to move swiftly by. Christine sent me letters to help my morale and sometimes she would send tapes from home.

If I got hung over, I would go downstairs in Building 21000 and get a large tomato juice from the snack bar. At this young age, I bounced back quickly and was ready for the bar scene once a basketball or softball game ended. On Friday nights, I sometimes stayed on base and slept in the office chair, rather than go out to Marbo and wait for a race riot to develop. As it turned out, my number was to come up one night, and I paid a painful price.

Webster, Lehman, Butler and myself became good friends and sometimes went out together. One time, we went to Agana and had a great dinner. Webster looked around when the check came and said "damn, we're going to have to burn the door." I had a puzzled look on my face until I realized what he meant. The meal had cost way more than we figured and there wasn't enough money to pay the bill. So, we went to the bathroom one by one and hit the front door the second nobody was looking. I expected to get caught pulling this caper, but the police never came after us. The next time the four of us went out, it was to the Airman's Club on base. It was a night that ended on a horrible note.

The night began innocently enough with me trying to get Lehman to hurry up and get dressed. "Ease up man," Willie told me. "You're too damn pushy." I needled Butler about a couple of things while I waited for Lehman and Webster. "Hey bird chest," I shouted across to his bunk. "You going to have your mouth fly open again in the bunk?" Carl just gave me a big grin and said "I'll tell big Sarge (Lehman) you're bothering me." Butler sometimes got this condition where the bones in his jaw locked and his mouth got stuck open. Sometimes he had to go to the hospital to get the jaw to close.

We sat at a table in the Airman's Club and were having a good old time draining our drinks and joking about military life. I saw a table of blacks, close to us, and they seemed to be staring us down. "What the hell is up with those guys?", one of us said. To my recollection, I don't recall any racial comments being said at our table. I could be wrong.

We hopped the Marbo bus and rode back out to the barracks to get some well-needed sleep. I remember walking down the steps of the bus but don't recall my foot ever hitting the ground. Instead, everything became a blur as I felt myself on the ground and being kicked in the head. There was a big black guy and some of his friends standing over all four of us and giving us the "boot jobs" of our lives. We were outnumbered and had been dead ducks as we walked into a planned ambush.

Several men shouted and ran from barracks porches to stop the assault and the attackers evaporated into the dark Guam night. I lay semi-conscious and felt the blood running down my face and into my eyes. My forehead had been kicked wide open and I tried to breathe until help could arrive from the base. One of my front teeth had been booted in and it was loosened in the vicious beating. Lehman had also been hit on and he was down on the ground as well. The other two, Butler and Webster didn't get it as badly and didn't require medical attention.

Sirens wailed in the night as we were transported from Marbo to Andersen. "Don't fall asleep," a medic told me. "You have a serious head injury." Willie took a couple of stitches in his lip, but I required 11 to close my wound. When I finally made it back to my bunk I was a shell of a person.

The next day, my face was swollen and an ugly black and blue. Friends came by the bunk to make sure I was alright and the reflection of the horror in their eyes told me how bad I looked. There would be no work and no food or drink for a couple of days. I touched my tooth from time to time, making sure it was still in the gum. At the hospital, they had told me to leave it alone and it might tighten back up (which it did).

I had to file a report with the Air Police on base. An Airman from Georgia wrote out my paperwork and asked me lots of questions. He said an investigation would be started in an attempt to find the perpetrators. "We think the guys that attacked you were here on temporary duty from Westover AFB, Massachusetts," he said. "They have already gone back to the states. It will be very hard to arrest anyone."

It was surmised that someone from the table at the Airman's Club had phoned Marbo and told their buddies what our descriptions were. The friends lay in waiting for us to arrive on the bus and carried out the attack. Meanwhile, those on temporary duty were close to leaving Guam for the states. I had been in the wrong place at the wrong time.

It was softball season on Guam and I walked outside building 21000 and felt the sun hit my healing face. The Philippine sea was a deep blue and the palm trees swayed in the breeze. Around to the front of the huge building, several of my co-workers had bought their coffees and were taking their morning break by walking parallel to the green railing that bordered the top floor. They looked down from time to time, seemingly non-chalant, but actually with a purpose.

Cars were parked down below the walkway and the bunch of us were professionals when it came to viewing pretty legs in vehicles. Sergeant Ferguson was the sharpest of us all. The lanky fellow with the light brown skin was an eloquent and intelligent individual. "Gentlemen," he would say. "I have to say that without a doubt, the legs on this fox are so fine they defy description." Every morning, with much chagrin, we would have to leave the skirts behind and return to our duty stations.

Down the hall from my bunk, in another open bay, lived a guy named

Jack Zea. Zea was a tanned Californian who dripped with competitiveness. The wiry yet powerful athlete, was our squadron softball coach and had me playing my customary centerfield and batting second.

Jack had this sign in his possession that spelled out the letters SCSOG. When I asked him what that was all about, he proudly announced, "Southern Californians Stranded On Guam." Jack, Ray Fleenor and some other West Coast Airmen were charter members of the club.

Like in basketball, we had a winning unit that always found a way to prevail. Neil Camburn from the Poughkeepsie, N.Y. area, pitched for us. The well built blonde and crew cut Camburn was fast and had great control. The team was loaded with stars and there was no weak part in our lineup.

While I handled the outfield with grace and speed I also contributed at the plate. The boot job had probably contributed to the blurring of my vision and I suddenly couldn't pick up the location of the ball as quickly. It seemed to be kind of fuzzy and I found myself suddenly struggling at the plate and flying out a lot. Being a line drive type hitter, I knew something was radically wrong. A Lieutenant on the team let me borrow his glasses every time I came to the plate and it got big results. As if by magic, I began pounding the ball again.

While going to the movies, bowling or watching the Andersen AFB Bombers football team play were pastimes on base, softball drew many spectators. They were treated to some of the finest softball played anywhere. I faced some of the best pitchers the Air Force had to offer but always held my own. At bat, I could adjust to any given situation. I would punch the ball to right field to move a guy from first to third or drop down a bunt on third basemen if they were playing too far back. I was very quick and so if I was on base, the question wasn't whether I was going to steal or not, but when.

One day a fellow named Bob Andrus processed in from the states. He was a serious kind of guy with the look of an athlete. I found out that he was going to work in the base gymnasium. I also learned another thing and that was that he had tried out for the Houston Colt 45s, a Major League baseball team. "They say he has an arm like a rifle," one of my teammates said. "And he is a centerfielder."

I had played center most of the time, since competing in city recreation softball in Port Jervis. Suddenly a very real challenge had been issued. I knew Andrus would be after my position but there was no way I was going to be unseated without a fight. "He is real good, Bill," Zea said. I'll put both of you out in center at practice and see what happens."

For the first time in my young life, I was beaten out for a position. I played capably but Andrus was simply out of this world. He hit his cutoff men with pinpoint accuracy, got to everything hit to him and had a throw to home plate that came screaming in at a low trajectory. It had been a fair and square battle for the position. I shook my head is dismay and congratulated this talented guy from Texas.

Zea met me as I came off the field and crossed the first base line. "How about third base?", he asked. "There is a lot of action over there." I ventured over to "the hot corner" and kicked the bag. It felt strange and very foreign but by the time I left the island, I was regarded as one of the best third basemen around. I became a student of the position, had a good arm, learned how to apply tags and played in dangerously close.

My reflexes were good and that preserved my front teeth. Sometimes, I got gut feelings that somebody was going to lay down a bunt, so I moved a step or two closer to the hitter. "Any closer and you'll be shaking hands with me," one batter said to me. I fielded some wicked liners down there and sometimes wonder how I emerged unscathed. When I finished a game, there was dirt all over my uniform from the completed battle. I would dive for grounders, throw from my knees and mix it up with base runners. I became a crowd favorite at Andersen and it felt great hearing the cheers or my name being called. All was well with this scenario, with one exception. There was a fan who came to all my games and got on my case big time.

He stood in the area of a restraining fence near third base and watched my every move. After one play at the base raised the infield dust, I not only put on the tag while getting down and dirty, but acquired a nickname. "Hey pig pen," the needler said. "I love the way you roll around in that dirt." I ignored this heckler for a few games but the constant banter was starting to get to me.

Finally I could absorb no more of this verbal barrage. Between innings of a game, I fielded grounders and listened to his yapping mouth. "You going to make an error this inning?," he yelled. "You're due to make some mistakes, pig pen." I walked past the third base bag and right to the fence as he swiftly backed up. "I'll see you right after the game," I said. "You really don't know me. But we can get acquainted real fast." His mouth suddenly became sewn shut as the contest progressed. I thought about "Branch" Wadsworth in Plattsburgh, and the limb he ripped down. Maybe it's a good thing there were palm trees on Guam and I couldn't reach the branches.

Of all games to make a silly blunder, this was the one. Cliff Coty, a slick shortstop and fine hitter from Connecticut, found a way to get into my head. He was coaching third base and there were two outs and a runner at second.

The next batter lofted a fly ball behind me at third. I back peddled and the ball came into my view. "I got it, I got it," I heard at the last instant. Thinking it was our shortstop calling me off, I ducked out of the way and let the ball go. There was no shortstop behind me, the ball dropped and a run scored. The guy that called me off, was none other than Cliff Coty. I felt about one foot tall as I slowly walked back to my position. "Sorry man, I had to try anything in order for us to score," Coty said. I glared out at the "pig pen" fan who previously ragged on me. He was too petrified to even think about uttering a word in my direction.

When I think about softball blunders, Jack Zea immediately comes to mind. Jack hated to lose and was a tactician who had his head in the game at all times. Well, almost all of the time. There was one occasion where we were competing in an important game and nothing seemed to be going right. We were trailing in a contest that would affect our seeding in the upcoming base championship playoffs.

Close plays went the other way, strikes and balls went against us and we seemed to be sleepwalking and just barely going through the motions. The intense Coach Zea paced the dugout and fumed at umpires and our players. Zea couldn't stand to lose and his neck turned a deep shade of red as the later innings approached. Softball games were seven innings long. After we batted in the top of the sixth, we trailed, 5-1. During our woeful performance, our dedicated coach had lost track of the inning and thought we had gone down in the seventh frame, without a rally of any kind.

After the third out of the sixth, Jack Zea went into a rage. Jack screamed at the top of his lungs "you guys robbed us" as his eyes shot daggers at the umpires. He slammed his fist against the dugout wall then threw all of our bats, one by one, onto the field. He fired our practice softballs into the outfield with a fiendish look on his face.

After tossing his softball cap on the dugout floor and stomping on it with his spikes, he happened to glance up and see us, in our defensive positions, as the game entered the bottom of the sixth inning.

Embarrassing moments? Think how he felt walking around the field to help retrieve softballs and bats. The crowd got a real charge out of it and became electrified. The temper tantrum had loosened us up. I looked at Zea, then the field and laughed into my glove at third. We retired the opposition 1-2-3 and then mounted a furious seventh inning rally that produced five runs and a nail biting 6-5 victory.

A certain defeat had become a stirring triumph. We gathered our belongings in the dugout and walked confidently away from the field. From that day forward, whenever we saw Jack Zea on Andersen, we would yell "you guys robbed us" and pretend we were throwing bats and balls on a field. Zea was a great sport about the whole thing though. He was a classy and fair individual who loved to succeed. The antics of that important night game has stayed with me now for 34 years.

Andrus turned out to be a real nice guy. He kept us loose on the softball field and in the barracks. Someone said that one day he was playing golf at Palm Tree Golf Course and missed a short putt. It is said that he calmly announced to his playing partners, that golf just wasn't the game for him anymore and that he would never swing another club.

They say Bob walked over to the edge of a cliff and the Pacific Ocean became the proud new owner of a an entire set of golf clubs, bag included. Andrus completed his activities by removing his golf spikes and throwing them far out into the deep blue water. That story could just be one of those old fictitious tales from the island of Guam, but if I was a betting man, I'd say it did happen.

The most fun, was playing beer softball games on Sundays. I even got a shot at pitching and developed blazing speed and a wicked curveball. Captain Stillman pitched and sometimes caught for us and Bill Ferris played first base. Ferris wasn't a great athlete, but he did a pretty good Lehman imitation. In fact he impersonated many of the workers in Building 21000, including the officers.

You would figure playing a beer softball game on Andersen AFB would be a risky thing. The keg glistened in the tropical island sun and the players refilled their glasses many times. What would happen if the Air Police caught us? And what would be the consequences if our commanding officer should happen by? Well, there was no sweat in either case. A group of Air Policemen were on the other team and the commanding officer? Well, he was playing the outfield for us.

Speaking of the Air Police, I did have one little experience with them. Willie and I worked some overtime one weekend and nipped on some Johnny Walker Black, while we went about our duties. I was located in a different section of Building 21000 from Willie. From time to time, I'd call him up and disguise my voice. "Are you from Rolling Hills, Oklahoma?", I asked during one of the crank calls. "Yes sir," he said. "I am from Rolling Hills and damn proud of it." (Willie was from Mooreland, Oklahoma).

As we became increasingly intoxicated, the calls became funnier. I played some songs that Chris had sent me from home (on a tape recorder) and was a happy camper. The song "Darlin" by The Beach Boys played and I blocked Guam completely out of my head. Out of my head, would have been a perfect description of how my condition became. Willie had sense enough to leave long before I did. I finally departed the office in an unsteady gait and made my way to a nearby bench. Waiting for the Marbo bus seemed to take forever.

I remember not being able to sit on the bench for any length of time. I was not used to Johnny Walker and it was taking a big toll on me. Three or four times, I kept sliding off the bench and onto the ground. The Air Police, who had an office in Building 21000, must have seen me teetering and falling. They came on the scene and escorted me to that office.

There was a real high desk in the room I entered and the Desk Sergeant looked down at me and asked for my military ID card. I quietly fumbled in my wallet and produced the document. While he left the room, I quickly moved down into duck walking position and exited the AP office, on my haunches. Once outside, I ran for all I was worth. I never comprehended that they now knew who I was and could find me easily.

I reached an oval field across from the bench I had been at and tried to sprint across it. This had to be the dumbest thing I pulled off during my escaping caper. While I set my sights on the other side of that field, an Air Police car was riding the roadway at the same time. When I arrived at my destination, the arm of the law was waiting for me.

"Get in, the Sarg can't wait to see you again," the fellow said. I got in the back seat and suddenly felt real sick to my stomach. Can you guess what happened next? I pleaded with the guy to let me out of the car but he wouldn't. Finally, I let loose and Johnny Walker appeared on the back seat and floor of the patrol car. To say the driver was livid, is the understatement of the year. His yelling nearly sobered me up.

I figure three things saved my ass from being arrested that day. I listened to what the two had to say, they probably cut me some slack because guys did get smashed on the rock and I indicated I would "fix" and Airman's records check for the driver of the car. He was slated to come into my office the following week and I told him I would sign him off, so he could take a little bit of free time.

The fear of God was instilled in me when the Sergeant dialed the number to my barracks, in search of the First Sergeant. He wasn't there or at his house, so he redialed the barracks. He was going to release me into the custody of the barracks CQ (charge of quarters), if they would come to get me on base.

I caught a big break when I found out the CQ was none other than Neil Camburn, from the softball team. "You are a wreck," he told me when he picked me up. "Let's go to a bar." And so, somehow I drank beer for an hour or so, before finally arriving back at the barracks. "Where the hell have you been?", Lehman inquired. "You don't want to know," I replied, as I fell in my bed, fully clothed.

The next day, I struggled to get out of bed and make it to work. I felt like Johnny Walker was doing a dance on my head. I walked past Christoff's bunk on my way out to the bus. The smile on his face, told me he was sleeping with the knowledge that his area was clean.

I caught up to Camburn by phone, on May 9, 2001, in Grand Forks, North Dakota. The 1957 high school graduate, had spent 25 years in the Air Force and was retired. He had been on Guam two times during that stretch, but couldn't place me. I told him the story of how good he had been to me that day in 1968. "We probably stopped at Mussels bar on our way to the barracks," he said.

My second escape from the island came in June 1968. I took a few days leave and decided to take an R&R (rest and relaxation) to either Australia or Taiwan. Australia seemed like too far of a plane ride, so I decided to go to Taipei, Taiwan. Sergeant Red Hitchings had told us that the women and drinking there, were just awesome. An Airman who worked in data processing, went on the same flight and we hung out together for awhile.

We went in a bar and immediately saw wall to wall girls. They were all angling to get picked up and had all their comments expertly planned. My blue eyes and blonde hair was immediately noticed by many of them. "You buy me drink?", they would ask with those big brown eyes shining. I already knew that the high-priced "drink" was probably some type of non-alcoholic juice. Any money that changed hands, was handled by the head honcho of the bar.

Taipei was not primitive as Thailand had been. The women were dressed well and establishments seemed pretty clean. Things became a selection process and you literally were shopping for a girl. They sat in a long line of chairs and looked up with pleading eyes. It put me in mind of animals in humane society cages, sporting expressive eyes that begged for freedom. Servicemen walked up and down the line as if shopping for a nice cut of meat. I realized I was messing with the culture of a country, but still found this practice to be degrading and barbaric.

In a way, I felt like I was freeing a woman from her bonds when I picked her out and quickly adjourned to a nearby booth. A GI and his girl shared the same booth and were getting along fabulously. I came across him later, and he told me they took a bath together and she walked on his back, to take away any tension he might have.

Securing a girl for her "date" was another thing straight out of Saturday Night Live. The owner of the bar (and probably the girls), made me fill out a questionnaire of sorts. On the paper was the date, girl's name, reason for the date and when the girl would return. Reasons included dining, movies and bowling. After consulting her, I checked the box for bowling and she smiled sweetly.

The tops of the pins appeared fuzzy to me and served as a reminder of the kicking to my head, which was probably affecting my eyesight. We arrived at my room in an impressive hotel in Taipei. I had already been tipped off that some of the Taiwan girls were famous for wanting to double their money. Seeing as though this lady had already sealed our transaction, she quickly came up with a convenient excuse to make her getaway. By giving me "the bum's rush" and getting off the hook, she would be free to hook up with another guy.

The official excuse in this case, was a sick grandmother. Rather than argue the point, I let her hustle me. It was the eyes of this person that continued to haunt me. She was trapped in life and had to use sex in order to eat. I considered my situation and how freedom to me, was firing down beers and being away from Andersen.

I flicked on the radio and heard some awful news from the U.S. On June 5, 1968, Robert F. Kennedy had been gunned down in an assassination attempt. Kennedy, 42, had won the California primary as he was actively seeking the presidency. He had just delivered a speech at the

Ambassador Hotel in Los Angeles, and had been shot in the hotel's pantry.

Sirhan Sirhan was charged with murder, when Kennedy, one of Joseph P. Kennedy's nine children, died the next day. Martin Luther King had been shot and killed in April and now Kennedy was the third major figure to die this way, in less than five years. RFK, a senator from New York, had managed John Kennedy's successful presidential campaign in 1960 and had later been Attorney General under his brother's administration.

I returned to Guam for the second time and the days began to go quicker. The last time I came back (1967), the Bob Hope Show had come to Guam. The famed comedian, who took his show all over the Pacific during the war, had appeared along with Barbara McNair and Raquel Welch. A friend gave me a glossy picture of Hope and Welsh (she wore a miniskirt) that would knock your eyes out.

On August 25, 1968, I went to the Flip Club to celebrate a year overseas. I ate a plate of "choppa steak" and washed it down with cold beer. I hoped a typhoon would suddenly bombard the island and keep me at the bar for a few days.

The flight over Vietnam in November, (war zone) had clipped 30 days from my assignment, or sentence, depending on how you looked at it. So, I was scheduled to arrive back at Travis AFB, California, on January 23, 1969. Christine was overjoyed with the news, and when I sent letters home, the number of days that I wrote (next to that outline of the island on the envelope), was dwindling.

Lehman's day in the sun finally came. He got his orders and would be going back to Plattsburgh again. I saw him off at the terminal and with a firm handshake told him I would look him up in Plattsburgh after I got back to the states. Butler and I said our goodbyes to "Big Sarg" as Tube used to call him, and I shouted some words to him as he walked to his plane. "Take care, you ungrateful bastard," I said.

Two big things happened in October of 1968. Pitcher Denny McLain and the Detroit Tigers won the World Series over the St. Louis Cardinals (four games to three) and I became a double digit midget (99 days or less left).

The brash and flamboyant McLain had a 31-6 season in 1968. He struck out 280 batters and was the first 30-game winner since Dizzy Dean (1934). The Tigers secured their first title since 1945 although McLain lost twice, but won game six. Before 54,692 people, the Tigers rode Mickey Lolich's pitching to victory over Bob Gibson and the Cards. I had pulled for the Red Sox in 1967 and they came up short. This time the Tigers, of baseball's American League, had shown the world.

I kept a short timer's chart on the inside of my locker. It started with 99 days to go, on October 16. I would meticulously begin coloring in all 99 sections of a gorgeous girl a day at a time, with a bright smile fixed on my mug.

One of the ceremonies for cracking 100 days, was to polish off a bottle of VO and affix the yellow and black ribbon from its neck, to a button hole of your shirt. This happy and drunken bash took place at Mussel's one evening. "Hey, you're the same guy that drank those six bottles of beer, aren't you?", a guy down the bar said. I was beginning to be a living legend in Mussels, which told me I had been on the island long enough.

Although Willie was already gone, I thought of him a lot. I began asking people if they were "authorized" and planned for the day we would party again. I saw that Pan American plane every morning as I cut my way through the jungle and out into the wide open land that is Andersen AFB. "It won't be long," I had said to myself day after day. Now that fantasy thinking was beginning to turn into reality.

My immediate boss was now John Erdmann, who I had known in Plattsburgh, and hadn't particularly cared for. Whether John changed, I did or we both did, it was for the best. For me, it was another case of judging a book by its cover. Erdmann wound up being a good guy and excellent boss. We used to tease the hell out of Peter Rooney all the time. Peter visited my parents when he was on leave from Guam. He read constantly and was on the nervous side. He was good at comeback lines and kept things light in the personnel section. Ferris was also a comedian who made the rigors of Guam pass quickly. He had sunk to a new low, by imitating Captain Stillman in his presence.

One time Erdmann had to drive down the island to deliver some paperwork. He selected me to accompany him and we decided to stop at a watering hole on the way back to base. We had left Air Force territory and were now south of Andersen, where Navy and Marine personnel were located.

I will never forget this day or the song Indian Lake by The Cowsills. We ordered up two beers and were in light conversation as a jukebox played in the background. Down at the end of the bar, was a solid and well-built fellow who looked a bit on the wasted side. I noticed that he kept staring at our uniforms and faces. "Wow, look at the flyboys," he said suddenly. "I hate anyone from the Air Force."

This trouble maker went on to say he was a Marine and that it was the only branch of service that existed in his mind. We tried to calm him down, but he would have none of it. "The Air Force sucks," he said. "And after this drink, I'm going to stomp both your asses."

I recalled the boot job I had received and thought "damn, not again." Erdmann and I quietly decided to put a wall at our backs and be ready for this obviously disorientated and fearless warrior. As we moved away from the bar stools, Indian Lake started playing near us. "And you keep on driving till your out of the city," could be heard as the Marine advanced.

Suddenly he got a puzzled look on his face, turned and walked away. "I apologize," he asserted. "Sometimes I get carried away. Let me buy you guys a drink." As the words "Indian Lake is a scene you should make with your little one," played, we settled down for a beer. We left in one piece and wondered if the guy later pulled his Jekyll and Hyde trick again.

My heartbeat quickened considerably, when an Air Force directive came down that stated anyone who served in Southeast Asia (between certain dates) and had less than a year to go in service when they hit the states, had the option to be honorably discharged from the Air Force. I thought this had to be too good to be true, because it looked like I qualified for an early out.

When I would arrive at Travis, there would be less than seven months left in my enlistment. When I found this applied to me, I was ecstatic to say the least. My days were chopped even further and it would be early in 1969 when I would be going home. There was a written document that indicated if any flights could be secured prior to Christmas, and was approved by appropriate people, I could be off the island and discharged in time for Christmas of 1968.

I quickly filled in a bunch more of my short timer chart and inquired at the terminal about December flights to California. I was lucky enough to find a seat on a plane leaving Guam December 23, but needed approval to make the flight. Wiley Price had been a thorn in my side since the second I walked into Building 21000 in August of 1967. He sat at his desk and smugly told me that he wouldn't allow me to go home for Christmas and that I would not be leaving until January.

I pleaded with his sense of fair play and found that when it came to me, there was no fair play to be had. I had never done anything to this man, (other than my shaved head) and instead had done a very credible job in personnel. He had tossed obstructions in my way countless times and I resolved that this time I was going to win. I refused to take "no" for an answer and prepared to wage a tooth and nail battle to the wire.

Although I made no bones about the fact that I wanted out of the Air Force and back into civilian life, I never rocked the boat with him. I was an unpretentious type person and had a "live and let live" demeanor. If you didn't know I was the guy that had a 25-point night or went 4-for-4 at the plate, you would never suspect I was a fine athlete. I didn't brag, tried to treat people fairly and yet had nothing but grief from this man.

I thought carefully about what my next move would be. In my mind, I remembered a mental note I believed in. "It's not what you know but who you know," I thought. It was a big decision, but I had the courage of my convictions and scheduled an appointment with Colonel Collins. In my final Airman's Performance Report, he wrote what he thought of me. "Airman Tangen has been a definite asset to this organization," the Chief, Military Personnel Branch said. "He is the type of individual needed in the career force. Promote as soon as eligible."

He was proud of the way I represented myself in a war zone and I always got along fabulously with him. We played softball side by side as men, not as Colonel and Airman. When I explained my predicament, he thought for a second and then said. "Don't worry about it. Make sure you get your flight and I will take care of the rest." I thanked Richard Collins up and down and felt like I was on cloud nine. I had just been "authorized" to return into civilian life. In the end, all my tough days on the rock had really been a test for survival. There were some suicides on this island and I had kept myself busy and felt for those who didn't make it off of this island. I was going home to the East Coast. This Airman was going to give Chris the surprise of her life. I was not going to let her know that there would be a brand new civilian making it home for the holidays.

I had one last altercation with good old Sergeant Price. When he found out that I had pulled strings to leave, he tried to make me work right up until the end. I flatly refused and said I was entitled to a certain amount of time to process out. This last confrontation resulted in me sitting at my desk and doing the bare minimum to get by. Finally, I hit my last work day and arrived at 21000, in a splendid mood. "Guam is good", I said several times. As the cobwebs cleared and I looked out at the Philippine Sea, I pictured my arrival back at JFK Airport in New York. I was filled with anticipation and it was tough to comprehend that my time here, this nightmare, was nearly over.

When I think of Guam now, Jack Heckman Jr. immediately comes to mind. Jack, his brother Bill and late dad Jack Sr., have been written up in Sports Illustrated as world class softball pitchers. One time I saw Jack Jr. in the New Bauer and told him all about Guam and the coral snakes in Thailand. He was mesmerized by my stories and anytime I would see him, he'd say "tell me about Guam again and those Thailand snakes."

Jack worked for the phone company and climbed plenty of telephone poles. He had never come across snakes on the job. One Sunday we were discussing the serpents in the Bauer Inn. The next time he saw me, he blurted out. "I saw a snake, I saw a snake." He then related how the next day, he went to work and came across one. To this day we both laugh before we even get to say a word.

I processed out quickly and my last few days were spent laying around at beautiful Tarague Beach and drinking ice cold beer. This area of ocean is still known throughout the world as a diving destination. I met a guy named Francis Gubler from Philadelphia, who was going home on the same Pan Am flight. We caught the bus from base a couple of times down to Tarague and delighted in the fact that we were so "short" (very few days left).

Pransky got off the island before me. He said he would be waiting for my phone call from Travis to give me a ride to San Francisco Airport. He had shipped lots of stuff home but the weight cutoff came and he couldn't send his stereo speakers. So, I told him I'd get it back in Port Jervis and re-ship them to California.

My last full day on the island finally arrived and I looked out the louvers at Marbo with the satisfaction that this test was about finished. It was so hard for me to believe that the next morning, I would board a plane and look down on the island for the final time.

I personally "processed out" of the watering holes I had frequented during my time there. I stopped by Carman's and Mussels and said goodbye. I blasted the jukebox and daydreamed about getting back to "the world." That night, a big bash was scheduled for the Filipino Club. I thought how ironic it was, that my first night was spent there and my last would be too. "Guam is good," I told the barmaid. "Choppa steak, choppa steak."

The evening of December 22, 1968, I partied with friends far into the night and into the early morning hours of the 23rd. My day had arrived and before I knew it, I would be by Chris' side again. It had been 16 long months since I had told her not to look back. I had survived race riots, a boot job, the Marbo bus, and harassment that I thought only existed in boot camp. I was ready, willing and able to fit back into everyday life as a proud and happy American civilian.

The only obligation I had left, was making damn sure I arrived at the terminal in time to make my flight. In a way, I understood the feelings of guys who were set to leave Vietnam after a 12-month tour and were paranoid about something happening to prohibit their departure. I never had to fire a rifle or lob a grenade, but I felt the same uneasiness, when it came to something going wrong, when freedom was so close.

I knew I would be stopping at tiny Wake Island and then Honolulu Airport on the way home. A few days sooner, I had seen a picture in the Stars and Stripes (military) newspaper, that made my blood run cold. Before my eyes, was a picture of a plane's wing, just above the surface of the ocean at Wake Island. A plane had overshot the short runway there, and crashed into the ocean. I didn't exactly love takeoffs and landings to begin with, and started to fear the time I would have to spend near or on, Wake Island.

I mixed beer and hard stuff at my party and got all fired up. I gave the guys pep talks about how they would make it to the day they would be leaving. "If I can do it, you certainly can," I had said. "When I got here, they told me I had 547 days to go. Now I have none. I have just a few hours."

I walked from the Flip Club to the barracks for the final time. Although higher than a kite, I took in the sights and sounds of an evening on Guam. Although sedated by alcohol, I knew there was no way in God's green earth that I could calm down enough to sleep. In about five hours, I would be phoning a taxi cab to come and get me at Marbo. I was definitely going to leave in class. There would be no damn Marbo bus for me.

All my stuff had been packed earlier. Dress blues hung in my locker for the trip home. After one last shower, that would be all she wrote. The clothes on my back would be good enough for me. I ascended the stone steps where I had gone up and down a million times. Opening the door to our bay, I slowly walked to my cube and opened my locker. I removed contents, including an olive green duffel bag that contained all my belongings. As I got ready to head up the hall to the shower, it appeared as if everyone was fast asleep. Tamba, Tadpole and Tube all seemed to be in dreamland. Then I looked up on my bunk.

My mattress was filled with numerous palm tree branches and I couldn't help laughing in a low chuckle. "You sons of bitches," I said. "You had to get me one last time." Butler stirred a bit and I had to think he was awake and getting a charge out of this, much like the night I brought Lehman the cheeseburger.

I removed the heavy branches from my bed and headed for a hot shower. I sang the words "This could be the last time," from the Rolling Stones hit of the mid 60's. Before I knew it, my day in the sun had arrived. A lot of the guys said they would be skipping out of work for awhile, to see me off at the terminal. I figured most weren't serious but was amazed later on, by the rousing sendoff I was given.

The cab left me off while it was still dark out and I took a short walk from the terminal. I went near the softball field where I learned to play third base. I had to take a leak, but rather than wait until the terminal, I went behind a bush near a building where the Base Commander was located. Somehow on this day, of all days, it seemed like the proper thing to do.

As the departure time neared, I was hung over and overcome with emotion at the same time. It seemed everyone I had ever known at Andersen, was there to see me off. Tube Butler was there with his smiling face, while close by, Stillman, silver Captain bars shining in the sun, wished me a safe trip and good luck in the future. This guy had the rugged good looks and demeanor of a movie star. I always knew where I stood with him, and couldn't have worked for a more dedicated officer. Even Colonel Collins dropped by to give me a genuine handshake and farewell.

This had turned into a real sizable bon voyage sendoff that sent goose bumps down my back. There were so many people saying goodbye, that they formed a very large circle around me. I didn't want to ignore any of them, so I rotated around in a smaller circle of my own, carrying on a bunch of conversations while addressing folks eye to eye. I felt like I was the central figure in a fantasy type storybook and none of this seemed real.

Ferris cracked everyone up by doing his Willie Lehman imitation and shouting out "choppa steak." This awesome display of brotherhood made me realize that in one respect, Guam was good. I had made countless friends here, on this small Pacific island.

At the barracks, our common denominator had been the obstacle of completing an assignment. We were bonded by the goal of making it through and resembled a basketball team that wouldn't quit, even when the chips were down. Although we were each jealous when one of our buddies finally left the island for good, we were happy for them at the same time. It gave us hope that the Pan Am on the runway, would be ours, eventually.

I recalled Lehman saying "Tangen, you will make it out of here, someday." Butler shook my hand and we promised to keep contact with each other. "For a Yankee, you're okay in my book," he said. I cracked a few jokes about the South rising again, just for his benefit. We have kept in touch now for over 34 years. He wound up spending 30 years in law enforcement (Portsmouth, Va.) and his hero is Al Bundy from the TV show "Married With Children." He has two grown boys and as of 2001, said he wasn't a grandparent yet. "When the kids are gone, I'm going to downsize this house and move to the woods or swamp," he told me. "I think I'd be a pretty good hermit."

Years back, I talked to him on the phone one afternoon (early 1970s). He always remembers that call for a good reason. "It was the same day I got into a hostage situation," he recalls. "I had to kill a man."

I walked to the big bird that glistened on the runway, turned back one last time and waved. Finding a seat, I could still see things out the window. The gray terminal dominated the scenery although I could view the blue sky and palm trees in the distance. I had clung to hope for all these months and always kept Chris in my heart. Nobody had ever meant so much to me in my 21 years. The long months of waiting was over and a new chapter of my life was unfolding.

As the plane increased altitude, I could see the whole island below me. It was a real pretty sight down there, a blend of colors that would put a postcard to shame. A Guamanian passenger sat near me and I smiled to myself. "Even Guamanians are glad to get the hell out of here," I thought. We cheered when we leveled off and began our long journey. Wake Island was next on our list of obstacles to reach "the world."

From what I understand, Building 21000 is still on Guam. The population, in the early 21st century, was 157,557. Men there, could expect to live 75.66 years and women 80.55 years. There was an election November 7, 2000, and a Democrat, Carl Gutierrez, remained governor. More than a million people a year visit, as tourism and fishing in the area's clear water, are big business. The island has built up and now sports luxurious high rise hotels, resort complexes, malls, restaurants and golf courses (nine 18-hole courses).

When I was on Guam, snakes were not a problem. Now the serpents (brown snakes) infest this tropical paradise. They slither onto the roadways at night (nocturnal), hang from tree branches, drop from the tops of doors, and extinguish the native bird population. The snakes apparently began their habitation here, by being transported on boats that docked on Guam. They hang by the thousands from trees and when there is a typhoon, they are blown out by typhoon winds. Residents have been known to spend days scraping dead snake remains from houses and cars.

July 4, 2002, Typhoon Chataanm ripped into Guam. More than 1,500 people in 13 villages, wound up in shelters. More than 105 homes were destroyed and over 400 were damaged. The people of this historical island continue to deal with any adversities tossed their way. And you just know that "Hafa Adai" can still be heard every day.

When the aircraft banked down toward Wake Island, I gripped the back of the seat in front of me. After seeing Guam from the air, this place was just a tiny dot that looked like a postage stamp. The landing gear creaked into place and I heard the wheels bump hard onto the runway. Ahead I saw two things that placed my heart nearly in my throat. The runway disappeared under me and all I saw ahead, on this short and scary runway, was blue ocean. Let me take that back. There was one other sight that just warmed the cockles of my heart. Out in that blue ocean, was the wing from that plane I saw in the paper. I closed my eyes tightly and prayed for the best.

When the plane had taxied to a stop, I knew I was 50 per cent of the way there, when it came to Wake Island. We weren't there long and before I could scream "help", we were airborne again and headed for Honolulu. For the second time, I wandered around on Hawaiian soil, if the lounge floor qualifies as soil.

The price of beer, even way back then, was through the roof. I couldn't care less as I fired down two or three bottles before resuming the trip. For the second time on this journey, I became paranoid with an uneasy feeling.

I was so close to being back in California and was so afraid something was going to go wrong. I was ripe for the plucking and a couple of pilots swooped down and terrified a few of us who were headed to the West Coast. They sat at the bar swilling down drinks, with loosened ties, hats off and much joking. "Hey, you guys going to Travis (AFB)?", one of them asked. When we answered yes, the pilot turned to his friend and said "these unlucky people are on our flight. Sure as hell hope we make it okay. Maybe we'll just put it on automatic pilot and let her rip."

We were sure as hell hoping these people were kidding around. Regulations prohibited them from consuming alcohol within so many hours of making a flight. Even though it sounds absurd, I thought there could be an outside chance that these pilots were really going to be on our plane. When we left the cocktail lounge, they must have cracked up and said something like "those dumb bastards, they believe anything."

217

I could envision putting on our seat belts, looking at the no smoking sign and hearing the pilot come on the intercom. "We gonna be cruising somewhere up in the wild blue yonder," he would say in a slurred manner. "Put on your parachutes just in case. And stewardess, bring us another drink before we take off."

En route to "the world" we eclipsed the International Dateline, which would be a sure fire way to screw up our body clocks. By the time we touched down in California, we had been flying well over 11 hours, and still arrived in the morning (of the day we left Guam).

I had on a long sleeved shirt and military dress blues. I never thought of California being a cold place, but it was in the 30s when we came off the plane. My blood was real thin from being in hot weather for all those months and I shivered uncontrollably. "This is nothing," one of the guys said. "Wait until you get to New York in December."

I foolishly forgot that I was still the property of Uncle Sam. In an uncomplicated world, you would sign for your pay, check a box on the paper that said "civilian" and be on your way. I thought I saw Rod Serling lurking around the terminal though, and soon I was to enter "The Twilight Zone". I was transformed to a place where you attended countless meetings, viewed films until your eyes fell to the floor and rolled under your desk, and you wanted to beg for mercy.

"We want to make sure you want to get out of the Air Force," a Sergeant told me. "Once you sign the paper, you can't get back in." All I could see was somehow turning temporarily insane, reenlisting and getting sent back to Guam on the next available plane.

We had to hang out at a barracks until the next scheduled meeting and our military pay was taking forever to be processed. I had eight days pay for untaken leave due me, plus separation pay. The films we were forced to watch were designed to snag any Airman who wasn't totally sure about getting released from active duty.

One movie showed a man sitting on a step in an alleyway with his head in his hands. He was upset because he had no home, no money and no friends. This poor soul obviously decided not to reenlist. We laughed about that film as some career types gave us icy stares. We were turned every which way but loose, for hours on end. Finally, the agony was over as I signed out of the Air Force and picked up my pay. As I phoned Bernie Pransky for a ride to San Francisco International, the thought crossed my mind to stay in California for awhile. I quickly dismissed that idea as being a result of delirium from the long flight and brain washing administered by those who wanted us to reenlist.

My records showed I had earned medals and ribbons including a good conduct medal, national defense service medal, Vietnamese service medal and outstanding unit medal. Those and a quarter, might get you a cup of coffee, especially in our country, which was divided during the Vietnam "conflict."

My honorable discharge came early, due to a "convenience of the government" directive. I was in the continental U.S., single and absolutely free. My thoughts drifted to the East Coast and how getting back there was my major goal since day 1. Chris could always look back now, because I would never leave her again, for any substantial amount of time. I had seen some of the world and its cultures. I was tired of taking orders. It was time for home.

Dad never knew I was back in the country until I had been discharged. Pransky and I joked and carried on, all the way from Travis to San Francisco. "We made it out, Bill, we got out of that place," he said. "The lifers don't have us to harass anymore. We beat them at their own game."

It was a smooth flight east, and five hours later, I was happily walking the floors of Kennedy Airport. I shivered when I hit the frigid New York air, but those familiar license plates and "New Yawk" accents, told me I was close to home. When I met Dad, it seemed like I had never been away. He hadn't aged much at all and we talked about the service and things at home, on our train ride from New York to Port Jervis.

The city looked very strange to me. I had been used to palm trees, rain nearly every day and a tropical climate. Being reunited with my family, Chris and Fish were top priorities on my list. I couldn't wait to start partying and telling tales of Guam. I appeared fit, tanned and content and as a brand new civilian, was filled with vitality and enthusiasm. I put on some weight in the Pacific, (nothing drastic) once I returned from Thailand.

I remained wearing my dress blues and felt flutters in my heart when the car pulled into the driveway at 6 Lyman Avenue. Out back, the basket was still attached to the backboard on the garage, just waiting for me to fire up some shots. That would have to wait until spring, I knew. Taffy the dog (French poodle) raised a ruckus when I walked in the side door. Mom went crazy when she saw me, showering me with hugs and kisses. My sister, now 16, and a sophomore at Port Jervis High, welcomed back her number one nemesis.

I had kept my discharge an absolute secret from Chris. She had no inkling that I was back home and standing in my West End home. She had kept close contact with Mom and Dad while I was gone. Many times Chris would go over to the house and have take out "chicken in the basket" from Jack Scully's impressive restaurant in Sparrowbush. Scully's was famous for its great food, charismatic owners and outstanding atmosphere. Papa and Jack Scully went way back, and Jack's sons were now a vital part of the business.

Chris was preparing for a Christmas Eve church service, when Mom placed a phone call and asked her to drop by the house. I became tense as I realized the magnitude of what was going to take place in a few minutes. I walked over to a floor heat register in the living room and waited for her to come in the side door.

My bride to be, entered, and walked through the kitchen and dining room. Turning the corner to the living room, she came face to face with me. For a second or two there was no movement, and no sound. Then she let out an excited shriek and was in my arms. "I couldn't believe it was you," she said later. "It was like I was looking at a cardboard cutout of you. I just couldn't believe it."

The long haul had been completed and my Air Force days were over. Chris and I were inseparable except when I hung out with Fish, drank in the Silver Grill on Pike Street, or both. Long pork chop sideburns were in during 1969. "Hair" became a phenomenal Broadway show. "Aquarius Let The Sun Shine In" by the Fifth Dimension wailed on the Silver Grill jukebox. It would go on to win two Grammy Awards.

Life became manageable to say the least. I was free of the service, plus had my girlfriend, family and friends back. I realize now, what a transition it was not only for me, but my family as well. They weren't used to me living with them anymore. Dad enforced rules, just like he did when I was in high school. I wanted total freedom and the luxury of coming and going as I pleased. Dad wanted for me to get a job.

I slept until noon, was constantly on the go and spent nights with Chris and at "the Grill." I dabbled into some part time work at my dad's insurance agency on Jersey Avenue, but really had no clear direction. I was tired of asking my folks for money and wanted a real job.

Just about everyone from the area worked at one time or another, at world famous Kolmar Laboratories (cosmetics). I nailed a job there in 1969 and being a material handler, supplied ladies on the assembly line, with eye shadow. Kolmar had one location way up a hill (Skyline Drive) in Sparrowbush and another in the middle of town. I wound up at the latter, and was pleasantly surprised to see that there was a gin mill, The New Bauer Inn, right across the street.

I began dabbling into liquid lunches at the Bauer and not too much time passed before I became acquainted with the owners, Ben and Marie. About 15 years later, I took Penny Ann the dog, out of this establishment.

I rapidly began fitting back into society again and was now earning a weekly paycheck. Most of my money went for food and drink and it's a good thing Mom and Dad didn't charge me room and board. If a heated discussion revolving around the Vietnam war ever occurred, I defended the war effort, seeing as though I had been in that area.

It was at the Bauer, that the name Muhammad Ali came up, in reference to him being drafted and refusing to go in the service. The former Cassius Clay was stripped of his heavyweight title and suspended from the fight game. He said he wouldn't go in the service because of his religious beliefs. Although I had served, I could kind of see his point. There was a gray area involved, but try telling that to a distraught father who lost his son in Vietnam.

The only good thing that came out of Kolmar, was a girl named Liz.

Lots of the young guys were after her, but I acted on my feelings and got a date with the dark-haired girl. She was a quiet and petite individual and had a nice smile. She gave off mysterious vibes and the curiosity got the best of me.

I drove Liz's yellow Camaro out to Buckley's Tavern in Huguenot and played pool with her. We had something to eat and some drinks. It was great to be home from the service.

In the television spotlight was a comedy show called "Rowan and Martin's Laugh In." Dad and I roared our heads off watching this ridiculous show that aired from January 22, 1968 until March 14, 1973. Meanwhile, I was bored stiff at Kolmar's and knew there had to be another job out there. My eventual goal, was to earn enough money to buy an engagement ring for Chris. If anyone asked me if I would someday get married, I more than likely would answer "you bet your bippy."

After awhile I bought a cool looking used 1966 light green Pontiac GTO. It was a smooth riding vehicle, despite the fact that it probably had been in an accident, since the bottom of the car kept banging the road. Now I had the necessary means to travel, should I find a suitable job.

That opportunity came when Fish and I secured jobs after he got out of the service, in September, 1969. We worked at Arrow Shirts in Chester, N.Y., around 35 miles from home. The distance we had to travel for our night shift was fine with us, just as long as we could speed home and get some drinks before the Silver Grill closed.

I had finally attained civilian status and it felt good not to be over a barrel on Guam. There was no more Marbo bus or lifers making life miserable for me. Sorry, all you Air Force retention people, I didn't sit on a step in some alley with head in hands, down and out, because I didn't reenlist.

In some respects I was mature for my age and in others I was still just a kid getting his feet wet in the real world. One of my least favorite sayings is "grow up." Anyone points at you and says that, has three fingers pointing at themselves. I never intend to grow up, and take great pleasure in the simple things life has to offer.

I always liked the song "Born To Be Wild" by Steppenwolf. Years and years later, Neil Diamond recorded "Blue Highway" on the Tennessee Moon CD. Both songs exude the feeling of being free from any restrictions life can bring. I was now free as a bird and knew it. I chirped about the champion Mets, Jets and Knicks in 1969. The Woodstock festival happened right up the road in August (Bethel, N.Y.), and I damn near went to it. I lived life to the fullest and the glass was always half full. I was back home in New York and loving every second of it.

I drove my toy steamroller through town and to Papa's insurance office when I was only 3 years old.

When I moved to West End, Penny the gray cat, came to live with us.

"Big Bill" and "Little Bill" were loyal N.Y. Yankee baseball fans. "Papa" read to me when I was small and made me sports minded.

Another trophy

Howard Griffin stands in front of me back in the early 1950s. I used to play in the canal (background)

Anne and I are joined by Penny the cat during one of our first Christmas holidays in our West End house.

My 11th birthday party featured a visit from Alex Osowick, my Port Jervis High basketball hero. My sister Anne observes, as I show Alex the scrapbook I compiled on him. He still holds the single season Port scoring record of 62 points in one game.

Thailand house girls at
U-tapao, 1967.

Our West End sixth grade teacher, Richard Donald, poses with our softball team. That's me, in the second row (far left) with the first baseman's glove. At the end of the row, is Roger Duryea who became a New York State Trooper. Next to me is boyhood friend, Jack Tedrick.

With Thailand friends, front of hootch.

Gary Weyant of Middletown came up against me in the long jump.

Dad has his coffee cup in hand, one early morning in the mid 1960s. My look, tells the story of an Airman about to end his military leave.

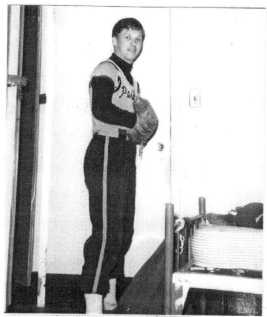

I wore my gold and black Plattsburgh AFB Panthers uniform proudly in 1966 and 1967. I patrolled centerfield and batted over .300.

Christine and I had a month together before Guam

Filing a sports story, 1973.

The Port Jervis High gymnasium was nearly packed when the Union-Gazette played WDLC Radio in March 1977. At the age of 29, I still had the ability to drive toward the basket. Photo by Pad Kroger.

I connected with this pitch during a softball game in Port Jervis in the mid 1970s. I played third base for Harding Insurance.

Easy points come from the foul line

Port Jervis guard Rich Saul was a scoring threat in this 1971 game and throughout his shiny high school career. Pound for pound, I regard Saul as the finest teenaged basketball player to ever come out of this area of New York State. Photo by Bill Tangen.

"The Rock" where America's day begins

I am posing out on the veranda of building 21000, on Guam, in 1967. The Philippine Sea can be seen in the background. I spent 14 months on Guam plus two months in Thailand.

My buddy, Willie Lehman, relaxed when he left Guam.

Fish and I were very close buddies through our school years and on into adult life. We were in the Air Force at the same time and somehow survived. We are close friends to this day.

I was cool, in the summer of 1967

Heavyweight boxing champ Muhammad Ali goes through his paces under the watchful eyes of trainer Angelo Dundee in September, 1976. Ali trained at the Concord Hotel and then went on to retain his championship with a decision over Ken Norton at New York's Yankee Stadium. Photo by Joseph Robles.

There are never dull times with Gary "Fish" Scales. He got wide-eyed for the camera prior to a Bruce Springsteen concert in Philly.

On August 16, 1997, Dawn came to sister Tracie's wedding in Pa.

Sometimes Chris and I sing duets together. Our favorites include Bruce Springsteen's "Bobby Jean" and "No Surrender." Most Friday nights we can be found at Doc's in Hamburg, New Jersey.

229

Mom and I both knew that after my 1967 leave, I would be off to Southeast Asia for a long time.

Chris had her future husband home in summer, 1967

Bill Tangen
Oct. 2003

After nearly 35 years, Plattsburgh buddy Tony Sewall and I reunited in Maine. The June 2002 reunion proves that friendship can pass the test of time.

Barely into April 17, 2004, at NY Nick's Springsteen bash in Pensacola, Florida, I hopped up on stage to sing "Glory Days" backed by the famous B Street Band. Formed by Willie Forte (far left) in 1980, the group is the longest running Springsteen tribute band in the world (24 years). Photo by Chris Tangen.

My wife and myself have been through thick and thin together. We were married on September 12, 1970 and continue to cherish our marriage.

CHAPTER 9

The Repo Man

I was in a new world where I was no longer counting down the final days of an Air Force enlistment. There was no more "23 days and a duffel bag drag" or "15 days and a wake up." I did watch the clock at Kolmar Labs in anticipation of quitting time, when I could see Chris again and slug down a few beers.

After awhile I grew bored of my job and had figured out that there was no future here. The women on the line were on an incentive program and some of them acted like lunatics as they screamed for us to "hurry the hell up." We had to supply them with eye shadow or other materials and at times it became real hectic. I unloaded trucks, scurried back and forth to the lines and lived for liquid lunch at The New Bauer and then for the day to end. In my time off, I continued to party but also began searching for another job.

While Fish was still screwing with Uncle Sam, I nailed employment at Pri-Jay Cleaners, driving a laundry route. My first obstacle was learning to drive a green colored standard transmission truck, which I accomplished in time.

The year 1969 was going to be a mixed bag for me. It was my last year of being single and I must say I went out in a blaze of glory. Pri-Jay's was owned by partners Preston Price and Jay Mack. These two men were a mind boggling study in contrast. Price had been in Price and Son cleaners with his dad for years. Mack, who is an accomplished dancer and owns a studio, was an animated motivator, a mover and shaker of sorts. From this job, I would move on to Arrow Shirts and then to Empire National Bank in Middletown, where I was known to swipe cars at 2 and 3 in the morning. Technically, I went from eye shadow to loan collections in less than a year.

Music was still great in these times. "Hair" by the Cowsills, "Everyday People" by Sly and the Family Stone, "Easy To Be Hard" by Three Dog Night and "Time of the Season" by The Zombies, hit the airwaves. Elvis tossed out "Suspicious Minds" while "Tracy" by The Cufflinks and "In the Year 2525" by Zager and Evans could be heard.

This was a big time in New York professional sports. The Jets, Mets and Knicks all surged to championships beginning in 1969 with Joe Namath and the Jets shocking the Baltimore Colts, 16-7, in Super Bowl III. Namath, a slick and mod quarterback, had been a standout at the University of Alabama. "Broadway Joe" took New York by storm and his good looks and brash, confident attitude was eaten up by the media.

The Colts were a veteran team that kicked ass and took names. Johnny Unitas (QB) had been their golden boy for years but he was in the twilight of his career. He saw late game action and eagerly tried to bring the Colts back, in this monumental upset. The rally proved futile though and the New York Jets of the AFL, had reached the top.

Namath had shaken up the football world during the week before the big game. At the Super Bowl Awards Dinner he dropped this bomb on folks. "The Jets will win Sunday, I guarantee you."

On January 12, 1969, 20 days after I was discharged, Namath made good on his word. The Jets, 19 ½ point underdogs, used Matt Snell's 4-yard touchdown run, an extra point and three field goals to secure the win. At 5:49 p.m. and under cloudy Miami skies, Namath left the field with an index finger in the air, indicating that the Jets were indeed number one in the professional football world.

The stunning win captured everyone's imagination. Being from New York State, we were all very proud of Joe Willie and the rest of the Jets. At Dick Jewel's Silver Grill, we partied and bragged about how "our Jets" had pulled off the upset victory.

The laundry route was relaxing, in that I could get out on the road and away from people. I picked up dirty clothes and scooped them into bags while also delivering clean laundry, making out slips and collecting money. I liked the feeling of being in charge and not having to listen to bosses screaming in the background.

One of the drivers, Bob Ferry, was a real joker and genuine nice guy. He laughed at the mistakes of my youth in good humor and taught me the ropes. Many times we sat in Pri-Jay's at the end of the day and sucked down some Fife and Drum bottled beer. Some stories from the routes were funny ones and in a way, I received a psychology lesson each and every day. I related to people well and was much happier at this job than I had been at Kolmar's.

The Silver Grill was definitely the happening establishment in town. It was the place that you hung out at, after finishing your military time. Bill McCormick talked about the tenseness of leaving Vietnam, John Zachary and Jim Perrego were hell on the bowling and fooseball machines and Jewel, a Navy recruiter, had a great sense of humor. The busting of cookies went on constantly and this became my second home. Sports topics were tossed around and everybody seemed happy in this atmosphere.

The Grill was located on Pike Street across from Blimpie's, where you good get a real good sandwich. There were many Blimpie and beer combos consumed at Dick Jewel's place. The juke box added to the overall package and girls came into the bar, mostly at night.

Jewel had nearly snagged me away from Sergeant Stone at the Port Jervis post office when I began the procedure to enlist in the Air Force. One day I was to meet "Stoney" but he wasn't in his office yet. "Hey," Jewel said. "Come on in here and I will have you all set to go in the Navy. That is where you want to go."

Inside the Grill was a lower and upper bar area. I used to go in the upper section to the left, as you had a birds-eye view of everything. One time I went in and found nobody tending bar. Activities went on as usual and I noticed guys were serving themselves from the beer tap and leaving money on the register. "Where's Dick?", I asked while heading for the bar. "He's up there," someone said, while pointing (at the upper bar).

While the Grill was lively and people laughed and communicated, Dick was in deep slumber, on the floor with a blanket over him. There was nothing like life at the Grill. P.C. Hess, Bill Collins, Jerry DeMarco, Joe Nolan and the rest of the gang hung here at one time or another.

Shortly after getting out of the service, they bought me drinks in here. I had a whole row of Peppermint Schnapps lined up in front of me and made short work of the shots. "To the Guam guy who is back with us," one of them shouted. And I toasted the night away. When I left the bar, I couldn't find my car. "It was right here," I said incredulously. "It is a green GTO." Guys came out to help me and I explained my predicament. "It is right there where you parked it," one of them said. I received a well-needed ride home from Jim Goetzman and retrieved the vehicle later on.

The Grill had been a well-known place long before I called it home. They used to have musicians perform there and the Union-Gazette newspaper was located next door. Mike Kowal, a superb sportswriter used to try banging out stories while his buddies partied at the Grill. "They would come by the front of the Gazette and motion for me to come over," Kowal jokes. "But I had lots of work to do and couldn't go."

I worked at the Gazette with Mike and he was a real inspiration to me. It was Kowal who had given Alex Osowick and his Port basketball teammates such great write ups in the late 1950s. I golfed with him many times and he used to call me "the people's choice." When Chris was due with Tracie, I told him "If it's a boy, I will name him Mike."

Perrego was one of the finest high school football players I have ever seen. He played in the backfield on the fine Raider teams that included Spears, Nolan, John Bell, Brian Seeber and Bill Oliver. He was called "the leash" and was a competitor from the word go.

"Per" was another of the comedians and was good at needling you or having swift comebacks. In this era, he sported the pork chop sideburns of the day and was a good bartender. One day we were in the Grill and he peered out the front door, looked to the left up Pike Street and said "Here comes Aunt Mary." I was bracing for some type of joke, but that is all he said.

I focused my eyes up the street and did see a woman walking our way. "Yes, the old bitch is on her way," I laughed, figuring it was another Perrego comedy act. The woman reached the Grill, Perrego went out and the two continued walking. I sank back on my stool, felt about a foot tall and wished I could be invisible.

As time went on, some of the regulars here, were known to travel from bar to bar (and there were many) in Port searching for a good time. From the Black Bear Inn at Sparrowbush to Len & Joe's in West End, there was never a shortage of places to go. Several men from the Grill began eating glasses, just to have something different to do. They would order up drinks and when finished, ate their glasses.

On one occasion, at The Hut, they chomped away on the glass shards as bewildered patrons eyed them in disbelief. DeMarco didn't partake in this glass feast and one of the guys asked him how come. "I'm full," he said matter-of-factly.

The laundry route maintained my interest, especially in view of the fact that I swiftly learned where to stop for liquid lunches on the road. If I got thirsty or had to take a leak, I had certain taverns on my route where I would stop. I sneaked into the New Bauer every now and then, plus hit Club 209 and Buckley's out in Huguenot. Those two places were damn near next door to each other and just to be fair, I hit both of them every time. If I went out Otisville way, Gambini's was a certain pit stop.

When Fish got out of the service, his old man was on him to get a job. Roy kept harping about the post office, where he worked as a janitor. "It is $3.06 per hour (decent money then) and all the benefits," Roy would say, regarding postal delivery. Fish would shake his head in horror and beg off throwing in an application.

To quiet down his dad and also to partake of the frothy suds of beer, Fish began going on the route with me. I would load up my truck with dry cleaning to be delivered, and then head up to West End to pick him up. I tossed him a few bucks and we chuckled all the way around the route.

That job ended when I got tired of the usual grind and wanted more money. One day Jay asked me to go up to Eddy Farm Hotel to pick up some laundry. I was ready to head home when he hit me with the request. I refused to go and instead quit right on the spot. My laundry delivery days were suddenly over and I was ready to turn another chapter in the book of life.

One important lesson was learned on the laundry route. Never swill down beer and not have a plan for a pee stop. I was driving in to Pri-Jay's from the road, bouncing up and down in the driver's seat one day, when the horrible feeling of having to urinate came upon me. I was in the city of Port Jervis and there was no place to pull the truck over and run in the woods.

I tried to ride out the involuntary feeling and parked the truck in front of the laundry. Of all days, Preston was there to greet me out front and my face must have been deep red. I got out of the truck, tried to take a couple of steps and stopped. Can you guess what happened next? As Preston and I talked, a flood was taking place on the sidewalk. He looked down and was at a loss for words. I simply said "I can't believe I did that." I felt a mixture of relief and embarrassment all at the same time. When Bob Ferry got word of this happening, he howled until passing motorists looked out of their cars. I learned to take a large container on the truck from that day forward.

Back in the summer, before Fish escaped the rigors of Watertown, New York, there was plenty going on. A man walked on the moon July 20, 1969, Woodstock took place almost in our back yard in August, and last but not least, Fish, some friends and I, staged a memorable drunken extravaganza at a nearby Sullivan County lake.

Chris and I were at Yankee Stadium that July day when Neil Armstrong of Apollo 11 became the first man to walk on the moon. The scoreboard flashed up a message that said "they're on the moon." Armstrong said these words. "That's one small step for man, one great leap for mankind."

Back in 1961, John Kennedy had made a challenge to put a man on the moon before the decade ended. Although JFK was long gone, his mission had been accomplished.

During the Yankee game, rookie Yankee Thurman Munson cracked his first major league homer. He would go on to become a Yankee captain and hit 113 homers while having a .292 career batting average. Mantle had retired on March 1, 1969 and Munson would be the guy who would assume team leadership for the Bronx bombers (Yanks). Mantle went on to make the Hall of Fame in 1974, the same year that Hank Aaron broke Babe Ruth's home run record by hitting his 715th on my birthday, April 8. Sadly enough, Munson, the former American League rookie of the year, died when he was the pilot in a plane crash, during the 1979 season.. Mantle, my favorite player ever, passed away in Dallas, Texas, August 13, 1995, not all that long after a liver transplant.

I tried my hand at working in a store that first year after the service. I snagged a day job way up in Liberty, New York, about 40 miles from home and was anxious to finally be making good money. Sullivan's Department Store stood right off exit 100 of Route 17 and I could make it to work in under an hour.

My first day of work, I had to put on a maroon sports coat like the rest of the employees. I walked out into the large store and took a look around. I would be working in the sporting goods department, so at least I was familiar with some of the sports.

After having to help lug some bulky merchandise from one place to another, my boss, a short and disciplined white-haired tyrant, began to tell me what the job entailed.

"Walk around the sports department, up and down all the aisles," he said. Look at all the items, because I want you to know where everything is. If a customer asks a location, you have to know it. In a few minutes we'll see how good your mind is."

My mind wasn't doing real well at that moment, as I had immediately been put on the spot. I don't even think this guy said hello or told me his name. He would be the first of many bosses who would try to play God with me. Those who looked down their noses at me or went on power trips, all got the same treatment, and still do to this day. If forced to, I can manufacture disappearing acts that make professional magicians seem like rookies.

While I perused the aisles, the boss man was watching my every move. He walked up to me and said "okay, I want to find a hunting knife, where do I find one?" I felt like saying "in a Tarzan movie" but instead looked around and tried to picture where I had seen hunting equipment. "Aisle 4," I said with uncertainty. "No, no, no that isn't right," he bellowed. "They are in aisle 3. Now go back and look at everything again."

This exercise in frustration went on all morning long. Some things I got right and some wrong, but he wasn't happy with my progress. "If we have to do this all day we will," he promised. Soon the noon hour approached and he caught up to me near the football goods. "You want a noon or 1 o'clock lunch?", he queried in an unfriendly tone. I gave him his choice and he took the 1. That was a big mistake.

I walked to my locker and neatly hung up my maroon coat. Walking out the front door to my car, I asked myself if this harassment would be worth my time and aggravation. The answer came back "no, no, no."

It was a happy ride back down home and I wasted plenty of time arriving at my house. "How did the job go?", Mom asked me. "Fine," I said in a simple one word answer. "Do you have a nice boss?", she asked. "Yeah," I retorted.

Sometime in the evening hours, the Liberty blowhard called my house, but I was gone on "important business" at the Silver Grill. "He never came back from lunch," he told my father. Of course Dad quietly pressed me about details the next day (that Grill business took a long time). "You are going back to work up there, right?", Dad asked. "No, no, no," I thought as I shook my head in a negative fashion.

Back in the summer, Fish had set up a Saturday when his buddies from Watertown would be coming down to Port Jervis. We prepared by getting all the essential things we would need. Money, beer, booze and gas were high on the list.

Don Pedin (Texas), Bill McMurray (Staten Island, New York) and Denny Dennison (Ohio), were three guys who were the perfect combination. Fish and I went over town in the morning and bought some wild looking hats and shades to wear on a ride over the Hawk's Nest and into Sullivan County.

It was a beautiful day and we didn't have a care in the world. We took two cars and found a nice looking exclusive club on one of the area's beautiful lakes. A sign on the establishment said "private club" and "members only." We all agreed that this must be the ideal place to party.

We entered, somehow got served, chugged beers, laughed and told jokes and played loud music on the juke box. The elderly patrons sat in total shock as a bizarre stage show was taking place in front of their eyes. One time, three of us had to pee at the same moment, so the sink came in handy. We swilled beer all afternoon and I think there was more alcohol spilled than entered our mouths. The customers found out we had lived up to our obligations to Uncle Sam and took a liking to us.

I have never had such a good time in all my life. The afternoon ended with Fish's friends peeling out on our new hats in the parking lot. We took the tattered head wear and proudly wore the shredded material into the next bar, which happened to be the Bel Air in Glen Spey.

Reeking of alcohol and slurring our words, we had a snowball's chance in hell at securing more beer. Instead, we stumbled out to our cars and wound up at The Black Bear. I think Lefty Barth owned the place in 1969 and it was a really cool place. The Culver brothers were in a talented band and played "Celebrate" by Three Dog Night, to perfection.

I remember being in "The Bear" one night, with Henszie, Fish, Bob Liptak and a couple of other friends. The band was playing while some New Jersey guys began to needle and insult us. The drinking age was 18 in New York then, while the Garden State youths couldn't get alcohol in their state until they were 21. They came across the border to the Port Jervis area, got drunk and became belligerent. Picking fights and settling things out in the parking lot was nothing new on a Friday or Saturday night.

I didn't start fights but was not one to back away from a confrontation. It was going to be a five on five situation and when the Jersey crew stood up at their table, we did too. Enter Gene King.

"Gino" as he is known these days, was a wiry ex-Marine who was a bouncer at The Black Bear. He tried to settle differences diplomatically and kept peace in the enjoyable hangout. He could smell trouble from a mile away and suddenly appeared near our table. "You guys have a problem with them?", he asked us. When we nodded yes, he motioned for us to sit back down. We reluctantly agreed and watched as he advanced to the nearby table where the New Jersey guys remained standing.

"You guys just calm down and enjoy your drinks and the music," he said with a smile. He got resistance right away, although he tried to avoid trouble. These idiots were hell bent to find a fight and they found one that night. "Okay, out into the parking lot," he told the fools. "Where are the five we want to fight?", one of them asked. "I am the five," Gene said in a Clint Eastwood voice.

Gino is an ex-Marine boxing champion who possessed blinding speed and fast fists. While a crowd gathered in the lot, he took on the bullies one at a time. After three had become acquainted with his vicious punches and the parking lot gravel, the other two were more than happy to walk away in one piece.

Gene never talks about these days when danger was constantly lurking near him. He chooses to champion causes for the handicapped, because he wound up in the fight of his life and survived. He was the passenger in a car that was in a horrible accident. He was badly hurt and it is a miracle that he didn't die. Gino had to learn to walk and talk again and has walked in various marathons (including the New York Marathon).

Gene has also staged his own private walks to hospitals that he spent time in. He has helped raise funds for worthy establishments and pushes forward with an uncanny and stubborn confidence. You could be having the worst day of your life and a smile and good word from Gene King will turn things around. The people who are fortunate enough to be friends with Gino are truly blessed. He has become an unbelievable inspiration to countless individuals and organizations.

The year 1969 was bittersweet for Chris. Her grandmother passed away in early January, just days after I had talked with her. There came the August morning when Chris and I hopped in her 1968 burgundy Barracuda and were going to head up north to the Woodstock Festival.

When we arrived at the top of Pike Street, we encountered bumper to bumper traffic that proceeded northward to a yellow caution light and up a hill leading out of town. The thought of driving up to Monticello in this mess and then continuing another few miles past Monticello Raceway, didn't set well with me. We gave our original plan the hook and instead headed north to good old Plattsburgh .

Willie Lehman met us at Filion's and I was ecstatic that an old service buddy and my future wife, finally had met. "Bill mentioned you all the time in his letters from Guam," Chris told him. "I am so glad to meet you." Lehman grinned back at her, mug in hand and offered a toast. "To Guam, that tropical paradise," he said with a laugh. "Yeah and you talked me into going there, you son of a bitch," I shot back. Lehman used to call me "pushy" and "mouthy" when we were back on "The Rock." So I said "hey pushy, you ready for another beer?" The song "Time of the Season" came on the jukebox and all was right with the world on this August night.

Fish, Chris and I came to "The Burgh" later in 1969 while Fish and I made the trip one or two more times while Lehman was still there. I still remember Fish getting all fired up and puking in broad daylight, next door to a bar. "It serves your right," a neighborhood woman had shouted to Fish.

We were known to stage all night parties at Plattsburgh motels and lived life to the fullest. I still see Bill Vokolos, Lehman, Don McKinney and Fish drinking the night away. McKinney was stationed on base and remembered me from before I went to Guam. I think it was his sister he set me up with once, but I blew the opportunity by getting smashed on my ass.

I have been to the Woodstock monument several times. The festival took place up in Bethel, New York, right in the middle of farms and beautiful rolling meadows. The scenery still takes my breath away as I gaze in the distance and see all the greenery and blue sky.

Here at the intersection of West Shore Road and Hurd Road, at the former site of Max Yasgur's farm, music history was made. It is very hard to comprehend that this place of serenity and tranquility was where over 400,000 people congregated for a celebration of peace and love. They swam nude in a nearby lake, enjoyed some great music and slogged around in a driving rain. Most of all, my generation showed the world that people could get along if they tried hard enough. We grew up when 18 year olds were getting gunned down for no good reason, in a foreign land. Unlike our parents' generation, we asked the question "why?". Country Joe McDonald, who appeared here, asked that very question in the start to one of his songs. "Well it's 1-2-3 what are we fighting for? Don't ask me I don't give a damn, next stop's Vietnam."

At this historical 1969 event, there were three deaths. The causes included one heroin overdose, a ruptured appendix and a tractor running over someone. The average festival person had to abandon a vehicle (highways were swamped and came to a standstill) and walk 15 miles to the site.

There was a total of 31 musical acts. For 45 minutes of work, Santana was reportedly paid $1,500. The Grateful Dead earned $7,500 and The Who raked in $11,200.

Only 60,000 people were expected at this get together and 186,000 tickets were printed. This festival was to have taken place in Woodstock, New York, over 50 miles from Bethel. When things fell through there, Bethel became the place to go. Kids and young adults (including hippies and flower children) got through restraining fences, entering for free. State Police worked tirelessly, medical personnel were kept busy and most in the community of 2,366 folks, welcomed the polite and energetic young people. While a few jackasses charged festival goers for water, the majority were great hosts to what would become the most memorable festival in the history of music.

Three days of love, peace and music took the world spotlight. Vassmer's Store was a favorite place for visitors to drop by and enjoy.

Residents ran hoses from their houses to quench thirst and the police were tolerant. People shared, cared and demonstrated what life could be like without the ravages of war. The event began at 5:06 p.m. August 15, 1969 when Richie Havens took the stage. By that time, I was viewing the Adirondack Mountains.

Fish and I nailed jobs at Arrow Shirts and were on a night shift. My buddy actually was hired while I had been turned down. Fish talked to the big boss though, and the next thing you know, I was in the door.

It was a long shift of packing shirts in the big warehouse near the New York State Thruway. We had a favorite bar, Carson's Corners, to stop off at, on the way to work. We enjoyed the homey atmosphere and would quaff down beers in a hurry. The shift was an hour shorter on Friday nights, so we had longer to hang out at the Silver Grill when we got home. Lots of times Chris was there to meet me, when I got into town.

While the Jets were Super Bowl champions, the "Amazing Mets" had captured the heart of not only New York, but the country. The Mets came from a humble background of futility where they would always find a way to lose. I had seen the first game ever played in Shea Stadium (1964) when Willie Stargel hit a homer to help beat the locals. While the Yanks were always looked up to, the Mets were the butt of cruel jokes in the past.

Like the Jets, the Mets were supposed to get trounced when all of the marbles were on the table. The Mets had gone 100-62 under manager Gil Hodges, a former Brooklyn Dodger first baseman. The New York team went from ninth place in 1968 (in the 10-team National League) to first place in the newly formed East Division. Few gave them much of a chance against a Baltimore Orioles squad that had won 109 games. The bleak situation was magnified for the Mets, when pitcher Tom Seaver and his mates lost game one to the Orioles.

However, the "Miracle Mets" came off the deck to surprise a whole country. While Fish and I cheered wildly, they came on to win the next four games in a row, to upset Baltimore and win the World Series. The Mets had been 9 ½ games back in August, but got hot and won the pennant. Tommie Agee had smacked 26 homers and knocked in 76 runs, to spark the world champs, in 1969.

Agee had two incredible catches during the World Series, preventing five runs from scoring. Pitchers Seaver (25-7), Gary Gentry (13-12) and southpaw Jerry Koosman (17-9) helped get the Mets to the big dance. From that point, the team with the futile background did the impossible, by overcoming big obstacles en route to the big prize.

It was flamboyant Mets relief pitcher Tug McGraw who coined the optimistic rallying cry "you gotta believe." The Mets did just that and a baseball world became real believers. Again, the Silver Grill crowd celebrated the satisfying accomplishment. We could always find some reason to celebrate, as I recall. Friday night, the first day of spring and the initial snow storm of the winter were always altruistic reasons for hoisting a cold mug.

The Mets had shocked everyone with a talented squad that included Cleon Jones (.340 batting average), infielder Bud Harrelson, catcher Jerry Grote and outfielder Ron Swoboda. After Baltimore won game 1 4-1, the Mets rallied for victories by counts of 2-1, 5-0, 2-1 and 5-3. In the clincher, Koosman twirled a five-hitter while Donn Clendenon and Al Weis poked home runs.

When pro basketball got its chance in the spotlight, the New York Knicks emerged as a force to be reckoned with. The hometown Madison Square Garden crowds were treated to spectacular performances from a team that was destined to reach stardom. They did it with tenacious defense, pinpoint shooting and a never-say-die attitude.

Coach Red Holzman was blessed with a lethal mixture of talent that included smooth as silk guard Walt "Clyde" Frazier and gentle giant Willis Reed. Earl "The Pearl" Monroe complimented Frazier in the backcourt while Dave DeBusschere and Bill Bradley (Rhodes scholar and later senator from New Jersey), completed the starting five. Phil Jackson was a big plus off the bench during this glittering season. Jackson went on to win world titles as coach of the Chicago Bulls and was Michael Jordan's coach through the glory years in Chicago. Scottie Pippen and the outrageous Dennis Rodman helped make Jackson's team fun to watch.

The Knicks played air tight defense, shot the eyes out of the basket and were a group of intelligent players. Frazier, out of Southern Illinois, was my favorite player. When the guy wearing uniform number "10" laced up his sneakers, he meant business. He was the most graceful player I have ever seen play basketball. Nicknamed Clyde because of some of his wardrobe (Bonnie and Clyde era) that included a cool hat, he had a smooth jump shot, quick hands and an elegant touch from the free throw line.

The Knicks had 60 regular season wins and an 18-game winning streak. They downed the Baltimore Bullets and Milwaukee Bucks in the playoffs before colliding with the favored Los Angeles Lakers for the championship. Like the Jets and Mets before them, this New York contingent wasn't expected to take the jolt of Laker players such as Jerry West and Wilt Chamberlain. West was a super scorer and floor leader while Chamberlain seemingly scored at will (once scored 100 points in a game) and pulled down vital rebounds.

It was David versus Goliath again. The glitz and glamour of the West Coast squad against the New Yorkers, blue collar type guys that are the brand that Bruce Springsteen writes about, sings about and relates to. This nail biting series went all seven games.

Reed, the courageous captain and center, had injured his leg in game

5 and sat out game 6 (135-113 defeat). The Knicks, 60-22 during the regular season, seemed to be headed to defeat when they hit the court for game 7 at Madison Square Garden.

Some of the television games were blacked out in the New York area, so Dick Jewel, Fish, myself and others from the Silver Grill, drove to Rudy's Tavern in East Stroudsburg, Pa., to watch the action. The establishment was always packed for these games and the experience was one I will never forget.

Reed had been the regular season NBA Most Valuable Player and All-Star Game MVP. When he was all finished, he would add another trophy to his list, the NBA Finals MVP.

The sight of Reed limping onto the court for game 7 is a lucid picture in my mind and is one of the most famous images in sports history. He had led his team with rebounding, defensive and scoring skills all season long. Now hobbled and hurting bad, his leadership had been tested. He rose to the challenge by giving the Knicks heart, hope and courage. Wearing his number "19", Reed scored just two hoops in game 7. His gutsy presence did the rest.

On May 8, 1970, the New York Knicks reached the zenith of the organization's being, by clubbing the Lakers, 113-99. Frazier was simply marvelous. He splashed 36 points, piled up 19 assists and was 12-12 from the free throw line. The Knicks were now big news in professional sports, joining the Jets and Mets as champions. While the refined Frazier gunned down the enemy, it was Reed who stood tall as an emotional leader. People viewing the game at Rudy's, went bonkers when it was over. Back in Matamoras, my former boss, Jay Mack (a big Knicks fan), was probably ecstatic.

Less than a decade later, as sports editor of the Sullivan County Democrat in Callicoon, New York, I sat down with Willis Reed and did an interview with him. Reed was the Knicks coach, and he liked to escape "The Big Apple" and do some hunting in the Callicoon area. I found Reed to be a humble and easy going man who was down to earth and acting far from the superstar he had been. Co-worker Sally Keith and myself were impressed with Willis and his lack of boastfulness. She took a picture of Reed and myself on the front steps of the Democrat office. Lacking height, I tried to sneak up a step higher than Reed, but he noticed. "Bill, get on back down here," he laughed.

That 1969-70 Knicks team left an indelible mark on NBA history. Frazier retired on October 15, 1979. The fellow with the catlike moves was a seven-time NBA All-Star and chalked up 4,791 assists in his sparkling hardwood career. He was elected to the NBA Hall of Fame in 1986 and is joined in the hall by teammates Reed, DeBusschere and "Dollar Bill" Bradley, a former Princeton star. Their uniform numbers hang from the rafters at Madison Square Garden as a constant visual reminder of days gone by.

The year 1969 had been a great one. Some of the movies that year included "Easy Rider", "Hello Dolly", "True Grit" (John Wayne), "Butch Cassidy and the Sundance Kid" (Paul Newman and Robert Redford) and "Alice's Restaurant" (Arlo Guthrie).

Three big things happened to me in 1969. I got engaged to Chris on December 16, 1969, I became interested in Port Jervis basketball again and I nailed a job at Empire National Bank, in Middletown, New York, as a loan collector. A big part of that job was repossessing vehicles.

I had purchased an engagement ring at Decker and Struthers Jewelers in Port Jervis and gave the ring to Chris following a Port home basketball game. Two things were ironic about the evening of December 16.

Port had a slick shooting guard named Rich Saul who had impressed me since I watched him for the first time, a year sooner. "This is some ballplayer," I told Chris back in 1968. "I see him becoming a real star next season. It's a shame the local newspaper (Union-Gazette) doesn't give him some nice write-ups." A year from the engagement, I was a sports writer covering Rich Saul and giving him his due. The ring was given on Reservoir Avenue near where my grandfather used to work at the brewery. Right across from the area I gave the ring, was 54 Reservoir Avenue. Two years later we'd be renting an apartment in that house and awaiting the arrival of our first born.

Working at Empire National Bank was an experience that still makes me smile. I was a single guy, free of Arrow Shirts and working a day shift, plus picking up some vehicles, usually at night. From my usual work garb of shirt and decent looking pants, I now was wearing a shirt and tie. I had entered the business world and had to look the part. The men I worked with were a mixed bag of personalities that would have been more suited to a 3-ring circus.

A short, stocky Italian fellow named Frank Pizza was my boss. He had the ability to smile and be humorous but also had a serious side to him. I got along fine with Frank and he did his best to get me acclimated to my new surroundings. The other loan collectors included Fred Crist, Les Rosenbloom (who would become a mayor of a small town), Ted Brown, Bob Duffus and Jim Stack. Ted savored doing cloak and dagger repossessions, while Bob was a good-looking musician and a close friend of Frank's. Jim was a tall and rugged individual who tackled the toughest cities in our area and who sometimes got results through intimidation.

I noticed right away that nobody particularly cared to work with Ted. He was a doting and meticulous man who seemed insecure about certain things. Everything had to be "just right" for him to be reasonably happy. If you wound up picking up a car with Ted, he wanted the repossession to be pulled off to his specifications. Many times, he wanted to get vehicles late at night and that didn't sit well with the other guys. It was easy to see that they were happy to have me arrive on the scene, because Ted began snagging me for repos, instead of them.

Fred actually helped me become accustomed to the job. "You have to watch out," he warned me. "You can get stabbed in the back, in this office." We went for coffee and he more or less told me to keep my nose clean, hold delinquency percentages down and all would work out well.

Bob handled Middletown and some other areas including across the Hudson River. His percentage was the lowest in the office, so I set out to challenge him right away. He and Fred usually ignored Ted, while Jim and Les broke Ted's spirit constantly. Bob was a little bit younger than me, was dressed immaculately and it seemed every dark hair on his head was in place.

Les or "Rosie" as he liked to be called, was a needler from the word go. Ted would begin complaining about something and Les was right there to stoke the fire. "Listen to me Ted," he used to say. "You are very upset and have to calm down or you could have a heart attack. We don't want you dying on the bank's time." Ted's face would turn a crimson red and he'd start yelling and waving his arms. "I feel bad for you kid," Les would say to me in front of Ted. "Keep as far away from Ted Brown as you can."

Stack was the kind of man you wanted to avoid at all costs. His rugged fiber and no nonsense attitude made him a perfect fit for Newburgh, a city with a large minority population. Jim could joke around with the best of them and could act as though he didn't comprehend things. In reality, he was dumb as a fox.

I got to watch his style up close and personal more than once. I went to the meanest streets of Newburgh with him and one day saw guns and knives displayed right in front of me on Water Street. "Don't give me that crap," he told one customer who was swilling beer as he participated in a card game at his rented room. "Get up that God damned money right now or I'm leaving with your car. You scumbags are all alike."

It was broad daylight and we were outnumbered 6-2. Stack, a few years older than me and rock solid, stood in the doorway and waited. Meanwhile, I set some kind of record getting my ass out of that dwelling and down the front steps. Moments later, Stack returned to our car. "The son of a bitch gave me just one payment," Stack said. "He knows if I don't have another by next week, his car will be gone. Now we'll head up the street to this next idiot's place."

I was in charge of several areas including Port Jervis and some Sullivan County places such as Woodridge, Rock Hill and Fallsburgh. Usually I was in the Middletown office three days and on the road two. The two days were also reserved for working Port Jervis accounts in that territory. I wish I had a quarter for every phone call made while working this job. As I acquainted myself with the tasks at hand, I became a lone wolf, toiling alone.

I would get printouts of those who were behind in their vehicle loan payments and go from there. I never began pushing people until they were behind 30 days or more. To have someone hit 60 days was a no-no and you had to keep your eyes open for the subtle signs that showed you someone was starting to slide.

My main thrust was to make damn sure none of my customers ever reached 90 days. Once the loan is late 90 days or more, a car or truck goes off repurchase and the bank absorbs the loss. Up until that time, the vehicle can be picked up and returned to the dealership from which it came.

It was not out of the ordinary for someone to never make a first payment and simply skip to another part of the United States or even leave the country. More than one customer and his wheels have wound up in Puerto Rico, never to be heard from again.

I had large file cards for all my accounts and kept them bound with an elastic band. On these cards were documented entries about contacts with customers. The date of the contact was written and comments such as "promises payment November 18th" or "says he will get account current August 10", would be written down. I was good at noticing certain patterns in working the accounts. I met the people halfway and those who really tried to get caught up, got plenty of help from me. I would take partial payments and encourage them to keep the credit history satisfactory. The ones who tried to screw me, wound up taking shoe leather express.

I was single in those days and was out to do my job. I didn't know what it felt like to feed and clothe a family of five. I didn't feel the pressure of mortgage payments and dealing with school taxes. It still bothered me though, to have to walk up and get in someone's car and drive it away. Sometimes a mother and her kids stood nearby as I took their only mode of transportation. It was a tough job but someone had to do it.

Rosenbloom used an effective spiel on the phone that never ceased to make me bust out laughing. He would quietly dial a phone number and his voice abruptly changed into that of the kind and gentle uncle who cared so much about you. "I know it's been very tough," he would begin. "But you just have to help yourself out. I have gone to bat for you and because of that, I may lose my job. They are threatening to fire me if I don't have a payment from you by Friday. If the payment isn't made, I have no choice but to phone the sheriff and have him come to your house."

While Frank Pizza shook his head at these tactics, "Rosie" did get results. I pictured the panic-stricken customers cowering inside their front door and dreading a sheriff's car pulling into their driveways. "You have the right to remain silent....."

While Jim Stack sat at the desk behind me and read the riot act to his people, I was diplomatic in my dealings. "I'm letting you off the hook for a few days," I would tell them. "But then you have to show me some results." Most of the time being honest with the customer was the best policy. But each and every case was different and you had to be a psychologist to be a step ahead of what they were thinking.

Ted didn't take long to swoop down and try helping me. I tried to keep him at arm's length but he would have none of that. He did have a kind and generous side, but seldom did you see that makeup. Most of the time, he enjoyed working an account to the max, and became obsessed with either getting a payment or repossessing the vehicle. He enjoyed sneaking around in the darkness of night and whispering in the bushes. "Okay, you go around the passenger side and see if the door is unlocked."

Sometimes I gave him the slip and breathed a sigh of relief. One time I brought Fish along just to see what Ted was all about. "He's crazy," Fish said when the two of us were alone. "He wants you to help him get this car and then you have to drive back to Middletown in it and he is going to drive your car. What sense does that make? Then he is talking about going to get another car. Why can't he just take the repo back himself?" After talking it over, we decided to leave the situation. "We have to go, Ted. You drive the repo back," I said. He was still bitching and moaning as he walked away from us.

The absolute worst part of this job was having to go on the road with Ted in the daytime. The script was always the same and I quickly got tired of it. First you checked into the office and worked accounts for a couple of hours. Around 11 o'clock we would head out to whatever area we were going to. Usually that meant out near Coldenham (by Newburgh) where he lived. Ted always had to eat lunch before we really got busy.

He had a few favorite diners where he ate and believe you me, the owners and customers knew Ted very well. Lunches always began with these questions from Ted to the patient waitresses of our land. "What is good today?", "Is the food good and hot?", and my all time favorite, "Is the food fresh?" He always examined whatever food was delivered with fork in hand. At least 50 per cent of the time he would wrinkle up his nose, summon the waitress and send the food back.

I'm not a fussy eater and this procedure quickly got on my nerves. One day I had enough of this rubbish and simply refused to go in the diner. "And another thing," I said to Ted. "We leave the office by 9 a.m. and will be back at the bank by noon. Then you can go get your lunch."

I hated picking up cars of people I knew. Once I had to pick up cars of two guys that I was friends with, on the same day. The second was a blue Corvair that was parked out near a beautiful lake, in Huguenot. The car belonged to a former Port football player who was having a tough time of it. There is no way he could ever get current and he was close to 90 days in arrears. Ted and I made sure nobody was around when we pulled our car off Route 209 and across from his. Most of the times we simply got a customer's ignition key number out of their file and had a key cut. This file had no key number written down, so Ted was going to hot wire the car.

I was the lookout this day and leaned against the fence that led down a road to the lake. I still see Ted quickly popping the hood and going to work. His tie was flying in the breeze and sweat poured down his face. While he couldn't get the engine going, I gave him this great news update. "Hey Ted, guess what?" He never looked up and began shouting. "Willie, damn it, I have no time to talk now." I began walking toward my car with these words of advice. "Ted, either get that thing going now, or get in my damn car. He is walking up the street."

The customer, fishing pole in hand, was walking and noticing that someone was near his automobile. "Hey," he yelled. "What are you doing?" At that moment the engine turned over. Ted ran to the car and peeled gravel all over as he squealed from the scene of the crime. The two of us put Bo and Luke Duke to shame in how we recklessly maneuvered back out onto Route 209 and out of harm's way.

It wasn't long before my trusty 1966 GTO dragged on the ground worse than ever. It was time to get rid of this cream puff, so I began looking around for a new car. The bank dealt with Galloway's on Broadway in Newburgh (Ford dealership), so that is where I nailed a brand new 1970 Ford Maverick. It was a small aqua (black top) automatic transmission vehicle and fit my needs just fine. I left behind a gas guzzling car and saved money in that area.

The day I traded "the goat" in, Ted Brown was right there, riding with me. As we neared Galloway's, he got all excited about the new car. "I want to drive the Maverick out of the dealership. Is that alright with you?", he said. "Sure," I answered. "And when the payment booklet gets to me, I'll put it on your desk."

It was tough enough going to pick up a car for the bank, when the customer knew you were coming. The real challenges included skip tracing and outfoxing someone who is trying to hide the vehicle from you. I have cruised darkened streets at 4 a.m., peered at bars from a block away and lay in waiting, to scoop up the merchandise.

One guy near Washingtonville, had evaded me for quite awhile. The Plymouth Duster was close to going off repurchase and I dropped everything else and concentrated on bringing the unit in. In the meantime, this customer and his wife had split up. Nobody seemed to know where our boy was.

I went to the Salisbury Mills post office to ask some questions. The people there were tight-lipped about customers, which was their policy. "I know you can't give me information," I smiled at a girl behind the counter one morning. "Man, I wish I could get just a little bit of help on this, without getting you in trouble."

Then I began craftily finding a way to pursue the matter. "Tell you what, I'll ask a question and you nod yes or no," I said. "Does the man I'm looking for get his mail here?" She nodded her head left and right. "Does the wife have a post office box here?" She nodded in the affirmative. "Is she short? Long hair? Nice looking?", were questions that followed.

I camped out across the street for three days watching for her arrival. On the third day, I reached my immediate goal. I got her to talk to me, pieced together a few things and began tightening the noose. A couple of days later, Ted and I drove up a hill and into the front yard of a house that had a blue car in the driveway. Bingo, I was looking at the car I was after. "She is all yours," the delinquent customer said. "You found me."

While I talked with the fellow, Ted popped the hood. "Damn it," I heard him shout. "There's no engine in this car." Our customer gave us a view of his pearly whites. "Oh yes," he said. "I forgot to tell you, I made some changes." You may not have been able to drive this vehicle, but it came back all the same, on the hook of a tow truck.

The skip tracing took patience, cunning and nerve. I became very proficient at this little game and felt great satisfaction at capturing my prey. I searched for clues, used the phone, talked to relatives, friends, police chiefs and bar owners. And, most of the time, I found the vehicle, no matter where it was.

I became a master at bluffing and fibs. I would go to damn near any length to trap my quarry in a net that was dropped so securely, there was no getting away. I made a few mistakes on my path to success, but learned from those blunders.

One of my cases, which I tackled first thing on a Monday morning, went something like this. It is a situation that arose when a customer left the area and was in the great state of Texas, with a best friend who had moved there. "Hello, is Ralph there?" After the receiving party answered and asked my identity, I said "this is Fred (Ralph's brother) back in New York. Put him on for just a second would you?"

When Ralph came to the phone he was greeted by this. "Ralph, this is Empire National Bank. I need two truck payments mailed to me today and I'm not kidding." "I sold the truck," he shot back. "No you didn't," I piped up. "It was spotted this morning. Now you're going to pay, or I will pick it up. If I don't see the payments here Friday, you won't see that truck Saturday morning." The customer asked if I was in Texas. "No", I said, "but some of my people are and they are watching you like a hawk. When I get the payment, I'll tell them to ease up." Of course, "my people" were a figment of my creative imagination.

Friday, I received my mail and saw a post marked envelope from the Lone Star state. Two payments had been sent from Texas and my mission had been accomplished. Intimidation and lies? Yes. Results? Yes. No runs, no hits, no errors. And, I didn't even have to send the sheriff.

The antics inside the room at the bank were a pure study in psychology. Everyone would smile it up and share jokes like one happy family. Then one of the guys would leave for a few minutes and the back stabbing would start. I ignored all of it and pursued my accounts.

Stack busted everyone including Frank, but got on Fred most of all. "Are you still smoking those cigarettes?", he would say as he put a pencil in his mouth and pretended to smoke. Fred gave him a blank stare, got up from his desk, and proceeded to dance for us. I couldn't believe my eyes as he boogied around the room in a Fred Astaire fashion. Maybe this hoofing was his defense mechanism against stress. The old "soft shoe" was a sight to behold and Fred acted as though everyone in the world took dancing breaks at one time or another. Later, Crist quit smoking and Jim had to stop smoking pencils.

It wasn't always nose to the grindstone at the 135 North Street bank. We were up a couple of floors with real large windows on the side of the building. We could see the building next door, the outdoor banking window below us and a bar on the corner of North Street. Next to the bar, was a telephone booth, and we noticed one of the guys that hung at the bar, used that booth a lot.

If my memory serves correctly the bar was named "Jules" and the man's name was Rudy. He played some drums at the place, sometimes out on the street. I'm not so sure that all the bricks were in the building.

One day we went out to lunch and walked past the phone booth. A great idea came to my mind and I ducked into the booth and wrote down the phone number. A couple of days later, Frank had a meeting and as luck would have it, Rudy was outside and standing right next to the booth. I called the number and he went in and answered. I disguised my voice and asked him some ridiculous questions. Every time he hung up, I'd redial and he'd pick up. Tears rolled down our faces in the bank each time he slammed the phone down, because we could see his every move.

We were a pretty tight knit group, in the collection office. In fact, Frank suggested we form a bowling team (which we did) and compete in a league at a bowling alley in Walden. Ted pounced on the golden opportunity immediately. "I will meet you at the bank and you can ride to the bowling alley with me," he said. "Then after bowling, we can go pick up a car." This obsessed collector, who used to drive a taxi, nailed me just once on that tactic. From then on, I drove my own car to Walden.

Fish and I made the trek up to Plattsburgh again in 1970. Lehman offered to put us up at the barracks, but we got a motel instead. His reenlistment date was coming up soon and he shrugged it off like it was no big deal. I got real serious with him though and looked in his eyes. "You are going to get out Willie, right?", I said. "Your going to go back to Oklahoma and be free of the Air Force." He gave me a grin and said "I sure am, boy." I pursued it further and he contended that he would not be reenlisting for a third hitch (four year commitment).

Lehman knew Chris and I were going to be getting married in September and he wished us the best once he knew. To this day, I am so happy that my bride to be and Willie, met eye to eye.

At the bank everything was going smoothly. One day, Ted sat at his desk and scratched his head with an irritated look on his face. When I asked what was wrong, he shuffled his paperwork and stood up. "I'm having trouble with this account," he said. "I'm going to have to reach this Harry Dingle." As I laughed uncontrollably, I managed to tell Ted not to sweat it. "With a name like Harry Dingle, he shouldn't have to make any payments," I asserted.

Summer changed to fall and area kids began going back to school. The leaves were raked into piles to be burned and the crisp nights were filled with football at Port Jervis High School. A year later, I would be a big part of athletics in my home town. But for now, my time at home on Lyman Avenue, was drawing to a close. On September 12, 1970, I would take the hand of Christine Goble in marriage. My bachelor days were coming to an end and a lifetime of happiness and commitment, was right around the corner.

CHAPTER 10

Wedding Bells

It was Christine who was sold on a September wedding right from the start.

Between the two of us, we were working a total of four jobs. While I was putting up with Ted Brown's shenanigans, Chris was toiling full time at Sparkomatic Corporation, a company that made car speakers, gear shift knobs and the like. She also had a part time job at the Atlantic and Pacific Tea Company (A&P) and was a church organist on Sundays. At Sparkomatic, in Milford, Pa., she was a computer programmer. Chris worked in the office and part of the job was making printouts from the computers of the day. By comparison to today's technology, she was working with office machines that would look good in Herman Munster's cellar.

We decided the wedding would be September 12, 1970, at Matamoras (Pa.) United Methodist Church. I was leaving the Catholic faith to marry a Protestant girl and no doubt, the forceful Father Leddy probably agonized for months over how he hadn't gotten through to me. I no doubt, was going to wind up with a one way ticket to hell.

While many prospective grooms think about forgetting the ring, passing out from nervousness or not being able to repeat the wedding vows, I worried about health issues. I had always been smacked around by hay fever, ragweed and pollen during the summer. I pictured myself, nose running, eyes itching and sneezing up a storm on this, the most important day of my life.

Pad was to serve as my best man while Fish, Henszie and Frank Ott (my nightly money source on Guam) would be ushers. Chris selected her cousin, Margaret Outwater, as matron of honor while attendants included Ann Davis, Cathy DeMarco and my sister, Anne.

Frank came up from Mineola, Long Island for the ceremony and fit right in perfectly with Fish and Henszie. The night before the wedding, we all adjourned to Bamberger's to drink away the waning hours of my bachelorhood. I had sewn my wild oats overseas and was ready, willing and able to settle down. While growing up, I had the same worries as many men and women. I agonized that I would never find anyone to

252

marry. In Chris, I thanked my lucky stars that I had found a true love, a genuine companion and a soul mate for life.

Christine was the most beautiful bride I had ever seen, it was a sunny day on the 12th and there wasn't a hint of hay fever in the air. Chris' shiny burgundy Barracuda delivered her to the church at the corner of Avenue H, for the noon wedding. The place of worship was nearly packed as Reverend Thomas Skyler performed the noon ceremony. My shirt sleeves, under a black tuxedo, seemed long, but other than that, all went well. Margaret wore a green gown while the other three bridal attendants were attired in blue.

My parents, plus Marion and Ernie Goble all beamed with pride. Chris' mom was not a big joker, and I was just the opposite, always kidding around, fibbing and working the room for laughs. Marion once told us that she didn't like to dance, so I, of course, pounded away at that fact. A couple of days before the ceremony, I sat in at her kitchen table with a straight face and discussed the wedding.

The reception was to be at the Matamoras grange hall, across and down the street from the Matamoras Elementary school. Mr. And Mrs. Coleman, well known for their excellent food, would be catering the affair, while the band Bob Duffus played in, would be providing the music. "The parents will walk into the hall and immediately start the reception by dancing," I told Marion. Chris gave me a look that would sink a thousand ships.

We walked down the church steps to the traditional rice shower and our lives as Mr. And Mrs. William Tangen had begun. I had done well, asking Ernie for Chris' hand in marriage as a gesture of respect and tradition. That eye-to-eye meeting was one I put off day after day. Finally, I couldn't take it any more and went over to his house.

Ernie was an intelligent and hard working individual. He had served in the Army during World War II and knew what serving overseas was all about. When I had gotten home from the Air Force, the Gobles saw their daughter being taken away from home time after time. However, I proved to them that I was a responsible person who would love and provide for their Christine. I came out with the question "I want your permission to marry your daughter" and quickly got an okay. We sealed the deal with a can of beer that I had brought from home.

The reception was spectacular. My dad and mom really got into the swing of things and the Gobles smiled radiantly. While Chris' guests were mostly of the quiet variety, many of mine nearly swung from the chandeliers as the afternoon gave way to early evening.

We had purchased beer from Meloi's Liquors in Montague, N.J. Rocky Meloi and his wife were friends of my parents and joined in to have a good time at the reception. There were some heavy hitter beer drinkers at the event and soon the beer supply began to dwindle. Everybody got their second wind when Rocky made a quick trip to his store for additional suds and more money kept the band playing another set or two.

This day is one that can never be duplicated. The memories return to me as if I got married yesterday. Aunt Pat and Uncle Bob came up from New Jersey and smiled as I danced with Mom and Chris with Dad. We wanted time to stand still but the hands on the clock whipped around quickly. The celebration, complete with some great oldies music, continued as night began to fall.

My dad had given us a fantastic wedding present in the form of a honeymoon in St. Thomas, U.S. Virgin Islands. Our plane was to take off the next day from Kennedy Airport in New York. We would be relaxing in the beautiful weather of the Caribbean, far away from the site of our marriage. Overnight we would be lodged not far from the runways of JFK. Those pretty blue runway lights would be entering my life again.

The year 1970 was a fine one for music. "Raindrops Keep Fallin' On My Head" by B.J. Thomas, was ranked first by Musicradio WABC, New York City. "Close To You" (The Carpenters), "The Rapper" (The Jaggerz), "Mama Told Me" (Three Dog Night), "In The Summertime" (Mungo Jerry) and "Ride Captain Ride" (The Blues Image) all made it big. Elvis was on the scene with "The Wonder of You" and Crosby, Stills, Nash and Young checked in with "Woodstock". I knew that in this, our first year together, Chris and I would combine to make beautiful music..

Marrying Chris was a dream come true. I knew that any roadblocks in our life together, could be conquered. Our ceremony had been an emotional one and I had fought back tears when I heard the "in sickness and in health" and heard Christine say "I do." She was the rock of Gibraltar in most cases but couldn't stop the steady flow of tears when Ernie walked her down the aisle.

Two potential obstacles emerged right away on "our day." As luck would have it, we would be flying the friendly skies, with the knowledge that there were airline hijackings going on in our country. The other fly in the ointment was a minor one, attired in a long polka dot dress.

Chris had changed her clothes at her parents' house but it would be awhile until I could be alone with my brand new bride. It seems an elderly friend of the Gobles happened to live in Middletown (N.Y.), which was on the way to the airport, and was in need of a ride home. While "Only You" by The Platters was "our song", it was "only me" who faced the prospects of driving away from the reception with my new wife and the little old lady from Pasadena.

Freda Stamm was a nice old gal. She cut a rug at the reception, dancing up a storm in front of the crowd. Now she conspicuously sat in a dark blue and white polka dot dress in the back seat of my 1970 Ford Maverick. This 16-mile jaunt to Middletown is one for the ages. I steered the car carefully and then helped the lady exit at her house. In the blink of an eye, we were free at last.

The green and white signs whizzed by as we proceeded south on Interstate Route 87 to the big city. The realization of total freedom was overwhelming and I never wanted that feeling to go away. We checked into our hotel happy, but whipped from the long day. Chris had been awake for many hours and was faced with her first plane ride the next day. Meanwhile, all the excitement, a long night at Bambergers and a heart-wrenching September 12th were taking their toll on me.

The only time we left our room was to tip toe out into the hall to a candy machine. I watched the corridor like a hawk. I trusted absolutely nobody in this place. For all I knew, hijackers were lodged in the next room. We wondered what the next day would bring. Would St. Thomas be a nice place? And what about the weather, is it warm there?

After eating breakfast, we embarked on our first long trip as a couple. The plane touched down and was dwarfed by the nearby majestic mountains. Everything was green and blue. The sight of the crystal clear ocean, lapping up on sandy beaches, was too much to comprehend. Our first sensation upon exiting the aircraft, was the sudden blast of heat. I had left the tropical warmth of Guam and shivered in San Francisco less than two years earlier. Now the trend was being reversed.

Later, a golf cart transported us to our accommodations at Pineapple Beach. Chris was feeling dizzy and I felt like a truck had just run over me, as we wobbled to our door, opened it and fell on the bed. We were in paradise but were too exhausted to even enjoy it. Once the air conditioning was turned on and our bodies began to recover, all was right with the world.

My father had given us a tremendous wedding gift. All of our meals were already paid for and signing a check was the only responsibility. There were several places to eat within walking distance and the food was excellent.

Back home, the Gillinders, Chris' neighbors, had just come back from Pineapple Beach. They raved about the place and told us to make sure to look up a fellow named Yves. They said Yves could be found at one of the salient outdoor bars that dotted the landscape. We swam at two nearby pools with palm trees swaying in the warm breeze. If we felt like hopping in the pool at 4 a.m., that is what we did.

We went to the main town, Charlotte Amalie, located right on the ocean. Ships were docked there and people on cruises flocked to nearby shops. One time we rode with another newly married people in a rented car. They drive on the other side of the street in the Virgin Islands and I tried to steer the car from the back seat. This was the land of beaches, water, steel bands producing invigorating music, and rum. It seems that everyone here enjoyed rum. To have it poured on my corn flakes wouldn't have raised an eyebrow.

We were adjusting to our new environment quickly and never wanted these precious days to end. The two of us hit the outdoor bars in the afternoon and had turkey sandwiches with mayonnaise and drinks. I favored bottled Heineken beer while Chris socked down "Donkey Kicks." Some of the ingredients in a Donkey Kick included lemon juice, grenadine and what else?, rum. It was Yves, a constantly smiling guy, who mixed us up some Donkey Kicks to wash down our sandwiches. He tended bar almost daily and we always looked for him.

Yves proved to be a fine guide. He remembered the Gillinders and said he would show us all around. He was a man of his word, making good on that promise. Chris and I climbed up and down hills like mountain goats and had our pictures taken together, by Yves. In one photo, my wife was sitting on a donkey. That shot came out real blurred and I have to think that Yves may have imbibed in too many of those Donkey Kicks, himself.

One night, Chris saw a skinny little cat outside our room and smuggled him in for the night. I loved married life right from the start, even though I knew that we would be going back to work when we got back home.

I recall one of the afternoons when we stayed too long at an outdoor bar and dragged ourselves back to our room. Both of us were shot to hell and decided to skip dinner and sleep instead. We woke up in time to shower and still get to the restaurant in time to eat.

This particular night we perused the menu through bleary eyes and decided on cornish hen, something we had never eaten in our lives. I dug right in and was shocked to find that the food had a gamey taste to it. I tried like hell to swallow it but couldn't. I quietly transported the food to a napkin and looked across the table at Chris. Her horrified look told the whole story. Neither one of us liked this dish at all.

Suddenly our appetites were totally gone. I looked around the room, saw my waiter walking the other way and decided we should get out of there fast. We left a tip and then tried to slink away into the St. Thomas night. We nearly made it to the door undetected.

Out of nowhere, our waiter was at our side. He placed a hand on my shoulder and said. "You have to sign this check before you can leave." I scribbled out my name and felt 1,000 eyes on me as we finally exited the eating facility.

Chris set the tone for how she would be, on most of our vacations over the years. She started getting sad the night before departure and asked if I was interested in staying another day. Like a jackass, I said that we should really be heading home. I have regretted that decision since making it and know it was the first major blunder of our marriage. I promised her we would come back to the Virgin Islands real soon. So far, it has been over 32 years since we were there. Pineapple Beach is long gone but St. Thomas is still there. I would love to go back there in 2003.

We had left the Ford Maverick at JFK Airport and Frank Ott had come and driven the vehicle back to Mineola so we would save money on the parking. The car was there when we touched down at JFK, and instead of going home, we wound up driving north on Route 87, all the way up to Plattsburgh.

After arriving in town, I pulled into the Dawn Motel and secured us a room. We had just come from absolute paradise and were now faced with the realization that the honeymoon was over. Those salty droplets cascading down Chris' face weren't tears of joy. It was a downer leaving St. Thomas, and my wife to this day, still brings up the fact that we sacrificed an extra day in the Virgin Islands.

We had managed to rent the upstairs at a gray house on Mill Street in Milford. We parked our cars in a lot across from the structure and began day to day life as husband and wife. I continued to work at the bank while Chris plugged away at her three jobs. We had a nice kitchen and Chris cooked us meals right from the start.

In our early days of marriage we liked the commitment but despised the lack of privacy at the Mill Street location. The landlords were nosy types who waited for us to leave for work and then went upstairs and delved through our property. We knew invasion of privacy was taking place because Chris noticed that candies began disappearing from a dish on our coffee table. "Are you sure?", I asked her. And then we set a trap. We counted out the number of candies in the dish and checked each day. Either people were coming up the stairs and having a good old time, or the mice had a sweet tooth.

We resolved to get another place as soon as we could and that break would come in 1971, when we grabbed an apartment on Reservoir Avenue in Port Jervis. In the meantime, we had to make due with the situation.

My father had developed a keen interest in art and pushed forward into getting his own art gallery. On October 4, 1970, there was a grand opening and open house at the Les Trois Art Display Gallery on East Main Street in Port Jervis. Less than a year later, on June 6, 1971, the gallery was dedicated in memory of local artist John Newton Howitt. Howitt (1885-1958) lived in Port but had studios in New York City. He did landscapes in Canada, New England, Bermuda, Florida, Tennessee, New York, New Jersey and Pennsylvania. His paintings hung in some of the most prestigious places there are, including the West Point Military Academy Museum. His widow, Bertha Howitt, was on hand for the dedication to her late husband, and a plaque still adorns the side of the building.

My dad helped bring arts and culture to Port Jervis. The gallery was dedicated to the growth of arts in the tri-state area. Hanging from the walls were original oils, water colors and graphics by professional artists from the surrounding area.

Chris and I loved spending time together. Sometimes we would go with her parents on picnics, or even climb nearby mountains. We would lie in bed in the morning when the clock radio came on and listen to the "Imus in the morning" radio show. Don Imus, tame as compared to Howard Stern, was still pretty outrageous. He liked to play the George Harrison song "My Sweet Lord" and the rhythmic beat of the tune, had us tapping our feet under the covers. Every time we heard that song, I would say "Tapper Tully" and we'd tap our feet and toes against each other. Where I came up with the words "Tapper Tully" to describe "My Sweet Lord", is anyone's guess.

October gave way to November and I realized that soon, high school basketball would be rolling around again. Rich Saul would be a senior on the Port basketball team and would probably still receive little ink when it came to his awesome ability. I brought that fact up to Chris and she said "you have the talent, do something about it."

I never realized that writing was really in my blood. But that unknown fact was to be drawn out quickly, by a "stop the presses" kind of editor who guided the Port Jervis Union Gazette. Gene Michael Casey was, and still is, the best editor I have ever had the pleasure to work under. For the hell of it, I dialed up the Gazette to see if there were any part time writing openings in sports. I was happy to be referred to my old track teammate John Kinney, who was writing there (when not in college at Georgetown University).

After Gene had left the Gazette, John became my editor and was another fabulous leader. Under Kinney, I was named sports editor in 1973. It was that phone call to John, that would change my life forever. "I was a catalyst," John, said in the middle of 2002. "Does that mean you raised cattle?", I joked. He is currently way up the ladder, in Ottaway newspapers, after having been a newspaper publisher in Massachusetts.

That fateful day, John told me that Gene Casey was looking for somebody in sports and that my timing was perfect. "Come on in and see Gene," John had said. "Who knows, you could wind up working here."

I arrived at the Gazette on Fowler Street and was taken into Gene's office. Casey was an animated, energetic person who stood around 5-9", had blue eyes and wavy blond hair. He was forceful in a pleasant kind of way, and his body language exuded raw and unbridled power. He was a positive individual who wasn't afraid to make decisions and get desired results. In his tenure at the Gazette, he was not a "good old boy" and wasn't afraid to take on those in the public eye, who figured they were above being observed. Gene was a fair and just man, who believed in what he was doing, and was totally loyal to his family and fellow reporters.

"What makes you think you can write?", he queried while grabbing a couple of pieces of blank typing paper. "I don't know Mr. Casey," I replied. "It is easy for me to write down what I'm thinking. The words come easily."

Gene rolled his sleeves up, loosened his tie and handed me the papers. "There's a typewriter in there, lad," he said, pointing to a nearby room. "Write about any kind of sport that you want to. I'll be here when you get done. And by the way, my name is Gene."

It didn't take me very long to rap out a story about a fictitious basketball game. Soon, I was back at his office to turn in the copy. Gene got up from his desk and was amazed when he realized I had completed the task quickly and impressively. He was ecstatic at what he was witnessing and let me know so, immediately. "Lad, I don't know what you are doing working for a bank. I do know, that you have writing ability and am offering you a part time job right now." I thanked him vigorously and headed for Milford, knowing that I had been hired on the spot.

I would be employed with an office staff that included John Kinney, Tony Krzczuk, Harry VanInwegen, and Stan Hojnacki (pronounced Hynowski). I would be working nights during the winter sports season, covering basketball and wrestling. I had made sure of one thing, Rich Saul would be getting some great basketball coverage.

While I continued my bank job, I shied away from doing many nighttime repossessions. Ted Brown was now on his own, to sneak around until all hours of the morning. Instead, I would be in the friendly and warm confines of gymnasiums at Port Jervis and Delaware Valley high schools.

At the start of my writing career, I was blessed with talented teams and performers from both schools. At the age of 23, I was only about a half dozen years older than the athletes I was covering. I showed enthusiasm for my new job, became respected quickly and gained the trust of those I came in contact with.

I was presented with challenges from the outset, and was eager to observe an event and take people behind the scenes. Writing was lots of fun for me and going to sporting events for free, was an extra added bonus. By the time this venture had taken me full time, I was totally hooked on sports writing. One call to John Kinney would snowball into pages and pages of fantastic local sports coverage. People at our sister newspaper in Middletown (Times-Herald Record), also owned by Ottaway, saw what was happening in Port Jervis, and some stated publicly that they wanted me to wind up on their staff.

I had gotten my wish to write sports stories but quickly was informed that photography and darkroom work would also be part of my job. In addition to never having photographed sports, I knew very little about high school wrestling and had to learn about it.

It is so ironic that basketball was my first love, yet wrestling coverage is what would win me a New York State Sportswriter of the Year award. I used a Yashica box 2 ¼ camera and a large gray flash that had to be plugged into an electrical outlet in the darkroom, to recharge. I found, to my relief, that I had a knack for stopping action with my camera. I caught basketball players in mid air, captured facial expressions and knew how to click the shutter at the precise moment a wrestler was getting pinned or executing an action packed move.

Later in my career I looked for the story behind the scenes in photography, as well as writing. Over the mountain, at Minisink Valley High School, each mat maid was responsible for getting pictures of one wrestler (for a scrapbook) as he competed. At one event, all the mat maids came to the edge of the mat and watched the progress of the wrestling match. I blended into the woodwork and got a great shot of the whole line of girls on their knees, including the girl closest to me, as she photographed. She had no idea that she was becoming an image, herself.

Shooting athletic events was never a problem for me. The real fun began back at the Gazette office, when I was faced with going in the darkroom, turning off all the lights, opening the camera and threading my film onto black and clear holders that would be placed in film chemicals. While I was filling sports pages with great pictures and long local stories, the real task to me, was conquering the challenge in that darkroom.

A quiet and deep thinking dark haired guy by the name of Doug Gore was a part time photographer for the Gazette. He had a natural instinct for the camera and possessed a barrel full of talent. He could capture droplets on a rose or a player diving into an end zone. He had the knack of bringing out emotion in his subjects and was a professional in every phase of photography. The two most stubborn individuals I have ever met in my 55 plus years of life, are my father and Gore. Doug is about five years older than I am, and has taught me much about life.

My first venture into the darkroom was a nightmare. "I'll show you how to thread that film," Doug said. "Watch and listen carefully because once that light goes out, you are on your own." Gore was the type to see a project through from start to finish. When he clicked the light off, he moved into a corner of the darkroom as I opened the back of the camera and took the exposed film out.

I tried to rush things, panicked and started screwing everything up. The film just plain wouldn't fit into the grooves on the holder. "Take a deep breath, and think about what you're doing," a voice said. "This is only as hard as you make it. I have all night and you aren't going anywhere until you get it right."

My mind quickly rewound back to Sullivan's in Liberty. But this time, instead of saying "no, no, no", I was determined to master this part of my new job. I persevered under the expert guidance of Gore and not only mastered the darkroom, but became a fine photographer of sports.

That first introduction to Gore wouldn't be the last. In later years he helped me obtain a job as parts counter worker in a dealership where he was the number one mechanic. I have seen him patiently build and fly model planes and ride a Harley motorcycle with the wildest of them. One day, he simply put how he felt about life, into words. "Don't tread on me," he said.

From that first darkroom meeting, evolved a strange but real friendship. We both seem to have healthy egos. If someone tells us that something can't be done, we will do it, just to prove a point. Come to think of it, I may be the third most stubborn person I've ever known. It was Gene Casey who saw the talent in both Doug and me.

Gore and I socked down suds together, stood on the same football sidelines, helped bury a friend and wrestled to the death on broken glass, near the Erie Railroad tracks. That little tussle happened one evening after we'd consumed much alcohol in a neighborhood bar. We call that altercation the night of "the mud, the blood and the beer." Incidentally, this individual is strong as a bull and won that event. We walked wearily past spectators at the tracks, recaptured our bar stools and continued to drink. I noticed that nobody in the tavern came near us for awhile.

You don't plan dates and times with Doug Gore. You may not see him for 10 years and one day he will either arrive at your house in a vehicle or on a cycle. "Hey snake," he'll say. "What's new, toad?", will be my response. He and Gene were close friends and those two "toads" were known to crack open a bottle or two of whiskey.

By becoming a writer, I would be going back into the Port Jervis school system. My boyhood idol, Alex Osowick, was the head basketball coach while Al Wilgard, who called me "T-Bone" and "round baller" in high school, was still the varsity wrestling skipper. Once football rolled around, I would be sitting in the locker room with Joe Viglione. I thought about how I bombed his history class but was quickly put at ease. "That was history then and this is football now," he said, as we shook hands.

I had the right idea about writing from day one. I am the type of individual who doesn't like last second surprises. I am organized in most things I do and covering athletic events would be no different. I did my homework on events to be covered and never went in cold. I put my heart and soul into this job and got tremendous intrinsic reward from my efforts. The words flowed easily, like the tumbling spray of a waterfall. I showed those fans who couldn't see the winning basket how the ball slithered through the net, under that brilliant orange rim.

The first coach I ever phoned was DV wrestling mentor Ned Bushong. Ned, Osowick, Al Holtzer and Angelo Matz (DV coaches) plus Ali (of course), were the easiest interviews I have had in my 32 years as a scribe. DV was loaded with freshmen and sophomores that first year and posted a 5-8 record. Bushong helped launch my career.

Over at Port, Wilgard's Raiders won the Orange County League title (5-0). Port took third in the OCL Tournament and later, Steve Saul (115 pounds) and Dan Simmons (215) won Section 9 mat titles and advanced to the New York State Intersectional Wrestling Tournament (states) at Syracuse's Onondaga War Memorial. Chris and I went up to cover the event and in quarterfinals, watched Saul drop a close decision and Simmons get pinned.

Across the river at DV, Paul Dedea (120) won a District 12 mat title and advanced to the Northeastern Pennsylvania Regional Tournament. He dropped a 10-4 decision in the semifinal round.

The two local basketball teams experienced rewarding 1970-71 seasons. DV, under first year coach John Watson, shrugged off a slow start to surge to the District 12 championship. The Warriors were sparked by Paul Samide, Walt Losee, Jeff Foss, Bob Orben, Rick Krause, Dee Losee, Mario Piccolo, John Gillinder, Jim Luhrs and Ed Gavalla.

It had been at the DV gym, where I had gone for my very first assignment. My December 2, 1970 byline appeared the next day and I looked at it again and again. "Pocono Mountain Likes New Delval Gym" the headline read. Next to my career-starting first story, was a photo of Orben, taken by Kinney, plus a large picture I took, of Foss up near the rim. The Warriors had dropped their opener, 57-47, but got hot from the middle of the season on.

DV copped the Class C Public School title over Waymart, 52-45, as Dee Losee's foul shots near the end, iced the game. The Warriors grabbed their eighth win it their last nine tries, by copping the District 12 title over Mountain View, 56-54, at the Scranton Catholic Youth Center. DV was down by five points with 2:09 to go, but used Rick Krause's late game heroics and Piccolo's 23 points to advance. The Warrior dream was shattered to pieces in a 62-59 Regional Semifinals loss to Forest City. DV had accomplished a lot in finishing 12-5 and winning the first District 12 crown since 1957, the school's first year of existence. Meanwhile, Orben was named a Wayne County League all-star as a junior.

Gene was real happy with my sports coverage. "Groovy", he would say as he maneuvered around the newsroom. Meanwhile, Saul and the Raiders captured the fancy of local basketball fans, who had waited many years for a decent team to represent Port Jervis.

Chris had not been interested in basketball since I played in high school. However, she, Fish and Pad became big time Raider cage fans. Port had an intelligent squad that season and could find a way to beat you. Decked out in their home whites or away black and reds, the Raiders looked and played like a confident high school squad.

Saul had led the Village DUSO and DUSO League in scoring his junior season and was back to strike terror in the hearts of opponents again. Port was now in the Orange County League and celebrated by running off a five-game winning streak. Port had won its opener over Washingtonville, 72-54, behind 33 points from Saul.

In addition to Rich, Port was led by Earl Sheard, Doug Wilson, Kevin Birmingham, Harold Ulbrich, Gary Spears, Jim Pollard, Curtis Grice, Jim Butler and Wilson Gardner.

As the season progressed, there was no doubt in my mind that Saul, pound for pound, was the finest high school basketball player our area had ever seen. It has been over 30 years since Rich Saul graced the Port gymnasium and my opinion hasn't changed. Saul was smooth as silk with his fluid jump shot or drives to the basket, had catlike defensive moves and could handle the ball exceptionally well. He faced double teams constantly but his leadership would still find a way to beat you. "No one can go one-on-one with Saul," Osowick used to say.

Port was an underdog, but remained confident when undefeated Highland Falls came to town for a February 9, 1971 game. Coach Jerry Kaplan's charges entered at 12-0, had won 24-straight games and was ranked fifth in the state of New York. Port, 9-3, was aware of the tough assignment it faced. "If we can put it all together, we could cause a major upset," Osowick predicted.

The next day's headline was in the form of a big banner over the top of the sports page. It read, "They Said It Couldn't Be Done." A smaller headline exclaimed "Saul, PJ Cagers Top Highland Falls, 77-76."

This story ranks right up there with personal training camp Muhammad Ali stories I've done, plus my coverage of Lou Banach and Port Jervis capturing New York State wrestling titles in 1977. The night Saul gunned down Highland Falls, is permanently etched in my memory bank.

The story began: "A fantastic display of guts and determination coupled with the terrific scoring power of super star Rich Saul put Port Jervis in the basketball spotlight Tuesday night." Saul had gone wild to splash 43 points in the stirring upset. Port had to overcome the antics of offensive threats Guy Oakes (21.3 points per game) and Gil Peoples (22.8). Meanwhile, the 5-11" Saul, played a dazzling game. He tied the game, 73-73, with a high arching jump shot and added two free throws with 37 ticks left on the clock. The ball was in his hands when the final buzzer went off, as he held the ball away from the frantic and desperate Highland Falls players.

My work at the Gazette was being watched by those in supervisory positions. One of my pages made its way back to Gene from Ottaway headquarters in Campbell Hall. The group's president, James Ottaway Jr., wrote on top of one of my sports pages "good action photos", while Casey and others in responsible positions, (including Milton McLean, publisher) initialed the page.

I got along fabulously with Gene Casey and knew it was just a matter of time before I quit the bank and went full time at the Gazette. One night I was in the newspaper office, got ready to leave and said "see you later Gene." He gave me a wink and said "you will." He would give that two word answer frequently to answer people.

Saul and the Raiders continued to flourish. Port made it into the OCL title game but was bounced by Highland Falls this time, 75-46. In the Section 9 Tournament, Saul popped in 31 points in a narrow 70-69 win over Onteora, but the end of the line came in a 69-61 loss to Highland Falls (again). Saul gave it everything he had, and scored 22 points, but it just wasn't enough. Port had finished at 15-5, the best Raider record since Osowick and his mates went 14-2 during the regular season, back in 1957-58.

Overall, Saul had averaged 26.6 points a game in his senior season. He grabbed the OCL scoring crown (26.3) and was a shear pleasure to watch. After he graduated, I ran into him one night at the Black Bear Inn. We kidded back and forth and I challenged him to a one-on-one basketball contest the next morning at a Port playground. That game, thank God, never took place.

Pad was a hard core Port basketball fan. He really got into the games with all four feet. Opening his mouth at the inappropriate time and in the wrong place, got him into trouble one night at a Port basketball game (this was a good five years before he worked for me). Gary Spears (Rick's brother) was a fine basketball player and a hard worker on the court. Pad hadn't really become all that familiar with Gary though and voiced his opinion during the course of an intense Port game. The Raiders called a timeout and Spears came off the bench and reported into the game.

Pad was sitting in a packed gymnasium and came out with this gem. "Oh no, here comes that selfish, grabby Spears again." Sitting behind Pad, was none other than Chet Spears, Gary's rough and ready dad. "How would you like a punch in the mouth?", Chet asked Pad. "If it makes you feel any better, go ahead," was my buddy's response. Talk about bloopers. As the season progressed, Pad admitted that he had been wrong and that Spears was a fine ballplayer. I don't know for sure, whether he made that statement honestly, or through a degree of intimidation.

Saul wound up his high school career (52 games) with 1,146 points and a 22.0 points per game average for his three years of competition. This honor student, who later went on to become a tax lawyer, was the toughest interview I have ever conducted. He was extremely quiet and let his cage expertise do the talking.

I continued to be lucky in that the Raider football team of 1971 was also a winning crew. Viglione's players ended a 24-year title drought by winning the outright OCL grid title with a 7-1 league mark. Quarterback Jim Butler, backs Kevin Nicolette and Jerry Stellato (who I labeled touchdown twins), linebackers Bohdan Pawlicha, and Joe Rybak, plus Dave Kowal, Len Ey and the rest, got the job done. It was easy to be a sportswriter in Port Jervis during these times. The athletic teams I covered were laced with excellent athletes.

I had made the decision in early 1971, to walk away from banking and move into the field of journalism. "You will never regret it, lad," Casey had told me. "You have way too much writing talent to let it go to waste."

Before I left the bank, Duffus and I went to Monticello Raceway to view the March 8. 1971 heavyweight boxing title match at Madison Square Garden, between champion Joe Frazier and challenger Muhammad Ali. Ali had been reinstated to boxing and decked in red trunks, was after Frazier's title. It has been billed "the fight of the century" and featured Ali being knocked to the canvas in the 14th round, by Smokin Joe, who gained a decision victory. Duffus pulled for Frazier and I wanted "The Greatest", who was 31-0, to prevail. It was one of the finest and most brutal fights I have ever witnessed. Muhammad later won both Ali-Frazier II and III, (1974 and 1975) by decision and 14th round TKO respectively.

I went to the Gazette as a full time reporter whose beats included sports, police and city court. I walked into this new world with an open mind and patience to learn from the seasoned Gene Casey. There had been quite a bit going on in Port Jervis during early 1971. On February 12, a holiday for some (Lincoln's birthday), a tragedy struck the city, when a three-story brick building collapsed on a next door diner, killing four people and injuring 20. This happening was ranked more serious than the 1955 flood, which didn't claim a life.

Chris and I had spent our first Christmas (1970) together in the Milford apartment, kidding around and happily taking pictures of our skinny Christmas tree. At this point in time, we were working five jobs and resembled two ships passing in the night. The year 1971 brought plenty of promise for us, as we delighted in our marriage and thanked God that we had found each other. Little did we ever suspect that the new year would begin on such a horrible note.

The holidays were over and the past, including my time in the military, started seeming as if it had been a dream rather than reality. From time to time, my bride and I would talk about Willie Lehman, though. We figured he had gotten discharged from the Air Force and was now attending "Sunday Mass" in his native Mooreland, Oklahoma. All was right in the world, until the telephone rang on January 3.

Rosie, a bartender in Plattsburgh, was on the other end of the wire. How she had found out my last name or tracked down my phone number, was a small mystery. What she had to say was serious, to the point, and made me squeeze the receiver in a death grip and stare at the wall in horror. "Bill, I have some awful news," she said. "Willie Lehman is dead." I felt as if I had been pounded in the stomach with a powerful fist. I tried to clear my mind and recover from the cutting words I had just heard. In a state of semi-shock, I had a typical first reaction, by refusing to believe the heartbreaking words.

"Willie drowned in Thailand," Rosie said. "They found his body, but he had a closed casket." Rosie and Willie had been good friends and I remember them having a good old time in Charlie's bar. "There was a picture of Willie in uniform at the funeral," she said. "I found out from his family and I have a picture." I never hesitated in telling Rosie that I would be up to Plattsburgh to speak with her.

"He swore to me that he wouldn't reenlist," I told Rosie. "God damn him, why didn't he listen to me?" There was silence on the other end and it didn't take an Einstein to figure out that both our hearts had been shattered by this dismal happening. I felt guilty that I hadn't pressured Willie more about civilian life, on my trips up north. I rationalized that he simply made his decision and stuck to it. Although he had been four years older and a brother figure to me, in later years I have shaken my head sadly and said to myself "damn, Willie was only 27 years old (born May 13, 1943). He never really got to experience life."

I could have just felt fortunate to know Willie's fate, shrug it off and go on with day to day life. While many people would have done just that, it is not my makeup to react in that fashion. I was realistic enough to know that nothing would bring Willie back. He had been a loyal and genuine friend. I had been terrified to meet him at Plattsburgh but wound up following him to Guam. I couldn't just let it go.

I made the trip north to Charlie's and found Rosie. We consoled each other and shared a common misery that featured a powerless and empty feeling. I felt sick in the pit of my stomach as a result of life delivering a cruel and lethal blow. "They say Willie was fishing, fell off a boat and drowned in November," she noted. Our eyes met instantly and I spewed out some angry words. "Who is to say some son of a bitch didn't push him overboard?", I said. It hurts to know I will probably never glean the real story of how William D. Lehman perished. Military cover-ups have been known to occur from time to time. In my heart, I hope this isn't one of those instances.

Years later, I made it my business to seek out Willie's family in Oklahoma and explain my relationship with their late son. I talked a few times to his mother, Letha Lehman, and she was very happy to have contact with one of her boy's friends. After one such call, I tearfully retreated to a bedside drawer and found a picture of Lehman. I wrote a short note, put it in an envelope and mailed it to his mother. Letha passed away in 1997 at the age of 77. She had been the widow of Willie William Lehman, my buddy's dad.

William Dean Lehman was the second oldest of six children. The oldest (now deceased) was Robert, while others include Kenneth Wayne (slightly younger than Willie), sister Cleta, Ronald, and Jim, the youngest. Only Cleta and Jim remain in Oklahoma and live only about 10 miles apart.

In later years, I began talking to Jim on the phone, chuckling over old military stories involving one of his big brothers. I sent him some pictures of Willie also, and got a strange feeling that my old boss was aware that I had bridged a gap between Oklahoma and Pennsylvania.

Jim was only 13 years old when the Lehmans got the glum word from Thailand. "We (family) never really talked about it (Willie's death)," Jim told me the evening of November 22, 2002. "A lot of time has gone by now," he said. "It doesn't bother me as much as it used to."

The youngest Lehman remembers some of the circumstances surrounding the death of his brother. "Dean (as Willie was called at home) was in Thailand and they were shipping him back to Arizona to testify in a court case," he asserts. "He was on a boat in the Mekong River and they said he got drunk and fell overboard. How do I know that happened for sure?" There was a moment of total silence at the other end of the phone, before Jim continued. "I wondered about this story right from the beginning. He died November 10, 1970 and the first word we got, was that he was missing. They recovered his body three or four days later."

Jim focused his mind back to that bleak day over 32 years ago, when the oldest brother, Robert, got involved. "He was the one who had to go and identify Dean," Jim explained. "Robert never talked about that." In reference to Willie's closed casket, Jim offers this thought. "For all I know, there were bags of dirt in it." Lehman recalls that although his brother used to sport a flat top crew cut, his hair was naturally curly. "He had to get that haircut to hide the curls," he laughed. He has many memories of William Dean Lehman that were seen through the eyes of a young kid. "Dean and Ken used to get in some pretty good fights," he says.

Jim's dad, Willie William, was a jack of all trades. "He did all kinds of things like construction, driving a truck and farming," Jim asserted. "Hell, I'm even trying some farming now, myself. Our mother taught us to dress neatly, and keep ourselves and the house clean." That little tidbit explained to me how Willie was always so immaculate, even if we were just heading for the neighborhood tavern.

Jim has a daughter, Emily Anne, 9, who he says is "daddy's girl." The Oklahoman explains that calling Emily a "girl" isn't a great idea. "She doesn't want to be called that," he explains. "She sometimes comes hunting with me and even helps cut deer meat with me."

The next day, Jim Lehman was going to rise at 4 a.m., to take advantage of deer season. "I will be using a Remington 270 rifle and I've killed some deer with it," he says. "That rifle belonged to Dean."

I know that Willie is gone, but the fact that I keep him in my heart, is kind of a selfish comfort to me. Before all is said and done, I'd like to meet some of the other Lehman "kids." For years, I just let that go, in respect for the family. Life is a one day at a time proposition and perhaps down the road somewhere, the young Airman that used to accompany Willie Lehman to "church" at Carman's on Guam, will set foot in Oklahoma.

I had dropped Chris back at work the afternoon of February 12, 1971 and was en route to my dad's insurance office. As I approached the underpass on Pike Street, I made the choice to turn right and get there via Front Street and Jersey Avenue, rather than going up the hill on Pike.

Had I decided on taking the Pike Street route and approached the underpass five minutes sooner, I could have been smothered in a wall of debris and bricks that showered down in a tremendous building collapse. As I exited the underpass, my eyes saw a huge wall of what looked like black smoke ahead. Just a few feet in front of me, there was zero visibility. I figured I was witnessing a giant fire, when in reality, 113-123 Pike Street had come toppling down on the Strand Diner next door. There had been an accumulation of heavy, wet snow on the flat roof of the big brick building and that is said to have helped cause the collapse.

The building toppled down crushing cars and leaving shattered glass, bricks and the like, all over the place. Doug Gore, Hojnacki and Krzczuk were three of the Gazette people who wound up on the scene. Gore got some unbelievable photo angles from the roof of a building across the street. Photographers from the New York Times arrived in Port Jervis and used the darkroom facilities. Meanwhile, the Gazette reporters shot 20 rolls of film.

With school being closed for Lincoln's birthday, the State Theater, just two doors up from the fallen building, was to be featuring a 2 p.m. matinee, Walt Disney's "Aristocats." Theater owner Irving Hulst expected 200-300 children for the movie. The young folks always lined up down the street from the theater and many of them would arrive prior to the 2 p.m. show. Some of the kids would probably have been standing in front of the ill-fated brick building, had the show been just over an hour earlier.

Mayor Sidney Sakofsky was at a meeting in New York City when all hell broke loose in Port Jervis. He returned to his home city to find the rubble of a disaster, fatalities, injuries and some tireless rescue personnel who made residents of the city proud.

In the next day's edition of the Port Jervis Union-Gazette, the events of the day before, were captured in words and pictures. Casey's crew had done a monumental job in springing into action and unleashing a huge dose of professional journalism. One of the stories brought out the fact that this horrible happening could have been worse. "Fate works in strange ways," the story said. "Fortunately, it smiled on the city's children, Friday."

UPI and the Associated Press joined the New York Times in Port Jervis, and the nightly news made those in this section of the country aware of where Port Jervis is. The city was now known for a major flood and building collapse. It was very satisfying in later years, to report on state wrestling championships and twins that grabbed Olympic gold medals in 1984. From the pall of disaster came the glitter of athletic accomplishments.

Once I went full time, I settled in to the constant grind of putting out a daily newspaper. The late Elsie Kayton had a nose for club news and wrote about down home kind of events. She gave the place a woman's touch as she attacked her job with gusto. The rest of the guys in the newsroom were great. I relished my role as a sportswriter and once I got out of covering the police beat and city court, I took the sports section straight to the top.

Back during my "hard news" reporting shifts, I began my day by phoning all the police agencies in the area. A couple of times I rode in a police car late at night, observing how the cops went about doing their jobs. I saw street fights, barking dogs, domestic quarrels and intoxicated drivers and pedestrians. The police trusted me, and I wrote behind the scenes stories that told the public how dedicated their police force was.

While John Kinney named me sports editor in 1973, years and years later, when I worked part time, Stan Hojnacki, returned to Port as the editor. We talked about how we had both worked for Gene and learned so much about journalism from him. Stan smiled and recalled a performance report Casey gave him early in his writing career.

"I had to cover this children's play day down at West End Beach and I took some notes and shot some art (pictures) of the event," Stan said. "I wrote the story and figured the assignment went well. Later I saw how I had begun the story. "Balls, balls, balls," were the first three words. You can guess what Gene thought of that." The last I knew, Stan, one of my three best editors ever, was still guiding a paper, this time in North Carolina.

The 1970s were known for lots of things. Television shows "All In The Family" (1972-79) and "MASH" (1972-1983) came on the scene. There were pet rocks, the Rubik's Cube, John Travolta, The Bee Gees and disco. On a more serious note, Richard Nixon resigned the presidency on August 9, 1974. That is the same year that Kinney (another in my top three), nailed a job up in Albany, as bureau chief for Ottaway News Service.

In 1971, "Joy To The World" by Three Dog Night, topped the WABC Musicradio list. Some other memorable tunes of the year included "Go Away Little Girl" (Donny Osmond), "How Can You Mend A Broken Heart" (The Bee Gees), "Rainy Days And Mondays" (The Carpenters), "Brown Sugar" (The Rolling Stones) and "The Night They Drove Old Dixie Down" (Joan Baez).

I began learning about wrestling and saw Port Coach Wilgard motivate his Raiders time after time. During his nine year tenure as coach, this pioneer of Port Jervis wrestling molded 11 Section 9 champions including 1970 senior Art Trovei. Art, who graduated with my sister, Anne, became known as "Party Arty" at Wilkes College, where his wrestling expertise helped him gain a 134-pound Wilkes Open mat title as a freshman.

Trovei was a terror on the mats as a high school grappler. Once I saw him pick up a guy, and bear hug him to the mat for an 18-second pin. He was a three time DUSO League champion, finished second in Section 9 twice, took second in New York State in 1969 and had an overall career record of 75-8-2.

Chris and myself traveled with his dad and mom, Lum and Margaret in 1971, to watch him compete at Wilkes College. Collegiate wrestling was much more refined and I watched the matches intently. Through exposure, I was becoming acquainted with, and getting hooked on, wrestling. I never suspected that this sport would take me to the zenith of scholastic athletic coverage and that just six years later, I would be named New York State Sportswriter of the Year.

Port's Wilgard and DV's Bushong were as opposite as two coaches could be. Al was a strapping tall and physical mentor with a black crew cut and Marine demeanor. If you went out and lost a bout because of some mental mistake, God help your ass when he greeted you at mat side. In one match at rival Minisink Valley, he became so upset that he tossed a chair against a wall, just like temper tantrum champion Bobby Knight. He was banned from the gymnasium and later, you could see his eyes, peering through door glass, to see how the Raiders were faring.

Bushong was a former wrestler with glittering credentials. When Wilgard found out that Trovei had broken team rules and smoked (as a senior), he wouldn't let Party Arty practice with the team. Trovei still competed in Port matches, but it was Bushong who let him attend DV practices to stay in shape. It was also Bushong's patience and caring attitude, that helped the talented and charismatic Raider matman with his confidence and moves.

"I never read your stories," Wilgard told me one day. "I have no idea what you are writing and couldn't care less." I shook my head and thought "yeah, and I'm a jet pilot." Wilgard was tough as a ruthless drill sergeant, but he had his lighter moments when he could fire off a joke or start needling. His intimidation got results.

I put my heart and soul into sports and lived the job. A typical winter day, had me arriving at the office at around 5 a.m. to rip down the UPI wire, and finish whatever work hadn't been completed from local sports the night before.

I had to measure and lay out local and national sports stories on miniature pages (dummies) and write headlines for them. I learned different sizes of headlines and whether to use italic or bold letters. The sports pages were like jigsaw puzzles in that you had to make all the pieces fit correctly. When all the pictures, stories and headlines were laid out and pasted down, you had successfully completed another edition. I had an 8:30 a.m. deadline and usually hung around to help in the newsroom and check out the actual pages downstairs.

Usually I left the office around 10 a.m. and headed home for a few hours of rest and lunch with Chris. By 6 p.m., I was off to the gymnasium again (split shift). My evening would begin with coverage of an event (taking notes and recording final statistics), and photographing the event. I got quotes from coaches and headed back to the Gazette office to begin developing film and to call other local coaches for results. I developed one to three rolls of film a night, plus helped out with film on the general news side, as well.

After all this, I had to hang negatives, print them onto photographic paper, select which pictures would be used, measure them and write captions. These tasks went on between writing my sports stories for the night. Many times I never left the office until 2 or 2:30 in the morning. Then the whole cycle began at 5 or 5:30 the next morning.

I was young and vibrant in those days and working all those hours became commonplace. One lunchtime, I began feeling dizzy, my palms sweated and I felt like I was going to pass out. I went to the emergency room of Saint Francis Hospital in Port for an EKG test and was afraid I was suffering a heart attack. The general conclusion was that I was feeling the results of stress and I was told to slow down. I informed Casey that I had to cut back on my hours and he gave me a puzzled look. "Bill," he said. "Just learn to pace yourself a little better. Writing is in your blood and you have to attack it each and every day."

Back when I reported hard news, I had photographed and written about lots of subjects. The toughest came one morning when the police scanner informed us that a truck had hit a little boy who was waiting to attend school that morning, over near Kingston Avenue. "It sounds like a fatal," Gene said. "You may have to take some police pictures."

I took regular pictures for page 1 of the paper and then a patrolman asked me to come over and shoot some official photos for the police. The little boy, who had been playing on a nearby wall, was under a blanket near the wheel of the truck. I returned to the office, knowing that sports is where my expertise was and that I wanted no more general news exposure.

Chris and I finally found another place to live, on Reservoir Avenue in Port. Our final night in Milford, we adjourned to a corner bar and celebrated our departure from the gray house on Mill Street. Maybe now, our candies would all stay in the candy dish while we were at work. All we needed was a little bit of sleep and we would be gone from Milford, lock, stock and barrel. Upon walking back to the apartment, a terrible realization hit us between the eyes. It was very late at night and we had locked ourselves out, leaving our keys in the house.

We could have tried to sleep in one of the cars but that would have been cramped. Gazing at the house from the shadows across the street, my eyes spotted a trellis at the end of the dwelling. It climbed up the house and past the front roof. If I could make it to the roof, there was a window there that would open to our bedroom.

You've heard the old "bull in the china shop" statement, but what I attempted under the cover of darkness, must have resembled a bear trying to be light on his feet, as he ascended the fragile wooden trellis. The trellis was no match for my weight and it pulled away from the house as the bottom two or three rungs smashed. We were forced to knock on the front door at an ungodly hour and gained entrance after a few hearty knocks on the door. Incidentally, the landlord found the smashed trellis and yelled his head off the next day.

We had to cross a brook that was bordered by cement walls, to gain access to a macadam parking area on Reservoir Avenue. We had an upstairs apartment that was small but had a great kitchen with a booth to sit and eat. It was a cozy little place and the downstairs landlords stayed out of our business for the most part.

Chris found out at her Sparkomatic job, that a kitten was available for anyone who needed it. We talked our landlords into allowing "Charles" the cat to come live with us. Charles was a gray manx kitten (no tail) who had unbelievable intelligence. He would run up the front of you without putting his claws out and was a loving companion. Chris' mom took Charles' sister, Chloe, and two gray kittens now had new homes.

Later, we brought in a second cat that we named "Blackie", even though I called him "Daffy." He was midnight black, had real big feet, and was lovable but possessed very little intelligence. We would let Charles and Blackie out from time to time and they'd roam the big mountain behind our apartment. When we whistled for them, they would both come running. One day only Charles showed up though and for days we combed the side of the road and portions of the mountain, thinking Blackie had gotten caught in a trap.

One of the landlords seemed very evasive and nervous when I asked if he'd seen the cat. He and his wife took to Charles but paid little attention to Blackie. Their son would drive over the brook every now and then to visit and we figured it was possible he, or another motorist, had run over Blackie.

"Try looking by the side of the road over there," the landlord said to me, as he pointed across the street. "Maybe he is over there." That weird statement kind of told me that Blackie had been nailed and disposed of in the bushes. However, despite our tireless attempts, we came up empty and never found a trace of the cat. I am convinced that years later, when the landlord and his wife died, the mystery of Blackie's disappearance went to the grave with them.

My hours at the Gazette were exhausting but I continued to love the reward of seeing an impressive sports page. I was drawing raves at the paper, in the community and throughout the Ottaway group. "So what do you think, lad? Did you make the right choice by leaving the bank?", Gene asked. When I answered "yes" he rolled up his sleeves, looked at me and said "groovy."

About once every two months, a guy named Charles King, from

Ottaway headquarters, would drop by and try blending into our daily routine of putting out a newspaper. King was a disciplinarian from the word "go" and he loved to critique the way things were done and the end product. I was respectful of this crusty, nitpicking and stubborn person, but resented his comments and the way he strong armed his way around the office.

He ripped my sports page apart, questioned how I did things, injected his own opinions and generally made life miserable for me. He sat at my desk for what seemed like forever, and never seemed to leave. One morning he was present when I grabbed my coat and bid the newsroom farewell for the day. I was going on two hours sleep and wanted to get some sack time before a rigorous sports schedule later that day.

"You aren't leaving are you?", King said. "I prefer that you stay here all morning and check out your sports pages downstairs," he said. I explained that I worked some demanding hours but that did no good.

Finally, after figuratively banging my head against the wall, I simply turned on my heel and exited stage left. When I returned that night, Gene had a sheepish grin as he greeted me in the newsroom. "Take it easy lad," he said. "Charles is from the old school. Just yes him to death and keep on doing things your way. I know the hours you put in and the work being done, so don't change a thing."

It was in August of 1971 that I ambled a little bit away from the sports desk and sank my teeth into major page 1 news. A 37-year-old area man was the subject and before all was said and done, he would appear on the FBI's top 10 most wanted list.

James Ellsworth Jones lived in Milford and Fish recalls him from when they worked an assembly line at Sparkomatic together. "He (Jones) was a real quiet guy," Fish says. "He never said much, and I just can't believe he did all those things." The list of "those things" began in the heat of that summer in Port Jervis.

He had been stopped in his car, by two local police and when asked to produce a license and registration, reached under the seat and pulled out a gun instead. After handcuffing the cops and tossing them in some nearby bushes, he was charged with taking their walkie talkies, pistols and keys to the police cruiser. Jones took off in his vehicle but that wasn't the last he would be heard from.

My page 1 story in the August 14, 1971 Gazette ran on the top of the page, under a banner headline that screamed out "Jones, Accomplice Rob Pike County Couple." Another headline on the page said "Armed Pair Takes Money, Drives Off In Stolen Car." Later that day, I was on Gene's front porch when he took a gander at the edition and said "Oh God, no." His short outburst was explained quickly. "Look at that headline," he said. "We convicted him (Jones) already. We should have put the word 'allegedly' before the word rob." I felt fortunate that the headline didn't come from my typewriter. However, just for good measure, I made the same exact mistake in the lead to the story.

My first major hard news story was factual, but the lead had to be among the longest in journalism history. I didn't come up for air once in spewing the words of this story.

"A 37-year-old fugitive, the prime suspect in the daring armed robbery of two Port Jervis policemen Saturday evening, and the object of an intensive manhunt, struck again Friday morning when he and a young long-haired companion tied and robbed a Pennsylvania couple seven miles from Milford and made a getaway in the couple's 1971 automobile."

The piece went on to say that it was believed Jones was armed with pistols taken from the Port police, six days earlier. Jones had worked as an electrical contractor at the Pike couple's house and was familiar with the husband and wife. He apologized as he tied them to kitchen chairs. Phone wires were cut, and the men made off with a wrist watch, $280 in cash, a .38 revolver, case of beer and 1971 vehicle. There was a 13-state alarm out for the 5-10" 170-pound Jones, who had a prior armed robbery at Ann Arbor, Michigan in 1961. This incident in Milford, happened on Friday the 13th.

This little episode, did not end the Jones saga. He was far from finished.

Casey had departed and Kinney was the new editor when Jones made the news a year later. The page 1 story was by Kinney and Tangen and appeared under a headline that said "Year-long Search Ends With Jones' Arrest."

By this time, Jones had a whole list of charges, one of them super serious. He had been a busy man in the time he spent on the loose. Not only was he wanted for the armed robbery of the Port police and armed robbery of the Pike County couple, but a kidnap-murder charge down South was on his list. He was charged with the kidnap and murder of a young (high school senior) Virginia service station attendant, (May 25, 1972) whose body was found 120 miles away, in West Virginia. The young man had been shot in the back twice, with a .38 caliber pistol. This crime apparently originated in darkness, when the victim phoned to check on Jones' credit card (he had purchased tires and gas). When the call was made back to the service station, nobody answered.

Jones, as the story stated, "fell from a tree in Milford Sunday night, right into the arms of the law." He had been spotted earlier in the day in Milford and a barking dog, on Bennett Street (8:30 p.m. at night) tipped off young State Police officer Michael Chaplin, that someone was in a nearby tree.

Chaplin saw Jones atop a 45-foot tree and ordered him down four times. Five minutes later, the suspect started down, and wound up falling 30-feet to the macadam below. He ended up in guarded condition, in more ways than one, at Saint Francis Hospital. He suffered a severe compound fracture of the left arm and broken left hip. Meanwhile, Federal Marshals had Jones guarded heavily when days later, they escorted him from the hospital to a correctional facility in Manhattan.

The Union-Gazette was there to photograph a sedated Jones as he was transported on a stretcher, to a nearby ambulance. Steve Rago and I focused our cameras on the drugged figure of Jones and it was hard to believe all the terrible things he was charged with. He was slated to be extradited to either Virginia (kidnap) or West Virginia (murder).

Rago and I became fast friends and three years later, when he became city editor, we both arrived in the Gazette at ridiculous hours. We ripped down our UPI wires while tossing jokes and barbs around the room. "It says here that Frank Sinatra's mother died," Steve said one morning. Frank, known as "old blue eyes" was in mourning but Rago showed no mercy. "He is old red eyes today," he said of Sinatra.

It was Rago and I that formed the little known "Delaware River Hall of Fame" for the headstrong jerks that challenged the Delaware without using life jackets. Every summer rescue personnel are summoned to the river to save lives of visitors to the area, who foolishly don't exercise safety. "Here's a guy that stood up in a rowboat while fishing, flipped the boat and drowned," Rago pointed out one day. "The dumb son of a bitch was wearing hip waders. He probably sank to the bottom like a rock. He is definitely a candidate for The Hall of Fame."

You would figure that the exploits of James Jones would finally fade into the past as he served his hard time. As it turned out, he had an encore performance in 1973. Jones had become a model prisoner and under little supervision, escaped from the Augusta County (Virginia) Jail on October 16, 1973. He became one of the FBI's most wanted fugitives (top 10) and remained free for about eight months.

Jones, who had already gotten a life sentence on the kidnap charge, was awaiting trial for the 1972 murder when he took off. I got on the phone and conned myself into speaking to the jail guard who had let Jones make his escape. He was afraid of losing his job and I guaranteed him that I wouldn't make him look bad in the story. Meanwhile, Jones, now sporting a moustache, was captured for the second time when an off duty cop spotted him in a Coral Gables, Florida restaurant. He had been working in a health store in Florida and when confronted, denied his identity. He wound up in maximum security at Dade County Jail.

Most of the time I covered only sports at the Gazette. An exception was during local elections. In 1971, I did a story on the dynamic Joseph Ricciardi becoming the new mayor of Matamoras, Pa. He showed up at the newspaper office after the victory with his son, Billy, in tow. Later, I covered Bill in DV basketball and the two men ran the popular "Mayor's Corner" store near the Delaware River bridge. When I was doing some local television reporting, Ricciardi had a tip for me. "You have to smile more," he said. "People want to see you grinning from ear to ear." The good natured mayor has been a vocal, yet fair politician and married tons of people in his time. He was a colorful baseball umpire for years and years.

Ricciardi showed me that good guys can finish first. Once the Port Jervis Softball League limited the amount of players per team that came from outside the Port city limits. "Someday, we will have a beautiful park in Matamoras where softball is played," he said. "There will be no restriction on how many players from outside Matamoras compete." He made good on his word and the beautiful Airport Park, nestled in our picturesque valley, is a site that makes Matamoras people beam with pride. "Mayor Joe" retired December 31, 2002, after 31 years of service.

Back in the spring of 1971, I began coverage of the Port track team. Although the Raiders absorbed some losses, the personable Joe Sweeney was a standout in the 880-yard run. Late in the season, he managed to clock a fine time of 2:00.4 in that half mile event. Now, over three decades later, I have covered his two boys as they competed for the DV basketball team. Both boys tower over the former track and field star.

My first year of football was a memorable occasion as I experienced the thrill of a title team. Coach Viglione molded some competitive teams from 1957 through 1983 and left Port with a career record of 155-72-5. He retired from coaching at Warwick High School in the early 1990s.

I had become exposed to Port football again in 1969 when I saw Port shock Middletown, 20-14, in the final Thanksgiving Day game played between the teams. I was headed up the bleachers and out to my car for the ride to Port Jervis when I noticed time had expired but players were still on the field.

A piling on penalty was assessed against the Middies and since a game can't end on a penalty, Port got one more crack at the end zone. The score stood 14-14 when quarterback Earl Sheard hooked up with Randy Senkiew who dived into the end zone and into the history books of Port-Middie grid tradition.

I looked at Kinney's chilling headline the next day in the Gazette. "Time Stands Still" it said. Just for a split second I envied Kinney because he got to cover high school athletics. One year later, I would be the person covering events and getting quotes. I figure fate had a big part in how things worked out for me.

That game winning 20-yard pass reception was the most exciting high school football play I've ever witnessed. From time to time I come across Sheard and he'll give me a wink. "We aren't going to talk about that play again are we?", he'll joke.

Port-Middletown began in 1897 and is one of the oldest rivalries in the country. While I was sports editor, the Raiders won the clashes in 1974, 75, and 76. In the 1974 victory at Middletown's Wilson Field, Joe Klemm scored three times and gained 128 yards in a 21-6 win. I wrote the story and Gore produced a fabulous picture page for me. Klemm was a bruising back who rushed for 996 yards his senior year.

I tried like hell to find four more yards to give Joe so he would be a 1,000 yard rusher. I reviewed each and every play of the season (I diagrammed the game on a sheet of paper) but the total stayed at 996. I wondered if I was right by not giving the kid four more yards. I knew in my heart that I made the correct decision. Klemm, who wore uniform number 32, was a fine football player. His whole family was proud of him, but realized that I was being honest and ethical.

Phil Dusenbury wrote a riveting book on Port Jervis football entitled "The Red And Black" in 1997 that covers a century of Port football. It was Phil and Minisink Valley coach Carrozza who picked up my New York State Sportswriter of the Year trophy while I was at Danzer's in Syracuse (1977). Phil, who has a teaching background, is now the voice of Port football (radio) and is respected as an authority on Raider grid history.

In 1971, Rick Spears played in the 35th Masters Golf Tournament at Augusta Georgia. The 23-year-old amateur practiced with Doug Ford, Steve Melnyk and Bob Murphy and 72 were in the field. My former basketball teammate at Port, had already played in the U.S. Open at San Francisco in 1967. In 1971 he was a Second Lieutenant in the Army, when he missed the Masters cut by four shots (two round total of 154).

The following year (1972) they demolished the YMCA on Pike Street along with my beloved Silver Grill. I had played basketball in "the Y" as a kid and remember the warmth of the place as you walked in the front door. There was a pool table near the lobby, where guys played for money and I recall the basketball court being in an ice-cold room. Now that is all just a fond memory of youthful days.

Wilgard had a fine wrestler in Hollis Farr (148 pounds). Farr and Minisink Valley's Dave Cherry waged some fierce battles on the mat and a whisker usually separated the two matmen when the final buzzer went off. Cherry had bowed to Farr twice in their wars, but got sweet revenge in the District I Section 9 championship bout by nipping Farr, 3-2. The blond Farr and dark-haired Cherry were crafty and physical grapplers who respected each other but weren't the best of pals. Years later they crossed paths as friends and always recalled their epic battles.

Port's Fred Merusi (112) took a 19-0 record into the Section 9 finals against defending New York State champion Joe Goldsmith of Ramapo. The likable Merusi suffered his first loss and Goldsmith went back to states. Across the river at DV, rugged Bill Schneck, Paul Dedea and Ray Schafer all won District 12 crowns for Bushong. Ned's wife, Lynda, kept the scorebooks for DV and was a real knowledgeable wrestling person. The Warriors were building a powerful team that would clip Port Jervis for the first time ever, in 1973.

The biggest event to take place since my marriage was to occur on March 29, 1972, when Tracie Lynn Tangen entered the world at 2:36

p.m. Chris and I lived for the day she would be born and prepared for the occasion months in advance.

One night in early 1972, I was at the office rapping out a winter sports story when the shrill ring of the phone broke the silence. Chris was on the other end of the wire and was crying hysterically. I thought something had happened regarding the baby, but after speeding home to Reservoir Avenue, I spotted the 1968 Barracuda down in the canal brook.

Chris had been watching a scary movie at her mom's house and upon arriving home, parked her car in a hurry and proceeded to the outdoor stairs, nestled against the mountain. In her haste, she figures the car was never taken out of gear. As she headed toward the apartment, she heard a rustling out near the driveway. She turned her head in horror, to see the vehicle rolling down an incline and into the back yard.

Her reaction was to stop the car from reaching the brook and as she sprinted toward the vehicle, she fell on the macadam, scraping her knees and cutting the palms of her hands. The next sound Chris heard, was the sickening clatter of her car going over the walls and into the brook.

"I could have been killed running after that car," she said after the fact. "My only thought, was to stop it from reaching the brook." She ascended the stairs, entered our small abode and frantically dialed my number at the Gazette. The plastic dialing device broke as she dialed and increased her anxiety even more. Finally she held the circular plastic to the phone and dialed again.

My dad and hers were contacted as we tried to figure a way to pull the car out of its bizarre location. Finally a tow truck came and pulled the Barracuda back up where it belonged. The beams of flashlights illuminated the cold, dark night, as this memorable happening progressed.

My wife felt pain throbbing in her hand and finally had to go to the hospital emergency room to treat the infected palms. From that night on, our cars have always been taken out of gear before getting out, scary movies or not. I look back and shudder to think that Chris and our baby were in serious jeopardy while I typed about a basketball game or wrestling match.

We enjoyed our cozy apartment as we waited for the arrival of our newborn. Sometimes Fish would drop by for awhile or my sister Anne, would happen by. One night Anne was at the house and for a joke I went in the bedroom, put on a long raincoat and stuck a pencil in my hand to represent a cigar.

Imitating the popular Peter Falk character Detective Columbo, I said "Mam, this probably isn't important. This won't take long, but my boss wants me to ask you a couple of questions." I looked at Anne and said "Well?, what do you think?" She thought a second and said "Great Groucho Marks imitation." That brought my career in doing impressions to a screeching halt.

In 1972, "Alone Again (Naturally)" by Gilbert O'Sullivan topped the WABC radio charts. Other songs of the day included "American Pie" (Don McLean), "First Time Ever I Saw Your Face" (Roberta Flack), "Brandy" (Looking Glass), "Daddy Don't You Walk So Fast" (Wayne Newton), "Taxi" (Harry Chapin) and "Garden Party" (Rick Nelson).

The afternoon of March 29, 1972, Tracie was delivered by Dr. Seymour Weiner. I donned the hospital greens and the white mask but wasn't present for the delivery. Chris was given pain killers prior to Tracie entering the world. My legs turned to jelly when I was informed that we had become three and that a daddy's little girl was breathing and alert in a nearby room.

Tracie had dark hair at birth and squinty little eyes. She was bundled in a little pink and white blanket and was living proof that there are miracles in this life that defy description. Chris and I used to laugh when we saw all the babies being wheeled out of the maternity room to visit with their parents. In those days, hospital rules were strict and you had to adhere to them. At certain times during the day, the babies were on the move being pushed in their little buggies. "Babies in….babies out" I used to say, and Chris would smile in agreement.

Holding my daughter was a thrill that I will always remember, although it is still tough to comprehend that something so small can be so precious. That night, I kissed my wife, told her to get some rest, and walked toward the Union-Gazette where I had left my car.

I was suddenly a "bachelor" for the first time since September 11, 1970. Gene Casey's big white and green house, on East Main Street, was located between the hospital and newspaper. He had told me to stop by to celebrate the birth of our first born. As I recall, his pretty dark-haired wife, Jana, wasn't home that night when I knocked on the door. "Come in lad," Gene said. "How is the new Papa doing tonight?"

Gene clutched a drink and went to the fridge to get me a beer. I sat down in his living room and the television was on. "I'm just watching "All In The Family" and it's hilarious," he said. "Carroll O'Connor is really funny." I wasn't familiar with this show yet and figured Carroll was some girl on the program, rather than the bigoted and cantankerous character Archie Bunker.

"There is no feeling in the world like being a dad," Gene mused, as he raised his glass in a toast. "Here is to your new little baby daughter. May she live a long and happy life."

Gene had small children so he knew what he was talking about. He always called his boy, Sean, "son." You could see the pride reflect in his eyes when the subject of children came up. This hard-boiled news hound, not afraid to take on the establishment, had a soft side to him. I felt like I was walking on air and drifting along in a make believe dream of fantasy and fun. I had a little daughter named Tracie and she would be coming to live with us. We were now three. I decided to hand out a few cigars and celebrate.

With no serious obligations on the home front, I headed for the Black Bear Inn in Sparrowbush. There I ran into fellow Port athlete Dick Pepper who was also shaking hands and beaming with pride. He also had a baby girl March 29, and beat me to fatherhood by a few hours.

Toasting the night away, I finally drank my fill and headed for home. When I used to drink a lot of beer I'd end the session by chowing down big time. Being the gourmet cook that I am, I popped a couple of TV dinners in the oven and promptly passed out. I awoke during the night, to the smell of smoke and ran out to the kitchen to turn off the oven. Inside were a couple of red-hot TV dinners that were glowing like red hot coals. I shook my head in disgust, thanked my lucky stars I hadn't set the house on fire, and went back to bed.

It was an experience watching Tracie grow into a toddler. She had a great disposition and loved to be held. She and Charles the cat hit it off wonderfully and the feline guarded her religiously as she slept in her bassinet. When she got older, she ran about our small apartment, playing with her toys. One night Chris and I were both home, when we got the scare of our lives.

Tracie had gone through the living room and into a small hall that connects to the bedroom and bathroom. She proceeded toward the bathroom on the run and we heard her start screaming and crying. Our little tot had run into the edge of an open door and cut her forehead wide open. Blood gushed into the air as my heart pounded a mile a minute. We wrapped her in a towel and I drove a million miles an hour to the emergency room. This precious little girl solemnly laid on a hospital bed as they stitched her head up. The nurses fell in love with her and I was just happy that a major tragedy hadn't occurred.

The new year (1973) began in the Reservoir Avenue apartment. My job was perfect, in that it gave me time with Tracie when Chris was working (days). I was in my mid-20s and life couldn't be better.

In 1973, Roberta Flack's "Killing Me Softly With His Song" topped the charts. Other songs that year included "Tie a Yellow Ribbon Round the Ole Oak Tree" by Dawn, Jim Croce's "Bad Bad Leroy Brown", "Sing" by The Carpenters and "The Monster Mash" by Bobby (Boris) Pickett.

At DV, Jeff Foss cracked 1,000 career points in basketball (wound up with 1,163), Hollis Farr of Port got ripped off at the Section 9 Wrestling Tournament, Ron Semerano was named the Most Valuable Athlete at Port and mat coach Al Wilgard resigned in May to take a job in Columbia, Maryland. He left behind a career record of 80-47-4, seven title teams and 11 sectional champions.

In 1973 riding time counted in New York State wrestling and a "drifty" riding time clock cost Farr in his Section 9 (138 pound) loss (2-1) to Suffern's Fred Boy. I thought Farr had the riding time point (a minute or more riding and controlling the other wrestler) and that the bout should have been tied, 2-2, and require overtime. The officials thought otherwise and Farr only had 59 ½ seconds in their eyes (and no point was awarded).

In basketball, Port's defending Tri-County scoring champion Rusty Smith returned. In 1973-74 he wound up with 1,133 points (13 shy of Saul) as Port went 13-5. In wrestling, DV beat Port for the first time ever, 30-17, with the likes of Aaron Balch, Fred White, Ray Wagner, Bill Schneck and the rest of Bushong's talented team. Kinney became editor and the positive newsroom spirit that Gene Casey had built, remained solid under John. The news staff went through thick and thin as a team. Every Friday after work, we all adjourned to the Hotel Carroll for some cold drinks and pool playing. Not only were we a big, happy family, we were excellent at our jobs. Gene had hand picked a spirited and accomplished crew and John continued the great award-winning journalism tradition the Union-Gazette was known for.

I learned how to dig for stories under adverse conditions, never giving up, no matter how big the odds appeared. When truckers got upset over gasoline prices, they blockaded the interstate highways and once, I was trapped in a traffic jam on westbound Route 80, en route to a Delaware Valley boys basketball game. I wound up escaping the mess by turning around and going eastbound on the shoulder of the road. Reaching the basketball game had become impossible but shooting a flash picture of all the trucks plus filing a story wasn't.

One time it rained all night and poured the day of a track meet. The oval cinder track was one large mud puddle and the meet was postponed. Having a news hole to fill, I took my camera to the site and shot pictures of tree tops reflected in the puddles. Some birds were on the soaked grass nearby, so I included them too. The headline to my story about the wet weather said that the rain was "for the birds."

On another occasion, Jeff Foss was nearing the 1,000 point career scoring mark in basketball and DV had an away game scheduled. Chris and I got in the car, bound for the new Western Wayne High School in South Canaan, Pa. We were out in the Pennsylvania backwoods, got lost and totally confused. Mayberry seemed like New York City compared to the desolate towns we rode through. I asked directions many times and followed them all. Still, no Western Wayne High and the game had already begun.

This eptic journey brought me back through a small town for the third time. I went into a small grocery store to continue my search. There was nobody behind the counter and I could have walked out with the contents of the establishment with no problem. The predicament was becoming a personal challenge to me and I was going to find the site or die trying.

These rural farmlands are a good distance away from major roads. In fact it was here, that kidnapped publishing heiress Patty Hearst was hidden away from authorities. Major news stories recounted how Patty, granddaughter of famous newspaper publisher William Randolph Hearst, had been kidnapped by the Symbionese Liberation Army, brainwashed and took part in crimes including armed bank robberies.

By the time I finally found this school, hidden on top of a hill and not visible from the road, the game had ended. Foss had not reached 1,000 points, but I had no game coverage. Instead, I fired off a column on the futility of the evening and used the headline "Western Wayne Where Are You?"

In 1973, DV's Schneck, the slick and pinning wrestler, was recognized for his outstanding soccer ability. Schneck, a personable blond, was one of only 33 players to be named to the All-American High School soccer team. His coach, Ron Robacker, would go on to become one of the winningest high school coaches in Pa. Schneck, meanwhile, is one of the most persevering and talented athletes I have ever covered.

Early in the year, I had come out with a scathing column that was highly controversial and had all of Port Jervis buzzing. I was young, enthusiastic and showed plenty of Gene Casey influence when I took on the Port Jervis athletic director in print.

Pat Farace was an excellent athletic director and I had a great working relationship with him. He did an outstanding job at his post and was still the animated disciplinarian he was when I went to school. However, the day came, when I had to take him to task.

There had been problems between Pat and his former basketball super star Alex Osowick. In addition to basketball, Alex coached the Red Raider baseball team. Alex told me that the baseball field hadn't been lined properly for home baseball games (crooked lines) and that it was affecting the morale of his Raider team. He said he tried to talk with Farace but was getting no results. His implication was that this baseball problem, was virtually being ignored. When I talked to Pat in his office, he indicated that school workers were too busy to take the necessary time to put the straight, white chalk baselines down. When I saw that this rift between Alex and Pat was not going to close, I told him a column was coming. "I wouldn't do that," he said with a stone face.

I figured I had to do my job and let the pieces fall where they may. So I rolled up my sleeves, dug in and went to work on a column that I hoped would resolve the matter once and for all. The two men had their own principles to stand for and I respected that. However, it was time to take action.

I fired out a dynamite story on how the two men should bury the hatchet and take care of the field lining problem in a professional type manner. There was a Port Jervis home baseball game the next day and I found out first hand that the Union-Gazette had already hit the streets, that afternoon.

I arrived on the scene of the game and walked down the grassy hill leading to the baseball diamond. Among the spectators, stood a disciplined man in a jacket and tie. In his hand he held a folded Union-Gazette newspaper.

I was heading to the bench to secure starting lineups for the two teams. I approached the area Pat Farace was in and noticed the absence of his usual greeting. He said nothing to me and as I passed he simply dropped the newspaper at my feet. I ignored that act and instead continued toward the field.

I respected the fact that Farace had held his ground in this ticklish matter. I also was to be impressed by the class that this individual would show, throughout the rest of my time at the newspaper. There came a day when I walked away from full time sports writing and that day was March 18, 1977. That is also the date on a letter of recommendation, typed on Port Jervis High stationery and signed by athletic director Patrick Farace.

"At all times, Bill was responsible, energetic, polite, eager to learn, cooperative, loyal and enthusiastic about completing assignments," some of the letter said. "As a sportswriter he blended all of these characteristics with hard work and long hours to become the most respected writer in the Tri-County area. His coverage of all local sports was concise, accurate, honest and broad in scope." The part that caught my eye the most, followed. "He was always fair to express both sides of the story on controversial athletic issues."

Anne Farace's husband and the dad of football standouts Dave, Rick and Franklyn Farace, had told me in certain words, that I did the right thing by meeting a touchy subject head-on. To this day, I look at Farace, now in Florida, as one of the fairest and most sincere people I ever had the pleasure to come in contact with.

In October 1973, at Pinehurst, North Carolina, Rick Spears launched his third try at a PGA card. This fantastic golfer just didn't produce at the right time, as he missed the cut by five strokes. A month earlier, he had put on a golfing exhibition at New Jersey's Rock View Golf Course (for $100). Mike Hylas and myself arranged the performance and Spears came through with a fine round of 65. In a practice round (with no out of bounds markers) he has carved out a blistering round of 59 on the par 68 course. A year later, and again in 1977, Rick would fall short in his attempt at a PGA card. It just wasn't meant to be.

In September 1973, a former Port Jervis athletic standout (wrestling, football) came back to his home town to teach Mathematics. Mark Faller, a 1971 Harvard graduate, and Ivy League wrestling champion, would be teaching at Port and taking over for Wilgard, as Red Raider wrestling coach.

Faller had placed fourth in the state of New York (1966) at 154 pounds under Wilgard and was an intelligent student-athlete (accelerated level) in high school. He returned as an accomplished collegiate grappler who was a proponent of upper body wrestling. At Harvard, he had won two matches at the NCAA Tournament two times (158 pounds).

Prior to the Port assignment, Mark had been mat coach at Tabor Academy in Marion, Massachusetts. The 5-10" 180-pound Faller had guided his grapplers to the New England Prep School championship (1972-73) and was bringing his knowledge and expertise to Port Jervis.

Wilgard and Faller were in sharp contrast. While Wilgard was fiery, vocal and physical, Faller was laid back and patient. He viewed matches not from the seat of his coaching chair, but from the top of it. He drifted into town virtually unnoticed. Seven years later, he departed with two New York State team titles (1977, 1978), two individual state champions (Lou Banach, 1977, Ed Banach, 1978), five Orange County League and Section 9 team titles and a career mark of 91-13-1.

I remember the day I ambled into the locker room to interview Mark about his arrival and plans as the Raider skipper. He smiled and shook my hand in an easygoing manner. He wore a long pony tail and sported baggy clothes with sandals. I thought to myself "the Port fans are going to go nuts when they see Al's replacement."

Wilgard had his grapplers wrestle down on the mat while Faller liked the upper body techniques. "I will let the seniors wrestle the way they want to (unless they want to change) and the younger kids learn upper body," Mark said matter-of-factly. "It will take some time for them to learn."

When I mentioned the coaching accomplishments of Wilgard, Faller gave a quick smile. "It will take about three years for the program to reach where I want it to be," he asserted. "By then, people around here will know who we are." No truer words have ever been uttered. Three seasons later, the three terrific Banach brothers epitomized Port Jervis wrestling and the Raiders were a New York State powerhouse.

Mark's first team included Bill Norris, Dan Howey, Tom Masanotti, Harvey Freeman and Ernie Jackson. That team posted a credible 8-7 overall record. Two seasons later, Port was headed for the stars by vaulting to a 14-1 overall record plus crowning Ed Banach and Jackson as Section 9 titlists. The duo was the first two sectional kingpins from Port, in five years.

The year 1974 would be a memorable one, not only in sports, but in my family. Tracie Lynn was a little under 22 months old, when a little sister, Dawn Melissa, came to live with us. Dawn was born at 7:36 p.m. on January 11, 1974 and Dr. Weiner again handled the delivery. I kept my amazing drinking and cooking record alive by swilling down suds that night and then burning two more TV dinners.

The top songs of the year included "Rock The Boat" (The Hues Corporation), "The Way We Were" (Barbra Streisand), "Your Having My Baby" (Paul Anka), "The Entertainer" (Marvin Hamlish) and "Cat's In The Cradle" (Harry Chapin).

Chris and I had attended Lamaze classes in preparation for Dawn's birth, so I was present when she was born. Tracie and her little sister made our lives complete and brought us great joy. While Tracie liked being the center of attention, Dawn was content to play by herself. Tracie shared her toys and took on the role of a "little mother" to Dawn.

Although sports was my life, I never pushed either girl toward athletics once they began attending Delaware Valley High School. I am reasonably sure that both were coordinated enough to have made fine athletes. Tracie ran a season of cross country (junior year) for DV Coach Angelo Matz, and was a constant point producer. She wasn't a star harrier, but helped provide the Warriors with depth. She had to skip her senior year of competition due to a knee injury.

At the hospital, babies were still being wheeled in and out of the maternity room and we were so happy that Dawn had entered the world. At night I held her in her solid pink blanket and thanked God that she was a healthy baby. While Tracie was familiar with her Reservoir Avenue surroundings, Dawn had just one home while she was growing up, and that dwelling was in Matamoras.

We had left Reservoir Avenue and while living at Chris' parents residence, a deal on a house fell through when it was discovered that the owner had liens against him. We searched high and low for a place to live and finally lucked out when Marion (Chris' mom) found out that a red-and-white house on Avenue I was unoccupied.

The executrix of the estate (lady had passed away) took a liking to the young couple who were expecting their second child. On December 23, two days before Christmas (1973), we moved into this spacious house. That date already had a special place in my heart, because I had been discharged on that date, five years earlier.

There was plenty of land for us to enjoy here, including a large side lot, complete with a beautiful rose garden. The owners had care takers come by just to groom the land and tend to the roses. There would come a day when the newspaper would do a feature on the rose garden, complete with a picture of Dawn sniffing a rose.

In the sports world, Port Jervis began a girls softball program under the able leadership of Hugh Spangenberg. "I think there is a need for interscholastic varsity girls sports," Hugh had said at the time. He wound up guiding Port to many championships and had a prize pitcher, Nancy Lane, who went on to pitch at the University of Oklahoma.

In 1974, Bob Semerano, a strapping right handed pitcher-third baseman for Port Jervis, graduated. Bobby was a fine hitter, but he could throw that speedball by you just like Springsteen describes in "Glory Days." While Spears and Eddie Dunn (football) before him, had gone on to national notoriety, Semerano was destined to go farther with his baseball career. The year after graduating, Bob signed a major league baseball contract with the Pittsburgh Pirates.

285

There were many memorable moments during 1974. Rick DePoalo emerged as an excellent Minisink Valley wrestler, the Banachs were coming up through the wrestling system under modified coach Phil Chase, and a big rough and tumble guy named Joe Murphy walked into the Gazette as editor. "Murph" arrived straight from the docks of New Bedford, Massachusetts with an ego bigger than the newsroom. He wanted his word to be law, but soon found out that Steve Rago and myself would tolerate this pushy attitude, only to a certain extent.

Joe could drink with the best of them, I would find out. One night the three of us adjourned to Joe Dunn's place on Front Street for some heavy beer drinking. Before we knew it, the clock's hands had turned past 2 in the morning. We hit the street with gusto and decided to play some basketball in the middle of Front Street near a bank clock. We had a good old time dribbling and shooting, as sweat poured down our faces. We capped the night by attempting to let some air out of some guy's tires (he had made us mad) and then went to the Gazette.

Drunk, disorderly and tired, we realized it was a work day. "You will put your pages out now," Murphy roared at me. "I will do no such thing," I answered. "I am going home, to get some sleep."

In a cranky mood, Murphy threatened me with the loss of my job if I left. I waited until he went downstairs and then sneaked to my car and home. The next day, I arrived on the scene late, but that wasn't the worst of it.

Bob Widmer was the publisher back then. He was a nice guy and I'd even wound up golfing with him from time to time. It was Widmer who had helped me secure a mortgage on my house. "Wid" may have been a wonderful fellow, but when he got riled up, you better watch out.

During the late morning, the three of us were called on the carpet. Widmer had found out about our early morning basketball and reamed out all three of us. "This is bullshit," he wailed from behind his desk. From that day on, Steve and I greeted each other in the newsroom, with the words "bullshit, bullshit....yah yah yah."

Murphy and Widmer didn't see eye to eye and it wasn't long before good old "Murph" hit the gate. It seemed Steve and I were the official editor greeters. We helped the new bosses learn the ropes and showed them where the best watering holes were. One new boss never got to sit in his editor's chair. He was a nice bespectacled Polish fellow and we showed him an afternoon of good fellowship at a neighborhood bar.

His name was "Ray" and he seemed nice enough to us. There was one thing we didn't know about this jovial man though, and that was the fact that he wasn't a drinker and couldn't hold his liquor. He lived east of Port Jervis and had to take Interstate Route 84 to get home.

The last we knew, "wrong way Ray" was heading east in the west-bound lanes of 84. It seems he was traveling at a dangerous rate of speed and going through some police barricades. He escaped with his life and luckily didn't kill anyone in his drunken escapade. Steve and I viewed his empty editor's chair with great sorrow. "Bullshit, bullshit yah yah yah."

I wrote another controversial column in 1974, which pissed off DV athletic director Ron Robacker and half the high school. DV had recently been intimidated by Port Jervis in basketball and always seemed beaten before the teams ever took the court. I figured I would point this out to DV, as a way to make them competitive.

In the December 20 edition of the Gazette, my headline read "Raiders Keep Walking The Dog." In the story, I explained all of the DV woes on the hardwoods. "About the only real question surrounding tonight's basketball rematch between Port and DV is how large the point spread will be," I said. "The family dog probably offers more resistance by trying to cut a walk short on a cold day."

These words of wisdom got "errant" basketballs tossed at me during DV's layup drill that night. Robacker sarcastically approached me with these words "nice story William (I am always called Bill)." After calling him "Ronald", I covered my ballgame. Incidentally, Port only won the game by four points, 52-48. I took some verbal abuse, but my point had gotten across. DV could now hold its head high. Robacker and I got along fine (in time) and a sportswriter could never ask for more than a Farace-Robacker-Carrozza (Port-DV-Minisink Valley) combination in athletic directors. All three were top shelf.

The young DV basketball coach was a guy named Nick Valvano. Nick was a class act from day one and was always available for interviews after the game. His dad and brother had been cage coaches, so he came from a knowledgeable basketball family. His brother Jim, got his first job at Rutgers and I remember Nick talking about how proud he was of Jimmy. This is the same Jim Valvano that reached the heights with a 1983 NCAA title at North Carolina State (over Houston). Jim had hit the big time and people remember his infectious personality, his radiant smile and the way he ran around the basketball court after the championship win, looking for a hand to shake.

You could tell Nick and Jim were brothers. The face and hair were similar and the teeth in the men, looked the same. Big brother Nick didn't have a title type team while at DV. He rolled with the punches though and it became obvious that he enjoyed teaching his charges about the game of basketball.

Nick liked to win just as much as the next guy. But when defeats reared their ugly heads, he was durable, realistic and open minded despite the reversals. He never dodged an interview and approached me with an open mind.

After a home game, I would head down the locker room steps and hang a left into the coach's office. There Nick would be, ducking and hiding in there like some kind of fugitive. "I don't like my team smoking and want to be a good example for them," he blurted out between drags. "I hope they can't see me in here."

Nick has a younger brother named Bob, who became a college basketball analyst for ESPN-TV. He is also the commentator for the University of Louisville basketball team and is the author of a book entitled "The Gifts of Jimmy V."

While Jim Valvano will be remembered as the NCAA winning coach in 1983, he went on to contribute much more to humanity. The guy with the great sense of humor, was diagnosed with cancer and after a courageous 10-month battle with that dreaded foe, he succumbed April 1, 1993. Jimmy is gone but far from forgotten.

He was and still is an inspiration to those battling cancer. After accepting the March 4, 1993 inaugural Arthur Ashe Award for Courage at the American Sports Awards (the ESPYS), he gave a now famous speech that brought tears to countless listeners. He said there were three things we all should do every day. Jim taught us to laugh, think and have our emotions moved to tears (happiness or joy). He went on to announce the starting of the Jimmy V Foundation (for cancer research). Less than a month later, Jimmy V was gone at age 47, a victim of bone cancer.

The Jimmy V Foundation has raised in excess of $26 million to aid in the fight against this disease that takes thousands of lives every year. It was never Nick Valvano's mission in life to become a high school basketball coach. Fate played a big part in his future and he wound up becoming the chief executive officer of the Jimmy V Foundation.

I communicated with Nick just before Christmas of 2002. "You brought back some memories (of DV basketball days)," he said. "When I left DV, I went into sales with Xerox and then spent the next 30 years in sales and marketing. My last position was VP of Sales and Marketing for Olivetti North America, a software company owned by Olivetti."

Nick helped Jimmy select the original Board of Directors of the Jimmy V Foundation. He continues his valuable service to a worthwhile organization. "I moved to North Carolina three years ago to manage the day to day operation of the foundation," he says. "The job takes me all over the country."

On March 19, 1974, I ran a column on Port Jervis modified wrestling coach Phil Chase and a goal he had set. With the story, was a picture that showed three impish brothers, two of them looking at the camera. They all had long hair and confident looks on their mischievous faces.

Three years later, this trio would head to Onondaga War Memorial in Syracuse as Section 9 champions. Their combined record (1976-77) heading to the New York State Intersectional Wrestling Tournament (states) was an unbelievable 86-0. Before all was said and done, the three Banach brothers would bring fame to Port Jervis. Two of them, Ed and Lou, would win Olympic gold medals (freestyle wrestling) at the 1984 Olympics.

Chase, son of legendary Port football coach Al "The Old Fox" Chase, coached golf and baseball at Port High. He started under Al Wilgard (wrestling) and then was a vital cog in the Raider powerhouse wrestling wheel when Mark Faller assumed varsity coaching duties for the Red Raiders. "Al (Wilgard) was tough and rough but good for the kids," Chase says. "He was so well prepared, he would tell you 'I don't run the practice my manager does' ".

Back in 1974, Chase had just coached the Port seventh and eighth grade team to its second Orange County League mat title in three years. From there, he was shooting for the stars.

"Someday I hope to see one of the kids I've coached win a New York State wrestling title," he had said in the story. Chase had taken up coaching (1971) because the younger kids at Port were in danger of not having a modified program. "I read a lot of books about wrestling," Chase noted. "Of course Mark (Faller) was ahead of everyone in the East and coached Greco wrestling (upper body) to the high school kids as much as most of the western and mid western colleges did. It wasn't as much fun for the kids but was very effective. A ninth grader with no wrestling background could be successful. I tried to teach everything including down on the mat style and Mark's moves. I wound up coaching 10 years."

Chase had the three Banach boys for two years and hauled them to tournaments in Pennsylvania and Long Island. Little did he know that the twins would go on to fulfill his wish for not just one state champion from Port Jervis, but two.

Current Raider coach Dave Simmons was guiding even younger wrestlers (fifth and sixth grades) than Chase was. "I asked Mark what he wanted and went from there," Simmons said. "Meanwhile, Phil did a phenomenal job with the modified wrestling program. I don't think he ever lost a match." Simmons has also kept Raider mat fortunes alive as the Raiders continue to be league and Section 9 contenders. In 2001, Jason Jones gave Simmons his first state champion (Port Jervis has four).

In 1975, Elton John had five songs in the top 100 published by Musicradio WABC. Checking in at number three was "Philadelphia Freedom" by Sir Elton. Some of the other tunes of the day included "Love Will Keep Us Together" (The Captain and Tenille), "Mandy" (Barry Manilow), "Feelings" (Morris Albert), "One Of These Nights" (The Eagles) and "Sister Golden Hair" (America).

We had a toddler and a baby under our roof and the two of us continued to work our jobs. We were a happy young family and couldn't be more content. Every now and then Chris' parents would baby sit for us so that we could go out and get dinner together.

Sports kept me on the go during busy seasons and Tracie learned to read while I was out covering sports. Up in Eldred, Fran Kean was molding a powerhouse girls basketball team. Kean, a former All-DUSO outfielder at Port, had five brothers (Bernie, Cy, Cary, Kevin and John) who had all made their mark as Port athletes. Their sister, Kathy, was a beautiful girl who became a Thanksgiving Football Queen. The Keans joined the Keys (wrestling) and Simmons brothers (wrestling, football) as household athletic names in Port.

Some other big stories were crafty Rick DePoalo (25-0) winning his second Section 9 mat title at Minisink under Frank Carrozza, and Jim Finlay, John Werner and Bob Chase being leaders (71s) in the Rock View Open after the first day. Dave Farace quarterbacked Viglione's Port gridders to an 8-0-1 mark while backfield ace Harvey Freeman rushed for 1,047 yards. Mighty might back Mike Barber, Ernie Jackson and Scott Taylor were also on that team. In wrestling, Port knocked off DV 36-18 as a New York powerhouse was being built.

The biggest story locally, revolved around 1974 Port graduate Bob Semerano. Bobby, one of the most competitive athletes I've ever covered (baseball, football, basketball), was drafted in the 22nd round by the Pittsburgh Pirates (signed contract June 9, 1975). Bob went to college at Orange County Community College (Middletown, N.Y.) and Southern Connecticut and also played baseball for the Minisink Valley Orbits (rookie league).

Pirate scout Murray Cook apparently liked what he saw and signed Semerano. The Royals, Mets, Yanks, Reds and Twins were all interested in the well-built kid who could throw the ball 100 miles per hour. Bob had an offer of a scholarship at the University of Miami but opted to take his shot at the majors. In June of 1975, Bobby headed for Sarasota, Florida to begin his career. Just a few days prior, I went with my wife and two small children to Bob's house to do a story. His parents' Frank and Eleanor, plus grandmother, Flora, brother Ron and sister Sharon were all happy as can be. Bob gripped a baseball for a picture and told me "my dream has come true."

In 1976, he was in Pirate City (Bradenton, Florida) and rubbing elbows with some of the star Pirate players such as Willie Stargel and Dave Parker. "They were real nice guys," Semerano had said. "Some of the biggest stars in baseball helped me from the second I got there." In 1976, Bob had fired strikes for a Pirate minor league team, Niagara Falls (Class A). But tragedy was waiting around the corner for Bob Semerano.

His elbow snapped in a game against the Cubs and it would prove to be the beginning of the end. The Pirates refused to give up on Semerano, even though he had suffered a stress fracture of his pitching elbow. Bob pitched in Charleston, South Carolina and Niagara Falls in 1977, after having rehabilitated his pitching arm while back at his Port Jervis home. I remember Bobby and friend Glenn Talmadge loosening up out near the Erie Railroad tracks and Semerano hoping that he could wind up back at 100 per cent again.

In 1978, Semerano was given his release from the Pirates. A year later, he was given a tryout with the New York Yankees but was released after spring training. Bob had received a bad break, tried to deal with it and ran out of time. He is married to former Port athlete Mary Ann Kowal and the couple has two children, Marcie and Robby. Robby followed in his dad's footsteps and played baseball for Fordham University.

Things were pretty much the same back at the office. I had the same enthusiasm for the job in 1975 that I had five years earlier. I covered some fine high school teams back then and the stories seemed to write themselves. After the Joe Murphy and "wrong way Ray" days, a new editor named Joe Richter arrived at the Gazette.

Joe was a slender dark-haired guy that was single. He had a good sense of humor and an eye for detail at the Gazette. It didn't take me long to figure out that he was a decent editor who was on his way up in the Ottaway group. Steve and I showed him around the town, so of course he fit right in to the Friday afternoon Hotel Carroll scene.

I continued to run the sports section the way I saw fit. The reading public was happy with the sports coverage and when Pad Kroger came aboard to cover Delaware Valley, we were producing a professional product that happens just once in a lifetime.

Port wrestling and its fabled Banach brothers would soon be capturing the fancy of hard-boiled New York State wrestling fanatics. I sensed a state title would be coming someday soon and began gearing for it. These three mat sensations were nice young men who were respectful of their elders. I still remember Ed and Louie watching cartoons with my two small daughters while Steve was getting his hair cut by his mother, who he called "sarg." By that time, the boys had already reached the heights in high school wrestling and were collegiate stars.

For the most part, when the Banachs started making headlines, DV wrestling followers began exhibiting jealousy and wanted equal coverage. I slammed the door on that kind of thinking from the beginning and knew that the Warriors were getting adequate stories. But it seems that some DV supporters were forcing the issue and Richter couldn't help but hear all the bitching coming from the other side of the bridge.

In 1976, songs that made it big included "I Write The Songs" (Barry Manilow), "Kiss and Say Goodbye" (The Manhattans), "You'll Never Find Another Love Like Mine" (Lou Rawls), "If You Leave Me Now" (Chicago) and "Welcome Back Kotter" (John Sebastian).

In early 1976, Lou Banach couldn't even crack Port's powerful starting wrestling lineup (he was a spot starter). Eddie (five minutes older than twin Lou) and his brother weighed in around 160 pounds each. Steve Banach, the rugged center on the football team, was an inspiration to his younger brothers. Meanwhile, Ed called Mark Faller the toughest grappler he had ever met on the mat. "He is by far the best," he had said.

Steve lost a heartbreaking Section 9 finals bout to Tappan Zee's Steve

Nevins (10-8). Nevins advanced to Syracuse while Steve rode north in a car with myself, my wife, plus Gary (Fish) and Nancy Scales. "Next time I won't be riding up here in a car," Steve said as he stretched out in the back seat. "Next year I'll be going as a champion." The oldest Banach brother made good on his word in March of 1977.

At states, Ed lost to Mount Vernon's rugged Tony Crawford, 9-5, in semifinals (Ed took fifth place) while Ernie Jackson surged to a sixth place finish. Jackson wouldn't be back (senior) but the twins and Steve Banach would, and they wowed the wrestling world in Syracuse a year later.

At work, Rago and I continued our morning comedy shows. He would wind up falling for one of his reporters (Pam Hart) and eventually the two would be married. In the twilight of my full time writing career, Pam and Mary Welch were reporters out in the newsroom. To say my eyes were always on the typewriter would have been an out and out lie.

Joe Robles was a fine production supervisor downstairs and was an excellent photographer as well. When September rolled around, he would accompany me to the Concord Hotel to photograph a picture page on Muhammad Ali and to Grossinger's in Liberty, to do the same with Ali's opponent, Ken Norton.

One memory I have of Joe, is back when I photographed Pete Rose against the New York Mets, at Shea Stadium. I had some great action photos of "Charlie Hustle" including one, where he was sliding safely, head first into third base, with unbelievable intensity on his determined face. The infield dirt flew in the air from Rose's grinding and gleaming spikes and I couldn't wait to see the prints of these fabulous shots.

Unlike the early days of my writing career, I no longer was responsible for doing darkroom work. Fred Stanton (from production) was one of the guys developing film and all I had to do, was wait for the finished product to come upstairs.

On this occasion, I just couldn't wait for Monday morning and went to the Gazette during the weekend to do my own film. I moved the film from canister to canister and waited for the procedure to finally be done. When the timer clock went off, I was right there to view the negatives.

What I saw, left an awful pain in the pit of my stomach. The film came out totally clear, with no images showing. Had the film been defective? I felt sick with the realization that my Pete Rose pictures would never be viewed. I got to Joe first thing Monday and asked him if something was wrong with the chemicals.

A lot of guys would have lied through their teeth, but Joe isn't like that. He told me that the chemicals had been dumped and that the canisters had been cleaned out for the next work week. What it amounted to, was my film being placed in nothing but tap water and soap suds. No sign warned anyone that there were no chemicals in the containers. The loss of the film pissed me off, but I figured there was no sense crying over spilt milk.

I continued to enjoy my job as a sportswriter. I hit most of my deadlines but every now and then pleaded with production for "just a few more minutes" (to get a story done and sent downstairs). Richard LeFrenniere, a real comedian, could turn serious, when you approached deadline time. He called me "BT 1" because of my initials, that became one of the slugs I used to identify stories. I would ask nicely for more time and he would shout upstairs "it's going without." These words became a way of life and we actually greeted each other outside the Gazette with those words. "Hey BT 1," he would say. "It's going without," I would answer.

Elsie Kayton had been the first woman I worked with at the Gazette and later Pauline Mateyak came across the street from her house, to toil in the newsroom. Pauline was a super worker and great person, who kept us loose, as we dealt with the pressure of deadlines.

In early 1976, Bob Cronin and Jerry Gray qualified for the New York State track meet, and Hugh Spangenberg's Port girls softball team went 19-2 and won a Section 9 crown behind the pitching of sophomore sensation Nancy Lane. Gray was a speedy sprinter who was a hard-hitting football player under Viglione. As fate would have it, I would one day be working side by side with Jerry, at his father's funeral home (Gray Funeral Home) in Port Jervis.

Rago and I continued to play tricks and were practical jokers in the newsroom. Once I phoned reporter Bob Couture from my office and watched as he picked up the phone. I identified myself as "Bob Moosic" and began discussing a recent story with him. "Well Mister Moosic, I'm glad you took the time to call," a serious Couture said at the end of our conversation. Rago and I absolutely peed our pants when he hung up the phone.

May 9, I left in the trusty Ford Maverick, bound for Reston, Virginia. "Welcome Back Kotter" by John Sebastian was playing on the car radio when I pulled out of the driveway. It was the first time since getting married, that I would be separated this long from my wife. The sports editor's seminar was slated from May 9 through 21.

This was the trip that ended with a major league baseball job offer in Oakland and a severely sprained right ankle. I attended the American Press Institute as a representative of a very small daily newspaper. "I do everything at the paper, including emptying the trash and making coffee," I explained to the other sports editors, as they laughed it up.

I stayed at the Sheraton Reston Inn, and attended cocktail hours and dinners daily. The seminar itself was very informative and I learned lots of things that I could use in my sports section. Malcolm F. Mallette was the director of the Institute while James Ottaway was the chairman of the board.

On August 16, 1976, I entered the Rock View Open and shot 88-94

(182) in B Flight. That sounded about right for me, since I seldom cracked 40 for nine holes. Just think, I finished only 49 shots behind tournament champion Gus Steiger. The lowest round I ever shot was a 38-39 (77) on the par 68 course.

The dog days of August turned into the brilliance of September and the hopes of another good Port Jervis football season, plus the smell of fall's colorful leaves, took center stage. On the 12th, Chris and I celebrated six years of a wonderful marriage. We had our pair of girls, ages four and two, who made our days very happy ones. We had a house, good jobs, two cars, two kids and some cats. Sadly enough, Charles had been hit by a car on a rainy Sunday morning back in 1971, and was killed. Many kittens and cats have passed through our doors since then. We were realizing the "American Dream" except for the white picket fence.

I was a respected and trusted writer and athletes from Port, DV, Minisink Valley and Eldred felt privileged when I showed up at their school, to cover an athletic event.

The reception and cooperative attitude I received out at Minisink was second to none. Frank Carrozza had developed into a top-flight athletic director and the well being of the school's students was his top priority. It was always a pleasure to hit Route 84 East with Minisink as a destination.

Up the road at the famed Concord Hotel resort, at Kiamesha Lake, Muhammad Ali was whipping himself into shape for a heavyweight boxing title defense against muscular ex-Marine Ken Norton. The Concord had been a famous site over the years, as professional entertainment came there to perform. The list of well-known people who appeared here in the Catskill Mountains, was mind-boggling. Now the former brash Louisville kid, who had become a world icon, toiled daily to get his 34-year-old body ready for the Yankee Stadium fight.

The Concord Hotel was less than an hour from Port Jervis on Route 42 North (through Monticello). It wouldn't be long before I was pointing my trusty Ford Maverick northward. I would watch Joe Louis signing autographs every morning during continental breakfasts. I wound up viewing Angelo Dundee, Dick Gregory, writers Roger Kahn and Dick Young (New York Daily News), ex-boxer Jimmy Ellis, and of course the heavyweight champion and his entourage.

I would sit in the bar and have drinks with Angelo Dundee as he spun some stories about his proud champion. And, I would talk and joke with my boyhood boxing idol, who had become a living legend. I would get to watch, interact with, write about and get to know the real Muhammad Ali.

CHAPTER 11

Muhammad Ali: Man Behind The Mask

My first glance of him, came at King Arthur's Court, a training facility at the Concord Hotel. He appeared taller than on television and was all business, on this September 1976 morning.

He perspired freely and approached his work schedule with the professional demeanor of a man on a mission. There would be time later, to kid around and make light of Ken Norton. But for now, Muhammad Ali reminded me of a "hit man" in training. The person he was targeting was training at Grossinger's Hotel in Liberty, just about 14 miles up the road.

Ali wore his customary white boxing trunks with the black stripe and took swigs from a water bottle every now and then. The heavyweight boxing champion, regarded as the greatest of all time, was eager and possessed with achieving another goal.

Back in March of 1973, Norton had beaten Ali (non-title) on a split decision in San Diego (12 rounds), in the first of their three fights. To Ali, the only thing worse than being beaten in the ring, is losing respect. He had gotten that back later that year (September), when he defeated Norton in Inglewood, California, on a split decision (12 rounds). Still the win hadn't been decisive and "The Greatest" was out to deliver a punishing message. As Cus D'Amato had told me while watching Muhammad spar, "Ali is too much of a man for Norton."

Ali projected such a positive image and his quiet and charming charisma this morning, seeped through the dead serious workout. It was easy to see why so many people loved and admired him. Muhammad sure knew how to "talk the talk." But he also knew how to "walk the walk" as well. Beads of sweat poured off his handsome brown face and toned body. Nearby, Angelo Dundee looked at the scene with the pride of a father.

Whenever the champ would halt this workout, he would quietly look into the distance and then meet the gazes of his adoring fans. People observed his every move and he acknowledged them with a quick wink. Then he went back to work.

It was hard for me to comprehend that my dream had come true. As a professional writer, I was intently watching the former Cassius Clay. I blended into this amazing and addicting boxing game, as if I was always meant to be part of it. A few days later, some of Ali's entourage were pleading with me to be near Ali's corner, when he came face to face with Norton at Yankee Stadium.

In the few days I made the trek up to the Concord, I would observe many Ali personalities. He could change that mature and serious exterior to become a laughing joker, in mere seconds. By the time I shook his hand in his hotel room (following an interview), I had a satisfying feeling that I had gotten to know the real man behind the mask. Ali is a genuinely kind human being, who wants to be loved and respected, just like anyone would.

I was interacting with the man who had been through three brutal fights with Joe Frazier. In his 1971 struggle at Madison Square Garden, he had been knocked down once and lost the 15-round decision to "Smokin Joe." However, Ali came back to decision Frazier in January of 1974 (New York) and battered him (TKO 14th round) in the "Thrilla In Manilla" (Quezon, Philippines) in October 1975. That epic battle was considered one of the greatest in boxing history.

Prior to his punishing win over Frazier, he had shocked rugged George Foreman in Kinshasa, Zaire (1974), the "Rumble In The Jungle", by laying back on the ropes (Ali called this tactic the "Rope-A-Dope") and letting Foreman punch himself out. Then in the eighth round, he unleashed a savage punching barrage that knocked Foreman out, as he regained the heavyweight crown.

The man that entered the world as Cassius Marcellus Clay Jr., on January 17, 1942, had begun boxing at age 12, in 1954. Six years later, he won the gold medal (lightweight boxing) at the Rome Olympics. He changed his name to Muhammad Ali in 1964, a month after taking Sonny Liston's heavyweight boxing title. He refused induction into the Army in April 1967 (religious grounds) and was found guilty of draft evasion and sentenced to five years in prison and a $10,000 fine. He went free, pending appeal and in June 1971, his conviction was reversed by the Supreme Court, on grounds the Selective Service System improperly refused to give Ali conscientious objector status.

Ali had overcome every pesky obstacle to reign as the king again. His positive attitude had gotten him a long ways not only in the ring, but outside it as well. At 34 years of age, this dynamic champion was embarking on another journey, this one to quiet Norton once and for all. Norton had broken Ali's jaw back in the first 1973 fight. Now just imagine Ali not being able to talk and jive with people. He wasn't sweeping this bad memory under the rug by any means and knew how dangerous Norton could be.

My dreamlike visit to Ali's training camp came about because I read an Al DeSantis story in our sister newspaper (also owned by Ottaway), the Times-Herald Record in Middletown, N.Y. Al was a fantastic and veteran writer with a heart as big as all outdoors. I had seen him many times at area athletic events and respected the man. I thought about phoning Al to find out how to get permission to cover Ali for a training camp story. With Port football in its early season stages, I thought better of that idea, then quickly reconsidered and gave him a call.

"Irving Rudd is the guy you want to talk to, Bill," Al asserted. "Just mention my name and you should get in alright." I am not the type of person that is a name dropper, but in this case, I figured what the hell, we are talking about Ali here. It took forever to finally catch up with Rudd, but I was glad I didn't give up. Irving was a real nice guy who had been around sports all his life. He was in charge of publicity for this title fight and told me how to reach King Arthur's Court and what I would need to get credentials. Before all was said and done, I would toss Irving some favors and he reciprocated by allowing me to penetrate the exclusive Ali circle.

I drove up to the site in that same Ford Maverick that I had purchased back in the Ted Brown days at the bank. Wheeling into a Concord Hotel parking lot, I viewed the building and said to myself "this is it, in a few minutes I will be watching Ali train." What would happen to me the next few days, is a transformation from high school to professional sports that couldn't be helped. I threw myself totally into this assignment and was on the scene all week, to write stories and observe Ali's every move.

I know it's an oxymoron, but I found Ali to be a complex, simple man. I would be watching the most famous athlete in the world, a person who was recognized everywhere by just one name, "Ali." He was known for his non-stop verbal ramblings, the "Ali Shuffle", "Rope-a-Dope", and his brutal battles with Frazier. In the 1971 fight which Ali lost, Frazier wound up in a hospital from the beating he took. An eye witness described Frazier's face. "It looked like raw hamburger," he had said.

Back when Ali was Clay, he won his gold medal, but reportedly wound up tossing it in the river, because he was so disgusted with racism in America. "I'm so pretty. Just look at this face, there's not a mark on it," he would say lots of times over the course of his career. He and the late sportscaster Howard Cosell, had many humorous interviews on camera and Ali cut Howie down every time.

Police patrolman Joe Martin had started young Clay working out in Louisville's Columbia gym. Ali had his bicycle stolen in Louisville and wanted to learn how to defend himself and become a fighter, in case he would come across the type element that scarfed up his bike. Black trainer Fred Stoner taught Clay the science of boxing and the future world champ took to it, like a fish to water.

Clay was quick, strong and witty. Later he would predict victories by reciting poetry and humorous rhymes regarding his opponents. He called Liston "the ugly bear" and Patterson "the rabbit." He was the flamboyant boxer who would "float like a butterfly and sting like a bee," as entourage member Drew Bundini Brown would often say. If Clay said a mosquito could pull a plow, you better hook him up.

Clay knew how to throw jive and leather too. At age 22, he became the unlikely titleholder. His technical knockout of Sonny Liston on February 25, 1964 in Miami Beach, Florida, shocked the boxing world. He had entered with a 19-0 record and few people gave him a whisker of a chance against the rugged brawler Liston.

Clay was lightning fast and doggedly went after his dream. Liston quit on his stool an embarrassed and beaten fighter, while Ali ran around the ring like a madman. The changing of the guard had been accomplished. The fight nearly didn't take place, because Clay's blood pressure had been sky high when he went through the pre-fight medical physical. He raved, ranted and got everybody's attention. Liston said Clay was "scared to death."

The Ali I saw more than 25 years ago, was a "Sybil" of sorts. He had many different personalities including the deeply religious person, the family man, the joker, the warrior and the kid that never grew up. Ali trained rigorously but at the same time, was enjoying the experience and the people around him.

The pungent smell of liniment pervaded King Arthur's Court as Ali hit the punching bag, skip roped, and strengthened his stomach muscles by bracing for the force of a medicine ball. Later in the week, he would enter the ring and spar. The sweat flew off him as he threw punches and moved around the ring with his speed. I saw with my own eyes, the quickness and punishing jab that had become Ali trademarks. I also viewed his reactions to pressure and his ability to take punches and pace himself.

Before he broke camp for his big test, I saw a man of peace, tranquility and serenity. Those qualities pierced through his humorous tirades like a flashing knife carving up a roast. He was a rugged fighter for sure, but this gifted and down to earth boxer, was a man of peace. He was a great comedian and poked fun at himself constantly. This super salesman, who could sell snowballs to the Eskimos, would get a chance to kid with me and enjoyed every second of it.

Every morning I would see Joe Louis "The Brown Bomber", former heavyweight great, signing his autographs with a smile on his face. I was drinking coffee and chomping on donuts with some of the most famous people around. I was in awe, but didn't show it. After awhile, I felt comfortable around the boxing game and settled in for the experience of a lifetime. Years and years later, Irving Rudd was to refer to his dealings with Muhammad. "I never knew Ali not to be accessible," he had said.

Ali exuded confidence in his title fight preparation. He dealt with the task at hand and yet after some of his session, he indicated that he was getting tired of the fight game. Norton had claimed he was ripped off in his second fight with Ali, and the champ shrugged that talk off like a gnat on a hot summer day. "Norton is a sucker," he said more than once.

Rudd started getting used to seeing me hanging around and sidled up to me one day. "How about doing me a favor?", he asked. Irving pointed out a couple he said was from England and asked if I could drive them to Grossinger's to witness a Norton workout. Joe Robles was with me to photograph an Ali picture page that day, and the four of us squeezed into the little Ford Maverick, for the ride out on Route 17.

The British people were big fans of Ali and thanked me up and down for the transportation to Norton's camp. "Don't thank him now," Robles said. "This car didn't make it there yet."

Joe got a chance to shoot Norton in action and that also wound up a picture page in the Union-Gazette. Our coverage of the training camps was top notch. We were bringing big time boxing to the Port Jervis area people, and they liked it. On the way to the camp, I thought of way back when Ali was the cocky Cassius Clay. Once he said "I'm so fast, I can turn off the light switch and be in bed before the room gets dark." I looked forward to seeing Norton, but couldn't wait to get back to the Ali camp.

Norton sparred, went through his paces and then had a 15-minute question and answer period. "Ali is in top shape for Tuesday," Kenny said. "He may act like he's taking it easy, but when you don't see him, he's getting ready." Dundee had mentioned to me that behind the closed doors of his hotel room, Ali did exercises.

The two training camps were a study in contrast. Norton trained in a small homey ski lodge room with an informal atmosphere. Ali was living in the lap of luxury by comparison. While Ali was running six miles mornings and appearing at noon for his public workout, Norton's regimen appeared more leisurely, although he worked just as hard.

Ali had been made aware this day, that some people were going to be going up the road to see Norton. "All of you who are going to see Norton, raise your hand," he suddenly bellowed. Nobody was brave enough to come clean.

Norton was loose in his approach to the impending battle. He waved to people as he sharpened his skills and declared himself equal to the challenge. "I'm physically ready," he said. "And I'm working on the mental part. I believe that the mind controls the body. By Tuesday, I'll be all set."

I asked Norton if Ali was feeling the most pressure about the upcoming fight. "I have nothing to prove," Norton said. "The pressure has got to be on him. All I know is I'm going to take care of business. I don't care about the odds and I'm not reading any papers. The age difference (Ali 34, Norton 31) isn't a factor. He's the same old Ali, except he isn't moving as much." Both pugilists had been around the boxing game for quite awhile. Ali had climbed through the ropes for 108 amateur bouts by the time he was 18 years old.

The day of fight, September 28, 1976, I ran my final stories and quoted legendary manager D'Amato. Cus had patience and an eye for the type of talent that transcended the normal boxer.

"Ali is an ageless fighter that comes along once in a lifetime," he said. "The only thing that can hurt Ali, is a loss of interest. He has an inner belief in himself and actually thinks he has never lost a fight."

The large bald man had been around boxing for all his life. At the time, he already had managed world champions Floyd Patterson and Rusty Torres. He watched Ali flick jab after jab and then cover up, to take some punches. "He is an amazing man," D'Amato asserted. "Nobody can take a punch like Ali."

Some fight fans choose to remember the big-mouthed braggart that came on the horizon and took care of Liston. They close their minds not only to Ali's dazzling talent and will to win, but pegged him as a selfish know-it-all. Those people put blinders on and never saw the forest for the trees. This generous symbol of confidence and power, has a heart as big as all outdoors. Many of these same critics have seen with their own eyes, the good that he has done and have changed their minds completely.

Ali could have stayed super serious at the Concord and have very little interaction with his fans. Instead this famous person chose to give of his time. He had already been through his regular workout toward the end of his training and was headed for a shower. Instead, he decided to tape his hands again, slip his boxing gloves back on and give an 18-year-old kid the thrill of a lifetime.

Jay Bright, of Catskill, New York, was just over half of Ali's age. He got the real life experience of going two full rounds with the heavyweight champion of the world. Ali didn't even cork him a good one, but left jabbed him until blood spilled from Bright's face and nose. Through bleary eyes and the dripping blood, the kid smiled back at Ali. He was living an experience that would be a fantastic memory, for the rest of his life.

"You didn't have to take the time to fight that kid," D'Amato said to Ali, later. "Yeah, I know that," Ali replied. "The kid has a long way to go. But when I was 18 years old, I sure would have wanted to fight the champ." When it was time to get his workout, Ali was as disciplined and regimented as a guard at Buckingham Palace. He knocked around sparring partners Randy Stevens and Rodney Bobick like they were rag dolls. He also went three rounds with former champion Jimmy Ellis. He worked daily on the speed bag and heavy bag and skip roped in three minute sessions. In one set, he skipped over the rope 404 times with just one miss. More remarkably, he walked away without breathing hard. He was in shape and ready for his test.

After one session, I sat with Dundee at the bar and Joe Robles took a picture for the paper. Dundee was bespectacled and dapper as always. I wore a white and black sports coat and had long hair, almost to my shoulders. When I got home from Southeast Asia my father had asked me what I planned to do, now that I was out of the service. "I plan to do lots of partying and grow my hair real long," I had said.

"Keep bringing your stories every day," Angelo said more than once. "Ali keeps asking me for them and he reads them all." Angelo seemed content that his champion boxer had gotten through another session and was now up in his room taking it easy. "Norton doesn't know the guy he faces Tuesday," Dundee asserted. "I'm not trying to act like there's a big secret. But I'll just say that Ali will be fighting differently."

Angelo proudly offered more. "Ali is in the ultimate physical condition. He had plenty of physical work. In fact he does exercises in his room. I'm sure Norton will be in good shape. He boxes like this (he demonstrated Norton's stance), with his foot in the bucket." Dundee said he was "scared" when he saw the golf driving range out in back of the Concord.

"When we fought Norton the first time, out in San Diego, we trained at a nice place--a motel located near a golf course, and Ali would spend plenty of time in the coffee shop talking to people. One day, someone wanted a picture of Ali swinging a golf club. Ali said he wouldn't just swing the club, but he'd run with the club and hit the ball. He did that once. On the second try, he fell down a hill and hurt his ankle."

Dundee said he tried to get Ali to pull out of that first fight, but Ali insisted he was alright. He fought that time with a badly injured ankle that was all taped up. In the rematch, the controversial Ali decision, Angelo said the shrewd Muhammad still wasn't 100 per cent. "Ali's hands were hurt and he punched with no feeling in them," the genial trainer asserted. "He couldn't feel his punches land and so his timing was off. Ali won the fight anyway."

The afternoon I sat with Angelo and a few others at that bar, I was really learning some background on "The Greatest." Angelo hadn't been the slightest bit presumptuous and related stories in a relaxed kind of way. "Ali is a boxing promoter's dream," he said. "It will end in the ninth, 10th or 11th round." That morning, Roger Kahn, author of "The Boys of Summer" (about the Brooklyn Dodgers), white-haired Dick Young from the Daily News and other notables had been around. They saw the champ in action and had to like what they viewed.

I knew that the next afternoon, I was going to be able to actually meet and interview Muhammad Ali. I didn't do a helluva lot of sleeping that night, as I jotted down possible questions to ask. I figured there would be some heavy hitters around me when I got to dig in and get a behind the scenes column. The only way to tackle such a big story was to just be myself. I figured it had gotten me this far and I didn't want to blow things at the worst possible time.

Terry VonIgnatius went up with me the next day and I told him I'd try to smuggle him in the room. He posed as a fellow writer from my newspaper, although he looked like he was going to pass out from the prospects of hanging out with Ali.

We were in the bar after Ali's training session, when a discreet hand sign was given to us. We ascended many flights of stairs and were greeted by security guards at each landing. One guard was going to perform an ID check, but a voice from the back said "It's okay they are with Ali." We continued up the steps, as my heart began to pound out of my chest. I walked down a carpeted corridor and entered an open door on the left. Inside, lying all sprawled out in a white terrycloth robe, on a big bed to the right, was the heavyweight champion of the world.

It was obvious how drained he was, from all of his physical conditioning. I went and sat in a chair almost directly across from Ali, but didn't want to be conspicuous, so I kept my reporter's notebook in my pocket for awhile. "People will know how great I am after I knock Norton out," he said in a quiet tone. "Everything is so perfect here at the Concord. I have this whole floor to myself. There are no phone calls, no TV and no beggars taking up my time. I am ready."

There were six writers (and a writer imposter) who peered across the room at Muhammad Ali. The champ was a master at handling people and he had no script or schedule, regarding what he was going to say to us. He was understandably proud about what he had accomplished in and out of the ring. He looked around the room, as if in deep thought. I could detect that he wanted to forget about boxing for awhile.

"I'm a fearless man--a warrior," Ali said. "Even if I get hurt, I come back dancing. Boxing just introduced me to the real arena. Fighting for minorities and worshipping Allah is what it's all about." I knew instantly, that this great fighter had gotten a bum rap, from many Americans. He was known as a braggart, big mouth and draft dodger. That image he projected in his younger years, was totally false.

He was exhausted from fighting nine rounds with three different sparring partners, but made time for us. He wasn't setting anyone up for a slanted news story. He just wanted to talk sincerely from the heart. "That picture up there (on the dresser) is of me and my oldest daughter," Ali said. "Her name is Maryum and she's eight years old," he said with a fatherly smile. "I also have a baby, six weeks old. Her name is Hana Ali. Hana means "happiness and peace of mind" in Arabic."

Reporters from a handful of big city newspapers, in addition to Reuter's News Agency, listened to Ali's words. They wanted to talk about the rapidly approaching fight at Yankee Stadium. Ali reluctantly got back on the subject of boxing and once he returned there, he seemed to get a second wind and relished being the center of attention. He was enjoying his role, took a breath and began firing out a spiel that reverberated around the room and brought smiles to our faces. This was the vintage Muhammad Ali at work.

"I'm the world's most famous person," the champ shouted. "Joe Namath and Willie Mays aren't known in England, but the name "Ali" is known everywhere. All of black Africa knows me and loves me. I'm a world man more than an American man. Little Korean girls walk up saying "Ali, Ali" and in Istanbul, more than 160,000 people waited to see me."

I looked at the rest of the people who were listening to Muhammad speak. No pens moved on the notebook pads and nobody interrupted Ali as he went on. "If I lose to Ken Norton Tuesday, I'll shoot myself. I do what I say I'll do. I'm used to clowning around and making predictions and Norton isn't. I was kidding him about being in an x-rated movie, but he came back and attacked my family and the way I live--that isn't fair."

Ali had gotten his own dander up, by delving into the morals issue and seemed to know it. He took a couple of breaths and focused his piercing eyes at the clock on a nearby table. "This thing rings at 3 a.m.," he said incredulously. "I'm out running at 4 a.m. with Dick Gregory and I'm in great shape. I take 32 different kinds of vitamins and Dick makes me some good things for my health. I don't drink coffee like I did out in San Diego."

The popular champion held up a tall pink tumbler filled with juice. "This is made of six squeezed grapefruits, honey and lemonade and believe me, it's really good."

It was obvious that Ali was ready for the approaching title defense and wasn't afraid to tell the world. "Boy am I glad I trained for this fight," he mused. "I went 15 rounds today and there was no jiving around. If I lose to Norton, I'll be the one that has to live with it the rest of my life. I'll have to tell my grandchildren some day--'kids, I lost to Ken Norton.' "

Ali began to rebound from his rough and tiring day over at King Arthur's Court. He began to curl his lips and give the satisfied look that the boxing world was used to. He was obviously enjoying the expressions on the newsmen who sat across from his bed. "Just look at this face," he said as he ran his hand over his smooth complexion. "Look how pretty I am."

Muhammad was on a roll now and went with the flow. "I've never been so ready in my life," he explained. "When I was training in Michigan, people were bothering me all the time. I couldn't train seriously and one day I said to myself, 'I'm gonna lose this Norton fight.' It's a good thing I left there, because the Concord is perfect."

He showed us how Muslims pray, on a prayer rug he had unrolled from near his bed. Ali had hopped up off the mattress and Terry helped him spread it out on the floor. Ali welcomed the relief from boxing talk and methodically showed us how his religion worships. He returned to the bed and suddenly caught my gaze. "Where do you live?", he asked me, as my heart began pounding through my shirt. "Near Port Jervis, New York, champ" I said. "It's a small town in Pennsylvania, called Matamoras." Ali mentioned that he owned some land along the Neversink River and then put his hand to his face in deep thought.

"What kind of a car do you drive?", he continued. "It's an old one, a 1970 Ford Maverick," I answered, as my fellow writers allowed a low laugh to escape their mouths. "Tell you what," the world champion said. "I'll drive your Maverick to your house and you fight Ken Norton." Everybody broke out in laughter. "No thanks, Muhammad, you can do that," I replied. I knew my face was a shade of red and hoped nobody noticed.

A movie projector was visible on a table next to Ali's bed. "I watch all of Norton's fights," Ali asserted proudly. "You know something? 6 million dollars is a lot of money." The champ would be getting all those bucks for climbing through the ropes at Yankee Stadium.

"God gave me all this money," Muhammad said. "I use some of it to help people. Houston McTear, the great runner, was living in a shack with 10 people. I sent him 30,000 dollars. I give money to the poor and old people and I wish my example would rub off. People should help other people."

Ali tugged on his white robe and stared into space. "I enjoy critics," he noted. "I like Dick Young cause when he criticizes me, I fight all the harder. I'm going to be 'terrible' Tuesday. Time is catching up with me I know, but I've changed a lot. I'm not like I used to be. I'm cool now, I'll knock Norton out."

It had been a mesmerizing and memorable interview for all inside of Ali's room. He yawned and mentioned that he had better get some rest. As we filed past him, he sat on the end of his bed and shook hands with each person who passed. Terry got an autograph from him and I looked in Ali's eyes as I shook his hand firmly. "Good luck champ," I said to him. "Drive that Maverick carefully," he winked, as I began heading to the door.

Sometimes that interview seems like it was just last week. I had started getting some grief back at work, because some of the high school athletic events were going uncovered. I figured this was a once in a lifetime thing though and readers in our circulation area, were waiting anxiously for my daily stories.

The newspaper clippings I keep in scrapbooks are slightly yellowed with age. Perusing them, causes me to flash back to those unbelievable September days. I see Ali with those dark eyes darting around the room, his sincere, determined demeanor and that pretty face that he loves to talk about.

I hated to have to walk away from Ali that afternoon. It meant going back to the daily seven day a week (no rest for the weary) grind that had become my life. Just a few months earlier, I had turned my back on a possible career covering major league baseball. I'm sure that with a little bit of maneuvering, I could have wound up writing about boxing and other big time sports, in a large city.

I bid farewell to professional boxing and headed the car back down Route 42 to Port Jervis. On the way there, I wondered if Ali would be retaining his heavyweight title. Norton had muscular arms and was in phenomenal shape. When I shook his hand and looked into his eyes, I saw an extremely positive man who was ready to find a way to beat "The Greatest." And that nearly happened.

Ali's preparation was barely enough to get him through. In famed Yankee Stadium in the Bronx, New York, Ali captured a unanimous 15-round decision over Ken Norton. Newspaper accounts said Ali pulled out the fight when "nothing was left." He surfaced in the 15th round, with the fight on the line. Two judges, Barney Smith and Harold Lederman, had Ali winning the fight by one round (8-7). Referee Arthur Mercante went with Ali 8-6-1, on his scorecard. United Press International gave Norton the nod, 8-7.

When it was all over, Ali walked away with bruises and a scraped nose. Norton thought he had won the fight and when the disturbing decision was announced, he crumbled into a sobbing hulk. "I won the last two rounds," Ali was quoted as saying. "That's what proves the champion from the trial horse." He gave Norton lots of credit, then turned to Dundee. "Wouldn't it be wise to get out now, get out as champion?", he said. "So many times I could feel age catching up to me. In my wind, in my endurance. I'd be wise to quit."

He had been shown up in six of the first eight rounds by Norton, but his left jab changed the tempo of the event and Ali assumed control of the battle. A total of 42,000 people ($3.5 million gate) watched the proud legend fight not only Norton, but "Father Time." Norton's manager, Bob Biron, felt for his boxer, but figured that the ref and judges wanted to keep Ali competing, because he was good for the boxing game. "I hit him three times to his one," Ali said, of the competition that had just occurred.

Although immediately talking about retiring, Ali is the type that loves adulation. He was intelligent enough to know that repeated blows to the head, had ruined the health of more than one fighter. I think the lure of the spotlight, the love of his fans and the thrill of competition and how far he could push his body, all made Muhammad Ali stay in the boxing game.

The late and great sportscaster-writer Dick Schaap was professionally and personally involved with Ali for many years. They were friends, and Schaap reportedly sensed when Ali should have walked away. The host of ESPN's "The Sports Reporter", was hoping Ali would retire following the 1974 "Rumble In The Jungle" bout with George Foreman. However, Ali had more challenges ahead and stuck with his profession for a few more years. Even now, I run into Terry VonIgnatius in Joe's Coffee Shop and he'll say "Ali still reigns supreme."

The real beginning of the end, can be traced back to Ali's February 15, 1978 bout against Leon Spinks. There was a time when Spinks wouldn't have belonged in the same ring as Ali. But on this evening, in Las Vegas, Ali appeared unprepared and dropped a 15-round decision. When I saw that result, I thought back to what D'Amato had pointed out at the Concord. He had stressed that a loss of interest, would be the only thing that could beat Ali. Seven months later, in New Orleans, Ali gained the title for the third time, by carving out a 15-round decision. Following that fight, Ali announced his retirement and didn't box again for two years.

This hero to the common man, had been competing in the greatest era in heavyweight boxing history. Like Joe Louis, Ali came back after retiring as champion. His entourage had never abandoned him for many years. From Dundee to corner man and fight doctor Ferdie Pacheco, they all adored Ali, yet feared for his well being.

On October 2, 1980, in Las Vegas, Muhammad Ali climbed through the ropes again. It was the beginning of the 1980s, which meant that Ali's time in the fight game, had taken place in parts of three decades. He was shooting for the vacant WBC title, but lost to Larry Holmes on an 11th round TKO. In his 61st and final fight, December 11, 1981, at Nassau in the Bahamas, Ali dropped a 10-round decision to an opponent named Trevor Berbick. The colorful fighter from Louisville, who used to "float like a butterfly, sting like a bee", had wound up his illustrious ring career with a record of 56-5 with 37 knockouts.

Dick Schaap wasn't the only fellow that wanted Ali to call it quits long before his 1981 finale. When I followed the champ in 1976, I wanted the Yankee Stadium battle against Norton to be his final appearance as heavyweight king. When he hinted at retirement, I wanted him to follow through. There was still time to push his daughter on the swing and spend time with his children.

In the twilight of his career, Ali was a shadow of his former self. His pride though, helped carry him through to the end of the line. Whenever I hear "The Boxer" by Simon and Garfunkel, I think of Muhammad.

"In the clearing stands a boxer
And a fighter by his trade
And he carries the reminders
Of ev'ry glove that laid him down
Or cut him till he cries out
In his anger and his shame,
"I am leaving, I am leaving."
But the fighter still remains."

Ali was, and still is, a guy who knows boxing history pretty well. One time, Ali said the 10 fighters that most impressed him were Jack Johnson,

Jack Dempsey, Gene Tunney, Joe Louis, Ezzard Charles, Jersey Joe Walcott, Rocky Marciano, Joe Frazier, George Foreman and Larry Holmes.

Ali is the second Louisvillian to ever hold the title. In 1905, Marvin Hart knocked out Jack Root, at Reno, Nevada, in the 12th round, for the title vacated by Jim Jeffries. When Ali gave Liston the surprise of his life, the then Cassius Clay, was just out of Central High School for four years.

The kid whose bike was stolen when he was just 12, went on to give boxing the national exposure it was sorely lacking. Instead of thinking of shady deals and the brutal underworld life that seemed to define boxing, Ali got everyone involved. Who was this brash kid who was yelling like a lunatic and shouting out predictions? Some, like me, got hooked on him right away, while others wanted his mouth shut permanently. Either way, Clay had come in and captured everyone in his intelligent and well-planned ambush. He inspired anger, hate, pride, love and most of all well-deserved respect.

Since I began writing this book, Teresa Martin of Kentucky, has been right on top of what is going on. She is a big Ali fan and has glossy photos of him in her home, a stone's throw from Louisville. "They are building a Muhammad Ali Museum in Louisville," she says with boundless pride. "He will always be the greatest."

In 1982, Ali was hospitalized for neurological tests, after showing minor symptoms of Parkinson's disease. He started treatment and was diagnosed in 1984, the same year that he proudly carried the Olympic torch through downtown Louisville. It is thought maybe the repeated trauma to the head (punches) could be a factor in his condition. Ali admitted to his health issue in 1988. He has decreasing motor skills and is on medication. There are slowed reflexes and neurological damage. Well-known-actor Michael J. Fox shares the same affliction.

If you think Ali is sitting around feeling sorry for himself, you have another thought coming. "The Greatest" continues to meet every challenge thrown his way, and helps his fellow man whenever possible.

On July 22, 1996, Muhammad lit the Olympic caldron at the opening ceremonies in Atlanta. Three billion TV viewers watched Ali, in a white gym suit, approach that unlit saucer with a flaming torch. He was trembling from the Parkinson's, but completed the task as observers began seeking out boxes of tissues. A person without tear ducts would have found a way to cry.

Ali raises money for worthy causes and is even more spiritual than he used to be. He travels 275 days a year from his home in Berrien Springs, Michigan. The dwelling, understandably enough, is protected by strict security at the gate. As Ali battles to keep Parkinson's at bay, he is into world politics.

Ali was 61 years old on January 17, 2003. That really blows me away, as he was just 34 when I got to know him.

He walks slowly and talks in a barely audible whisper, yet still possesses that crackling charisma that illuminates a room when he comes in the door. He was named United Nations "messenger of peace" in 1998 and visited war ravaged Kabul, Afghanistan in November 2002. In February 2003, he was due at a Fort Wayne Komets (Indiana) hockey game at Memorial Coliseum. There, he was slated to drop the opening puck at center ice, for the Komets-Kalamazoo Wings game. He would be mingling with children, who are battling life threatening diseases and signing autographs. Money earned from the event, was planned to go to charity.

When we think of Muhammad we envision the loud mouthed young man in the white and black Everlast boxing trunks. We see him taunting Liston, calling him an "ugly bear" and then going out and asserting ring supremacy. "He is too ugly to be champion," he had told us. Then he went out and changed things.

We see a flamboyant individual who was slowed by a disease and was recognized as "Sportsman of the Century," by Sports Illustrated magazine. In 1999, USA Today newspaper ranked him as "Athlete of the Century." The movie "Ali" was a screen hit, with Will Smith playing the part of Muhammad. For some reason, the exploits of Muhammad Ali remain fresh in people's minds. They refuse to let go of this national treasure.

He resides at that 100-acre farm in Berrien Springs with his wife, Yolanda, who is also his business manager. Ali values his privacy but is in such demand, that his free time is very limited. On the property, is a custom made boxing ring. Ali still hits the punching bag, as he battles his disease with the same vigor that made him the greatest to ever lace up the gloves.

Ali's list of the 10 most impressive heavyweights changes from time to time. Included with Foreman, Frazier, Johnson, Marciano, and Dempsey, are Ali himself (on top of the list), Liston, Floyd Patterson, Archie Moore and "my third wife."

In some of the great athlete lists that Ali has headed, he beat out super performers including Babe Ruth, Jesse Owens, Jim Thorpe, Jack Nicklaus, Jackie Robinson and Michael Jordan. Ali figures Sugar Ray Robinson is the finest fighter that ever lived. "Even better than me," he reportedly once said. It really is hard to comprehend that I met both of these legends. Playing pool with Sugar Ray and hanging out in Ali's hotel room, are truly rewarding experiences.

Ali wants to be remembered as "a black man who won the heavy-weight title and who was humorous and who treated everyone right."

The guy that shows all this grace, wit and joy is the pride of Louisville, Kentucky. Ali entered the Kentucky Hall of Fame in 1999. He grew up on Grand Avenue and as a young teenager, carried a bible, and didn't smoke or drink soda pop. He ran the city streets to train, including jaunts down Greenwood Avenue toward Chicksaw Park and the Ohio River. He worked at Nazareth College Library and at a roller skating rink. Cassius Clay could be seen racing buses to school and boxing out in the yard of Tucker's Grocery Store, two blocks from his house.

It is said that Leonard Tucker gathered up some old and worn boxing gloves from the YMCA and tossed them out in the yard. Soon Clay, his brother Rahaman and their friends would be out there slugging away at each other. Cassius was obsessed with boxing at an early age and was determined to excel at the sport. City resident Bettie Johnson was quoted as remembering a day that Clay and a Great Dane dog played. "He was running around the yard dodging it (the dog), jumping out and running some more," she said. "He ran the dog ragged. Cassius wasn't even fazed, wasn't even out of breath. But that dog lay down and never got up for two or three hours."

There are countless interesting stories about the champion that I was privileged enough to meet. One occurred in 1960, when he went to Rome to represent the United States at the Olympics. He was afraid of getting on an airplane and was scared stiff of flying to Rome. People tried to calm him down and get him to deal with his fear. He finally gave in, but not before he went to an Army surplus store and bought a parachute. It is said that he actually wore the parachute on the plane.

One of Clay's hobbies was photography. The gold medal winner happily snapped countless pictures while in Rome. People don't really remember how he got back home, but they do say he refused to take the medal off for a couple of days. Once back in Louisville, the 18-year-old was greeted at Standiford Field by Mayor Bruce Hoblitzell, six Central High School cheerleaders and about 200 friends and fans.

After six years as being an amateur boxer, Clay turned professional. His first pro fight was a six round decision over Tunney Hunsaker in Louisville, on October 29, 1960. The 6'3" Clay, who would weight 210 pounds in his prime, reportedly received $2,000 for his efforts.

On April 19, 1961, he predicted a second round knockout over Lamar Clark, and made good on his statement. This boastful newcomer, with the speedy footwork and blazing fists, was on his way to a fabled career, that would make a power packed storybook or movie, pale by comparison.

He gave us humorous poems, predictions and sayings along the championship path and beyond. "The man who views the world at 50 the same way as he did at 20, has wasted 30 years of his life," he once said.

When he was illuminated under the glaring bright spotlight, he never blinked. "I am the greatest," he shouted to anyone who would listen. "I am pretty. I am baaaad man." Some people were sick and tired of hearing the "Louisville Lip" flapping. But he backed his boasts. "I predict that he will go in eight, to prove that I'm great" he said prior to the first fight against Liston. "And if he wants to go to heaven, I'll get him in seven. If you want to lose your money, bet on Sonny." He dethroned Liston, then took him out in the first round at Lewiston, Maine. He towered over Liston and as he looked down at Sonny lying on the canvas, he shouted "get up and fight, sucker."

Before one of his fights against Joe Frazier, he offered this gem. "This is the greatest event in the history of the world. Joe's gonna come out smoking and I ain't gonna be jokin'. I'll be peckin' and pokin' and pourin' water on his smokin'. This might shock and amaze 'ya, but I'll retire Joe Frazier." Of course boxing fans came running with cash, and the boxing promoter's "dream" had sold another fight.

In 1978, Louisville honored Ali by renaming a street in his honor. Walnut Street became "Muhammad Ali Boulevard." Though he hasn't been hanging out in his hometown in many, many years, he hasn't forgotten where he came from.

In 1999 he told a USA newspaper writer, "wouldn't it be beautiful, Ali coming back; it would give the press something to write about. I'll have new poems and predictions. It's worth a try."

We will always have a mental picture of Ali, as the animated athlete who impressed us, upset us, made us laugh, made us cry and touched every human emotion known to man. For a long time now, he has been spreading the word of Islam and is a proponent for peace in the world. And to think, so many folks thought he was using religion as an excuse to dodge the draft. How sad! When it comes to describing how the everyday person viewed Ali during his glittering career, I don't have to go any farther than Teresa Martin. She lives about 40 miles from Louisville and Ali's fellow Kentuckian bubbles over with pride, in talking about "The Greatest."

"I remember hearing more about the 'Louisville Lip' than I did about Cassius Clay," she explains. "For years, I never realized that they were the same person. I guess I never really paid attention to him, until he became known as Muhammad Ali. The very first time I remember watching him, he was fighting Ken Norton. I think I was about 11 or 12."

At first, Teresa wasn't impressed with what she heard and saw. "I thought he was the most arrogant black man I had ever heard of, and thought of him as being just a loud mouth," she notes. "My friends and I were always going around saying 'float like a butterfly, sting like a bee.' I think he made a huge impression on Louisville, mainly because of the fact that a kid from "that" side of town, could make a name for himself, like he did."

It is obvious that Teresa's initial view of Ali changed dramatically, just like so many opinions had across America and beyond. "He is living proof that if you want something bad enough, and have the determination to succeed in what you are striving for, then any dream is possible," she asserts. "Finally, with the completion of the new Muhammad Ali Museum (2004), there is hope that he will get the recognition he so richly deserves from this town. He proved not only to this city, but to the nation, that if you believe in something and have the courage to stand beside what you believe in, achieving your goals is possible."

She sums up this living legend perfectly. "There was something about him (Ali) then, and even more so today, that causes you to almost become entranced...or hypnotized by him. Today when he speaks, my heart is filled with pride and I hang on every word. The way he has dealt with his disease and refuses to give up or give in to it, has spoke volumes to this nation. He is to be admired and respected for being the man that he is. I am a huge fan and am enthralled by anything that is ever written about him. Muhammad Ali is 'The Greatest' ."

Ali's sayings are laced with humor but sometimes are dead serious. "It isn't the mountains ahead to climb that wear you out; it's the pebble in your shoe," is one of them. Of course back when he was a brash, younger fellow, he came out with some like this. "If you even dream about beating me, you'd better wake up and apologize."

It seems the cream always rises to the top when it comes to being great. These exceptional people have talent in common and sometimes wind up finding each other. Such is the case with Ali and Elvis Presley. I wanted to meet both these men, far away from their adoring throngs. I thank my lucky stars that I batted .500. Ali met "The King" in February of 1973, out in Las Vegas, Nevada. As Presley's song title of 1960 said, they both had "Fame and Fortune."

The two who started out as poor kids in Louisville and Tupelo, Mississippi, became fast friends and wound up exchanging gifts. Presley had an elaborate robe made for Muhammad while Ali gave Elvis signed boxing gloves. The gloves have been on display in many locations, thanks to a mobile vehicle that became "Graceland on Wheels."

Ali had a profound message to share when he came out with this gem. "People don't realize what they had till it's gone. Like President Kennedy...nobody like him. Like the Beatles, there will never be anything like them. Like my man Elvis Presley...I was the Elvis of boxing."

My three most precious professional writing thrills include coming face to face with the one and only Muhammad Ali, watching Lou Banach and Port Jervis win state wrestling crowns in 1977 and being named New York State Sportswriter of the Year (scholastic wrestling) that same March evening, up in Syracuse, New York.

Muhammad Ali has touched many generations and countless lives. His contributions in and out of the boxing ring, can never be duplicated and will be etched in American history, with more impact than a gaping cut caused by a flicking, stinging left jab. Like the kid who smiled back at Muhammad when he was bleeding at King Arthur's Court, I am proud to have been part of Ali's amazing life.

"Look at this face. Look how pretty I am. I am 'The Greatest'."

CHAPTER 12

15 Minutes of Fame

The monumental difference between covering professional and high school sports, had become evident to me. For the first time since becoming a writer, I didn't feel all that excited about covering the early part of the 1976 football season.

Coach Viglione and his Port Jervis Red Raiders got my interest back though, by surging to seven consecutive victories. Dave Farace was a splendid quarterback and used his intelligence to spark the Raiders on offense. However, Port experienced a bad day at Valley Central in November, and was upset, 12-6. The Banachs, Joe Amato, Bob Cronin, Nick Nicolette, Rick Farace and the rest, saw a chance for an outright Orange County League title squelched with the defeat.

Vig rolled with the punches like he always did and prepared his talented squad for a showdown with Monroe-Woodbury. Port would have to knock off the Crusaders to share the OCL top spot. In the six years Port had been in the OCL, they had won or shared four titles. Viglione worked his troops hard in preparation for the big game. On the practice field, he kept the team until dusk telling them "we are going to do this thing until we get it right."

Port did get it right. The Raiders knocked off the purple-and-white clad Crusaders, 20-13, to grab a share of the top prize. Farace was to receive an appointment to West Point and an invitation for a June party at the Farace house, arrived in my mailbox.

Things happened in a blur during the early part of 1977. Port would experience a spectacular 1976-77 wrestling season and I reached the top of my writing game. By the time the Farace party rolled around, Christine would be attending with a former sportswriter. Perhaps I was a bit burned out, or the daily grind started to wear me down. I know when I left the Gazette, the weight of the world went off my shoulders.

I had been constantly taken for granted and got damn tired of it. The Gazette saved money by not having to pay my salary. However, a shimmering sports page became a boring and dull product. I had taken pride in what I did for a living and it sickened me to see what happened when I walked away.

Six days a week, I was present to lay out the sports pages. I didn't take time off and when I tried to secure a day away from the office, I was usually met with resistance. I always got the same old story that nobody could get free enough, to do my pages.

One day I asked Joe Richter (editor) what would happen if I smashed my car into a tree and wound up in the hospital. "We'd have to figure something out with the sports pages," he said. I thought for a moment and said "pretend I smashed into a tree."

Joe was a fine editor and we had always gotten along, but our relationship was to become somewhat strained. That would occur after Port Jervis had won the New York State Intersectional wrestling team title and Lou Banach had become Port's first state champion. I look back at March 1977 as an exciting time in my nearly 30 years of life. But on March 18, 1977, I walked out the door and into total freedom. As far as sports was concerned, it is "the day the music died."

Mark Faller was about to make good on building a wrestling power-house. His grapplers had gone 14-1 the prior season and the Raiders came back with awesome talent and depth. Before all was said and done, this team became regarded as one of the finest high school teams anywhere.

This team lifted weights together, practiced at fever pitch and was great on its feet. Port wrestlers would give you a one point escape and quickly sail in and take you down for two points. It was always "give one and get two" and the Banachs were masters at this strategy.

I loved writing about "Mark's Maulers" and how it was "feeding time at the zoo" when teams tangled with Port Jervis. The three Banach brothers usually pinned and gave the Raiders 18 team points, time after time.

Faller kept his pony tail and continued to sit on the top of his chair, next to assistant coach Ray Holyk. Mark was knowledgeable, patient and consumed with wrestling. His charges listened to his every word and attacked when they hit the mat. Home matches were standing room only and there was a huge sea of red and black clothing everywhere you looked in the packed bleachers. The frenzied Port fans, including ladies, knew their wrestling inside out. If a referee missed a takedown call or waited too long to slap the mat for a pin, he heard about it. Some officials dreaded working a Port match, because of the intense crowd participation.

To say that Port Jervis was the hot bed of New York State high school wrestling is the understatement of the century. The whole town ate, drank and slept wrestling. Football had been king for years and years in this city, but even the proud and traditional grid program had to move over, when Mark and his talented squad made big waves.

I began my career with basketball player Rich Saul. I achieved my goal of getting him the proper coverage that he deserved. Nobody has ever surpassed Saul in my mind and when I reached the twilight of my full time writing years, I would leave with an explosive wrestling team that was a shear pleasure to watch. There is really no adjective to adequately describe what I witnessed and felt, during that 1976-77 season. The closest I can come, would have to be the word "awesome."

In 1975-76, number one ranked Brentwood had given Port its lone loss in the14-1 season. A campaign later, Port went 14-0-1 with a tie with Pennsylvania power Bethlehem Catholic being the only non-win. Port took the mat with graceful splendor and ripped through every other opponent on its schedule. Each home match resembled a championship type atmosphere. Visiting teams found themselves intimidated but left with all the respect in the world for the grinding, energetic wheels of the Port Jervis wrestling express.

The Banachs were simply magnificent. In the past, Lou (177 pounds) looked very intelligent off the mat as he wore his glasses and didn't appear aggressive. On the mat, he possessed brute strength, countered every move and turned lights out on bewildered and outclassed opponents. Eddie (155) went non-stop from the opening whistle. He was an aggressive grappler and was called an "animal" many times during the course of the season. He shot for the pin immediately and was a master at taking you straight to your back.

Steve (167) was the oldest brother. He was mature and cunning as he viewed you eye to eye. He had a herky jerky kind of style that had opponents on the defense from the beginning. He was lean and mean and his arms and long legs would tie you up and swarm you from the outset. He was accomplished at noticing a weakness and then exploiting it. A dogged hard worker, he inspired his brothers and teammates to reach the top. When it came time for states, it was Steve who was favored to become Port's first state champion.

Port had opened the season by thumping Rockland County's North Rockland (52-11). Port, the defending Orange County League champs, had lost six wrestlers to graduation but had reloaded and was ready to take aim on destroying anyone in sight.

The rugged Raiders shocked Kingston in an away match, 35-18, and followed that up with wins over Suffern (33-10) and Newburgh (39-15). Taking a break from dual matches, Port did well at the prestigious Bethlehem Catholic (Pa.) Wrestling Tournament. With two starters out sick, Port still managed a fifth place finish as all three Banachs won tourney crowns. While Freedom High won the team title, Ed Banach downed a rugged Billy Williams of Freedom, 9-5 in the finals. Williams was seeded first, and Eddie, who wore a white mask to protect a broken nose, wound up being named the most valuable wrestler of the two-day event.

Port returned to the mat wars by knocking off Valley Central (39-15) and Minisink Valley (33-17), to become 6-0 on the season. Port crowned six champs in winning the Kohl Wrestling Tournament at Suffern. Sophomore Eric Savacool (114), Rick Farace (134), Ron Simonson (140) and the three Banach brothers all copped championships in the Rockland County tourney.

Port next took care of Washingtonville (54-2), Monticello (60-3), Monroe-Woodbury (32-25), Cornwall and Middletown (65-0). Port put the unscathed 11-0 record up against East Penn League powerhouse Bethlehem Catholic at West Point's North Gym on February 12, 1977.

The two talented teams wrestled to a 25-25 draw that afternoon. Savacool, Simonson and all three Banachs won while Port's Rick Farace and Tom Deiter fought to a 1-1 draw. Port led 25-19, but Bethlehem secured the tie when 270-pound Pat Brown pinned a Raider foe who was outweighed by 80 pounds.

In interstate competition, there was no weight limit for the heavy-weight class and that favored the Pennsylvania squad. Also, in the Keystone State, there was no 91-pound weight class (there was in New York), so when Barry Chase whipped his Bethlehem opponent, 12-4, no team points were awarded. The battle may have ended in a 25-25 tie, but if you read between the lines, Port had taken care of Bethlehem Catholic.

Port completed its second straight 9-0 Orange County League season, by clinching the title over Goshen, 33-21. Then on Wednesday, February 16, 1977, the Raiders rallied past neighboring Delaware Valley, 39-21, in front of more than 1,100 screaming fans. That intense conquest over 7-7 DV, completed Port's regular season at 14-0-1, the best in school history.

Pad had been covering DV all season long, but I handled this much anticipated clash between Coach Ned Bushong's Warriors and Port. Pad had indicated that DV 167-pounder Tyrone Presto would give unbeaten Steve Banach a tough bout. "In all fairness, I haven't seen Tyrone," I told my co-worker. "But I have seen Banach many times. Get ready for a pin." Pad scratched his head thoughtfully. "I don't know boss, Tyrone is strong enough to do it," he asserted. I glanced his way and said "we'll see, and by the way, I'm not boss, I'm Bill."

Presto entered with a 14-1 record and was a rugged and muscular grappler. Banach took him down with a slick single leg move in the first period for a 2-0 lead, but surrendered four points, including a Presto takedown, early in the second chapter, to fall behind, 4-2.

Steve, ever the tactician, patiently waited for his chance and roared from behind, 5-4, on an escape and takedown. Banach then gracefully tripped Presto to the mat and nailed him with just 12 seconds left in the second period (3:48). The Raider, like his brothers, remained unbeaten (21-0) and Port had completed its unbeaten season.

The OCL Tournament was next and Port, as expected, defended its crown and dominated by crowning six champs. Eighth grader Barry Chase (91), Savacool (112), Simonson (140) and the three Banachs (155, 167, 177) all came through for Faller.

Next on the agenda for state-ranked Port, was the 30-school Section 9 Wrestling Tournament at Orange County Community College in Middletown and Suffern High School. That tourney served as a state qualifier and champions would advance north, to the 15th annual New York State Intersectional Wrestling Tournament at Syracuse's famed Onondaga War Memorial.

The individual Section 9 (Hudson Valley area) champs would become a team and then go up against the best grapplers the rest of the state had to offer. The first two rounds (preliminaries and first round) were contested in Middletown and the remainder of the tourney took place at Suffern, March 5.

Tappan Zee, ranked 14th in the state, grabbed three top seeds and was installed as the Section 9 team favorite. However, 10th ranked Port Jervis, who also had three grapplers ranked first (Savacool, Ed and Steve Banach), was chomping at the bit to prove it was the cream of the crop.

Undefeated Tom Habel (177) of North Rockland, landed the top seed while Lou Banach (24-0) was second. Habel and Banach had heard about each other and a clash of the titans shaped up, from the second the tournament began. When the two went eye to eye, Habel tried to be intimidating while Banach appeared laid back.

Tappan Zee pulled 11 of 13 matmen through the first two rounds while Port advanced 10. In team points, Port went to Suffern in first place with 70 ½ to 65 for the Rockland school. The Section 9 finals at Suffern is an event many fans will never forget.

Port had sent two to Syracuse the year before (Ed Banach and Jackson). But in front of an enthusiastic mob, Port surged to the team title and crowned five champions who would make the trip to Syracuse. Barry Chase (Bruce Chase's twin), Savacool and all three Banachs racked up top prizes.

The first four Raiders all claimed decisions. Chase, wrestling in just his 14th varsity match, downed Newburgh's Ted Casey 6-2, while Savacool zipped Clarkstown North's John Lynch, 5-0. Ed Banach beat Ramapo's Chad Flayhan, 4-1, and Steve Banach handled Monroe-Woodbury's Harold Sumter, 6-3.

Habel and Louie came to the center of the mat during pre-match introductions. Habel looked strong, stern and unbeatable. Lou wore his glasses out to meet Habel for the first time. As it wound up, Lou was doing his best Clark Kent impersonation because he was to suddenly become Superman. It was billed as a "grudge match" and started just that way. The two wrestlers got to know each other by slapping each other around.

After the referee had a word with the grapplers, the bout resumed. Lou trailed 2-1 but was muscling with the burly Habel. Lou manufactured a two-point takedown in the second period and forced a shocked Habel to his back for a fall at the 3:24 mark. Just like that, Louie became the third of the ferocious brother act to prevail in a sectional final and earn a trip to states. The gymnasium was filled with deafening applause as Banach showed Habel the ceiling lights. The noise level never dropped but stayed at fever pitch, when his hand was raised in victory.

Moments later, Lou went out to receive his first place award to an enthusiastic standing ovation that rocked the bleachers. The brilliance of the red and black clothing of Raider fans appeared everywhere and Port Jervians beamed with pride at what the gutsy wrestling team had accomplished. Meanwhile, Habel refused to shake Lou's hand, and instead stalked off. This brought the boo birds out of the woodwork and tossed even more electricity into the wired crowd.

Ed Banach was making his second trip up to Onondaga while his brothers would be under the shimmering lights of the war memorial for the first time. Christine and I would be heading to the site for the third time and we had hopes that Mark's Maulers would be in the hunt for individual and team crowns. As it turned out, this talented squad would be blessed with both.

Neil Kerr from the New York State Sportswriters Association had contacted me through the mail. He admitted the association was probably underrating the Banach brothers. He indicated there were other reasons to be present for the intersectional. I just never picked up on the fact that I entered into the mix.

Before heading to Syracuse, I was to set foot on the Port basketball court as a player, for the first time since 1964. The Gazette had started a basketball team and we were to play radio station WDLC as a preliminary game to the Port Jervis teachers and Port police department.

The gym was nearly packed for our game and it was an exhilarating feeling to be playing in front of people again. We were coached by Joe Richter and whipped WDLC easily (68-28) while the teachers won, 50-37. We had quite a few players on the team so I didn't play the whole game, but more like half of it.

I contributed 11 points to the cause and drove the lane for a couple of pretty baskets. Pad wrote the story, and for the first time ever, my picture was in the paper as a basketball player. Pad clicked the camera when I was firing up a foul shot during the first half.

Mike Chardullo led the Gazette with 18 markers while Mike Mikulak tossed in 16. The three-pronged scoring attack led us to the easy victory (we led at halftime, 27-12 and 47-18 through three quarters). Our team, including Roger Maltby, John Brundage, Fred Stanton, Mike Murray and Tim Dodson, wore white and red uniform tops with our last names printed on the back. Tracy Baxter sparked WDLC while Joe Sanchez, Marty Shaw, Bob Wein, Oscar Wein and Doctor Michael Parmer also saw action. The referee was former Red Raider athlete Bob Semerano.

The next weekend we motored up to "The Cuse." The trick in having fun in Syracuse was to have weather forecasts that were free of snow.

This location gets pounded in the winter and the final test used to be following the tournament when you made you way up the first big hill of Route 81. Sometimes there was snow, other times freezing rain or fog would be the obstacle to overcome.

The war memorial is a big oval looking place that sits on a corner in downtown Syracuse. You get a feeling of history when you walk through the doors. That history is replaced by anticipation on a Friday afternoon when a champions procession occurs. All the sectional champions come out to be recognized, before the first bout takes place. Some grapplers look up in awe at the seats up in the second level. Others look straight ahead or gaze at the floor. Every color in the rainbow is represented here and many wrestlers have been psyched out and defeated before they ever stepped foot on a mat. You could wrestle back for a place here (after losing) but it was a tournament of champions in every respect, as the two finalists in each weight class had gotten through their two days unbeaten.

Reed F. Hawke was the tournament director and was a distinguished and helpful person in every way. On Friday, I went into his office at the war memorial to get my press credentials. The efficiency of this tournament was mind-boggling. Reed left no stone unturned to make sure the prestigious event was a success for all involved. The referees were top notch, crowd control was efficient and the press was accommodated.

After exchanging pleasantries with Mister Hawke, I was on the way out of the office, when a writer from Section 11 (Long Island) asked if I was from Section 9. When I nodded that I was, he had these wonderful words of wisdom for me. "In the quarterfinals tonight, John Plante (Brentwood-Ross-Section 11) will beat Steve Banach with no problem." I chuckled to myself at what a pompous ass this guy was, and simply replied. "I don't really think so."

The scribe didn't let it go at that. "Plante is undefeated (27-0) and competes in a tough wrestling section. Your guy (Banach) hasn't wrestled anybody." I collected my thoughts and exited the room with these words. "Guess what? Plante gets his first loss tonight. Don't cry on your note pad."

Reed Hawke was probably relieved to see this little conversation end. After all, the battles were supposed to take place on the mats, not in an upstairs office. The braggart's big mouth made me enjoy the excitement of Onondaga all the more and I thirsted for the battles to begin for Port's five grapplers.

Section 9 matmen wore robin's egg blue uniforms. I was so used to seeing Port in its customary red, white and black, that blue looked very foreign to me. The white "9" on the back of the uniform top indicated Section 9. I looked up at all the seats in this auditorium and envisioned how packed the place would be for the finals the following night. "God, I hope all three Banachs make it to the championship round," I thought.

Christine filled in all the information for the 14 weight classes, as bouts were contested on four mats. The announcer was a real pro and was on top of the action at all times. He informed folks of who won and lost, scores and what mat wrestlers would be performing on. I can still hear that authoritative voice booming "Plante, Section 11 and Banach Section 9, your on deck on the black mat."

Steve Banach had received a bye in the preliminary round at 167 pounds. Meanwhile, Barry Chase at 91 pounds (the only eighth grader in the 154-wrestler field), and Lou Banach (177) also got byes and automatically advanced to quarterfinals.

Port also got the other two grapplers into the quarterfinal round. Savacool (112) clamped Eminio DeAngelis (Spencerport-5) in 3:55 of prelims while Eddie (155) dominated Rich Patterson of Babylon (Section 11). A takedown, reversal and two near falls paved the way for an easy 9-1 win.

Savacool (25-1) fell in the quarterfinals when unbeaten Bob Bury (Calhoun-8) prevailed. Meanwhile, Chase had advanced to the semifinals with a shocking 5-2 win over Bob Buscher (Westlake-1). The young son of Phil and Merle Chase, seemed like a composed veteran as he headed into the 10 a.m. semis the next morning.

The battling Banachs all won their quarterfinal bouts and joined Barry in the next round. While Ed zipped Ron DeSanto (Section 1), 6-0 and Lou Banach beat Rich Potter (Carey- 8), 12-7, the most satisfying win for me, was watching Steve Banach suck it up and defeat Plante.

That clash was a knock-down drag-out affair and several times I felt nervous about Banach possibly losing. I knew what Steve was made of though, and had a gut feeling that he would be the wrestler that had his hand raised in victory. Steve racked up two takedowns, a one- point escape and two-point near fall, for a 7-5 decision. My eyes searched in vain for the bragging writer from Section 11, but I didn't spy him anywhere. While Plante fell to 27-1, Steve hauled a shiny 30-0 record into the semifinal round. The New York State Sportswriters Assn. had predicted that Steve would be Port's lone champ. While Port did get one champion, it wasn't to be oldest brother Steve.

Chris, myself and the Scales' (Fish and Nancy) adjourned to Danzer's on Erie Boulevard West, for some good food and drink. Visions of a couple of state champions from Port danced in my head. I was really happy with how Steve Banach had come through in a pressure situation. While I was proud of the lanky and good-natured senior, what he did the next day, is what I will always associate with the class that is Steve Banach.

We drove back to the Dinkler Motel on James Street and an hour of some much-needed rest. The wrestlers, coaches and some parents, preferred the city's oldest hotel, The Hotel Syracuse, on South Warren Street, just a stone's throw from the war memorial on South State Street. Chris had discovered the Dinkler when she worked for Sparkomatic and attended an IBM computer class in Syracuse. The location was out of the downtown, yet only about 10 minutes from the wrestling action.

When they play the star spangled banner under the lights on a Saturday morning at Onondaga, you feel American patriotism sweep through your body and settle in your heart. The realization that there were only 28 wrestlers left in the quest for state titles, was hard to comprehend. It became even more overwhelming for me, to see four Port Jervis wrestlers, a quartet of Mark Faller's boys, still in the hunt.

I thought of how far Mark had brought this team and recalled that first day in the locker room when I interviewed him. His wrestlers had been taught and digested his upper body style, then persevered in a fearless and optimistic manner. The culmination of all the hard work came in the form of a state championship. Port went up to Syracuse and began proving right away, that it was a full-fledged state powerhouse.

Suddenly Mark's ponytail wasn't a big topic, but getting involved in, and following Port Jervis wrestling was taking center stage. All of Section 9, had its eyes on the Raiders and soon, all of New York State was watching the 1977 state champion in waiting. At the crack of dawn Saturday, I had been on the phone to the Gazette, transmitting my story from Friday night. This was before the luxury of countless laptop computers and the speed of typing out a story at the scene and sending it to a newspaper. It was tedious writing the story longhand and then reading it out loud four or five words at a time, until it was totally sent.

The war memorial was nearly packed for the semifinal round and signs were visible in the upper deck. I was with the rest of the writers, coaches, wrestlers and officials, inside a plastic partition that keeps the fans outside the main battle area. My eyes saw all the sweat, and my ears heard all the grunts and groans. I viewed through an invisible window, the sights and sounds of victory and defeat. The pressure level on those mats was through the roof, as the young grapplers tried with all they had in them, to advance to the evening's championship finals.

I gazed way up to the top of the war memorial and saw Chris filling in her wrestling program brackets. I hoped that she could pencil in four Port Jervis names for the finals round. As it turned out, the twins, Ed and Lou, advanced to the championship. Barry Chase lost a tough 10-8 decision to Dave Parisi of Section 4-Windsor and Steve Banach suffered a heartbreaking 3-2 loss at the hands of Glen Falls (Section 2) grappler Mike Vermette. Parisi and Vermette both went on to win state crowns.

Ed Banach beat Terry Miller (Portville-6), 3-2 in overtime, while Louie blanked John Doherty (Tioga-4), 7-0.

At Danzer's, the four of us dined on thick roast beef sandwiches and cold liquids. Fish and I were drinking Heineken and discussing the upcoming finals. Meanwhile, at Onondaga War Memorial, I was being called over the public address system, to report to center mat to receive my New York State Sportswriter of the Year award. I had no inkling that the award was coming, I was never told to be at the sight at a certain time, and my 15 minutes of fame never came. Instead, I still look back at the high school basketball game against Ellenville as the night I basked in the spotlight of victory. That was my 15 minutes to be recognized and I was present for them.

Steve Banach's high school wrestling career ended in an ocean of tears. Steve was wrestling on an adjoining mat to Eddie in the semifinals. When he sneaked a look at Eddie's match, Vermette took him down to lead 3-1 late in the contest. Banach managed an escape to chop the deficit to 3-2, but the lapse in concentration earlier, cost him a shot at the 167-pound state crown.

The final story I wrote as a full time Union-Gazette writer appeared on March 18, 1977, and was headlined "Steve Banach--Maturity In Motion". At the bottom of the story was a picture of the three Banachs, mat side, prior to a regular season match. Two of them were clapping, as Ed walked out to center mat in pre-match introductions. That is the way I will always remember these three polished and talented grapplers. Always, they were side by side. Although miles now separate the trio, they will forever be together, as one, in my memory.

In the finals, Ed locked horns with Dom Macchia (Island Trees-8) while Lou had the dubious task of taking on undefeated (34-0) Section 3 (New Hartford) strong boy Charbel Karrat.

Eddie was mere seconds away from his state crown, when he made the mistake of getting up too high on Macchia. Banach tabbed a takedown with 36 seconds remaining to lead 4-3, however disaster was about to strike. He rode Macchia too high, Macchia notched a two-point reversal and a near fall to pull out an 8-4 title decision.

Lou Banach not only had Karrat to contend with, but he went on the mat knowing that Eddie had just suffered a tear-jerking decision loss. I have to believe that Lou wrestled for Banach pride when he went out an manhandled Karrat, 11-3. He threw in the legs and nearly had Karrat pinned a couple of times. When the exhausting battle was over, Lou went to his corner of the mat where he was embraced by Mark Faller and Ray Holyk. I caught the moment perfectly with my Yashica camera and the picture appeared in the package of the state wrestling story, Monday afternoon.

Somebody said that Tom Habel was present prior to Lou's match with Karrat and that someone had indicated that Banach would lose. It is said that Habel sided with Lou and said "anybody that can beat me, can beat anyone up here."

Lou was on cloud nine when the final buzzer went off. Port's first state champion ever, was breathing heavily as he reached Faller. I asked how he felt and his answer came quickly and from the heart. "It's a dream come true," he said simply. Lou wound up 31-0, Ed 32-1 and Steve 31-2 for 1976-77.

Section 9 finished sixth out of 11 sections. Lou had a title and Ed a second place. Steve Banach wound up in fifth place while Barry Chase grabbed a sixth. Section 11's Brentwood-Ross was favored to win the state team crown but instead, it came down to a two-team battle between Port Jervis and Locust Valley (Section 8, Nassau County).

A year later, Mark would send six champs back here to Syracuse and successfully defend the team title. Ed became Port's second state champ in 1978 when he decisioned East Rochester (Section 5) strong boy "Big John" Zito.

I took my sportswriter of the year trophy back to the room that night and put it on a table. I sensed that I had reached the top in high school wrestling coverage. All those hours of dedication had paid off. I felt real proud of Lou and the team that night. Three great things had happened to us up in Syracuse.

Great things were destined to happen to the Banach twins. Collegiate wrestling legend Dan Gable, the coach of the powerful University of Iowa, came to Port Jervis to recruit the twins. He sat on the back porch of their Ball Street home and didn't leave until he had secured them.

Iowa flourished with Gable and the Banach boys. They became worthy champs in collegiate wrestling and helped Iowa to NCAA crowns. Ed won NCAA mat titles in 1980, 1981 and 1983 (second in 1982), and was Big Ten Athlete of the Year in 1983. He was ranked first at Iowa in career pins (78), seventh in winning percentage (.937), and wound up 141-9-1. He called Lou "the toughest opponent I have ever wrestled." Eddie wound up at Iowa State, where he is a student athlete counselor. He was in Port Jervis to talk to young wrestlers, in 2002, prior to the NCAA's in Albany, N.Y.

While Steve went to Clemson University and later transferred to Iowa, Lou grabbed NCAA crowns in 1981 and 1983. He got a Masters degree in business administration and was a graduate assistant at Penn State. He is now a banker back in Iowa. Like Ed and Steve, Lou is married and has kids. Years ago, Chris and I received an invitation to Lou's wedding. He married the former Kim Thomas of Northbrook, Illinois. Lou had a stint as a Second Lieutenant in the Army and Steve made the Army a career.

The Banach twins left a wrestling legacy at Iowa, but were far from finished with freestyle wrestling. Both of them qualified for the 1984 summer Olympics in California and each would reach the zenith of wrestling, by raking in Olympic gold at the Anaheim Convention Center. The Russians had boycotted the Olympics in 1984, but I had a funny feeling that the Banachs would have prevailed, no matter who their foes were. Like in high school it was "feeding time at the zoo."

Ed was the first to garner the gold. While Penny Ann (the dog) and I watched in the wee early morning hours of August 9, 1984, Eddie whipped 27-year-old 198-pound foe Akira Ohta of Japan, 15-3, on a bout stopped at 4:01 on technical superiority (ahead by 12 points). Ed used single and double leg takedowns to dominate throughout the Olympics, where he outscored opponents, 52-7.

Two days later, at 220 pounds, Lou earned his gold by pinning Syria's Joseph Atiyeh in 1:01. Atiyeh, formerly of Louisiana State, had split two matches with Banach in his career. The prior loss had been by a dominating 28-5 count. In all, Lou surrendered just one point in the Olympics. On television, channel 7 covered the twins and showed Eddie carrying Lou on his shoulders after Lou won his gold. They also panned their cameras in on Al and Stephanie Tooley, the Banachs' proud parents.

Port Jervis Mayor Art Gray was willing to loan out Port's Banach brothers to Iowa and then the world, but wanted folks back home to be mentioned. He interacted with veteran ABC sports commentator Curt Gowdy as the Olympics progressed out in California. "Hey Curt, there are 8,700 people in Port Jervis that are upset at not being mentioned," Gray said. "We don't mind sharing Ed and Lou, but we don't want to give them up altogether." Gowdy reportedly gave this reply: "Okay, I'll mention Port Jervis on the air and help you get reelected."

After the "gold dust twins" had surged to their medals there was a party in the Tooley's room back at the Magic Carpet Motel. The proud parents and Mayor Gray were present at the celebration.

The Banachs had been household names in NCAA wrestling circles and then went on to represent their country in a proud manner. The United States garnered seven wrestling gold medals in 1984 under American coach Gable. When competitive wrestling is discussed in this country, Gable's name immediately comes to the forefront.

Dan went 64-0 at Waterloo High School (Iowa), then competed at Iowa State (130 through 142 pounds). His combined record was an amazing 182-1 as he lost in his last bout, as a senior in 1970, in the NCAA Tournament finals. He posted two NCAA titles and won his first 117 bouts as a collegiate grappler.

He is a gold medal winner (1972) who proved equally as proficient as a coach at Iowa. Gable won 15 national crowns in 21 years and copped nine straight NCAA titles from 1978-86. His Hawkeye matmen won Big Ten championships in all 21 seasons. His career coaching record was 355-21-5. This is the caliber wrestling enthusiast, that came to Port Jervis and made sure he signed the Banachs.

Steve Banach was destined to be a leader. He entered the Army and became an airborne ranger for three of his first five years. He ranked first out of 150 in an advanced course, was used to running 10-15 miles a day and leaped out of planes and into danger without batting an eye. Married to the former Marge Gines, Banach was back in Port Jervis, as a Lieutenant Colonel in June of 2002, to speak to fifth and sixth graders about his experiences in Afghanistan. He was introduced to the kids by high school teammate Ernie Jackson, the former Section 9 champion

(1976), who is a retired Colonel.

At the time, Banach was commander of the 3rd Infantry Ranger Battalion at Fort Benning, Georgia. He had commanded a company in Desert Storm in 1990-91. In October of 2001, Steve took a battalion to Afghanistan where they did combat parachute assault and conducted operations that assisted in the destruction of Taliban forces and their facilities. The brother who sacrificed himself instead of advancing to the New York State finals, wound up commanding 736 U.S. Army rangers.

Mark Faller guided his Port teams to records of 15-0 (1977-78), 14-1 (1978-79), and 14-1 (1979-80). Holyk took over for the following season while Faller wound up as head coach at Franklin and Marshall University in Lancaster, Pennsylvania. While in Port, he guided the team to a second place finish at states (1980) and had state runner-ups in Kevin Troche (140) in 1978 and John Stewart (134) in 1980. In 1978, six Raiders went to states. The grapplers included the Banach twins, Troche, Bruce Chase, Ron Simonson and Bob Masters.

Mark is currently assistant professor of Philosophy at Alaska Pacific University in Anchorage, Alaska.

On September 1, 1984, Port Jervis honored the Banachs with "Ed and Lou Banach Day" and a parade complete with marching bands, waving flags and speeches. It is said 10,000 people lined the parade route to catch a glimpse of the twins. The 24-year-old boys signed hundreds of autographs on everything from tee shirts to casts. Fire hydrants were spray painted gold and the city gave an outpouring of love to Ed and Lou. Banach Olympic Circle was dedicated (near the underpass) and a historical blue and yellow marker tells of the Banachs' exploits.

Port Jervis High School's senior high gymnasium became Ed and Lou Banach Arena. The Tri-State Gazette (former Union-Gazette) came out with a 24-page tribute to the brothers. The New York Times covered the event in story and photos and Sara Rimer interviewed editor Ken Books and myself.

In the September 3 edition of the New York Times, the headline read "Port Jervis Holds Party For Its Olympic Twins." Following the parade, Rimer, Books and I adjourned up to Holiday Inn where the two of us were interviewed.

Rimer wrote "Bill Tangen, who was sports editor at the Gazette during the Banach-Faller era, remembers those days in the late 1970s as the good old days in Port Jervis." And then she quoted me. "It was the greatest time of my life. This town was a wrestling powerhouse. It happens in a community once in a lifetime. Eddie and Louie were awesome, awesome."

The three Banach brothers, sometimes smiling and kidding while lending their team much-needed morale, were excellent students in high school. Their mom was seeing to that, while their father followed their every move on the mats. They were exciting to watch and captured the hearts and imagination of a whole town here in the northeast. If there are two lessons to be learned in regards to the Banach saga, it is that adversity can be overcome and dreams realized, plus the ingredient of love is the most powerful thing in the world.

There was a time when the future looked bleak and dark for this trio. They had 14 brothers and sisters and lived in Wilbur Junction, New Jersey. Tragically, their house caught on fire, and just as tragically, the kids were farmed out to adoption agencies when their dad took off and their mother was no longer capable of raising the brood alone. Enter Stephanie Jashembowski Tooley and Alan Tooley.

Janice McCann (now Janice Osborne) wrote a terrific story on the boys' past, in the August 31, 1984 tribute to Ed and Lou Banach tabloid that appeared in the Tri-State-Gazette. That tab, with Eddie and Louie on the front, was seen everywhere on the day of the Port Jervis parade. Now, years and years later, I am a freelance writer who does work for the Tri-State Gazette, under the editorship of Janice Osborne.

Janice pointed out that it was Steve who first came to live with the Tooleys, who were on an adoptive parents waiting list. On September 8, 1964, five year old Steve Banach arrived at his new home.

He was getting ready to start kindergarten and was already tackling responsibility at a tender age. Janice wrote about Stephanie's first actions with her new son. "He (Steve) acted like he had just been away on vacation and was returning home," Stephanie asserted. Then she explained a serious part of the new relationship. "I said you can call me Mrs. Tooley, Stephanie, Aunt Steph or mom." Steve's answer was "okay mom."

The new member of the family went over to Alan, who was watching television, and said "whatcha watchin' pop?" Suddenly the Tooleys were three. It doesn't end there, though. Soon, specifically on November 8, 1964, the Tooleys became five. Four year old twins Ed and Lou Banach were brought to the Tooley home and awaited older brother Steve, who was arriving on a school bus.

Janice's story pointed out that Stevie usually bounded off the school bus and ran up the driveway shouting "hi mom." But on this particular day, he had spied the caseworker's car and somberly shuffled toward his house, eyes riveted to the ground.

Steve looked his younger brothers over, and touched them. "Ed and Lou are going to stay with us for awhile," Stephanie explained to the older sibling. Christmas was the most joyous that Stephanie and Al had ever experienced. Presents were everywhere and three kids had the time of their young lives. The obstacle had been overcome and the miracle of love pervaded the Tooley home.

Stephanie never figured the path these boys would take. "I wanted them to be ballet dancers and gentlemen, not wrestling hoodlums," she told Janice. "They'll wrestle over my dead body," she told Alan. She didn't like wrestling one bit and was afraid her boys would wind up getting hurt.

The Banachs' mom changed her opinion of the sport later, although she never saw Steve Banach wrestle until he was a senior. Stephanie had wanted dancers for sons, or boys who could play the piano. Instead, they would go on to dance in the victory circle and drop pianos on over-matched foes.

"I was wrong," Stephanie had said. "They learned self respect, sportsmanship, sacrificing, respect for their opponents and how to control their tempers."

When the boys first went to Iowa, I had a phone call one day from Steph. "The boys are home for the holidays and they want to see you," she said. "Bring the family." And so, Chris, myself and the girls, Tracie, seven years old, and Dawn, five, hopped in the car.

Louie answered the door and our two small fries looked up at the imposing figure above. "Come on in," he smiled. Inside, Steve was in the kitchen clutching a mirror and getting a haircut from his mom. "Don't take too much off, sarg," he said. Steve always called his mom sarg. Bob Simonson, whose son had wrestled with the Banachs, was at the kitchen table with Alan. They were discussing an upcoming tournament in Michigan.

Ed and Lou, who often displayed a fiery sibling rivalry, were arguing over who drank the last soda in the refrigerator. Our daughters seemed uneasy around all the adults and Lou picked up on that vibe immediately. "Do you girls like cartoons?", he queried. Soon, Lou, Ed, Tracie and Dawn were laughing it up with Daffy Duck and Bugs Bunny.

These were the same young men that were dropping opponents like bad habits. They had rippling muscles and big upper arms from the hours of weight training and dedication. Sweat and good old fashioned hard work would one day bring them to the top echelon of freestyle wrestling. They honed their skills with the stubborn demeanor of mules and were never satisfied with the results. Individual New York State wrestling crowns would not be the top rungs on the ladder for these twins. Someday the pedestal to be gained, would be trimmed in a glittering gold sheen for the world to see. But for right now, Elmer Fudd was the focus of their attention.

Some tough NCAA mat tests lay ahead at Iowa for the twins. These two physical specimens of athleticism were the same little boys who let Steve touch their faces so many years ago, when they were only four years old. They had grown into men in every way, mature beyond their years. The twins were on a mission that would someday launch them into the outer space flight that ended with glory and accomplishment.

In 1984, the pot of gold at the end of the rainbow, the pirate's chest filled with gold, was located at the Anaheim Convention Center. They had gone a combined 166-11 (Ed 97-8, Lou 69-3) as Hawkeyes under

Gable. They were ready for the challenge that loomed ahead and were never intimidated.

When I covered the boys back in high school, I sensed there would be something great in their future. I just knew that all the greatness would not end on the mats up in Syracuse. Onondaga War Memorial was merely a stop on their road to success.

In August of 1984, Penny wagged her tail to answer my whoops of joy. I felt in my heart, a great pride for the Banachs, their parents and the city of Port Jervis. Again, it had been feeding time at the zoo. Mark's "animals" had satisfied their hunger for Olympic gold. Their mission had been accomplished.

Art Gray was the mayor of Port Jervis when the Banachs struck gold. Chris and I ran into him in Joe's Coffee Shop on April 9, 2003, a day after my 56th birthday. "I remember that after they won the gold, I went to work getting a sign up in the city (at Banach Olympic Circle)," he said. He looked out the front window of Joe's at the sign and plot of green grass that still serves as a proud Olympic moment to Port Jervians. "I told Dick Onofry (head of public works), we had to get a sign up quick. I swear, it was still molten hot when it went in the ground."

As a modified (seventh and eighth grade) wrestling coach, Phil Chase helped to shape the mat future of the three Banachs. The son of legendary Port Jervis High School football coach Al Chase saw the boys blossoming when he made the prediction about one of them grabbing Port's first state mat crown.

"I had the luck and thrill of having Lou, Eddie and Steve on the team for two years," he recalls. "I hauled them to many tournaments including Pennsylvania and Long Island (N.Y.) for off season matches as kids. It was also a great treat for our four boys (Phil and Merle had four sons, Bruce, Barry, Al and Bob) to wrestle in the same room with them."

Phil is as well rounded an individual as you will ever come across. He taught Physics, Earth Science and Chemistry for 34 years at Port, plus coached baseball, football, golf and modified wrestling. He stressed academics first and athletics next and had Section 9 mat champions in his twins Barry (1977) and Bruce (1978).

Barry is a certified public accountant in Pittsburgh, and Bruce passed away from cancer. Meanwhile, Bob is a computer expert in the banking field, Al, a former New York State golf champ, is a licensed surveyor and daughter Carol is a biology teacher who with camping gear, has traveled to locations such as Russia, Africa and Australia.

While Phil's dad won six DUSO grid titles and tied for another as a football coach, Phil excels in many fields. He went 62-0 as modified wrestling coach before losing to Valley Central. He is a professional fisherman and was named "man of the year" by the federation of fly fisherman (national, 1970). An avid environmentalist, Phil has dedicated his life to improving reservoir releases for area rivers in the Delaware

River watershed. He won two Orange County League baseball crowns at Warwick High School before coming to Port in the fall of 1959. And, he has rubbed elbows with some political and sports heavy hitters.

Phil fished for trout with former President of the United States Jimmy Carter and his wife Rosalyn, below Lordville in the Delaware River (1984) and also became a fishing buddy to New York Jets football tight end Mickey Shuler.

"Jimmy was a real nice person and I was a guide to his wife," Chase said. "I really didn't want to get in his way, so I fished some distance away from him. We fished in ice cold water for about four hours and Rosalyn got a rainbow trout." Chase netted the trout for the former first lady and had an observation about the two famous people, who are from Georgia. "They were very much in love," he said, without going into detail. "I sent Jimmy some flies and got a nice picture out of it," he concluded.

Al DeSantis (the same fellow I spoke to about watching Ali train) asked Chase if he'd take Shuler trout fishing. Mickey, a tight end for the New York Jets (1978-1989) and two-time pro bowl selection (1986, 1988), and Chase became tight.

"The three of us, Mickey, Alex Osowick and myself went to the gorge," Phil noted. "Alex and I rode down (three miles) to the river in a two-man jeep while Mickey ran about 2.5 miles. It was too hot to do any good fishing and I wound up telling Mickey about my son, Bruce, having cancer. I asked if he would like to fish the Delaware River at Eddy Farm for small mouth (bass) the next day. I was playing golf with a relative at Rock View and got home late. Mickey had already arrived at the house by the time I got there. Bruce told me that when Mickey came to the door, the two of them stood facing each other for a minute, without speaking, and then hit it off."

Chase says Shuler and the father-son team went to Eddy Farm in what proved to be Bruce's last walking trip. "Mickey was 6-3" and 234 pounds and wound up carrying Bruce on his back," Phil told me.

Shuler had become attached to the younger Chase and was there for him. "Mickey visited Bruce in Sloan Kettering and it was a real treat for Bruce," Chase asserted. Perhaps athleticism is what bonded the burly Jets player and the son of Phil Chase. From fourth grade on, Bruce never lost an Orange County League match.

It took Phil a long time to even watch a wrestling match where a grappler resembled Bruce. "Some looked the same as Bruce did and used some of the same moves. I just couldn't bring myself to watch. It hurt too much."

Chase explains he fished for three days with Shuler in western Pennsylvania and noted the pro football player, who had 76 catches and seven touchdown receptions in 1985, also liked to archery hunt. "When I received the man of the year award from the Federation of Fly Fishermen in 1970, they presented me with a beautiful 6-foot Orvis bamboo rod," says Phil. "Mickey had a son who was five years old in 1985. And he was liked a little man who had it all. One time his whole family was vacationing in the Catskills (mountains) and had come to the house for some home made maple syrup and pancakes. I wanted to do something for Mick, after Bruce died. He had been so nice to Bruce and all of us."

Chase wrote a note to Shuler's son, that was to be read when he reached about 14 years of age. "I wanted the boy to appreciate a good rod (the Orvis) and told him how wonderful his father had been to Bruce. I had put the note in the rod case and given it to Mickey."

These stories aren't meant to glorify Phil Chase, but to show the type of individual who helped to mold the Banachs into famous wrestlers. We sat down in the Port Jervis Burger King in late March 2003 and rehashed some of these old wrestling and non-wrestling tales. My obvious question to Phil, was how he had any type of inkling that one of the three Banach boys would more than likely garner Port's first state crown.

"It was the competitiveness," he answered quickly. "All three of them were super kids to watch. Even in football, it was a pleasure to see them. Eddie would go downfield on a kickoff and they got out of his way."

Phil had Ed and Lou in his Physics class and noted they were "dynamite" in the classroom, too. "I kept their lab books behind glass to display," Phil asserts. "Art Trovei's book was great too." Trovei was a state runnerup wrestler for Port in 1969 and made all his lab notes in color.

"When I had the Banachs, the goal was to be competitive. We were working in the direction of a state title and discussed the Olympics maybe once. Our teams were excellent because we used upper body throws."

Chase thinks back at the younger versions of the battling Banachs. "Eddic was the biggest hypochondriac," he laughs. "He was always screaming but I paid no attention. When the Banach twins were in ninth grade, we went to a match in Bethlehem, Pennsylvania. I felt tired, but said to myself 'I can't fall asleep because I have some great wrestlers in this vehicle.'"

At the match, Ed Banach showed a rip roaring preview of what was to come in later years. "He beat a kid so bad, they came with an ambulance, put a sheet over him and took him to the hospital," Chase remembers. "Eddie didn't even blink. That's when I knew he was over the hump."

The Port Jervis powerhouse was forming way back when the Chase twins, Bruce and Barry, were in sixth grade. "We went to Bennington, Vermont and the whole team placed," says Chase. "Eddie was intelligent on the mat and off. Later, he got a 96 per cent in my Physics class."

Chase has kept in touch with the Banachs over the years. In 2002, Ed gave a wrestling clinic in Port Jervis (on the way to the NCAA tournament in Albany, N.Y.) and visited with Phil and his grandson, Joe Chase. "Can you imagine a 5-year-old headlocking Eddie?", he joked. "I gave Ed a driver (Phil dabbles into working on golf clubs) and later got a letter from him, telling me he was hitting the ball better," Phil asserts.

Chase also got something in the mail, signed by undefeated (159-0 career) Cael Sanderson of Iowa State (Ed and Cael are friends). "It was a Wheaties box that Cael had signed for me," Chase notes. "He wrote that Eddie said I was 'da man'".

Eddie didn't steer Sanderson wrong, because Chase is "da man." He guided young and impressionable boys with his trademark patience and understanding. Three of the athletes Phil knew well, went on to become Colonels (Steve Banach, Ernie Jackson and Dave Farace).

As for the Banach men, this veteran sportswriter is very proud to know them so well and am ecstatic at the example they have set for thousands of others.

In August of 2002, Ed found out that I had labeled he and his brothers "animals", for the book. He wrote "My mom (Stephanie) probably had a hand in "taming" us boys. That is why Steve and Lou referred to her as "sarge!"

These happy and heart warming things that happened to the Banachs are an inspiration to say the least. The lanky kid riding in my back seat to Syracuse, had vowed to win a Section 9 title the next year. He made good on the prediction and returned as a champ. Years later, he wound up commanding Army personnel involved in life or death situations. His twin brothers were the two young boys who were waiting for the school bus to arrive, so many years ago. One wore glasses and initially couldn't crack Port's starting varsity lineup and one was yelling about all his ailments. They both went on to wear Olympic gold as Port Jervis' "gold dust twins."

It has been more than two and a half decades since I stood in my Syracuse motel room, in the early morning hours of March 6, 1977, and focused on the New York State Sportswriter of the Year trophy that sat on the brown dresser. The dark bronze colored object showed two wrestlers tangling in ancient Greece. I wondered just what this symbol of my hard work in sports writing really meant. Where would I go from here?

When I got home and began filing the stories, I was met with the forceful orders of an editor. I was told to cover Delaware Valley wrestlers in the regionals or else. I took the "or else." And you know what? If presented with the identical situation again, all these years later, I would do the exact same thing. I would walk away with pride.

Soon, I gave the one week notice, put my feet up on the desk and cruised. I viewed the headlines of Monday, March 7, 1977, with great happiness. "Lou Banach, Port Cop New York State Crowns", "Tangen State Champ In Wrestling Coverage." I rest my case. Four days later, my final headline read "Steve Banach--Maturity In Motion."

I felt the burden of deadlines and stress begin to lift. When I shook fellow staffers' hands, I felt a sad twinge to my heart. I didn't go near the editor's office. I had too much pride for that. Bob Couture said he would be "right behind me", exiting that front door. I still smile when I picture "Coutch" leaving years and years later. Tim Dodson was the city editor when I left and Mike Kowal was still the amiable advertising manager.

I carried a box with my belonging to the car, pulled away and watched the big gray Union-Gazette building disappear from my rear view mirror. "One door closes and another one opens," I thought as I viewed the bright, sunny day.

For me, the open door was located at Gray Funeral Home

CHAPTER 13

Life is for the Living

After a few days of soul searching, I began thinking that walking away from the newspaper may have been a mistake. Writing was so much in my blood, that I missed it instantly. The editor was phoned, in hopes that something could be worked out. Apparently, close to six-and-a-half years of loyal service was being swept away, because I was no longer welcome at the Union-Gazette.

My children were just four and three then, and there was the house mortgage and other bills hanging over our heads. Chris continued to work her jobs while I searched every day for employment. I had a personnel and writing background and tried to find something that matched those vocations. I failed to connect and felt a giant burden being placed on my shoulders. I recalled that old saying "God will provide" and said to myself "yeah, sure he will."

The days flew by and soon it was time to go to Dave Farace's party out at his dad and mom's house. I balked at going, because I realized that I was no longer on top of the sports writing world. Many local people thought I had taken another job at a newspaper. Simply put, I considered myself a "has been" at the age of 30.

We conversed with folks we knew out by the Farace pool. I talked to Dave, Port's spectacular quarterback, about his appointment to West Point, located just about an hour from Port Jervis. He maintained his disciplined demeanor of a winning quarterback and seemed more than equal to the task at hand.

I clutched my beer and gazed off into the warm evening air, feeling a little bit out of place and yet, kind of welcoming the excitement of being around sports types again. Pat and his wife were great hosts and it was a memorable evening of celebration.

My whole life changed at this party. I had never taken a formal Psychology course, but because of E. Arthur Gray, I would be taking my first. Many years prior, the tall and distinguished Gray once pitched college baseball in Colorado, but gave up what could have been a major league career, to join his dad in the family business, Gray Funeral Home. He was the fellow that watched me play junior varsity basketball in the early 1960s and I had covered his son, Jerry, on the football field and as a Port sprinter. Art was a friend of the family and he and my folks went way back.

Art looked like a politician and possessed the charisma and positive attitude to earn plenty of respect. He was a leader from the word go. Just a year later, he would become the new mayor of Port Jervis and hold that title for years. He eventually became a New York State Democratic Senator representing the 39th district.

"How are things going Bill,?" he asked in his easy going manner. "Well, I left the Gazette in March and don't have another job yet," I admitted. The future mayor thought for a few moments and offered these words. "I know you have to put bread on the table," he began. "You have two kids to feed anyway you can."

After I nodded in agreement, he went on. "No matter how far down you go, how tough it is, you can never let people know you are struggling. Even though it is hard, you have to smile and be optimistic. Some people like to see someone having a hard time. But when you act like everything is fine, they will leave you alone."

Those words of wisdom have stuck with me now for nearly 26 years. Chris and I refer to Gray's idea as "the old E.A." If things aren't going our way and we begin to be pessimistic or start complaining, we will catch ourselves. "We have to do the old E.A.," one of us will say, and we'll both laugh.

"There are some jobs to be done at the funeral home," Art said. "There is some outdoor work, like painting and mowing grass, that can help keep you in shape. Are you interested?," Gray asked. I couldn't get the word "yes" out quickly enough.

"Come to the front door of the funeral home Monday morning and Jerry will be there to let you in," Gray asserted. I thanked him up and down and was happy to get the chance to go back to work and earn a paycheck. I left the party in an optimistic mood, although the words "funeral home" seemed to hit me between the eyes and conjure up visions of sadness and dead bodies. I figured that beggars couldn't be choosers and decided to make the best of the situation. Besides, I told myself, I will be working outdoors and probably would never even see a dead person.

Two places that I tried to avoid at all costs, were hospitals and funeral homes. While hospitals did offer some type of hope for the sick, the finality of death and the setting of a funeral home, seemed to me, to be the absolute end of the line. I mean what do friends and family of the dearly departed say, as they pay their final respects? "Hey Charlie, I sure hope Jeter shakes out of this batting slump", or "Joe, looks like we're getting more rain tomorrow." If you asked me back in June of 1977 to describe a funeral home in one word, that word would be "uncomfortable."

People have pre-conceived ideas drilled into their heads regarding death and I was no different. I had a morbid fear of the unknown at this place, and wanted no part of being anywhere near the prep room. I shuddered at the thought of where I was headed that Monday morning. I would be employed again, but at what cost? All I could visualize was a loaf of bread on the table and E.A.'s inspiring words about appearing happy, even when things weren't going real great. I got out of the car, rolled up my sleeves and approached the front steps of Gray Funeral Home.

Jerry Gray came to the door before I got there and we walked to the front steps. He was a solidly built athletic kind of person who loved to make contact on the football field. He was a quiet type until you really got to know him. This guy could raise hell with the best of them and yet he could turn humor on and off like a faucet. He was a great kidder and practical joker but could quickly become dead serious (excuse the pun). Jerry Gray, who I covered in sports, would be an absolute riot to work with. We mowed grass together, raked leaves, painted indoors and out, clipped grass around gravestones and markers and did whatever odd jobs there were to be done.

His cousin, Pete Misczuk, worked with us that summer and the morale among the three of us couldn't have been better. When we worked we worked, but when we played we played.

I still see Jerry and Pete getting a sheet of paper out first thing in the morning and listing all the things we had to do that day. Don Parker, who later became a partner at Gray-Parker Funeral Home, was our immediate boss and tried to make us toe the line. Don is a fair man who is dignified and professional. Every hair on his head is in place and he is a well-respected member of the community. His wife, Esther, is an attractive woman who knew the funeral business inside out, but always had time for a joke or wisecrack. I could see right away, that this setup was going to work out. As long as I was kept away from that damn prep room, I was satisfied.

I was always nervous in the morning, when we went down in the cellar to get our mowing equipment. Pete and Jerry simply put their stuff on an elevator and rode upstairs, into the prep room, and then exited the funeral home. I opted to go down some back cellar steps from the outdoors and return that way too. A couple of days into the job, Jerry tricked me into coming over near that elevator. You can probably guess what happened next.

Suddenly, I was headed upward toward that dreaded room. I silently shook in the dark, thinking of where I was headed and resolved to look away from any bizarre objects in the room. There were no bodies in the room that day and I thanked my lucky stars about that. "Before you know it, you will be used to all of this," Jerry said. "They are dead you know. They aren't going to hurt you."

The day came when I did come through this room and there were people in there. I forced myself to look and tried to put it in perspective. The bodies were covered with sheets (there were two), and the people seemed to just be sleeping. The smell of the prep room, which includes the products that are used for embalming, permeate the area. It is a clean yet odd scent that I could recognize and identify, as easily as the smell of marijuana.

I did draw the line on one thing, regarding death and the prep room. Every day Jerry would enter the room first and make sure there were no children in there. I just know I couldn't have dealt with seeing a young person like that.

Like E.A. Gray had said, I was getting into even better shape because of the muscles I was using and the activities involved in the daily work. And the real highlight came when Don Parker would come and hand me my pay envelope. I wasn't going to get rich at this job, but my bosses were decent and paid me a fair wage. I was getting a break from the pressures of writing deadlines and getting healthier at the same time.

The employees at this establishment were split into two groups. There was the younger crew, which I readily joined, and the older people who took their jobs super seriously. Every morning, we would have coffee in a room with Bud Hunter, and the late Jack Bohan. Both of these guys worked their asses off at gravesites and poured cement foundations for the headstones. They wore heavy work boots and returned in the late afternoon, dotted with cement and dirt.

Jackie was just a few years older than me and possessed a great sense of humor. He was prudent about the way he carried himself and was as nice a fellow as you could find. Bud was disciplined, from the old school and was a bit gruff. This played right into Jerry's hands and he busted Bud whenever he got a chance. Bud would just puff on his cigar and shake his head about how silly the youth of the day acted.

Jerry would talk about Bud when we headed off to do our day's chores. "He's a good worker," Jerry would kid, as he gave me a wink. "He is a better man than I." That became a rallying cry of sorts for us that memorable summer. I would say to Jerry, "what am I?" and he would reply "you're a better man than I."

Sitting around the funeral home in the morning was some experience. Jackie would be sipping some coffee, Nancy, the small and foreign cleaning lady, would be tidying up and Bud would be paging through the Times-Herald Record morning newspaper. He would digest some of the stories and then give his view and opinions on world happenings. Jerry took that all in and came up with a name for the early summer mornings at Gray Funeral Home. "Bud's Bitchathon" was really good today," he would say and then laugh his ass off.

Sometimes Cappy Jaggie worked with us, whether it be repairing things inside and out or painting. He was a demure kind of guy that wasn't the joking type. And so, of course, Jerry and I used that fact to break off some jokes during the workday.

Upstairs, Don and Esther were in the main office with Jack Wilsey and Ed Furchak. Jack and Ed spent lots of time in the prep room getting people ready to be viewed. I got along fabulously with both of them. Jack, a good looking guy, got a charge out of the shenanigans Jerry, Pete and I pulled. His family owned a funeral home in Saugerties and Jack stayed in that line of work. He also became a really competent high school football referee.

Furchak, a thoughtful and laid back person, spent his lunch hour watching "The Gong Show" which featured Chuck Barris, Gene Gene The Dancing Machine and The Unknown Comic. When we returned to work, we discussed that day's show and it was a welcome relief from the day to day activities. On the show, the audience would throw vegetables and fruit at Gene Gene The Dancing Machine as he danced. Ed had that dance down pat.

One day, Nancy was looking at some lady in her casket and commenting on her hair. Jerry remembered that and the next morning he began a list of "programming" for the day. "First is "Bud's Bitchathon" and then "Hairstyles With Nancy," he said. "Then we have "Report From Renie" and "People Patrol.""

"Report From Renie" was one of my favorite activities. We'd be painting or mowing in the sun and decide to take a break. Usually, we would have a gray El Camino car with us and would simply hop in and head for downtown Port Jervis. Renie was a bartender at Bob's Grill on Front Street, near the center of town. We would find a good hiding place for the car and sneakily enter the bar.

There was a jukebox against the wall and usually a few people downing shots and beers. We would have two or three beers and ask Renie what was happening around town. After we got updated on the day's happenings, we returned to our tasks at hand. Usually we took two breaks like this during the day but every now and then we took off three times for a total of about 45 minutes. We made our own free time during the course of the day but didn't abuse our job all that much.

For "People Patrol", you had to be extremely alert and ready to quickly shout out names. We played that game mostly while riding in the car. From the second Jerry said "the game has officially begun" we would look for people, either walking or riding in cars. The first one to recognize the person shouted the name and got a point. These games were usually close as both of us knew many people from Port Jervis.

One time we were in Bob's and there was a thin white-haired guy slowly walking to his stool. He looked a lot like Cap Jaggie and so he immediately was labeled "the Cappy impostor." If we saw him on "People Patrol" one of us would blurt out "Cappy impostor" and receive a point.

Back at the funeral home I was getting used to my surroundings. That elevator that came up from the basement to the prep room was called "the Frankensteiner" and the dead bodies were known as "Snideleys." My day would begin by asking Jerry two questions. "How many Snideleys are in there?" (prep room) and "Are there any young people today?"

From time to time, Art Gray's brother, Billy, would stop by the funeral home. He is a fine golfer and could joke with the best of them. Sometimes I would see him over at Gino's Restaurant in "The Acre" section of Port Jervis. With Billy, there was never a dull moment and he was fun to be around. It is his wife, the former Judy Riker, that was one of my babysitters, way back in the mid and late 1950s. Sometimes, Billy would be around for "Bud's Bitchathon" and would join in laughing with Jerry, Pete and me.

There is no doubt that Jerry, nicknamed "C.J." by his friends, was the one that made the days pass quickly. He could take a certain amount of authority, but if he didn't agree with hard and fast orders he was given, he would simply do it his way. And, he had a knack for sinking the hook in nice and deep when he wanted to play games.

One day E.A. mentioned that the garage down on Barcelow Street needed to be painted. Jerry nodded in agreement and when specific colors weren't mentioned, he got an impish look on his face. "He (Art) didn't say what colors to use, so we will pick our own," he noted, as we drove up to see Bill Yennie, for supplies up at Sherwin-Williams.

It doesn't take a rocket scientist to figure out what was on the younger Gray's mind. He selected a light robin's egg blue and a putrid looking green and yellow mix for the two-tone job. While Art, Don and the rest of the funeral home crew may have been expecting a gray or brown shade, they instead, were going to see weird and bright colors that threatened to jump right off the structure and chase you down the street.

Equipment and a large truck were kept in the garage and we looked around for ladders, rags and other painting items. We spent many hours completing this job, although we always managed to sneak off for Renie's report, some cold beer and people patrol. If we used brushes in a difficult area, we called it "nook and cranny" painting.

The garage was a tall one and I looked way up to the peak and shuddered when I thought of teetering off a ladder way up near the top. "You start at the top and I'll handle the lower parts," I blurted out right away. Jerry is the type of guy who shows absolutely no fear when it comes to heights or any other dangerous situations. One day, Art took me aside and said "do you know what the C.J. stand for?" I shook my head left and right and the future mayor explained it to me. "I personally don't much care for what it stands for," E.A. said. "It stand for Crazy Jerry."

The painting arrangements worked out well for the first couple of days. I would return home after a long day of work, smelling of latex paint and turpentine. The hot sizzling summer sun beat down on us during the afternoons and we replenished the lost liquid at Bob's Grill a couple of times a day.

On the fourth day of garage painting, "C. J." suggested we switch positions and that I start a second coat of paint up near the peak. "You have to prove that you're a better man than I," he said with a twinkle in his eye. I looked up there and began heading up the ladder rungs. I hesitated about three quarters of the way up and looked down at him. "Hey you know what?", he said. "I think you have a case of scaredy catness." I laughed so much at this new description, that I nearly fell off the ladder.

Craftily, I quickly suggested a "coffee" break for people patrol. I dodged the bullet for that day, but not for the next one. The following morning, after coffee in the funeral home basement, we hopped in the El Camino and went back to Barcelow Street. As I turned the corner of Pennsylvania Avenue and Barcelow, Jerry had this advice. "Don't be getting any scaredy catness today. Remember, you're a better man than I."

I ascended the ladder to the heights with reckless abandon. It felt like a big weight came off my shoulders and it reminded me of the day I climbed up the thick rope in gym class and touched the gymnasium ceiling.

When summer changed to fall and the brilliant leaves began to flutter down from the trees, Jerry and I went on "leaf raking patrol" at Art's house on East Main Street. Art's wife, Helen, would pour me coffee every morning to start the day. We raked near the outdoor pool and out toward the Neversink River. I continued to work myself into shape and was getting paid at the same time. I knew that this job was temporary though and still longed to go back to a football field or basketball court, where I belonged.

While working at Gray's, I played for Gray Funeral Home in the Port Jervis City Recreation slow pitch league. I handled third base and pitching chores for a dark blue and white clad team that suffered through a 2-13 record. In one of the games, I got the 14-7 win on the mound over Horn's Lumber and that was a highlight. I continued to bat over .300 and was adept at getting on base and scoring runs.

Many of our losses were by close scores, so we were a better team than the record indicated. I seldom pitched but competed from my third base position where I wasn't afraid to play in real close to the hitter. I had learned to be fearless at the "hot corner" about 10 years earlier on Guam. My daughters were little girls in the late 70's and used to come to West End Field with Chris. She would push the kids on the swings and watch "daddy" play ball.

The toughest hitter to get out, was Dick Felter, a slender former Burke Catholic (Goshen, N.Y.) athlete. He would guard the plate, get into a crouch and dare you to hit the heart of the plate with your pitch. I worked him inside, outside, up and down, but just couldn't retire him. He walked a couple of times and reached on a fielder's choice in one game and I got tired of looking at him over there on first base. He possessed speed on the bases and was a constant threat to steal. He was a pesky, living, breathing softball pest. About four years later, I was working a parts counter with him at Austin Auto Parts.

Probably the highlight of pitching for Gray's, came when I struck out power hitters Ken Smith and Rusty Smith (brothers) back-to-back. I threw them a variety of junk and got both of them on off-speed pitches. Both of these players had glittering credentials and I silently wondered if I could get them out when they stepped in the batter's box again.

That question was answered soon enough when Ken clubbed a double off the fence and Rusty launched a rocket into the brisk night air that soared toward the outfield lights and disappeared over some car roofs. I have never seen a softball hit so hard and so far. I stood on the mound and wished I was back over at third base.

At the funeral home, the summer was gone and the feeling of football was in the air. When there wasn't a funeral or visiting hours, we washed the El Camino, plus the sleek gray limousine and hearse. When there was activity at the establishment, we learned how to blend into the woodwork by making ourselves scarce. Our saying, a password of sorts, on those days, was "family and friends."

We would go into the rooms after funerals and remove the flowers and help Nancy clean up. Jerry was always kidding with her and making her life miserable. Meanwhile, Pete kept making up morning lists of things that had to be done during the day. Usually that list was disregarded which gave him a red face and raised his blood pressure. Jerry and I were a solid 1-2 punch for Pete and at times he had a tough time putting up with our antics.

Don continued to be a good boss and Esther was a decent person and was fun to talk to. He was an Orange County coroner for years and years and displayed commitment and devotion to a thankless job. It takes a special type of person to climb out of bed and race to an accident scene while also consoling distraught families.

Jerry did a great Cap Jaggie imitation and we had countless pranks and jokes going on for most of our work shift. C.J. was a master at listening to people and then acting like he didn't comprehend what they were saying, just to piss them off. At work sites, Jerry would always be prodding me to tell some Guam and Thailand stories. I told him about the 32 mile long "rock" in the Pacific and how we were stuck over there with screaming lifers and no escape. "How did you make it through all that time?", (16 months overseas) he asked me more than once. "Athletics and drinking," I told him. "Your body can belong to them (the military) but they don't own your mind. That can be somewhere else," I said. C.J. is now an attorney with three kids, living on Guam. He is retired from the

Navy.

E.A. had been compassionate and caring in offering me this job at the Farace party. He would go on to become a respected and effective mayor of Port Jervis and was destined for bigger things. In 1989-90 he was to become the New York State Senator from New York's 39th district. Later, powerful politics had him defeated by William Larkin, who as a Republican Conservative, won his seventh term in November of 2002.

I had been away from athletics for quite a few months and felt the pang that signified a void in my life. I admitted to myself that I missed sports writing and began looking for employment in the journalism field again.

One of the newspapers I investigated, was the weekly Sullivan County Democrat, way up in Callicoon, New York, about 45 miles from my home. My friend from way back, banker John Werner, had married Kathy Stabbert, the daughter of the newspaper's editor. The paper was in a small town up Route 97, along the Delaware River. Snowmobiles, hunting and fishing were big up there in Sullivan County. I took my shot at a job and was accepted.

I drove a big old green Fury II back then, a car that friends Les Helms and Sue Helms had given me after my car punked out. Soon, my days at the funeral home were all finished. There would be no more Snideleys, Frankensteiners and people patrols. I had learned plenty of lessons about life that summer. I saw everything from high grass to prep rooms and gained a wealth of knowledge about things other than sports.

Once I had to be a substitute pall bearer at an area church. I don't like getting all dressed up to begin with, and didn't have a big wardrobe of sports coats and suits. I somehow squeezed into a sports coat, barely got the buttons to fit into the holes and arrived at St. Joseph's Church in Matamoras. Art Gray was there and gave me a thumbs up for helping him out. Later, he told C.J. I looked like an Irish bartender from the Fordham University section of New York. I had to agree that I'd feel much more comfortable pouring beers than carrying a casket

Fred Stabbert was a well known man up in Sullivan County. He is a mountain of a man, gentle in his dealings with people, yet firm in making decisions. He was involved in politics and seemed to know everybody in the world. He was to be my boss up at the Sullivan County Democrat, located in one of the prettiest areas I have ever viewed.

The ride up north was breathtaking, although I would later find out, that winters were tough in Callicoon. When it snowed up in this small town and when ice was involved, there was no way to make it to the top of that first steep hill up Route 97. One time I tried getting out of there in the snow and slid sideways into the deep ditch. I gave up the notion of making it home that night, turned around and slept in a chair at the newspaper office.

I got paid every two weeks at the Democrat and Stabbert was a fine boss. My immediate supervisor was Tom White, who had worked at the Times-Herald Record in Middletown. Tom was laid back, flexible and intelligent. He was the kind of guy you could talk to and he was out to do his duties with perfection. I tackled the job with vigor and my co-workers and readers were impressed with how dedicated I was to local sports.

The local high school basketball team, the Delaware Valley (NY) Eagles greeted me with a fine season that landed them in Section 9 post-season play. Fred's son, Freddie, was a guard on this dynamic team that played cohesive basketball and nearly always found a way to win. I traveled the Sullivan County roads all over the place to follow DV basketball and baseball. I hit locations like Jeffersonville, Grahamsville, Narrowsburg, Eldred, Livingston Manor and Roscoe. Being up there was like turning the clock back a couple of decades into the 1950s, especially in Eldred, where you expected Fonzie to come walking down the street any minute.

When I got my paycheck, I would adjourn to the bank, cash it, hit a bar in Callicoon for a couple and head home in the afternoon. On the way home, I stopped at Rohman's Bar in Shohola, Pa., a historical place that was run for many years by area legend Art Rohman. People happily flocked into Art's place for his appealing low priced beer.

There were folding stools at the bar and a view out the windows of the railroad tracks. Many famous people, including Paul Newman, came to this landmark and had experienced the large draught beers that were served here. On the jukebox was a song called "Springtime In Shohola." During basketball season, I had a few afternoons and evenings off, and so I relished free time to sit and slug down a few before going home. Sometimes I would get involved in the great atmosphere of Rohman's and forget I had a home. Christine made me remember though, and she was intelligent enough to know I was tossing some big money over the bars that I frequented.

It wasn't long before she was driving north on Route 97, headed for Rohman's, to get a large chunk of my cashed paycheck. To this day, I see that she is the one that kept things financially afloat. Without her and with my obvious lack of discipline regarding bills, it wouldn't have taken me long to fall way behind on my responsibilities.

I was soon named sports editor at the Democrat and worked with a nice girl and fine writer in Sally Keith. Sally sat at the desk right across from me and we reported and wrote the local sports with professionalism. She was nice looking, happy and a great worker. The only thing we ever disagreed on, was when I used the word "kids", in a story. She always preferred the word "youngsters." She, Tom and a few others, always congregated at coffee break time. Instead of firing down caffeine-laced java, they opened up Tupperware containers of healthy fruits and salads. I knew they had some type of clique going on at the newspaper, but really didn't figure it out for awhile.

I was an outsider to begin with. Later, I learned that they all lived in the same community and had several things in common, including being real healthy. There was a vegetarian type lifestyle going on around me and I thought of that, many days, while wolfing down a juicy cheeseburger and washing it down with beer, at a local bar.

It wasn't long before I got a bit paranoid over this situation and was not only trying to cover up the beer smell with mints (after lunch), but didn't want to get caught chowing down on that God-forbidden red meat. I wondered if my co-workers sensed the sports editor was sneaking off for the passions of wicked alcohol and dreaded meat. I pictured returning to the office after lunch all fat and sassy and being confronted by a lynch mob. "But, I never meant to hurt anyone in eating burgers," I would say in my own defense. "Guilty," this biased jury would say, "off with his head."

While I traveled around Sullivan County covering sports, I also decided to finally take advantage of the GI Bill. Because of my military service, the government would pick up the tab for any collegiate courses I would take, plus the cost of the books. The best part is, after those expenses were paid from the check, there was plenty of money left, to be spent on golden life sustaining fluid (beer).

It was a perfect thing for me, because Northamption Community College (Pennsylvania) had an annex that was coming to Matamoras and would be located just a few blocks from my house. I didn't have any clashes with sporting events and so I took advantage of this deal, although I approached the challenge with less than a fiery and positive attitude.

After being exposed to college level courses, I found that I actually applied myself and got some decent results. Unlike high school, when my focus was on romance and sports, I began tearing into the material and tried real hard.

My grades, dated Jan. 11, 1978, included a mark of B in General Psychology, plus A's in English I and Journalism. On June 5, 1978, I pulled B's in English II, World Geography and Introduction to Sociology. While the other classes were a good test, I liked Psychology the most.

The professor, Glenn VanWarrebey, was a cool kind of guy, arriving in his Corvette with sunglasses on and a coffee in his hand. His class was off the beaten track and I enjoyed teasing my mind with the material.

He had little exercises that helped you learn about yourself. I was wary about being led around the block with a blindfold on and just plain couldn't bring myself to trust another human being when it came to falling backwards and letting myself go (for someone to catch me).

VanWarrebey is a black belt in judo and karate and has broken 600 pounds of ice with his bare hand. He has tried to reach the Guinness Book of World Records and is an accomplished author. He has published books on many different subjects and already had one out on hypnosis when he was my teacher.

The thing that bothered me about taking college courses, was the fact that I didn't pursue earning credits years earlier. The GI Bill was only good for 10 years after discharge from the service. I had been separated on December 23, 1968.

While I did a good job up in Callicoon, I lived a considerable distance away. Tom White and Fred Stabbert pointed this out to me many times and the tone at work suddenly looked as if I was going to be forced to move up north to be closer to the job. To me, this idea just plain didn't cut it. I had turned down a chance to cover major league baseball because I wanted to stay put in the nice house on the corner of Avenue I and Fifth Street in Matamoras.

The wheels turned in my head and it occurred to me that if I relocated, I would be at the beckon and call of the Sullivan County Democrat. I would be too available to cover things (probably including non-sports) and wouldn't fall for the trick. My resistance to moving, didn't go over well with my supervisors and a friction began to develop.

I still remember Tom, eyeglasses hanging around his neck from a chain, as he talked about my responsibilities. "When you are off, I don't care what you do," he had said. "Go fishing, get drunk. That is your time." I liked that kind of maturity and logic on his part, but felt the pressure of riveting eyes on me, regarding relocation.

I admit that the trip did start being a big burden. It put lots of wear and tear on me and the car. I would even drive up to Callicoon on Sundays, to cover baseball games involving the adult town team. "On your way up here or while heading back home, stop at the river and take some pictures of people fishing," Tom said one day. He was always out after news and pictures and I couldn't blame him. By the same token, I didn't want to begin living this job, the way I had lived it at the Gazette.

After awhile I tired of the constant grind. One day, when I refused to listen to the prospects of moving anymore, things suddenly came to a head. I listened to Tom go on and on about how I could contribute more, if I resided within close proximity to the newspaper office. I walked into Fred's office with bitterness in my eyes. I told him I wanted out immediately and asked him to arrange for my final check, so I could head down Route 97 for good.

Tom had been unusually forceful and pushy on my last day in Callicoon and I had to figure the subject of where I lived, and how much I contributed to the job, had come up plenty of times, behind my back. For all I know, the topic was discussed the second I left the office and the tupperwear lids came off the healthy salads.

"The hell with this," I told Fred as he sat at his desk. "I'm packing up my belongings and getting out of here."

Fred tried to calm me down, as Tom had finally gone too far. He gave me advice not to act too hastily and to think over my decision. "You can't burn your bridges behind you," he said. Twenty minutes later, I cleaned out my desk in a whirlwind, set the bridge on fire and exited the front door.

The Gazette and Democrat had one thing in common. Instead of going with the flow and enjoying the rewards of a top notch sports section, they chose to take that fact for granted. Nobody in the world is indispensable, but in these cases, the sports pages took nosedives and never looked the same again. These publications had used a "what have you done for me lately?" kind of approach. In the end, both had cut off their noses to spite their faces.

At the Gazette, sportswriters like Ernie Arico, Monty Tyner, and Lisa Miller were compared to me many times. They probably got sick of hearing my name after awhile. I worked (part time) with Lisa, a real nice lady, and also Skip Leon, who brought the color and enthusiasm back to the Gazette readers. Without a trace of conceit, I regard Skippy, Ralph Fredericks, Mike Kowal, former Times-Herald Record writer Lou Hansen, and myself, as the finest five sportswriters to ever come out of this area, during my lifetime.

The highlight of working up in Callicoon, was meeting and writing about former New York Knicks player Willis Reed. He was one of those dazzling Knicks stars that I had traveled to Rudy's Bar to watch play on television, way back in the 1969-70 season.

Big Willis used to go turkey hunting in the Callicoon area and had many friends, far away from the roar of Madison Square Garden, where he was the current Knicks coach. He had a calm demeanor and was a gentleman, when Sally and I interviewed and took pictures of him one afternoon.

Willis had already entered a turkey (shot in Pennsylvania) in the Democrat's Annual Spring Turkey Shoot. At the time he came in for an interview, he was trying to bag a New York bird to enter.

Reed admitted that playing on title teams in high school, college and the pros had all been big thrills in his lifetime. The 6-10" Reed had just completed his rookie season as head Knicks coach. His team had made the playoffs but was eliminated by the Philadelphia 76ers. On this Monday afternoon in late May 1978, he and friend Henry Austin sat in Fred's office and were very relaxed with us.

He was decked out in a jeans outfit and displayed a contagious smile while he sipped coffee. He had recently nailed a 14 pound 3 ½ ounce turkey, but was now ready to talk basketball. "They (the press) were indifferent much of the time (to Willis as coach)," he explained. "They have pre-conceived notions about me coaching and wondered why I didn't serve an apprenticeship under Red Holzman (Willis' coach)."

The physical education major out of Grambling college in Louisiana, said he thought nothing of hopping in the car at 3 a.m. in New York and heading up to Callicoon. "Lots of times I'll head up here for the day and drive back at night," he asserted. "I've always been an outdoor person. It's a way of life." Reed first hit the Sullivan County area in the fall of 1966. He liked what he saw and continued coming back.

The father of Karl (then 14) and Veronica Marie (13), told me about what it felt like to be hobbled and still make an appearance in game 7 at Madison Square Garden (1970) during that run to the NBA title against the Lakers.

"It wasn't the best game I ever played, but it was the most important," he said. "I could hardly walk and it was a heck of a position to be in. I'd always wanted to be in a championship series, but not this way. When the fans saw me, they figured 'hey, everything's alright, Willis is back', but they just didn't realize what it was like to play on one leg. There was a lot of pressure involved and the fans went wild. We won the championship at Madison Square Garden on my daughter's fifth birthday."

When he first entered the office doorway at the Democrat, Willis had ducked down and walked to a chair. "Look at this," he said, while feeling his chin. "I even shaved for you," he kidded. He talked about hunting dogs his dad had owned, basketball, turkeys and the outdoors. The glitz and glamour of a big city like New York, hadn't affected this laid back man. Instead of just answering our questions, he reversed roles, by asking about things Sally and I enjoyed doing in life. It was evident early on, that this interview with Willis Reed, was going to be a pleasant conversation and that the story and column I did, would write themselves.

Willis came from a town of 1,600 people and identified with Callicoon. "I do some bass fishing when I go home," he had said. "Here, I like it during the hunting seasons and the bow season. That's a real sport, a real art (bow and arrow). Wind conditions and everything else are important."

The calm man who was used to sitting on and walking near a team bench in a venue filled with close to 20,000 people (Madison Square Garden), noted that he could survive all alone in the woods, far away from the Big Apple. "I'm a better person for having been an outdoorsman," he said.

"Those people who aren't for the killing of deer just don't understand," Reed explained. "I wish they could walk in the woods with me and see the deer that have starved. But the way I feel about it, is that everyone has a right to his own opinion."

Sally had her picture taken with Willis and your truly, all 5-7" of him, stood next to Willis for an outdoor snapshot. That's when I tried to sneak up on the first step to look taller and Willis caught me. "Hey, I see you doing that," he laughed. "Don't be trying to make yourself taller."

When it came to being tall, nobody stood any taller than Willis Reed.

And I'm not talking about his height, I'm talking about him as a person. You will never find an individual with more class than Reed.

The day I walked away from the Democrat, I stuffed my check in my pocket, hopped in my car and took off for the bank. Soon, I was heading south on Route 97, bound for Rohman's. Chris had known I had grown discouraged with the job and hated tackling the trip north. I hadn't told her I was quitting, but she had a pretty good idea the end was near.

I wheeled into Rohman's parking area and headed for the door. A couple of hours later, calm and happy, I finally took off in the direction of home. There were a couple of more pit stops en route to Avenue I. I finally reached home in the dark, tired from the draining day that had transpired. There would be no more long drives and pressuring about relocation. There would also be less bread on the table (E.A. had taught me well), unless I nailed a job somewhere. I wanted something closer to home and wanted to tackle a non-sports job where I could punch a clock everyday and have plenty of free time.

In 1979, I went on to do some other things, in addition to writing sports. After taking college courses, I worked with Calvin DeMond at PJTV (television), on Route 6, in Port Jervis. This was a tiny station, but it was fascinating learning this branch of the communication field.

Calvin was great with a camera and was intelligent in his approach to packaging a TV program. We had already done some top-notch softball work together. I had done play-by-play coverage of local softball games at West End Beach. However, one of my most satisfying projects was putting together a special on the Banach brothers. They were going to be coming home from college, and so we entitled the show "Good To Be Back Home."

We rode the interstate and had his camera trained on the picturesque valley below, that Port Jervis is located in. The two of us drove down Route 84 west, from up in a nearby mountain, 1,272 feet in elevation. We photographed some of the places the Banachs used to frequent, including Port High School and their home on Ball Street. As the pictures showed on the screen, John Denver's song "Back Home Again" played in the background.

The one hour documentary aired at 7 p.m. Saturday, June 2, 1979. I was the producer-host and Calvin was the executive producer. All went well with this project, except when the show came on, the picture kept jumping up on the screen (at certain times). It was enough to make me rip my hair out, but I had to roll with the punches.

When longtime radio sportscaster (and Port teacher) Ralph Zelno saw what I did to prepare a football broadcast (Port games), he was amazed. I had cue cards for the pre-game shows and interviewed players. "You worked very hard," Zelno told me once. "It really showed." Later, I got to cover Port High School basketball games with Ralph. We each handled radio play by play (WDLC) for half a game and it was lots of fun covering a basketball event from that vantage point.

When I left the Democrat, I looked for full time work and it didn't take long to get discouraged. I was used to having money in my wallet and suddenly there was very little. I finally went to the unemployment office in Port Jervis and got lucky.

"You ever work a parts counter?", the late John McGoey asked me. "Well I was dealing with people in personnel, while in the Air Force," I replied. "It can't be that much different."

Boy was I wrong.

At a car dealership, the parts guy secures parts for the general public plus supplies mechanics in the shop with parts to do their jobs. I was about to learn many valuable lessons regarding being employed in a family business. The main thing was that getting salary increases to boost your morale and being recognized for doing a decent job, just weren't in the cards. I would become a necessary evil in the conveyor belt of parts distribution. While the college course in Psychology gave me lots of information, it was the real life situation of this type of job, that taught me about people.

I dealt with all types of individuals and was usually flexible enough to weather whatever storms were on the horizon. At Case Motors, a Chrysler dealership, I worked with an older guy named Floyd VanAken. Floyd was a friend of the owner, Doug Case, and was real easy to get along with.

Floyd wasn't around on my first working day and I was immediately thrown to the wolves. The first phone call I ever took at this job, was one I will never forget. On the other end of the wire was a fellow who sounded southern to me. He was trying to get a message across to me regarding his job and I tried to interpret what he said, a word at a time. "Tell Coby, I got a few things I gotta do today and I will be in tomorrow," I managed to write down.

Corby Case was Doug's son and with his dad, ran this dealership. I had played basketball against him in high school and for the most part, I would get along with him in the time I was employed here. I went to his office and told of the call. "Oh that's just Willie," he said. "He must be drunk and can't make it in."

I learned through mechanic Doug Gore, that Willie was a black man who got the new and used cars ready to go out to new customers. "Wait until you meet him," Gore said. "There is nobody like Willie."

Little did I know, that black Willie would someday become one of my greatest friends in the world. He kept the morale bearable at Case's, was a practical joker, worked on cars until they shined and was known to sneak around the corner for a beer or two during working hours.

At the time, Gore, who was the guy who taught me darkroom work at the Gazette, was into Harley motorcycles. He was a member of the "Asphalt Brotherhood" and could party with the best of them. He was an accomplished and thorough mechanic who wanted jobs done exactly right.

One time he showed up to work all cut to ribbons. He had bloody scrapes all over his chest, side, back and palms. He explained that hours earlier, he had slid on loose gravel at a club function and skinned himself to pieces. "Somebody poured booze on it and I had a drink or two to calm down," he said. Then he walked to a car near his tall red tool chest, hopped inside and caught some sleep until it was time to punch in.

Doug Case was from the old school. He regarded most college graduates as educated idiots and had no use for them. I explained that I was a sports writer who had some college credits, but never got a degree. He ignored that statement, spit bits of his cigar on the cement parts room floor and told me "when you're resting, sweep the floor." This was the type relationship I would have with this man. He was an expert hunter who often took off on trips, including to Montana, where he went after Elk.

One of the mechanics, Bob Heimbrook, was also an avid hunter. He and Doug often talked about their exploits and had an unspoken bond. Being an ex-athlete and writer, I had little in common with Doug Case. For the most part, I tried to avoid him and do my job to the best of my ability.

Gore had dark, bushy hair and a black moustache. He had big arms, was a no-nonsense type and was an expert at photography, model airplanes and motorcycles. Heimbrook was a solidly built man with a blonde beard. The third mechanic was Harold Stearns, a slender man with glasses, who methodically worked on whatever car or truck was assigned to him.

The service manager was Joe Schreiner, a transplanted Seaford, Long Island guy, that still possessed traces of a New York accent and attitude. While Willie got the cars ready to roll, Harold Simpson, in his sports coat, hat and slow moving sales pitch, was selling vehicles. He would pursue prospective buyers to the end of the earth, like a bounty hunter, and his objective was getting you to sign on the dotted line, at any cost. Willie knew how to get under Harold's skin and pulled practical jokes on him, much of the time.

Corby's wife, Dolores, and Doug's wife, Sue, worked in the office, keeping the books up to snuff. Meanwhile, once Willie knew me, he would begin giving most of the employees pet names, that he threw around regularly.

My second day at the parts counter, I had met William Burton. "Willie" was a short and muscular man who always wore a hat. He had short hair, was graying at the temples and had one eye that seemed to be looking away a bit. He was very hard to understand at first, but as time went on, I got in tune to his speech and his zest for life.

When Willie wasn't fishing, he would frequent a few of the city's bars, making small talk and enjoying the company of fellow patrons. He was a down to earth man who had a million stories to share. I learned a lot about life from this simple, yet lovable man with the joking demeanor.

It was Willie who first bounced the word "gizmo" off of me. This was his name for beer, whether it be in a can or bottle. If someone at work dragged in under the weather, it was Willie who would say "he had too many gizmos."

There was never a dull moment with this fellow. When he worked he worked, but when he was suddenly absent from being in or around a car, you could bet there was some caper going on. One of his favorite things was slipping around the corner, to the "House of Characters" bar on Pike Street, during the morning coffee break.

"Bud, if anyone comes looking for me, tell them I went to the telephone company to pay a bill," he would say. The telephone company was located nearby, and Willie used that place as an excuse continually.

One day, I tracked him to the bar. Soon, there were two of us going to pay telephone bills.

While I was putting bread on the table again, I still competed in sports. During the winter, I played in the Port Jervis Adult Recreation Basketball League (for Schields Brothers Tire). Two of my teammates were Dick Felter, who I would share a parts counter with down the road, and Tom Redmond, a former Orange County League player of the year (football) for Minisink Valley High School. Redmond is beyond a doubt, the most competitive athlete I have ever covered in any capacity. He had the heart of a lion and the drive of Pete Rose.

At the beginning of one season, we won seven of our first nine games, with the seventh coming over Karsten's, 101-70. We were a tough team that was spearheaded by the scoring of big Walt Lederhaas, who had been a star at Port, back when I played ball.

One game, the tall and ruggedly built Redmond became so upset on the court, he was given two technical fouls by the referee, and tossed from the game. He went into our locker room and started punching out lockers. You could hear the echo of the gray lockers being smacked all the way from the gymnasium. Nobody could stop this violent rampage except for Felter, who calmly talked to him and got him under control.

I covered Tom, affectionately known as "Red Bone" when he caught for P.J. Electric in the Port and Matamoras softball leagues. He was an intense player who could connect for doubles and triples with regularity and spark a team to victory from his catcher's position.

One time when he was playing for a team (not P.J. Electric), he was fuming behind the plate. The pitcher couldn't find the plate at all and began walking batters. Suddenly Redmond had seen enough and asked the umpire for time out. He then rolled the ball back out to the pitcher and said "now throw the damned ball will you?"

Another time an opposing player was getting on him from first base, where he had just reached. The concession stand at Matamoras' Airport Park is located right behind home plate. As the player flapped his gums at Tommy, he called time out. He turned around to the ladies working the concession stand and asked for some paper plates and plastic spoons and forks. "I'm going to need these to scrape him off the God damned ground," he said as he glared down to first base. "They knew how to start needling Tom," Felter said. "But when it came time to back up their big words, they looked like little pipkins, trying to back down and get away from him." Dick and Tom have played plenty of softball, basketball and racquetball together, and are fast friends.

"Tom Redmond plays any game to win," says Felter. "You should see him when we play racquetball. He gets this intimidating look in his eyes. Tom loves competition and doesn't care much for losing. He looks like Rowdy Yates out there on a softball field, basketball court or in racquetball. (Clint Eastwood character). Nobody tries harder, or can lead a team better, than Tommy Redmond," Felter adds.

Since I first saw Redmond on a basketball court or bracing himself for a collision at home plate, I figured him to be a cross between Eastwood and Pete Rose. He was cool under pressure and yet his fiery make up, led to many victories.

Currently, Red Bone coaches a Little League baseball team up near Kingston, New York. He is married to the former Carol Hissam and has four sons who are learning from the best. What few people realize, is under that rugged exterior, beats a heart of gold. I still envision him with that mouth full of chewing tobacco, slowly walking out to the mound to settle a pitcher down. Once, some players on a basketball team we were playing, dared any of us to drive down the lane. "Give me the God damned ball," Redmond said. And with that, he drove the lane like an out-of-control railroad train. "He's crazy," one of our foes said. "Get out of his way."

The days at Case's seemed to be long ones, especially on Monday nights when we went home for supper and then had to come back to work for three more hours. People who couldn't make appointments in the daytime, were fit in at night. Some always seemed to grin at us, knowing they were tampering with what could be free time for us.

I learned from Floyd, and then when he retired, I had the parts counter all to myself. There were very little parts sales over the counter, but the three mechanics kept me busy. If I got in a bind, any of the three would pitch in and help me out.

Willie kept me loose and in stitches. He would sneak through the back of the garage and peer in the rear parts room door window. "What's up Bud?," he would say. "You look like you ate too much bull moose puddin." Many times he would tell me real stories of the deep South and about the perils of growing up with discrimination all around him. He loved the music of Elvis Presley and from time to time, I would loan him music by "The King."

Willie took his gizmos very seriously and if I was a little hung over he could spot it in an instant. "You look rough today," he would say. "Do you want a gizmo?" I asked how that would be possible, and he pointed to the bathroom. "Just lift up the back of that toilet and there's a present for you in there," he would say. I would turn on the sink water, pop the top off a beer can and slug down the suds in two or three gulps. The hair of the dog, squared me away on more than one occasion.

This gentle comedian used to look for the right time, slink around behind cars and deposit pictures of funny faces or animals in the mechanics' tool boxes. When they would find these "gifts" they would either ignore them, or say "Willie, you put this here?" He would look crestfallen and lie through his teeth. "Bud, I have never seen that before in my life," he'd smile. "What you got there?"

Willie called Doug Case "Pow Wow", his wife "Sweetie Pie", Corby "Baby Boy", Doug Gore "Moustache", Bob Heimbrook "Whiskers" and Harold Stearns "Warsaw." I never did find out if he ever had a name for me.

Gore was a piece of work. Determined to get jobs done correctly, he was sometimes hell bent on getting parts quickly. Once I went to a parts store for a tailpipe (none were in stock for the truck he was working on) and took it to his lift. He brought it back and said "Go back there, this is wrong, it's for a different wheel base." I returned to the store and they said the part was indeed correct. I called Gore on the phone to try figuring out what was wrong. "What is this off of, Doug?", I asked. "A truck...a big fucking truck," was his reply. Sometimes he would walk into the parts room with a saying on his lips. "Changes in attitudes, changes in latitudes," he said one day, looked me in the eye and returned to his area.

This is the same guy that photographed droplets on a flower and horrible automobile wrecks. He was up front about everything and took no guff from anyone. "Don't tread on me" was one of his favorite statements.

I will always recall the night of "the mud, the blood and the beer." That was the evening we left the Captain's Quarters in a disagreement and proceeded to fight out on the railroad tracks and returned to our beers disheveled and bleeding. If we didn't have respect for each other before that, we did after.

I saw Doug Gore up at Poli's Garage (his job) in Monticello, December 7, 2001. He had turned 61 years old the day before, and had just over a year to go until retirement. I finally located him outside the garage and he seemed very surprised to see me. "Hey snake, I thought that was you over there," he said. It was commonplace for he and I to go four or five years without coming across each other, then get an impulse and seek the other guy out.

Doug's moustache and curly hair were gone. His hair was shorter and be was missing a couple of lower teeth because a tool had slipped and slammed him in the mouth. After we went to a nearby pizza joint, I told him about this book and said I'd be back shortly before his retirement, the following December.

Chris and I went up there again a year later. We went out to the Woodstock Festival sight in a drizzle and snapped some pictures. Then we headed just a few miles away to look in on Gore. The man that used to be voracious when it came to Harley bikes, showed little excitement about this chapter of his life coming to a close. He was taking everything in stride and would be moving on to what I knew would be a very action filled retirement. This is not the type individual who plops in a rocking chair and watches the world go by.

Back at Case's, we had been through thick and thin together. When the Colonial Inn Hotel was still open, we would meander over across the street after work on a Friday, and quaff a few in the cocktail lounge. They had some good songs playing in there and a pool table sat in the corner. The time flew by in there and only good memories stick in my mind.

At the dealership, I had been equal to the task at hand. I became more seasoned and knew the job pretty well. There were bad and good times inside the walls of 20 West Main Street. My daughters were little kids then and I managed to spend as much time with them as possible. Tracie had learned to read when I was on the road covering basketball and I wanted to make up for lost time.

It was my job to check in new cars when they rolled down the ramps of a car carrier. I had to write up any damages or flaws to the vehicle, before the driver could go on his way. Sometimes there was a barely visible scratch or two that I knew Willie could get out with some compound and elbow grease. Sometimes I would let the drivers skate on these minor damages and they would reciprocate later. Although I had responsibilities at work, my pay check stayed the same. I began growing restless, had no goals and began thinking about getting the hell out of this dealership life.

Many of the times, Chris and the kids would be outside in the car at noon, when I was to have lunch and be able to see them. A car carrier would come around the corner and I would be stuck checking in cars while they either waited or went back home. This started to happen more and more. It got on my nerves and I let my feelings be known. Still, these frustrating situations went on. My complaining fell on deaf ears. It was very obvious that I was trapped in a place where the unwritten motto was "what have you done for me lately?"

I got along with most of my co-workers and was amazed at the diverse human beings who shuffled in and out of this place of business.

Willie would walk directly behind Simpson, imitating his slow gait. He could also mimic his halting style of talking, perfectly. Harold would get agitated with Willie's shenanigans, stare off into space and say "So, how you been? Nice day out there." Willie would not bat and eye as he went into his answer. "It's a…well ummmm….a nice…a day."

One time Willie had deposited a picture of some cats in one of the tool boxes and a doll in another. Harold Stearns confronted him with the doll and shook it in front of his eyes. "That's a mighty nice doll you got there, Warsaw. Where did you get it?", he asked.

On another occasion, Willie sneaked around from the back of the garage carrying a large rock. "That damn Simpson's gonna have something to ride with him today," he laughed. He went out to the salesman's car and craftily placed the rock on the passenger seat.

Soon, a woman representative from Chrysler happened by, and went into Corbin Case's office. It was just before noon and Simpson sat out in the showroom while Willie peered through some door glass at him. Corby and the rep came out of the office and it became apparent that she was going to go to lunch or something, with Simpson.

The two walked out to the car and I laughed until I cried. Simpson returned directly and began bitching Willie out. "Now…ah…that lady is ah in the car and there was a rock in her seat," he said. "You should be ashamed of yourself, Willie." My buddy stared down at the floor and then looked up at Simpson and the rock. "That's a fine looking rock you have there bud," he blurted out. "Where did it come from?" All Simpson could do was shuffle back outside and toss the heavy rock on the ground in disgust.

Before I knew it, Willie came around from the back of the garage and was peeking in the parts room. "Whatcha got goin for you bud?", he queried. "Looks like you could use a gizmo." And with that, he exited the garage bound for "the telephone company."

There was a lady who did some odd jobs at the dealership and her name was Florence. She was a masculine appearing person who wore a long dress and heavy looking shoes. One day Willie happened by and was looking for her. Sometimes they went fishing together on the banks of the Neversink River and apparently he was planning on a fishing experience that night. "Hey, you seen big foot around?", he asked. All I could do was grin and watch Willie put on another performance.

I tipped many a gizmo with Willie. We were really tight and he is the main reason I made it through the day at Case Motors. The word "gizmo" went with me to Austin Auto Parts when I left Case's, on to Milford Motors and everywhere I showed up. I still use that word to this day, to describe beer.

I always remember Chris DeVries popping in the side door of the parts room, beer in hand. The slender parts man from Milford Motors was a happy-go-lucky guy who was happy to be working in Milford.

"My bosses are great to work for," he told me more than once. "Someday you have to work there. You would be a good fit." I heard those words many times and years later wound up at that location. Chris was a good guy who was a loyal employee. When I had a part in stock that he needed, or the other way around, we did business.

If Doug Case's friend, business owner Phil Wells dropped by, they would toss barbs back and forth. "If I had your money, I'd burn mine," Case would tell him. Meanwhile, Simpson kept chasing prospective customers, badgering them until they finally gave in and bought a car. "There's an ass for every seat," he used to say.

Around Christmas time, we would have a little party at Case's. Corby would stock his vehicle with cases of beer and bring them to the dealership. Soon we were all standing around the showroom, loosening up with cans of Miller in our hands.

"These are good gizmos," Willie would say, and then go and get another. "Look at Pow Wow over there," he's getting ready to do the gooch." Willie called dancing "doing the gooch" and got great delight in talking about his boss that way. "Hey Lobo," he said to me. "You going to a bar when you leave?" When I nodded affirmatively, he said "don't forget me."

Former Mayor Sidney Sakofsky was a customer at Case's and he would stop by the parts room and tell some really inspiring stories of how he grew up poor and worked hard for everything he got. Sid owned half the town of Port Jervis and was always smoking or carrying a big cigar with him.

One day I was talking with him while Willie super-glued a quarter to the cement floor outside the parts room door. When Sid left, he saw the quarter, got down on his haunches and learned the shiny coin was glued down. He worked on that quarter for a good 10 minutes before finally giving up and walking away.

Sometimes I would have to hop in the jeep and take a ride down to Austin Auto Parts on Orchard Street. Charlie Roeder, the red-haired owner, and his workers, seemed really loose and constantly fired out jokes to customers. It was easy to detect that the morale in this place was through the ceiling. Although being the owner, Charlie rolled up his sleeves and worked right alongside his employees.

He, Mike Radzikowski and Dick Felter got to know me pretty well and one day, Charlie tossed this one out to me across the counter. "How would you like to work here?" At first I thought he was kidding, but he looked serious. "Drop by and we will talk about it," he said.

Visions of walking away from Case's filled my head and I knew instantly that this was my ticket out. Charlie paid a real fair wage, but you had to work every other Saturday. I felt like there was no real choice to be made here and loved the idea of suddenly holding all the cards at Case's.

"Well, good for you, bud. Pull up your britches and go to where you will be happy," Willie said when I told him. I informed Corby, gave him a one week notice and thought of the future. Corby wasn't pleased with me. He wanted two weeks and stated that his father was in Montana and wouldn't be back by the time I left. I looked at the cement floor where Corby's dad spit his tobacco and stuck to my guns. A week later, I punched my time card for the final time and nearly floated to my car. I would miss Willie's antics but little else about the job. I was leaving a dealership behind in favor of a busy parts store. I still regard that change of employment as a good move on my part.

I have always liked comedy.

Since my younger days of laughing at Red Skelton and "The Honeymooners" and on to Richard Pryor, Eddie Murphy and George Carlin, I get a charge out of laughing. It's not that I walk around giggling 24 hours a day, but that I feel many people take life too damn seriously. Lighten up folks, it's later than you think. Life is for the living and call it selfish if you like, but I am in the process of living it to the fullest.

The customers at Austin Auto Parts weren't just getting their parts at decent prices, they were getting a free comedy show nearly every time they walked to the gray counter.

I went from a job where the look on people's faces reflected strain, to a happy environment where professional parts people completed transactions in a carefree way. I instantly felt a part of this team and was accepted the second I walked through the door.

There were six of us working at Austin's, Charlie, Mike, Dick, Vinny DiNapoli, Russ Skinner and myself. Mike and Dick didn't get along all that great although the rest of us did. Russ was an old school kind of guy, short and bespectacled. He was a warm-hearted sort who mixed paints most of the time. He moved very quickly once he got started and that alone was worth the price of admission. It's a wonder this nice person had time to put lids on the paint cans. All of us admired and respected the late Russ Skinner.

Vinny was a good looking wiry and dark-haired high school kid who worked part time. He was on the counter Saturdays, when the place was a bee hive of activity. Vinny ran around the place squinting a lot, because he needed glasses. This was one of the jokes in the place...watching Vinny try to read the printing in parts books. He said little, took in lots and could bust cookies with the best of them.

We used to get a charge out of his dad phoning the store on Saturday mornings. His dad, Mickey, was a hairdresser and big time New York Yankees baseball fan. When he phoned it meant that "Vincent" as he called him, wouldn't be in. "Vincent had too much fun last night, he won't be in," the elder DiNapoli would say.

Charlie was a former musician who has a great sense of humor. He can get moody, just like anyone, but for the most part, the atmosphere was very light in his store. He used to work for owner Gene Austin and then one day, bought the business and became a boss. He was one of the guys, but I imagine the pressure of operating a successful business got to him. He complimented good work and bought gizmos for us at the end of the work day.

Mike Vicchiariello and John Curry would stop by around quitting time and it was usually me that walked up the hill to the store, for some bottles of Michelob light. Mike, who was a cookie-buster, sipped his gin, which he called "witch hazel" and all was right with the world.

Dick took his job seriously. He gave 110 per cent to Austin's and was a perfectionist when it came to giving out the right part and keeping accurate inventory records. He wasn't a big fan of shoddy work or shoddy people. When loud, unruly or silly customers came to the counter, he would go over, sit down and plug his ears with his fingers as they rattled on and on. Refusing to wait on them until they acted civil, he usually got results.

At the counter, Dick and I usually hung out together while Mike and Charlie were tight. Those three people taught me valuable things concerning the parts game. This was a whole different game than it was in a dealership and I was happy to play it.

The customers are what kept us loose and made the days fly by.

"Slim" ran a garage and had a southern drawl. Felter used to chuckle when he came in, because he used to say "know what I mean", "know what I mean" just like the cartoon character "Foghorn Leghorn." Dick cracked up when he saw Slim come through the door. "Chicken hawk...I said chicken hawk," he used to say, as I tried not to laugh my ass off.

Another customer had the last name Martino. When he came around, Dick would start singing Al Martino's "Spanish Eyes."

Saturdays were a lesson in Psychology that no textbook or professor could possibly teach. Most of your Saturday morning mechanics didn't have a clue what the hell they wanted to begin with. It's a miracle that they knew how to tie their shoes, let alone have the correct information to obtain a part.

Usual gems we heard tossed across the counter were things like "it's an eight-banger" (eight cylinder engine), "it's off an old pick-em up truck" or "how come you need to know the engine? The part should fit them all. They are all the same." If we didn't have what they were after, they simply wouldn't take "no" for an answer. These creatures would refuse to leave the store, probably hoping that some miracle shipment would suddenly arrive.

This exercise in futility was so ridiculous you just had to laugh. Some customers trucked into the store with a greasy, oily rag that contained some unknown part. "Guess your best", Dick used to say, when he saw this transpire. The would-be mechanic would slam the part down on the counter, open the rag and say "you got one of these?"

One Saturday, Dick showed me how to cope with this type of hair-brained thinking. In came a babbling fool, with the infamous sludge part in rag. "Got one of these?", he asked, obviously enjoying his role as keeper of the parts. Dick reached under the counter and pulled up an old, greasy starter wrapped in a rag. "Have one right here," he said, and plunked it down next to the other part.

On another occasion, another Albert Einstein was hassling me about a wrong part he had received earlier that morning. He had supplied the wrong information ("they are all the same") but blamed the mistake on me. I gave Felter a wink and told the guy I would go in the back and get him the correct part. I walked back where our parts stock sat on shelves and hung a left out the side door. As I drove to lunch, I thought of the jerk standing at the counter waiting for his part. I think the part may have been off an eight-banger or was it a slant six?

There were some good customers for sure, but we had our share of arrogant and obnoxious types also. We insulted them right to their faces and they still didn't get it. "Oh no, not this guy," Felter would say when seeing a familiar face coming across the street. As the fellow went on and on, Dick would retreat to that chair, plug his ears and either say "play it again Sam" or simply whistle a tune.

"Here comes another engine head", he would say to alert me. We made a good team, were efficient and helped bring money into Austin's. The two of us, plus Charlie and Mike, kept folks happy and satisfied for the most part. The fact that some of the "mechanics" had IQ's rivaling a grapefruit, made the time pass quickly.

I knew I would never become opulent at this job, but going to work wasn't drudgery. Charlie was fair for the most part, and I enjoyed my time at Austin Auto Parts.

I was in the midst of selling a part one afternoon when Dick ambled up to me and indicated he wanted to talk after the sale was completed. "Did you hear about your friend from Case Motors?", he asked cautiously. When I said I hadn't, he had to be the bearer of bad news. Harold Stearns was Dick's father-in-law and had given some very disturbing news to Dick.

William "Willie" Burton had drowned while fishing on the Neversink River. Apparently he had slipped on some rocks, fell in the water and went under the surface. Roughly a decade apart, I had lost two close friends, who were non-swimmers, went fishing and drowned. One was a 27-year-old white guy that I served in the Air Force with and the other was a wise and simple old black man who kept me smiling all the time. They were both named "Willie" and I miss both of them to this day.

Saturday afternoons were usually boring at Austin's because the customers dwindled after high noon came. Charlie, Mike and I devised ways to pass the time until the afternoon was over.

Sometimes we played indoor golf with a wiffle ball. We would tee the ball up on a green mat and hit toward the back of the stocked parts area. If you hit the mat instead of the ball, it was called a "rugby." There were many laughs during this indoor sport. Once a guy came in and asked for Charlie. "He is back there on the fourth hole," I said.

Another time it had poured rain overnight and there was a huge pond in the field across the street. When I went home for lunch, I had a brilliant idea and returned to work with some plastic duck toys that my kids had lying around the house. I placed the "ducks" in the pond and watched people drive by and slow down to look at them.

One winter, Red O'Hanlon, owner of a garage up in West End, came to the store and we all engaged in a late afternoon snowball fight. I still remember the jovial, overweight Red running down the street chasing Mike Raz. Mike had ambushed Red, nailed him with a snowball when he had arrived at the store. Red was determined to even up the score, slipped and fell on his ass. These were the funny times, the memories that stick in the mind.

We used to call Red "Arafat" and "Fatty Arbuckle." Sadly enough, Red and Mike are no longer with us. They died as young men in their 20's, way too soon.

Mike, Charlie and myself used to play golf about once a week at nine-hole Eddy Farm Golf Course up in Sparrowbush. "Lets fire up some green meanies," (drinks) Charlie used to say at the store, before we drove to the course. Mike had his witch hazel, I had my gizmo and life couldn't have been rosier.

We had a bar on wheels out on the course. I packed some cans of beer in my golf bag and Mike had the gin in a container. We noticed our golf games started coming apart as the round progressed. Charlie and I would stand behind Mike when he hit a fairway shot and broke up laughing if he sliced the ball or took a huge divot as the ball rolled a few feet. "Man he took a rug on that one," Charlie would say seriously, after Raz had screwed up. Charlie was worth the price of admission. If he hit an awful shot, he would stand back and say "yup, that was a beauty."

Back at the store, the days went pretty quickly. My kids were growing up some and making friends. Dick Felter continued to make me smile. One morning a pack of people exited their cars at the same time, bound for the front door. He began singing Judy Collins' "Send In The Clowns" (they're already here). If Slim was there, he would have said "that's a joke son, that's a joke."

My days at Austin's ended because of a problem between Charlie and I, that revolved around time off. Dawn was going to be 10 years old on January 11, 1984 and it was a Saturday party that was planned for Carmine's Restaurant out on Route 6 in Greenville.

Dick had agreed to switch Saturdays with me so that I could have off and help at the party. A few of Dawn's friends were invited and I thought it could be a once in a lifetime thing, to see her reach double digits in this type of setting. All I had to do, was clear the switch with the boss. Usually, Charlie was really fair about things like this and there would have been no problem. This time it was different.

I tried to explain the situation to him, but he flatly refused to yield and said I would absolutely be at the store on January 11th, not at a party. He was wrong.

I seethed for a half hour, ignored him and finally came out from behind the counter. I grabbed my coat, walked across the front of the store and nearly neglected to say hello, goodbye or go to hell. I thought better of that though and simply said "I quit", as I walked toward the door. I figured once cooler heads prevailed, I would probably wind up back on the job. This just plain didn't happen. If faced with the same situation again, I wouldn't change one thing. I had the courage of my convictions and even though it cost me a job, I refused to be a damned robot.

One door closes and another opens. I was destined to wind up at Milford Motors and that happened just after Labor Day in September of 1984. Chris DeVries offered me a job and I accepted. I was back to punching a time clock again and working in a Chrysler dealership. The bosses, partners Bill Strong and Bruce Earlin, were great to work for.

I got along with mechanics Don Antcliff and Mike Pranga and worked with a seasoned veteran named Bill Brundage, in parts. It was a bit confusing, with two Bills in parts and we made light of it. Brundage was a quiet kind of guy who had owned a garage in the past. He got a charge out of the younger workers and many times, walked away just shaking his head. He called me "Willie" and I thought it ironic, because of Lehman and Burton.

I worked with a kid named Eddie Murphy (no kidding) and he was wild as they come. We had a get ready (for sold cars) guy, who was an absolute riot. One time he came to work with dirt all over hands and arms. "Man you got to wash up some," he was told. "No," he said. "I will only get them dirty again, so what's the use?"

Chris was easy to work with and sometimes the bunch of us stopped at the Penn Grill in Matamoras or the Milford Inn, on Fridays, after the week had ended. We had a service manager named Bill Hofeldt, who conducted his area like a drill instructor. It didn't take long for me to label him "Sarg."

Shirley Strong (Bill's wife) was the head honcho in the office and made out the paychecks. She could be a real disciplinarian, but under it all, she had a caring heart. "What's up Willum?", Bill Strong would say to me as he walked through the parts room. Bill was an easy-going friendly type of guy while Bruce was the charismatic extrovert. They gave us a top notch dinner and sizable bonuses at Christmas time and it was easy to be motivated under these people. A couple of times I played golf with Bill, in New Jersey.

Bruce had an infectious sense of humor and made you feel like you were part of a team effort. He knew how to use the media to advantage, made some excellent radio commercials and was well-known in and out of the area. He was into antique cars and has owned many in his time. Fair and easy to talk to, Bruce Earlin was a pleasure to work for.

When Frank Heater came aboard as a salesman, the happy family grew larger. The morale was through the roof in 1984, 1985 and 1986. I actually looked forward to arriving at work in the morning and earning a decent paycheck.

We were a bunch of comedians at coffee break time and often listened to Howard Stern on the radio. Brundage used to sit at his desk, pipe in mouth, and wonder how our IQ could be this low. At noon, Christine would sometimes come by or I would walk down the narrow back roads to the Milford Inn for a liquid lunch. Charlie Albanese ran the place in an efficient and easygoing manner. He had a beer softball team and I was asked to join.

One Sunday, we played a double header against another bar from a lake community. I played third base and had a 7-for-8 day including homer, triple and double. I handled every chance at third base and absolutely enjoyed myself to the max.

Beer flowed from a keg and I figured this is how life was always going to be. Charlie was impressed by what he saw and told me so. "I never knew you could play softball like this," he said. Pranga was also a good ballplayer who slammed the ball hard and played in the outfield. The next morning we arrived at work with bleary eyes. My arms and legs ached and I suddenly got a wake up call that said I wasn't 18 years old anymore.

Like Billy Joel's song says "Only The Good Die Young" and I figure Bill Strong, although not young, sure wasn't old and feeble. He passed away on January 27, 2002 while my parts partner Bill Brundage passed away after that. He used to travel to Florida in a big beautiful motor home and loved smoking his pipe. His wife Audrey's sister lives two doors down from me and Brundage would drop by the house or call every time he was in the area. I will miss his dry wit, always present pipe and his enthusiasm for traveling.

The year 1987 wasn't a good one for Chris and me. Her dad, Ernie, died on July 1, 1987, in Castle Point Veterans Hospital and her mom, Marion, passed away 94 days later, at the hospital in Port Jervis. Although a heart attack claimed her at age 73, Dr. Craig Brown told us that she died of a broken heart. She counted on Ernie for everything in life and needed his strength and support. When he died, she put up a good front. But underneath it all, she was heartbroken.

Earlier in 1987, I walked away from Milford Motors. I was bored with punching a time clock and slinging parts over a counter. Bruce said he would give me an excellent letter of recommendation and pointed out that I had to try finding employment where I would be happy. He was so right, and eventually the road led back to sports.

Milford Motors is the last place I punched a time clock. I had some long gaps of unemployment but continued to dabble into the writing field. It seems every time I tried the old 8-5 workday routine, I would have the lure of writing waiting for me in the background.

I have always liked wolves because they are beautiful, intelligent, majestic creatures. They have expressive eyes and are a natural and picturesque figure under the spotlight of a shimmering moon. They are simply mesmerizing.

Like a wolf, I heard the call of the wild and responded through instinct. Writing was in my blood and always will be. Once I went back to writing sports, I felt content, fulfilled and appreciated by the reading public and athletes.

I was a "Lone Wolf" back then, choosing to go through life alone much of the time. That was my CB handle while Wolfie and variations on "wolf" are now used sometimes on the internet. I am even contemplating my first tattoo and if I follow through with that idea, it will be of a wolf with expressive yellow eyes.

It wasn't until I stopped drinking, that I left behind the empty pangs of loneliness and joined the pack.

CHAPTER 14

We Come This Way But Once

I sit here and mull over what has become the story of my life.

There are happenings and names that jar memories and thoughts that I figured were lost forever. Instead, I find that those occurrences and recollections were put away in some far away file cabinet of my mind, just waiting to be discovered again.

I can't comprehend all that has happened to me in more than 56 years of life. That would be too complex. I figure that the facts in this book, are very close to being accurate. Everyone is fallible and can make mistakes…it is only human. I take comfort in knowing that anything that isn't totally true, is trivial and unimportant.

If I unnecessarily hurt anyone in these pages, rest assured that it was purely unintentional and I apologize. I have never been a rabble rouser who purposely goes out and starts trouble. However, if someone starts on me and wants a battle on their hands, they came to the right place. I will never back down when a pompous ass tries to control me. Just ask the many bosses who looked down their noses at me, or tried to play God. In the end, most of them wound up paying the price.

It is May 18, 2003, a brilliant Sunday morning in Northeast Pennsylvania. Someone down the block is sawing down tree branches and a few cars pass by on their way to churches or the stores.

I have now been totally sober and free from the clutches of alcohol, for just over two years, 10 months and two weeks. I sit on the back porch gray steps and feel the breeze slide through my dark blonde hair. I used to sit here on Sunday mornings with the shakes. I was hung over, sweating, and dying for noon to come, so I could walk over town and get my fix.

I just returned from a nice ride up along the Delaware River to feed my oldest daughter's two cats. Tracie, Mike and the kids, Sarah, Ashley and Kyle, are in Amish country (Lancaster, Pa.) for a couple of days. They are staying at Willow Valley Farms, a place we took the kids when they were growing up. Chris started a family tradition way back in the early 1970s, going there when Tracie was a baby. Ashley and Kyle were born after this book began.

On the ride to their home, located in the seclusion of the woods, I listened to a Bruce Springsteen song entitled "Waitin' On A Sunny Day" off "The Rising" CD. The tune tells me "don't worry we're gonna find a way" and that "everything'll be okay." I did find a way and it is okay.

When I got home, I remembered how futile, lonely and bleak things used to be, especially on a Sunday. My song selection changed to "Sunday Morning Coming Down" sung by Johnny Cash. The hopeless pangs of this song are in sharp contrast to Bruce's optimism. I know I have to hear Johnny's tune, because that is where I came from and I can never forget that. Like the two songs, my life shows the contrast from pessimism to optimism and from sickly to healthy.

"The beer I had for breakfast wasn't bad, so I had one more for dessert" and "there's something in a Sunday makes a body feel alone" seep into my mind and I remember, all too vividly.

One day I was that forlorn figure, walking the city streets on a Sunday morning. I heard the lonely church bells ringing and felt how desperate, alone and hurt I really was. As time went on, I started believing there was no way out of this horrible trap. One day I needed that beer fix and the next, I was totally freed from my hallowed prison walls.

I have changed dramatically.

In less than a week, Chris and I will be flying to London, England. There, we will visit with a female pen pal she has been writing to for 39 years. She will come eye-to-eye with Mary Allchin and I know Chris will dissolve in a sea of tears. On May 26 and 27, we will see Springsteen and the E-Street Band in concert, at London's Crystal Palace. We have already seen "The Boss" three times, including December 8, 2002 in Charlotte, North Carolina, five days later in Albany, New York and March 4, 2003, in Jacksonville, Florida. In one word, Bruce Springsteen is "phenomenal."

Sixteen days ago, Chris and I met him and his violinist, Soozie Tyrell, at Asbury Park's Stone Pony. Soozie put on a May 2nd concert there, to celebrate the release of her first CD "White Lines." Bruce, New Jersey's favorite son ("Glory Days", "Born In The USA" and many more), was on a break from the European segment of "The Rising" tour. He lives just a half hour from the Stone Pony in Rumsford, New Jersey.

Christine and myself figured that since Bruce's violinist had a special night planned, he probably would show up at the establishment, which he views as his favorite night spot. We hit the nail right on the head with that logic. When home, Bruce feels extremely comfortable in the Stone Pony. He has dropped by there plenty of times and hopped on the stage to jam late at night. Although he is a rock star, Springsteen blends in at this place and is just known as "Bruce", the guy down at the end of the bar, having a drink.

Before the concert, we had a couple of cold ones (soda for me) at Phil

D's Golddigger bar on Ocean Avenue, across from the boardwalk. Back in July 2002, Bruce had been out near that boardwalk, in Convention Hall, singing on the early morning "Today" television show, hosted by Katie Couric and Matt Lauer.

He belted out "Glory Days" and I had looked at Chris and said "man, this guy is great, we just have to see him in concert." We did just that, catching his performances in Charlotte, North Carolina (December 8, 2002), Albany, New York (Dec. 13) and Jacksonville, Florida (Mar. 4, 2003). The E Street Band, including Max Weinberg, Nils Lofgren, Garry Tallent, Roy Bittan, Soozie, Clarence Clemons, Steve VanZandt, Danny Federici, Bruce and Bruce's wife, Patti Scialfa, were tremendous.

During the morning TV concert, Bruce had joked that he had his pajamas on under his clothes and was going back to bed. As he rocked the roof off Convention Hall, he shouted out these words. "We come this way but once." No truer words have ever been spoken in my lifetime. From that moment on, in late July of 2002, I have gone through life with that message firmly on my mind. I will try not to put things off, because there are no guarantees.

Chris went up to Soozie and said "I'd like to congratulate you on your CD" and asked to snap her picture. Soozie was down to earth and decent, said "sure" and so, Chris got the picture. Later, Soozie signed this on her CD for Chris "see you in London." (we were slated to see Bruce in Crystal Palace, England, May 26 and 27).

There was heavy security the evening of May 2nd, in the Stone Pony. There were three bars in this intimate one-story structure, that was run by Domenic Santana. You could feel electricity in the air, as Patty Blee performed as well as Soozie. Then it happened.

A poster of The Boss hangs over a cigarette machine and there are pictures of him all over the wall. The proud New Jersey native digs the loose atmosphere at the Stone Pony and just couldn't let Soozie Tyrell down.

Bruce, wearing a gray Miami Dolphins baseball cap, was suddenly in the house. He and his wife, Patti, were asked by Soozie, to come on stage. "This is my favorite song of the album," Soozie had told the crowd, in explaining the song "Ste Genevieve." Then she looked straight ahead and said "I have two friends to help me."

The Springsteens were decked out in leather jackets and smiled their way up to the stage. Christine got in step with Bruce and security and rode that wave to the front of the stage, where she snapped pictures of Bruce and red- headed Patti.

Bruce and his wife soon gave the spotlight back to Soozie on her big night. They stood off to the left of the stage (as you faced it), applauding and swaying to beat of the violin and piano music. Bruce sipped water from a clear bottle as he watched and every now and then, he would put his left arm around Patti.

The Boss and Patti were beckoned to the stage again and Bruce belted out "It's All Over Now", a song recorded by the Rolling Stones. He played guitar and sang in his easily identifiable voice. The place crackled with unbridled electricity. The Boss had come home.

After he sang, Bruce was escorted by security to the back of the Stone Pony. I tapped him on his left shoulder as he passed and said "nice going, Bruce." Christine went a step further. She talked to Bruce and shook his hand. "Bruce, you are so good," she said. And then, Springsteen firmly shook her hand.

"His (Bruce) hand wasn't very big, and it was cold," Chris joked. He had been playing his guitar near a door that was opened from time to time (to let in cool air). The rock and roll legend had been guarded closely and it was obvious that he wanted to mingle with his fans more.

The Boss was charismatic as he kissed a lady and made small talk. "It seemed so possible that he (Bruce) would be there that night," Chris notes. "It was strange to see Bruce in a different light...as part of an audience," she explains. "He did go up on stage and sing like he usually does, but it was evident he didn't want to be in the limelight this time. When he walked back to the bar, some people cornered him for a minute and it gave me my only chance to shake his hand. Then he was whisked away by security. He hung out for awhile in the back, while some people just glanced his way and within minutes, he was gone. It was an awesome night."

I thought about what question I would ask Bruce, if I ever got the chance to talk with him. He writes and sings songs about the underdog or loser overcoming odds. He tells us of faith and hope even when things look bleak. And he passes on his teenage memories in the Asbury Park and Freehold areas on to us. I guess I'd say "Bruce, does the mood have to be right for you to sit down and write a song about your memories of years gone by? Do you go back to those areas where you spent your young years and look around?"

While Bruce is a complex person who has brought joy to millions, I am still trying to figure out and solve the mysteries of the universe. Where do paper clips go in the course of their existence and how come the sun sets in the west?

My mind wanders from Bruce Springsteen back to reality. I glance to my left at the blue gazing ball in the side yard, past the picnic table and patio. A dog used to eat out here when I would bring her out for a little while on a sunny day. I miss the red and blue dishes, the wagging tail, the big brown eyes. Penny Ann is no longer with us.

Chris is at church and it's a laid back Sunday. A yellow plastic boat rests near the picnic table and reminds me of its owner, my oldest grandchild, Russ, who lives in South Carolina. Now, in 2003, he has a brother, Jeremy and sister, Brooke.

I can't get my mind off the dog today. Sipping coffee instead of beer,

I think of the loyal spaniel mix dog that nearly made it to 18 years of age. We had to put her to sleep on January 21, 2002, because she developed a tumor and couldn't go to the bathroom. I had 32 pages of this book done when she was taken over to Doctor Roeder. I had been sober for over a year and a half. I still can't bring myself to shed tears for Penny because I figure I am beyond grief. She was my best friend in the whole world and she will always have a place in my heart.

I used to joke about Penny outlasting me. In time, that suddenly wasn't so far fetched. She was a loving dog who expected nothing but a pat on the head and caring people around her. She robbed the cats of their food, watched sporting events with me and jumped from the couch to the floor when she had to go out. In later months she had some "accidents" inside the house and looked at us with sad eyes.

Chris would wash her in the sink, wrap her in a towel and sit in the living room with the dog on her lap. Penny licked her hands and face in appreciation because she sensed my wife was helping her and extending her life. Suddenly Penny stopped eating and howled in pain. The sheen was gone from her coat and the sparkling eyes that used to follow my every move, appeared dim and filled with hurt. It was time.

My last words to Penny were "It will be alright" while Chris' were "I'm so sorry, Penny." As I type these words I do feel strong emotions. Maybe someday, out of the clear blue, tears will fall down my cheeks when I recall the life and times of a wonderful dog named Penny Ann.

I still return to the house from football or basketball games, expecting her to be at the back door, wagging her tail because she is happy to see me. Many times I have been driving home and realized that there was no real reason to go there (Chris works nights).

She came to us as a little brown and white fur ball in 1984 and captured our hearts. When I patted her on her head for the final time, my heart was broken. The brown circle on her loyal head, resembling a penny, was larger than when she was a pup. God, I miss her so.

Within seconds, Penny's suffering was over. I felt sadness and relief at the same time. Life can really suck sometimes, but life does go on. As of today, July 3, 2003, my third anniversary of sobriety, Penny hasn't been replaced. Another dog may live here someday, but replacing Penny is impossible.

My friend Teresa, in Kentucky, said it best, back when the dog's life ended. "She (Penny) has done her job well, and faithfully," Teresa said. "She has earned the right to rest."

When the tears come, I will prove to myself, that I am not a cold or callous person and that I do have feelings. People cope with grief in different ways and I was prepared for the day Penny was given a needle. It was one of the most difficult decisions we ever had to make. We suddenly were in the position of playing God, ruling on whether an animal continued to breathe or not.

Penny did suffer quite a bit, because her downward spiral occurred on a weekend. We got her to the vets as soon as possible and did the humane thing. Her yips in the night, tore my heart apart and I had to put a pillow over my head to drown out the desperate shrieks that she put forth. We gave her water from an eye dropper, stroked her face and talked soothingly to her. We didn't want Penny Ann to face these final hours alone, and we were visible and made her as comfortable as possible.

Right now, a young Penny is romping on the grass, chasing a ball. We cuddle her like we always did and give her bones, which she proudly accepts. She sits at our feet with those big brown eyes, pleading for attention and of course, getting it. She is eternally young here and there is no such thing as pain.

Like "Jim" in an Elvis Presley version of "Old Shep", I was called on to make a gut-wrenching decision, regarding my best friend. I helped ease a faithful dog's burden and hurt. Now Penny wags her tail happily, is stealing cat food again and jumps off a heavenly couch when she hears the back door. Penny is home where she belongs, in a land of tranquility and eternal sleep. She has attained her well-deserved reward and is resting peacefully up in paradise, watched over by the keeper of the stars.

I read a story recently, that quoted the National Institute of Alcohol Abuse and Alcoholism, noting that one in 13 adults (14 million Americans) has a drinking problem (as of April 2003). They say that alcohol is involved in 50 per cent of all homicides and 50 per cent of all fatal accidents. It contributes to the risks of cancer, heart disease, brain damage and cirrhosis of the liver. There is no cure for alcoholism but various therapies can improve the situation.

Alcoholics Anonymous and detoxification programs (such as rehabs) have helped people cope with the misery of alcoholism. I am not alone in the day to day battle to stay clean and sober. If you think you may have a problem or know someone who does, I urge you to act now, not tomorrow. For me, the tomorrows nearly ran out.

Today, I have a zest for life. I always worried that quitting the booze, meant entering a holier than thou phase, a boring and tedious lifestyle that would kill me quicker than beer. I am here to tell you, I was dead wrong.

Last night, I belted out three songs at karaoke in Annie's Lounge at Best Western in Westfall Township, Pennsylvania. I used to sing just in the shower as the cats eyed me suspiciously. When I drank, I would be tempted to go up on stage and see if I had any kind of voice. I always felt eyes on me though and in the end, chickened out.

Karaoke DJ's like Joe, John, Mary and Laura know who I am, now. The other night, when I headed toward the microphone, someone in the back shouted "the boss is in the house." The people knew that a Springsteen song, like "Glory Days" or "Dancing In The Dark" was coming. I will never be the best singer in the world, but I do pass the test and get a feeling of satisfaction, escape and self-confidence, entertaining others. Who would have ever thought my life would change this much?

I have no craving for beer and am surrounded by people who are relaxing with drinks. While some in the alcohol field would worry that I was exposing myself to temptation, I know better. When alcohol nearly costs you your life, you simply don't have a choice anymore. That burden was lifted from my shoulders on July 3, 2000. I was told by a supreme power, that my time on earth wasn't up just yet. And so, I walk up front, take the microphone and give you "The Wanderer" by Dion. I definitely qualify as a former wanderer.

Through all my trials and tribulations, I still figure myself to be a demure human being. Christine, my beloved bride of close to 33 years, is my reason for living. It seems I just can't really come up with the words to tell her how much I love her. There are no appropriate words that are worthy enough for her. She is a gift from God, given to me way back when the 1960s became the 1970s. She took a broken down and worn heart and gave it life. She is love.

I have a routine of sorts, that usually begins at the Matamoras Turkey Hill store. The manager, Cathy Lemke, and workers like Ilona, April and Patti, see me come and go with my coffee mug, at least twice a day. Ilona, a resident of Dingmans, Pa., is always telling me little humorous anecdotes about her daughter. "You won't believe what she did this time," she will say of her offspring, who is just past her teens. "I gave her my credit card and you can guess the rest." Her favorite saying as she hurries from task to task is "never a dull moment." We talked about "The Boss" one morning and she said she liked his music. "But he has those veins that pop out in his neck when he sings," she says. "I'm afraid something is going to happen to him." Ilona is humorous, conscientious and a hard worker. She also now owes me a free coffee, for saying all these nice things. When I begin to leave Turkey Hill, the words "have a good one" are usually said.

I fuel our two cars up at Dick Mai's Exxon on Pennsylvania Avenue. I covered Dick when he was a fine southpaw pitcher for Delaware Valley in the early 1970s. I realized many years had gone by, when I covered his son, Richie, who was a feared DV hitter all season long. The coverage of another generation has spread to the Spears', Stellatos and Semeranos. Their dads were excellent athletes, and sometimes their moms, like quarterback Matt Semerano's mother, Doreen (Winters, softball, basketball), were star athletes as well.

Chris and I usually eat lunch either at Joe's Coffee Shop in Port Jervis or Stewart's in Matamoras. Joe Foss, a former neighbor of mine in West End, has top flight food at his Pike Street establishment. Karen (who cooks and waitresses and loves the band "Bad Influence"), Bill (cook), Joe's brother, Dave, plus waitresses Dee and Teresa have great sense of humors. Karen is amazed that we are going to so many Springsteen concerts and I tell her Bruce's words, "We come this way but once." Stewart's is not only convenient because it is close to our house, but owner-cook Jim Martowicz and his crew do a bang-up job in the restaurant department. We also go to Homer's in Port Jervis, for great food.

The cars go to DG Pontiac in Port Jervis. John DiGiantomasso bought my dad and mom's West End house and his son Tony, keeps up the tradition of excellence when it comes to dealing with the public. The parts manager is none other than Bob Heimbrook, the guy Willie Burton labeled "Whiskers" at Case Motors. My plumbers have included Al Tooley, Jim Ellison, and the Cheshire boys who I knew through softball. Jerry and George are intense athletic competitors and should form their own comedy team when not working. Both have been bartenders and have the ability to stay a step ahead of smart-assed customers, most of the time.

I notice these days, that I have some sparse specks of hair that my wife keeps telling me are gray in color. I refuse to accept the fact that my blonde hair is being invaded, as the years go by. Sometimes I wear colorful bracelets and neck chains, especially if I happen to be singing at Best Western, the Tom Quick Inn Sports Bar or the Flo-Jean.

I visited John VanGraafeiland near Buffalo recently and later wore those black and aqua colored rubber spike bracelets to Jamestown, N.Y. where I experienced two great nights of karaoke at a place called Stravato's. Rich and Wayne do a great job handling the karaoke there, and I was impressed with a classy lady named Ethel, who did a superb job on "Sad Movies" and "You Light Up My Life." Christine figures I am reliving my teenage years all over again, while I simply tell her "I'm cool and always will be."

I know I will never be a great singer but I definitely pass the test. The Springsteen songs seem to be going over big in my area. I just delight in passing on to the people, some of the fantastic accomplishments that The Boss has given all of us.

I have pet names for my wife, such as Malone, Kinjla, and Sparky. How I come up with these names is anybody's guess. By now, my mate has gotten used to my bizarre sense of humor and the names that go with it. We have five cats, named Binky, Becky, Cinnamon, Tiger and Tony. Cinnamon showed up one day on my dad's back porch and must have belonged to a family, because he had been altered. Tiger was a little kitten, found wandering around in the rain at a blasting site next to the A&P in Vernon, New Jersey.

Over the years I have compiled quite a list of likes and dislikes. I never use the word "butt", preferring "ass" instead. I say "swearing" not "cursing", "bathroom" not "John", and "ice box" or "fridge" instead of "refrigerator." I am sometimes still known to call pants "dungarees" instead of "jeans" which cracked my daughters up for years. When the girls used to be on the run nights and weekends, I used to refer to their absences as "running it." They got poker faces when I used to confront them and tell them "hey, you girls are running it. Why don't you hang around home sometimes. We forget what your faces look like." I believe Dad used these same expressions on me.

Some sayings I like, are "you only live once", "one day at a time" (an AA expression, which I believe to be true in almost everything), "nothing is forever", "what does that have to do with the price of tea in China?", "what's the point?", "I can't take it anymore", "I'm outta here", "go easy", "your running it", "the last guy that said that would have been 35 tomorrow", and the Danny Webster gem from Guam, "I feel so damned good I might reenlist."

I chuckle at the strangest things. When retired A&P employee Joe Piccolo used to say "what time does the balloon go up?" to customers in his check out line, I would just die watching the customer reactions. One guy even looked out the front of the A&P store, in case the balloon was going up from out in the parking lot.

When Joe would ring up an order, that came to say $35.77, he would tell the customer "I kept you under 36 dollars." Other times he would simply walk around the store muttering "Mahwah" again and again. Mahwah is a town in the great state of New Jersey. I am convinced that these diversions from the everyday A&P grind, helped Joe cope and reach retirement with his mind still intact.

From time to time, a pretty female will catch my eye and I'll appreciate her grace and beauty, big time. I know that I possess charisma and I don't mean that in a boastful way. I use that charisma wisely and usually can manage to initiate conversations, should the situation arise. On occasions, Christine has been known to stop me in my tracks. "Put your eyes back in your head," she'll say. "Behave yourself, she's young enough to be your daughter."

I am big on sports and music nostalgia, dig action movies and enjoy ice cream at night. There is nothing like a driving rain storm and I go right out into it, enjoying the drops pouring down on my face. The rain cools things down on a hot summer's night and I feel refreshed and invigorated by the world around me. Polka music instantly makes me happy and the Yankees, Mets, Knicks, Jets, Giants and Miami Dolphins are still teams that I follow. I am constantly writing down things to do or buy, on scraps of paper that wind up in most every room of the house. I feel sad that Dan Marino never won a Super Bowl, love watching Drew Barrymore on television and think the Red Green Show is the funniest thing on television (Canadian show on PBS). I like Chris Martin of Cold Play, a person Christine got me to enjoy. And, I think Dean Martin had a velvet voice and was a real showman.

I like some country and western songs except when she done him wrong, broke his heart, took his money and shot his horse. I dislike most rap and heavy metal music, especially the vulgar crap, so I guess you could say I am set in my ways. I still believe in opening a door for a lady, being respectful and honoring the American flag.

Painting a house, inside or out, gives me a great feeling of accomplishment. I despise raking leaves the most and get no big thrill out of trudging outside in the dead of winter to shovel the sidewalks.

I am nauseated by loud, obnoxious people who think they know it all, yet are as shallow as a dried up creek at the height of a drought. Possessing IQ's that rival that of a cucumber, they let their kids run in the street, throwing litter and other trash in homeowners' lawns. Simply put, these creatures, masquerading as parents, possess no class and don't know their ass from third base.

I shudder when I read the words in a newspaper "the car suffered extensive damage", wondering how the hell a car can suffer and feel pain. Also, I am irritated by the words "a good time was had by all", figuring there had to be at least one person that had a really rotten time.

I just shake my head when I see pictures in a newspaper that have 20 people standing there smiling with their shark teeth gleaming in the noonday sun. Pictures of people being themselves (like Candid Camera) are the best, while the posed and ridiculous pictures, just beg for permanent residence on a dart board or in a garbage can.

Watching the weather is one of my favorite things, especially if heavy rain, electrical storms or heavy snow is predicted. I am the guy who goes out to the garage and has snow shovels all ready on the front and back porches. I believe that you can't look too far ahead in life. Former A&P employee Bill Roberts drove that point home with these words of wisdom "a plane could hit your house tomorrow."

Here in my native Port Jervis, I look around and see people of my age, and younger, holding responsible positions. While I look up to people like Don Parker and Art Gray, younger guys like Port Jervis City Court Judge Robert Onofry and retired Port police chiefs Gary Lopriore and Bill Wagner have made all of us proud. Onofry won his seat in 1996 and was unopposed for his second term on the bench. Wagner retired in 2003.

I used to drink a lot of milk, but my taste has changed since quitting alcohol. I have to watch my intake of sweets and get back to vegetables and grains more. If you have your health, you have everything, and I will never forget that. I started 2003 at 225 pounds and still have hopes of someday seeing 155 pop up on the bathroom scales.

I know I will never work for "the man" again as being a puppet on a string just isn't my bag. Impatience is something that I am having a real tough time with. If I consult my list of things to do, and there are still many tasks that haven't been tended to, I get anxious. Chris points out to me that "there is always something you want done. When you cross something off your list, you are asking right away, about the next thing."

Maybe I should write "chill out" on my list, as a very important item.

In regards to journalism, I just don't see the commitment from writers anymore. The "stop the presses" mentality, by editors with their sleeves rolled up and sweat pouring from their brow, just isn't there. Some college graduates, armed with degrees, arrive on the scene with blinders on. Doing things by the book, is tedious, mechanical and most of all, boring. Compassion for your fellow man and behind the scenes looks at the core of our very existence, is sorely lacking these days. If you can't touch emotions, I feel an important ingredient is lacking.

This new regime, spills over into the coaching field. That eye-to-eye "sacrifice your soul" type of dedication, is seldom seen anymore when it comes to coaches and their athletes. I realize part of this observation is caused by my aging, but much of it is just a gut feeling I have. The writers, coaches and athletes seem to have come off an assembly line...mass produced and armed to the teeth with trite sayings they can utter to cover any given situation. The "new breed" does have hope, dreams and goals. But it takes old fashioned dedication to get steady results and achieve intrinsic and extrinsic reward.

Getting back to likes and dislikes, spaghetti, meat loaf and Springsteen, top the list of great things. Fonzie, rain on the roof, chili, and ketchup on bologna are all fine with me. So was Dick Young, Jim Bishop, teenage rides across the Hawk's Nest (a curvy road near Port Jervis and featured in TV car commercials), and my discharge out in California.

I like Dave Berry, Mike Lupica, and Phil Pepe, tolerated Howard Cosell and enjoyed the old Monday Night Football broadcasts. I think John Madden is a hoot, enjoy the velvet tones of Pat Summeral and like the humor of Terry Bradshaw. I think Bruce, Billy Joel, Neil Diamond, Anne Murray and Three Dog Night gave me great live entertainment. I like the saying "don't just stand there with your teeth in your mouth."

I don't like twist off caps that seem to be cemented onto the jar, onions, pork, liver, kale, olives, lamb and rhubarb. I despise the words "I have a bone to pick with you."

I do believe the saying "one day at a time", know for sure that honesty and trust help form a solid marriage, realize that life can be over in a heartbeat, and that it should be savored and cherished. This isn't designed to scare you, but to help explain that every chance you get to pet a dog, look at a sunset, give a loving touch or feel love in someone's eyes, are priceless gifts from the keeper of the stars.

The clock of life is ticking fast, like an out-of-control race car. Nobody can stop time and that can be both beneficial (when you are getting through a dental visit) or detrimental (when a visit with a loved one is coming to an end). I hate doing things twice (as in reconnecting to the internet), looking for something that is lost (where was the last place you remember seeing it?), lunatics who tailgate out on the highway, New

York City people who come up here and bitch that there is no nightlife like in "the city" (then what the hell are you doing here?), vicious dogs, pushy people, and hot, humid days in July and August.

I will try most anything except for bungee jumping, riding a Ferris wheel, walking around on the roof of my house, or dealing with my wife before she has her first cup of coffee.

I try to hang on to precious moments in my life. September 12 (marriage), January 11 (Dawn's birth) and March 29 (Tracie's birth) are dates I will never forget. Back on April 8, 2002, Sarah, Tracie's oldest daughter and barely three years old, stood near the back steps of my house and sang these words to me. "Happy birthday to you, happy birthday to you, happy birthday dear Poppy, happy birthday to you." It brought tears to my eyes, not only because she was so sweet, but that I was alive to hear those words. This little pixie had capsulated what had happened with my life in just 21 short months.

I have had the fortune to meet wonderful people in my life. Folks like Joe, Wanda and Jamie Rickard, Ned Bushong, Delores Brennan (DV teacher), Trevor Woodruff (basketball coach), Angelo Matz (DV girls softball coach), Al Holtzer (DV athletic director), George Rollman (Port softball coach), Alex Osowick (my idol), Phil Chase (former Port teacher), Chris Ross (DV wrestling), Keith Olsommer (DV football), Mel Durrwachter (DV coach) plus Bob and Ron Semerano. These are just some of the decent people who sports has connected me with.

Jamie Rickard is a hard throwing right handed pitcher for the West Scranton High School girls softball team, an opponent of Delaware Valley's. I have written about the red-haired girl a few times, even though she competes for an opposing team. Her maturity as a hurler and star basketball player stood out to me. The talent was there and so was the attitude. Jamie is an amazing lady and familiarized herself with our area of the state, by playing for Coach Matz' Tri-State Angels (when school wasn't in session). She formed relationships with the same DV players she was trying to strike out during the scholastic season. Athletics is an education in itself and it is a vehicle for human relations. Friendships have taken place on athletic battlegrounds that have lasted a lifetime.

Too many times, young people are categorized as being lazy, boisterous or troublesome. I never group people as if they were cattle. Each human being is an individual with needs. A friendly word or story to show that a young person is on the right track, is a justified reward. Jamie's mom, Wanda, sends me heart warming cards of appreciation in the mail. This is a wonderful family and just another reason that I know my observations and words, are making folks feel good about themselves. I am making a difference by showing that I care and that reward surpasses any paycheck I could ever earn. As I said earlier, it just wasn't my time to leave this earth.

I never set out to meet or watch famous people perform. And yet, I have come in contact with some well-known entertainment types. In my 56 plus years, I have seen or interviewed President Kennedy, Muhammad Ali, Angelo Dundee, Willis Reed, Three Dog Night, Johnny Maestro and the Brooklyn Bridge, Jimmy Sturr, Neil Diamond, Billy Joel, Anne Murray, Bobby Vinton and Pistol Pete Maravich, plus his dad Preston. Also, Joe Louis, Bruce Springsteen, Sugar Ray Robinson, Mickey Mantle, Dick Young, Pete Rose, Ken Norton, Dick Gregory, Cus D'Amato, Jimmy Ellis, Cold Play, Cher and many more.

Family tragedies have never really reared their ugly heads. I am fortunate that things have pretty much been on an even keel. However, on September 11, 2001, the day before our 31st wedding anniversary, Tracie's husband, Mike, was as close to a major catastrophe as a person can get. He stood and watched in person, as the second hijacked plane hit the World Trade Center in New York City.

Four planes took off from United States airports with innocent passengers aboard. These aircraft were used in attacks on our country. Two planes took off from Boston, one from Newark, New Jersey and the other from Dulles Airport, outside of Washington, D.C. The planes were hijacked by terrorists who had more than violence on their minds. They were out to kill people and accomplished their aim.

There were victims and heroes on this dark day in American history. Heroic firefighters and policemen gave their lives for their country that day. This horrible happening, tightened the bond of Americans who reside in different geographic areas. Folks from California, Florida and everywhere else, spilled tears for those in New York City, Washington, D.C. and southwestern Pennsylvania.

Two of the planes, American Airlines flight 11 (bound for Los Angeles from Boston) and United Airlines flight 175 (also Boston to LA), were forced to crash into the World Trade Center twin towers. Meanwhile, United Airlines flight 93 (Newark to San Francisco) crashed in southwest Pennsylvania while American Airlines flight 77 (Washington to LA) crashed into the Pentagon.

Rough estimates say that about 2,749 people perished in the twin towers while 184 died at the Pentagon and 40 in Pennsylvania. At Ground Zero at the WTC site, it took nine months and 2,300 workers (and 1,600 trucks) to clear away debris and human remains. Nobody was found alive under the debris and Americans and the whole world walked around in shock and disbelief. A total of 19 terrorists hijacked the commercial jets and pulled off what amounted to suicide missions. The North tower (the one with the antenna on the top) was struck by flight 11 (carrying 92 people) at 8:45 a.m., while the South tower (flight 175, carrying 65 people) was hit at 9:03 a.m.

The Twin Towers, in lower Manhattan, were elegant buildings that represented freedom to Americans. Our sense of security was shattered, but amazing spirit came through when the chips were down. A picture snapped by Thomas Franklin (staff photographer for The Record, Bergen County, New Jersey) showed three firefighters raising Old Glory at Ground Zero, in what epitomized that American spirit. The United States had been dealt a cruel and severe blow, but its people refused to throw in the towel and give up. Instead the resolve and perseverance of Americans, shone through under the bleakest of situations.

The towers had taken awesome hits and eventually crumbled to the ground in a fiery inferno. Innocent people had tried reaching exits while enveloped in smoke, fire and debris. Some were lucky enough to make it to the street. Others simply perished inside or leaped from windows to their deaths. Heroism ran rampant and we showed how proud a nation we can be.

Nearby, my son-in-law, a native of New Jersey, looked on in horror.

He is an accomplished and well-respected field technician who repairs electrical objects such as intricate computers that supply major businesses. He was working about eight blocks from the WTC, at Globex, near Greenwich Avenue, and had come outside the building to get a cup of coffee. Sometimes he worked inside the WTC, as computer equipment was stored on the 110th floor. Today, September 11, 2001, wasn't one of his days to work in the WTC. Still, he would find himself imperiled by the dynamic and surreal happenings that morning.

"I saw the smoke in the North tower (the tower with an antenna on top) and stayed outdoors watching," Mike recalled, on Halloween night in 2002. "Then I saw the flames. I got on the phone with Tracie (my daughter) and she told me a plane had hit the tower. I was ready then, to take off for the Holland Tunnel."

Tracie had phoned me in a wavering voice and told me to turn on the television. What I saw, resembled a horror movie. I couldn't comprehend that this was actually taking place for real, in New York City.

She informed me that Mike was on the phone with her when the second plane approached the South tower. She watched on television and he viewed proceedings in person as the plane approached. "It's going to hit the building," he told her, in what had to be a voice to send a million chills down her spine.

When I talked to my daughter, she was obviously upset and worried that her husband could have been hurt or killed that morning. Flying debris, shards of glass, thick smoke and people in panic were a lethal combination.

"I went to my dad's (in New Jersey) and saw the South tower collapse," Mike asserted. "Cantor Fitzgerald (a brokerage firm) lost nearly 700 people (101st, 103rd, 104th and 105th floors). I knew lots of those people, they were really nice. I remember going up to the windows of the World Trade Center and eating $12 burgers with many of them."

Mike, a reticent individual, also knew two guys, who like himself, was spared that terrible day. "They were due up at Cantor Fitzgerald at 9 a.m. to work," he explains. "A fellow named Vince, convinced the other guy to stop for a bagel first. He said he didn't want to smell bacon and eggs from the windows of the World Trade Center. So, they stopped for the bagels and it saved their lives."

At Cantor Fitzgerald, the unofficial casualty tally showed that 657 of its nearly 1,000 employees perished in the terrorist attack. The 56-year old firm had been like one big happy family as they worked in offices that overlooked New York Harbor. Surviving employees moved to temporary Manhattan midtown quarters where dozens of American flags decorated the work space at the bond brokerage house's facility.

Firefighter Douglas Miller from near where I live (in the tri-state area), died that day. The 34-year-old Mill Rift, Pa. Fire chief left behind a wife, Laurie, and daughters Elizabeth, Rachel and Katie. I didn't know Doug Miller, but sure got to find out what a caring and wonderful person this Pennsylvania resident was. Laurie and the daughters were grand marshals for the 153rd annual Inspection Day Parade in Port Jervis. The parade is a tradition and Doug Miller's name and his heroism were a natural fit for this memorable day.

When the smoke had cleared, major league baseball games were postponed, Broadway shows were cancelled, major tourist attractions were closed and the Emmy Awards, slated for September 16, were postponed. The whole country, was basically on high alert. Osama bin Laden was named the mastermind and prime suspect in the tragic events. Afghanistan's ruling Taliban, was accused of protecting the suspected brain trust of the terrorist attacks. Soon, America began bombing Afghanistan. To date, Osama bin Laden has not been found.

Bruce Springsteen, who grew up in New Jersey, gazed out at the World Trade Center many times when he was in the East. Suddenly he felt the void that all Americans did. That symbol of freedom was no longer there, and instead, there was just empty space, just like the painful void that was occupying American hearts.

Bruce's area of New Jersey had the most casualties in the whole Garden State, and he felt the pangs of heartbreak just like his less famous countrymen. Springsteen has always been a blue collar type of guy and he is able to communicate with, and feel, the vibes of a regular Joe.

One day not too long after the attacks, "The Boss" was out driving his car near his hometown of Rumson. A fellow motorist recognized Springsteen and pulled up alongside. He didn't want an autograph or to talk to a star. He had a meaningful message he wanted to convey to Springsteen. "Bruce, we need you," the man shouted to him. Bruce resumed driving with that plea triggering the spinning of the wheels in his head.

Springsteen knew that America was hurting bad and was having trouble coping with what had happened. He wanted desperately to help a nation begin the healing process by licking its painful wounds and going on with a positive attitude. He began working on music that would have people relate to 911.

In the end, a CD entitled "The Rising" was released on July 30, 2002, the same day that he appeared on the Today TV show and gave a fine performance at Convention Hall, near the boardwalk at Asbury Park. On that CD, are such songs as "The Rising", "Your Missing" and "Empty Sky." Bruce was set to launch "The Rising" tour at Continental Arena (at the Meadowlands) in East Rutherford, New Jersey, August 7. Bruce had come through in the clutch. In 2002, he went on to perform (with the E Street Band) in 45 cities and nine countries.

If the WTC tragedy had any message at all to give, it is that life is fragile and that nothing is forever. As Bruce said on that TV show, "We come this way but once." I have rallied behind those powerful words and constantly keep them in mind, in my daily life. Knowing where I came from and knowing where I am, are two very important things.

Putting things off in life, is not a good idea. Most of the time, what you intend to do, gets put on the back burner and remains there. So, wanting to follow through with some of my ideas, I actively began to seek out my Uncle Buddy in Oregon.

I wound up speaking to his daughter, Jeannette, on the evening of June 19, 2002, and spoke with Buddy eight days after that. It had been 28 years since I had any type of contact with him. He asked about the family, wanting to know about his brothers and sister. Sonja was alive then, but has since passed away. To my knowledge there are five of the original seven Tangen kids (including my dad) still alive.

I reminded Buddy about how he used to scare me when I was a kid. "You used to say there were monsters in my bedroom," I said. "Oh, the old monster trick," he laughed on the other end of the phone wire. Someday, hopefully soon, I will shake hands with Uncle Buddy, out in Oregon.

Since I quit drinking, I have been through a root canal, an injured left shoulder, which an X-ray showed to be scar tissue (possibly drinking related), and the loss of my beloved dog. Nothing earth shaking has occurred, and I would be real happy if this trend continued.

I still am meticulous in my preparation to cover an athletic event. I refuse to go into a story situation, cold. Being organized comes from my dad. We both are constantly writing down lists of things to do. I am the type, that has to know what I am walking into. I can be difficult and bullheaded at times, but I figure if you're going to do something, you may as well do it right.

Jackie Beck, my social worker back at Montrose, continues to be proud of me. She never forgot the guy that came to her in July of 2000, and wound up being shipped to the Bronx.

I received a greeting card from her on July 3, 2002 (my two year anniversary of sobriety), that said "this special day is just for you. Congratulations." Yellow fireworks were shooting and spraying in the air on the card. And there were these words. "I am so very proud of you and your accomplishment! You allowed the powers that be, permission to give you a second chance! And look what you have done! Happy second sober year! Take care. Jackie."

A year later, I got an e-mail from Jackie. "Happy belated 3rd anniversary," it said. She went on to say she got married in May of 2003 (she is now Jackie Beck Bush) and that life was treating her well. "I continue working with my beloved veterans," she said. "Occasionally I run across another "Bill" who changes his life for the better! Having 1 in 50 turn around, makes all the stress and hard work worthwhile and very rewarding."

A coffee cup is my constant companion now, especially in the morning. Sports and music are still my passions these days and I am also enjoying traveling, especially to Bruce Springsteen concerts. I enjoy singing his material and have developed a following of "Boss" fans, when I sing karaoke. It isn't uncommon for me to hear the call "Bruuuucccceeee" when I enter a building or step up to a microphone.

On July 17, 2003, prior to a Springsteen concert at Giants Stadium in the Meadowlands, I walked over to a Bruce Springsteen Karaoke area, right next to Giants Stadium. Q104.3FM radio (Manhattan, New York City) was broadcasting from the site and sponsoring the karaoke event for all 10 Boss concert dates at Giants Stadium.

"Should I put in a slip (for a song)?", I asked Chris. We decided to, and I wrote out "Dancing In The Dark." I had to walk up a few steps to a stage and sang the song for over 500 people. Later, I returned and put in "Born To Run." There was a sea of faces at 7 p.m. and we planned to enter the stadium around 7:30. "I don't think I'll get a chance to do the song," I told Chris.

Around 7:25 p.m. or so, the well-known Q104.3 DJ, Jonathan Clarke, came on stage and said "we have time for one last song before going in to see The Boss. This next guy sounds more like Bruce than anyone we have heard today. He will be singing "Born To Run" for us."

I searched the crowd for someone to come forward. I wondered if the guy would look anything like Bruce. I looked forward to hearing how close the voice was to Springsteen's and how well he did the song. I didn't have to look very far. They were talking about me.

I didn't have time to get nervous. It seemed like a flash and I was at the microphone again. "Bill, Bruce is doing a sound check inside the stadium and can hear you," Jonathan said. That was too mind-boggling to comprehend. "Well, if he is, I apologize, Bruce," I said, as the crowd cracked up.

There were people everywhere, and those expectant faces were all looking at me. An adrenalin rush took over and I belted out the song with every ounce of energy I had. Three young girls ran up on stage and accompanied me. One of them planted a kiss on my cheek in front of God and everyone. Over 1,000 people saw me sing "Born To Run" that early evening in July. "You were in heaven up there," my wife joked on the way home.

She snapped a picture of me on stage and Gazette editor Janis Osborne ran it in the August 1 edition, on page 14. Over the top of the picture were the words (in bold headline print) "Sounds Like The Boss." While complete strangers came up to me at Giants Stadium and said things like "we saw you on stage, you were great" and "are you the guy that sang "Born To Run"? I also got kind comments after the newspaper picture appeared. I thought to myself "if singing Bruce is an addiction, it's a damn harmless one."

I often think of how dramatically my life has changed. I used to live for that $5.09 12-pack of Milwaukee's Best beer. Now I was chomping at the bit to entertain people with Springsteen music. Life can be so unpredictable and so rewarding. I guess the moral of the story is "never say never."

The "nothing is forever" philosophy came to light back on September 8, 2002. My old stomping grounds, my home base and source of many cold mugs of beer, burned down and claimed one life. It was Fish who told me the unbelievable words on the telephone.

"The New Bauer caught fire," Fish had said on this tragic Sunday evening. "I was across the street in the Erie Hotel, eating," he went on. "All of a sudden, smoke and flames were shooting out of the New Bauer."

I felt like someone had sucker punched me in the stomach and I instantly thought of owners George and Louise Noroian. I had so many laughs with them in the Bauer and with prior owners Ben and Marie Ozehosky. The happy memories came flooding back like it was yesterday.

I heard great music in there, watched Super Bowls, World Series games, stood in the doorway in the rain swilling down frosty Schaefers. This was just so unreal to digest and accept. It just couldn't be.

They used to have a fish head mounted over the bar (when Ben and Marie owned the place). After a few "gizmos" people would get frisky and begin tossing coins, trying to get them in the fish's mouth. You could hear errant coins clinking off the whiskey bottles below and people laughed their heads off.

We used to play practical jokes in here. Once Irv Rothschild (a super softball pitcher and teammate) went to the men's room and a couple of us placed a barstool under the doorknob so he couldn't get out. We sat at the bar grinning and chuckling, just waiting for him to pound on the door. The pounding never came. Irv executed a nifty escape through a small bathroom window (and Irv is a big man), located on the Front Street side of the historical three-story building. He walked around and entered the bar from the Jersey Avenue door. He acted like he was arriving for the first time, and that cracked us up even more. I know I've told this story countless times, probably including a time or two in this book, but that memory stands out so vivid and clear.

I still see tall and lanky Jay Bauer (a descendant of the original hotel owners), taking those fireman's mugs off the hooks (to wash them) that were screwed high up on wood over the bar mirror. The games of bowling, pool, hurrying up the street to place bets at OTB, eggs over-boiling and crackling loudly in the kitchen (good going George), and the kitchen where a puppy named Penny Ann waited for an owner to come into her life. Dearly departed souls Jay Bauer, Al Selemba, Randy Conklin and "Fast Eddie" Grau all had their days in the sun in this bar. Dad used to drop by here on Saturdays after work, to have a beer (when Larry Taylor owned the Bauer).

This building, which was located in the center of downtown Port Jervis (across from the Erie train depot), was originally constructed as a four-story brick structure in 1903 at a cost of $15,349. Jacob Bauer awarded the contract. Nearly 100 years later, at just before 2 p.m. on a Sunday, the building caught fire and a 55-year-old man, who was seen hanging out his third story window, perished. The fire reportedly began in a second story apartment. The New Bauer Inn was a neatly painted red brick structure and by night, it was a pile of timber and brick. Parts of the building that weren't destroyed by fire, were taken down by a demolition crew hours after the flames were extinguished. The fond memories are priceless. Nothing is forever.

I had entered the New Bauer Inn, back in 1969. I was just out of the Air Force, single and working a job at Kolmar Laboratories, across the street. I had no idea what the future held for me. What it held was a second engagement, a September 12, 1970 marriage, two daughters and six grandchildren.

The half dozen little ones are different and unique in their own way.

Tracie's children are native New York Staters. Sarah Nicole (January 1, 1999) is a quiet little girl with a creative imagination (as of August 3, 2003). She acts like a little mother to Ashley Sabrina (October 24, 2000) and Kyle Michael (July 19, 2002). She is a dancer who has performed at recitals (Rosemary's Dance) at Port Jervis High School.

Ashley is a little joker. She is mischievous and there is never a dull moment. However, in a wink of an eye she can turn serious and look at you with those big and expressive eyes.

Kyle is a tough little guy. He is destined to be an athlete and more than likely has hockey in his future. His dad, Mike, is a big New Jersey Devils (hockey) and New York Giants (football) fan.

Dawn's children are native South Carolinians. Her oldest, Russell Philip (May 3, 1995), is a typical all-American rough and tumble kid. He speaks in a thick southern drawl ("cut off the light Poppy") and loves race cars (lives near Darlington speedway). He is constantly climbing, throwing, jumping and breaking toys ("I busted it, Poppy").

Jeremy Ace (September 7, 2000) is a blond-haired little boy with big blue eyes. He is a real and live action figure as he runs, non-stop, from morning until night. Perpetual motion and playing are the names of his game.

Brooke Elaine (May 2, 2002) loves to be held and "dances" when Bruce Springsteen VCR tapes are viewed. She has to be the youngest "Brucer" in the country and perks up when "Glory Days" or "Dancing In The Dark" (from a Barcelona, Spain concert) come on the screen. She is quiet, smiles a lot, seldom cries and slugs down bottle after bottle of milk.

In writing this book, I don't want to appear vain. I realize I am leaving words for others to read, now and in later years. The lives I touched and the real emotions I exposed in people, may very well be my legacy. Two regrets I have, are never having connected again with Doug Smith (Smitty from Guam) and Mom never pursuing all the way, to learn more about who her real parents were. I realize that is her prerogative and I respect that. However, quitting the trail of her very existence, snatches that information from me, as well. I am a person who likes to follow things to conclusion, who likes to have answers. I may never learn which of my blood relatives (if any) fought the alcohol battle like I did. This trail may have a dead end...but I know the answer is out there somewhere.

Sometimes, I feel as if I am watching someone else rap out this book. It seems I stand back from the keyboard and go into another mode, as thoughts and visions intertwine. I have a distinct connection to the past and nostalgia. I remember how tall my grandfather was and things he said to me 50 years ago.

My parents are still alive as of August 2003, so maybe that means that I still have quite a few years left on earth. When the time comes, I want to be first, because I would hate life without Christine. On occasion she keeps me sharp and humble, by knowing how to get under my skin when I get too high and mighty. But there is no way to stay upset at her. It seems we have had a battle of wits since the day we met. We always try to stay a step ahead of the other guy. She is my companion for life and I will always be in love with her. There isn't a more loving and giving person on this planet, than Christine Diane Goble Tangen.

I have had the ability to touch and reach many people. People confide in me when they have a problem or need someone to talk to. Chris has that same gift, as friends and people she barely knows, seem to sidle up to her and trust any advice she may have.

I see myself writing a book on Bruce Springsteen as soon as this one is completed. I am not a Springsteen "fanatic" but I will readily admit that his music tears at my guts and inspires me. His words of struggle, lost hope, and gained faith, pierce my heart. He is a rocker, an icon, a once in a lifetime gift, a living legend. He is also down to earth, caring, compassionate and "real." More than likely, the book will revolve around what it is like to be a true fan. It will show what it is like to follow The Boss and the E Street Band in and out of the country on "The Rising" tour which began at Continental Arena in the Meadowlands (East Rutherford, New Jersey) on August 7, 2002. I have heard that in just under a year, he had sold about 3 million tickets to his concerts.

Someday, I may launch an alcohol seminar. This is both an employment venture and a way to "give back" and to help those individuals that are either afflicted with alcoholism or know someone who is. I will never stand on a soap box or in judgment of others. I will simply tell them the hell I went through and hopefully inspire them to walk away, or have a loved one walk away from the peril and lethal consequences of this dreaded disease. I would conduct this seminar (probably two hours in duration) in classrooms, banquet halls, colleges and anywhere that people can sit down and listen. My goal is to have the Springsteen book completed and the seminars begun, sometime in 2004 or the first half of 2005.

If neither of these goals are realized, I won't run off into the woods like a pissed off half-crazed lunatic. The real lunatic days ended over three years ago. I have learned, through bitter experience, that some things don't follow a precise and accurate time frame. As of August 2003, I remain in the area of 228 pounds but still think I can make 155. I have a white cardboard square with black flare numerals "155" taped to the inside of my closet door. I am going to look at that "155" more often and begin really shooting for the stars.

I am not afraid or intimidated by powerful or charismatic people. That was obvious when I grabbed that microphone and sang Bruce songs at the Meadowlands. My confidence level has really gone up since I used to crack open those beer cans.

One morning I drove to Middletown to see about ordering some tee shirts for Chris and me. Since we had been following Bruce, I figured to have the words "Touring With Bruce" (in white letters, black shirt) on the front and "We Come This Way But Once" plus "The Boss 2002-2003" on the back. The store I was going to check out, wasn't open yet, so I walked up West Main Street, clutching a coffee, wasting some time.

I couldn't believe how clean this city was. I remember when it began going downhill as the downtown area died and the malls grabbed all the business. There has been a revitalization in Middletown and I believe that Mayor Joseph DeStefano is a big part of the turn around.

The mayor is in the news quite a bit. He is a controversial and colorful subject, who says what is on his mind. He owns a couple of restaurants including the Olde Erie Brew Pub and Grill at 7-11 West

Main.

As I looked through a parking lot toward city hall, I noticed a guy in tan shorts hurrying down the steps and across the street. The man looked like, and turned out to be, the mayor.

Moments later, I was sipping a coke in the Olde Erie when he came in and sat two stools down. He is a busy man but always finds time to answer questions or converse with someone. When I saw the chance, I told him how impressed I was, with the way the city looked. "We really like hearing things like that," Joe said. Later we talked about Bruce Springsteen and he asked if I was going to Fenway Park to see him. The mention of Fenway in Boston, changed the short conversation to baseball. "Are you a Yankees or Mets fan?", he queried. When I said I was a pinstripe follower since my very young years, he gave a sigh of relief. "That's good," he exclaimed. "I didn't want to have to throw you out of here." In just 10 minutes, I had discovered the wit of Middletown's mayor.

I have learned to take the bad with the good. There are times when doing your best, will just not be good enough, in the eyes of those in power. I admit to having a strong ego when it comes to my writing ability. Each story is different and the way a piece is shaped and delivered, varies from writer to writer.

In over 32 years of filing stories, I had been heavily edited a minimum of times, and never had a story killed. That perfect record came to a screeching halt when I was working for a weekly newspaper in Pennsylvania. The editor there, is a disciplined type, who is as stubborn as they come. He has a huge ego and the power of the magic word "editor" has obviously affected the way he does business.

I felt the clash of egos a few times in over a year that I handed in my work there. He insisted on me calling him with the stories I planned for the week, which was fine with me. He was upset that I never called when he was in the office, but rather gave my budget on an answering machine. I knew that he wanted to discuss stories while I just wanted to go out and get the job done. I covered high school sports well, and had many favorable comments.

I typed a story on a new athletic director and got a tough time from the editor. He didn't like the slant of the story and wanted to concentrate on the duties of the new AD. I went for a background kind of piece on the type person that was assuming control of the position. Listing duties and the like, would have been boring with a capital B.

He e-mailed me that he was "spiking" the story and that it had to be rewritten. There was no way I was going to change the way this package was presented, and so I vigorously refused. When I saw his stubborn attitude and lack of decent communication, I "spiked" the job.

This control freak bitched because I didn't phone when he was in the office and said all planned stories had to be discussed. This may sound like a rule that more fits the New York Times, I told him. Nevertheless, he wanted all these petty things accomplished as he stood "tall" in his ivory tower of power. By the way, for all this turmoil, I was being paid the ludicrous wage of 30 dollars a story.

I laughed off his narrow minded demeanor and ridiculous attitude and moved on. Later, Janice Osborne, editor of The Gazette in Port Jervis, was happy to get the AD story. She not only ran it the way I wanted, she praised what I had done, like many other readers in the city. I had met an obstacle laced with complete resistance and refused to knuckle under. I overcame this situation with a positive attitude and the courage of my convictions. I learned from the experience and feel I am wiser because of it. I did not retreat or give in to a know-it-all...I did not surrender.

In the past, I had dealt with one of the greatest editors a writer could ever have asked for (Gene Casey). Can you guess who is at the other end of the totem pole?

In Janice Osborne, a fine editor and caring human being, I see a person who has writing ability, a keen feel for interacting with people, plus unbridled compassion. On July 23, 2003, she knew I had reached over three years of sobriety. I received an e-mail from her that tells it like it is. "Congratulations and I mean that sincerely," she said. "Just think of all those healthy organs inside your body. What you have done is an incredible feat of courage and bravery. It ain't easy being green."

I sing lots of Bruce Springsteen these days. In fact, at the Flo-Jean in Port Jervis, I am known as "Bruce." It is easier to fill out my song requests with that name, rather than my real first name. Besides, Bill Heckman is usually there with Tammy and he and I always head to the mike at the same time, when the name "Bill" is called out.

I see lots of my former athletes at karaoke events. Jim Andriac and Mike Polanis are two who played football at Port Jervis. Mike went to see Springsteen July 26, 2003 in Giants Stadium, while Jim, a rugged back under Viglione in the early 1970s, thinks The Boss is great. "Born To Run" is the best song I ever heard," he says. "I used to love hearing it when I was driving on the open road. It made me go 10 miles an hour faster."

Jim and his girlfriend, Diane, are fine karaoke singers. The former Raider athlete always brings the house down at the Flo-Jean and Doc's in Hamburg, New Jersey, when he belts out Toby Keith's "How Do You Like Me Now."

I run into Springsteen fans everywhere. At Krogh's, at Lake Mohawk, New Jersey, I sang some Bruce and found a table filled with Boss fans. They were getting ready to see him in the Meadowlands and one had a Bruce shirt on. I put extra effort into "Born To Run" and soon one of the guys was up next to me, singing into the microphone.

At Doctor Joseph Schwartz' place (dentist), Sally, who cleans my teeth, also was getting ready to see Springsteen, August 30, 2003. Sally is a personable lady who can bust chops with the best of them. I know it sounds strange, but I don't dread the appointments and instead enjoy talking with Sally, Barbara, Deana and Dr. Schwartz. "I saw Springsteen back in 1984," Doctor Schwartz said one day. "He put on a great concert."

Lately, the Guam nightmare that I kept having, is being replaced by another dream. I am sitting at a bar and I look in front of me and see that I have been drinking beer instead of soda. I eye my mug and see that about half of the contents have been ingested by me. It was an honest mistake, I think. I ordered beer and drank it before thinking clearly. I figure it's too late for me, now. I drank that dreaded beer and am no longer alcohol free.

I face the dilemma of whether or not to finish this mug. Do I stop drinking now? Do I order another beer and try getting straight tomorrow? How much alcohol can I have before it threatens my life again? I feel total relief wash over my body when I awaken to find that it was only a dream, I have not slipped and my official date of sobriety is still July 3, 2000.

I find it hard to actually comprehend how much my life has changed. I am happily married to the greatest lady in the world, enjoy covering sports and entertaining at night. I have met fabulous people including karaoke company owners Mary and Joe plus disk spinner John from Hi - Note Karaoke (Tom Quick Inn, Milford, Flo-Jean, Port Jervis and Best Western, Westfall Township, Pa.), Loody, a pretty and classy lady from Loody and Pat's Karaoke (Krogh's, Lake Mohawk, New Jersey and Mama Roni's, Branchville, New Jersey), plus Bill and Cindy of Bill's Karaoke (Doc's, Hamburg, New Jersey).

I sing alongside some decent people and performing seems a natural fit for me. I am a late bloomer at some things and this is one of them. I know in my heart, I could have sung in a rock 'n' roll band way back in the 1960s. The opportunity just never did materialize.

I never figured I'd ever enjoy such a wide range of music. While I sing some non-Bruce songs such as "Margaritaville", "City Of New Orleans", "The Wanderer", "Lyin' Eyes" and "Eve Of Destruction", there are all types of tunes out there.

A guy nicknamed "Spike" sidles into Flo-Jean's or Doc's and one look at him tells you he is a weight lifter. Although short in stature, he has bulging arms and a confident demeanor. He doesn't back down from confrontations should they arise, but takes on a very different personality when he steps to the microphone and belts out Meat Loaf, Bon Jovi or AC/DC material. There are all types who drift into the karaoke lounges and bars of our land. Jay and his wife dance to some of the music at the Tom Quick, Bill Heckman aces "Daddy's Home", Frankie at The Black Thorn, is a born rocker (used to live near The Boss), Katie, the lovely bartender at this bar, digs "Thunder Road" and Mark, who has done some

DJ work, likes Springsteen and music in general.

Since becoming sober, I have formed some solid relationships. One is with my brother-in-law Jeff, a merchant marine type. He is another weight lifter who is in superb shape. When he isn't out to sea, he is home with my sister and his pride and joy, Willow, his chocolate lab. When not at the house, he is more than likely taking his intelligent dog up to Jeff Masurack's garage. The other Jeff shares my brother-in-law's love of Willow.

My brother-in-law has seen me at my best and at my worst. One Sunday morning, I sat shaking at his kitchen table as I went through the agony of waiting for noon to arrive. There was no beer in the house and I was absolutely desperate. He had some wine in the fridge and so I asked if I could have some. He surrendered the alcohol with a look in his eyes that told me he understood the hell I was going through. I do believe I have earned a great degree of respect from him. When I see him in a store or restaurant he gives me a look that speaks volumes. I know he is glad that I found the right way out, before it was too late.

Back on March 30, 2003, in Lancaster, New York, (near Buffalo), I came to the door of one John VanGraafeiland III. It had been nearly 17 years since I had seen Van and I knew he had been through some serious health problems. His girlfriend, Teri, answered the door. Van lives upstairs.

I had spoken to Teri a few times on the telephone and she impressed me as a mature and gracious person. I already knew, that she was the best thing that ever came into my Air Force buddy's life.

Van was upstairs and Teri said she would call him down. "He is going to be so surprised to see you," she said. "He has been through so much and has lost some weight. I am so glad you came."

I figure I know my old roommate as much as anyone. He treats any crisis with a low key demeanor. Many times over the years, I recall that day of the surprise room inspection at Plattsburgh and Van still high as a kite in his bunk. While I scurried around the barracks trying to paste our room together, Van simply laughed. "Screw them if they can't take a joke," he had said.

Van is not a quitter. He had become thin and obviously had been to hell and back. His spirit was still intact though and that winning smile of his, appeared the second he walked into the living room where Teri, her mom, Joyce, and I waited. The two Airmen, who initially didn't like each other, hugged like long lost brothers. His soft voice (I swear he still has a southern tinge to it) was identical to what I remembered.

He had on a hat like Robert Redford wore in "The Sting", plus a blue and white athletic outfit and white sneakers. "Well I'll be," he managed to blurt out. "I don't believe it. Where's Chris?"

Van had suffered from pneumonia, a fungus infection and emphysema. The only thing I could think of, at the time, was the song "Only

The Good Die Young" by Billy Joel, and quickly decided that Van was too much of a rebel to be taken from us this early. I do believe that my old sidekick has many trails left to blaze. He, like I, had cheated death. Who could have known what the two of us would have in our futures, way back in the 1960s in Plattsburgh?

"Back in January, John had a fire upstairs," Joyce said. "Yes," Van said, "I tried to put it out with a spray bottle. I saw that this idea wasn't such a great one and later the firemen were here." This is vintage Van, for sure. "It was no big deal, they got it out," he explained.

Teri looked from across the room and shook her head in amazement. "John, we were outside, freezing in the middle of the night. Do you remember that?" Van shot that smile at me again and predictably enough said "they put it out fast and then we went back inside."

Van continues to have a heart as big as all outdoors. He gives of his time to mow neighborhood lawns in the nice weather. This charismatic person, is probably known throughout his area of New York state as "John, that guy who helped us out."

These three people were a delight to be around on this memorable afternoon. I was there for about an hour or so and then had to head back south toward Salamanca and then Jamestown, New York. The session ended too fast, but then again, I knew it would. I hugged Teri and Van very tightly and realized that decent people in this lifetime, aren't a run of the mill and routine thing. Van and I shook hands a couple of more times before the three of us walked outside to my waiting Pontiac Sunfire.

"Take care of my buddy," I had said to Teri when Van wasn't around. But I already knew that this loving and caring person would be there for him. I drove away with misty eyes and a confused mind. My heart was bursting with pride though, at the man who didn't know the word "quit", the man who has had my respect for over 35 years. If I ever had an older brother, I would have wanted him to have the heart and compassion of John VanGraafeiland III.

Sometimes I'm not the sharpest quill on the porcupine. Although I have lost a few bucks at the Indian casino at Salamanca, I would inevitably show up on the doorstep again, ready to at least get even.

I had to smile at this on the way down the road to Salamanca. It reminded me of an old joke about the Lone Ranger and Tonto. I heard it somewhere, maybe on television. It is no secret that the Indian Tonto (Jay Silverheels) of the Lone Ranger show in the 1950s, would go to town from time to time and wound up getting beaten up. "You would think after awhile, Tonto wouldn't go back to town," the punch line says.

I really enjoy the Salamanca area and as luck would have it, I won a few dollars that night. I figure I am only down around 40 bucks at this professionally run establishment, nestled in the pretty New York State mountains.

After I began singing some karaoke, I happened upon a couple of bars in the Jamestown area that had singing at night. A favorite one is Stravato's, which has karaoke Thursday through Sunday evenings, beginning at 9:30 p.m. Rich, who spins the disks and is a fine singer, does a phenomenal job as a charismatic DJ. He possesses personality, humor, a great taste in music and a refreshing knowledge of rock and roll's history. Although many years younger than me, he has become an authority, by pouring himself into the history and roots of rock and trivia.

Rich is very familiar with the New Jersey shore background and current scene and so, Bruce Springsteen (native of New Jersey) is a subject he knows well. He smiled when I stepped to the microphone one night and belted out "Dancing In The Dark."

Another time, I started with Arlo Guthrie's "City Of New Orleans." When I was all finished, Rich picked up his microphone and said "great job, Bill. That is one of my favorite songs." I love this area of New York State (south western), out near Lake Erie, and the next time I head up that way, I'm sure he will be slipping the "City Of New Orleans" CD out of its holder.

When Rich takes a break, Wayne does a fine job in his place. He sings along with such names as TJ, Debbie W., Barbara, Cowboy Willie and Ethel. TJ has a fine voice, Debbie has Creedence Clearwater Revival (CCR) down pat and Ethel is a delight to listen to. This dynamic redheaded lady can reach your emotions which such tunes as "Sad Movies" and my personal favorite of hers "You Light Up My Life." She used to play in a country and western band years ago and has made a singing comeback. The comeback is successful with a capital "S".

Chris and I saw our lives change dramatically back on December 8, 2002. That is the night that we experienced the dazzling Bruce Springsteen and the E street Band, live, at the Charlotte Coliseum (North Carolina). It had been four months since Bruce began his "The Rising" tour in East Rutherford, New Jersey. Our plan was to fly down to Charlotte, drive to Gatlinburg, Tennessee (to experience Dollywood), hit South Carolina to see Dawn and back up to see The Boss.

This trip began on a sour and dangerous note. The forecast for Charlotte and into Tennessee showed freezing rain and slick roads. Southerners aren't used to this type of driving and they panic on the area highways. Since salt trucks aren't commonplace in the south, people slide all over hell's creation. Fender benders and chain reaction accidents are the order of the day.

I tried making Tennessee in our rental car but it wasn't meant to be. I saw cars and trucks sliding into guardrails and into each other. People were sliding past exit ramps and into ditches. In early December, this area was to experience ice storms that would cut power, strand people and paralyze cities.

I had seen enough by the time we were a few miles past Spartanburg,

South Carolina. I got off an exit at about five miles per hour and we parked the car. We turned around and headed back to a Spartanburg Holiday Inn Express for the night. The place was beautiful, complete with great coffee and internet access. When it was time, we drove back to North Carolina and accommodations a few miles from the Charlotte Coliseum.

It was our first live exposure to The Boss and he blew our doors off. We hoped and prayed that the show would go on, although Charlotte was in a state of emergency. It always seems that Bruce comes through with a needed boost, when people are down or depressed.

Outside, people tried to cope with the adverse weather conditions that had turned their worlds upside down. Prior to the concert, North Carolina Governor Mike Easley went on a three-city tour to survey the damage from one of the worst winter storms in state history.

Hundreds of thousands of customers were blacked out by the major ice storm. Temperatures climbed into the 40s to help melt the ice. The storm had taken a path from the southern Plains into the Northeast December 4 and at least 29 deaths were blamed on the storm and its aftermath. More than 200 people sought medical help for carbon monoxide poisoning. Over 300 National Guard volunteers fanned out to knock on doors. December 6, 2,028 people stayed in 67 shelters across the state as temperatures hit the teens and 20s. Over a million utility customers (homes and businesses) remained without power for days.

People buzzed inside the Charlotte Coliseum while they waited for a music legend to take center stage. When he and the band made their appearance at about 8:22 p.m., the joint went nuts.

Bruce began by moving up to the microphone and belting out the cover song of the CD and namesake of this tour "The Rising." This song is The Boss' musical response to the September 11, 2001 terrorist attacks, and was released by Columbia Records on July 30, 2002.

It seems whenever Bruce decides to head out on tour, he has a purpose in mind. He talks in a laid back and clear voice that touches people from eight to 80. This tour would go on to become the sixth biggest of 2002 (and remember he never started until August 7) by generating $42.6 million in 39 shows. The album (CD) was the first by Bruce and the E Street Band in 15 years.

Physically fit and sometimes exhibiting his oratory skills, Bruce captivated the Charlotte crowd. He was assessing the emotional fallout that was connected to the September 11 events. He is a street poet who shows raw emotions and he has a keen talent for shifting those emotions to those listening to his material.

Springsteen fans, many of who had left darkened, cold homes, banded together to appreciate arguably the finest performer in rock history. While he performed "Candy's Room" and the tear-jerking terrorist-related tune "Your Missing" early in the set list, it was the ninth song that had the crowd going wild.

"Darlington County" got the folks revved up for the rest of the show. He went on to include "Badlands", "She's The One", "Where The Bands Are", "Dancing In The Dark" and crowd favorite "Born To Run" (1975 song that really ignited his career). He then delivered a raspy and powerful "Born In The USA." While some people figure that song is a patriotic one, it really explains the feelings and repercussions of war and hardship (Viet Nam).

There is a very humorous side to Springsteen. He gets big, wide eyes and a look of confusion on his face as he exhibits that brand of humor. He also delights in teasing not only his band mates, but the crowds that flock to see him. He enjoys the reactions of fans and plays off them expertly. It is as if you are hanging out in his living room one-on-one, rather than being in a stadium or arena.

He was a master at bringing wide smiles to the faces of concert goers on this particular night. While Charlotte and the surrounding area was licking its wounds from a horrible ice storm, Bruce hit them with this gem. "I know why you are all here tonight," he said. "You came for the heat and electricity." This brought the house down.

Bruce did supply his own brand of "electricity" in the form of "Bruce juice" that changed attitudes and united all as one. He sang "Land Of Hope And Dreams" and wound up the show with a spectacular version of "Ramrod" followed by "Santa Claus Is Coming To Town."

I am one of those people who instantly became a fan. When you listen to Bruce, Clarence Clemons' saxophone, Soozie Tyrell's violin, or Max Weinberg's drumming, there is no turning back. Chris and I had been entertained to the highest level in Charlotte. We boarded our flight back to Allentown-Bethlehem-Easton's Lehigh Airport (Pennsylvania), as enlightened people. We were now Bruce fans (not groupies) for life.

Five days later, we drove north to Albany, New York, about 120 miles from home, to see Springsteen and the band perform at the Pepsi Arena. We parked in a garage and walked down to the show. The Boss didn't disappoint by tossing out "My Love Will Not Let You Down", "Darkness On The Edge Of Town", "No Surrender" and "This Hard Land." Again, "Ramrod" was a crowd-pleaser as the band marched around, single file, while blowing our doors off with their musical genius.

We became full-fledged "Brucers" in early March. For concert number three, we attempted to score some tickets for Atlantic City, New Jersey, but that proved to be fruitless. Loyal Bruce fans were all pissed off because the ticket availability was nearly non-existent. Big money people from the casinos and the like, scarfed up tickets while countless Springsteen fans came up empty. This is what happened to us, and we were annoyed to say the least.

One day, Chris sidled up to me with these words "what about Jacksonville?" This came out of left field and I didn't know what she meant. "Ummmm, lets see, that is in Florida," I said. The way she looked at me, told the story. She was serious and was thinking about nailing tickets for Bruce at the Jacksonville Coliseum on March 4.

While Atlantic City just didn't pan out, heading down to Florida would serve as a dual purpose for me. I had always wondered what Florida was really like. I had seen it in television movies and read stories about the place. People from up where I live, go down there during brutal winter weather. I pictured the palm trees, laid back lifestyles and a warm breeze coming off the ocean. "Go for it," I said.

With a "we come this way but once" attitude, the two of us made arrangements to head down to Jacksonville, Florida, and would be attending the March 4 concert at the Jacksonville Coliseum.

Florida had been calling me since way back in 1969. This is the place that "Ratso" Rizzo never got the chance to hang his hat. Ratso, played by Dustin Hoffman in the 1969 movie "Midnight Cowboy", was a con man who was trapped and hustling, in the seedy sections of New York City.

Joe Buck (Jon Voight) was an out-of-towner cowboy, who befriended Rizzo. Ratso, seriously sick, was persuaded by Buck to travel by bus with him to Florida. Rizzo was decked out in a Florida type shirt, near the back of the bus, heading south as the movie soundtrack "Everybody's Talkin" by Nilsson, played in the background. Ratso Rizzo never saw Florida, because he perished on the bus. Hey, now you don't have to see the movie.

The words and music to the song were intoxicating in a positive kind of way and I had imagined myself going south to Florida. "I'm going where the sun keeps shining, through the pouring rain." After nearly 56 years of life, I touched Florida soil on March 1, 2003. I watched the flat land and greenery come up to meet the airplane and my heart skipped a few beats. So this is the place that Ratso never got to see.

While my curiosity about this place just had to be satisfied, like a nagging itch that had to be scratched, there was another major reason why I wound up here. That reason was Bruce Frederick Springsteen.

"The Boss" was back to perform in Jacksonville for the first time in 27 years. This talented, dynamic and dedicated rocker had a rugged New Jersey shore fiber. His songs, sung in his trademark raspy voice, told of love and loss, overcoming odds, of never giving in and finding a better life. Born September 23, 1949, at Monmouth Memorial Hospital (New Jersey), the son of Adele and the late Douglas Springsteen was to reach rock stardom. He entered the Rock and Roll Hall of Fame, in Cleveland, Ohio, on March 16, 1999. His musical genius in writing, pleasing twang and awesome guitar playing, brought him here to the land of hope and dreams.

Bono, of the group U2, gave the keynote address in Cleveland that night, and said "Bruce owns our heart." From "Glory Days" to "Dancing

In The Dark" Bruce is the real deal, the complete package. By March of 2003, he had over 350 songs to his credit.

Chris and I accomplished our mission in reaching Florida. We loved Jacksonville and marveled at the history and romantic charm of cities such as St. Augustine. We walked the white sands of Bradenton Beach, hung out in Daytona Beach during "bike week" and saw one of the greatest musicians that ever lived.

At the start of the Florida concert, Bruce joked with the crowd by asking "where's all that sunshine?" It was raining outside, but for a jam packed Jacksonville Coliseum crowd, there wasn't a cloud in the sky. Everything was going to be okay.

Bruce has been called arguably the best live performer in the history of rock. He used to give four hour (and longer) performances throughout the land. He idolized Elvis Presley and once, in his mid 20s (in 1976), leaped a fence at Graceland, hoping to see Presley.

A guy like Springsteen comes along once in a lifetime. He tossed out his heart on a silver platter like 8-pound test line rippling the calm waters of a lake or river. I was snagged, hook, line and sinker.

I was on my way to becoming a full-fledged "Brucer" when I attended a fantastic pre-concert party the night before the show, at Jacksonville's London Bridge restaurant. The concert is where I officially joined the "Bruce Club" for a lifetime. We are a legion of loyal and diehard Springsteen fans forever. I not only dig his music, I believe in what Bruce stands for. He is an inspiration to countless people here and abroad.

Bruce Springsteen is unselfish, talented and most of all sincere. If he comes back out on another tour in the future, and you can't get off work, or don't have money for tickets, here is the answer to the dilemma. Take out a loan and call in sick. I promise you won't be sorry.

I started delving into Springsteen's music and his fans before the Jacksonville show. Chris found a site on the internet that brought people together on a message board. We found one that revolved around the upcoming Jacksonville show and I was off to the races. The thread was started on December 18, 2002, by a real nice guy (I met him) who went by the name "I Spybeeper." In time, I was writing and reading things on the board and getting more excited by the second, about heading to Florida.

A fellow from Jacksonville (formerly of Edison, New Jersey), with the board nickname "Turnpike 64" was a fantastic organizer of the party that was to take place at the London Bridge, a restaurant-bar in the downtown section. The evening of March 3, 2003, about 200 of us "Brucers" congregated at the site. Two of the owners, Martin and Virginia, smiled continually as we drank, ate, watched Bruce videos, listened to his music and sang Springsteen songs.

Most of us bought black and white London Bridge tee shirts that were inscribed "The Rising By The River Tour Jacksonville, Florida" and "The Boss Returns 3-4-03." There is an American flag on the lower right front and numbers in a black flair pen's writing is there too. Of 200 shirts dispensed that night, my shirt has the number "88" on it. The shirts are unique, in the respect that only so many were made. Many of us, wear the shirt to other Bruce concerts in and out of the country.

The money taken in from tee shirt sales went to feed the hungry of Jacksonville. For years now, it has been Bruce's passion to help those less fortunate than himself. Whatever city he happens to arrive in, he donates big money to the local food banks and encourages concert goers to give of themselves to help.

The Jacksonville group collected $4,000 (which translates into about $32,000 in canned goods, etc.) and presented a check to the Second Harvest Food Bank in Jacksonville. A representative of the group picked up the money at the London Bridge the night of the party. "Turnpike" had these words to say on that occasion. "We are fulfilling some of our dreams and will be feeding hungry folks we never met."

"Turnpike Mike" Dugan turns 40 years old on May 3, 2004. He is one of the most unselfish and genuine people I have ever met in my life. He helped out-of-towners with hotel arrangements (Omni Hotel), and pulled people from different sections of the country together at a dynamite Bruce concert.

"The first concert I went to, I swear Bruce was singing to me," says Mike, who is in management for Maxwell House Coffee in Jacksonville. Mike, his wife, Sharon and children, Mickey, 8 and Chelsea, 13, are hardcore Springsteen fans and Mike has been to at least 24 Bruce shows, so far. Mickey sat on his dad's shoulders in "the pit" (close to the stage) at Jacksonville and actually interacted with Springsteen. The look in Bruce's eyes told you that he enjoyed the presence of one Mickey Dugan.

Mike's father was a supervisor for the New Jersey Turnpike and one snowy night, Bruce drove up to the toll. "The toll collector called into my dad and said 'guess who I got at the toll?' My father told him to hold Bruce there. Mike now has a New Jersey Turnpike ticket with Bruce's signature on it and a note that says "happy holidays" to him.

Dugan, a former second baseman and New Jersey all-state baseball selection (1982), remembers Bruce filming "Glory Days" in a bar called "Maxwell's" in Hoboken. He spent 12 hours trying to get into a closed bar, didn't get in, but heard Bruce sing. By this time, Mike was already bitten with the Springsteen bug.

"I saw Bruce in 1983 in Greensboro, North Carolina, and we chartered Piedmont Airlines," Mike notes. "The pilot of the plane, played Bruce songs over the airline speakers."

The London Bridge party was just great. Gail, from the Jacksonville thread, and her husband, Bill, had the idea to get a shirt to Bruce, and have it signed for an auction. Bruce signed the shirt in Duluth, Georgia, sent it down to Jacksonville, and "Red Headed Woman" won the drawing.

People from all walks of life have become friends because of Bruce's music. Board names like Raisncaine, Nightgirl, Lake 612, Boss Luvsda Steelers, Tn Fan, Little Frog (our daughter), McCarthy, Red Headed Woman, Miami Silvio and ghalti, fill the Jacksonville thread. Bridge Brother, Sunfire (my wife), Lesluii, NY Nick77, No Retreat, Har-MonyCa, BillyM, The Shot, First In Line and of course I-Spy beeper (the Jacksonville thread's originator), all have a common denominator. And that denominator is Bruce Springsteen.

"We accomplish a lot as a team," Turnpike Mike Dugan says. "We met and remained friends. We are like a family. Bruce was the catalyst and now we're growing together through sicknesses, reunions, concerts and births. I can't tell you how many times a person on the Jacksonville thread comforted another in need. There have even been trips to other states to help out."

Mike reflects on what life means to him. "I love my wife and love my family," he says. "The Jacksonville thread isn't an addiction or phase. It's just pure enjoyment to stop in, say hello, and go back to your daily life. It's just like stopping by a coffee shop or tavern." Mike likes songs such as 1978's "Darkness On The Edge Of Town."

"Turnpike", the solidly-built guy with the awesome smile, is one of the most sincere people I have ever had the pleasure to meet and befriend. He has glowing qualities and is an inspirational leader. Possessing compassion and heart, he is a shining example and has very similar beliefs as "The Boss" when it comes to life and helping out his fellow man. In Mike Dugan's case, to know him is to love him.

While the Charlotte concert on December 8 was a ground-breaker for us, and Albany added to the Springsteen mystique, it was Jacksonville where Chris and I jumped in with all four feet. When we saw Jacksonville leaving our eyesight in the rear view mirror, we would take our experiences on the road for 17 more Boss concerts.

Our ambitious itinerary took us to the following locations in 2003: Crystal Palace, England (May 26 and 27), Giants Stadium in the Meadowlands, New Jersey (July 17, 18 and 24, plus August 28 and 31), PNC Park, Pittsburgh, Pennsylvania (August 6), Lincoln Financial Field, Philadelphia, Pennsylvania (August 11), Fed-Ex Field, Landover, Maryland (September 13), Keenan Stadium at the University of North Carolina, Chapel Hill (September 14), Rentschler Field, East Hartford, Connecticut (September 18), Six Flags, Darien Lake, New York (September 20), Comerica Park, Detroit, Michigan (September 21), Invesco Field, Denver, Colorado (September 25) and Shea Stadium, Queens, New York (October 1 and 4). The tour ended at Shea Stadium with powerful musical legend Bob Dylan as a special guest (on October 4).

Back at Jacksonville in March, Bruce created an electrical connection bctwccn himsclf and his loyal fans that is hard to explain. The day after the concert, I described what I felt and saw, to my fellow "Brucers" on the Springtseen board's Jacksonville thread.

"The Boss was in town last night," I said. "He rocked Jacksonville with his raw, teasing New Jersey charm. He slapped hands with Turnpike Mike's son, Mickey (on dad's shoulders in the pit), gave some beads to Mickey, put them over his head and continued singing. He slid across the stage on his knees twice and held the microphone out for us to contribute."

I began finishing my thoughts like this. "The Boss delivered time after time with his trademark charisma, professionalism, impish sense of humor and genuine smile. I will remember Bruce leaping up on the piano, sharing the microphone with his wife, Patti, and band member Steve Van Zandt. I see him grinning ear to ear as he slides gracefully across the floor on his knees…in shape, fulfilled and involved in enriching the lives of others."

And then the finish. "He is a rock and roll icon…a national treasure. We at the Jacksonville concert regarded him as a friend. He seems like a buddy that lives just down the street. Thanks for being you, Bruce. Thanks for the memories."

The concert had lasted two hours and 35 minutes and we entered the Florida night knowing we had seen the best performer since "The King" did his thing. Our seats had been good ones (fourth row, Clarence's side of the stage).

Florida Times-Union newspaper music writer Nick Marino was also impressed with Bruce's performance. He educated readers about what The Boss was all about.

"Whether at football games or rock concerts, Jacksonville audiences have a tendency toward sedateness," Marino wrote. "Any Jags season ticket holder or regular concert-goer can testify to that."

Marino went on. "But the roar that came forth as Bruce Springsteen and the E Street Band finished playing Born To Run Tuesday night at the sold-out Coliseum was nothing less than a soul cry. It may have been the loudest sound I've ever heard from a Jacksonville crowd at any public gathering."

Marino made his feelings known. "People went nuts for this show. I saw grown men hugging in the aisles. I saw air guitar. I saw a group of fans in the seats unfurl a giant American flag, and I saw a fan on the floor waving the flag of Brazil. I saw a father bend over to his young son and point to the stage, as if directing the boy to the messiah himself."

For Turnpike and his son, it was an unforgettable evening. "Bruce hugged Mickey," Mike says. "He (Mickey) had seen him (Bruce) three times already and hooks up with him every time. Last time, Bruce said 'I know you.'"

Bruce is for the underdog and that comes through in his songs. He wants folks to rise up when things look bleak and depressing. He wants you to find some kind of faith and hope. "Perseverance" is The Boss' middle name as he is no stranger to struggles. In the early days, it seemed nobody was interested in the young musician, Bruce Springsteen, and his New Jersey sound. My how times have changed.

There are stark messages in Springsteen's music. He gives free expression and is a throwback to the 1960s when my generation asked "how come?" He is a live and let live kind of guy who is real, down to earth and genuine. He is a complex person and is a deep thinker. Bruce is a pure rocker who leaves everything out on the stage. He illuminates the rock and roll world with his refreshing attitude and style. He is known to tease his audiences from time to time. "I think it's quittin' time," he often says during a concert. He does this to stir up the audience and get them even more involved in the show. "I think it's time to go back to the hotel and eat some friend chicken," he sometimes quips.

Springsteen has reportedly been known to show up at his children's schools for meetings (three children), goes to stores and shops just like an average person, and appears at roadside bars to relax and maybe play a few songs.

Decked out in his St. Christopher's medal and with a left wrist filled with colorful bracelets, he demonstrates that "it ain't no sin to be alive."

He generously donates money and time to food banks at different stops on his tour. At Jacksonville, it was the Second Harvest Food Bank that received some help. At each concert, Bruce tells his crowds that workers for food banks are in the establishment and to "help them out any way you can."

I was in heaven in Florida. The white paved highways, palm trees, blue water and mild temperatures caused a relaxed and content feeling. You could zip along the road at 70 miles per hour and not worry. I would often see cars parked in the median on spongy, green grass. I figured somehow these vehicles ran off the road and sank into the soft ground.

Bradenton Beach and its white sand was something right out of a postcard. People built sand castles near the water and cars were parked between palm trees. "So this is what Florida is all about," I said to myself. "I bet these people laugh their asses off while we are getting pounded with snow, up north."

At the London Bridge, the night before the concert, Chris gazed over in front of where people sang on stage, and said "I know that guy over there. I saw him on television." I shrugged off the statement, but she persisted. "He was right in the front row, near Bruce, in Asbury Park, for that live morning television show that we saw."

Soon, my bride returned with Frank Holler, a well-known DJ. He had on the same shirt from that TV show and was the nicest guy in the world. "You knew every word to the songs," Chris marveled. "Well, I have seen

Bruce many times," Frank said. "In fact, I was a DJ and played lots of Bruce music in the early days."

Frank wasn't the only person we would meet from that TV show. There was a guy outside on the Asbury beach, in shades and baseball cap, who was singing with The Boss. After Jacksonville, we would be going way over to London, England and would be meeting colorful Jim McCarthy, who was in the London Bridge at the same time we were. We would also come across the jovial, good guy "Mac" in Philadelphia and at the Meadowlands.

Bruce, who has been known to encourage people to read the book "History Of The United States", had given us a fabulous concert at Jacksonville. He makes no bones about the fact that he strives to give people "a good night out." He has said that he hopes guys can bring their dates (or wives) to his concerts, and that his music can change how you feel about life. His music gets to people quickly and as he nods his head side to side, you can hear the tapping of feet on the floor or ground. He captured the music world with "Born To Run" in 1975 and has been a musical icon since. "Tramps like us...baby we were born to run."

The Jacksonville event renewed friendships and started others. We met so many Bruce fans who are still our friends to this day. In fact, NY Nick (originally from Syracuse, N.Y.) owns a bar in the Pensacola, Florida area (with his wife, Deb) and hundreds of us will be arriving there for a reunion on April 15, 16 and 17, 2004. One of the main organizers, along with Nick, is none other than the one and only Turnpike Mike.

Since way back in high school, my wife had been corresponding with a girl from England, named Mary. They had talked on the phone a couple of times, but never met eye to eye. That was about to come to a screeching halt in May of 2003.

Bruce was going to be playing over in the London area (Crystal Palace) for two nights, May 26 and 27. We knew his touring schedule and began plotting what would be the trip of a lifetime. I balked at first when I thought of taking an eight hour flight from New York to London. "It will be a big plane," Chris had said. "We will be there before you know it. And don't forget what Bruce said. 'We come this way but once'"

In 1964, when Chris was 16 years old, she experienced the wonder and excitement at the New York State Fair, near where Shea Stadium is. She went with parents Marion and Ernie and was impressed with what she saw.

Inside a pavilion, the Delaware Valley senior used a computer to spit out the name of a would- be pen pal from England. It was Parker's International Penfriend Program that matched up Chris and Mary. The friendship spanned nearly 39 years of letters. The fabulous friendship journey included marriages, births and deaths.

Mary Christine Saunders was in another area of the globe but the young girls hit it off right away. Although their cultures were somewhat different, they shared a love of cats and other things.

A miracle of sorts occurred on May 26, 2003, when Christine and Mary looked into each other's eyes for the first time at London's Gatwick Airport. Mary's husband, John Allchin, and she, had waited for us behind rope barriers.

Mary held a sign with our name on it, from that vantage point. Chris knew, even before seeing the sign, that the lady was Mary Allchin. "It's her. I just know it," Chris had said.

John showed us castles and other points of interest and we genuinely liked the couple. After being dropped off at our hotel (we would see each other again and Chris would get the grand tour, complete with dinner), we began exploring England.

We rode the trains to Victoria Station as we passed tidy homes made of clay, rock and thatched roofs. The houses were uniform and set close together, usually separated by fences. Most backyards had a small garden and place to park their small car.

Some of the towns we experienced included Canterbury (home of Canterbury Cathedral), Ashford, Faversham and East Croydon. We saw Big Ben in London and rock and rolled at a pair of Springsteen shows.

Chris went with the Allchins (I had a cold) and experienced English pubs, castles, a ride over the Thames River and the breathtaking sights and sounds of historical England.

She stood on the beach at the White Cliffs of Dover and collected some of the famous white pebbles. To the left, were ferries going to Paris, France. There was the Motorway Highway, where a Eurotrain will go under the English Channel and connect London with Paris.

The last time we saw Mary and John, was at the East Croydon train station. "I told myself not to cry," Chris said. "It happened so fast. But I know we will meet again."

The two shows in Crystal Palace were simply awesome, as Bruce and the band put on phenomenal performances. The Boss gave his customary 110 per cent and Crystal Palace came alive when he walked on stage. It is estimated that 44,000 saw the opening night show.

A delightful lady named Maxine plus England thread (Springsteen board) fellows AndrewNet and Andy C., led us through a maze of people and toward the stage. We were directly behind the pit, got within 70 feet of Bruce and he looked at us and smiled several times.

We had e-mailed Max a few times before actually meeting her at a pub called The Blue Bottle, just up the hill from Crystal Palace. This is where we also met McCarthy and his sidekick Miami Silvio.

We brought an American flag for Max and she proudly wore it on her head as we walked toward the stadium. Maxine was one of the classiest ladies I have ever met. She breathes Bruce Springsteen and she made the night even more magic.

What we saw that evening and the following one, was a national treasure. Bruce charmed the English people with his wit and intoxicating music and over 40,000 people seemed to become one.

This train carried saints and sinners...losers and winners. We had hopped aboard the Springsteen express and the engine was running smoothly and throwing out crackling energy and power. The train speeds down the track and if it stops, it's only to board new passengers, who quickly love this ride they are experiencing. We had wound up in the land of hope and dreams.

On the 26th, people lined up for blocks to get into the impressive stadium. Later, at his "house party" The Boss offered up songs including "Darlington County", "Thunder Road", "Badlands" and "Land Of Hope And Dreams."

Springsteen tee shirts of every color in the rainbow dotted the lush green countryside. People who had never met, traded Bruce stories as they walked down through a park to the stadium. The Boss hung upside down on the microphone stand and was the picture of perpetual motion. He got the crowd involved in "Mary's Place" and "Waitin' On A Sunny Day", and delivered a somber and emotional "Your Missing." All three songs are off "The Rising" CD.

During one of the songs, Bruce was running all over the place but darted behind some band members to get a mouthful of water. Soon saxophone player Clarence "Big Man" Clemons got a free shower from The Boss.

According to Bruce, a house party has to have certain ingredients. Two of those vital parts include being "righteous" and rising from your seat to stand. "Get off your English asses," Bruce joked, and the crowd went wild.

He closed both Monday and Tuesday's shows with a stirring "Dancing In The Dark" in which he jumped up and down on center stage with guitar in hand.

Tuesday (27th) Bruce began by walking out before the people all alone, and performing an acoustical version of "Born In The USA"

There were some changes in the set list including "Sherry Darling" and "Atlantic City." Bruce mocked seriousness many times, looking out into the crowd with brown eyes as big as pies. He slid on his knees, and indicated that Clarence was royalty. During a short version of "Rescue Me", he danced up behind his wife, Patti, displayed some animated movements and told the spectators "this works at home."

Earlier in the concert, fans started singing the beginning of a song, before Bruce did. Bruce twanged his guitar strings, stopped and said "let me start it." After doing so, he smiled and exclaimed "that's better."

After performing his sixth song, Bruce said "thank you, good evening. It's nice to spend another night in London. Anybody here last night?" When hands shot up and people said "me", he laughed and said "get outta here, come on. We'll play some different things."

For "Mary's Place" he said "alright get your voices ready" and prior to "Sherry Darling" he said "are you ready to sing?" He captured the primarily English audience with his wit and talent and nobody wanted the concert to end.

"Big man on the move. Big man walking. Please keep back 500 feet," Bruce teased Clarence during the playing of "Ramrod." Later, he began kidding with us that he was getting ready to leave for the hotel.

"I do believe that it is quittin' time. Yes it is. It's quittin' time right about now," he teased. VanZandt shot back "say it ain't so," and Bruce looked at him. "I think I hear Big Ben chiming, baby," Bruce went on. "Does Big Ben chime? Well I thought I heard it chiming."

Even the queen of England didn't escape Bruce on this evening. "I think the queen is in her pajamies and she has gone to bed, baby," he noted. On the subject of returning to his hotel room, he kidded that he was going back to the room and "watch some of those fine English adult films."

It proved to be a memorable evening. Max Weinberg had pounded his drums in a stirring solo during "Born To Run", and Bruce had delivered a powerful and dynamic performance. "If it ain't quittin' time, Steve, I wanna know what time it is. What time is it?," he had exclaimed earlier. Then he answered his own question, "it's Boss time."

Bruce tossed out 25 songs on May 27 and after "Dancing In The Dark", said "thank you London. We love you. We'll be seeing you."

From "Lonesome Day" to "Seven Nights To Rock", Bruce had been on fire all night. His loyal followers had been treated to an extraordinary show. Suddenly, they were hit with reality. The show was finished. All the anticipation and months of waiting was over. The Boss had taken them on a wild roller coaster ride and that ride had concluded.

The sight of tears rolling down cheeks, signified that this big occasion was now history.

I walked back up to the Blue Bottle and sat at an outdoor table. Soon McCarthy stopped by and was rapping with some English men and trying to talk them into coming to America for Meadowlands shows in July and August.

As we flew back from London to LaGuardia Airport in New York, Chris and I realized we had been to the top of the mountain. We had met the Allchins, experienced England and seen Bruce twice, all on the same trip. During all of this, we kept in touch with our oldest daughter, Tracie, from an internet café in London and she was rapidly becoming a Springsteen fan.

Bruce had launched The Rising tour at Continental Airlines Arena in East Rutherford, New Jersey, on August 6th. That arena is located on 750 acres of land at the 450 million dollar Meadowlands Sports Complex (includes Giants Stadium, eight miles from the George Washington Bridge).

The name of the indoor facility was changed from the Brendan Byrne Arena (after a former governor of New Jersey) on January 1, 1996.

It was Bruce Springsteen who was the first musician to play here, officially christening Brendan Byrne Arena back in the summer of 1981, when he performed the first of six sold out shows there. On July 17, 2003, Chris and I were bound for Giants Stadium for the first of 10 sold out Springsteen shows. "The Rising" had won three Grammy awards in February and now The Boss was bringing his incredible show to his native New Jersey, where he is worshipped by throngs of loyal fans.

Bruce had performed 44 times in the arena and six times at Giants Stadium, before July 17. Now, 1,100 part-time employees would be hired and working each of the 10 nights. There would be a 175,000 square foot boardwalk area next to Giants Stadium where refreshment stands, souvenirs, Ferris wheel, carnival games, beach volleyball, music and Bruce Springsteen Karaoke would be. This is where I would sing "Born To Run" in front of over 1,000 Bruce fans (karaoke).

The blacktop surrounding Giants Stadium was transformed into a gigantic tailgate party, the warm night of the 17th. We were to meet many friends we had seen in Jacksonville and some we would meet for the first time. At an RV (tailgate party organized by Turnpike Mike, of course) we met a delightful Kanie for the first time. She had come all the way from Australia. We renewed friendships with No Retreat, Nightgirl, Lake 612, Red Headed Woman, MonyCa, NY Nick, McCarthy, Miami Silvio, Spy, Gail and Bill plus met Rosie, a lady from Pennsylvania. Mike's wife, Sharon, brother Darren, and Bridge Brother, were also among the folks that listened to great Springsteen songs, ate hot dogs, burgers and sausage and drank, before and after Bruce performed.

All I can say about the five Meadowlands shows we saw, is that after seeing Bruce, you could win millions of dollars in the lottery and it would be a downer.

On the 17th Bruce was relaxed, loose and smiling. He did the upside down microphone stand act again, and performed for just under three hours in front of more than 50,000 people. We had good seats in Section 129 and the place really rocked.

Bruce mentioned that his friend and fellow rocker Joe Grushecky (from Pittsburgh) would be playing in the Stone Pony two nights later. He then brought fans to their knees with "Born To Run", "No Surrender", "Thunder Road", "Rosalita" and "Dancing In The Dark."

Bruce, in a vest and sporting his bracelets, had gotten the record-breaking 10-night engagement off on the right foot. There is no show on earth like a passionate Springsteen show. He sings of hot cars, even hotter girls, New Jersey shore life, dying factory cities, heartbreak, overcoming adversity and odds, faith, hope and the promised land. Some

401

say that when Elvis died, Bruce kept the music alive. I concur wholeheartedly.

On July 17, he had mentioned how great it was to be back in New Jersey. He talked about the humidity, the stadium boardwalk and how folks should take the time to drive down to a revitalized Asbury Park.

When it was over, we walked back to the RV. While passing the parked cars, vans and trucks, we heard every imaginable Bruce song in the world. Our Jacksonville crowd began to dwindle as vehicles snaked out of all the parking lots at this fabulous complex in the swamps of Jersey. Turnpike Mike kept on singing, fighting the late night tiredness. He still had South Carolina looming in front of him before returning to home in Florida. I thought about how strange life could be, with all its ups and downs. Christine and I had enjoyed Bruce's Meadowlands show. I watched Mike, his wife and his kids, so happy as a family. Soon it was over. Chris, Red Headed Woman and I hopped in the car and returned to our hotel. I fell asleep with "Dancing In The Dark" pervading my head.

I awakened with unbridled happiness. It was a new day and we'd be seeing The Boss again, that evening. He had opened his Meadowlands shows July 15th and so we had been to the second event, the night before. Back home, Dawn and one of her children, little Brooke, had arrived from South Carolina for a visit, on July 13, and were staying at Tracie's home. We knew when we headed back up the road, both of our children were back in the area where they grew up.

It was estimated that in the 10 nights Bruce played Giants Stadium, he cleared about a million dollars a show. He drew about 55,000 fans a night, and the tickets averaged out at just about 70 bucks each . Reportedly, tee shirt sales were projected to reach the $700,000 mark per show. It was Bruce's first time back at Giants Stadium since 1985 and the glowing smile on his face, told everyone how happy he was to be back in New Jersey.

While Springsteen belted out 25 song a night at Crystal Palace, he sang 24 the night of the 17th and 26 on the 18th. That second perform-ance was another great one (as all Bruce appearances are). His facial expressions and kidding was infectious fun that spread into the audience. It had rained at the start of the concert and Bruce began by delivering "Who'll Stop The Rain", a Creedence Clearwater Revival tune.

It was prior to this performance, that I had my day in the sun, singing in front of over 1,000 fans at the Bruce Springsteen Karaoke, sponsored by Q104.3 FM in Manhattan. Jonathan Clarke was master of ceremonies and I got along with him well. Singing in front of more than 500 people in the afternoon and twice as many that night, was something I will never forget. I still hear Clarke's words "this guy sounded the most like Bruce, today" and then I began looking around for someone to come forward. I had only been singing karaoke for 36 days, but the adrenalin put me over the top. There was no time to experience a bout of nerves and the three young girls who jumped up on stage and sang with me, made my day. One gave me a kiss in front of God and everyone.

On the 18th, The Boss was to fire up a three hour show. After singing "Something In The Night", he said "welcome…raining out in Jersey. That's nothing, just slows you down a bit." Later he talked about downtown Asbury Park and how it was reviving. He spoke of the Community Food Bank in New Jersey and how any help they could get, would be appreciated.

That evening, Bruce tossed in some different songs from the night before, including "The Ties That Bind", "My Love Will Not Let You Down", "Something In The Night", "You Can Look But You Better Not Touch", "She's The One", "Racing In The Street", "Cadillac Ranch", "96 Tears" (with Garland Jeffries), "Bobby Jean", "Glory Days", "Hungry Heart", and "The Detroit Medley", which included "Devil With The Blue Dress On", a Mitch Ryder and the Detroit Wheels song.

After delivering "My City Of Ruins", Bruce was serious when he said he had to "make my public service announcement." The Boss had written "Born In The USA" back in the 1980s and most people figured this was a patriotic song that reflected Springsteen's love for America. While Bruce makes no bones about the fact that he is patriotic, he had tried to point out the injustice and attitudes regarding the Vietnam war, a senseless war that many figure never should have taken place.

This July 18, 2003 announcement, which he gave at many of "The Rising Tour" shows, gave his opinion on the war in Iraq.

"We get all kinds of different people coming up to the shows," he noted. "People with all kinds of different political beliefs…and we welcome all." He continued, "there's been a lot of questions raised recently about the forthrightness of our government and I think that playing with the truth, has been a part of both Democratic and Republican administrations."

The Boss indicated that masking the truth during wartime is always wrong and noted that real lives were at stake. He said sons and daughters were asked to die for their country and that it is our "sacred trust as citizens" to demand accountability from our leaders. He said it was "our job as Americans" and that it is "the American way." He capped the statement with the words "so may the truth will out" and then blasted out "The Land Of Hope And Dreams." He also gave us stirring renditions of "Rosalita" and a show-concluding "Dancing In The Dark."

Dawn and Brooke came to stay at our house for awhile on July 22 and two days later, we were back at the Meadowlands. When I got a chance to baby sit Brooke, she stood in her play pen, smiled and "danced" while we watched an October VCR tape of the Barcelona, Spain concert. When Bruce sang, little Brooke cooed happily. At less than 15 months of age, Brooke Elaine may have been one of the youngest Springsteen fans on this earth.

Back on the 18th, Bruce had ended his performance by saying "we love you, New Jersey, see you next week." On the 24th, we headed back down to New Jersey and pulled into the vast parking lot that surrounds Giants Stadium. The big stadium, which seats over 70,000 for football games, sat in its majestic glory with a big Springsteen banner attached to the east side of the building.

We pulled into post 17A and for the second straight time, it appeared very empty without Turnpike Mike and the rest of the Jacksonville crew. I sang "Glory Days" and "Born To Run", in front of over 300 fans at the Springsteen Karaoke. Then we went inside for another terrific show.

Bruce began with "The Promised Land" and after singing "Prove It All Night", he looked up at the sky, hopeful that rain was going to stay away. "Looks good. Looks good up there," he said. "I'll keep them crossed (fingers). Looks good, I won't say a word."

After "Badlands" he shouted out "is anybody alive out there?", three times. He referred to Clarence Clemons as "the emperor of the Garden State." Bruce acted very loose and content with this intimate meeting with his fans. On this beautiful evening, he did an extra verse of "Dancing In The Dark" and said "I'm going to run out of moves."

A fellow in a suit and tie sat to the right of me, as we gazed down from our third deck seats, located on Patti's side of the stage (right side as you look at the stage). We were right in the front row and there was a plastic shield in front of us, to keep people from falling over the edge. When spectators stood up from this vantage point, you could hear the music just great. It was muffled a bit when you sat down in your seat.

"Mister Suit" became irritated when the show didn't start promptly at 7:30 p.m. "What is the hold up, my ticket says this starts at 7:30?", he asked nobody in particular. Not able to resist that comment, I told him that Bruce hits the stage at about 8:17 p.m. He wanted to pry further, but decided to keep quiet. "He is worth it," I said. "Have you ever seen him (Bruce)?" The man looked at me and said "no, but I heard Springsteen puts on some kind of a show."

"Mister Suit" sat for the first few songs and stood for a couple. About 60 per cent through the show, he was screaming, yelling, singing and into the sizzling performance with all four feet. With my own eyes, I had seen another "Brucer" being born.

Bruce did a powerful "Jungleland" and was totally involved in his music. The E Street Band was fabulous and people were very impressed.

Bruce knows he has the finest band around. They had been apart for 15 years before they came back together in 1999. The time was right for this magnificent combination to reunite and the results were awesome.

The Boss calls the E Street Band "the greatest little house band in all the land." He proceeded into "Mary's Place" with great vigor and paused during the song to introduce each and every member of the band. When he was all done, shouting out the introductions in a Brother Love's

Traveling Salvation Show type voice, he summed it all up.

"Ladies and gentlemen, that's the heart stoppin, pants droppin, house rockin, earth shakin, booty quakin, viagra takin, love makin, legendary E Street Band."

When the event was nearly over, Bruce had these words. "Thank you, New Jersey. See you Saturday night."

We didn't return for that show, but daughter Tracie and son-in-law Mike, did. Mike is originally from Parsippany, New Jersey, is a staunch New Jersey Devils and New York Giants fan and liked The Boss. Tracie became a full-fledged "Brucer" that night.

She had Springsteen albums from back in the mid 1980s, but had never actually seen him. She and Mike had seats down on the floor and had walked into the Meadowlands through the football players' entrance. Before the tour concluded, Tracie would see Bruce four times on "The Rising" tour, twice in the Meadowlands and two times at Shea Stadium, in October.

Springsteen doesn't live all that far from the Meadowlands. He called his loyal fans here, "Mister and Mrs. New Jersey" and every time he would say the words "New Jersey" or "Jersey" he would get a big crowd reaction. The Garden State's favorite son was getting a spectacular welcome home and he was having a ball.

Our ninth concert on the tour occurred at PNC Park in Pittsburgh, Pennsylvania, on August 6, 2003. Chris and I agree that the intimate sandy brown ballpark, built in 2001, was one of the finest sites and hosted one of the greatest concerts we saw on the tour.

PNC, the home of the Pittsburgh Pirates baseball team, has a capacity (for baseball) of close to 39,000 people. Outside, there are statues of Pirate heroes Roberto Clemente and Willie Stargell. Stargell had been kind to Bob Semerano when the former Port athlete was working out with the Pirates back in the 1970s. Willie passed away the morning that the Bucs hosted their first baseball game at PNC.

This venue gives customers a spectacular view of both the Pittsburgh city skyline (beyond the center and right field fences and across the Allegany River) and the Roberto Clemente Bridge. From home plate to the Allegany River, measures out at 443 feet, 4 inches.

We arrived in the early afternoon of August 6th and parked in a lot across the street from the park. Restaurants were within walking distance and paved walking paths next to the park and river, were awesome. We both pulled up the legs of our jeans and waded with others in a multi-tiered water fountain, next to the park. Riverboats passed by on this lazy and sunny afternoon and despite the heat, we felt like we were in heaven.

This park, adjacent to Federal Street, cost around 200 million dollars to build and it was impressive, to say the least. During the afternoon, Bruce did a sound check and we heard songs like "The Rising" and "Fade Away." PNC and Crystal Palace, England, are forever tied in my mind, as the nicest areas that we saw Bruce perform.

When I think of Pittsburgh, I think of the Pirates and their great tradition. The Bucs have been located in Pittsburgh for more than 115 years. We had seats down on the natural grass turf, in the right field area, and looking at the lights of Pittsburgh and the colorful Clemente bridge, sent chills down my spine.

The night before the show, I sang karaoke at a place called Elwood's Pub, in Rural Ridge, Pa., one exit west of Monroeville. On the wall of this happy place was a sign that read "live well, laugh often, love much."

The barmaids were Judy and Kathy and the DJ was a lady named Cindy. Kathy was a big Bruce fan and even played some Boss tunes on the jukebox before the karaoke. "My roommate (in college) had a shrine to Bruce in the 1980s," Kathy said. There were no Bruce songs at this karaoke, but I vow to return there with my disks someday soon. Pittsburgh and western Pennsylvania is absolutely beautiful and it is only about six hours from home.

The night of the concert, there was a calm atmosphere outside the park. It was a serene kind of evening and in the distance, you could see those breathtaking buildings and pretty Pittsburgh lights. Nearby, more lights shimmered off the Allegany River, the walkway and the fountain. I felt a magical tug that this was going to be a real dynamic performance. I wasn't disappointed.

Bruce began the actual concert with a raucous and rocking "Jackson Cage" and threw out a tremendous "Prove It All Night." His friend, rocker Joe Grushecky (of Pittsburgh) and his teenage son, John, accompanied Bruce on "Glory Days." Grushecky often comes to the Stone Pony in Asbury park and some of the times he performs there, Bruce emerges from the audience of his favorite neighborhood night spot, and hops up on stage with him.

A total of 47,000 fans showed up to see Bruce and his E Street Band, in the first concert ever, at this ballpark. "It's nice to be in Pittsburgh in a brand new ball park," The Boss said. "We gonna try to hit a home run for ya."

The Pittsburgh Post Gazette covered the event and was impressed by what Springsteen brought to the table.

Reporter Ed Masley described what his eyes took in. "For a concert that featured no fewer than nine selections from "The Rising", the overall mood of the show was one of healing and redemption, of coming to terms with the horrible hand your sometimes dealt and moving on. Like any decent wake, it felt more like a celebration of life than a wallowing in despair."

The Pittsburgh Tribune-Review had a headline that read "Springsteen wows 'em at PNC Park Concert" and ran a front page color picture of Clarence, Bruce and Steve Van Zandt entertaining the crowd.

In his review, reporter Regis Behe wrote "Let the record show that the first song at a rock concert at PNC was "Take Me Out To The Ballgame."' He added "It was a sweet opening night and anyone who was at the show will be talking about it for years to come."

The PNC event began around 8:25 p.m. and included a long set list of 28 songs. "Working On The Highway" and "Blinded By The Light" joined "Further On (Up The Road)", as some tunes that Bruce brought out of his magical, musical bag. Meanwhile people out on boats on the river, strained to catch a few of the stray notes that escaped the ballpark.

You could feel the intense energy and emotion in "The Rising". Bruce leaped on Roy Bittan's piano, flirted with wife, Patti, and acted more like 20 years old than in his 50s. Not many folks Bruce's age care to even sit through a three hour rock show, let alone orchestrate one, but that, among other things, is what Bruce has become famous for.

For many years, diehard Boss fans have followed him in and out of the United States. Loyal and hard core "Brucers" camp out for days just to get tickets to his shows. While Chris and I aren't quite that frenzied, we too, have walked the extra mile for Bruce Springsteen.

In the first 85 shows, Bruce had given his fans 103 different songs. By the time the 120th show had ended, in New York, Bruce and his band were totally spent, drained and ready for some rest. It had been a memorable tour and during it, CBS television aired a February 28th special, that showed Bruce and the band at their October 2002 Barcelona, Spain show. It was the first time he had ever appeared on network TV, although he already had been on an HBO special.

Many fans differ on whether the Pittsburgh or the three Philadelphia performances were better. To me, trying to rate Bruce's shows is like comparing apples and oranges. To compare is fruitless.

We had good old Fish with us when we motored from our home to Lincoln Financial Field in Philly, on August 11. Gary Scales, the bass guitar player and part-time comedian, is a Jon Bon Jovi lover. While he grooves to Jon, guitarist Richie Sambora and the rest of the band, he is very open minded when it comes to music. "Bruce is a rocker," he said simply. "I know he is going to be great."

Bon Jovi and Springsteen have appeared on stage together (helping charities) and in the past, lived close to each other in New Jersey. They are similar, yet very different. Jon has no wife on stage, while Bruce only has to look down to his left to see his red-headed wife, Patti Scialfa, strumming her guitar. By the time the evening was over, Fish had these words. "That is the greatest band in the world (E Street Band), the best I have ever heard, and The Boss is just great. Can I go to Denver with you?" The Denver concert took place the following month, and Fish would have gladly packed himself away in the luggage. He was stuck home though, to work his job and take care of our cats.

Fish never fails to make me laugh. He has a contagious sense of humor that could make a guard at Buckingham Palace break down with laughter. Once, way back in our teens, Fish told me about a dream he had.

"I was over at the sink," he had said real seriously. "And these eyes were looking up at me from the drain. Soon, there was a knock at the kitchen door and it was this wolf, who lived in the basement. He had a cup in his paw and asked me if he could have a glass of water. I gave him the water and he walked away happy."

I wonder how many dishes of ice cream Fish had the night of that dream.

We had a real easy time getting to Philly on Route 95 and parked our car out near the Spectrum. Bruce had a sound check going on inside of the brand new 512 million dollar Lincoln Financial Field and people stopped what they were doing, to listen. You couldn't locate any food until you got inside the gates and so, we had to wait for awhile. Radio stations were camped out in the vicinity and the place became more energized as time went by.

Our seats were located on the field for this concert, also. We didn't sit in our seats though and walked up closer to the stage. Fish really got into the spirit of the evening and found himself totally involved. The seed was planted in Philly for Fish, and it would grow to full blossom on October 1, at New York's Shea Stadium.

The Boss delivered 27 songs on August 11th. Before it all began, I was standing on the second floor of the stadium, looking down over a railing, when a familiar face looked up at me. I don't know what the odds were, but I was eye-to-eye with good old Jim McCarthy. Whether it's Florida, London, New Jersey, Manchester, Dublin, Philadelphia, or New York, chances are that McCarthy and Miami Silvio were somewhere in the vicinity.

In Philly, Bruce gave us "Be True", "It's Hard To Be A Saint In The City", "Incident On 57th Street", and "Atlantic City". He also did "I'm Goin' Down" for the first time on stage since 1986 and Manfred Mann's "Pretty Flamingo" for the first time since 1978.

Bruce sent people into hysterics when he started the song they had been waiting for in the city of brotherly love. He delivered the epic "Streets Of Philadelphia" with feeling and compassion.

This 1993 motion picture, starring Tom Hanks and Denzel Washington, won many awards. It earned Bruce an Oscar in 1994 for the best achievement in music (original song). He also got Grammy awards for song of the year, best rock song, best rock vocal performance and best song written specifically for a motion picture or TV show.

For Philly's three shows, they had a stage with a massive gray canopy. The fans packed in all three nights to see Bruce, the venue's first concert performer, ever. Soon, the Philadelphia Eagles (NFL) would call this place, home.

Bruce had been in Philly on this world tour, back in October 2002

(First Union Center) and folks were ecstatic to have him back. After the concert, workers sold the Philadelphia Daily News which had a color front page picture of The Boss with his guitar held high in the air. Bruce is the picture of durability and his music remains timeless.

After singing "Atlantic City" The Boss said "good evening, good to see you on this balmy Philadelphia evening. Thanks for coming out." He thought for a minute and then said "Got a question. About 10 minutes after we stopped the other night, did it rain like hell, here?" When fans told him "yes", he said "oh it did?", whistled, laughed and offered this. "Lucked out on that one, thanks."

During the "Mary's Place" intro of the band, he told folks "I'm feelin' a little too sexy for my vest" and later belted out a "Ramrod" that went nearly 11 minutes. During that song, he said "I think the werewolf is on the prowl. I said I'm on the prowl...ahhhooo. Everybody howl now...ahhhooo." You could hear howling going on all over the dazzling, majestic stadium. People danced, laughed, sang and enjoyed this dynamic show to the max.

Bruce blended "The Rising" music with his past hits and the mixture shot the lights out.

We had heard "Darlington County", "Thunder Road", "Born To Run", "Rosalita" and the finale "I'm A Rocker."

Fish was at a loss for words when we got in the car. He had seen a show to end them all. Earlier, I looked over at him and noticed a tear escape from his eye. "I always get emotional when I hear this song," he said, when describing the 911 tune "Empty Sky."

Chris and I were back at Giants Stadium August 28, and saw Bruce do "From Small Things" with Bobby Bandiera. A beach ball appeared during the show and was tapped around in front of the stage. "If you see one of those beach balls that's going around, slice it to shreds," The Boss said. It was muggy out that night and Bruce did a lot of slow songs. Like we did many times on tour, Chris used her cell phone to call "NY Nick" (from the Springsteen thread) down at a Florida bar he owns. The name of the bar, is none other than "NY Nick's" and has all kinds of Springsteen memorabilia displayed. Much of the Bruce things came from fellow Brucers who Nick has made friends with, all over the globe.

At this concert, I bought an olive Bruce shirt that says "Bruce Springsteen & The E Street Band" on it. There is a drawing of a ferris wheel and roller coaster and a big white number "8" is on the back, representing the 8th of 10 Giants Stadium concerts.

The one thing that New Jersey crowds were waiting for, was the song "Jersey Girl." Bruce hadn't sung that selection at all at Giants Stadium, but that was to change three nights later when he concluded his Meadowlands appearances on August 31.

Daughter Tracie was with us (for her second Bruce show) when we arrived in the Meadowlands parking lot for the final time.

She and Chris sat in Section 115 while I was on the floor. Bruce began with "Cynthia" a tune he performed the only time on the 120-show 82-city tour.

He did "Lucky Town", "Lost In The Flood", "Kitty's Back" and "Spirit In The Night" (McCarthy likes that song). "Can you feel the spirit?", Bruce said. Later he shouted out "Is she out there tonight?", and followed with an unreal "Rosalita."

Bruce had hit the stage with the song "Summer Wind" playing in the background. He looked very serious and wasn't cracking any of his usual jokes. It was somber early in this performance because Bruce had realized that this was the grand finale of a great 10-show summer extravaganza at Giants Stadium. "Welcome to the last New Jersey house party of the summer," The Boss said near the start of the concert. I think I'm going to cry. We'll try to ring it out in style."

When he got to "Jersey Girl", Giants Stadium went absolutely wild. People literally cried while hearing Bruce deliver this classic song in a soothing and gentle voice that crackled with images of the Jersey shore, boardwalks, salt water taffy, dancing and the strong emotions of a true love.

When it was all over, Bruce Springsteen looked out at us and showed what he is made of. "We love you Jersey," he said. "Thanks for a great summer. We'll be seeing you."

McCarthy and some friends were near pole 17A when this final show concluded. "He (Bruce) didn't hold anything back," Jim McCarthy said. "These concerts at the Meadowlands were the best."

Chris and Tracie enjoyed the event too. Chris called Nick in Florida to let him hear some of the performance and dabbled into some hard lemonade and hard rock as well. It was tough seeing Giants Stadium disappear into the rear view window, but we took comfort in knowing that we (Chris and I) would be starting a whirlwind Boss schedule that would take us to eight of Bruce's last 11 shows including stops in North Carolina, Detroit and Denver.

The first two stops would be Fed-Ex Field in Landover, Maryland (Washington, D.C. area), on September 13 and then on to Keenan Stadium in Chapel Hill, North Carolina, the next night.

The night before the Fed-Ex event (September 12th) was our 33rd wedding anniversary. We spend part of it at a karaoke in an indoor tent-like structure at the Holiday Inn at Greenbelt, Maryland, where we stayed two nights.

Bruce had recently lost two friends in Warren Zevon and Johnny Cash and so it was with a heavy heart, that Springsteen and his E Street Band, took the stage the next evening.

When we arrived at Fed-Ex, we marveled at the beautiful stadium, located up a hill. Tailgating was going on in the area and we were walking away from a shirt vendor when a pretty blonde walked toward us. It didn't add up right away, but sirens went off in my head when I realized this was "Greendoggy", a hard core Brucer from Florida, who we had seen in the London Bridge. When you follow Bruce, you come across friends everywhere, in this fine land.

She had flown in alone from the Sunshine State and was all excited about viewing another Bruce show. We hung out in the parking lot, listened to Boss music and then went inside to see the real thing.

Bruce started by playing a Johnny Cash song entitled "I Walk The Line." This Stadium, home to the Washington Redskins, was beautiful. The outside colors of the building included purple, orange and green and the parking lots were color coded in these shades, also. Brightly lit torches surrounded the structure and it almost seemed like on this night, the place was a shrine to The Boss.

Just to illustrate the perseverance of a Springsteen fan, Greendoggy is not fond of flying. She not only blocked that fear out and flew from Jacksonville to Baltimore, but she did it on a scary date...September 11.

Bruce fired up "Pink Cadillac" a song he said he hadn't done "in about 20 years." Bruce joked about how Clarence should be president, howled and wanted the crowd to howl along. In 13 days, we would be in six different locations. It was going to be a hectic schedule, but I wouldn't have traded it for all the tea in China.

We were up bright and early and left for North Carolina (270 miles away) at 8:22 a.m. Our arrival was at 3:10 p.m., and we ran smack dab into some ungodly humid weather down there, complete with an invasion of mosquitoes at the University of North Carolina (Chapel Hill), site of the show.

On the way down to North Carolina, Chris talked about our impending trip to Denver, Colorado. She said we'd be staying in a Holiday Inn at Estes Park, and added this. "Out back, there will be wild animals, and they won't be squirrels." I laughed off what I thought was a cute joke. Little did I know, that less than 10 days later, I'd be walking through the motel parking lot, surrounded by the beautiful Colorado Rockies and a half dozen Elk.

I picked up a Sunday paper, the "News Observer" of Raleigh and saw the headlines "Bruce Is In Town." We parked on campus and walked up some streets and into the woods. It was unbelievable that a stadium was located here in the wildness and hills. Mosquitoes made almost every inch of me itch. Sweat poured down my face and we trudged up a hill and sat down on a bench as college students walked by. I silently wondered if Michael Jordan ever walked up this sidewalk that led to Keenan. There were trees all around us and I was positive that we were lost. There was only one thing to do at a time like this...call NY Nick in Florida.

Nick is one of the most loyal and enthusiastic Bruce fans I have ever met. He proudly points to Syracuse as his favorite collegiate basketball team. When they won the NCAA championship in 2003, he was ecstatic. This man, who attended six Bruce concerts on "The Rising" tour, may reside down in Florida, but his heart is back up in the Northeast.

There was no alcohol allowed at the concert, as many students under 21, study here. The curfew is 11 p.m. for the students and many were in their dormitories the evening of the show. People the age of their parents were on hand to see The Boss, plus some students came because they were either curious about Bruce or wanted to get a few chuckles about some "old guy" trying to rock to some music they didn't understand.

It is safe to say that Bruce converted many young people on September 14, 2003.

When we had arrived at the Holiday Inn at Durham, North Carolina, I noticed we had put 560 miles on the car since leaving for Maryland. The time spent and the miles and miles of traveling, were well worth it.

At Chapel Hill they are proud of their athletic program. Light blue and white Tarheels bumper stickers could be seen everywhere and you could sense the pride.

Springsteen began with "I Walk The Line" again and did a superb "Jungleland" as part of his 26-song show. He also offered "Living Proof", a tour premiere. After "Darkness On The Edge Of Town", mosquitoes began to attack The Boss. "I thought the mosquitoes in New Jersey were bad," he said. "This is worse."

Following the 911-based song "Your Missing", he saw a huge bug near him, gently latched onto it and then let it go. "What in the hell is this?", he said, holding it up for the crowd to see. "What's that? The school mascot? Oh man", he said as he chuckled about the situation.

Bruce referred to "big man" Clarence Clemons as "the honorary emperor of North Carolina" and made a further observation. "Tonight, there's only one big man on campus," he asserted.

We were in the very first row of seats, next to the field, (Row A, seats 21 and 22) and although quite a distance from the stage, saw the band real well. There were quite a few empty seats at Keenan, which we weren't used to. At prior shows we had seen stadiums packed with people.

Some of the critical students, were won over by Bruce. Down on the field, they danced in the back as The Boss rocked Chapel Hill. When it was over, they clapped, whistled, screamed and pleaded for Bruce not to leave. He hung around and for the final two songs, gave them a stirring "Rosalita" and aggressive "Dancing In The Dark." He left the stage with these words..."see you further on up the road."

At show's end, we walked back through the woods and past equipment trucks. Those big trucks logged many miles, toting some of the band's musical equipment. Keeping up with The Boss isn't easy, in more ways than one.

We left Durham at 12:05 p.m. the next afternoon and wound up on the beautiful Blue Ridge Parkway (Virginia). We went through a tunnel and up to the Bluff Mountain Overlook, in George Washington National Forest, (1,820 feet up). On the way there, Chris saw a turtle in the middle of the road, slowly creeping a couple of inches at a time. She decided to turn around, go back and deposit it in the woods, so it wouldn't get hit by a car.

I got off at the overlook and gazed at all the beauty, as the car sped away. Then it suddenly occurred to me that there was nowhere to run, should a wild animal suddenly appear out of the wilderness and decide to attack me. Perhaps it would be a huge bear that would lumber up to me. "Hey, Bruce sang "Jungleland" last night, he likes you animals," I could say. "Let's be friends." He would extend his paw, I would offer my hand and all would be well.

I looked back at the road and waited for the car to reappear. Maybe this tour was taking a toll on me, because now I was thinking of what it would be like to communicate with a ferocious bear.

In Virginia, we stopped at a place called Gert's Country Store. They were bracing for Hurricane Isabelle, which was heading in that direction. A lady in the store told me that 100 people were killed here, in a storm in 1969. We hopped in the car and were glad we were heading away from the impending rain.

People back home were worried about us, but we were well ahead of the upheaval that loomed ahead.

Chris and I had already seen 14 Bruce concerts but still had a half dozen waiting on the horizon. That final big push, started on Thursday, September 18, 2003, when we headed the Pontiac Sunfire in the direction of Rentschler Field in East Hartford, Connecticut.

We would witness the Connecticut show, then drive all night to the Buffalo, New York area (for a September 20 show at Six Flags, Darien Lake, New York), and then drive the morning after that concert, for a performance the next night at Detroit's Comerica Park. The journey would continue the next morning, when we'd fly west from Detroit's Metropolitan Airport, to Denver, Colorado. We would be spending a few days (with the Elk) at breathtaking Estes Park, before going to Denver's Invesco Field (mile high area) to see Bruce, September 25.

In Connecticut, you could see the band walk to the stage from an area behind the stadium and The Boss came out appearing young and vibrant. They had discussed a potential problem with "loud noise", regarding this concert, but local radio stations laughed that off, probably realizing that a Springsteen show isn't exactly an exercise in loud rap or heavy metal.

There was a cool night breeze and I was decked out in a black tee shirt with the word "Springsteen" in white letters on the front. The parking lot attendants were very professional and people were tailgating in parking lots that looked like airplane runways.

The Boss was his usual dynamic best and the crowd responded

positively. The hurricane would be headed into the area but the rain held off for us. Bruce highlighted his guitar expertise in this show and whaled on many tunes including "Because The Night."

He began with "Souls Of The Departed", and later went to "Leap Of Faith". Those songs, he would wind up doing only four times each, on the tour. He delivered "Factory" for the only time on tour and "Living Proof", which he did two times. Late in the show, Bruce offered "Seven Nights To Rock" and following it, told the crowd "after tonight, we only got seven nights to rock," in reference to only seven shows remaining on "The Rising" tour.

He labeled Clarence "the emperor of the universe" and tossed out a great "Janey Don't Lose Heart." His rapport and interaction with his fans was pleasing to watch and listen to. He kept the beat, twanging his guitar to the familiar strains of "Glory Days", the song that had captivated me way back on that TV show in July of 2002.

"Are you with me kid?", he asked boyhood friend and fellow band member Steve VanZandt. Stevie, with his familiar bandanna on his head, nodded and answered affirmatively. The Boss gave his million dollar smile and went on. "Is the band with me?", he queried. Then he took it a step farther. "Are the Connecticans with me?", he said. He laughingly repeated "Connecticans" and then added, "the people of Connecticut."

Bruce was enjoying his banter with the faithful crowd. "That's right," he asserted. "That's what I'm talkin' about, baby. Cause I got just one question, I gotta ask you right now and I need an answer, real loud. And that question is, what time is it?". The frenzied fans screamed "Boss time" in unison and the spectacular song, from the mid-1980s, continued.

Springsteen ended the event with the classic "Dancing In The Dark", a song he performed 113 times in 120 shows. "One more time," he shouted, as he went into one final verse of the song again. People hopped up and down, sang, hugged. It was a sight for the ages. When he was done, the brown-eyed and animated "kid" from Jersey, looked out at the happy faces, raised his guitar and said "We love you. Thank you for two beautiful nights in Hartford."

We shared driving responsibilities up to the Buffalo area. Bruce's show was moved from Buffalo to Darien Lake and he seemed real happy to be singing in an amusement park rather than in a large stadium. Springsteen virtually grew up on the boardwalks and in the amusement parks of New Jersey and it was like old home week for him.

I had some great experiences in New York State, like dropping the entire contents of an ice chest all over the bathroom floor at a Holiday Inn in Cheektowaga. Of course a glass bottle was shattered in this misadventure, but those kind of things are minor when a Bruce show lies ahead.

Chris and I met up with Ethel at the entrance of the Six Flags. She is the charismatic lady that told me to go out and give singing a try. We have sung at Stravato's and the Crescent in Jamestown and also in Cheektowaga.

It had rained the day before, but the sun came out and the temperature was comfortable. Ethel, her kids and grandchildren, have been to the Six Flags amusement park at Darien Lake many times. It had been an easy ride from Cheektowaga, via routes 90 and 78 and it felt great to be back in New York State again.

The night before, I had sung "Glory Days" and "Born To Run" at Cheektowaga's Garden Park Café. The two Boss songs had gone over real well and I was anxious to hear Bruce do these songs again in this country setting.

The three of us walked around looking at the impressive roller coasters and Ferris wheel. People screamed from a ride called "The Predator", a band played nearby, there were places to get temporary tattoos plus eating booths were everywhere. This seemed like a different kind of world from the one we would be walking into that night.

Bruce would perform under a big pointy, white tent with lots of chairs under it. There were rolling green hills farther back, where spectators watched him sing. Three big color picture screens gave everyone good views of the concert. When The Boss peered out at the crowd, he could see all the big, exciting rides, bathed in the dazzling and shimmering lights of a foot stomping country fair.

Being from New Jersey and hanging out at boardwalks like at Asbury Park in his younger years, Bruce was no stranger to this type of atmosphere. After being in large stadiums, he seemed invigorated and relaxed by what he saw. "I feel right at home here," he said, and then chuckled about how he and the band, should be going on a tour of amusement parks.

He began the show with "Tunnel Of Love" a favorite of Karen, the waitress and cook, back at Joe's Coffee Shop in Port Jervis. Bruce hadn't performed this song since back on September 23, 1988, in Oakland, California.

"Hello Buffalo, hello Rochester, Darien Lake and Niagara Falls," Bruce said. "I like the way this feels (playing an amusement park)." For a seventh selection of his 26 songs, he did the beautiful "Mansion On The Hill", and later, he reached into the past for another memorable song.

"Get out your accordion, Dan (Federici), Soozie (Tyrell), get out your violin," Bruce said. The Boss indicated that the band wasn't real familiar with the next song ("man, they can do it") but said they would do just fine. "Here's a song I wrote I guess about 10 years ago," he asserted. "It's appropriate for the night."

Bruce twanged his way into a stirring version of "County Fair" that had everyone tapping their feet. Chris and Ethel were mesmerized by what was taking place before their eyes. If there was any doubt that Bruce was a humble and down to earth person, that doubt was quickly dashed on this evening.

He referred to Clarence as "the king of Buffalo, the prince of Darien Lake and the emperor of Niagara Falls." He looked around and offered this tidbit. "Impeach the president and put in a man that knows what he is doing. I nominate "Big Man" Clarence Clemons. Get that fool (the president) out of there."

Bruce did "Glory Days" with Willie Nile and said there were "six nights left to rock". As the evening grew chilly, he teased his loyal fans after finishing the song "Land Of Hope And Dreams."

He began singing the 1959 number one hit from Lloyd Price "Stagger Lee", as many in the crowd, scratched their heads in wonder. "The night was young, and the moon was yellow and the leaves came tumbling down", he sang. Quickly, Bruce shifted gears and began ripping his guitar to the strains of crowd favorite "Rosalita." In the old days, Springsteen ended many of his concerts, with this song.

When the show was over, Bruce waved and said "thanks for the great night." He had adjusted well and changed his environment from large cities to a country setting and smaller crowd. Originally, this performance was to take place at Ralph J. Wilson Stadium (Orchard Park, near Buffalo), but the site was changed. I feel that Bruce would come back again, in a heart beat, to the down home flavor of Darien Lake.

While Chris and I continued to be impressed by this musical icon, named Bruce Springsteen, Ethel had seen The Boss for the very first time. Decked out in a black Springsteen shirt with a colorful car on it, she said "Bruce is really awesome and I am so glad I got a chance to see and hear him." We parted ways with this red-headed woman, just outside the main gate. She walked to her car with pleasant thoughts of the upbeat concert, she had just witnessed. She was now officially a full-fledged "Brucer."

We had talked about this show for months and now, in what seemed like the blink of an eye, it had become history.

Morning came soon enough and it was time to take a 364-mile drive to the "Motor City." We would be going to a place called Comerica Park where the Detroit Tigers were suffering through a horrible baseball season.

It took about seven hours to reach Dearborn, Michigan, but the trip hadn't been all that bad. On the way, we saw signs in Cleveland, for the Rock And Roll Hall Of Fame. We just didn't have time to stop, because we wanted to get settled in at our new surroundings and that night, we would be seeing Bruce again.

We did have time to pop into the Greek Casino, located just a few blocks from the concert venue. We put the Sunfire in a parking garage and walked to the casino where one armed bandits quickly gobbled up my quarters.

It was only a few blocks to Comerica Park and when we arrived, there were long lines leading to entrances. There are two big tigers on top of the stadium and Ford Field, where the Lions play football, is across the street.

As luck would have it, we sat in Section 213 (foul territory, right field area) and encountered a jackass with a loud mouth. Bruce performed in the center field portion of the pretty, but confusing park. It had taken me considerable time to locate our seats as I wound up walking back and forth in nearly abandoned hallways, looking for a way to go up another floor.

The jackass was one of those blowhards that shouts "down in front" every two seconds, because fans are standing and getting involved in Bruce music. If you have every seen The Boss sing, you know that people stand and really get involved in the show.

When he insulted a lady by shouting calling her an "ass", I stared at him in disgust and we promptly moved over to Section 212, where there were empty seats.

Bruce played a great harmonica during "The Promised Land" and a fabulous guitar on "Because The Night."

Special guest was Martha Reeves of Martha and the Vandellas, who Bruce introduced as "one of the great ladies of Motown." She did the famous "Heat Wave" with Bruce singing backup. "We love you Bruce," Martha said, before leaving the stage.

On this night, Clarence became "the emperor of Detroit" and Bruce tried to helped the baseball team, which was on track to set a major league record in futility, for the most losses in a season (set by the New York Mets). "I'm going to chase all the evil spirits outta here," Bruce said, as the crowd cheered. The Boss must have accomplished just that, because the Tigers recovered enough, not to set the dismal record.

The ninth song of the night was "Local Hero" a tune he did for the only time on tour. The weather was turning windy and chilly, but nobody seemed to care. Bruce was taking Detroit by storm. He noticed some signs on the field that proclaimed that he was hot. That cracked him up and he walked across the stage saying "I'm hot. I'm hot, baby."

We all sang "Happy Birthday" to Bruce and he thanked us for supporting his music throughout the years. He made mention that just a buck (dollar), buys 16 meals for those who are in need and plugged the local food bank.

This was the 115th show out of 120. Chris and I were attending our 17th out of 20 and knew this once in a lifetime venture, was winding down to a close. It wouldn't be fun when these bills had to be paid, but we figured what the hell, "we come this way but once."

The next morning, we were airborne, headed for the picturesque Denver area. My eyes took in the fabulous vistas as we circled in for a landing. All the pictures I had seen of Colorado over the years, hadn't lied. This place was heaven on earth.

We arrived on September 22 at around 10 a.m. and secured a convertible car from Hertz. Jan, at the Hertz desk, was a Bruce fan and said he had passed through the terminal in the past. I gave her a note for him (in case she saw him), explaining that I would be writing a book about the tour and had pictures (in the Stone Pony) to give himself, Patti and Soozie.

We pulled the white Mustang into a North Glenn, Colorado Cracker Barrel and couldn't believe we were here. We took Route 34 West through the mountains, and near trees, rocks and streams, to the Estes Park Holiday Inn, where we arrived at 6 p.m.

We both felt quite a bit lightheaded and a bit weak from being in such a high elevation, and the order of the day was to drink plenty of water. The first couple of days we found ourselves out of breath. I could feel a tightness in my chest and was huffing and puffing, especially when I walked uphill. We took things easy, paced ourselves and soon enough, our bodies began adjusting to the high elevations.

On one occasion, I came out of the Holiday Inn door and into the parking lot, to find seven Elk walking all around the cars. The big creatures seemed docile enough as they sniffed shrubbery and seemed to mingle well with people. The sight of an Elk standing next to our rental car, was real hard to fathom. I was seeing wild life outside of a Colorado hotel...and that wild life wasn't squirrels.

I can see why people visit a place like Estes Park and decide to live here. Spectacular scenery is everywhere and most of the people who live here, are neighborly and genuine. Former Denver Bronco quarterback John Elway is still a king here. He is plastered all over billboards in the Denver area, with his sparkling teeth shining out at you as you drive along at a 70 mile per hour clip.

It was sunny and an unseasonable 64 degrees at 9:34 a.m. on the morning of Tuesday, September 23, 2003. We ate breakfast in Estes Park (at The Egg And I) and headed out, under crystal clear blue sky, to a horse riding stable. We cruised along east and west Elkhorn Street (now where could that name come from?) as we breathed clear, cool air.

Estes Park is just at the edge of the Rocky Mountain National Park and the downtown area is filled with stores and tourists. The streets and sidewalks are immaculate here and it isn't hard to figure that the locals take pride in this town. You can find leather, beads, Indian articles, sweatshirts and fine restaurants here. But on this day, Chris wanted to saddle up and ride. I saddled up the Mustang and headed back downtown, looking for a place that might have an evening karaoke, complete with Springsteen songs.

The stable, called "Sombrero's", was easy to find on Route 34. The elevation here is 7,522 feet and Chris and her horse, "Face", headed up the trail for a couple hours of relaxation. I have already agreed to saddle up (I am no Clint Eastwood) the next time we come here, which I hope is in 2005.

The next day, we photographcd thc Stanley Hotel, where the 1996 movie "The Shining" starring Jack Nicholson, was filmed. It was slightly cooler when we regretfully left Estes Park, bound for Denver. We left behind unspoiled countryside and a tranquil atmosphere, for the hustle and bustle of Denver highways. Chris was not thrilled by the change of location and neither was I.

We arrived at the Radisson Hotel on Quebec Avenue and saw that the mating calls of Elk was being replaced by honking horns and many people. Chris had loved going across the street from the Holiday Inn at Estes Park, to watch countless Elk walk around the golf course as dusk began to set in. Now, those placid times, were just a pleasing memory.

The morning of concert day, we ate sweet rolls and drank coffee at nearby Panero's. Back at the hotel, you could see the city of Denver from the right side of our balcony. It made some kind of picture with the tall snow-capped mountains serving as a spectacular background to Denver's tall buildings.

We drove to the famous "Red Rocks", in the mountains. This historical outdoor amphitheater has hosted countless famous entertainers over the years. For awhile, rumors were going around, that Bruce would be playing here, instead of at Invesco Field. We climbed 30 steps and then 12 more, to get to the main area of this place. Looking at all the red rocks was another mind-boggling sight. A sign, next to a walkway, said "No Climbing On Rocks $999.00 fine or 180 days in jail or both." You can go inside this facility and down a hall where plaques line the walls, engraved with the names and dates that entertainers performed here.

The Greatful Dead led the pack with 25 appearances here. Benny Goodman was here on July 27, 1951 and some other performers included Nat King Cole, Rick Nelson, Ray Charles, Peter, Paul and Mary, The Beatles, Johnny Cash, Simon and Garfunkel, Sonny and Cher, John Denver, Neil Diamond, Wayne Newton, Bob Hope, The Eagles, Bob Dylan and Bon Jovi. Bruce Springsteen is on a plaque dated June 20, 1978 plus August 16 and 17, 1981.

Bruce took the stage at Mile High's Invesco Field that night and immediately charmed the people of Denver. He started out with "Get Out Of Denver", which was the only time he sang that song in 120 shows. After that, he pointed out that the last time he played here, it "snowed a few days before and it was about 36 degrees."

The Boss offered "Across The Border" (he did that a half dozen times on tour) and sang "Tunnel Of Love" for the second time in three concerts. He did explosive renditions of "Brilliant Disguise", "Darlington County", "Rosalita" and "Kitty's Back."

Gazing out at the audience, Bruce said "we don't play this much" ("Kitty's Back"). He had seen signs requesting that amazing and instrument-rich song and responded. "We'll give it a shot for these guys here." Bruce and his fabulous E Street Band tore into that bluesy song for over 11 minutes.

On this evening, Clarence was "the emperor of Colorado." Patti, Soozie, Nils, Clarence, Garry, Max, Stevie, Danny, Roy and of course, Bruce, blew the Denver crowd away.

Bruce urged the crowd to support the Food Bank Of The Rockies, who were on the premises. "They distributed more than 11 million pounds of food last year in Colorado and Wyoming," he said. He pointed out that 42 per cent of those receiving the food, were children. He asked the fans to support the food bank with donations to "help the struggling citizens of Colorado and Wyoming."

We sat and watched Bruce do his thing for the 18th time, in a Colorado setting that some can only dream of. People had worn extra layers of clothes to this event, expecting a cold evening. Instead, temperatures were comfortable and the crowd got very involved.

I sat near a jovial and humorous guy named Jerry Allen of Orange, Texas. He had driven to Denver for the show and he and his wife, had been to casinos in the area. "She (his wife) is 700 bucks ahead," said the fellow who said he has panned for gold. He hadn't seen Bruce since the "Tunnel Of Love" tour and watched in awe with his brother (who would be going to Shea Stadium also) and the rest of the fans.

Bruce had arrived for a sound check, in a limousine at 4:50 p.m., but didn't have time to roll down the window, talk with fans or sign autographs. He does this whenever possible, as he loves mingling with people. After one of his concerts, Gail, a real nice person from the Jacksonville thread, not only talked to Bruce and Patti who were in a limo, but gave Patti a scrapbook she had made.

The band smiled a lot and this wound up being one of the finest concerts of the tour. The special guest this night, was Brendan O'Brien, who produced "The Rising." Bruce introduced him prior to "Rosalita" and immediately began teasing.

"You better know all these chords," he asserted. "You better know them." Just before swinging into Rosalita, Bruce said "here's a little end of the summer treat...until we meet again."

We took off from Denver at 3:05 p.m. on September 26 and arrived back in Detroit at 7:40 p.m., local time. We searched for a karaoke but had no luck. The next night, Bruce would be at Miller Park in Milwaukee, but we would skip that show and drive to a Holiday Inn at Amherst, New York, and then into Niagara Falls (Ontario), Canada.

A beer garden, behind a pizza place on Clifton Street, (up from Casino Niagara), was a great outdoor karaoke (it runs seven nights a week). You could get on stage, look out at all those people and belt out songs while televisions, out on the front sidewalks, were being viewed by those that passed by.

This karaoke was put on by Moe V Entertainment (Maurice). A guy simply called "DJ" was a real rocker and threw out some Bon Jovi. My Springsteen material was very well received. While Chris ate a piece of pizza at a table, and the brilliantly lit falls roared in the background, I blared out "Dancing In The Dark", "Glory Days" and "Born To Run."

We arrived back home on Sunday, September 28, and had two more shows left on the agenda. We would be going to the October 1 Shea Stadium show with Fish and Tracie while Tracie and Spike accompanied us three days later.

Bruce played Shea three nights. We took the Bronx Expressway for the first show and arrived at the home of the New York Mets around 7 p.m. While Tracie and Chris walked across the parking lot to check out the future site of a Springsteen party (fans), I put in a song slip with the Bruce Springsteen Karaoke people.

Fish had never seen me sing before. He was in the band (Invaders) I had wanted to sing with all those years before. Not only did he get to see me sing in front of people ("Glory Days"), he watched a reporter (the pretty and charismatic Toni Senecal) and her cameraman run up to the stage to record me for the 10 o'clock news on WB-11.

Toni was really a cool person and you could tell she loves her job. She got totally involved in my performance, sang along, and referring to me, told the viewing audience "I love this guy."

For the second time in about two-and-a-half months, the New York City media was watching and listening to me do Bruce Springsteen material. I figured that this and a buck, would get me a cup of coffee. God knows how many people saw me on TV that evening. I do know that my parents and Ethel, up in Jamestown, were among them. She had to be getting a real kick out of this scene, since she is the one that told me to pursue singing in public.

It rained before Bruce hit the stage and he made sure to include CCR's "Who'll Stop The Rain" on his list of songs. The Boss displayed some great guitar playing and appeared to be happy in New York.

The concert had begun with a taped voice of President Bush talking about the war on terror and weapons of mass destruction. Bruce started his evening by answering that message with "Souls Of The Departed."

Bruce performed "Johnny 99" and later said "it's twang time", following with "Man's Job", a tour premiere. He began doing "Mary's Place" and stopped to read part of a short letter he had received backstage. The letter indicated the writing was from John C. Hughes, principal of PS 48, in the Hunt's section of the south Bronx.

The Boss explained that the principal said he was bringing three of his students (a third grader and two fourth graders) to the Wednesday, October 1 show. He read some of the words.

"Given their tender age (the students), I don't know if it is such a great idea to be making comments regarding sexualization, natural viagra, booty quaking and eating Philly cheese steaks while watching adult films (as Bruce had said in some of the previous shows).

Bruce went on with the letter. "On the other hand, while I am the principal, I understand you are The Boss." Springsteen had all he could do to contain his laughter. Bruce went on. "I gotta figure…this sounds a little tongue in cheek to me. Either somebody has hijacked Principal Hughes' stationery or maybe while not running PS 48, in the south Bronx, Principal Hughes resides in a galaxy far far away. The man has never heard of Britney Spears."

In answer to the communication, Bruce offered this. "I can't really compromise my artistic integrity." He agreed to leave out the sexualization and viagra, but as for rest, The Boss made his point clear. "Principal Hughes," he said. "If you're out there, these things are gonna happen within the next eight minutes." Later, during the song, Bruce smiled and said "booty's about to quake."

Springsteen said it was the last stand of the tour and asked folks to help the Coalition For The Homeless, who were in Shea Stadium. "Tonight, in New York City, 39,000 people will sleep in shelters," he asserted.

Bruce sang the controversial "American Skin/41 Shots" and "Born In The USA", in a show that ran two hours and 45 minutes. We left the Shea Stadium parking lot in a content mood from another great Boss show. We only had one performance left to attend.

Bruce's final concert on "The Rising" tour came on Saturday, October 4, 2003. I thought how ironic that date was, in that Chris' mother, Marion, had passed away 16 years ago, to the day. I silently wondered if Marion Goble had ever heard of Bruce Springsteen. Being that she was well-versed on TV news, she probably did know who The Boss was.

Being that this was Bruce's final show, he wasn't the usual rollicking and carefree singer-musician in the beginning of the event. The keyboard sound, bluesy sax and Nils' fiery guitar, vital parts of the E Street Band, were still as smooth as silk, though.

It was chilly and overcast on the way to Shea and that weather gave way first to a spitting drizzle and then heavy rain, before the show. It's almost as if God above, was crying big tears because this was the last time Bruce was strapping on his guitar.

As if by magic, when Bruce walked on stage, the rain totally stopped. I knew this artist controlled a lot of things, but did he have the power to turn the rain on and off?

Bruce began with "Code of Silence", a song he did just twice on "The Rising" tour. He tried to be energetic on this sad evening, but appeared somber in this last stand. During the evening he sang "Roulette" and "I Wish I Were Blind" (only time on the tour). After an emotional, tearjerking "Your Missing", The Boss addressed us.

"Welcome to the last dance," he said. "I'm getting a little misty right about now. Steve, cheer me up will you?" Bruce, Stevie and the rest of the band swung into "Waitin' on a Sunny Day" and later, Bruce did "Back in Your Arms" (tour premiere).

It was the 120th concert of the tour and 20th show for Chris and me. We had been to 14 arenas and stadiums stretching clear from Jacksonville, Florida to London, England. Bruce knows how to throw a party and on this final evening, he resorted to some heavy ammunition. Bruce's mood got better with each song and by the time he hit the home stretch, he was jamming to "Quarter To Three" with Gary U.S. Bonds and "Twist And Shout" with a group of guests. He acted more like being in his living room, than performing at a major stadium.

Following "Seven Nights To Rock", Bruce introduced a musical icon. "A great friend and inspiration (is) with us tonight," he explained. "Mister Bob Dylan." Shea Stadium, of course, went wild when Dylan walked on stage. To see Dylan and The Boss on the same stage, belting out "Highway 61 Revisited", was a historical sight for the ages .

Later, Bruce got real personal with the fans. "I wouldn't be here tonight without him (Dylan)," Springsteen asserted. "It was Bob's work when I was first trying to write songs, (that), a particular time in our country's history. He was one of those fellas who came along and has been willing to stand in the fire. I remember when I was growing up in my little town. He just made me think big thoughts. His music really empowered me and got me thinking about the world outside of my own little town. I don't know if great men make history or history makes great men, but to me, Bob's one of the greatest. Now and forever."

The Boss was paying homage to one of the biggest influences in his life. "I want to thank him (Dylan) for gracing my stage and for being such an inspiration," Bruce continued. "And ah, when I wrote this one (song), I was trying my best to follow along in his footsteps."

Springtsteen gave his "public announcement" about the war in Iraq and then gave a chilling rendition of the song he dedicated to Dylan, "Land Of Hope And Dreams".

By this time, everybody at Shea was into the concert with all four feet. Before "Rosalita", Bruce shouted out "Rosie, I'm home." John Landau and Willie Nile did "Dancing in the Dark" with the band. "Let's hear it for management," Springsteen said (Landau is his manager).

When it came time to do "Quarter To Three", a song made famous by Gary U.S. Bonds, Bruce looked around. "Anybody seen Bonds?", he queried. He called for Mrs. Bonds to help sing backup and was obviously enjoying the moment. "Come on up, kids," he said. "Ladies and gentlemen, it ain't been done in a long time ("Quarter To Three"), but this is the man (Bonds) that did it. Let's do it."

Bruce loved throwing 30 songs out to the people. He rocked to "Twist And Shout" and Shea reverberated from the ground to the rafters. Bruce was closing the tour New York style.

All good things come to an end, someday. As Dad had pointed out to me countless times, nobody can stop time. That clock keeps right on ticking. This festive mood was about to come to a screeching halt. You could see it in Bruce's eyes when he prepared for his final song. And then, like a giant wave of love and emotion, the band wound up standing on the front of the stage. Their Boss and ours, delivered a tear-jerking "Blood Brothers." It was the first and last time he would do this song on the record-smashing tour.

Tears were visible on "Big Man" Clarence Clemons' cheeks. Most people in attendance, choked back their emotions. The Boss put lumps in our throats when he hit the words "I close my eyes and feel so many friends around me."

The lonely harmonica sounded the inevitable and waning moments of a tour that struck the hearts and souls of people all around the world. Bruce had been there for America in its hour of need. He had looked at the awful terrorist attacks and found a way to begin the healing. We were a proud nation again, largely due to the effort, compassion and caring of Bruce Springsteen and his E Street Band.

He (Bruce) left us with a huge gift in 2002 and 2003. His last words on the Shea Stadium stage were "until we meet again. We love ya. We'll be seeing you. Thanks."

I realize that I have written a lot about The Boss. The simple fact is, he became a big part of my life, after I had stopped drinking. He showed me that life can be good and filled with meaningful music. He inspired me, unbelievably. These days, I carry the melody, words and messages of his music almost everywhere I go. When I walk into most New York, New Jersey or Pennsylvania restaurants, lounges or bars, I am known as "Bruce", even though some of the places know my name is Bill.

In Maryland and Virginia, people loved my Bruce material. Chris and I went to the wedding of Christopher and Veronica Crim in November 2003, at Bolling Air Force Base, Washington, D.C., and had two late nights of great karaoke at a place in Alexandria, Virginia, called "The Rock It Grill." They have karaoke there every night and I appeared alone the first night and with Chris "No Surrender" the second evening. Both times there were over 300 people crammed into this cool place, that caters quite a bit to college-aged people. I wore a black and white Springsteen shirt, a bunch of bracelets on my right wrist, and a chain.

Many from the first evening came back less than 24 hours later. I was greeted with calls of "Bruuuucccceeee" and "what are you going to sing tonight, Bruce?" I must make it clear that karaoke singing has not become a replacement addiction. Although I have sung many times during the course of a normal week, I don't need karaoke to survive and never climb the walls when I am not on stage. There was only one addiction that ever got to that point.

Some karaoke sessions have grown on me, while I continue to check out new places from time to time. Four karaoke businesses have caught my attention with their professionalism, music selection and good attitudes.

I can be found at appearances by Hi-Note Entertainment (Joey and Mary Migliorino, John Adamo), Loody & Pat Entertainment (owner Loody Tamboer and Pat Ferrante), Bill's Karaoke (Bill Pauling) and Entertainment by Randy (Randy Ringleben). All eight of these DJ's can sing real well. Loody, who has a velvet voice and reminds me of Cher, has a couple of CD's she made at a Parsippany, New Jersey studio. Mary really should make a CD as her voice is a pleasure to listen to. Pat can give you a wide variety and great oldies, while John does a perfect John Mellencamp and Latin beat type songs. Joey's claim to fame is Chuck Berry's "Johnny Be Goode". Bill is great on country material, while Randy can bring tears to your eyes with his rendition of "Why Can't Every Day Be Like Christmas", an Elvis masterpiece. When he hits the stage, his voice is very close to that of The King.

"Glory Days" continues to be my favorite Boss tune and I plan to do that song April 17, 2004, down at NY Nick's Restaurant in Pensacola, Florida. Nick, Turnpike Mike and hundreds of Springsteen fans will be gathering at "Springbreaksteen" a three-day event that will include former Boss drummer Vini "Mad Dog" Lopez.

As of today, January 16, 2004, I have done 22 different Springsteen songs and always introduce new material when I figure its ready.

This morning, The Gazette editor Janice Osborne's feature story on me, appeared on page 3 with a picture of Chris and me in front of Fed-Ex Field in Landover, Maryland. The story recounts my struggle with alcohol and how I was fortunate enough, to find a way out. By doing this compassionate and professionally written story, Jan not only touched the hearts of myself and my family, but reached countless others who have been affected by alcohol. By showing what I have been through, she gave the still-afflicted and their families, a flickering of hope that could become a shining and never ending beacon of light to recovery.

Mentioned in the story, is how Jackie Beck Bush (my social worker) was of great help to me, and how I will be going back to FDR Montrose Veterans Hospital, to speak with 28-day rehab people and sing Bruce songs, the end of this month (Monday, January 26, 2004). Randy (who is volunteering his time and use of his equipment), Christine and I will be making the trek across the Hudson River.

To me, I will be going back "home" as I come full circle. This is the place where my real life was beginning back in July of 2000. I have gotten great cooperation from Amy Hahn, who deals with alcohol cases and possesses great wit. She is a big asset to the Montrose facility. I know my heartbeat will quicken when 6 p.m. January 26 rolls around (start of at least a two hour show), because Jackie Beck Bush will be there.

When Mary Migliorino learned I was going to sing for the vets, she shot me off an e-mail. "You are a wonderful person for using your time and talent to help other people," she said. "I know they will enjoy your singing and it will lift their spirits during a tough time in their life."

Loody and Bill Pauling echoed those kind of comments, and both of these people burned me CD's containing Bruce music, so that they could be available for the Montrose performance. These are the type of individuals that put themselves out and walk the extra mile to help someone. Their generosity will always be remembered.

I realize that in the past 42 months, I have become a different type of human being. I am more laid back now, although at times I still want things done "yesterday." One of my favorite statements is "keep your wits about you" and I sometimes wonder if I am saying those words to myself.

I have grown to appreciate the strong message that music can bring. I saw a band whose "The Rising" tour hit the top in 2003, with gross ticket sales of 115.9 million bucks. Celine Dion was second (80.5) and The Eagles third (69.3). Still, Bruce puts things in perspective and is still very much that lonely Jersey boy, from back in the 1960s.

I look around and see Port Jervis and the Matamoras area changing constantly. I am a proud resident of Pennsylvania, but Port Jervis, New York, will always be my hometown. Although I am not a technology freak, I am realistic enough to know that certain changes in life, are good. Laws like "flying kites on Sunday is illegal because it scares the horses" are hopelessly outdated.

Over in Port Jervis, former police chief Gary Lopriore has become the mayor. He is younger than I am and his brother Mike and myself, played basketball on the same team with Eugene Drew back in the 60s. We were three of the clowns laughing it up on the school bus as we headed home from away basketball games.

I know there are many horrible stories revolving around alcohol addiction. I lived through some of them. So has Denny Balch, the guy who I played Little League baseball with (for the Yankees), way back in the 1950s.

Back on May 6, 2001, I went up to Fish and "Balchy's" trailer in Sparrowbush, New York, and learned that Denny had experienced the same type of nightmare hallucinations that I did. After all this time, he is the only person I can relate to, although I admit I don't go out on the street corner and ask people if they ever hallucinated.

A few years earlier, Denny had spent five months at a Westchester, New York Hospital. His kidney, liver and other things had begun to break down from alcohol abuse and he wound up with seven operations on his pancreas.

"I hallucinated that I was in the Hotel Minisink (a hotel that no longer exists in Port Jervis) and was looking down at Orange Square (a park across Pike Street)," he explained. "People were being shot and executed over there," Denny continued on. "I remember seeing Frank Bell (former athlete and current Port politician) and they were doing away with him."

Dennis Balch continued to remember the hallucination. "My ex-wife came by, said 'it's time' and was going to take me to Orange Square. I didn't want to go with her." Denny and myself, both figure that the "it's time" was an instant in his tenuous life, when he was facing a life or death situation. He was at the crossroads and was trying to ward off death and stay alive.

"They were going to kill me," Denny said. "In fact, I had lots of hallucinations and they were all violent." I could identify with this, and told him about hallucinating about having some of my limbs sawed off. Up until this time, Denny and I had only two things in common: playing baseball and having Fish as a mutual friend. Now I was finding another common denominator.

Both of us stood at death's door but didn't want to see what was on the other side. We had scrapped to stay on this earth and obviously had wills to live. Denny diets, exercises and feels fortunate to be alive.

Like "Balchy", I was always the life of the party. I was humorous and outgoing, felt amorous after many "gizmos" and drank until the well went dry. I smiled on the outside but was agonizing on the inside. I masked the hurt with jokes and didn't want to face up to reality.

Denny's hallucinations and mine were very similar. "I blubbered to my brother...telling him not to let them kill me," he said. "It seemed so real, like it was really happening," he concluded.

While the hallucinations were harrowing, dreams that I have these days, take on several dimensions. I don't believe all that much in fortune tellers, premonitions are crystal balls, but I figure some things that occur, aren't coincidences. What I'm trying to say is somehow, some way, I think there is a possibility that the dearly departed can contact us through daily happenings and especially in dreams.

Back on the morning of December 8, 2003, I had a dream that left me shivering with how real it seemed. As in the past, the site of this dream, was the island of Guam.

I was back there in the barracks...where I vividly saw the drab walls, dark brown floor, silver louvers, gray lockers and double beds with pink bedspreads on them. I hopped out of my rack (bed) and knew I had just one day left in this tropical paradise. Not being able to contain my excitement, I shouted "I only have one to go."

Garland (Carl) Butler watched me bound out of my bunk and Willie Lehman, across the aisle, was sleeping in his bottom bunk. He seemed perturbed that I had awakened him and slowly walked over to the louvers, which suddenly changed into the screens that are in the back bedroom windows, here in Pennsylvania.

Willie glanced out the window, turned his head and told us it was going to rain. He then pulled the screen up, went out the window and sat on the roof, wearing only a pair of white boxers (underwear). As the precipitation began, in the form of a gentle, then steady rain, Willie continued to sit there and didn't even budge when a downpour occurred. I could see his feet and legs but nothing else. I told him I was going to a place on Andersen Air Force Base, to get a bite to eat, and asked if he wanted anything.

He declined the offer with the word "no" but the gentle inflection of that simple word, told me that he was happy to be where he was. He was fulfilled, serene and very content.

I awoke with the strange feeling that the screen Willie opened, was the entrance to his death, 33 years before (he would be 60 years old now). The tranquility of the rain and in Willie's voice, told me that he was sitting comfortably in heaven and had no desire to come back here or to eat mortal food again.

In my doubting mind, I felt I was slowly admitting that there could be something out there that we, here on earth, don't understand. I am convinced that through a dream, William D. Lehman made contact with me and told his younger sidekick, that all is well, where he is.

I know it is inconceivable, maybe even crazy, for those "on the other side" to contact us. Nevertheless, I feel Willie reached my thought processes. I do believe that daily happenings and dreams, are perfect places for those departed souls to tweak our senses and trigger our minds. I know I lost some brain cells when I used to swill that alcohol, but Willie, you reached me, man.

While I currently sing close to two dozen Bruce songs, I know that the list is going to be growing. Life now, is really fulfilling to me. I have never been happier.

When I walk into a place that has karaoke, I see people like Ramone, Bill Heckman, Tammy, Annie, Elizabeth Katz, John Adamo (DJ), Cheryl and Bob Sauschuck (Flo Jean's Port Jervis), Randy, Jeff, Kathy, Anita, Tim, Christian, Rose, Country Joe, or bartender Sue (Mama Roni's, Branchville, New Jersey) and I know I am home.

My daughter, Tracie, is now belting out plenty of songs, including a great rendition of Pat Benatar's "Hit Me With Your Best Shot." Christine has been known to sing "Yellow" and "The Scientist" by Cold Play, or to team with me for Bruce's "No Surrender" or "Glory Days."

At Doc's, in Hamburg, New Jersey, the lady bartender (another Sue) does a mean "Lyin' Eyes" by The Eagles. Bill Pauling is laid back...he is a 60s kind of guy (with ponytail) who rides a motorcycle and hits big time venues where bikers congregate. He and I rap out The Rolling Stones' "The Last Time" every now and then, as the crowd rocks. He also whales on "Hot Rod Lincoln." Diana (with an elegant, velvet voice), Jim and his Diane (the Toby Keith guy and his pretty girlfriend), and a young lady named Dawn (nick-named Spazz) all give this place character and make Friday or Saturday nights a delight. Jeff goes to the microphone and gives us Hank Williams Jr., and the place is totally alive.

These days I am either grabbing a notebook, to cover a sporting event, or putting on a Bruce shirt, chain, and colorful wristbands (made by Tracie) to head for a karaoke. In just six days, I will be singing (January 26, 2004) at the FDR Montrose Veterans Hospital (with Chris and Randy Ringleben) and I am beginning to become excited about it. I have 12 Bruce songs picked out and will speak to rehab patients and explain that I am one of them. I will hold up a pair of blue slippers to prove it to them. I wore those slippers back in July of 2000.

I love walking through a verdant meadow to see a waterfalls, going and looking for lighthouses and covered bridges with my wife and wolfing down ice cream at night. I enjoy the simple things in life now, and sometimes just breathing the outdoor air, invigorates me with the contenting happiness that life can give.

I look at that screened window in the spare room (the former "drunk tank") and realize it is the one that Willie Lehman went through in the dream. That's the same window where angels buzzed around and talked to me in high pitched voices, way back on July 3, 2000. Through that window, I was afforded the crispness of cold air and the smell of a downpour, to help me cope with anxiety attacks as I lay sweating from alcohol. My heart would beat like a bass drum, a million times a minute, and I would worry that I would never see another day. Then I would get up, put on my cleanest dirty shirt and struggle downstairs and out to keep the merry-go-round in motion.

I know I am a changed person and that the other man is gone forever. He wasn't a bad individual and was looking for ways out of a deadly trap. Day by day, the escape routes narrowed though and were diminished until none were left. Suddenly, as if by magic, the inevitable became reality. I could no longer stop drinking on my own.

For years, I have told Jackie Beck Bush that whenever she needed any type of help with a person involved in alcohol, I would be there. I got my chance to help on December 8, 2003.

"I have someone I would like you to call," she said. "His wife is similar to Chris (my wife) in that she loves her husband very much and is supportive of his sobriety. But, she is afraid he will relapse again. I think you can help him and Chris can help her. I think he can pull a "Bill Tangen" but will feel better if he has Bill Tangen on his side."

I called the person that night. He lives across the Hudson River from me and we became friends on the phone. The next day, he decided to enter rehab at Montrose. He was determined not to give up and to finally succeed. I kept in touch with his wife and was ecstatic when I found out he had made it through the rehab. Just like the feeling I will get going back to sing at Montrose, I feel like I gave back to the people (Montrose personnel) who had helped me, when things looked so bleak.

You get quite a lot of time to think when you aren't swilling down 12-packs. Sometimes I wonder what we are really here for. You get born, you live and you die. End of story. But there has to be more to it than that. There has to be a more meaningful feeling you can cling onto while you are here on earth and maybe even after.

I want to be looked back on, as a sincere person who cared about people and would walk that extra mile, when others wouldn't or couldn't. If my example, compassion or caring helped someone or sparked an individual to spring into action, then I did my job.

Sports is my first love (even before beer) and I still thrive on watching athletic competition. I am resigned to the fact that my days of playing one-on-one basketball are over. Like Bruce's "Glory Days" I can always sit back and recapture those colorful days.

Most of the time, I feel much younger than my 56 years. I feel like life is a dazzling light show, so lets get on with it, and enjoy the brilliance of the colors. It actually translates to a New England autumn day of the mind. Some days I do feel my age. I'm not saying I'm old, but my social security number is 4. I take pleasure in realizing that the beautiful Cher is older than me. There is justice in this world.

It all began laughing with Gene Drew and the rest of my basketball teammates at Port Jervis. Now, I get a kick out of former athletes I have covered, seeing me on the street and stopping to thank me for what I did when they played sports. "I still have my scrapbooks," they will say. Some pay tribute by saying "you are the best sportswriter I ever saw in my life."

The greatest form of flattery is seeing my style or terms used in a local story. Skip Leon, who I have worked with in Port Jervis, uses "stanza" sometimes, to replace the word "quarter" in football stories...just like I do. I covered Skip under the lights at Glennette Field (softball title) when he was a teenager. He blossomed into a fine writer, who can take you behind the scenes or give you a humorous story.

I feel I have become wiser over the years. I put every ounce of energy into my fiber and being for something I believe in. I continue to be a rebel of sorts, always fighting for the underdog and not giving up. I think everyone has a certain degree of insecurity in their lives and I am no different.

Speaking of rebels, I worked for a guy named Stephen Witt, editor of The Young Sport newspaper which was a colorful and well-read sports newspaper in Port Jervis (initiated in late 1990s, but no longer in existence). Stephen is a complex kind of a guy...a dark-haired guitar playing, singing, journalist, who just happens to be one hell of a writer (he sings a mean "Hit The Road Jack"). Steve can never be accused of going along with the rest of the cattle and instead, chooses to be a rebel and rock the boat at times. His wife, Dorreth (publisher), is a professional artist and is an ad and layout wiz. The Witts and their four children made this attractive paper a family venture and it was starting to really take off, when controversial stories in the colorful tabloid, backfired.

I saw the Witts spend countless hours putting out this weekly publication and there was plenty of pride involved. I sharpened my writing and computer skills at The Young Sport, and was sad when it wound up folding, due to a decrease in ad revenue. At first, other area publications scoffed and laughed at The Young Sport, but the Witts came in like gangbusters and started to become a force to be reckoned with. They took the bull by the horns, covered the school districts tirelessly and began kicking ass not only in Port Jervis, but throughout the area.

I'm not saying that I totally agree with the way Stephen and his wife perceived things. I am saying that they didn't just talk the talk, but walked the walk. These people got me to believe again, in the excitement and pride of writing.

I look out the window and see the homes of neighbors Paul Bertino, Dutch Weigel and Dennis Reilly. Paul is a former New Jersey athlete, Dutch was a Port Jervis football player under Coach Al Chase and Dennis moved up here from down near New York City. They are decent folks who I am proud to call my friends.

I look at the end of the couch and remember the day when Penny lay there wagging her tail. The other day I looked at her leash hanging on the back porch and smiled when I thought of her heading out for her nightly walk. I still can't let my emotions pour out, even though she has been gone just over two years. I don't know if I will ever bring another dog into this house. I realize that no animal can replace my Penny Ann and that Chris and I would be sacrificing a degree of freedom to bring in this responsibility. All I need is to recall Bruce saying "we come this way but once" and I will probably be headed up to the Humane Society to look for a browned-eyed canine.

I have been through a grueling and draining fight. I was dazed, stunned, battered and out on my feet. I covered up somehow, weathered the storm and heard the final bell. I was exhausted and my strength was totally sapped. I know that I nearly died and even though it seems like that was another person, I do know it was me. There were people in my corner who helped me keep going and survive. My wife, kids, grandkids, parents, Jackie Beck Bush. They were all there, hoping I would survive against the odds. I battled the vicious perils of alcohol addiction and made it through. I went from my back porch steps to heights I never would have thought possible. This complex turn of events is mind boggling to say the least. I will never question what I have been through, but will always be grateful to The Keeper Of The Stars.

Reality can hit you between the eyes. It isn't all peaches and cream when the drinking stops. Doctor Schwartz (dentist) discovered a tooth abscess last year (September 11, 2003) and I was referred to Dr. Seth Pulver over in Central Valley, New York, for a root canal (my second).

Pulver is a real nice guy, a former wrestler, who is as classy as a person can be. He put me at ease and got me through this tough time, with compassion and professionalism. It was the second time I had secured Dr. Pulver and I told him it was nothing personal, but I never wanted to return to his office. There are decent people in this world and the former grappler is one of them.

I am impressed by people who overcome long odds. Teresa Martin, my "Kentucky Woman" (we are going to see a Neil Diamond Concert someday) had surgery and wound up getting rid of many, many pounds . She always had a pretty face and now she has a remarkable body to go along with it. For a long time, the real Teresa was hidden away, but when I saw her up in Rhode Island, it was obvious she was thrilled with the happiness that life can bring. Her condition was life-threatening, just like mine was, and I figure we share a common denominator. That bond, is being a survivor. Another we share, is helping other people. She gives people hope in their struggle with weight.

Sports writing was and still is my passion. I shudder to think of the dangerous times I had repossessing cars back in the late 60s and early 70s. My wife to be, discovered the writing ability and the rest is history.

When I think of how I want to be remembered as a writer, the evening of September 5, 2003, comes to mind. I was covering a Port Jervis-Saugerties football game under the lights at Glennette Field. Over near the Port bleachers, I began talking with Scott Taylor. Taylor is a former football player (under Coach Joe Viglione), who kicked a 43-yard field goal in a 26-0 win over Cornwall in 1975, on the very field we were viewing the game. He played alongside guys like Dave Farace, Mike Barber, Jerry Gray, Bob Cronin and Harvey Freeman (this Port Jervis team went 8-0-1).

Anyway, Scott's late father, Bill Taylor, was an avid sports fan, extremely proud of his athletic children and was a die hard Red Raider fan.

"One time, my dad was talking about you," Scott told me. "He said 'when Bill Tangen writes, you can smell the sweat from the locker room.'" I regard this, as the greatest compliment I have ever received from a reader.

The other night, I went down to the cellar and wound up looking through some old notebooks that I kept. On the white and blue-lined pages I had kept a diary of daily happenings. This diary, which covered most days between September 10, 1996 and September 29, 2001 (over five years), peeked out at me and jogged my memory. It was hard to believe that the person who took these notes (especially up to July of 2000), was me.

The pages were filled with how much beer I consumed every day and the times I took the last sip at the end of the day. The beer ounces usually totaled 144 and the times I quit were usually 11:47 p.m. (my flight number at basic training in Texas) and 11:59 p.m. (the last available minute of the day and seconds before I could get a fresh start and a new day). My objective was always the same: to quit drinking and stay sober.

These accounts totaled 451 sober days (July 3, 2000 through September 29, 2001). It must have taken that many days to realize that I had actually begun a new life and didn't need a diary to tell me where I was headed.

For August 16, 1997, I wrote this: "It's a proud day. Our first born (Tracie) is getting married (it was my 16th consecutive day of drinking, but I didn't even get high at the reception). It is oppressively hot and the heat index is supposed to reach 100 degrees."

This jarred my mind back to that Saturday morning when I kept playing the Wayne Newton song "Some Sunday Morning". Even though Sunday was in the title, the theme of the song surrounded marriage. I liked the song and I loved the fact that Tracie was marrying Mike. To this day, I am proud of him and his beautiful family.

On December 31, 1998, I noted that Christine had gone to the hospital to be with Tracie, who would be giving birth for the first time.

And on New Year's Day, I penned these words: "Chris called at 3:15 a.m. Sarah Nicole is here. She was born at 12:49 a.m. after 50 hours of labor." I pictured the happy little dancer, Sarah, our second grandchild, who entered this world weighing in at 8 pounds 11 ¼ ounces.

On October 23, 2000, I tipped the scales at 208 pounds and was in my 113th day of sobriety. The next day, Tracie delivered her second daughter, at 12:09 p.m., Ashley Sabrina, who weighed in at 8 pounds 8 ounces. The prior month, on September 7, 2000 in South Carolina, Dawn delivered her second baby, Jeremy Ace, who was 8 pounds 12 ounces. Since then, Brooke Elaine (Dawn) and Kyle Michael (Tracie) have joined the family. I thought how quickly our daughters had become moms and how their families had grown.

One of the most chilling entries that met my eyes, was the Sunday, July 2, 2000 account. The writing was large, sloppily scribbled and I swear it just screamed out the words "frantic" and "scared".

"My sister drove to Rite Aid for (12) 12 ounce cans of beer," it said. "Consumed approximately 144 ounces of beer. Drinking ended at approximately 11:47 p.m. Hearing music through my ears."

The next day, Monday, July 3, 2000, was even scarier. "Weighed in at 172 pounds (had lost lots of pounds). Got the DT's around midnight."

I glanced over the thick pile of paper and put it all in a pale blue binder. Maybe someday, I will write a book about what a drinker's diary looks like. I wouldn't have to inject much into it, other than picking out certain days and presenting them word-for-word.

While those days are done and over, the futility and seriousness of the situation is still very evident. The writings are from a confused and lonely man who had hit a brick wall at every turn in the road. After awhile, it becomes apparent, that total sobriety is not going to happen without the writer securing some type of help.

I shiver when it hits me that this diary could have been all that was left for my widow to cling onto.

Plans to go back to Montrose, began in the summer of 2003. I wanted to come full circle and go back across the Hudson River, to where this odyssey all began. Jackie Beck Bush was ecstatic about me returning to Montrose to sing some Springsteen and talk to the rehab patients. My burgeoning stardom was a gift from God, much like my writing ability, and I didn't want to waste it, but to use it to help get a message across. That message is to never surrender to alcohol or to give in. I wanted those battling this deadly disease, to see first hand, with their own eyes, that it can be conquered.

"I would LOVE you to do "Bruce" for the guys (and staff)," Jackie wrote, on July 30, 2003. "Having you come to tell these guys what you have gone through the last 3 years PLUS entertain them...WOW!"

The FDR Montrose VA Hospital campus had a 70-bed psychiatric inpatient unit, 116-bed residential drug and alcohol treatment program and 105-bed nursing home. In all, the Montrose campus, which serves Rockland, Dutchess and Orange counties (New York State), had a very vital 291-bed psychiatric hospital.

The facility had been in the public eye, in that some people were trying to close this Montrose healthcare system and related services. The plan was to combine services on fewer VA hospital campuses. It would leave Montrose with just an outpatient clinic at the 180-acre campus. The proposal would also reduce services at the VA hospital in the Bronx.

About 200 veterans and family members attended a hearing in late October 2003, to fight the proposed transfer. Opponents said that going through with this action regarding this 53-year-old campus, would be "breaking moral contract with veterans." New York State legislators Senator Charles Schumer and Senator Hillary Rodham Clinton got involved and Senator Schumer noted that "the decision to limit veteran access to these hearings is highly disturbing."

Schumer, a Democrat, had said he was drafting a proposal to restore $1.6 billion that had been slashed from the VA's budget allocation. "Congress is being asked to approve $87 billion to pay for war in Iraq, yet the White House is shortchanging veterans with cuts in health care and pension benefits," Schumer asserted.

The Montrose facility and its services were still alive and well on Monday, January 26, 2004. That morning, Chris and myself, drove our two cars to a parking lot behind the Spring House Restaurant in Newton, New Jersey, where we met Randy Ringleben.

Randy had just begun his own business "Entertainment By Randy" in the Sussex County area of New Jersey. I had met this fellow at Mama Roni's in Branchville, New Jersey, at a Loody and Pat karaoke. He is a thoughtful quiet guy with a subtle sense of humor. When he sings "Why Can't Everyday Be Like Christmas", by Elvis, it sends shivers down my back. Randy has Elvis down pat and puts 110 per cent into his songs. When I approached him about lugging all his DJ equipment across the Hudson River, he never blinked an eye. He is a compassionate person, who believes in lending a helping hand and was only too glad to sing with me at this event.

The plan was to have a total of 23 songs, 11 of them by Randy. I would speak (not preach) to the veterans, between some of the songs. I made out set lists and plans that showed two Springsteen songs beginning the 6 p.m. performance and then Randy following with two songs of his own. We would dodge back and forth with 2-song sets, throughout most of the show.

A major snowstorm was forecast in our area and we were hoping to get the event in and reach home before any heavy accumulations. On this day, Chris and I would be on the go for 14 hours and cover 249 miles. Once the equipment was loaded, we hopped in the two cars (three of us) and proceeded to a Fishkill, New York Cracker Barrel for lunch.

I wore a pair of brown Texas Steer work boots, tight black levi jeans and a black and white Springsteen shirt, covered by a long-sleeved gray top. I had bracelets made of rubber and other colorful material on my right wrist and a silver chain on my neck. By the time this show began, at 6:05 p.m., I was Bruce Springsteen. The adrenalin and energy began pumping when we went through the hookups and sound checks.

A brand new large flat-screened color television adorned the stage at the second floor conference room at Montrose's building 25. Amy Hahn, who organized the Montrose show, was there to greet us at 3:30 p.m. and help us up a ramp and to an elevator, where the equipment was moved up to the second floor.

It was a cold day and the sky was turning dark. I began wondering if veterans who had been through a rigorous day already, would be ready for this kind of format. I kept thinking "what would Bruce do in this situation?" I answered my own question swiftly. He (Bruce) would go before these people, give them every ounce of hope there was in the world, and rock the joint. And, when the time came, that's exactly what I did.

Lots of chairs faced me and they began filling up at 5:30 p.m. Chris played the piano while Randy and I went through a sound check and got things ready. Prior to the actual start of the two-hour-and-10-minute performance, he sang a great "Please Release Me" while I worked on "Cadillac Ranch (The Boss)", "Have You Ever Seen The Rain (CCR)" and "Margaritaville (Jimmy Buffet)".

I began to feel the electricity in the room when Amy Hahn talked with patients and I saw Jackie Beck Bush with her husband, Jon. She sat to my right and she was beaming with pride. I pictured Clarence

Clemons, decked out in black hat and gloves at the cold October 4 Shea Stadium concert and realized he and the E Street Band sacrificed their souls nearly every night. It was with that spirit and determination that I heard Randy introduce me and then I glided into a pretty version of Bruce's "Jersey Girl."

As the concert progressed, there would be about 75 people in this room. I would entertain, talk from the heart and laugh with these people. Many of the patients were undiscovered comedians who could also sing well. They were here to receive help and many positive thoughts and happy faces were in this room. The feeling of brotherhood quickly emerged on this night and I knew for sure, that I had come home.

Before delivering "Jersey Girl", I spoke to our audience. "Believe it or not, this is like coming home to me," I began. "I failed so many times trying to quit drinking. I did 12-15 cans of beer every day, baby. Beer came before anything. I had to have that $5.09 every day (for a 12-pack). That went on year after year. You guys know that story. That lady (pointing to my wife) brought me over here to Montrose on July 3, 2000. I almost died in the Bronx, but for some reason I got lucky, it just wasn't my time yet. I fought to stay alive. I got the second chance."

My people were silent as lambs and their eyes were as big as pies. They were realizing that I was one of them. "I'm not scared of alcohol," I went on. "But I'll tell you what, I respect that stuff. Outside of these doors there is a good life. Good things happen to you. You really got to trust me on that one. Jackie is my angel of mercy. She believed in me when a lot of people gave up on me. It gives you a helluva feeling when you get control again. Drinking will definitely take me out (if I drink again). This (Montrose) is where it all began."

There was thunderous applause and many patients were on their feet. This evening was off to a successful start and I hadn't sung a note yet.

I would go on to hear calls of "509" from the audience and I happily shouted back "I get high on orange soda now." I told them the story of Chris seeing me rifle through her pocketbook one morning. She had peered through a clear shower curtain while taking a shower, and caught me. I knew many of these people could identify with that.

After I sang "Tougher Than The Rest", Randy delivered "Suspicious Minds (Elvis)," and "If I Can Dream (Elvis)." Randy, who is about my height, sounds so much like "The King", it makes me shiver. He is a quiet and decent man, who the patients accepted and liked, almost immediately.

Prior to my third song, Bruce's "No Surrender", I told these upbeat people "I have the upper hand now and it feels good. So don't give up. Never surrender. You can beat it…I know you can."

Just before Chris joined me for the "No Surrender" duet, I looked into the crowd and reached into a brown paper bag at my feet. I retrieved the pair of blue slippers that I had brought home from Montrose, back in July of 2000. "I kept these for a souvenir," I said, holding them in the air. "I keep them in a top drawer of the dresser. I'm one of you guys, there's no doubt about it. It is a powerful feeling being out there (outside Montrose) and yet not "out there (drinking)." Drinking didn't solve a damn thing. A lot of wives would have walked away. For some reason, she (Chris) didn't give up."

As we sang together, I looked over at Chris and was affected emotionally. I suddenly realized what she meant to me, not only on this night, but throughout my life. She has been with me through thick and thin, good and bad. She was by my side on this evening, as I returned to the scene where my sobriety really took off. She sang four songs with me including "No Surrender", "Born To Run", "Glory Days" and "Twist And Shout."

As I stood across from her, singing in front of these veterans, it dawned on me that I loved this woman, much more than life itself. Sometimes we sit together and laugh at "Seinfeld" or she will set up a card table in the living room and work on figuring out the bills. Usually, Bruce or Cold Play DVD's will be playing in the background. When she is impressed or startled by something, she'll say "Holy Toledo." We still have a running battle of wits, constantly trying to stay a step ahead of the other. Our marriage has not only survived, but been very fulfilling.

Chris is a genuine person who is always there to listen and help, even if she doesn't know you. She brings joy to countless parishioners who listen to her play the organ at church each week. These days she sometimes walks up to the microphones with me and sings in front of various crowds. The veterans at Montrose were captured by Randy and me. But it was Christine who they watched closely and wound up falling for.

She had love in her eyes at Montrose and she reflected pride as she watched me perform. I am an organized person and she marvels at how everything fit into place for this show. Randy was meticulous in his preparation and his voice was one to behold. These people got Elvis and Bruce all rolled into one.

Amy and Jackie didn't miss any of the show. They were the two key people I was in contact with, to prepare this special evening. I looked out at these folks who now occupied most of the chairs in the impressive room. They were escaping for awhile and guess what? They were doing it, without a drink in their hands.

While Randy continued to impress with songs like Roy Orbison's "Pretty Woman" and Neil Diamond's "America", I sang a total of seven Springsteen songs including "Dancing In The Dark", and "Darlington County".

Our daughter Dawn lives down in the Darlington County, South Carolina area, and I made note of that fact, before the song. "That's the land of grits," I told the spectators. "They got some partiers in South

Carolina. The only bad thing is on Saturday night at midnight, they put a bar across the doors (where beer is kept in convenience stores). So, when I visited down there, I used to stock up with 24 cans on Saturday." I marveled at how the locals could take the wilting heat during the summer, down there. I mentioned the very real southern hospitality and said "You all come back down here now." in a corny southern accent. Those words and the "509" were shouted to me throughout the rest of the event.

I decided to revise my set list and tossed in five non-Bruce songs. While Randy offered "The Wonder Of You" by Elvis and Bobby Darin's "Somewhere Beyond The Sea", I came out with Buddy Holly's "Oh Boy", back-to-back Rick Nelson tunes "Lonesome Town" and "Poor Little Fool", plus Dion's "The Wanderer". For the grand finale, I selected "Twist And Shout" by The Beatles.

Several men came up to thank me during the course of the night. But one stood out more than the others. A young guy named Joe Vasquez approached me as I sat at a table off to the left side of the singing area. He wore a dark blue New York Yankee baseball jersey top and a backward baseball cap. What he said, struck me right through the heart and told me why I had come here to share with these folks.

"I have another 45 days of rehab because I'm not ready yet (to leave). You are an inspiration to me," he said, as he hugged me. "I have a wife waiting for me on the outside. I just know that when I go home, I will be ready."

I gave him some encouragement and glanced in Chris' direction. It was hard for both of us to hold back the tears. Joe had joined me for "Poor Little Fool", before I met him. Later, he and some others all came forward as we wound things up with a rousing "Twist And Shout."

I had addressed the crowd and talked about Amy, Jackie and the people who help run the Montrose facility. "They are definitely in your corner," I explained. "Jackie has been my friend for over 3 ½ years. I have a friend for life over there (as I looked in her direction). I owe my life to Jackie Beck Bush."

The place went absolutely wild. The younger veterans were on their feet clapping while older people, some who would be living in this facility for life (nobody on the outside to care for them), stood in the back and applauded. Chills went down my spine. I looked at my colorful wrist bracelets and the silver chain around my neck. Somehow, I had put Bruce's type of energy into this performance and reached many people with my messages of hope.

Before swinging into "Twist And Shout", I addressed these coura-geous veterans, one last time.

"Dream some happy dreams tonight," I said. "Before you know it, you guys are going to be outta here. You're going to be on the outside and able to drive past those neon signs and wave 'hasta la vista amigo', and say 'I ain't gotta worry about you anymore.'"

During "Twist And Shout", the place went bonkers. Randy was putting Chubby Checker to shame and veterans went wild. "We got a twist contest going on here, honey," I said to Chris, as spectators clapped in agreement. I looked at this happy throng and sacrificed my microphone for a guy who wanted to be a star for a few minutes. Then suddenly, with a deafening ovation, the event was officially over. We were thanked a zillion times for giving a hoot and making the trip across the Hudson River. Randy, the efficient "Elvis guy" was smiling as he began to tear the equipment down. He was now a true friend, who came through for us in the clutch.

We drove snowy roads in two cars and unloaded at Randy's house. The three of us were dog tired, and operated on the adrenalin from the show we had just put on. "They loved having us there," I told Randy. He agreed.

Chris and I arrived home and were greeted by five cats who began shaking us down for food. Reality was setting in rather quickly. We couldn't wait to turn off the lights and head upstairs to our bed. I closed my eyes and thanked God for pulling us through the veterans show. Somewhere up in the heavens, he was smiling along with any of our friends who have left this earth.

The next day, I received an e-mail from Jackie Bush. "Your show yesterday was wonderful," it began. "The guys really enjoyed it and in a weird way, I felt like a proud mom. You and Christine looked great and are clearly happy and in love. Thank you so much for coming 'home' and giving back. Your music selection was excellent! The lyrics spoke of recovery and hope with a little fun mixed in! Hope you had a safe trip home! PS Thanks for the article! (Janice Osborne's story in The Gazette). I made copies for the patient advocate and the director so they can see for themselves your success story! Your forever friend - Jackie"

The night before, I had met her husband, Jon, after the show was over. He is a professional caliber bass fisherman who was warm and kind. His good humor showed through to me right away. I hugged Jackie tightly and thanked her for coming. She said husband Jon (Montrose employee) helped to move me into the ambulance when I was transferred to the Bronx. I apologized to him for any bizarre behavior that may have occurred that day. Jackie said simply: "That wasn't you that was here. It was just your body."

I think of all the people I have touched during the past few years and it is very hard to comprehend. Janice Osborne helped to pass the message of hope with her compassionate story. I know that piece reached many people who can identify. Many of them have called me up or stopped me on the street.

"Keep up the good work," my editor, Janice, wrote in a January 29, 2004 e-mail. "You are touching many lives and are a hero in my eyes." A lump comes to my throat when I read these words. Me? A hero? Hell, I'm the guy that needed that $5.09 every day...just had to score to survive. The transition has been mind-blowing.

On February 7, 2004, I sang "Glory Days" and "Jersey Girl" at the Erie Hotel (Port Jervis). Port businessman Dick McKeeby (his son is involved in the ownership of the establishment) stopped by our table at the beautiful and spacious banquet hall, next to the hotel, and said hello. He is the fellow who has staged record-breaking fundraiser events to fight cancer. His progressive attitude and pro-Port Jervis business ventures, with partner Lenny Miglionico, are well documented.

Dick isn't the only one who stopped by to compliment me on my Springsteen singing. Les Buchanan, Nancy Buchanan, Sidney Quick, Ray Kahmar, Ted Kuykendall, Jeff Masurack, Bob and Cheryl Sauschuck plus Bill Heckman and his lady, Tammy, also made contact with us. Lester, Sidney and Ted are three fellow classmates who graduated with me from Port Jervis High School in 1965.

Rich "Elvis" Wilson, a local guy who made good singing Presley material, came in and sang a couple of Elvis songs. He is well-known in many places and has The King down pat. It was just before he sang, that I performed "Glory Days." The presence of Rich helped to push me into a dynamic rendition that had everyone in the place, hopping. Many who were present this night, had seen the story in the local paper and were seeing me sing for the first time. Most of the time, I had gone to karaoke in New Jersey, where crowds really get into the music.

Places like Mama Roni's are really into the tunes. A guy named Bill Rowan, who works as a Port Authority cop, loves Bruce and I have heard him do "Thunder Road" while he has watched me sing lots of Boss stuff. Recently, we teamed up to give a dynamic presentation of that classic which had the whole place in an uproar. Sue, the bartender, put down her glasses to clap after that one. The pretty Loody was all smiles and Pat, who has done some New Jersey high school football officiating, gave me a positive sign of approval that isn't in any books on refereeing signals.

I know one thing. When it comes to getting pumped to sing karaoke, I have no problem. I just throw on some "Bruce juice" in the house...either a VCR tape, DVD or CD, and start getting real positive vibes. The TV performance that really gets me fine-tuned, is the Barcelona concert (2002, The Rising tour). When Bruce rocks to "Dancing in the Dark", I challenge you to not have something on your body, move to his rhythm.

I may not be the sharpest quill on the porcupine, but when it comes to doing Springsteen material in front of restaurant and lounge spectators, I am as cool as the other side of the pillow.

On the way to some of the New Jersey karaoke venues, I sometimes find motorists tailgating me and it is irritable to say the least. You see, in a 45 mile per hour zone, I am the guy doing 50 and sometimes 52 or so. That is still not good enough for some people. Rather than stop the car and get involved in road rage, I will pull off the road until the jerk goes by. I must admit that sometimes, I have been guilty of hopping right back on the road and tailgating for a few seconds just to get some revenge. Traveling to out-of-town karaoke, comes with a price.

Sometimes I just simply think of some happenings in the past. The other day, I was flashing back to Willie Burton, the black comedian from Case Motors. I still see him sneaking some toy dolls into the mechanics' toolboxes. Sometimes he'd tiptoe to the parts room door and look in at me. "Hey bud," he'd begin. "You look like you had a rough night. You been out kissin' geese again?" He'd laugh into his hand and then go around the corner to that "telephone company" to pay a bill. The "bill" he paid was actually money spent on a frosty glass of beer.

I remember the song (Richard Rogers score) from the TV show "Victory At Sea", that Dad watched in 1952-53, when I was just 5 and 6 years old. That really sticks in my mind, like it was yesterday. This is the action-filled show that won Peabody and Emmy awards and had that compilation of footage from the most famous battleship encounters of the Atlantic and Pacific in World War II. When that program began, Dad was totally silent as he took in the scenes and the commentary. Obviously, I had no idea that Dad was a tail gunner way back in the 40s.

I recall the 1957 movie "Fear Strikes Out" starring Anthony Perkins (think "Psycho" and Bates Motel) and Karl Malden ("Streets Of San Francisco" TV show with Michael Douglas). It was the story of Boston Red Sox great Jimmy Piersall and Papa was with me to watch that movie. I was only 10 years old then, but can recall how scary mental illness and nervous breakdowns looked. I felt the pressure put on by Jimmy's father, who was never satisfied with his boy's play on the baseball diamond. Jimmy just never seemed to measure up in his dad's eyes.

And, there was the movie "Frankenstein" at the Strand Theater in Port Jervis. I was scared beyond belief, but was also getting sick at the same time. When I literally got sick in the movie theater, I was close to panic. On the big screen, Frankenstein came to life and in reality I was heaving my guts out with the start of the flu.

Of course there is always that Guam dream and about being in my first day on "The Rock". I guess being "trapped" there for 14 months, did take a big toll on me, even though I was just a young guy then. I still see the sands of Tarague Beach and that blue bus that took me from Marbo, past palm trees and on to Andersen AFB.

I see myself arriving in Thailand and chomping at the bit to go downtown where the wine, women and song awaited me. Sometimes I look back at these times as if it is another person I am talking about. In a way, it is.

I dreamed some intense images between 6 and 7:30 a.m. on February 11, 2004. The scene seemed so real and was like a blast from the past.

I was drinking (what else is new?) and my currency was sloppy and crinkled up in my jeans pocket (again, what else is new?). I straightened the money out to find I had 65 dollars in cash. I bought some beer for the bartender and a mug for a guy at the end of the bar.

I began feeling guilty when I realized that these two people might have read the newspaper story on me that said I quit drinking over three-and-a-half years ago. On the way home, I started looking for a store where I could stop and buy a 12-pack. I resolved in my mind, that following that 12-pack, I would stop drinking again. I pictured the 12 empty cans being tossed one by one into the blue recycling tote that is located in our garage, next to the 1968 Barracuda. I awoke with a start, cleared my mind and realized I was still sober. I heaved a sigh of relief, because my life was still alcohol-free.

Relieved that the dream wasn't real and that The Keeper Of The Stars was still watching over me, I began a new day. A couple of days earlier, I had stopped by The Gazette and talked about some business with Janice Osborne.

As I conversed with her near the front door, a guy walked toward us from the newsroom and I recognized him immediately. Tom Leek, a superb journalist, extended his hand. We had worked side by side at The Gazette in the days when the facility was located back on Fowler Street (it is now on Canal Street). I always marveled at the way his investigative abilities led him to tie up loose ends and bring baffling cases to conclusion. He had also worked at our sister newspaper, The Times-Herald Record, in Middletown, New York, and quickly fit into their news staff.

On one occasion, a body was found near a lonely road in Pennsylvania. There was no ID on the person and Tom began the task of trying to piece together who the man was, and why he met such a bizarre final resting place. He literally logged thousands of hours on this case, consulting everyone from the police to gifted people who can see situations that have happened in the past.

The male body was buried without a name. He was a "John Doe." Tom is a compassionate person who felt real bad about this, and continued his non-stop pursuit until "Roger's" identity was finally obtained.

I thought how strange it was, that after all these years, I came face-to-face with Tom and it seemed as if no time had gone by at all. Life can work in strange ways and many times sudden meetings can really jog the memory.

I realize that every day can't be a contenting walk in the park. It is a fact of life, that people go through all types of mood swings. Sometimes I will think back to Plattsburgh AFB and picture the small but mighty "Tiny" Tiedeman. He was a moody kind of guy, much like a small version of James Dean. Sometimes he would break his silence by simply saying "bite my ass." We all used to laugh at those words and I must say

I have used them many times over the years.

Once, Chris and I were traveling and we stopped at a rest area. A guy we saw there, had on a red shirt with white lettering, that said simply "blah, blah, blah." I chuckled for a long time, thinking about how moronic that shirt appeared. I just have to get myself a shirt like that, because it identifies the way I feel sometimes, regarding the general public. There is just too much chatter out there. People are talking just to be heard and their petty sentences are as boring as watching grass grow. These people should be made to sit down, adhesive over mouth, and look directly at a shirt that says "blah, blah, blah."

I have had some great times and met true friends, since I quit drinking. One time we were passing through Rhode Island, on the way up to Ogunquit, Maine, and ate dinner with new friends Joe and Liisa. Frances Murdock came in from Saranac Lake and Mindy flew in from Mississippi. There were a lot of laughs and some great music pervaded the impressive home. Joe plays a mean guitar, Liisa was a gracious hostess, Frances kept us in stitches and Mindy, possessing an elegant southern drawl, made us breakfast, the next morning.

Just a few miles away, more friends awaited our arrival. Lynnie and Tommy opened her house to a few people including Danielle, who flew all the way in from the state of Washington and Christy, from Ohio. Down the road of life a bit, I returned to this house and "pahked my cah" out behind this dwelling again. That is the day I talked with Lynnie and "Kentucky Woman" Teresa Martin (I promise we'll see Neil Diamond in 2005). I wouldn't trade these genuine times, with down to earth people, for anything.

Back on January 31, 2004, I covered a Delaware Valley-East Stroudsburg North boys basketball game. One of the players on the local team (Ryan Roa) reminds me of how I used to play the game of basketball in high school.

Roa is an exciting, versatile, energetic type who uses perpetual motion offensively and defensively to play inspiring and explosive basketball. He is blonde, like me, but is a taller version of the kid that played for Port Jervis back in the 60s. Like myself, Ryan knows how to draw fouls, ball-hawk on defense and shoot the eyes out of the basket. In all my years of covering basketball (34), Ryan Roa resembles my basketball style the most.

Happiness to me, is lunch at Joe's or Stewart's, going over new songs for karaoke (I'll be coming out with "Light My Fire" real soon), a nail-biting basketball game or a soaking rain that pelts down on the roof.

On cold nights, we'll turn up the heat and the five cats, Binky, Becky, Tiger, Cinnamon and Tony, will come out of the woodwork to be petted and held. This amounts to contentment for the furry felines and us.

What lies on the horizon for me? Planning too far ahead never seems to be a good idea, but being totally dormant or somewhat remiss in this world, just isn't in the cards for me. It just isn't my style.

Season after season, I write about female and male teenagers as they take their pursuits to the athletic fields and courts of our land. I keep getting older and older, but they always remain the same age. That cold, hard fact keeps me young. Many of them can't believe that an old guy can be this cool.

Youth is never more evident than on the karaoke stage. Dion, Elvis, The Boss and Rick Nelson all are presented to you in various stages of their fabled lives. When I do "The Wanderer" by Dion DiMucci, you are transformed back to the 1960s, right along with me. Times were simpler then, contenting, to say the least. New generations of music enthusiasts appreciate this kind of music and the roots it came from. There is no way to feel old when you are cranking out "Born To Run" or "Thunder Road."

Up at Jamestown, New York's Crescent Inn, John and Deb throw out a rocking karaoke on Friday evenings that never fails to have toes tapping in a heartbeat. You'll hear everything from Ethel's "These Arms Of Mine" to Lee Ann Rimes and Toby Keith material. John, a rocker if I've ever seen one, always starts this karaoke with "Leave This Country Boy Alone" a Charlie Daniels standard. That driving beat, loud guitars and pounding melody, get me more than ready to bring Bruce Springsteen into the mix.

I very seldom travel way up this way to see John Van Graafeiland and experience western New York karaoke, but when I do, the John from the Crescent, usually tells the crowd "Bruce is in the house" when he sees me arrive. Deb even gets plugged into The Boss, by doing a great rendition of "My Hometown."

Tomorrow is Thursday, February 19, 2004 and I will probably begin my book on Bruce Springsteen. I will show what it is like to travel all around creation while watching this incredible man and his E Street Band perform. I know for a fact, that I can look back at when I was in my mid-50s, and say those were truly "Glory Days."

On February 27th, Chris and I will be going down to the Stone Pony to see a second Soozie Tyrell concert and to help celebrate the Stone Pony's 30th anniversary.

It doesn't take a rocket scientist to figure out that a certain New Jersey guy and his guitar playing red-headed wife may show up at this event. If that pans out, Chris will probably give Soozie, Patti and Bruce some color pictures we took of them, at the same site, back in May.

I think the real Bruce comes out at intimate gatherings like this. Behind the superstar tag is a real decent person. This compassionate and deep-thinking human being likes to have impulsive fun, just like the rest of us. For him to hop on stage after Soozie's show and jam into the early morning hours, wouldn't surprise me at all.

It is Friday, February 20, 2004.

It is two years and seven months since I typed the first word to this book. I took my sweet time in trying to wrap up nearly 57 years of my life between two book covers. I didn't want to rush at all and there were no deadlines. With this freedom, my real feelings came out about what it has been like to walk in the shoes of Bill Tangen.

In the professional sports world, Derek Jeter and the rest of the New York Yankees are going to be joined by former Texas Rangers baseball star Alex (A-Rod) Rodriguez. They say he'll be moving over from shortstop to third base and Jeter, the Bombers' team leader, will stay put.

In local sports, the Delaware Valley wrestling team will be competing in districts and the Port Jervis girls basketball team will be having a home game against Valley Central. The Port team has fallen on tough times this season and I feel bad for the young girls who keep trying so hard, but come up short most of the time.

Here at the house, there will be some major home improvement going on this spring. A section of the living room ceiling crashed down some time ago and there is water leakage going on in the shower area.

I sit on the back porch steps and gaze out to the side yard which is now covered with snow. There is still no dog trying to get her cold, black nose under that crusted snow. With the home improvement right around the corner, any thoughts about a new dog joining us, has been put on hold. We have enjoyed our freedom and being able to travel, but I will "never say never" when it comes to a canine with big brown eyes, hopping on the couch.

I miss my Penny Ann more than anyone will ever know.

Back when I drank, there was a show on TV called "Highway To Heaven", starring the late Michael Landon. Michael played Jonathan Smith, an angel, who from time to time was sent back to earth to help mortals who were in tough situations. When Jonathan had something to say to his boss (God), he would look up at the sky and converse. I really liked this show and many times, especially at night, I would look up at the heavens and say "thank you for keeping me alive. Please help me get well." This was not foxhole praying but was a way of connecting with the being that had all the power.

Even just before passing out, way back in that "drunk tank" I would say "I love you" to my wife. Sometimes I would have to raise my voice for her to hear me in our bedroom. The reason I did this, was to have loving words to say to my mate. If I passed away in the night, she would know that I really did love her with all my might.

Now that I am well, you would think I would abandon talking to The Keeper Of The Stars. Instead, I will still look up and thank him or maybe even compliment him on throwing me curves and making situations difficult. "Nice one," I'll say. "What a sense of humor you have."

Needless to say, one of my favorite songs is Vince Gill's "Keeper Of The Stars."

When I was climbing the walls for a drink, I could be cold, callous, nervous and extremely difficult. I know I was an anxious, irritable and very difficult person to live with. Now, I happily take notes at a basketball game or hop up on stage and howl at the end of "Glory Days." I don't take myself so seriously anymore and enjoy my new friends and my life. We are looking forward to NY Nick's at Pensacola, where I will sing in front of 200 people or more.

I am genuine, real, caring, humble and satisfied. I can give and receive love these days. I am living life to the fullest.

This body has been to hell and back. I've experienced the mud, the blood and the beer. It is The Keeper Of The Stars, my wife Christine, medical personnel at Montrose and the Bronx, plus family and close friends who believed in me and are the reason I am here today.

It is those six small grandchildren who will experience what life has to offer for years and years to come. I wish all of them happy, rewarding and fulfilled lives. I hope they can experience at least a fraction of the gratitude I have and the feeling of hope and contentment that fills my soul. They will know, through words, who I am.

Chris and I are heading for 34 years of marriage. Last night at Mama Roni's, a nice guy named Joe Mango guessed we were in our mid-40s, which was a great compliment. A lady who sat next to me (Carol) has me by a year and also looks a lot younger. It looks like a good attitude and karaoke are leading to the fountain of youth.

I don't fear death like I used to. Like most happily married men, I don't like to think about passing away and want to be first, so I don't have to deal with the heartbreak and loneliness of my beloved spouse perishing first.

The Keeper of the Stars will have the final word on that. If I am second, I will know she is with a real straight shooter who will shower her with eternal love.

Tonight I will put on my bracelets and chains, because there is some rockin' to be done at Doc's in Hamburg, New Jersey.

I'll listen to some "Bruce juice" before I leave the house, just to get psyched for the evening ahead. Maybe I'll sing "Rosalita" and "Streets of Philadelphia" tonight. At any rate, my wife will be meeting me at 11:30 p.m. She comes right by Doc's on her way home from work at the A&P in Vernon, New Jersey.

There was a time when I used to paint the town red. Now the colors are more subdued...like an ice blue or serene green.

I dipped my brush into that paint can for over two-and-a-half years. I squeezed every drop out of that can to put my life on paper. The can is empty now, but sits there with a humble and proud majesty.

My picture, my masterpiece, is all done. It is a portrait that exudes happiness and hope. It is my living legacy.